★ ★ ★

THIS DAY IN
ROCK

★ ★ ★

★ ★ ★

THIS DAY IN
ROCK

★ ★ ★

Day by Day Record of
Rock's Biggest News Stories

★ ★ ★

by John Tobler

This book is dedicated to John Fogerty, Emmylou Harris, Van Morrison,
Tom Pacheco, Bonnie Raitt and anyone who ever really understood 'Do You Believe
In Magic', and to Joe, Jac, Isobel and Alex, in the hope that their lives
will be worth living.
JOHN TOBLER, 1993

A CARROLL & GRAF/CARLTON BOOK

Text and design copyright © Carlton Books Limited 1993

First Carroll & Graf edition 1993

Carroll & Graf Publishers, Inc.
260 Fifth Avenue
New York, NY 10001

Library of Congress Cataloging-in-Publication Data

Tobler, John.
   This day in rock : day by day record of rock's biggest news
      stories / John Tobler.— 1st Carroll & Graf ed.
      p. cm.
   ISBN 0-88184-860-3 (paper) : $19.50
   1. Rock music—Chronology.   2. Rock music—Miscellanea.
      I. Title.
ML3534.T64   1993
781.66'09—dc20   93-24665
                                                          CIP
                                                          MN

Project Editor: Lorraine Dickey
Project Art Direction by Russell Porter
Designed by The Design Revolution
Editor: Geraldine Christy

Manufactured in Great Britain

CONTENTS
INCLUDING SELECTED HIGHS AND LOWS THAT MADE THE NEWS HEADLINES

1953

HANK WILLIAMS DIES ON THE ROAD

Somewhere between Tennessee and West Virginia, *en route* to a gig in Canton, Ohio, legendary country performer Hank Williams died of heart failure brought on by a lethal cocktail of alcohol and pills. He was a tragically young 29 years old.

Hank Williams Senior – a legendary country superstar.

Williams, author of a string of songs destined to become classics (among them 'Cold Cold Heart', 'Jambalaya' and 'Your Cheatin' Heart') was apparently asleep in the back of his powder blue Cadillac when chauffeur Charles Carr stopped for gas in Oak Hill, West Virginia and touched Williams' hand, which he found icy cold.

Born in Mount Olive, Alabama, on September 17, 1923, Hank formed his band, The Drifting Cowboys, in l937, and within nine years hit Nashville and secured a publishing deal with Acuff-Rose. With Fred Rose as producer, he signed to the newly formed MGM label and the hits began. In 1949, his *Lovesick Blues* was the year's No. l country disc, and he had become one of America's most successful performers, which resulted in a punishing tour schedule. This was only sustained with the help of chemicals, and in 1952 his unreliability led to his firing from *The Grand Ole Opry*, America's most famous and influential country radio show. Ironically, Hank was at No. 1 in the country charts at the time of his death with 'I'll Never Get Out Of This World Alive'.

ARRIVALS

1893 – Elizabeth Cotton
1900 – Xavier Cugat (band leader)
1917 – Johnny Young (vocalist/disc jockey)
1923 – Milt Jackson (Modern Jazz Quartet)
1928 – Frank Pourcel (orchestra leader)
1942 – Country Joe (Joseph) McDonald
1950 – Morgan Fisher, (Mott the Hoople)
1957 or 1958 – Grandmaster Flash (Joseph Saddler)

★ ★ ★

DEPARTURE LOUNGE

1953 – Hank Williams
1967 – Moon Mullican
1972 – Maurice Chevalier
1984 – Alexis Korner

★ ★ ★

1962

DECCA PREFERS POOLE TO FAB FOUR

Decca Records A & R chief Dick Rowe secured for himself an everlasting place in rock 'n' roll history when he turned down The Beatles, preferring to sign the Essex-based group, Brian Poole and The Tremeloes.

Failing their audition was an inauspicious start to 1962 for the Liverpool lads, but one that would turn out to be the best break of their lives – within months they would begin a long and incredibly fruitful relationship with record producer George Martin at EMI's Parlophone label.

Their manager, Brian Epstein, secured the Decca audition by using his influence as a major record retailer – he ran the family business, NEMS (North End Music Stores), in Liverpool and began to manage the group after receiving requests from local fans for copies of a record the group had made in Germany while resident house band at Hamburg's legendary Star Club.

RAVINGS

1960:
Johnny Cash played the first of many free concerts behind bars when he entertained the inmates of San Quentin Prison, California. Country star Merle Haggard was in the audience.

1964:
The Rolling Stones, Dusty Springfield and The Dave Clark Five were among the acts who appeared on the first edition of BBC's weekly TV chart show *Top of the Pops*, hosted by Jimmy Saville.

★ ★ ★

Cast off like an old shoe from Decca, The Beatles find a better fit at EMI.

1979

SID VICIOUS MURDER TRIAL OPENS IN NEW YORK

When his trial opened in New York, Sid Vicious, former bassist with The Sex Pistols, was formally accused of the murder of his American girlfriend, Nancy Spungen, in their Greenwich Village apartment three months earlier. Sid, born John Ritchie (or Beverly) in London, had recently embarked on a solo career and an eventually fatal heroin habit. Brought into the Pistols to replace Glen Matlock, Vicious had been an early fan of the group via his friendship with singer Johnny Rotten. Despite his inability to play bass (his most notable previous musical achievement was playing drums at Siouxsie and The Banshees' debut gig at the legendary punk rock festival at London's 100 Club in 1976), his nihilistic attitude was perfect for the band.

RAVINGS

1975:
Georgia State Department of Corrections honoured The Allman Brothers Band, naming them The Outstanding Community Organization of The Year.

★ ★ ★

1978:
Singing cowboy Tex Ritter died of a heart attack at a Nashville jail where he was trying to bail out a member of his band.

★ ★ ★

ARRIVALS

1930 – Julius La Rosa
1936 – Roger Miller
1942 – Chick Churchill (Ten Years After)
1948 – Kerry Minnear (Gentle Giant)

★ ★ ★

DEPARTURE LOUNGE

1974 – Tex Ritter
1977 – Erroll Garner
1980 – Larry Williams
1981 – David Lynch (Platters)
1989 – Eddie Heywood

★ ★ ★

Not a pretty sight . . .

1968

TWO VIRGINS IN COVER UP-ROW

Authorities at Newark Airport, New Jersey, seized the entire shipment of *Two Virgins*, the experimental album by John Lennon and Yoko Ono, which featured a full frontal photograph of the naked couple on its cover.

Copies of the album were only allowed into the US when Tetragrammaton Records promised to protect American sensibilities by wrapping them in plain brown paper before putting them on sale! Although under contract to Capitol Records in the US, Lennon had been forced to negotiate a deal with Tetragrammaton when Capitol refused to accept the album or its controversial artwork.

Few people doubt that the furore over the cover helped boost sales of what would otherwise have been a complete flop. As it was, *Two Virgins* sold very badly worldwide and reinforced the belief that the Lennon–Ono artistic relationship was too weird for most.

1974
DYLAN AND THE BAND – HAPPY TOGETHER

In a mixture of reunion and regeneration, Bob Dylan worked with his erstwhile backing group, The Band, on stage in Chicago for the first time in ages when they kicked off a 39-date US tour to promote Dylan's *Planet Waves* album. The reunion was an artistic and box-office smash, while the gold disc status achieved by the album a few months later was positive proof that Dylan's powers were not on the wane. Throughout the tour, Dylan played a solo set and performed another with The Band, who also had a set of their own. His first American No. 1, *Planet Waves* was the first album Dylan recorded for Asylum Records after almost 13 years signed to Columbia (now Sony), a deal that had soured for him when CBS released Dylan, a contract-filling album of shelved material and out-takes that would normally have been rightly consigned to a secure vault and forgotten.

His first for eight years, the tour grossed almost $5 million in ticket sales as hundreds of thousands packed auditoriums in 25 US and Canadian cities to catch a glimpse of the man who had been their voice in the 1960s. An indication of his drawing power is the fact that more than six million applications were received for the 660,000 available tickets. Dylan seemed unimpressed: 'It doesn't mean that much to me, really. I mean, who else is there to go and see ?', he was quoted as saying.

Parts of the tour with The Band were recorded and edited to create *Before The Flood*, Dylan's second and last Asylum album. Before the end of the year, Dylan was back in the Columbia fold and working on songs for his highly acclaimed *Blood On The Tracks* set.

1967
BEACH BOY CARL SAYS NO TO UNCLE

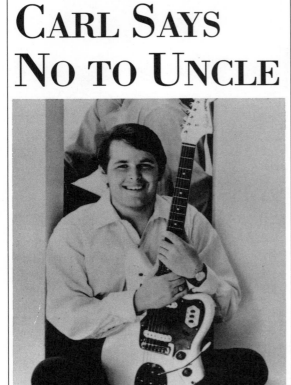

Beach Boy Carl Wilson – make love, not war

Beach Boy Carl Wilson hit American headlines when he turned down the 'invitation' that arrived in his mailbox from Uncle Sam. It suggested he report to his local draft board for induction into the armed forces. As this would inevitably mean a trip to Vietnam after a spell in tough military training, Carl decided to decline the offer. His decision set in motion a five-year legal battle that would eventually result in his triumphant acquittal on charges of draft evasion.

1954

ELVIS'S RECORDING DATE WITH DESTINY

1979

JAZZ GIANT MINGUS DIES

Charles Mingus, the influential jazz bassist, pianist, composer and arranger, collapsed and died from a heart attack in Cuernavaca, Mexico. He was 56 and had been ill for some time.

Born in Arizona, Mingus's career, which began in Los Angeles in the early 1940s and included spells working with the likes of Louis Armstrong, Miles Davis, Charlie Parker and Duke Ellington.

At the time of his death he was collaborating with Joni Mitchell on an album of material which she would complete without him and entitle (what else?) *Mingus*.

1936

BILLBOARD INTRODUCES FIRST-EVER POP CHART

America's leading music industry magazine, *Billboard*, published the world's first record sales chart. For the record, the first No. 1 single (then on a breakable 12 inch 78 rpm disc) was 'Stop! Look! Listen!' by jazz star Joe Venuti.

Elvis – the Hillbilly cat

History does not record how much Sam Phillips spent on the equipment he put into the Memphis Recording Service, the small but profitable sideline to his Sun Records studios at 706 Union St where locals could cut their own demos. No matter how much or little it was, it was the best investment Phillips ever made.

On January 4, 1954, a young truck driver employed by Crown Electric Co. stopped by with an acoustic guitar and his four dollars fee to record two songs – 'My Happiness' and 'That's When Your Heartaches Begin'.

The resulting acetates were to be given to his mother, for whom he had recorded another two songs a few months earlier. The boy's name was Elvis Presley, and within two short years he was to be the single most important performer in the world.

Intrigued by the unique blend of hillbilly and blues influences in Presley's voice, Sam Phillips took him in hand and put him in Sun's proper studios with bassist Bill Black and guitarist Scotty Moore. The results were startling, even revolutionary. A legend was born and popular music would never be the same again.

'FIFTH BEATLE' MAL EVANS KILLED

Mal Evans – that man behind The Beatles in this picture

Mal Evans, longtime friend, bodyguard, confidant and road manager to The Beatles, was shot dead today by Los Angeles police officers investigating a domestic dispute. When Evans refused to surrender a gun he was brandishing, LAPD's finest opened fire. Born in Liverpool in 1935, Mal Evans was working as a bouncer at The Cavern Club in 1961 when he first met and befriended The Beatles.

He joined their team as principal equipment and tour manager, acted as bodyguard for each member of the group in their leisure time, and in 1968 had his loyalty rewarded when the group appointed him Assistant General Manager of their new Apple Company. Mal had cameo roles in the Beatle movies *Help!* and *Magical Mystery Tour*, and a bit part in Ringo Starr's solo film, *Blindman*.

Co-credited with George Harrison with authorship of a song Ringo recorded, 'You And Me (Babe)', Evans managed the Apple group Badfinger before moving to Los Angeles. At the time of his death, he was completing work on his memoirs, *Living The Beatles Legend*. The gun he had refused to give up was found to be unloaded.

NOW HEAR THIS!

America's Federal Communications Commission heard the very first test transmission of the breakthrough FM radio, with its clearer, static-free signal.

It would be a year before the first public broadcasts were made to the few radio sets capable of picking them up.

RAVINGS

1978:
The Sex Pistols make their US concert debut with a gig in Atlanta, Georgia.

1979:
Saturday Night Fever, the movie soundtrack album that defined the disco boom and made John Travolta an international star, rang up its 25-millionth sale.

★ ★ ★

ARRIVALS

1923 – Sam Phillips (founder of Sun Records)
1940 – Athol Guy (The Seekers)
1946 – Don Hartman (Frost)
1949 – George Brown (Kool and The Gang)
1950 – Thom Mooney (The Nazz)
1950 – Chris Stein (Blondie)
1951 – Biff Byford (Saxon)

★ ★ ★

DEPARTURE LOUNGE

1976 – Mal Evans (Beatle associate)

WINCHESTER PREFERS CANADA TO FAR EAST

Unlike Beach Boy Carl Wilson, who decided to stay and successfully slugged it out with the draft authorities (see January 3), folk singer Jesse Winchester took a stroll across the Canadian border when his papers arrived, became a Canadian citizen and stayed that way even when President Jimmy Carter offered a blanket amnesty to draft dodgers.

Singer/songwriter Jesse – a brand new Tennessee waltz across the Great Lakes

ARRIVALS

1924 – Earl Scruggs

1929 – Wilbert Harrison

1935 – Nino Tempo

1937 – Doris Troy

1944 – Van McCoy

1946 – Syd Barrett
(Roger Barrett) (Pink
Floyd)

1947 – Sandy Denny
(Alexandra Elene Maclean
Denny)
(Fairport Convention)

1951 – Kim Wilson
(Fabulous Thunderbirds)

1953 – Malcolm Young
(AC/DC)

1959 – Kathy Sledge
(Sister Sledge)

1964 – Mark O'Toole
(Frankie Goes To
Hollywood)

★ ★ ★

**DEPARTURE
LOUNGE**

1980 – Georgeanna Tillman
Gordon (Velvelettes)

1977

EMI PULLS THE TRIGGER – PISTOLS FIRED

Faced with growing discontent from staff who had come face to face with The Sex Pistols, and a strike threat from employees at the company's pressing and distribution centre who were unhappy about manufacturing the group's debut single, 'Anarchy In The UK', EMI Records announced that they had dropped the group only weeks after signing them amid much controversy and confusion.

1964

ROLLING STONES HIT THE ROAD . . .

The north London suburb of Harrow (home of the élite British school) was the unlikely starting point for the first tour headlined by rock's *enfants terribles*, The Rolling Stones.

Supporting Jagger, Jones, Richards, Wyman and Watts at the Harrow Granada (in normal times, a suburban cinema), were hit US girl trio The Ronettes (protégées of Phil Spector, himself a buddy of the Stones) and fading Fifties rocker Marty Wilde, father of 1980s hitmaker Kim Wilde.

To coincide with the tour, the Stones released a five-track EP titled *Five By Five*, following it in February with their third hit single, a Bo Diddleyesque reworking of the B-side to 'Oh Boy!' by Buddy Holly and The Crickets, 'Not Fade Away', which became the first of thirteen Top 3 hits for the Stones.

Jagger and Co. in 1964 . . . and 1990

1990

. . . AND MAKE A COOL $100 MILLION!

Figures released today in the US by weary accountants showed that the recent American tour by The Rolling Stones grossed over $100 million – a new record for any rock act. Timed to promote the group's *Steel Wheels* album, the trek opened at Veteran's Stadium, Philadelphia on 31 August, 1989 and finished on 19 November at the Convention Center, New Jersey.

It marked a triumphant return to live work for the self-appointed World's Greatest Rock Band, and was especially notable for its vast stage set and lengthy performances and excellent value for money. One particular highlight included Eric Clapton joining the band on stage at Shea Stadium playing lead guitar on the Stones' 1964 No. 1, 'Little Red Rooster'.

1957

ELVIS BIDS ED BYE BYE

Taking time out from filming his first Hollywood movie, *Loving You*, Elvis Presley made his seventh – and last – appearance on televison's top-rated *Ed Sullivan Show*, the programme that had arguably made the young singer from Tupelo a household name across the USA when his debut appearance showed him from the waist upwards when singing anything other than ballads, not allowing his celebrated reverberating pelvis to be seen on screen.

The King signed off by singing four of his big hits, 'Hound Dog', ' Love Me Tender', 'Heartbreak Hotel' and 'Don't Be Cruel', plus the religious epic, 'Peace In The Valley', and a first performance of his new single, 'Too Much' as well as 'When My Blue Moon Turns To Gold Again'.

RAVINGS

1982:
Fun Boy Three's Lynval Golding required 20 stitches to his head and neck after being stabbed by white youths in a discotheque in Coventry, the city where the trio first emerged as members of The Specials.

★ ★ ★

1955

ROCK 'N' ROLL'S CHART DEBUT

Kiss curled King William

Ask most rock historians to name the five seminal records from the first decade of rock 'n' roll, the 1950s, and one title on their list is likely to be 'Rock Around The Clock' by Bill Haley and His Comets. Considering its prestigious position, it is surprising to discover that its success was mainly due to its use over the title sequence of a feature film about juvenile delinquents, *Blackboard Jungle*, which had little, if anything, to do with rock 'n' roll.

'Rock Around The Clock' had been recorded and released by Haley and his band a year earlier, when it sank almost without trace. It was saved from oblivion and became a rock anthem after its use in the controversial and highly successful movie. Although the record's initial chart run was for less than a month, with a peak position outside the Top 20, the film's success and the widely publicized riots it provoked all over the world rocketed the single back into the chart, making the chubby-faced country singer with the kiss curl the first rock 'n' roll icon.

RAVINGS

1958:
Gibson Guitars registered the US patent for their legendary and instantly recognizable Flying V model.

1963:
Gary 'US' Bonds sued Chubby Checker for plagiarism, claiming that the latter's 'Dancin' Party' was too close for coincidence to 'Quarter To Three', the 1961 hit by Bonds

1974:
A potentially stunning future vocal star, Sarah Maria, was born to parents from rock's aristocracy, James Taylor and Carly Simon.

★ ★ ★

1980

HUGH – BIRTHDAY BOY BEHIND BARS

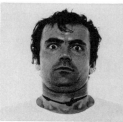

Hugh Cornwell – temporarily out of circulation

On his 31st birthday, Stranglers vocalist Hugh Cornwell was sentenced to three months in London's Pentonville prison after admitting possession of heroin, cocaine and cannabis, and was additionally fined £300 ($450). After a failed appeal, Cornwell only ended up spending from 21 March to 25 April behind bars.

Cornwell's enforced 'vacation' at Her Majestey's pleasure was put to good use. While in prison, he kept a diary of his time behind bars which was later the basis for a book he wrote entitled *Inside Information*.

ARRIVALS

1899 – Al Bowlly
1930 – Jack Greene
(The Jolly Giant in Ernest Tubb's band)
1941 – Jim West
(The Innocents)
1942 – Danny Williams
1943 – Leona Williams
(Helton Family Band, Loretta Lynn's band)
1944 – Mike McGear

(Michael McCartney)
(The Scaffold)
1945 – Dave Cousins
(Strawbs)
1946 – Andrew Brown
(The Fortunes)
1946 or 1942 – Paul Revere
(Paul Revere and the Raiders)
1948 – Kenny Loggins
1949 – Hugh Cornwell 1959
– Kathy Valentine (Go-Go's)

DEPARTURE LOUNGE

1964 – Cyril Davies
(Alexis Korner's Blues Incorporated/Cyril Davies All-Stars)
1980 – Carl White
(Rivingtons)

★ ★ ★

1975

ZEPPELIN FANS RIOT IN BOSTON

Boston, Massachusetts, had not seen the British cause so much trouble since the Boston Tea Party a couple of centuries earlier.

Thousands of Led Zeppelin fans started a riot while waiting for the box office to open at the Boston Gardens auditorium. Hours later – and with a hefty $30,000 bill for damage to be met – the show was cancelled.

Meanwhile, in New York, 60,000 tickets for three Led Zeppelin concerts to be held at the Madison Square Garden venue sold out completely in only four hours.

1960

COCHRAN TEMPTS FATE – AND LOSES

It was a recording session that seemed like any other, and just one of many attended by 21-year-old Eddie Cochran during his short but action-packed life. What Cochran and his sidemen on the session, drummer Jerry Allison and bassman Joe Mauldin (both members of The Crickets), did not know was that this would be Cochran's last recording session. It took place, as had most of the sessions that produced Cochran's hits, in Hollywood's Gold Star studio.

The major hit Cochran cut at the last session was ironically called 'Three Steps To Heaven', and it seemed little more than a gently rocking love song lacking the attack of his earlier classics like 'C'mon Everybody', 'Summertime Blues', 'Something Else' and '20 Flight Rock'. However, when Cochran died in a car crash in England three months later, its title assumed new importance and the track became his only single to cruise to the top of the UK charts.

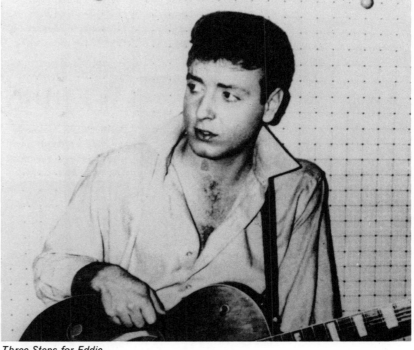

Three Steps for Eddie

1991

DEF LEPPARD AXEMAN'S LAST DRINK

Beleaguered Sheffield hard rock superstars were beset by tragedy when guitarist Steve Clark became the latest victim of misfortunes that had dogged the band, dying of alcohol-related problems. Fellow guitarist Pete Willis had been fired by the group for alcohol abuse in 1982, while drummer Rick Allen lost one of his arms in a 1984 car crash, but despite these and other setbacks, the group remained Britain's biggest Heavy Rock group and one of the biggest acts in the world during the 1980s with albums like *Pyromania* and *Hysteria* reaching multi-platinum status in both the UK and US.

1985

SWIFT SOLO SELL-OUT FOR GEORGE

Tickets for the first solo concerts by ex-Wham! star George Michael – two nights at London's 20,000 capacity Earls Court arena – sold out within hours of going on sale. To meet overwhelming demand, two more London dates were added to his debut tour, as well as seven gigs in other British cities.

RAVINGS

1982:
When Johnny Cash Parkway was opened in Hendersonville, Tennessee, the country singer became the town's first living inhabitant to have a road named after him.

1985

ELVIS LICKED AT LAST

In a controversial and unprecedented move, the US Post Office issued a set of commemorative stamps to mark the 50th Anniversary of the birth of the 'King of Rock 'n' Roll', Elvis Presley.

RAVINGS

1959:
First showing on TV of *Rawhide,* in which a young and little-known Clint Eastwood played the part of Rowdy Yates. Eleven years later, his recording of 'I Talk To The Trees' was released as a double A-side with Lee Marvin's 'Wand'rin' Star', as both were from the soundtrack of the feature film musical *Paint Your Wagon.* Marvin's track topped the UK charts for three weeks, Eastwood's was soon forgotten.

★ ★ ★

1959:
Cliff Richard's backing group, The Drifters (who changed their name to The Shadows six months later), auditioned for EMI at Abbey Road Studios, recording what would become their first single, 'Feelin' Fine'. It was not a hit.

★ ★ ★

1965:
The Beatles dominated the Top 10 of the US album chart with three entries: *Beatles '65, A Hard Day's Night* and *The Beatles' Story.*

★ ★ ★

1973

WEDDING BELLS PART 1

Punk Godfather Lou Reed married an unknown cocktail waitress named Betty in New York.

1981

FOUR HUNDRED FINES FOR SPECIALS STARS

Terry Hall and Jerry Dammers, leading lights in The Specials, Britain's foremost 2-Tone band, were each fined £400 ($600) plus costs by a court in Cambridge, England, after being found guilty of using threatening words during a gig in the city the previous October.

ARRIVALS

1889 – Gracie Fields
1928 – Domenico Modugno
1940 – Jimmy Boyd
1941 – Joan Baez
1943 – Roy Head
1944 – Jimmy Page (Led Zeppelin)
1944 – Scott Walker (Scott Engel)
1948 – Tim Hart (Steeleye Span)
1948 – William Cowsill (The Cowsills)
1950 – David Johansen (New York Dolls)
1951 – Crystal Gayle (Brenda Gail Webb)
19?? – Kenneth Kelly (Manhattans)

★ ★ ★

1979

BEE GEES, ABBA, ETC. PLAY FOR UNICEF

Billed as 'A Galaxy Of Stars', the 'Music For UNICEF' concert in New York featured performances by Rod Stewart, ABBA, Donna Summer, John Denver, The Bee Gees, Kris Kristofferson and Rita Coolidge, Andy Gibb (brother of The Bee Gees), Olivia Newton-John and Earth, Wind & Fire.

Apart from the hundreds of thousands of dollars raised by the concert, the United Nations children's charity also benefited by many millions more from the proceeds of the copyright fees from a song that each act donated to UNICEF. Rod Stewart, for example, donated his royalty cheques from 'Da Ya Think I'm Sexy', a number one single on both sides of the Atlantic. ABBA gave UNICEF the rights to 'Chiquitita', one of their biggest hits and with the massive Europe-wide sales of their greatest hits collection, *Gold,* in 1992, UNICEF are set to receive another substantial donation.

Although surprisingly an album released in 1979 featuring all the famous names who participated in the concert was a total flop, despite the inclusion of wall-to-wall superstars performing unique versions of their biggest hits, its sales raised hardly any funds for UNICEF.

1977

WEDDING BELLS PART 2

Former back-up singer to Linda Ronstadt, now country music queen Emmylou Harris, who was once romantically linked with the late country/rock pioneer Gram Parsons, married her record producer, Brian Ahern, in his Canadian birthplace in Nova Scotia.

Emmylou becomes Sally Rose

1976

WOLF HOWLS HIS LAST

Howlin' Wolf, one of the most distinctive and influential blues artists to rise from local popularity in Chicago bars and clubs to international stardom, died in hospital following brain surgery aged 65.

Born Chester Arthur Burnett at West Point, Mississippi, on June 10, 1910, Wolf learned his early music from blues giant Charlie Patton, whose guitar style he copied. Wolf's youth was spent picking cotton, and after a spell in the US Army during World War II, he returned to farming before moving to Arkansas and forming one of the first all-electric bands in the American South during the late 1940s.

Discovered by Ike Turner, Wolf recorded for Sam Phillips's Sun Records in Memphis, and the tracks were later leased to Chess Records in Chicago. Among these recordings were 'Little Red Rooster' (later covered by The Rolling Stones), 'Spoonful' (a subsequent classic by Cream), 'Back Door Man' (included on the first album by The Doors) and 'How Many More Times' (a staple of Led Zeppelin's repertoire). Covers by such acts led to Wolf's music reaching a huge new audience in the late 1960s, and many of his young white disciples, including Eric Clapton, Steve Winwood, Ringo Starr, Bill Wyman, Charlie Watts and others, backed him in 1969 on an album titled *The London Sessions*, becoming his only album to chart in the US.

Howl silenced as Wolf dies

ARRIVALS

1912 – Buddy Johnson
1927 – Johnny Ray (John Alvin Ray)
1943 – Jim Croce
1945 – Donny Hathaway
1945 – Rod Stewart
1946 – Aynsley Dunbar (John Mayall, Jefferson Starship)
1947 – Martin Turner (Wishbone Ash)
1948 – Cyril Neville (Neville Brothers)
1948 – Donald Fagen (Steely Dan)
1953 – Pat Benatar (Patricia Andrzejewski)
1955 – Michael Schenker
1965 – Nathan Moore (Brother Beyond)

★ ★ ★

DEPARTURE LOUNGE

1976 – Howlin' Wolf (Chester Burnett)
1985 – Anton Karas

★ ★ ★

1956

GOLDMINE IN LONELY STREET

Elvis Presley, newly signed to RCA Records, after Sam Phillips of the Memphis independent label, Sun, sold his contract for an unprecedented $35,000, cut his first tracks for his new label. A cover of Ray Charles' 'I Got A Woman' and a new song, 'Heartbreak Hotel'. Released as a single, the latter soon became Presley's first million-selling gold disc – over 50 more would follow in the next 20 years.

1963

CLIFF TAKES A BREAK

The premiere of Cliff Richard's fourth feature film, *Summer Holiday*, took place in London. With one single from the soundtrack, 'The Next Time'/'Bachelor Boy' having already topped the UK charts, the title track repeated this success, while the soundtrack album also reached No. 1.

By the middle of the year, Cliff's predomin-ance had been usurped by The Beatles, whose debut album, *Please Please Me*, knocked *Summer Holiday* off the top after the latter's 14-week residency in pole position. Over the next two years The Beatles went on to occupy the No. 1 album slot for an unprecedented 83 weeks, pausing only to allow the Rolling Stones a brief foray at the top.

RAVINGS

1948:
Loretta Lynn (née Webb) married her husband, Oliver Vanetta 'Doo' Lynn. The bride was 13 years old.

1958:
'Great Balls Of Fire', the latest of a string of Sam Phillips produced tracks, became the first US Number One hit for Jerry Lee Lewis.

★ ★ ★

1963

WHISKEY A-GO-GO OPENS IN HOLLYWOOD

Just as Liverpool's forward-looking music scene would not have been the same without The Cavern Club as its focal point, it is impossible to imagine rock in Los Angeles without The Whiskey A-Go-Go, the longest lived club devoted to the cutting edge of rock music in Hollywood.

Owned by one-time Chicago policeman Elmer Valentine, the Whiskey opened its doors on the world-famous Sunset strip (the portion of Sunset Boulevard that runs through Hollywood) and immediately became the meeting place and watering hole for the young and beautiful residents of Los Angeles.

It was the place to see and be seen, to hang out with the rich, the famous, the weird and the wicked, to score whatever turned you on – booze, birds, bullshit – and to be surrounded by the regiment of hot-panted, hot-blooded groupies who made it their domain. You had to play at the Whiskey if your band was going to make it – The Doors were spotted by Elektra boss Jac Holzman opening for Love (led by Arthur Lee and Bryan MacLean) in 1966.

Numerous live albums were recorded there, and Johnny Rivers used his almost resident status as house band as the basis for his career as one of America's most prolific and ingenious nurturers of talent, including Jimmy Webb, The Fifth Dimension, etc.

Meanwhile, back at the Whiskey – Johnny Rivers, King of Sunset Strip

---

RAVINGS

1964:
Ring Of Fire by Johnny Cash became the first country album to top the US pop album chart.

1987:
Frankie Goes To Hollywood's farewell tour opened at Manchester's G-Mex centre.

1988:
'So Emotional' became the sixth consecutive US Number One hit for Whitney Houston, following 'Saving All My Love For You', 'How Will I Know', 'The Greatest Love Of All', 'I Wanna Dance With Somebody (Who Loves Me)' and 'Didn't We Almost Have It All'.

★ ★ ★

ARRIVALS

1911 – Tommy Duncan (Texas Playboys)
1924 – Don Cherry
1924 – Slim Harpo (James Moore)
1933 – Goldie Hill
1949 – Frederick Dennis Greene (Sha Na Na)
1952 – Lee Ritenour
1960 – Vicky Peterson (Bangles)
1962 – Julie Roberts (Working Week)

★ ★ ★

1990

PAUL DISINTERS BEATLE HERITAGE ON STAGE

Having generally avoided performing songs associated with The Beatles during his solo career, Paul McCartney's first world tour in 13 years, with Friends Of The Earth information and merchandise at every venue, reached Wembley Arena and a delighted crowd relived their youth explaining to their children what 'fab' and 'gear' meant. Paul and his specially recruited new band devoted a considerable section of their show to his glorious past with John, George and Ringo on the 27th anniversary of the first

Paul – back on the Beatle beat

appearance by The Beatles on TV's *Thank Your Lucky Stars*.

As many of the songs he wrote with Lennon are certified classics (and the tour was an unqualified success both commercially and aesthetically), some asked the question why it had taken him so long to make this delightful decision . . .

1963

BOB DYLAN'S BOOT HEELS RAMBLE TO LONDON TOWN

Bob Dylan, whose eponymous debut album had been released during the previous summer, appeared in a play on BBC Radio, *Madhouse On Castle Street*, playing the part of a folk singer (typecasting or what?).

The former Mr Grunt in London, 1962

He also performed two songs, 'Blowin' In The Wind' (a hit later that year for Peter, Paul and Mary) and 'Swan On The River', reputedly a pro-IRA song, which he has never subsequently performed.

During his London trip, Dylan also played a 'floor spot' (so called because performers are from the audience – 'the floor') at Bunjies folk club after the club's owner had insisted that Dylan paid the admission fee: 'I didn't know who he was,' said the club's organizer. 'He was just another punter, as far as I was concerned.'

Perhaps the most enduring achievement of Dylan's visit was a recording session at Dobell's Record Shop (only yards away from Bunjies), where he sang and played harmonica (using the fascinating alias of Blind Boy Grunt) on a session with fellow American folk singers Richard Farina and Eric Von Schmidt.

1981

WHITE HOUSE ROCK

A dynamic duo – Ron and Maggie ponder each other's policies

The Recording Industry Association of America (RIAA) thoughtfully donated 800 albums to the record library at Washington's White House, the residence at the time of ex-movie actor President Ronald Reagan. His reaction to hearing such albums as *Alive* by Kiss, Bob Dylan's *Blonde On Blonde* and *Never Mind The Bollocks*, the genteel masterpiece by The Sex Pistols, was not widely reported, nor did his British opposite number, Prime Minister Mrs Margaret Thatcher, recommend a particular personal favourite track by the Pistols as far as can be ascertained.

ARRIVALS

1904 – 'Mississippi' Fred McDowell
1905 – Tex Ritter (Woodward Maurice Ritter)
1926 – Ray Price
1930 – Glenn Yarborough (Limeliters)
1936 – Charlie Gracie
1939 – William Lee Golden (Oakridge Boys)
1941 – Long John Baldry
1945 – Maggie Bell (Stone The Crows)
1946 – Cynthia Robinson (Sly and the Family Stone)
1949 – Abe (Abraham) Tillmon (Detroit Emeralds)
1953 – Michael Barker (Magnum)
1959 – Per Gessle (Roxette)
1967 – Mark Moore (S Express)

HERO'S WELCOME FOR CLAPTON'S RETURN

1973

With a lot of help from his friends, Eric Clapton made his long-overdue return to the stage at London's Rainbow Theatre after an absence caused by a combination of drug dependency, alcohol abuse and emotional problems. His rehabilitation was largely due to the efforts of fellow guitarist Pete Townshend (of The Who), who recruited a superstar band of musical chums and virtually confronted Clapton with the challenge of fulfilling an already confirmed and rather well-leaked booking.

The concerned friends who appeared on stage with the revitalized guitar hero were Townshend himself, erstwhile Blind Faith bassman Ric Grech and another Blind Faith colleague, Steve Winwood, on keyboards, drummers Jim Capaldi (like Winwood, ex-Traffic) and Jimmy Karstein, plus percussionist 'Rebop' Kwaku Baah.

The show, which was a complete sell-out and a triumph for all concerned, was recorded by master engineer Glyn Johns, and the evening's highlights, which included versions of J. J. Cale's 'After Midnight' and Jimi Hendrix's 'Little Wing' were remixed by Who sound engineer Bobby Pridden and appeared as an album appropriately called *Eric Clapton's Rainbow Concert* later in 1973. This was both a welcome return to activity from the viewpoint of many Clapton fans, and, more importantly, a personal giant step for Clapton out of his dark years in purgatory.

RAVINGS

1956:
Ballad singer Eddie Fisher (whose wives included actress Debbie Reynolds and film star Elizabeth Taylor, and whose daughter is actress Carrie Fisher) signed a 15-year $1 million radio and TV deal.

★ ★ ★

1969:
Elvis Presley returned to a recording studio in Memphis for the first time since he signed to RCA Records from Sun in 1955.

★ ★ ★

1980:
Grateful Dead, Starship and The Beach Boys headlined a benefit concert in Los Angeles in aid of victims of the Khmer Rouge in Kampuchea.

★ ★ ★

PISTOLS CLAIM A MILLION

1986

John Lydon (Johnny Rotten), now a member of Public Image Ltd, Steve Jones, Paul Cook and Mrs Ann Beverley (mother of the late Sid Vicious) sued Malcolm McLaren and his Glitterbest company for £1 million ($1.5 million) in unpaid royalties.

While hardly anarchic behaviour by the punk/rocking Pistols, they won their claim.

JAPANESE MOUSE ALERT

1990

Cats, the Andrew Lloyd Webber musical based on T. S. Eliot's feline poems and already a smash hit in London, where it is the longest-running musical ever, established a new Japanese record with 1590 performances in Tokyo. More than 1.6 million people had had a yen to watch the fur fly.

Biggest in Japan, 'Cats' creator Andrew Lloyd Webber

ARRIVALS

1884 – Sophie Tucker
1930 – Bobby Lester (Moonglows)
1938 – Richard Anthony (Ricardo Btesch)
1948 – John Lees (Barclay James Harvest)
1955 – Fred White (Earth Wind and Fire)
1955 – Trevor Rabin (Yes)
1961 – Suggs (Graham McPherson) (Madness)

★ ★ ★

DEPARTURE LOUNGE

1864 – Stephen Foster
1979 – Donny Hathaway

1973

GADD? RAVEN? GLITTER? WHAT'S IN A NAME?

The Leader who finally found the right name

British rock singer Paul Gadd who began his career in a 1950s skiffle group, Paul Russell and The Rebels, gathered all the mementoes of this and another of his alter egos, Paul Raven, including records, photos and everything else he could find, and consigned his less than world-shattering professional past to the waters of the River Thames in London.

The 'burial' took place from the deck of a floating restaurant/club, and also celebrated the birth six months earlier of a new star with the somewhat glamorous name of Gary Glitter (another of Paul Gadd's noms de plume).

1985

BAND AID BETTERS MACCA

Band Aid's chart-topping 'Do They Know It's Christmas' became Britain's biggest-selling single ever, with sales approaching three million only weeks after release.

The Ethiopian relief fund-raiser conceived by Bob Geldof and Ultravox main-man, Midge Ure overtook Paul McCartney's bagpipe-assisted singalong, 'Mull Of Kintyre', the previous biggest seller from Chrtistmas 1977.

1967

TUNE IN, TURN ON, DROP OUT, BUT . . . BE THERE

San Francisco has experienced an entirely new phenomenon – the Human Be-In. For weeks, exotic psychedelic posters had appeared in store front windows, on illegal billboard sites and on the walls of the city's music clubs. Designed by someone with the unlikely name of Stanley Mouse, they announced that at 1.15 pm on Saturday January 14, 1967, a Gathering Of The Tribes would take place – a Human Be-In.

Whatever else it might be, this event at The Polo Field, Golden Gate Park, was free, and the main attractions were to be LSD guru Dr Timothy Leary, beat poet Allen Ginsberg, black politico-comedian Dick Gregory and a bunch of other radical poets like Michael McLure and Gary Snyder. The tag line added that music would be supplied by San Francisco rock groups.

History has tended to diminish the importance of the first Be-In as a milestone and focal point of the drug culture that would lead to San Francisco's pre-eminence as an innovatory centre for pioneering music.

The music was little more than interludes between pro-dope and mind-bending hallucinogenic drug messages from the great and the good of alternative society, but for the record, the music that day was made by The Grateful Dead, Jefferson Airplane and Quicksilver Messenger Service (all notable Bay Area bands) and jazz trumpeter Dizzy Gillespie. The age of the rock festival had finally arrived.

1977

BOWIE HITS NEW HIGH WITH *LOW*

The latest face of the constantly changing David Bowie appeared with the release of his new album, *Low*. The title was proved inaccurate when the album soared high in the charts, becoming his eighth to reach the UK Top 3 in under four years. The album offered fans and critics alike the opportunity to keep up with the mercurial star's latest change of musical direction.

Recorded in the then divided city of Berlin, the spiritual home of Kraftwerk, the electronic combo admired by Bowie, the album was co-produced by Bowie with Tony Visconti, assisted by ex-Roxy Music synthesizer supremo Brian Peter George St John le Baptiste de la Salle Eno, whose own career involved what he called 'ambient' music – some said the tracks on the album that featured Bowie singing (the entire second side was instrumental) were 'ambient vocal' music.

Bowie was clearly determined to keep ringing those ch – ch – ch – changes . . .

Bowie (Berlin model)

1988

PAY FOR PLAY – OK OR NO WAY?

As newcomers Krush enjoyed a UK Top 3 single with 'House Arrest', a payola scandal exploded. Group manager Amrik Rai (an ex-New Musical Express writer), appeared on TV and admitted paying local pirate stations 'hundreds of pounds' to ensure blanket airplay for the single.

This was so successful that influential mainstream stations started playing it, helping it to become a hit. Rai, when asked about the morality of his move, was unrepentant: 'It was worth every penny,' he said.

1983

DOWN UNDER ON TOP

Australia's Men At Work achieved a first for any band from the biggest island in the world.

The Melbourne group's single, 'Down Under', a novel travelogue of the way things are in Oz, and the album *Business As Usual* from which it came, both topped their respective charts in America. Vegemite anyone ?

1972

CHIPMUNKS CREATOR DEAD BUT GROUP LIVES ON

David Seville in London, 1964

Ross Bagdasarian, the 'father' of The Chipmunks, a non-existent group that topped the US singles chart for a month over the 1958/59 festive season, died – but their sound lived on, with their creator's son, Ross Bagdasarian Jr, speeding up the tapes to sound like the small rodents.

Even before he created the Chipmunks Alvin, Simon and Theodore (each named after an executive at Liberty Records, the label to which he was signed), Bagdasarian had topped the US singles chart with 'Witch Doctor', released under the name of David Seville earlier in 1958.

1970

YOU CALL THAT ART?

The heavy hand of the law – eyes no doubt averted – came down with emphatic force when Scotland Yard's Obscene Publications Squad visited a London art gallery and confiscated eight lithographs. Such events rarely attract national headlines, but on this occasion the artist concerned was an ex-student of Liverpool College of Art named John Winston 'Ono' Lennon, singer and guitarist with the most famous group in the world, The Beatles. The works of 'art' concerned were a series of line drawings that included nude studies of Lennon and his partner, Japanese avant-garde artist Yoko Ono.

For the discontented Beatle, the whole charade was grist to the mill, adding a certain credibility to his desire for recognition as a serious artist rather than merely as a lovable Mop Top.

1957

CAVERN CLUB OPENS IN LIVERPOOL

Designed as a traditional jazz venue, The Cavern Club opened in disused property owned by British Railways in Mathew Street in Liverpool. After pursuing a 'jazz only' policy for several years, it eventually allowed some of the burgeoning local R & B acts to tread its boards, and it was only a matter of time before financial pressures forced a further relaxation of the 'no rock 'n' roll' stance and such Merseybeat originators as The Beatles, The Big Three and others effectively consigned the trad bands to the out tray.

Gerry and The Pacemakers rocking at the famous Cavern

ARRIVALS

1904 – Phil Harris
1937 – Bob Bogle (Ventures)
1942 – Barbara Lynn (Barbara Lynn Ozen)
1942 – Raymond Philips (Nashville Teens)
1942 – William Francis (Dr. Hook)
1944 – Jim Stafford
1946 – Ronnie Milsap
1960 – Sade Adu (Helen Folasade Adu)

1962 – Paul Webb (Talk Talk)

★ ★ ★

DEPARTURE LOUNGE

1972 – Ross Bagdasarian (aka David Seville)
1973 – Clara Ward
1975 – Paul Beaver (Beaver and Krause)
1980 – David Whitfield

★ ★ ★

1969

LED ZEP DEBUT DIVIDES NORTH AMERICAN CRITICS

Released during their first US tour, *Led Zeppelin* **was the debut album by the group that had played its first gig under that name only three months before.**

The group name was suggested by the rhythm section of The Who – drummer Keith Moon claimed that it was his idea, but bass player John Entwistle maintained that he had coined it during a conversation with Richard Cole, a chauffeur he knew who later went on to work with The New Yardbirds (as the group formed by guitarist and Yardbirds

Led Zeppelin, briefly The New Yardbirds

member Jimmy Page were originally known).

When the other members of the final Yardbirds line-up, Keith Relf, Jim McCarty and Chris Dreja, allowed Page to use the group name, he recruited bass player John Paul Jones (with whom he had

worked as a session musician) and two one-time members of Birmingham R & B combo Band Of Joy, vocalist Robert Plant and drummer John Bonham. This line-up toured as The New Yardbirds in Scandinavia and to fulfil

a handful of contracted British dates adopting the 'lead balloon' tag for the first time at a gig at Surrey University.

The Led Zeppelin album quickly became a major success, reaching the Top 10 on both sides of the Atlantic and being certified gold.

1965

DOUBLE CELEBRATION FOR STONES AT THIRD NO. 1

Two milestones – and two more desirable future acquisitions for Rolling Stones fans:

A just published book composed of drawings by drummer Charlie Watts entitled *Ode To A High Flying Bird* and dedicated to jazz saxophone giant Charlie Parker, who had died

ten years before; and the recording session for a brand new Stones single, 'The Last Time'.

By now the Stones' career was in full swing with two UK No. 1 hits under their belt: a cover

of the Valentinos' 'It's All Over Now' and 'Little Red Rooster'

The important difference with 'The Last Time' was that it was the first hit single by the group written by the 'Glimmer Twins' songwriting partnership of Mick Jagger and Keith Richards, and had been recorded at RCA Studios

in Hollywood with famed American engineer Dave Hassinger at the controls assisted by Phil Spector and Jack Nitzsche.

The single's success came as no surprise – it quickly made it a hat trick of consecutive UK chart-toppers for the Rolling Stones, a run that was later to be extended to five.

1981

POLICE PINDOWN FOR PLASMATICS PUNK

Wendy O. Williams, vocalist with US punk shockers The Plasmatics, had never been accused of being a shrinking violet, but police attending a gig by the volume-conscious group in Milwaukee felt that she had perhaps exceeded the entertainment brief when they arrested her for simulating masturbation on stage with a sledgehammer! In the ensuing fracas that followed as they tried to stop the show, police officers wrestled Williams to the floor of the auditorium and pinned her down. The singer received cuts to the head and face requiring twelve stitches.

Wendy O., a sweet old-fashioned girl with a sledgehammer

RAVINGS

1964:
The Beatles entered the US singles chart for the first time, with 'I Want To Hold Your Hand'.

★ ★ ★

1973:
The Rolling Stones held a benefit concert at Los Angeles Forum for refugees of a Nicaraguan earthquake. Mick Jagger's first wife, Bianca, came from Nicaragua.

★ ★ ★

1974:
Bad Company was formed by ex-members of Free, Mott The Hoople and King Crimson.

★ ★ ★

1978:
The first (and only) US tour by The Sex Pistols ended at San Francisco's Winterland Ballroom. Next day, Johnny Rotten publicly announced that the band was finished.

★ ★ ★

1978:
Neil Sedaka was granted a gold star on Hollywood Boulevard's 'Footpath Of Fame'.

★ ★ ★

1986:
The AIDS charity record by Dionne (Warwick) and Friends, 'That's What Friends Are For', topped the US singles chart, remaining at No. 1 for four weeks. The 'Friends' were Elton John, Stevie Wonder and Gladys Knight.

1980

THE DAY THE DISCO DIED

If the disco movement had a head-quarters, it was almost certainly in New York at Studio 54, the glitzy trendsetting nightspot where the rich, the famous and those who aspired to wealth and celebrity boogied the night away under the ever watchful eyes of owners Steve Rubell and Ian Schrager.

Style gurus for a generation, the duo were seemingly too busy taking care of business to take care of Studio 54 business, and were each sentenced to three and a half years in prison after being found guilty of income tax evasion, and also fined $20,000.

Doubtless many who were barred by doormen from entry to Studio 54 on the grounds that they were too ordinary felt that the duo's incarceration proved there could still be justice in the world.

Pundits point to this moment, when Studio 54 lost its directors (and thus its direction) as the day the disco age ended. However, it had made an impact sufficient for spin-off musical crazes like technopop, and eventually acid house music, hip-hop, rap and rave to develop in the later years of the decade and fill the pop charts on both sides of the Atlantic with dance music that by the early 1990s, simply was not universally popular – the ultimate contradiction.

ARRIVALS

1913 – Danny Kaye
1918 – Elmore James
1941 – Bobby Goldsboro
1943 – Dave Greenslade (Thunderbirds/Colosseum/Greenslade)
1957 – Tom Bailey (Thompson Twins)
1959 – Bob Rosenberg (Will to Power)

1962 – Jeremy Healey (Haysi Fantayzee/E-Zee Possee)

★ ★ ★

DEPARTURE LOUNGE

1990 – Mel Appleby (Mel and Kim)

★ ★ ★

INAUGURATION BALLS PART 1

1957

Boone - white and right for Ike

Pat Boone, the white 'Mr Clean' who covered original hits by such black acts as The Charms, Fats Domino, The Five Keys, The Flamingos, Little Richard, Ivory Joe Hunter and quite a few more, and in most cases scored a bigger hit than the original versions (largely because he was white and clean cut, and thus acceptable to white Americans, rather than because he was a superior vocalist, although he was an above-average vocalist with film-star looks) sang at President Eisenhower's inaugural ball.

INAUGURATION BALLS 2

1977

Linda Ronstadt, Loretta Lynn and Aretha Franklin were among the stars of a specially networked TV Special to celebrate the inauguration of former Georgia governor Jimmy Carter as the new President of the United States. Among the guests at Washington's Kennedy Center were Carter and his wife Roslynn, John Lennon and Yoko Ono, Paul Simon and Carter's local musician friend, Gregg Allman (of The Allman Brothers). At the next evening's Inaugural Ball at The White House, dinner-jacketed guests got funky on the dance floor to the music of two of the hottest 'Southern Rock' acts around, The Marshall Tucker Band and The Charlie Daniels Band – the latter raised a cheer with the anthemic song 'The South's Gonna Rise Again'.

RAVINGS

1974:
A Bob Dylan concert in Miami caused traffic jams said to be the biggest since the Woodstock Festival in 1969.

1976:
The Beatles refused an advance payment of $30 million to re-form offered by US promoter Bill Sargent.

1980:
Michael Jackson received his first gold album for sales of *Off The Wall*.

1981:
Chrysalis Records boss Chris Wright, chairman of the British Phonograph Industry (BPI) predicted the death of the 12 inch vinyl album and the future dominance of the cassette format.

INAUGURATION BALLS 3

1981

Old-timers Frank Sinatra, Dean Martin, and Charley Pride joined Donny and Marie Osmond among the entertainers who rocked out at the Inaugural Gala to welcome ex-film actor Ronald Reagan to his new elected post as President of The United States.

SUGARCUBES SOOTHE THROAT THREAT

1988

Iceland's first rock stars, The Sugarcubes, had to re-edit the video clip for their second hit single, 'Cold Sweat', after the producer of British television's Chart Show objected to a sequence in which vocalist Einar appeared to have his throat cut. The footage was filmed using a piece of raw bacon, and the band, with their wacky sense of humour, substituted shots of playful monkeys. Puzzled but content, the producer screened the new version of the clip.

ARRIVALS

1919 – Rollin' Oscar Sullivan (Lonzo & Oscar)
1939 – Phil Everly
1941 – David Ruffin (Temptations)
1943 – Janis Lynn Joplin
1944 – Laurie London
1944 – Shelley Fabares (Michelle Fabares)
1945 – Rod Evans (Deep Purple)
1946 – Dolly Rebecca Parton
1949 – Robert Palmer
1951 – Dewey Bunnell (America)
1951 – Martha Davis (Motels)
1957 – Mickey Virtue (UB40)
1963 – Caron Wheeler

★ ★ ★

DEPARTURE LOUNGE

1960 – Ralph Peer (famous country music publisher and talent scout)
1983 – Don Costa

1965

ROCK 'N' ROLL GODFATHER DIES AT 43

Disc jockey Alan Freed's death in Palm Springs, Florida, at the age of only 43, in some ways marked the end of an era.

Born in the Philadelphia suburb of Johnstown, Freed formed a jazz group known as The Sultans Of Swing while in high school, and after leaving school worked in radio before moving to Cleveland, where he worked at a station known as WJW. Encouraged by local store owner and sponsor Leo Mintz to include R & B hits in his show, Moondog's Rock 'n' Roll Party, Freed introduced black music to a white audience.

This led to a series of live shows promoted and compered by Freed, at the first of which 30,000 fans attempted to enter the 10,000 capacity Cleveland Arena.

1n 1954, Freed moved to WINS, New York, where his *Rock 'n' Roll Party* became the city's single most influential show. As the rock 'n' roll phenomenon gained momentum, Freed's influence grew, and he appeared in three early rock 'n' roll movies as himself, shared songwriting credits on hit records (his name appears on Chuck Berry's 'Maybellene'), and became one of the East Coast of the USA's biggest promoters of live concerts with racially mixed bills. He also made quite a few enemies, so it became inevitable that when the 1962 payola scandal broke in the US, Freed would face charges of accepting money for playing particular records. Found guilty, he received a suspended prison sentence and was heavily fined, and seemingly lost the will to live, dying of uraemia.

His story was fictionalized in the excellent 1970s feature film *American Hot Wax*.

1973

KILLER SHAKES UP OPRY

Officials at Nashville's Grand Ole Opry reportedly told Jerry Lee Lewis before he made his debut at the legendary home of country music, 'No rock 'n' roll and no cussin' '. By the end of his performance the Memphis firebrand who later adopted the nickname 'The Killer' had deviated from his approved set list, playing 'Great Balls Of Fire', 'Whole Lotta Shakin' Goin' On' and 'Good Golly Miss Molly' before announcing to the dumbstruck audience 'I'm a rock 'n' rollin' country and western rhythm and blues singin' mother****er!". No one argued.

Alan Freed, the first rock'n'roll disc jockey

REET PETITE STAR DIES AFTER EIGHT YEAR COMA

The late, great Jackie Wilson

On September 25, 1975, Jackie Wilson collapsed on stage in Cherry Hill, New Jersey, with a heart attack that led to an irreversible coma that only ended when he died over eight years later. One of the finest and most copied soul stylists of the 1950s' R & B explosion, Detroit-born Wilson was in his fiftieth year.

Discovered by band leader Johnny Otis in a 1951 talent show, Wilson replaced his idol, Clyde McPhatter, as lead vocalist with Billy Ward and The Dominoes in 1953 when McPhatter left to become a founder member of The Drifters.

After leaving Ward's ever-changing group in 1956, Wilson's solo career took off in 1957 with his first solo single, 'Reet Petite', a song written by his friend, Berry Gordy Jr (who launched his own Motown label not long afterwards).

A brilliant live performer (and an influence on such disparate artists as Elvis Presley and Rod Stewart), Wilson enjoyed over 50 US hit singles by 1972, among the biggest being 'Lonely Teardrops' in 1957, the double-sided hit 'Night'/'Doggin' Around' (1960), and perhaps his best-known release, '(Your Love Keep Lifting Me) Higher And Higher' (1967). In 1975, Wilson's 1968 classic, 'I Get The Sweetest Feeling', was reissued in the UK, returning him to the chart only months before the heart attack.

He would never be aware of the immense British success to be achieved by his old hits in 1986/7. A reissue of 'Reet Petite' topped the UK singles chart for a month at Christmas 1986, 'I Get The Sweetest Feeling' was reissued for a second time making the Top 3 in early 1987, and 'Higher And Higher' reached the Top 20 later in the year, although none of these hits achieved similar success in America.

ARRIVALS

1936 – Snooks Eaglin
1941 – Placido Domingo
1941 – Richie Havens
1942 – Edwin Starr (Charles Hatcher)
1942 – Mac Davis
1947 – Jimmy Ibbotson (Nitty Gritty Dirt Band)
1947 – Pye Hastings (Caravan)
1948 – Peter Kircher (Status Quo)

1950 – Billy Ocean
1959 – Vic Reeves
1966 – Wendy James (Transvision Vamp)

★ ★ ★

DEPARTURE LOUNGE

1984 – Jackie Wilson
1992 – Champion Jack Dupree

★ ★ ★

BONO, EDGE, ADAM AND LARRY TOP US BOX OFFICE CHARTS

Bono, The Edge, Adam Clayton and Larry Mullen Jr alias U2 became the biggest live attraction in the USA, according to Pollstar, the US information service for rock promoters. Ireland's finest were head and shoulders above all other acts as the most profitable act in the States during 1987, grossing a mind-boggling $35 million in box-office receipts.

RAVINGS

1961:
Elvis Presley signed a five-year film contract with veteran producer Hal Wallis.

1966:
George Harrison married model/actress Patti Boyd, whom he had met on the set of the Beatles movie *Help!*

1982:
Former disc jockey B. B. King donated his record collection to the University of Minnesota for their Southern Cultural Studies Center.

★ ★ ★

1959

BUDDY HOLLY MAKES FINAL DEMOS

Alone with his guitar in his New York apartment (apartment 3B, The Brevoort), Buddy Holly used a newly acquired automatic tape recorder to make demonstration recordings of a number of new songs he was considering recording.

As his solo single 'Heartbeat' was climbing the British and American charts and during the days before he left for the fateful Winter Dance Party tour from which he did not return, he laid down raw unfinished solo recordings of such songs as Little Richard's

'Slippin' and Slidin'' (recorded in both slow and fast versions), the 1906 chart-topper 'Wait 'Til The Sun Shines, Nellie', Mickey Baker's 'Love Is Strange', Bo Diddley's 'Dearest' and the Leiber/Stoller classic, 'Smokey Joe's Cafe'.

After his death, all

these (and many more incomplete tracks) were subject to overdubbing under the supervision of the producer of Holly's early hits, Norman Petty, and many became hits, thus keeping the Buddy Holly industry alive for much of the 1960s.

1971

COCKER'S MAD DOGS ON LONDON SCREEN

Sheffield soul star Joe Cocker

Mad Dogs and Englishmen, the feature movie capturing 1970's record-breaking US tour by Sheffield-born Ray Charles disciple Joe Cocker, premiered in London before a celebrity audience. Notably starring Cocker and American singer/guitarist/keyboard player Leon Russell , the touring party numbered 36, including musicians,

spouses and lovers, children and dogs, sound engineers, roadies and secretaries, and travelled in a large private aircraft. Lasting over nine weeks from start to finish and incorporating 65 shows, the tour was staged as a result of Cocker being obliged to embark on a pre-booked series of concerts at a time when his backing band had left him,

whereupon Russell volunteered to recruit musicians and singers.

1983

JAM JAMS UK CHART

Having announced three months earlier that the group was going to split up after a farewell tour, The Jam found themselves in the record-breaking position of having nine reissued singles entering the UK chart simultaneously.

All had been UK hits at least once before, and 'All Around The World', 'David Watts', 'In The City', 'News Of The World', 'Strange Town' and 'The Modern World' had charted twice before when there had been a similar burst of interest in 1980.

Sadly, the obvious interest of their numerous British fans did not make Paul Weller (vocals, guitar), Bruce Foxton (bass) and Rick Buckler (drums) change their decision.

ARRIVALS	
	(Journey)
1931 – Sam Cooke	1950 – Graeme John
1940 – Addie 'Mickie'	Douglas (Kursaal Flyers)
Harris (Shirelles)	1960 – Michael Hutchence
1949 – Nigel Pegrum	(INXS)
(Steeleye Span)	1965 – Andrew Roachford
1949 – Steve Perry	(Roachford)
	★ ★ ★

RAVINGS

1959:
British rock 'n' roll singer Terry Dene joined the army for an obligatory period of national service, but had a nervous breakdown and was discharged only weeks later.

1960:
Soul singer Sam Cooke signed to RCA Records on his 25th birthday.

1972:
Succssful songwriting and production team Holland, Dozier and Holland settled out of court with Motown Records, who had sued the trio when they left the label for which they had produced such major hitmakers as The Supremes and The Four Tops.

★ ★ ★

1978

CHICAGO AXEMAN BLEW HIS MIND

Terry Kath, a founder member and guitarist/vocalist of the group Chicago, paid the ultimate penalty for his carelessness in a bizarre accident – he pulled the trigger of the gun that he was holding to his head in a fit of bravado unaware that it was loaded. It went off, and his brains were scattered like scrambled egg. The foolish accident occurred only eight days before what would have been his 32nd birthday.

Chicago lose guitarist in gun game

Formed in 1967 in the city from which the group took its name, Chicago were originally known as The Big Three, but when they expanded to an eight-piece band and met producer James William Guercio, who had worked with The Buckinghams and Blood, Sweat and Tears, they adopted the name Chicago Transit Authority (abbreviated at times to CTA and eventually simply to Chicago). Initially a punchy jazz-tinged band with aggressive soulful vocals and a strong line in ensemble riffs from a three-piece brass section, the group soon abandoned such distinctive leanings, opting instead for a somewhat bland, but extremely commercial and radio-friendly, sound that had produced two dozen US hit singles by the time of Kath's Russian Roulette tragedy.

Later in 1978, after replacing Kath with Donny Dacus, the group stopped working with producer Guercio, but it made little difference, and by 1990 the group, albeit with somewhat different personnel after the departure of several more original members, including the rhythm section of Pete Cetera and Danny Seraphine, scored their 48th US hit single, making them the 16th biggest rock act ever.

1970

JUDY COLLINS SILENCED IN COURT

Folk star Judy Collins was denied permission – along with fellow folkies Pete Seeger, Country Joe McDonald, Arlo Guthrie and Phil Ochs – to sing as part of her testimony for the defence at the trial of the Chicago Seven. The latter were radical young political activists charged with a wide range of offences connected with the notorious Democratic Party convention held in Chicago when scenes of violent street fighting broke out after Chicago mayor Richard Daley ordered the police force and the National Guard to put an end to anti-Vietnam war protests in the city.

Singing disallowed for Judy Collins

ARRIVALS

1910 – Django Reinhardt
1944 – Jerry Lawson (Persuasions)
1944 – Millie Jackson
1948 – Anita Pointer (Pointer Sisters)
1950 – Billy Cunningham (Box Tops)
1950 – Pat Simmons (Doobie Brothers)
1952 – Robin Zander (Cheap Trick)
1955 – Earl Falconer (UB40)
1955 – Reggie Calloway

★ ★ ★

DEPARTURE LOUNGE

1972 – Big Maybelle (Mabel Louise Smith)
1973 – Edward 'Kid' Ory
1976 – Paul Robeson
1978 – Terry Kath (Chicago)
1978 – Vic Ames (Ames Brothers)
1990 – Allen Collins (Lynyrd Skynyrd)

RAVINGS

1974:
Alvin Stardust made his first appearance since changing his name from Shane Fenton at the Midem Festival, Cannes, France.

★ ★ ★

1982:
Daryl Hall and John Oates collected their first platinum album for *Private Eyes*. In the wake of its million-selling success, its predecessor, *Voices*, also reached the platinum mark.

★ ★ ★

1970

DR ROBERT LAUNCHES MINI-MOOG

The unveiling by its inventor, Dr Robert Moog, of a miniaturized synthesizer known as the mini-moog opened the door for many aspiring groups to proceed beyond the limited vista of two guitars, bass and drums. Even suitable for onstage work, its disposal of the spaghetti forest of wires that were previously the lot of electronic musicians, not to mention the remarkably low price of $2,000, put the mini-moog within the reach of all but the unambitious. The American Federation Of Musicians were uncertain about its advantages to the organization, however, and considered a ban on the instruments they were concerned might affect the ability of some of their members to earn a living as musicians.

ARRIVALS

1936 – Doug Kershaw
1936 – Jack Scott (Jack Scafone Jr.)
1941 – Aaron Neville (Neville Brothers)
1941 – Michael Chapman
1941 – Neil Diamond (Noah Kaminsky)
1941 – Ray Stevens (Ray Ragsdale)
1947 – Jim Rutledge (Bloodrock)

1947 – Warren Zevon
1949 – John Belushi
1958 – Jools Holland

★ ★ ★

DEPARTURE LOUNGE

1970 – James Sheppard
1972 – Gene Austin
1986 – Gordon MacRae

★ ★ ★

RAVINGS

1962: The Beatles signed a management contract with Brian Epstein, although Epstein never signed it himself.

1964: The Osmonds played a musical family alongside Mickey Rooney in *The Seven Little Foys* on American TV.

1979: The Clash released their first single in America, 'I Fought The Law', which was written by Buddy Holly associate Sonny Curtis.

1981: Country girl Dolly Parton topped the US pop charts with the theme song to the film *Nine to Five*, in which she starred.

★ ★ ★

1969

HOMERLESS AT JETHRO'S NEW YORK DEBUT

The only Jethro most Americans previously knew of was Jethro Burns, mandolin-playing half of the popular bluegrass comedy duo, Homer (Henry Haynes) and Jethro (Kenneth Burns), but the New York debut of hitmaking British rock group Jethro Tull made them aware of a second Jethro.

Named after an 18th-century inventor of agricultural implements – he was responsible for the introduction of the seed drill – the group opened for Blood, Sweat and Tears on a two month tour and quickly won over their audience with their unique onstage antics in support of

Tull's Ian Anderson – a balancing act?

lyrically and musically challenging, but remarkably accessible, music.

Fronted by Scottish singer and flautist Ian Anderson, whose one-legged stance during his flute solos was totally unique, the group's driving R & B-flavoured set made them instant favourites with the audience.

1984

YOKO AND SEAN IN LENNON'S LIVERPOOL

Penny Lane and Strawberry Fields were just two of the places in Liverpool visited by John Lennon's widow, Yoko Ono, and their son Sean. Their pilgrimage to the birthplace of the late Beatle provided the opportunity for first-hand experience of landmarks that had inspired some of the immortal songs he and Paul McCartney had written during his years as a Beatle.

DYLAN MISGUIDED OVER HURRICANE

1976

No one has ever doubted Bob Dylan's sincerity in his pursuit of causes in which he believes, but his support for boxer Rubin 'Hurricane' Carter, still in prison after nine years protesting his innocence of a fatal shooting conviction, was thought by many to be a misjudgement. In 1975 Dylan and the entire Rolling Thunder Revue band played a Madison Square Garden benefit concert to publicize Carter's plight and raise funds for his appeal.

Night Of The Hurricane II took place at Houston Astrodrome, with a bill pre-advertised as featuring Dylan and his Rolling Thunderers, Isaac Hayes and Stevie Wonder. Surprise guests included Ringo Starr, Stephen Stills and Carlos Santana – the two guitarist guests fought an instrumental duel on an extended version of 'Black Queen'.

Partly due to the short notice – the benefit had been planned for New Orleans but was switched to Houston with a week to go – and also due to growing doubts about Carter's innocence, the expected turnout of 60,000 fans willing to pay $12.50 was halved to a disappointing 30,000 in reality. Confusion over the intentions behind the event plus sky-high staging costs meant that the Hurricane Carter fund received only $10,000 from the night's show – and that a direct donation from the owners of the Astrodrome.

RAVINGS

1964:
Producer Phil Spector appeared on the panel of BBC TV's *Juke Box Jury* show in London, which gave its verdict on new releases.

★ ★ ★

1984:
Yoko Ono made a £250,000 ($375,000) donation to Liverpool old people's home Strawberry Fields, the institution that inspired the song written by her late husband, John Lennon, and Paul McCartney that became a massive international hit in 1967.

1989:
Bobby Brown was arrested in Georgia for alleged lewdness on stage and fined $652.

★ ★ ★

ARRIVALS

1899 – 'Sleepy' John Estes
1915 – Ewan MacColl
1938 – Etta James (Etta James Hawkins)
1943 – Anita Pallenberg
1946 – Ronnie Brandon (McCoys)
1954 – Richard Finch (K.C. and the Sunshine Band)
1956 – Andy Cox (Beat/Fine Young Cannibals)
1958 – Gary Tibbs (Roxy Music/Adam and the Ants)
1962 – Peter Coyle (Lotus Eaters)
1963 – Carl Fysh (Brother Beyond)
1971 – China Kantner (daughter of Grace Slick and Paul Kantner)
1982 – Chelsea Jane Crowell (daughter of Rosanne Cash and Rodney Crowell)

★ ★ ★

DEPARTURE LOUNGE

1976 – Chris Kenner

★ ★ ★

1956

Elvis's chart-topping hotel

PRESLEY HEARTBREAKER HITS THE STREET

RCA Records in the US released the first single by their new signing, Elvis Presley, coupling the echo-drenched 'Heartbreak Hotel' with 'I Was The One'. Having purchased his contract from Sam Phillips at Sun Records in Memphis for an incredible $35,000 (plus a $5,000 bonus to Presley himself), the label was understandably anxious about how quickly they could recoup such an immense advance, but there was no need to worry – on April 21 the single reached No. 1, remaining there for eight weeks.

1984

JACKSON'S CURLS CRACKLE

It would be difficult to believe that filming an advertising commercial for a soft drink could be described as a hazardous undertaking, but superstar Michael Jackson might disagree – and he has the scars to prove his point. During the shooting of an advertisement directed by Giraldi for his concert tour sponsors, Pepsi Cola, an accidental flare explosion ignited hair spray that had just been applied to the world-famous vocalist's crowning glory, and the conflagration that followed produced second-degree burns on his head and neck.

Jackson cheats fire

No one is precisely certain how the incident occurred, but it was only quick thinking of staff and crew that prevented a far greater tragedy.

Jackson was hospitalized following the incident, and a Jackson aide assured horrified fans and admirers in a press statement that his employer's injuries were neither as serious nor as potentially permanent as they might have been had the fire not been so swiftly extinguished, and that Jackson intended to return to work as soon as possible. While his desire to restart his activities so quickly was laudable, his commitments to Pepsi, which involved a $5 million sponsorship deal, may have somewhat forced his hand. Part of the agreement was that Jackson would always hold or drink a can of the soft drink in any promotional activity.

ARRIVALS

1900 – Clayton 'Pappy' McMichen
1934 – Huey 'Piano' Smith
1939 – Marshall Lieb (Teddy Bears)
1942 – Dave Rowland (J. D. Sumner and The Stamps, Dave and Sugar)
1949 – Derek Holt (Climax Blues Band)
1951 – Andy Hummel (Big Star)
1951 – David Briggs (Little River Band)
1957 – Eddie Van Halen (Van Halen)
1958 – Norman Hassan (UB40)
1963 – Andrew Ridgeley (Wham!)
1963 – Jazzie B. (Soul II Soul)
1966 – Pim Jones (Hipsway)

★ ★ ★

RAVINGS

1956:
Buddy Holly's first formal recording session took place at the Nashville studios of Decca (MCA).

1967:
Mick Jagger's verdict on a show by newcomer Jimi Hendrix was, 'The most sexual thing I've seen in a long time!'

1970:
The Ourimbah Festival, the first such rock event held in Australia, attracted more than 11,000 fans, only 26 of whom were arrested for misbehaviour.

1970:
John Lennon and Phil Spector wrote and recorded 'Instant Karma' in one day.

1980:
Prince made his TV debut on Dick Clark's *American Bandstand*.

★ ★ ★

1977

FLEETWOOD MAC FOUNDER IN MENTAL INSTITUTION

Peter Green, the gifted but sometimes unpredictable guitarist who with drummer Mick Fleetwood founded the internationally adored Fleetwood Mac, the British blues band that became Anglo-American stadium rock headliners after several years in the doldrums, was committed to a mental hospital. Green had attacked his accountant with an air rifle – the latter was attempting to deliver a royalty cheque for $30,000, but Green subsequently maintained that he did not want the cheque .

Green, who had left

Green – keeping royaltie[s] away with a gun!

the band in [...] effective[...] mu[...]

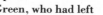

1981

BANKRUPTCY FOR CAPRICORN

Allman Brothers – Capricorn stars

Georgia-based Capricorn Records, the label that had championed and patronized the very popular 'southern rock' genre, filed for bankruptcy in Macon, Georgia.

Founded by Phil Walden, ex-manager of Otis Redding, to provide a local alternative for bands who would otherwise find it necessary to find record deals in New York, Los Angeles or Nashville, the label's first and biggest stars were The Allman Brothers, the brilliant R & B-based group launched by brothers Duane and Gregg Allman. It was Duane's quicksilver slide guitar work that first enthralled Walden and inspired him to launch Capricorn, and the label's catalogue was built around various Allman Brothers projects, both with the band and with solo albums. Duane's untimely death in a 1971 motorcycle crash, however, and the death in similar circumstances of bass player Berry Oakley, led the group to break up by 1976.

Among the other acts on Capricorn were the intriguingly named Wet Willie, the bluesy Grinderswitch, and ex-Delaney and Bonnie principal, Bonnie Bramlett. US President Jimmy Carter was a major supporter of his local hometown label and was interviewed in Macon before becoming President for BBC TV's rock show *The Old Grey Whistle Test*.

ARRIVALS

1919 – David Seville (Ross Bagdasarian) (inventor of The Chipmunks)
1920 – Helmut Zacharias
1930 – Bobby Bland (Robert Calvin Bland)
1931 – Rudi Maugeri (Crew Cuts)
1937 – Buddy Emmons
1944 – Kevin Coyne

1945 – Nick Mason (Pink Floyd)
1947 – Nedra Talley (The Ronettes)
1948 – Kim Gardner (Ashton, Gardner and Dyke)
1951 – Brian Downey (Thin Lizzy)
1951 – Seth Justman (J. Geils Band)
1961 – Gillian Gilbert (New Order)

1961 – Martin Degville (Sigue Sigue Sputnik)
1964 – Miguel (Migi) Drummond (Curiosity Killed the Cat)

★ ★ ★

DEPARTURE LOUNGE

1972 – Mahalia Jackson

★ ★ ★

1956

MARTIN PRODUCTIONS DOMINATE UK CHART

Productions by George Martin occupied three places in the Top 20 of the UK singles chart. Eve Boswell's 'Pickin' A Chicken' was followed by the monologue by Irish sports commentator Eamonn Andrews, 'The Shifting Whispering Sands', while dance band vocalist Dick James scored with the theme to a popular children's TV series, 'Robin Hood'.

Seven years later, Martin and James would be reacquainted when James became the publisher of music by The Beatles, Martin's most successful clients.

1976

GARY GLITTER RETIRES – OR NOT

Larger than life UK chart star Gary Glitter announced his retirement from live performances after a televised 'farewell show'. The one-time Paul Gadd/Paul Raven/Paul Monday opted for the name Gary Glitter in 1971 after adding vocals to the second half of a lengthy stomping instrumental with the inventive title of 'Rock 'n' Roll Parts 1 and 2'.

Clothed in tinfoil, he promoted the single in 1972 when it was released, and after popularity in discotheques had been followed by airplay on Radio Luxembourg and then on the national BBC Radio One, his career was finally off the ground after 12 years of failure as a recording artist.

With his new Glitter persona he enjoyed eleven straight UK Top 10 hits including three chart-toppers in around three years, but as the glamrock era, which had made him a star, tailed off, his weight and size increased, and he was made bankrupt in 1977 after non-payment of taxes. A comeback tour in 1980 was followed by cult success that continues today. There is nothing quite like a good retirement story to grab the headlines and provoke interest in a comeback . . .

Glitter – retirement only temporary

1984

Frankie Says he's at the top

RELAX FRANKIE – YOU'RE NUMBER ONE!

'Relax', the single by Liverpool group Frankie Goes To Hollywood, hit No. 1 and was destined to spend a year on the chart despite an extensive airplay ban for its allegedly obscene lyrics. Britain went Frankie mad, and the hottest fashion items during the summer were oversized T-shirts with either the single's title or the words 'Frankie Says' emblazened across numerous chests.

However, reports suggested that while the advantages of such wide-ranging free publicity were incalculable, so was the amount the band and their managers lost due to many of the T-shirts being counterfeit.

1970

STARS PLAY GIANT ANTI-WAR BENEFIT IN NEW YORK

A diverse bunch including Jimi Hendrix, The Rascals, Blood Sweat and Tears, Judy Collins, Harry Belafonte, Dave Brubeck, The Voices Of East Harlem and the cast of the musical *Hair* were among the many artists who appeared at New York's Madison Square Garden in an effort to raise nearly $150,000 for the Vietnam Moratorium Committee, organizers of the peace movement protesting against American involvement in the Vietnam war.

January

34 January

Boomto

1962

WARNER BROS SIGN NEW YORK FOLK TRIO

World-beating folkies Peter, Paul and Mary

Greenwich Village folk favourites Peter (Yarrow), Paul (Stookey) and Mary (Travers) signed with Warner Bros Records after being created as a trio under the auspices of Albert Grossman, manager of Odetta and other folk stars (later to include Bob Dylan).

Yarrow had been a solo performer, Stookey a stand-up comic and Travers had worked in the chorus of a Broadway show starring Mort Sahl. The combination of their voices created a magic sound that brought them 19 US hit singles during the 1960s. Among the biggest being 'If I Had A Hammer', 'Puff The Magic Dragon' (a song for children that was suspected by the suspicious and ultra-narrow-minded of being about marijuana), 'Blowin' In The Wind' (probably the first song by Bob Dylan to become a million seller), 'Don't Think Twice, It's All Right' and their only No. 1, 'Leaving On A Jet Plane', which was written by a then unknown John Denver.

1979

I WANT TO SHOOT SHOOT SHOOT . . .

San Diego teenager Brenda Spencer seemed stuck for a good answer when quizzed by police about why she had opened fire on her schoolmates, killing eleven of them. 'I don't like Mondays' was her excuse, and her objection to the first working day of the week made world headlines, six months later becoming the inspiration for Bob Geldof, leader of Dublin group The Boomtown Rats, to write a song titled 'I Don't Like Mondays', which topped the UK chart for a month later in the year. Maybe it was not so surprising that this huge British hit was a comparative flop in the US – it was, after all, about an American schoolgirl.

...wn Bob – inspired by teenage murderess.

1969

UP ON THE ROOF – BEATLES FINAL LIVE SHOW

The Beatles made their last live appearance with an impromptu 42 minute concert on the roof of their Apple Corps headquarters in London's Savile Row.

The show was cut short when a large crowd gathered in the street outside, and this, combined with the noise of full-blooded rock music, provoked complaints from the occupants of neighbouring buildings in London's high-class tailoring district, who called the police to stop the session.

The performance was being filmed for inclusion in the documentary about the recording of the Beatles album *Let It Be,* and the band were playing a new song, 'Get Back', with able support from black American keyboard player Billy Preston when the plugs were pulled and the show ended. It was a sadly anti-climactic end to a remarkable era in the history of rock music.

The previous live show by The Beatles had taken place at San Francisco's Candlestick Park back in August, 1966, a few days after their remarkable live concert at New York's Shea Stadium. The only authorized live album by The Beatles was *The Beatles At The Hollywood Bowl,* recorded in 1965 but not released until 1977.

1961

ROCK'S FIRST PRODUCERS LAUNCH INDEPENDENT PRODUCTION COMPANY

Mike Stoller (left) and Jerry Leiber flank a well-known rock star

Jerry Leiber and Mike Stoller, writers and/or producers of some of rock 'n' roll's greatest hits, including such Elvis Presley smashes as 'Hound Dog', 'Jailhouse Rock', 'Loving You' and 'Baby I Don't Care', many hits for The Coasters including 'Searchin', 'Yakety Yak', 'Charlie Brown' and 'Little Egypt', as well as songs for Dion, The Drifters, The Clovers, Sammy Turner, etc., announced plans to form an independent production company to make finished records for established labels. The company intended to undertake all aspects of creative management, from writing and publishing songs to producing and engineering completed masters. Among the labels immediately happy to sign acts produced by the new production hous[e] Atlantic (wh[o] enjoyed [a] Leib[er] [...] sign[...]

1967

SEEGER'S SHOW GOES AHEAD DESPITE POSSIBLE LEGAL ACTION

A New York Supreme Court dismissed a lawsuit brought by officials of Yorktown Heights High School who were attempting to cancel a concert by folk singer/left-wing political activist Pete Seeger to an audience composed of the school's students.

Pete Seeger – would this man incite a riot?

The officials feared that Seeger's appearance might incite students to riot, so inflammatory was his political stance – he had been blacklisted in the 1950s for sympathizing with victims of the McCarthy anti-communist witch-hunts, and had supported anti-Vietnam protests during the 1960s, when The Byrds had scored a major hit with their cover version of his setting of a biblical passage from Ecclesiasticus, 'Turn ! Turn ! Turn !'.

In the event, the concert took place five days later, and the paranoid fears of the school board were discovered to be completely unfounded. The 50 or more police officers hired to maintain decorum were left to twiddle their batons as the concert passed peacefully and totally without incident.

1988

BEASTIE BOYS BREAK-UP NOT PERMANENT

The controversial New York white rap trio The Beastie Boys denied widespread press reports that they had broken up. The news would have been most welcome to owners of Volkswagen cars whose vehicles had been stripped of the German automobile manaufacturer's distinctive trademark in emulation of the group's use of the symbols as medallions. However, the group members were pursuing individual activities at the time, perhaps in the hope of defusing a situation that seemed to have got out of control at times, with rioting often following their live shows - King

Beasties – holiday cooling-down period

Ad-Rock (Adam Horowitz) had been arrested in Liverpool on charges of Actual Bodily Harm after a concert at the city's Royal Court Theatre.

The son of respected playwright Israel Horowitz, Ad-Rock had formed the band with Mike D (Mike Diamond) and MCA (Adam Yauch) in 1981 to play at MCA's 15th birthday party. The individual projects that preceded the release of the group's *Paul's Boutique* album included Ad-Rock's cameo appearance in the TV series *The Equalizer*.

1986

HEART ATTACK CLAIMS MAN WITH GOLDEN EARS, DICK JAMES

Dick James – 'Robin Hood' led to Merseybeat success

Dick James. the former dance band vocalist who moved into music publishing when his hairline thinned and his waistline began to thicken, died at the age of 65 after a heart attack.

As a singer, James won the affection of a generation of British kids when he recorded the theme song for the top-rated 1950s TV series, *Robin Hood*. The producer of that theme had been an EMI Records A & R man named George Martin.

In 1962, Martin was heavily involved in another enterprise connected with James, who became the music publisher of The Beatles, the unknown Liverpool group who had just been signed by Martin to EMI's Parlophone label.

Although reportedly not over-impressed with 'Love Me Do', the first song he heard, James was impressed by the fact that, unlike most British groups at the time, this bunch wrote a large proportion of their own repertoire. He drafted a contract whereby he took 50 per cent of future profits generated by songs written by John Lennon and Paul McCartney, with the latter duo receiving 20 per cent each and the group's manager, Brian Epstein, the remaining 10 per cent. James also established a company with the appropriate name of Northern Songs to administer the immense income that soon began to flood in as Beatlemania became an international sensation.

After Epstein died and The Beatles split up, both Lennon and McCartney unsuccessfully attempted to wrest ownership of Northern Songs from James, but both lost out when Michael Jackson acquired the company for an immense amount (a reported $47 million) in 1985 from ATV Music, to whom James had sold it earlier.

Dick James was also shrewd enough to support a young songwriting duo, lyricist Bernie Taupin and singer/pianist Reg Dwight (aka Elton John), in 1966 when their compositions began to show promise. The small retainers he paid them, along with time in the company's demo studio, was a small price to pay for the vast income their songs would generate, but unfortunately this relationship also ended in law suits and, after a long and bitter court case, Taupin and John were awarded £5 million ($7.5 million) for royalties that the court decreed they should have been paid.

NOT IF – BUT WHEN

It was widely felt that the death of former Sex Pistol Sid Vicious was inevitable. If he was not executed for the murder of his American girlfriend, Nancy Spungen, he would overdose on some illegal substance. In fact, it was the latter method consigned the 21-year-old icon to his grave.

Sid Vicious – ex-Pistol

Sid, whose real name was either John Ritchie or John Beverley, had been freed on bail by a New York court after being charged with the murder in October 1978 of 'nauseating Nancy' (as his Sex Pistols colleagues referred to her) at the Chelsea Hotel.

Vicious's death, resulting from a heroin overdose, occurred at the Greenwich Village apartment of his new girlfriend, Michelle Robinson, and left many questions unanswered

about the the circumstances surrounding the fatal stabbing that caused Spungen's death.

Although Vicious had spent much of his time since her death attempting to free himself of his addiction to heroin, either in prison or in clinics for detoxification, it was presumed that the quantity of heroin he had used in his final fix was greater than the decreased tolerance level his body possessed after abstaining from the drug

for some weeks.

Vicious was not the original bass player with The Sex Pistols (and in fact was a total novice on

the instrument when he replaced Glen Matlock in February, 1977 - his only previous musical experience was on

drums). He was invited to join the group as a result of his friendship with vocalist John Lydon (Johnny Rotten).

TAB AND SONNY IN 'YOUNG LOVE' CHART BATTLE

Two versions of the same song, 'Young Love', were slugging it out in the Top 3 of the US singles chart. Written in 1956 by Carole Joyner and Ric Cartey, the song sold over a million copies for both country-and-western singer Sonny

James (born James Loden), and for film star Tab Hunter (real name Arthur Kelm). Eventually honours were more or less even – James hit the No. 1 spot first, but his version was outsold by Hunter a week later.

Tab Hunter, film star turned chart-topper.

ARRIVALS

1889 – Lonnie Johnson	(Gentle Giant)
1927 – Stan Getz	1947 – John 'Pugwash'
1934 – Skip Battin	Weathers (Gentle Giant,
1940 – Alan Caddy	Man)
(Tornados)	1948 – Alan McKay (Earth
1942 – Graham Nash	Wind and Fire)
(Hollies, CSN)	1963 – Dan Reed
1943 – Peter Macbeth	
(Foundations)	★ ★ ★
1946 – 'Whistling' Jack	
Smith (Billy Moeller)	## DEPARTURE LOUNGE
1946 – Howard Bellamy	
(Bellamy Brothers)	1979 – Sid Vicious
1947 – Derek Shulman	★ ★ ★

RAVINGS

1956:
The Coasters signed to Atlantic Records. They would score 17 US hits before the end of 1961.

★ ★ ★

1962:
Liberty Records was launched in the UK.

★ ★ ★

1967:
The Bee Gees returned to Britain from Australia, where they had achieved stardom.

★ ★ ★

1981:
Duran Duran's first single, 'Planet Earth', was released. The band took its name from the villain in the Jane Fonda movie *Barbarella*.

★ ★ ★

THE DAY THE MUSIC DIED

Buddy Holly, Ritchie Valens and The Big Bopper were tragically killed when the single-engined light aircraft they had hired to fly them from Mason City, Iowa, to Fargo, North Dakota, crashed in a snowstorm about ten minutes after take-off. The three artists were appearing, along with Dion and The Belmonts and Frankie Sardo, on a tour known as the Winter Dance Party, which had just played a sell-out date to 1,000 fans at the Surf Ballroom, Clear Lake, Iowa.

News of the tragedy spread worldwide within hours, terminating a highly successful career that had lasted only three years during which Holly (real name Charles Hardin Holley), from Lubbock, Texas, had carved himself a permanent niche in the history of popular music with a string of hits and a distinctive and unique style.

Among the songs that Holly wrote and/or recorded with his backing group The Crickets were 'That'll Be The Day', 'Oh Boy!', 'Not Fade Away', 'Rave On', 'Think It Over', and many more that later became rock classics.

The death of Ritchie Valens was also a tragedy, although the 17-year-old Los Angeles-based Mexican had only

scored two hits at the time, with the infectious 'Come On Let's Go' and the double-sided smash, 'Donna'/'La Bamba'.

The third victim of the crash, The Big Bopper, was in reality disc jockey J. P. Richardson, who had just scored a major hit with a novelty song, 'Chantilly Lace', and was touring to promote its follow-up, 'Big Bopper's Wedding'.

Buddy Holly – gone but not forgotten

JOE MEEK COMMITS SUICIDE ON ANNIVERSARY OF HOLLY'S DEATH

Visionary record producer Joe Meek, who was responsible for such worldwide hits as 'Telstar' by The Tornados, 'Have I The Right' by The Honeycombs and several

smashes for John Leyton, including 'Johnny Remember Me', shot his landlady before turning the gun on himself.

Meek claimed to have contacted Buddy Holly

during seances, and his penchant for making Holly-influenced records suggested that the shooting's occurrence on the eighth anniversary of Holly's death was more than coincidence.

RAVINGS

1969:
Beatles John Lennon, George Harrison and Ringo Starr appointed Rolling Stones manager Allen Klein as their new Mr Fix-It. Paul McCartney refused to sign with Klein, preferring his father-in-law, Lee Eastman.

1990:
For the first time, the Top 3 of the UK singles chart featured non-British and non-American acts: Ireland's Sinead O'Connor ('Nothing Compares 2 U'), Australia's Kylie Minogue ('Tears On My Pillow') and Belgium's Technotronic ('Get Up').

ARRIVALS				DEPARTURE LOUNGE
1940 – Angelo D'Aleo (Dion and The Belmonts)	(Hollies) 1945 – Johnny Cymbal 1946 – Stan Webb	(Melanie Safka) 1948 – John 'Ozzy' Osbourne	(Big Country) 1959 – Laurence 'Lol' Tolhurst	1959 – Buddy Holly
1943 – Dennis Edwards (The Temptations)	(Chicken Shack) 1947 – Dave Davies	(Black Sabbath) 1949 – Jim Lockhart	(The Cure)	1959 – Richie Valens
1943 – Eric Haydock	(The Kinks) 1947 – Melanie	(Horslips) 1957 – Tony Butler	★ ★ ★	1959 – The Big Bopper 1967 – Joe Meek

1983

TRAGIC KAREN'S FATAL HEART ATTACK

Karen Carpenter, who died at 32

Less than a month before she would have reached her 33rd birthday, the sweet-voiced Karen Carpenter, lead vocalist with the internationally successful brother and sister duo, The Carpenters, was found unconscious at her parents' home in Downey, California. She was rushed to hospital, but never regained consciousness. The coroner in Los Angeles who conducted the post mortem gave the cause of death as 'heartbeat irregularities brought on by chemical imbalances associated with anorexia.

Karen and her older brother, Richard, had become among the biggest acts in the world during the 1970s, when their immaculately crafted songs had given them chart-topping albums and 24 US hits, including ten that made the US Top 3. '(They Long To Be) Close To You', 'Top Of The World' and their revival of 'Please Mr Postman' all topped the chart.

Criticized by some commentators for the antiseptic nature of their records, the 'Downey Duo', as they were dubbed in *Rolling Stone* magazine, were nevertheless incredibly popular.

1989

GUNS N'ROSES PLACE TWO ALBUMS IN US TOP 5

There are various theories about how vocalist Axl Rose acquired his name. One version suggests that William Bailey did not discover that his real surname was actually Rose until he was 17, his father having left home soon after he was born, and his mother having remarried, while 'Axl' came from a group he had played with, presumably called The Axles. A slightly more likely version is that his adopted name is an anagram of the words 'oral sex', and the numerous controversies and disturbances in which he and the band he fronts, Guns n'Roses, give this some credence.

The anti-authoritarian stance of Guns n'Roses did not made them popular with concert promoters and the music business in general, but their immense following among younger record-buyers made them arguably one of the biggest acts in the world.

Two of their albums, *Appetite For Destruction* and an eight-track mini album, *G n'R Lies*, were both listed in the Top 5 of the US album chart in the same week, making them the first act to achieve this feat for 15 years. The last artist to do this was Jim Croce, who had sadly died shortly before his mega-success. Three years later, country star Garth Brooks would duplicate the achievement.

Guns n'Roses – two Top 5 albums in the same week.

1966

STAFF SERGEANT'S GUNG-HO SOLILOQUY SPLITS STATES

America was split by controversy over a single that entered the US chart by a former member of US Army Special Forces, Staff Sergeant Barry Sadler, whose leg was injured in a booby trap while he was on active service.

'The Ballad Of The Green Berets' was a narrative spoken over a martial rhythm extolling the activities of his unit in Vietnam, and it eventually topped the US singles chart, but peaked outside the Top 20 in Britain.

As flag-waving patriots and anti-war protestors lined up on opposite sides of the fence, Sadler's anthem, written with author Robin Moore, whose book *The Green Berets* had inspired the song, rocketed up the charts. Simultaneously, the identically entitled album that included the hit single burst into the US chart, eventually staying at No. 1 for over a month.

Sadler was not heard of again for some years, although in 1978 he was involved in the Nashville shooting of songwriter Lee Bellamy.

Then, in 1981, Sadler was also involved in the shooting of his erstwhile business partner – Sadler protested his innocence by saying, 'I was a Green Beret – if I'd shot him, he'd be dead'. Sadler himself died of a heart attack in 1989, the year after he was shot in the head during a robbery at his home in Guatemala.

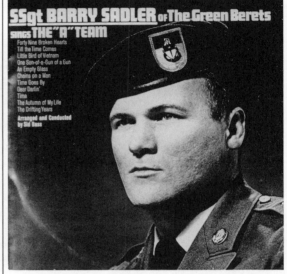

Staff Sergeant Barry Sadler's moment of glory (?) came in 1966

1957

HALEY'S ARRIVAL CAUSES LONDON RIOTS

Bill Haley, the shortlived first rock 'n' roll monarch

Thousands of British rock 'n' roll fans crowded into London's Victoria Station to greet American originator Bill Haley, whose 'Rock Around The Clock' was the first rock 'n' roll classic. Haley and his band, The Comets, had arrived by train from Southampton after crossing the Atlantic on the liner *Queen Elizabeth*, and fans at Victoria grappled with police in efforts to get closer to their hero. It was a suitably rowdy start to a concert tour that continued to make front page news in the British mainstream press for weeks, and consolidated Haley's position among his British following.

ARRIVALS

1933 – Claude King
1935 – Alex Harvey
1941 – Barrett Strong
1942 – Corey Wells (Three Dog Night)
1943 – Chuck Winfield (Blood, Sweat and Tears)
1943 – Sven Johannson (Tangerine Dream)
1944 – Al Kooper (Blood, Sweat and Tears)
1949 – Nigel Olsson

1949 – Norman Barratt (Gravy Train)
1944 – James R.Cobb (Classics IV)
1941 – Henson Cargill
1943 – Larry Tamblyn (Standells)

DEPARTURE LOUNGE

1976 – Rudy Pompilli (Bill Haley's Comets)

RAVINGS

1955: New York radio station WNEW announced the winners of a popularity poll: Perry Como, The Crew-Cuts, Patti Page and Ray Anthony were the biggest turn-ons for listeners to the station.

1961: 'Will You Love Me Tomorrow' by The Shirelles topped the US chart.

1976: 19 years to the day since he first set foot on British soil as a member of Bill Haley's Comets, sax player Rudy Pompilli died.

1977: Rolling Stones signed to EMI and Iggy Pop signed to RCA.

★ ★ ★

1981

SURVIVING FABS REMEMBER DEAD COLLEAGUE

And then there were three

On the same day that Yoko Ono's single, 'Walking On Thin Ice – For John', was released in the US, recording began on another single on which the three remaining members of The Beatles reunited under George Harrison's auspices to cut their own tribute to John Lennon.

John Lennon had been shot and killed two months earlier outside The Record Plant, the New York studio where he had ironically been mixing 'Walking On Thin Ice' that evening. George Harrison had written a song entitled 'All Those Years Ago' for Ringo Starr, who had actually recorded it for an album he was making at the time called *Can't Fight Lightning*. Ringo eventually decided not to include the song, which

also featured George, on that album, and to further complicate matters, the album was considerably revamped and finally emerged in late 1981 under the title *Stop And Smell The Roses*. All this meant that George had an unheard song whose lyrics he could adapt to make into a tribute to his late Beatle comrade. He apparently used the original instrumental track from Ringo's version (on which the

latter had obviously participated), and added his own lead vocal in place of Ringo's.

Shortly afterwards, Paul and Linda McCartney added backing vocals to those that already existed by Ringo, making 'All Those Years Ago' the first post-Beatles track to feature Harrison, McCartney and Starr – however, they were not all in the studio together at any time during the recording of the track.

RAVINGS

1986:
The mother and sister of Irish vocalist and erstwhile Undertones front man Feargal Sharkey were held at gunpoint by terrorists in Londonderry.

1971:
Conway Twitty and Loretta Lynn made their debut in the US country charts as a duo with 'After The Fire Has Gone', which became the first of their five duets to top that chart in less than five years.
★ ★ ★

1982

DEUTSCHLAND UBER (W)AL(L)ES

Synthesizer wizards Kraftwerk (known as perpetrators of so-called 'industrial' music) became the first German act to top the UK singles chart, when their insistent double-sided hit, 'Computer Love'/'The Model', overtook the Shakin' Stevens revival of the 1958 US hit by The Crescendos, 'Oh Julie', after the latter had become the Welsh rock 'n' roller's third No. 1 single in a year.

Originally 'Computer Love' had been the 'A' side, but the single fared badly. Then disc-jockeys started to pick up on the flip side, 'The Model', a track from their 1978 album *Man Machine*. At that point it became a dance-floor favourite, and in the last week of that year it re-entered the chart, going right to the top.

Kraftwerk – very efficient rhythm

ARRIVALS

1916 – Bill Doggett
1941 – Dave Berry (David Grundy)
1943 – Fabian (Fabiano Forte)
1945 – Bob Marley (Robert Nesta Marley)
1950 – Mike Batt
1950 – Natalie Cole

1950 – Punky Meadows (Angel)
1966 – Rick Astley
★ ★ ★

DEPARTURE LOUNGE

1960 – Jesse Belvin
1976 – Vince Guaraldi
1981 – Hugo Montenegro

BEATLEMANIA HITS USA AS FAB FOUR FLY IN

1964

Riots greeted the arrival of The Beatles in New York

It was official – Beatlemania was not a public relations hype dreamed up by record company executives and concert promoters.

The kids of America experienced it for real when Pan-Am flight PA 101 touched down at New York's Kennedy Airport, causing a near riot as John, Paul, George and Ringo set foot on American soil for the first time.

10,000 fans were there to welcome the group, with radio, television and newsreel crews to capture the moment and a few words from the mop tops at a chaotic press conference.

The group arrived to find their single, 'I Want To Hold Your Hand', at the top of the US chart, where it had climbed within three weeks of release, a remarkable feat for a previously unknown act, making it the fastest-selling single ever for Capitol Records. They had declined to release three earlier singles and the group's debut album *Introducing The Beatles* (the US equivalent of the British *Please Please Me* album).

RAVINGS

1959:
1,000 mourners attended Buddy Holly's funeral at Lubbock City Cemetery in Texas.

1965:
George Harrison endured a tonsillectomy at London's University College Hospital.

1980:
Pink Floyd premiered their live version of *The Wall* in Los Angeles. The first half of the show featured the building of a 30 feet high wall across the stage, which was then demolished after the intermission.

1984:
Columbia (CBS) Records threw a party for Michael Jackson at New York's Museum Of Natural History.

★ ★ ★

SIMON DEFENDS SOUTH AFRICAN RECORDINGS

1987

Paul Simon flew into London and was immediately forced to defend his decision to record tracks for his *Graceland* album in South Africa, a country that was the subject of an international political and cultural boycott because of its policy of racial segregation (apartheid).

Simon's use of local black musicians such as members of the vocal group Ladysmith Black Mambazo helped to make *Graceland* an interestingly different and most successful album, but his brazen breaking of the boycott aroused the ire of many anti-apartheid activists. However, Simon refused to apologize, and maintained, quite reasonably, that music can never have political frontiers – the end justifies the means, especially when great musicians are provided with a wider international platform on which to perform.

Paul Simon, who broke the UN boycott over South Africa

1990

DEL SHANNON SUICIDE TRAGEDY

Things had appeared to be looking up for Sixties rock star Del Shannon. He had all but completed his first new album for eight years, with production chores shared by two major contemporary stars, Tom Petty and Jeff Lynne.

Del Shannon, who committed suicide when his tribulations seemed to be over

Both had produced tracks for Shannon previously, Lynne, an obscure 1975 single and Petty, Shannon's previous album, the critically acclaimed *Drop Down And Get Me*, which included Shannon's only hit single since 1966, his revival of the Phil Phillips classic, 'Sea Of Love'.

Even more significantly, both Petty and Lynne were members of The Traveling Wilburys, the hugely successful 'occasional supergroup' that also featured Bob Dylan and George Harrison. The fifth original member, Roy Orbison, had died in December 1988, and there was considerable speculation about the possible identity of a replacement. A name frequently mentioned was that of Del Shannon, but he had not been invited to sessions for the group's second album, the amusingly entitled *Volume 3*. Shannon had recently remarried. Divorcing his first wife after over 20 years of marriage, his new wife was from the same generation as his children, who constantly fought with their stepmother. Shannon's schizophrenic paranoia was compounded by the fact that he was actually five years older than he had claimed when he had his first hit in 1961 with 'Runaway', which topped the singles chart on both sides of the Atlantic. He was rapidly losing his hair and had worn a wig for many years as Del Shannon, but appeared with thinning hair when he was off duty and used his real name of Charles Westover. Whether these were sufficient reasons for Shannon to turn his gun on himself at his home in Santa Monica, California is a difficult question to answer.

1969

BLIND FAITH ASSEMBLE

So-called 'supergroup' Blind Faith

The demise of Cream had left Eric Clapton without a group in which his mercurial lead guitar prowess could be expressed to best advantage, although he was reportedly unwilling to further tolerate the pressures of pop stardom. Surprisingly, he teamed up with Steve Winwood, whose group Traffic had recently fallen apart. Blind Faith was completed by Clapton's ex-colleague in Cream, drummer Ginger Baker, and bass player Ric Grech, previously with Family.

ARRIVALS

1889 – Lonnie Johnson (Alonzo Johnson)
1902 – Harold 'Pappy' Daily
1931 – James Dean (James Byron)
1932 – John Williams
1938 – Ray Sharpe
1941 – Tom Rush
1942 – Terry Melcher
1943 – Creed Bratton (Grass Roots)
1944 – Jim Capaldi (Traffic)
1946 – Adolpho 'Fito' de la Parra (Canned Heat)
1950 – Dan Seals
1950 – Ted Turner (Wishbone Ash)
1962 – Ken McCluskey (Bluebells)

★ ★ ★

DEPARTURE LOUNGE

1990 – Del Shannon

RAVINGS

1965:
US born, UK based P. J. Proby (real name James Marcus Smith) was banned from US TV's top rated *Shindig* show when producers read reports of the singer's repeated onstage trouser-splitting exploits in Britain.

1967:
Peter (Asher) and Gordon (Waller) discontinued their singing partnership that had produced 14 US hit singles since mid-1964.

1969:
The Move topped the UK chart with 'Blackberry Way'.
★ ★ ★

1981

CLOCK STOPS FOR HALEY

Bill Haley (William John Clifton Haley), the first white artist to score a pop chart hit with a rock 'n' roll record and the man who was probably the most influential performer during the music's infancy (until the arrival of a certain Elvis Presley), died in his sleep at Harlington, Texas, at the age of 56. He had been unwell for some time and had become a heavy drinker.

In many ways, Haley was an unlikely figure to be a central part of the biggest shake-up in popular music during the 20th century. When overnight fame occurred for him in 1955, and the *Rock Around The Clock* movie in which he starred provoked riots, he was already in his thirtieth year, and his chubby face topped by an eye-catching kiss curl hardly made him a role model for young black-leather rebels – it was no surprise when he was eclipsed by the arrival of the mean, moody and magnificent Presley.

Haley and his backing group, The Comets, were a huge international draw between 1955 and 1957, when 21 of their singles were listed in the *Billboard* pop singles chart, including 'Burn That Candle', 'See You Later Alligator', 'The Saints Rock 'n' Roll', 'Rockin' Thru The Rye', 'Rip It Up' and 'Rudy's Rock'. It was estimated that he had sold over 60 million records during his career.

The group also made appearances in such films as *Rock Around The Clock* and *Don't Knock The Rock*. By 1958, Haley's influence had greatly diminished, and while he occasionally continued to record and tour, he never again approached his mid-Fifties glories.

The late Bill Haley

1987

HOUSEMARTINS SCOOP BRITS AWARD

The Housemartins, a quartet claiming to be from the some-what unlikely Yorkshire city of Hull, won the Best British Newcomers title at the sixth annual BRITS Awards, no doubt strongly assisted by the chart-topping achievement of their cover of the Isley/Jasper/Isley hit, 'Caravan Of Love'. Within days, there were allegations in the British tabloid press that some group members came from the south of England.

Housemartins – from Hull or Horsham?

ARRIVALS

1914 – Ernest Dale Tubb
1939 – Barry Mann
1941 – Brian Bennett (The Shadows)
1941 – Carole King (Carol Klein)
1942 – Mark Mathis (Newbeats)
1943 – Barbara Lewis
1947 – Joe Ely
1947 – Major Harris (Delfonics)
1951 – Dennis 'Dee Tee' Thomas (Kool and the Gang)
1955 – Jimmy Pursey (Sham 69)
1960 – Holly Johnson (William Johnson) (Frankie Goes To Hollywood)
1970 – Percy Nathan Rodgers (B.V.S.M.P.)

★ ★ ★

DEPARTURE LOUNGE

1966 – Sophie Tucker
1981 – Bill Haley

★ ★ ★

1988

JOHNSON ESCAPES FROM HOLLYWOOD – ZTT ZAPPED

British High Court Judges, not widely renowned for their awareness of rock music, sent shivers up and down the spines of the UK Music Industry when one of their number ruled that the recording contract that had tied Holly Johnson, lead vocalist with triple chart-toppers Frankie Goes To Hollywood, to the record label ZTT (an abbreviation of Zang Tumb Tumm, or something like that, apparently), was 'nonsensical' and 'an unreasonable restraint' on the singer. The judge was particularly forthright when delivering his judgement, which allowed Johnson to accept the offer of a new contract as a solo artist offered to him by MCA Records, and with a final twist of the knife, he ordered ZTT to pay Johnson's court costs, a reputed $500, 000.

Holly Johnson – escape from Frankie's label

RAVINGS

1942:
The first gold record was presented. The recipient was Glenn Miller, for sales of his 'Chattanooga Choo Choo' single.

1974:
Record producer Phil Spector was reportedly seriously injured in a car crash somewhere between Los Angeles and Phoenix, Arizona. In a typically mysterious statement, precise details of the incident were vague.

1982:
Guitarist Mick Moody left Whitesnake, while drummer Kenny Hyslop departed from Simple Minds.

1990:
With her 'Forever Your Girl' debut, Paula Abdul became the first female artist with an album in the Top 10 of the US chart for over 50 weeks.
★ ★ ★

1963

BEATLES DECLARE INDEPENDENCE

The Beatles decided to take control over their own destiny following the death the previous year of their manager, Brian Epstein. They announced the closure of Beatles USA, their fan club and business office, and fired their press agents in America. They also severed all ties with NEMS, the management company previously headed by Epstein that had recently been joined by Bee Gees manager Robert Stigwood.

Instead, they announced the formation of Apple Corps, a company that would incorporate a record label, management and general patronage of young artists whose ideas needed initial investment, while also looking after The Beatles themselves .

1971

ALBERT BANS FRANK'S MOTHERS FOR OBSCENITY

Authorities at London's Royal Albert Hall banned a scheduled concert featuring Frank Zappa and his group, The Mothers Of Invention, with the Royal Philharmonic Orchestra, playing excerpts from Zappa's fictionalized musical account of a group's experiences on the road, *200 Motels*. Some of the lyrics of the songs that made up *200 Motels* were branded 'obscene' after officials had heard the soundtrack album to the *200 Motels* feature film, which starred Beatle Ringo Starr as Frank Zappa and Keith Moon of The Who as a nun.

The RPO had played on the album without apparent damage to their morals.

ARRIVALS

1902 – Chick Webb (William Henry Webb) (Ella Fitzgerald Band)
1932 – Rockin' Dopsie (Alton Jay Rubin)
1937 – Don Wilson (Ventures)
1939 – Roberta Flack
1943 – Ral Donner
1944 – Peter Allen
1946 – Clifford T. Ward
1951 – Cory Lerios (Pablo Cruise)
1961 – Robbie Neville
★ ★ ★

FEW DAYS IN THEIR LIVES

It should come as no great surprise that rock history includes a large number of dates involving The Beatles. Between 1962, when they scored their first hit in Britain with 'Love Me Do', and 1970, when they called it a day amid recriminations on all sides, The Beatles were busy. What follows are some highlights of the group's career that occurred on February 11 in the first three years after the group achieved fame.

1963

At a cost of £400, The Beatles undertook a ten-hour recording session at Abbey Road studio that produced ten completed tracks.

With the addition of the tracks already released as the A and B-sides of their first two singles, 'Love Me Do'/'PS I Love You' and ' Please Please Me'/'Ask Me Why', these tracks comprised their first album, *Please Please Me*. Among the newly recorded songs were 'I Saw Her Standing There', 'Misery', 'Do You Want To Know A Secret' and 'There's A Place', along with six cover versions of recent records by American artists, including 'Boys' and 'Baby It's You' (both originally by The Shirelles) and a cover of The Isley Brothers' 'Twist And Shout', recorded in one take as an afterthought. This was the final track they completed, after which John Lennon's voice was displaying considerable strain.

1964

The Beatles played their first US concert at the Washington Coliseum in Washington DC, topping a bill that included Tommy Roe, The Chiffons and The Carvelles.

The band was inaudible through a barrage of screams from the sold-out audience of 8,600 people. After the show, British ambassador Lord Harlech hosted a party during which an inquisitive guest snipped off a lock of Ringo's hair, which led the group to decide never to attend such a party again.

1965

Ringo was again in the news, finally marrying his childhood sweetheart, Maureen Cox, in London, with George Harrison and his then girlfriend, Patti Boyd, plus John and Cynthia Lennon in attendance. Paul McCartney was on holiday in Africa.

BUTTHOLE FANS RIOT IN HARLESDEN, LONDON

Butthole Surfers - dream tickets?

London-based followers of Texan string quartet The Butthole Surfers went on the rampage in and around Harlesden, North London, when tickets for the group's recital at local venue The Mean Fiddler, sold out.

ARRIVALS

1889 – John Mills (Mills Brothers)	1942 – Leon Haywood
1908 – Josh White	1946 – Ray Lake (Real Thing)
1918 – Wesley Rose	1949 – Johnny G. (John Gotting)
1935 – Gene Vincent (Eugene Vincent Craddock)	1950 – Rochelle Fleming (First Choice)
1939 – Gerry Goffin	1953 – Alan Rubin (Blues Brothers)
1940 – Bobby 'Boris' Pickett	1953 – Neil Henderson (Middle Of The Road)
1941 – Earl Lewis (Channels)	★ ★ ★
1941 – Sergio Mendes	

RAVINGS

1956:
Elvis Presley performed 'Heartbreak Hotel' on American television for the first time.

★ ★ ★

1969:
The Monkees set a record when their second album, *More Of The Monkees*, jumped from No. 122 to Number One in the US chart. It remained at the top for another 17 weeks.

★ ★ ★

1985:
Prince won Best Solo Artist at the fourth annual BRIT awards ceremony held at the Grosvenor House Hotel, London

★ ★ ★

1967

STONES BUSTED AT KEEF'S PAD

Acting on a tip-off by staff of the high circulation British Sunday newspaper *News Of The World*, police raided Redlands, the country home of Rolling Stones guitarist Keith Richards at West Wittering in Sussex.

Armed with a search warrant obtained under the Dangerous Drugs Act, the 15-strong police officers found Richards, vocalist Mick Jagger and his girlfriend, chanteuse Marianne Faithfull, plus a variety of substances that they removed for laboratory analysis.

Jagger and Richards were subsequently charged with a number of offences. Both were initially given custodial prison sentences and Jagger spent two nights behind bars and Richards one before they were allowed leave to appeal.

After an impassioned leader article in The Times written by editor William Rees-Mogg with the headline 'Who breaks a butterfly on a wheel?', which protested that the sentence was hardly appropriate to the rather trivial crime, public opinion (and new evidence) allowed the two Stones virtually to escape punishment, and to capitalize on the considerable press coverage that the case provoked.

Jimi Hendrix, born in Seattle, now with his own key

1968

HENDRIX'S HOMECOMING – SEATTLE CELEBRATION

Jimi Hendrix made a hero's return to his hometown of Seattle, Washington State, where he had attended school (from which he dropped out at the age of 14 to become a musician) before enlisting in the paratroopers at the age of 17 in 1959 to avoid being drafted. He played a free show for the students of Garfield High School. Hendrix was presented with a replica of the key of the city by the mayor of Seattle, and was clearly overcome by his reception.

ARRIVALS

1867 – Len Spencer (America's first recording star)
1902 – Will Glahe
1911 – Stephen Sholes
1935 – Gene McDaniels
1935 – Ray Manzarek (The Doors)
1942 – Kenny Dino
1944 – Moe Bandy
1946 – Cliff DeYoung (Styx)
1949 – Stanley Knight (Black Oak Arkansas)
1950 – Steve Hackett
(Genesis)
1951 – Gil Moore (Triumph)
1951 – Vincent James (Sweet Sensation)
1968 – Chynna Phillips (Wilson Phillips)

★ ★ ★

DEPARTURE LOUNGE

1976 – Sal Mineo
1983 – Eubie Blake (ragtime pianist aged 100)

★ ★ ★

1981

HARRY SOLO SURPRISE

Blondie vocalist Deborah 'Debbie' Harry cofirmed that she was to make a solo album without the other members of the group she had fronted to fame. Collaborators and producers of the album, *Koo Koo*, were Nile Rodgers and Bernard Edwards (aka Chic), and its poor chart performance was largely blamed on the sleeve shot of Harry with long steel pins sticking through her cheeks.

It was not the most satisfying Blondie-related event in a year that had brought the group two international No. 1 singles, 'The Tide Is High' and 'Rapture'.

After her solo effort Blondie never managed to hit the Top 10 again.

RAVINGS

1956:
'Screaming' Jay Hawkins recorded his seminal 'I Put A Spell On You' in New York for Okeh Records. The song would later be the 1966 debut UK hit for The Alan Price Set, the group formed by the ex-leader of The Animals.

1965:
London's Pye Records announced that they had signed 'the British Bob Dylan', singer/guitarist/song writer Donovan Leitch, professionally known as Donovan.

★ ★ ★

1981

FLOYD'S DARK SIDE SCOOPS CHART LONGEVITY RECORD

Pink Floyd – over 10 million units, but still not platinum

The remarkable *Dark Side Of The Moon*, the Pink Floyd album released in March 1973, became the holder of the title of longest-charted rock album in history when it completed its 402nd week in the *Billboard* chart. Only two other albums had remained longer on the chart – *Johnny's Greatest Hits* by Johnny Mathis and the original-cast recording of *My Fair Lady*. By mid-1985 *Dark Side Of The Moon* had accumulated over a staggering 560 weeks on the US album chart, making it the undisputed champion, but it had not at that time been certified platinum, despite selling over 10 million copies, because the RIAA (Record Industry Association Of America) did not make platinum awards to records released before 1976!

1974

DYLAN AND BAND CUT FLOOD AT FORUM

Bob Dylan ended his triumphant US tour with The Band by playing a concert at the Forum in Los Angeles. Many of the tracks that appeared on his live double album *Before The Flood*, were recorded at this concert.

1961

SINATRA LAUNCHES OWN LABEL

After many years signed to Capitol Records, for whom he made a string of classic albums including *Songs For Swinging Lovers*, Frank Sinatra launched his own Reprise label under the auspices of Warner Bros Records, which had been launched in 1958.

Hardly surprisingly, the first release on the new label, Reprise 20001, was by Ol' Blue Eyes himself, a single coupling 'Second Time Around' and 'Tina', which peaked exactly halfway up the US Top 100.

Given Sinatra's open and much-quoted disapproval of rock music, it was ironic that Reprise, in later years, should be the American label to which such rock icons as The Beach Boys, Jimi Hendrix, The Kinks, Neil Young, Joni Mitchell and Neil Young were signed. At a certain point, a decree was issued that all artists other than Sinatra were to be transferred to the parent Warner Bros label, but Neil Young refused.

1977

ALBERT APPLAUDS ABBA ARRIVAL

ABBA - Sweden's first international superstars

London's Royal Albert Hall played host to the final concert of the first British tour by Swedish chart sensations ABBA, the quartet who had topped the UK chart with three singles during 1976: 'Mamma Mia', 'Fernando' and 'Dancing Queen', the last of which also reached No. 1 in the US.

This was a significant breakthrough for a non-British, non-American act. While other artists from continental Europe had enjoyed brief chart success in the past, most of them were unable to follow it up. ABBA had displayed much more consistency since winning the Eurovision Song Contest in 1974 with 'Waterloo', which went on to top the charts in Britain and most of the rest of Europe, while also reaching the Top 10 of the *Billboard* chart.

After a period spent re-evaluating their status following several lesser follow-up hits, the ABBA songwriting team of guitarist Bjorn Ulvaeus, Benny Andersson (keyboards) and their manager Stig Anderson entered a purple patch when they could apparently do no wrong, and the added attraction of vocalists Agnetha Faltskog, who was married to Bjorn, and Anni-Frid Lyngstad, Benny's fiancée, resulted in a string of smashes that lasted into the 1980s in the UK and the rest of the world outside America.

RAVINGS

1970:
The Who recorded a live album at Leeds University in Yorkshire, released with the appropriate title *The Who Live At Leeds*.

1972:
John Lennon and Yoko Ono hosted The Mike Douglas Show on American TV while Douglas took a week's holiday. Among their guests were Chuck Berry and Black Panther leader Bobby Seale.

1981:
Billy Idol (real name William Broad) left punk group Generation X for a solo career. The group's co-founder, Tony James, later formed Sigue Sigue Sputnik.

★ ★ ★

ARRIVALS

1947 – Tim Buckley
1945 – Vic Briggs (Steampacket/Animals)
1937 – Magic Sam (Samuel Maghett)
1943 – Eric Andersen

1931 – Phyllis McGuire (McGuire Sisters)
1940 – Lillie Bryant
1950 – Roger Fisher (Heart)
1946 – Doug Simril (Steve Miller Band)

★ ★ ★

1961

PLATTERS SUE MERCURY OVER LEAD SINGER ROW

US vocal group The Platters sued Mercury Records, the label for which they had recorded over 30 hit singles, including such early rock 'n' roll classics as 'Only You', 'The Great Pretender', 'My Prayer', 'Twilight Time', 'Smoke Gets In Your Eyes' and 'Harbor Lights'.

The dispute was over which of the five-member group sang lead on new tracks recorded by them. Mercury claimed that they were entitled to recordings featuring the distinctive high tenor voice of Tony Williams, while the group and their manager, Buck Ram, who owned the rights to the group name, maintained that Mercury had perviously accepted tracks with other members singing lead. The fact that Williams had sung lead on all the group's biggest hits was not, they argued, a valid reason to reject new recordings made since Williams left the group for a solo career in June 1960, replaced by Sonny Turner.

1950 superstars The Platters

1965

THE KING IS DEAD

The above headline would be reused in 1977 when Elvis Presley's body gave up the unequal struggle against self-indulgence, but in many ways the death from cancer of velvet-voiced vocal stylist Nat 'King' Cole was an equally appropriate occasion to mourn a royal death, although Cole could not remotely be regarded as a rock 'n' roller.

Born Nathaniel Adams Cole in 1917 in Montgomery, Alabama, he was raised in Chicago, forming his first band, The Royal Dukes, at the age of 17. A jazz-styled pianist, he first recorded in 1936 with a band led by his brother, and formed his own trio in 1939, scoring his first hit in 1943. Even before the birth of rock 'n' roll, he had recorded several tracks that would transcend their age, including 'Route 66', which was covered by both Chuck Berry and The Rolling Stones, 'Mona Lisa', a major hit for Conway Twitty, 'When I Fall In Love', a Top 3 hit for Rick Astley, and 'Smile', covered by Eric Clapton.

Between 1955 and his death from lung cancer ten years later, Cole amassed over 50 US hit singles.

Nat 'King' Cole

1981

DANCE CRAZE HITS THE SCREEN

Coventry-based ska fanatics The Specials

The feature film *Dance Craze* was premiered. It featured acts who had risen to prominence via the 2-Tone movement, which sprang from Coventry in the midlands of England, and largely comprised inter-racial groups playing West Indian ska music. Leaders of the movement were The Specials (originally The Special AKA), led by keyboard player Jerry Dammers, and featuring vocalist Terry Hall. They were soon joined by Madness (named after a famous song by ska star Prince Buster) from North London's Camden Town, The Selecter, The Beat and The Bodysnatchers, all of whom appeared in the movie, which included live footage of many artists who had made their debut on the 2-Tone label, along with film of another similarly influenced London group, Bad Manners.

The soundtrack album featuring songs by the bands appearing in the film was catapulted in to the Top 5 of the charts.

ARRIVALS

1918 – Hank Locklin (Lawrence Hankins Locklin)
1941 – Brian Holland
1944 – Denny Zager (Zager and Evans)
1944 – Mick Avory (The Kinks)
1945 – John Helliwell (Alan Bown Set/Supertramp)
1947 – David Brown (Santana)
1952 – Melissa Manchester
1959 – Ali Campbell (Alastair Campbell) (UB40)
1960 – Michael 'Mikey' Craig (Culture Club)
1962 – Mike and David Milliner (Pasadenas)

★ ★ ★

DEPARTURE LOUNGE

1965 – Nat 'King' Cole
1968 – 'Little' Walter Jacobs
1981 – Mike Bloomfield

★ ★ ★

1978

SWEDES INVADE WEST END CINEMA

With six UK No. 1 hits under their collective belt in less than four years (and with a seventh, 'Take A Chance On Me', about to assume the top spot two days later), ABBA, the Swedish quartet that had broken the British and American strangle-hold on the UK and US pop charts throughout the rock 'n' roll era, attended the London premiere at the Warner West End cinema of the feature film in which they starred, *ABBA – The Movie*.

In many ways a fairly lightweight film with little in the way of a plot, *ABBA – The Movie* nevertheless succeeded in its main aim, which was to have the group on screen performing their hits for as much of the film as possible. The initial plan had been for a documentary based on the group's hugely successful 1977 world tour, during which they filled London's Royal Albert Hall for two separate shows on St Valentine's day (February 14), but this was later amended.

Set in Austalia, where ABBA had been immensely successful – at one point in 1976, the group had four singles and three albums simultaneously in the Top 20s of that country's charts – the eventual shooting script included a storyline about the tribulations experienced by a local disc jockey (played by Australian actor Robert Hughes) in his attempts to interview the group.

The film's executive producers were ABBA manager Stig Anderson and Australian entrepreneur and TV station owner, Reg Grundy (who was responsible some years later for the incredibly popular soap opera *Neighbours*, which featured teen idols Kylie Minogue and Jason Donovan).

RAVINGS

1957:
BBC TV broadcast between 6 pm and 7 pm for the first time. The 'toddler's truce' had been maintained to allow parents to send children to bed without the potential disruptive effect of continuous television. The show broadcast was the first British programme aimed at a teenage audience, *6.5 Special*.

1963:
Canadian hitmaker Paul Anka married Marie Ann Dezogheb in Paris.

★ ★ ★

1972:
Ricky Nelson, an American teenage idol who profited particularly from Elvis Presley's two years out of the limelight in the US Army, began his first British tour.

Nelson had forsworn his pop music past, turning instead to country/rock with a group calling themselves The Stone Canyon Band.

★ ★ ★

1991

SINEAD GRAMMY SNUB

Controversial Irish singer Sinead O'Connor, whose shaven-head and outspoken anti-Catholic pronouncements had gained her public notoriety, announced that she would not accept any Grammy Awards that she might win.

Four times nominated O'Connor decided to snub the ceremony. She shot to stardom at the age of 25 with the success of her worldwide No. 1 hit - a cover version of the torch song 'Nothing Compares 2 U', originally written by Prince for the Minneapolis-based band Family.

Nothing compares 2 Sinead....

ARRIVALS

1901 – Wayne King
1914 – Jimmy Wakely
1916 – Bill Doggett
1920 – Patti Andrews (Andrews Sisters)
1932 – Otis Blackwell
1935 – Sonny Bono (Salvatore Philip Bono)
1939 – Herbie and Harold Kalin (The Kalin Twins)
1940 – Leon Ware
1949 – Lyn Paul (The New Seekers)
1961 – Andy Taylor (Duran Duran)
1962 – Tony Kylie (Blow Monkeys)

★ ★ ★

1969

CASH AND DYLAN HOLD COUNTRY/ FOLK SUMMIT MEETING

'Spokesman for his generation' Bob Dylan and country music legend Johnny Cash collaborated on a recording project in Nashville at CBS Studios, owned by the label to which they were both signed. Both had expressed admiration for each other's work, but circumstances had made previous professional meetings impossible.

Although a number of songs were recorded during the session, only the Dylan composition, 'Girl From The North Country', was released on record, appearing on Dylan's *Nashville Skyline* album (a British number one album with sleeve notes written by none other than Johnny Cash). Another song cut at the same sessions, 'One Too Many Mornings', was included in the documentary film *Johnny Cash, The Man And His Music*.

Dylan also appeared on the first show of Cash's TV series in May that year, singing 'I Threw It All Away'. Dylan later remarked when asked about the session, 'I was scared to death'.

RAVINGS

1960:
Elvis Presley won his first gold award for an album with *Elvis*. Released in late 1956, the album included such notable tracks as 'Paralysed', 'When My Blue Moon Turns To Gold Again', 'Rip It Up' and 'Ready Teddy'.

★ ★ ★

1970:
Joni Mitchell announced that she would make no more live appearances during a concert at London's Royal Albert Hall, London. Before the end of the year, she was on stage at the Isle Of Wight Festival.

★ ★ ★

1972:
Pink Floyd began a three-night live season at London's Rainbow Theatre during which they premiered material that would appear on the following year's *Dark Side Of The Moon* album.

★ ★ ★

1979:
The Clash opened the US leg of their *Pearl Harbor '79* North American tour at New York's Palladium, launching their set with a spirited 'I'm So Bored With The USA'.

★ ★ ★

1975

LENNON'S ROOTS ALBUM RELEASED

John Lennon's *Rock 'n' Roll* album of songs that he recalled from his teenage years was released in the US. Recording for this project, whose original title was *Oldies But Moldies*, had started in late 1973, with Phil Spector producing, but disagreements between the two, followed by Spector's alleged involvement in a car crash and subsequent disappearance produced a hiatus of a year. When a TV advertised album titled *Roots – John Lennon Sings The Great Rock and Roll Hits* was released without Lennon's authorization in early 1975, the official *Rock 'n' Roll* album, containing many tracks that were identical to those on the unauthorized album, was quickly made generally available, even though Lennon's *Walls And Bridges* album had been released less than six months earlier.

Lennon-back pages album.

ARRIVALS
1905 – Orwill 'Hoppy' Jones (Inkspots)
1922 – Tommy Edwards
1933 – Bobby Lewis
1934 – Barry Humphries (Dame Edna Everage)
1935 – Johnny Bush
1939 – John Leyton
1941 – Gene Pitney
1947 – Dodie Stevens (Geraldine Ann Pasquale)
1966 – Melissa Brooke-Belland (Voice Of The Beehive)

★ ★ ★

DEPARTURE LOUNGE
1931 – Uncle Jimmy Thompson (first musician featured on WSM *Barn Dance*, later called *Grand Ole Opry*)
1982 – Thelonious Monk

1968

FLOYD FOUNDER FIRED

Following several weeks of uncertainty for psychedelic quartet Pink Floyd, during which guitarist Dave Gilmour, a friend of the band from Cambridge (where he had played in the group Joker's Wild), was recruited as a fifth member, he was finally invited to make the temporary assignment permanent. He replaced original Floyd founder, singer/guitarist Roger 'Syd' Barrett, who had conceived the group's debut hits, 'Arnold Layne' and 'See Emily Play', as well as masterminding their debut album, *Piper At The Gates Of Dawn*, but Barrett's heavy indulgence in psychedelic substances had rendered him unreliable and often incoherent.

Gilmour soon slotted in with the group, while bass player Roger Waters assumed Barrett's roles as songwriter and vocalist.

In later years Barrett was virtually forgotten, particularly in the US, where the group's success was somewhat limited until the release in 1973 of *Dark Side Of The Moon*, their first album to reach the Top 40 of the US chart and eventually becoming the longest-charting album in history (see February 13). In 1975 the group's *Wish You Were Here* album included a song written by Waters and dedicated to Barrett, 'Shine On You Crazy Diamond'.

It was said that during the creation of the album, Barrett visited the recording studio where it was being made, but subsequent sightings of the increasingly reclusive erstwhile star have been rare.

'Syd' Barrett (third from left), Pink Floyd's original inspiration

1980

WYMAN TO WALK IN 1982

In an interview with London's *Daily Express* newspaper, Rolling Stones bass player Bill Wyman declared his intention of leaving the group in 1982, after their 20th Anniversary. Wyman (real name William Perks) was the oldest member of the group – he was born in October, 1936 – but the last to join the quintet who achieved international stardom second only to The Beatles. In December 1962 – it was felt that his major attribute in the minds of the triumvirate of Mick Jagger, Brian Jones and Keith Richards was that he owned an expensive amplifier.

In 1992, a similar controversy existed – Wyman, by then closer to 60 than 50, but still a Stone, mentioned that he might not work with the band again; if the group fulfilled their recently signed commitment to Virgin Records, he would be the first member of a rock group with a free bus pass!

1977

'RUMOURS' MAKES MAC A MILLION (OR FIVE?)

Fleetwood Mac - an enduring sound

With their line-up stricken by personal angst, Fleetwood Mac, originally formed in London about 1967, but ten years later based in Los Angeles with two American members aboard, released their masterpiece album, *Rumours*, which became one of the biggest-selling albums of all time. By the end of 1991, it had spent well over eight years in the UK album chart, falling out of the list and returning on numerous occasions, while it spent an incredible 31 weeks at the top of the *Billboard* album chart.

The album was written and recorded at a time when two members of the group, bass player John McVie and his wife Christine, keyboard player/songwriter and one of the three main vocalists in the band, were separating (and would eventually divorce), and while the relationship between the two Americans who had been recruited in late 1974, singer/songwriter/guitarist Lindsey Buckingham and vocalist and songwriter Stephanie 'Stevie' Nicks, was also falling apart. Added to that, drummer Mick Fleetwood, the only remaining original member of the group formed by guitarist Peter Green (John McVie did not join until a few weeks after the group was launched) was also in the midst of divorce proceedings.

Four singles excerpted from the album reached the US Top 10: 'Go Your Own Way', 'Dreams' (a chart-topper), 'Don't Stop' and 'You Make Loving Fun'.

Fleetwood Mac fullfill their 'Dreams'

1980

AC/DC DRINK DEATH

Ronald 'Bon' Scott, Scottish-born vocalist with Australian-based hard rock group AC/DC, died in his car after an evening of hard drinking at Camden Town's Music Machine venue in London. The coroner noted that Scott 'drank himself to death'.

Like the group's founders, guitarist brothers Angus and Malcolm Young, Scott had emigrated to Australia with his parents as a child, and joined the group in 1974, after working in their road crew. The Young brothers apparently warmed to Scott when they discovered he had several convictions (for minor offences) and had been rejected by the Australian Army as being 'socially maladjusted'. His death came during the year when the band's *Highway To Hell* album became their first million seller.

Bon Scott, alcohol victim

ARRIVALS

1936 – Bob Engemann (Lettermen)
1940 – Smokey Robinson (William Robinson)
1943 – Lou Christie (Lugee Alfredo Giovanni Sacco)
1946 – Pierre Van Den Linden (Focus)
1948 – Mark Andes (Spirit)
1948 – Tony Iommi (Black Sabbath)
1949 – Eddie Hardin (Spencer Davis Group)
1950 – Andy Powell (Wishbone Ash)
1950 – Francis Buchholz (Scorpions)
1956 – Dave Wakeling (The Beat/General Public)
1957 – Falco (Johann Hoelcel)
1960 – Holly Johnson (Frankie Goes To Hollywood)
1960 – Prince Mark D. (Fat Boys)
1963 – Seal

★ ★ ★

DEPARTURE LOUNGE

1980 – Bon Scott (AC/DC)

1972

MCCARTNEY'S SIMPLISTIC SOLUTION

Paul McCartney surely could not have expected to escape unscathed after releasing a single suggesting that Great Britain should return the province of Northern Ireland to the jurisdiction of the Dublin government, which controlled the rest of the Celtic island to its south. At a time when the relationship between Britain and Ireland's nationalists was close to flashpoint, it was no surprise that someone of Irish extraction should wish to make his views known, but to release those views as a somewhat simplistic single aimed at the pop chart was another matter entirely.

Pop writers generally dismissed the single, 'Give Ireland Back to the Irish' as a nursery rhyme with lyrics that could have been written by a teenager, but the British national press were rather more critical – the single was regarded as inflammatory in the wake of 'bloody Sunday' three weeks earlier, when a civil rights march in Londonderry turned into a riot and British paratroopers opened fire, killing 13 people and wounding 17 more.

Three days later, the British Embassy in Dublin was burned down, after an IRA declaration that their immediate policy was 'to kill as many British soldiers as possible'.

Needless to say, British radio stations slapped an immediate ban on airplay, and the single lurched into the lower reaches of the UK Top 20 before vanishing, while in the US it peaked outside the Top 20. It was the first single by Wings, the group McCartney had formed with his wife Linda, singer/guitarist Denny Laine (ex-Moody Blues) and American drummer Denny Seiwell (ex-Jam Factory) along with new recruit Henry McCulloch from The Grease Band.

Paul McCartney - naive solution in dumb single

1974

SONNY AND CHER TO DIVORCE

Cher, the female partner in the Sonny and Cher husband and wife duo who topped the world's charts in 1965 with 'I Got You Babe', filed for divorce from Sonny Bono, her husband of ten years in Santa Monica, California.

Cher married Gregg Allman of The Allman Brothers Band a mere four days after her divorce from Bono was finalized, but the new liaison immediately ran into problems, and she was talking of divorce only nine days after marrying for a second time.

Sonny and Cher - pop aristocracy divorce

1976

WAYLON AND WILLIE WANTED

Country music stars Waylon Jennings and Willie Nelson topped the US country singles chart with 'Good Hearted Woman', a track from *The Outlaws*, the first album in country music history to be certified platinum for sales of over one million copies.

Outlaws Nelson and Jennings

Texan singer/songwriter Willie Nelson had not enjoyed his time living in Nashville when making his name as a top songwriter composing hits like 'Crazy', 'Night Life', 'Funny How Time Slips Away', 'Hello Walls' and many more.

In 1970 he moved back to Texas after his house in Nashville burned down, and began to operate on his own terms. His attitude to the Nashville establishment won him few friends in Music City, but gained him much support among other musicians who were similarly disenchanted, including fellow Texan Waylon Jennings, who had unwittingly avoided death by giving up his seat on the light plane that crashed in 1959 killing Buddy Holly (for whom he was playing bass on the fateful tour).

Jennings was also a free spirit, and the duo recorded *The Outlaws* with Waylon's wife, Jessi Colter, and Tompall Glaser, at the suggestion of RCA executive Jerry Bradley – the album title was certainly appropriate for the renegade duo. With a sleeve in keeping with the album's title – the participants were pictured as on a 'Wanted' poster in cowboy mythology – the album captured the imagination of a large number of rock fans, who certainly boosted sales.

Apart from 'Good Hearted Woman', which was ironically voted song of the year by the Country Music Association in Nashville, the album included the wry 'Put Another Log On The Fire', an ultimate song of male chauvinism, performed by Glaser.

1987

SIXTIES STAR SLY IN SLAMMER

Sly Stone (Sylvester Stewart), leader of 1960s psychedelic soul hitmakers Sly and The Family Stone, was jailed on drug related charges.

This was just one of a series of drug busts culminating in late 1989 in his being sentenced to spend nine to 14 months in a drug rehabilitation clinic to cure his cocaine addiction and placed on three years probation by judge Robert Altman.

Sly and The Family Stone during their glory years

RAVINGS

1964:
Three British Beat classics were released: Billy J. Kramer's 'Little Children', 'Just One Look' by The Hollies and 'Not Fade Away' by The Rolling Stones.

1970:
Simon and Garfunkel's *Bridge Over Troubled Water* album entered the UK chart at No. 1, where it remained for the next 12 weeks. In all, it topped the UK album chart for 41 weeks, returning to the top seven times before the end of 1972. No other album by any single act (including The Beatles) has topped the UK chart for more than 30 weeks.

★ ★ ★

1976

ORIGINAL SUPREME FLO DIES IN POVERTY

The death of Florence Ballard, the original lead singer of Motown's hugely successful female vocal trio, The Supremes, was a tragedy. Since her forced departure from the group in 1967 in search of a solo career, Ballard had reached rock bottom.

The original Supremes, with Florence Ballard

At the time of her death from a heart attack nine years after leaving the group with which she had recorded nine US No. 1 hits in less than three years, she was living on welfare with her three children. She was only 32 years old.

The trio of Ballard, Diana Ross and Mary Wilson began working together in 1960 as The Primettes. By the end of the year, they had been signed by Berry Gordy Jr, boss of Motown, but early releases were not big hits, and it was not until 1964, when the group, with Ross singing lead rather than Ballard, began working with writer/producers Holland, Dozier and Holland that any success accrued to them. Having made the breakthrough with 'Where Did Our Love Go', the trio topped the US charts with ten singles in under three years, including 'Baby Love', 'Come See About Me', 'Stop! In The Name Of Love', and many more. During this period, Gordy seemed to favour Ross to the detriment of Ballard, and an intense rivalry between the two group members developed, with Ross often winning arguments by invoking Gordy. Ballard then began drinking heavily, which led to her becoming increasingly unreliable, and in 1967 she left the group after singing on their ninth US Number One, 'Love Is Here And Now You're Gone'. She was replaced by Cindy Birdsong.

Ballard attempted a solo career, but little resulted, and an unhappy and shortlived marriage together with two flop singles left her at a low ebb. During the early 1970s she sued Motown for over $8 million, but lost the case, and the downward spiral eventually led to coronary thrombosis. She died in a Detroit hospital.

1989

OFFSCREEN RAPPERS SHUN SHOW

The year's Grammy Awards ceremony was boycotted by rap artists when they discovered that their award would not form part of the TV coverage of the event.

Among the winners on the night were Bobby McFerrin, who did not worry and was happy to have been selected, Tracy Chapman, George Michael and Jethro Tull,

Bobby McFerrin, a 1988 chart-topper

who somewhat surprisingly won the Heavy Metal Grammy.

ARRIVALS

1910 – Spade Cooley (Donnell Cooley)
1920 – Del Wood (Adelaide Hazelwood)
1936 – Ernie K-Doe (Ernest Kador Jr)
1938 – Bobby Hendricks (The Drifters)
1943 – Louise Lopez (Odyssey)
1943 – Mick Green (Pirates)
1945 – Oliver (William Oliver Swofford)
1953 – Graham Lewis (Wire)

1953 – Neil (Nigel Planer)
1962 – Michael Wilton (Queensryche)

★ ★ ★

DEPARTURE LOUNGE

1976 – Florence Ballard (Supremes)
1982 – Murray Kaufman (Murray The K)
1987 – Andy Warhol

★ ★ ★

1991

WHITNEY NECK AND NECK WITH MADONNA

Nine US No. 1s in under six years – that was the enviable record achieved by Whitney Houston, as 'All The Man That I Need', her revival of a 1982 minor US R & B hit by Sister Sledge, returned her to a position she had occupied in 1985 with 'Saving All My Love For You', in 1986 with 'How Will I Know' and 'The Greatest Love Of All', in 1987 with 'I Wanna Dance With Somebody (Who Loves Me)' and 'Didn't We Almost Have It All', in 1988 with 'So Emotional' and 'Where Do Broken Hearts Go', and in 1990 with 'I'm Your Baby Tonight'. She had a rather quieter year in 1989.

Houston, the daughter of Sixties hitmaker and Sweet Inspirations lead vocalist Cissy Houston and cousin of both Dionne and Dee Dee

Warwick, was signed by Arista Records boss Clive Davis in 1983 after a showcase arranged by one of the label's talent scouts. Prior to that

Whitney had worked during her teenage years providing backing vocals for such notables as Chaka Khan and Lou Rawls.

Whitney Houston – nine US Number Ones in under six years

1973

ABBA BABY APPEARS BEFORE EUROVISION

Having come close to the US singles chart in 1972 with 'People Need Love', a song they had written and produced together, Swedish pop stars Benny Andersson and Bjorn Ulvaeus, who had been accompanied on the single by Benny's fiancée, Anni-Frid Lyngstad, and Bjorn's wife, Agnetha Faltskog, had been invited to enter a song for a competition, the winners of which would represent Sweden in the 1973 Eurovision Song Contest.

With their manager, Stig Anderson, one of Sweden's most prolific lyricists, they assembled the catchy 'Ring Ring', with lyrics in English specially written by 1960s' American hitmaker Neil Sedaka.

Benny and Bjorn decided to perform the

song themselves with their lady friends. The name they chose – Bjorn, Benny, Agnetha and Anni-Frid – was rather unwieldy and Stig Anderson abbreviated it to ABBA (the initial letters of their first names). However, Agnetha was pregnant, and the baby was expected on the very day of the contest. Anni-Frid learned all Agnetha's vocal parts so that if the birth should coincide with the Eurovision heat, the show could go on, but in fact, the baby did not arrive until February 23, and Agnetha was able to appear with the rest of the quartet. 'Ring Ring' was clearly the choice of the audience, but a panel of experts placed it only third, and another song represented Sweden in the contest proper.

ARRIVALS

1944 – Johnny Winter
1944 – Michael Maxfield (Dakotas)
1946 – Rusty Young (Buffalo Springfield/Poco)
1949 – Tex Comer (Terry Comer) (Ace)
1950 – Steve Priest (Sweet)

1952 – Brad Whitford (Aerosmith)
1952 – Gary Giles (Stray)
1955 – Howard Jones
1955 – Zeke Manyika (Orange Juice)
1957 – Robin Gray (Dead End Kids)
1958 – David Sylvian (David Batt) (Japan)

1967

STIGWOOD INKS WIZARDS FROM OZ

Robert Stigwood, the Australian impresario who was Beatle manager Brian Epstein's partner in the NEMS organization, signed The Bee Gees to a five-year management contract.

Bee Gees – brotherly success

Although the trio of Gibb Brothers who front the group were born on the Isle Of Man (off the north-west coast of England), they had first achieved significant fame in Australia, where they had emigrated in 1958 with their musically inclined parents – their father led the Bill Gibb Orchestra and their mother, Barbara, was a vocalist.

Having topped the Australian charts with their eleventh single, 'Spicks and Specks', the brothers (Barry and his younger twin brothers , Robin and Maurice) decided to try their luck at conquering the British charts. On their arrival in the UK they played an audition for Stigwood at London's Savile Theatre, after which he offered to manage them. With all three singing (plus Barry on guitar and Maurice on bass), along with native Australians Vince Melouney (lead guitar) and Colin Peterson (drums), the group were almost instantly successful, and their debut single, 'New York Mining Disaster 1941', entered the UK chart within two months, eventually peaking just outside the Top 10.

Before the end of the year, the group had scored with three more UK hit singles – 'To Love Somebody' (a minor item in the UK, but the group's second US Top 20 single in three months), 'Massachusetts' (their first UK chart-topper) and 'World' – and were among the biggest groups in Britain.

1990

MILLI VANILLI FOLLOW FARIAN FAME RECIPE

Milli Vanilli – real or bogus?

Winning three Grammy Awards made Milli Vanilli one of the most successful new acts of the late 1980s. A duo comprising vocalists Rob Pilatus (from Germany) and Fabrice Morvan (from Guadeloupe), their records, which included three consecutive US Number One singles, 'Baby Don't Forget My Number', 'Girl I'm Gonna Miss You' and 'Blame It On The Rain', were supervised by Frank Farian, who had created the hugely popular Boney M group during the 1970s.

However, all was not as it seemed – when Pilatus and Morvan, who had taken the act on the road, insisted that they should participate in future recordings, Farian revealed that the duo had been hired only for stage work. The vocalists who had actually appeared on the records were as named Charles Shaw, John Davis and Brad Howe. Eventually, Pilatus and Morvan were forced to hand back the Grammy Award they had won for Best New Act of 1989.

RAVINGS

1956:
Bill Haley received a $250,000 guarantee for 21 US gigs.

1990:
Happy Mondays dominated the UK independent singles chart, with six entries in the Top 30.
★ ★ ★

ARRIVALS

1932 – Michel Legrand
1933 – David 'Fathead' Newman
1942 – Paul Jones (Paul Pond) (Manfred Mann, Blues Band)
1947 – Lonnie Turner (Steve Miller Band)
1947 – Rupert Holmes
1948 – Dennis Waterman
1959 – Colin Farley (Cutting Crew)
1965 – Nicky Hopkins

★ ★ ★

DEPARTURE LOUNGE

1988 – Memphis Slim (Peter Chatman)
1990 – Johnnie Ray
1991 – Webb Pierce

★ ★ ★

1989

ORBISON'S POSTHUMOUS SUCCESS

Although he had died of a heart attack during the previous December, after being absent from the US pop album charts for over 20 years, Texan vocalist Roy Orbison had participated in both the CDs that occupied the top two places in the US chart - his own *Mystery Girl* album and *Volume One*, the debut offering from The Traveling Wilburys.

Roy Orbison – gone but far from forgotten

However, Orbison had shown during the 1980s that he was not completely irrelevant to all but the middle aged. At the start of the decade, he had reached the Top 10 of the US country singles chart with 'That Lovin' You Feelin' Again', a duet with Emmylou Harris that was included in the film *Roadie* (the movie starred Meat Loaf in the title role and also featured Blondie and other New Wave stars).

In 1987, a re-recorded version of his 1963 hit, 'In Dreams', was heavily featured in the David Lynch film *Blue Velvet*, and only weeks later, a duet with Canadian country star k. d. lang on another of his past hits, 'Crying', was showcased in the movie *Hiding Out*. The single made the US country chart and was finally a hit in the UK in 1992.

1983

DOROTHY'S DOG BAND UP FOR FIVE GRAMMIES

Toto – named after Japanese bathroom furniture or a fictional dog?

Named (according to who you ask) after Judy Garland's dog in the famous *Wizard Of Oz* movie, the real surname of vocalist Bobby Kimball (supposedly Toteaux) or the major manufacturer of toilet bowls in Japan (less likely, but not impossible), Toto was formed in 1979 by a group of noted session musicians based in Los Angeles.

At the 25th Grammy Awards, Toto were winners in six categories, including Album Of The Year (for the double platinum *Toto IV*) and Record Of The Year (for 'Africa', the chart-topping single from the album) and Best Instrumental Arrangement for 'Rosanna'.

The group initially included brothers Steve and Jeff Porcaro (respectively lead guitar and drums), the sons of jazz percussionist Joe Porcaro, and their childhood chum David Paich (keyboards), the son of bandleader and arranger Marty Paich. When bass player David Hungate left the band in 1984, another of the Porcaro brothers, Mike, replaced him shortly before the group were commissioned to write the theme music for the 1984 Olympic Games held in Los Angeles.

RAVINGS

1955:
Irish songstress Ruby Murray had three singles in the UK Top 6 – 'Softly Softly', 'Heartbeat' and 'Happy Days, Lonely Nights'.

★ ★ ★

1957:
Buddy Holly recorded 'That'll Be The Day' at Norman Petty's studio in Clovis, New Mexico.

1965:
The Beatles began filming of their second feature film. Originally titled *Eight Arms To Hold You*, it eventually emerged as *Help!*

★ ★ ★

1983:
Successful 1960s folk trio Peter, Paul and Mary re-formed for a European tour, their first since 1967.

★ ★ ★

ARRIVALS

1927 – Ralph Edmond Stanley (Clinch Mountain Boys, Stanley Brothers)
1932 – Faron Young
1942 – Roy Michaels (Cat Mother and The All Night Newsboys)
1943 – George Harrison
1945 – Elkie Brooks (Elaine Bookbinder)
1950 – Emitt Rhodes

1957 – Stuart 'Woody' Wood (Bay City Rollers)
1958 – Jim 'Daryl' Gilmour (Saga)
1959 – Mike Peters (The Alarm)

★ ★ ★

DEPARTURE LOUNGE

1991 – Slim Gaillard

★ ★ ★

1987

DIGITAL BEATLES AT LONG LAST

The Compact Disc revolution was never going to be comprehensive and complete while nothing by The Beatles, the biggest rock group ever, was available in the new digital format.

It was not simply an oversight – renegotiation was required over royalty deals that had been agreed during the early 1960s, when CD was not even a twinkle in the eye of the electronics firms who later conceived a way to make the world buy another copy of what they had already purchased 20 years before, albeit with enhanced clarity.

Many Luddites who refused to upgrade their hi-fi equipment used the non-availability of Beatles albums on CD as a reason for their recalcitrance – 'I'll get one when *Sergeant Pepper's* on CD' was the cry of many, and 1987 was when they had to put up or shut up, as a dozen original albums by the group were released during the year after being remastered by George Martin, who had originally produced them.

The general consensus among critics seemed to be that the earlier albums had scarcely benefited from the new format, although they all reappeared in the UK album chart (albeit briefly in most cases). The only one of the dozen that remained in the chart for longer than five weeks was, of course, *Sergeant Pepper*, which reached the Top 3 during a 16-week chart residency, bringing its total stay on the UK listings to an impressive 164 weeks.

ARRIVALS

1928 – Fats Domino (Antoine Domino)
1930 – Chic Hetti (Playmates)
1932 – John R. Cash
1943 – Paul Cotton (Poco)
1945 – Bob 'The Bear' Hite (Canned Heat)
1945 – Mitch Ryder (William Levise)
1947 – Sandie Shaw (Sandra Goodrich)
1953 – Jim Crichton (Saga)
1954 – Michael Bolton (Michael Bolotin)
1960 – Steve Grant (Tight Fit)
1961 – John Jon (Bronski Beat)
1963 – Bernie Bremond (Johnny Diesel and the Injectors)

★ ★ ★

DEPARTURE LOUNGE

1990 – Bukka White
1990 – Cornell Gunter (The Coasters)
1990 – Sherman Garnes (The Teenagers)

1983

JACKSON'S 'THRILLER' REWRITES RECORD BOOK

Jackson's 12 Grammy nominations and sales of 40 million

Michael Jackson's *Thriller*, the follow-up to his hugely successful *Off The Wall* album released in 1979, reached No. 1 in the US album chart.

Widely recognized as the most successful album of all time, it amassed an incredible 37 weeks at the top of that chart, selling over 40 million copies worldwide (including over one million in Los Angeles alone!). In the UK, it became the first album ever to spawn six hits (five of them reaching the upper echelons of the Top 10). In the US seven tracks were released all of them Top 10: 'Billie Jean' and 'Beat It' (both topped the US singles chart), 'The Girl Is Mine' (a duet with Paul McCartney), 'Wanna Be Startin' Somethin'', 'Human Nature', 'P.Y.T. (Pretty Young Thing)' and the title track.

The album reached the No. 1 spot in every Western country and received a record 12 Grammy nominations, winning a total of seven.

1967

ARNOLD AND THE UNDERWEAR

Cambridge-based quartet Pink Floyd released their debut single (and first hit), 'Arnold Layne'. Supposedly named after two obscure bluesmen, Pink Anderson and Floyd Council, the group's personnel featured singer/guitarist Roger 'Syd' Barrett, keyboard player Richard Wright, Roger Waters on bass and drummer Nick Mason. Written by Barrett, the song was apparently based on an actual local occurrence, and according to those who listened closely to its lyrics, seemingly concerned a man who stole female underwear from washing lines.

Despite suggestions that the song might be about a transvestite, it still reached the UK Top 20. Unfortunately, Barrett's predilection for mind-expanding drug experimentation eventually made him unreliable. In 1968 he was replaced for live performances by Dave Gilmour, and two months later was asked to leave the band.

Reports of his eccentric behaviour over later years made Barrett a cult figure, which was expanded when the group's 1975 album, *Wish You Were Here*, included a track written by Waters and dedicated to Barrett, 'Shine On You Crazy Diamond'.

1956

YODELLING COWBOY STARTS FIRST UK TOUR

Adams beats Whitman's long-standing record

Slim Whitman, the Florida-born country-and-western vocalist, started his first British tour. His first UK hit single, 'Rose Marie', had established during the previous year a remarkable record that would not be beaten for over three and a half decades by topping the chart for 11 consecutive weeks. When the yodelling country singer's mark was beaten by Canadian Bryan Adams in 1991, with 'Everything I Do (I Do It For You)',

Whitman, by then in his late sixties, made a guest appearance at a Wembley concert by Adams. The Adams hit owed its success partly to its inclusion in the celebrated feature film starring Kevin Costner, *Robin Hood Prince Of Thieves*, although the song was only heard over the closing credits of the movie.

1955

SMALLER SEVEN-INCH SINGLES OUTSELL 78s

Billboard magazine, the 'bible' of the US record industry, announced that for the first time, sales of the recently introduced seven-inch 45 rpm single, the new format that was to dominate for the next 35 years, had overtaken sales of its heavier ten-inch 78 rpm rival.

1977

PISTOLS FIRE MATLOCK, RECRUIT VICIOUS

The Sex Pistols, who had been released from their EMI recording contract during the previous month, changed bass players when the constant bickering between vocalist Johnny Rotten and bass player Glen Matlock was finally resolved by Matlock's departure.

In retrospect, many suspected that this marked the beginning of the end for the Pistols – certainly, his replacement, Sid Vicious, was a far less able musician, and Matlock's songwriting ability exceeded that of the other group members. He received songwriting credits on nine of the dozen tracks on the group's debut album, *Never Mind The Bollocks*, which topped the UK album chart later at the end of the year, and those nine included the group's first three hit singles, 'Anarchy In The UK', 'God Save The Queen' and 'Pretty Vacant'.

Rotten's dislike of Matlock was said to stem from the latter's professed admiration for The Beatles, which Rotten clearly felt lacked street credibility. Matlock then launched a new group, The Rich Kids, which also featured James 'Midge' Ure, later the star of Ultravox and co-writer of Band Aid's 'Do They Know It's Christmas'.

1966

CAVERN CLOSES DOORS

The Early Beatles who played at The Cavern during their formative years

The venue where The Beatles performed over 280 times between March 1961 and August 1963 was forced to close with debts estimated at £10,000 ($15,000). The famous stage on which the chart colossi had stood was removed, and sold in small pieces to souvenir hunters.

Opened in early 1957 as a venue reserved exclusively for jazz, The Cavern expanded its musical horizons of necessity during 1960, and became the leading local venue for the burgeoning Merseybeat movement. In late 1961

Brian Epstein, who ran the local NEMS record shop, saw The Beatles on stage there for the first time in late 1961, and their resulting partnership made rock history. The Cavern reopened later in 1966, but in 1973 the owners of

the site, British Rail, demolished the building at 8 Matthew Street.

After the area had been cleared of the debris, a shopping centre known as Cavern Walks was built there. This complex contains The New Cavern Club.

Matlock – ex-Pistol becomes affluent

RAVINGS

1981:
Three successful 1970s groups split up, each spawning successful future hitmakers: Annie Lennox and Dave Stewart of The Tourists became Eurythmics; Billy Idol, vocalist of Generation X, became a solo star; and both Terry Williams and Dave Edmunds of Rockpile went on to work with bigger acts, Williams as drummer with Dire Straits and Edmunds as a major record producer.

★ ★ ★

1984:
Michael Jackson won a record seven Grammy Awards.

★ ★ ★

ARRIVALS

1939 – John Fahey
1940 – Joe South
1941 Marty Sanders (Jay and the Americans)
1942 – Brian Jones (Rolling Stones)
1944 – Barbara Acklin
1952 – Eddie Manion (Southside Johnny and the Asbury Dukes)
1955 – Randy Jackson (Zebra)
1957 – Cindy Wilson (B52's)
1957 – Ian Stanley (Tears For Fears)
1957 – Philip Gould (Level 42)
1967 – Marcus Lillington (Breathe)

★ ★ ★

DEPARTURE LOUNGE

1968 – Frankie Lymon
1974 – Bobby Bloom
1984 – Joe Vann (Duprees)
1985 – David Byron (Uriah Heep)

★ ★ ★

LEAP YEAR DAY NUMBER ONE SINGLES 1960 – 1992

UK	US
1960 – Why Anthony Newley	**1960 – Theme From 'A Summer Place'** Percy Faith Orchestra
1964 – Anyone Who Had A Heart Cilla Black	**1964 – I Want To Hold Your Hand** Beatles
1968 – Cinderella Rockafella Esther and Abi Ofarim	**1968 – Love Is Blue** Paul Mauriat
1972 – Son Of My Father Chicory Tip	**1972 – Without You** Nilsson
1976 – December '63 (Oh What A Night) Four Seasons	**1976 – Theme From 'S.W.A.T.'** Rhythm Heritage
1980 – Coward Of The County Kenny Rogers	**1980 – Crazy Little Thing Called Love** Queen
1984 – Relax Frankie Goes To Hollywood	**1984 – Jump** Van Halen
1988 – I Should Be So Lucky Kylie Minogue	**1988 – Father Figure** George Michael
1992 – Stay Shakespears Sister	**1992 – To Be With You** Mr.Big

LEAP YEAR DAY NUMBER ONE ALBUMS 1960 – 1992

UK	US
1960 – South Pacific Film Soundtrack	Artists/*Stars* Simply Red
1964 – With The Beatles The Beatles	
1968 – Greatest Hits Diana Ross and The Supremes	**1960 – The Sound Of Music** Original Cast
1972 – Neil Reid Neil Reid	**1964 – Meet The Beatles** Beatles
1976 – The Very Best Of Slim Whitman Slim Whitman	**1968 – Magical Mystery Tour** Beatles
1980 – The Last Dance Various Artists	**1972 – American Pie** Don McLean
1984 – Into The Gap Thompson Twins	**1976 – Desire** Bob Dylan
1988 – Introducing The Hardline According To . . . Terence Trent D'Arby	**1980 – The Wall** Pink Floyd
1992 – The Awards 1992 Various	**1984 – Thriller** Michael Jackson
	1988 – Faith George Michael
	1992 – Ropin' The Wind Garth Brooks

1980

PRICELESS ROCK ICONS RELEASED AFTER TWENTY YEAR STRETCH

Buddy with glasses

Don McLean apparently dubbed February 3, 1959, 'The day the music died', when a light plane carrying three rock stars plummeted soon after take-off from the airport at Mason City, Iowa. The plane's pilot also perished in the crash.

Twenty one years and a few days later, during perusal of the files at headquarters in Mason City, Police were astonished to find a dusty file with Buddy Holly's spectacles and a watch that had belonged to The Big Bopper.

ARRIVALS

1904 – Jimmy Dorsey
1940 – Gretchen Christopher (The Fleetwoods)

★ ★ ★

RAVINGS

1964:
The Beatles dominated the US album chart, with *Meet The Beatles* at No. 1 and *Introducing The Beatles* at No. 2. The pair remained back to back for nine weeks

1992:
Vince Neil left US hard rock band Motley Crue

1992:
It was reported that Anthrax had signed to Elektra for $10 million – shortly afterwards, lead vocalist Joey Belladonna left the band.

1936:
The title of Jimmy Dorsey's biggest hit of the rock era accurately described the frequency of his birthdays – 'So Rare'.

★ ★ ★

1969

MORRISON'S MIAMI MAYHEM

While fronting The Doors at Miami's Dinner Key Auditorium, 'Lizard King' Jim Morrison's ritualized cavortings ended with his arrest for 'lewd and lascivious behaviour'. According to the group's keyboard player, Ray Manzarek, Morrison was sending up his sex symbol status with a routine involving a towel, and accidentally exposed himself.

Jim Morrison – towel tactics

Backstage opinion intimated that the resulting charge was trumped up by local authorities, anxious to strike a blow for common decency against this anti-establishment group who, since 1966, had been inciting rebellion and corrupting their children. In fact, the children were often as shocked as their parents by the exhibitions that led to previous ructions between Morrison – a known stimulant abuser and heavy drinker – and the police.

Roaring drunk at the microphone during a concert in Connecticut in 1967, his foul language and dubious antics caused a riot averted only by the prompt action of the local constabulary in hustling the superstar off stage. On that occasion he escaped with a non-custodial sentence. He was also arrested for interfering with an air hostess, but the charges were later withdrawn.

The affair in Florida would have meant gaol for Morrison, had he not moved to Paris while his conviction was still being appealed. The Doors finally began to close in Miami that night . . .

1980

MC5 FRED WEDS PUNK POETESS

Patti – a rose by any other name

Former MC5 guitarist Fred 'Sonic' Smith married New York based punk poetess and recording artist Patti Smith in a civil ceremony in his native Detroit.

Since his group's disbandment after a troubled European tour in 1972, Fred had twanged the wires in several other local combos – but none of these produced a fraction of the impact generated either by his old band outfit or his new wife's Patti Smith Group, who had enjoyed a big international hit in 1978 with 'Because The Night', written for her by Bruce Springsteen (his first appearance in The American Top 20).

Though she and Fred planned to concentrate on raising a family, Mrs Smith hoped to find time for recording sessions with members of the Group as well as the occasional poetry reading. Her fifth book, *Babel*, was published in 1979. Suggestions that Patti chose to marry Fred on the basis that she would not have to change her name were unfounded.

1968

Otis Redding, who died before scoring his biggest hit

OTIS SCORES WITH POSTHUMOUS SMASH

At the funeral of soul star Otis Redding, the pallbearers included many of his colleagues and friends from the soul vocalist fraternity. Joe Tex, Solomon Burke, Percy Sledge and Don Covay were among them, along with Johnnie Taylor and Sam Moore (of Sam and Dave).

Redding's departure in a plane crash was shown to have been particularly badly timed when a track he had cut only three days before he died, '(Sittin' On) The Dock Of The Bay', topped the *Billboard* chart and earned the 26 year old his first gold record – posthumously.

1983

COMPACT DISCS: BRITAIN'S VINYL SOLUTION?

Spelling the possible demise of vinyl records and even cassette tapes, the compact disc and the laser-beamed equipment needed to play it were introduced to Britain's music-lovers. As their transatlantic cousins had known for some time, this was a format of such clarity that, straining your ears just a little, you could almost make out the impact of dandruff grains falling from a heavy metal guitarist's split ends – and you could certainly hear the quieter passages of classical music that previously tended to disappear in crackle and hiss.

The compact disc's detractors cast aspersions on its durability, and argued that, as techno games continued to supplant pop music as the fodder of youth, its marketing was a ploy by record industry moguls to recycle old material in a new package. Indeed, among the first such items to reach UK shops

Ringo – likes a bit of dirt

were reprocessed albums by The Beatles, whose Ringo Starr had already pontificated that CDs were, 'a bit too clean for me. I'm from the old school. I like a bit of dirt on the record'. However, the drummer would find that his own recordings and those of most other artists would be available only on CD ten years later.

1960

ELVIS McPRESLEY

En route to North America after completing his national service in Germany. The plane carrying Elvis Presley stopped for refuelling at Prestwick Airport, Scotland. Presley stepped on British soil for the first and only time in his life, and chatted with fans.

ARRIVALS

1900 – Kurt Weill
1923 – Doc Watson (Arthel Watson)
1939 – Paul Dino
1941 – Keith Potger (The Seekers)
1942 – Tony Meehan (Shadows)
1943 – George Benson
1944 – Lou Reed (Louis Firbank)
1948 – Larry Carlton (Crusaders)
1949 – Eddie Money (Edward Mahoney)
1949 – Rory Gallagher
1950 – Karen Carpenter
1955 – Dale Bozzio
1955 – Jay Osmond (Osmonds)
1956 – Mark Evans (AC/DC)
1962 – Jon Bon Jovi (John Bongiovi)
★ ★ ★

RAVINGS

1959:
Buddy Holly and The Crickets played their first British date.

★ ★ ★

1967:
Proving that schmaltz was very much alive, Englebert Humperdinck's 'Release Me' prevented the double-sided meisterwerk by The Beatles, 'Strawberry Fields Forever'/'Penny Lane', from claiming the No. 1 spot, ending their unbroken string of 11 No. 1s in a row (From 'From Me To You' to 'Eleanor Rigby')

★ ★ ★

1984:
Gold Star Studios in Los Angeles, where Phil Spector created many of his classic hits, was closed in preparation for demolition.

★ ★ ★

STILLS STARTS SPRINGFIELD

Singer/guitarist Steve Stills, a recent migrant to California, formed a new group with Richie Furay, another fretboard-picking friend from New York's Au Go Go Singers. A third singer/songwriter/guitarist in the group was another old mate, Neil

Buffalo Springfield – steamrollered into history by personnel peeves

Young, a Canadian folk singer with whom the pair became reacquainted by chance, so the story goes, when all three were stuck in the same Los Angeles traffic jam! Another version of the story suggests that Stills had been trying to contact Young without success until he found himself driving one way along Sunset Strip and recognized Young's distinctive hearse with Ontario number plates cruising towards him on the other side of the road. The combo came up to full complement with the subsequent recruitment of drummer Dewey Martin and bass player Bruce Palmer, an old associate of Young's in a Canadian group known as The Mynah Birds.

The quintet named itself Buffalo Springfield (after noticing the phrase on the nameplate of a steamroller). With rich resources of internal songwriting talent, Stills and Co. promised to provide an exciting fusion of country and rock for an audience biased against one or the other, but their first album was overshadowed by the timely release of a Stills song entitled 'For What It's Worth', a protest/commentary on the conflict between Los Angeles teenagers and the forces of law and order that had culminated in the celebrated Hollywood riots fictionalized in the *Riot On Sunset Strip* movie.

The single reached the US Top 10, but the group never again aspired to those heights and by May 1968 they had broken up, with Furay launching Poco, Stills joining ex-Byrd David Crosby and Hollies member Graham Nash to form Crosby, Stills and Nash, who sometimes co-opted Neil Young to become Crosby, Stills, Nash and Young when the latter was not working on his own account.

In retrospect, it became clear that Buffalo Springfield had been one of the finest Los Angeles based bands of the mid-1960s. Internal strife and leadership disputes had apparently been a fairly constant factor of the group's short life, however, and their third (and final) original album, *Last Time Around*, was completed by the group's bass player, Jim Messina, after the other band members had launched new careers.

1966

JOHN'S JESUS JIBES

Hot on the heels of the incident at Manila International Airport where The Beatles were jostled by an angry mob, a battering psychological rather than physical was expected to await them on their North American tour later in the year through John Lennon's off-the-cuff comments about the increasing godlessness of our times in an interview with London's *Evening Standard*.

When reprinted in the American teenage magazine *Datebook*, his opinions that The Beatles 'are more popular than Jesus right now' and that 'Christianity will go. It will vanish and shrink' might be interpreted as blasphemy – particularly by 'redneck' whites in the Deep South who strongly laced a right-wing militancy with God-fearing piety. A backlash of moral opprobrium might precipitate hellfire sermons vilifying The Beatles, bonfires of their records, their removal from radio playlists, picketing of shows by the Ku Klux Klan, hostile audiences and even the in-concert slaughter of Lennon by divine wrath – or by someone claiming to act on the Almighty's behalf.

Lennon's remarks were symptomatic of a recent tendency for Beatles

Lennon misunderstood, Beatles in trouble

press conferences to swing in seconds from zany merriment about mini-skirts to two-line debates on inflammable issues. One of these was over the sleeve of an album released in the US (but not the UK), *Yesterday And Today*, that portrayed the Fab Four as butchers gleefully going about their grisly business with dolls' limbs and heads among the bloody wares. This was hastily withdrawn from circulation, and a bland portrait of the group congregated round a cabin trunk was substituted.

1989

U2 VIDEO VICTORY

While topping the charts on both sides of the Atlantic with their latest multi-platinum album, the Grammy Award winning *Rattle And Hum*, Ireland's U2 racked up an unprecedented 400,000 sales for the disc's associated video. Footage for this movie-length offering was shot during the previous year's 110-date world tour. Among its *ad hoc* highlights were a free concert in the streets of San Francisco, and a session at the famed Sun Studios in Memphis.

The group planned a well-earned sabbatical for the rest of the year.

U2 – Grammy, then video explosion

COUNTRY DEATH COLLISION AFTER KC CONCERT

1963

The Grim Reaper came for Patsy Cline, Lloyd 'Cowboy' Copas and Harold 'Hawkshaw' Hawkins as well as Randy Hughes, pilot of the twin-engine Comanche aircraft hired to return the country stars to Nashville after their appearances at a charity concert in Kansas City for the widow of radio presenter 'Cactus' Jack Call who had himself perished in a recent road accident.

The plane crashed while flying low over steep hills in Camden near Dyersburg, Tennessee, between 6 and 7 pm. After a radio report that the craft was missing Roger Miller and Carl Perkins joined the party searching the area, where the wreckage was discovered around dawn.

Though popular on the *Grand Ole Opry*, Copas's recording career had been in decline until 1961 when he topped the country chart with 'Alabam'. Hawkins's hits included 'I Wasted A Nickel' and 'Slow Poke'.

Of all the departed, the artiste who was most missed by the general public was Patsy Cline, queen of the heartbreak ballad, who, it was said, could 'cry on both sides of the microphone'. Singer Loretta Lynn's reaction to the tragedy was typical of the profound grief felt by the country music community in Nashville: 'That just about broke me up, to think that someone as good as that was gone. Patsy was like a mother and sister to me'.

Patsy Cline, role model for k.d.lang

1982

GOODBYE TO BLUES BROTHER BELUSHI

John Belushi (33) died of an accidental drugs overdose that caused respiratory failure. This distinguished actor and comedian was also a competent if idiosyncratic rock 'n' roll performer as shown by his version of Barrett Strong's much covered 'Money' in the 1978 feature film *National Lampoon's Animal House*. From the same movie, his version of The Kingsmen's 'Louie Louie' entered the US charts.

Belushi will, however, be best remembered for his role in the 1980 smash-hit movie *The Blues Brothers*, but a selected few may also fondly recall less public performances such as an after-hours jam session in a Chicago club where, accompanied by *Blues Brothers* co-star Dan Aykroyd and members of The Eagles, his lengthy rendition of 'With A Little Help From My Friends' had the sweaty intensity of a Joe Cocker.

Blues Brother Belushi – idiosyncratic?

MURDERER MANSON MAKES MUSIC

Awareness Records had just released an album by Charles Manson. However, the artist would be unable to promote the disc in person because, after being found guilty of masterminding the Sharon Tate bloodbath by his 'Family' in 1969, he was serving a life sentence in California's San Quentin prison. Addled by drugs, demonology and group sex, The 'Family' had listened to The Beatles 'white double album' on instant replay as they prepared for the murders, having deduced revolutionary directives in such tracks as 'Helter Skelter', 'Piggies' and 'Revolution' as well as such innocuous songs as 'Rocky Racoon' and 'Blackbird'.

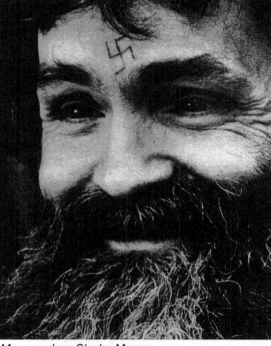

Mass murderer Charles Manson

As a petty crook and would-be pop star, Manson had been singing guitarist in the short-lived Milky Way, and had allegedly auditioned to join The Monkees. He had better luck when patronized by The Beach Boys – particularly drummer Dennis Wilson – to the degree that a Manson composition, 'Cease To Exist' (retitled 'Never Learn Not To Love'), appeared as one of their 1968 B-sides before he alienated them with his unstable conduct and heavy-duty pilfering. Nevertheless, 'message' songs he taped under the band's aegis were included on the new album, which was less remarkable for its content than a sleeve that reproduced the cover of *Life* magazine but with the title altered to read 'Lie' above a portrait of a haunting Charles Manson looking rather less than welcoming.

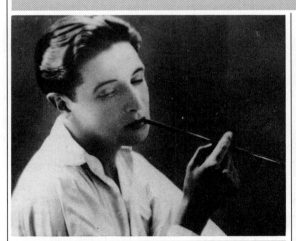

1951

NOVELLO'S HOME FIRE BURNS OUT

The distinguished British composer and film actor Ivor Novello died aged 58.

Born Ivor Davies, his most famous song was the patriotic 'Keep The Home Fires Burning', but he was also the creator of many revues for both the musical and legitimate stage. His plays included *The Truth Game* and 1929's *Symphony In Two Flats*.

Another Novello legacy is the prestigous annual British songwriters award named after him.

RAVINGS

1968:
The Filmore East auditorium opened in New York.

★ ★ ★

1968:
Sandie Shaw (née Sandra Goodrich) was married to fashion designer Jeff Banks.

1972:
Beatle John Lennon's US visa was revoked.

ARRIVALS

1893 – Furry Lewis (Walter Lewis)
1905 – Bob Wills
1925 – Wes Montgomery
1936 – Sylvia Robinson (Mickey and Sylvia)
1937 – Doug Dillard
1942 – Flora Purim
1944 – David Gilmour (Pink Floyd)
1944 – Mary Wilson (Supremes)
1944 – Mickey Jupp
1945 – Hugh Grundy (The Zombies)
1947 – Kiki Dee (Pauline Matthews)

★ ★ ★

DEPARTURE LOUNGE

1991 – Ivor Novello

1913

JOURNAL LEGITIMIZES JAZZ

Controversial classical composer Igor Stravinsky was sincerely loud in his praise of jazz (or 'jass'), the term describing the noisy, improvised extrapolations prevalent in negro dance music at the time.

This word was seemingly elevated from slang by its use in the *San Francisco Bulletin* in a feature concerning the hugely successful singer Al Jolson, whose recording of 'The Spaniard That Blighted My Life' was released a week before .

1976

ELTON'S EXHIBITION HONOUR

The celebrated London waxworks exhibition known as Madame Tussaud's displayed a model of Elton John, the only pop star at that time to be so honoured since The Beatles. This was warranted by a run of hits from 1971's 'Your Song' to 1975's million-selling albums, the autobiographical *Captain Fantastic And The Brown Dirt Cowboy* (the first album to enter the US chart at No. 1) and *Rock Of The Westies*. A further contributory factor might have been the singing pianist's flamboyant stage costumes and trademark flyaway-rim spectacles, which lent themselves to the making of a more intriguing figure than, for example, that of retiring Prime Minister Harold Wilson's designated successor, James Callaghan, a waxwork of whom was to appear soon afterwards.

ARRIVALS

1941 – Danyel Gerard (Gerard Daniel Kherlakian)
1942 – Hamilton Bohannon
1943 – Chris Taylor White (The Zombies)
1944 – Townes Van Zandt
1945 – Arthur Lee (Love)
1946 – Matthew Fisher (Procol Harum)
1946 – Peter Wolf (Peter Blankfield) (J. Geils Band)
1962 – Taylor Dayne (Lesley Wonderman)

★ ★ ★

DEPARTURE LOUNGE

1963 – Jack Anglin

1973

SPRINGSTEEN SHOWCASE

New Jersey born singer/songwriter Bruce Springsteen starred in a showcase at Max's Kansas City club in New York. Considerably less well mannered and artistically self-centred than the Melanies and James Taylors of this world, Springsteen's energetic performance, and a vocal approach described by one critic as possessing 'a Yogi Bear vibrato', reputedly coincided with a heart attack in CBS talent scout John Hammond.

Nevertheless, the man who signed Billie Holiday and Bob Dylan recovered sufficiently to persuade Bruce to sign a long-term recording contract.

With his backing combo, the E Street Band, which included Clarence Clemons (sax), Garry Tallent (bass), Vini Lopez (drums) and David Sancious and Danny Federici (keyboards), Springsteen's debut album, *Greetings From Asbury Park, NJ*, was due for imminent release.

Bruce Springsteen – The Boss

RAVINGS

1917:
The first jazz record was released in the US, 'The Dixie Jazz Band One Step' by Nick LaRocca's Original Dixieland Jazz Band.

1962:
The Beatles made their broadcasting debut on BBC Radio's *Light Programme*.

1965:
During a Rolling Stones gig at the Palace Theatre, Manchester, a girl fell from the balcony.

1966:
Brian Wilson's 'Caroline No' was the first solo single by any member of The Beach Boys.

★ ★ ★

1987

OLDIES HOLD THEIR OWN IN UK CHART

Thanks to snippet coverage in ITV commercials, Ben E. King's 'Stand By Me' from 1961 and 1966's 'When A Man Loves A Woman' by Percy Sledge occupied the respective first and second positions in the UK singles chart for three whole weeks, at a point when every fourth record in the Top 40 was either a reissue or a revival of an old song.

Percy Sledge could not be immediately located, but Ben E. King (by this time aged 49) was scheduled to appear in Britain later in the year to cash in on his unexpected windfall – by complete coincidence, his stage act included a version of Sledge's 'When A Man Loves A Woman'.

1973

McCartney's Marijuana Misdemeanour

In Campbeltown Magistrates Court, ex-Beatle Paul McCartney and his wife Linda pleaded guilty to cannabis cultivation after police officers discovered illegal marijuana plants growing in the greenhouse of the family's remote farm in Scotland's Mull of Kintyre, contrary to the provision of the 1966 Dangerous Drugs Act, section 42.

They were freed after paying a fine of £100 as there was no question of the narcotic being used for any purpose other than personal consumption. Nevertheless, the McCartneys reportedly showed little remorse as they left court.

It had been Paul who first revealed in 1966 that The Beatles had all 'tripped' on LSD. The following year, however, the group publicly repudiated the illegal taking of controlled drugs, although individually and privately they either continued or resumed the habit – as demonstrated by the respective 'busts' of John Lennon and then George Harrison.

National treasures and Members of the British Empire or not, The Beatles were no longer above the law.

McCartney – letting the grass grow

1986

Reaction to Ross Chain Mixed

Exactly 16 years after the first concert (staged in Framingham, Massachusetts) of her solo career that followed her departure from The Supremes, the trio that she had fronted to an incredible ten US No. 1 hits in less than three years during the mid 1960s, Diana Ross topped the UK singles chart with 'Chain Reaction'. This was only her second solo No. 1 in Britain – the first had been 'I'm Still Waiting', back in 1971. Critics quickly picked up on the single's heavily Motown-influenced sound, and British record-buyers evidently agreed with their recommendation to the point where the single ruled the roost for three weeks. Strangely, however, American record-buyers were clearly unimpressed by this retrogression to the sound of the label that Ms Ross (as she likes to be called, according to her unofficial biographer) had left over four years earlier.

Arrivals

1942 – Ralph Ellis (Swinging Blue Jeans)
1944 – Keef Hartley
1945 – Mickey Dolenz (Monkees)
1946 – Randy Meisner (Eagles)
1947 – Michael Allsup (Three Dog Night)
1947 – Shel Macrea (Andrew Semple) (The Fortunes)
1948 – Mel Galley (Whitesnake)
1949 – Dave Lambert (Strawbs)
1957 – Clive Burr (Iron Maiden)

1958 – Gary Numan (Gary Webb)
1958 – Pauline Murray (Penetration)
1960 – Peter 'Pedro' Gill (Frankie Goes To Hollywood)
1960 – Richard Darbyshire (Living In A Box)
1962 Steve Grantley (Eighth Wonder)

★ ★ ★

Departure Lounge

1973 – Ron 'Pigpen' McKernan (Grateful Dead)

★ ★ ★

Ross The Boss – Motown sound still viable?

1972

KLEIN CONCERT CONTROVERSY

Allan Klein, the New York manager and accountant behind George Harrison's Concerts For Bangladesh, presented UNICEF with $1,200,000, purportedly an agreed donation of $5 per unit from sales of the Grammy award-winning triple album documenting the charity events that took place at Madison Square Garden during August of 1971. However, it was estimated that, as the boxed set shifted more than two million copies hitting the top in the UK and No. 2 in the US, the amount given by Klein should have been considerably more. Headlines like 'Did Allen Klein Take The Bangladesh Money ?' in *Rolling Stone* were not reassuring. Unfortunately, as the shows had not been registered as a charity, the cash accrued was also at the mercy of the Inland Revenue in Washington as well as turgid bureaucracy on both sides of the Atlantic. Even personal appeals by Harrison failed to reduce up to £1 million tax liability.

Some sources had named a date in October 1971, when the ex-Beatle would repeat his Madison Square miracle in Britain for Shelter, but they failed to report the allegedly impossible conditions that Klein had stipulated as quid pro quo for this deed. One would require a revision of British law so that the drugs convictions of his clients, Messrs George Harrison and John Lennon, would be quashed.

RAVINGS

1957:
Rival versions of the calypso hit 'The Banana Boat Song' were released simultaneously by The Tarriers and Harry Belafonte.

1961:
Brian Epstein attended his first lunchtime session at The Cavern starring The Beatles.

1967:
Rolling Stone Brian Jones entered hospital with respiratory problems.

1974:
The last performance of the *Grand Ole Opry* took place at the Ryman Auditorium in Nashville.

★ ★ ★

1972

McGOVERN'S MUSICAL MONEY MAKER

A fund-raising concert for George McGovern's bid to become US president was staged at The Forum in Los Angeles.

Among its diverse assortment of stars were Barbra Streisand, Carole King, James Taylor and Quincy Jones, with singers Mama Cass Elliott (of the Mamas and the Papas) and Carly Simon (Taylor's wife), and movie actors Julie Christie, Burt Lancaster, Jon Voight (brother of 'Wild Thing' songwriter Chip Taylor), Jack Nicholson and Britt Ekland as well as record producer Lou Adler among the famous names on hand to show customers to their seats at the event.

Yet despite the support of such big names from the world of entertainment, polls suggested that McGovern's incumbent rival, Richard Nixon, would be elected for a further term of four years in the White House.

James and Carly – supporting McGovern

ARRIVALS

1925 – Billy Ford (Billie and Lillie)
1928 – Keely Smith
1933 – Lloyd Price
1936 – Mickey Gilley
1944 – John Lee (New World)
1944 – Mark Lindsay (Paul Revere and The Raiders)
1945 – Robin Trower (Procol Harum)
1946 – Jim Cregan
1948 – Chris Thompson (Manfred Mann's Earthband)
1948 – Jeffrey Osborne
1948 – Jimmy Fadden (Nitty Gritty Dirt Band)
1949 – Trevor Burton (The Move)
1958 – Martin David Fry (ABC)

★ ★ ★

1977

PISTOLS PALAVER AT PALACE

The gentlemen of the press had assembled outside Buckingham Palace where, so they understood, The Sex Pistols were to sign a lucrative recording contract with A & M records.

Punk at the Palace

At the appointed hour a limousine cruised past containing the group – with new bass guitarist Sid Vicious – who made vulgar signs at the waiting hacks before speeding off towards Victoria. Minutes later they returned and a rather cynical ceremony took place on a trestle table outside Her Majesty's London residence – a fitting location as 'God Save The Queen' was to be the title of their next single, following the withdrawal of their debut hit while it was still in the UK singles chart.

Scheduled for release in time for Queen Elizabeth II's forthcoming Silver Jubilee, the new single was not reflective of monarchist fervour – in fact, it was very much the opposite.

There was speculation about how long the outfit would stay with A & M in the light of EMI dropping them shortly after the release of 'Anarchy In The UK' at the end of 1976. EMI had not been prepared to tolerate the group in the light of the headline-hogging outrage that followed their cursing on an early-evening chat show and a public instance of alcohol-induced vomiting. All the same, The Sex Pistols and their manager, Malcolm McLaren, left EMI with the agreed £40,000 advance.

After only six days with A & M, due to pressure from the head office in Los Angeles, the band were let go - again with their advance of £75,000 intact. It is hardly surprising therefore that they were among nominees for a 'Young Businessmen Of The Year' award by one financial journal with a sense of humour.

1990

RUSSIAN ROCK RESULTS

The published results of a survey conducted amongst Russian teen-agers revealed that the Western rock acts they would most like to see in concert were Michael Jackson, Pink Floyd and The Beatles. While the last of these choices seemed rather optimistic in view of John Lennon's murder in 1980, since the formal end of the Soviet regime there was more likelihood of the other two appearing beyond the Steppes than ever before. Nevertheless, contemporary pop from the free world was not unknown in the USSR, as exemplified by regular concert tours by Gold (an outfit unknown elsewhere, even in their native England), a much publicized 1979 show in Moscow by Elton John accompanied by percussionist Ray Cooper, and Paul McCartney's *Choba B CCCP (Back In The USSR)*, an album of 1950s' rock 'n' roll favourites, initially available only in Russia.

RAVINGS

1956:
Johnnie Ray was mobbed on arrival in Australasia for his first visit down under.

1974:
David Bowie recorded an in-concert album, *David Live*, at Philadelphia's Tower Theatre.

★ ★ ★

ARRIVALS

1940 – Dean Torrence (Jan and Dean)
1945 – Pete Nelson (Flower Pot Men)
1947 – Tom Scholz (Boston)
1948 – Jethro Burns (Kenneth C. Burns) (Homer and Jethro)
1950 – Ted McKenna (Alex Harvey Band)
1955 – Bunny DeBarge (DeBarge)
1962 – Gary Clark (Danny Wilson)
1964 – Neneh Cherry
1964 – Patrick Kane (Hue and Cry)
1965 – Tina Charles (Tina Hoskins)
1967 – Susie Q. (Susan Banfield) (Cookie Crew)

★ ★ ★

DEPARTURE LOUNGE

1988 – Andy Gibb
1989 – Doc Green (Drifters)

★ ★ ★

1967

YESTERDAY'S NORTHERN SONG

It transpired that John Lennon and Paul McCartney's 'Yesterday' was the most 'covered' song of all time. The announcement was made by Dick James, director of Northern Songs, the songwriting duo's publishing company, a subsidiary of his own Dick James Music. As a vocalist, James's 'Robin Hood' had been the most successful of several versions issued in 1956. However, 'Robin Hood' swallows dust well behind 'Yesterday', which had elicited 446 different recordings by other artists since it was first released by The Beatles on the soundtrack album of the *Help!* movie and as a US hit single. Billy J. Kramer – also managed by Brian Epstein – was given first refusal but, said Billy, 'it was too nicey-nicey for me'. In Britain, renderings by Matt Monro and Marianne Faithfull each reached the Top 40, and the number was to be Ray Charles's Yuletide single later that same year.

The composition had been given the provisional title of 'Scrambled Eggs' until McCartney came up with the lyrics that he sang accompanied by a string quartet and his own acoustic guitar strumming. 'Yesterday' is an extreme example, but other tracks from *Help!* and later Beatles albums also went beyond conventional beat group instrumentation by employing sitars, flutes, horn sections, tape collage and other resources that the group did not use on stage during their 1966 world tour – a tiresome trek that they were in no hurry to repeat.

1976

SIMON SELLS A MILLION

Simon and Garfunkel – separate success

Paul Simon received a gold disc for his million-selling '50 Ways To Leave Your Lover' single excerpted from 1975's *Still Crazy After All These Years* album. This was the second such award for singer/songwriter Paul since parting with musical partner Art Garfunkel, who had himself notched up a UK No. 1 the previous September with his revival of The Flamingos' arrangement of 'I Only Have Eyes For You'.

While it reached only No. 23 in Britain, '50 Ways To Leave Your Lover' topped the *Billboard* chart for three weeks in February 1976, before being superceded by Rhythm Heritage's 'Theme From S.W.A.T.'

MOP TOP MCCARTNEY MARRIES

1969

Paul McCartney, the last bachelor Beatle, wed Linda Eastman, the pop photographer. A civil ceremony took place at London's Marylebone Registry Office but the marriage was blessed at a St John's Wood church local to Paul's Cavendish Avenue residence. To limit the possibilities of an outbreak of Beatlemania, none of the other Beatles were present at either location. George and Patti Harrison had intended to make the Ritz Hotel reception if George had completed production chores at a Jackie Lomax session, but a police raid on the guitarist's Surrey home and the subsequent discovery there of controlled drugs rather spoilt the day for the youngest Beatle and his wife.

A Beatle with a new wife

A random survey among those of McCartney's female fans who witnessed the newlyweds' exit from the registry office revealed they were not dismayed by his choice, though most had expected him to tie the knot with Jane Asher, the dashing young actress to whom he was once engaged. Linda coincidentally attended school in the same district as Yoko Ono, the Japanese-American performance artist who became the second Mrs John Lennon.

ARRIVALS

1896 – Jesse Fuller
1940 – Al Jarreau
1942 – Brian O'Hara (The Fourmost)
1942 – Mark Valentino
1942 – Paul Kantner (Jefferson Airplane)
1946 – Liza Minnelli

1948 – James Taylor
1948 – Les Holroyd (Barclay James Harvest)
1949 – Mike Gibbins (Badfinger)
1956 – Simon Booth (Working Week)
1956 – Steve Harris (Iron Maiden)

1957 – Marlon Jackson (Jackson Five)

★ ★ ★

DEPARTURE LOUNGE

1955 – Charlie Parker
1978 – Tolchard Evans

RAVINGS

1964:
The Beatles played in Washington, their first live show in America.

1966:
Los Angeles rock band Love released their first album, Love.

1971:
Jethro Tull's *Aqualung* album was released, as was the John Lennon's first solo single since the break up of The Beatles, 'Power To The People'.

1976:
Joe Stampley entered the US country charts with 'The Sheik Of Chicago', a tribute to Chuck Berry.

★ ★ ★

LA LOUT – LENNON TIRED AND EMOTIONAL

1974

Ex-Beatle John Lennon was ejected from the Troubadour club in Los Angeles, where he had been constantly interrupting a show by The Smothers Brothers with comments that included swearing and a recurrent 'I'm John Lennon!' There were also allegations that Lennon had assaulted both the duo's manager and, with a sanitary towel attached to his forehead, one of the club's waitresses, who consequently filed a complaint against him to the city's district attorney. Once outside the building, Lennon instigated a scuffle with a waiting photographer.

The 'Give Peace A Chance' hitmaker had been experiencing marital difficulties, and had been drinking heavily. In his cups, he also fulminated about the official harrassment that had hindered his efforts to settle permanently in the States since his arrival from England in 1971.

SLOWHAND SAYS 'SO LONG' TO THE YARDBIRDS

1965

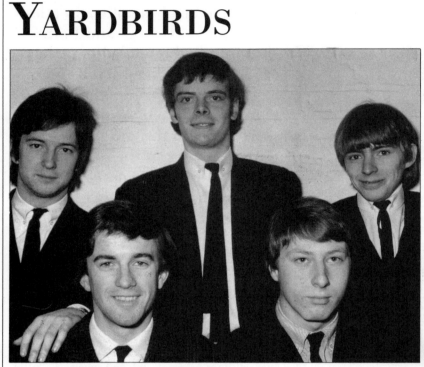

Yardbirds – Clapton off to Mayall's Bluesbreakers

Lead guitarist Eric 'Slowhand' Clapton left The Yardbirds on the eve of the release of their third single, 'For Your Love', which pundits predicted was destined to catapult the group from cult celebrity to national eminence.

Blues purist Eric was, apparently, at loggerheads with bass player Paul Samwell-Smith over musical policy. The main bone of contention was Paul's highly commercial arrangement of 'For Your Love', featuring bongos and Brian Auger's harpsichord. The song was composed by Graham Gouldman of Manchester's Mockingbirds.

Clapton was unavailable for comment, but Samwell-Smith reflected, 'had we continued to play just blues, we would, in the end, have broken through (but) we were desperate for a hit because you can't tour America without one.

You suddenly get on television – everything opens up for you. It's no good saying "we're a great blues band" when there's three thousand people in England who've ever heard of you. We'd have had to keep playing the Crawdaddy and Station Hotel otherwise'. While Clapton prepared for a debut with John Mayall's Bluesbreakers, The Yardbirds searched for a replacement. Top sessionman Jimmy Page was approached, but declined the offer.

1975

TAMMY AND GEORGE D.I.V.O.R.C.E.

The six-year marriage of country-and-western stars George Jones and Tammy Wynette ended in the divorce court. The couple had separated several times during a stormy espousal as Jones's drinking – initially to overcome stage fright – increased, along with underlying emotional turmoil. By coincidence, Alabama-born Tammy's follow-up to her UK 'sleeper' hit, 'Stand By Your Man', was to be the self-penned 'D.I.V.O.R.C.E.'

George and Tammy, now divorced

1972

REAGAN PARDONS STAR FROM SAN QUENTIN

Described as 'a fully rehabilitated member of society', Merle Haggard, the 'outlaw' country star, was granted an unconditional pardon by Ronald Reagan, governor of his home state of California.

The death of his father when Merle was nine had precipitated a battle against authority that culminated in January 1958 with a prison sentence of two years five months for burglary.

Haggard's stretch in San Quentin prison was notable for a spell in solitary confinement in a cell next to that of homicidal multiple rapist Caryl Chessman (the subject of a record by Canadian rock 'n' roller Ronnie Hawkins), and a 1960 concert by Johnny Cash that might have hardened Merle's resolve to go straight and make a go of it as a country-and-western entertainer when he was released on parole just over three months later.

Merle Haggard – a Presidential pardon

RAVINGS

1953:
Marty Robbins made his US chart debut with 'I'll Go On Alone'.

★ ★ ★

1968:
Elvis Presley's 26th movie, *Stay Away Joe*, was premiered.

★ ★ ★

1971:
The Rolling Stones played a Farewell Concert at The Roundhouse, London, before moving to France as tax exiles.

★ ★ ★

1981:
Roxy Music topped the UK chart with their cover version of John Lennon's 'Jealous Guy' released as a tribute to the murdered ex-Beatle.

★ ★ ★

1991

DOC DIES

Noted US composer Jerome 'Doc' Pomus died at the age of 66. Confined to a wheelchair from earliest youth, he had scratched a living as a blues singer in the style of Mose Allison from the end of the Second World War.

More lucrative than the records he made for various obscure labels were the numbers he wrote for such as Joe Turner and Ray Charles before a long collaboration with New Yorker Mort Shuman in 1957. Among their joint efforts was the much covered 'A Teenager In Love', a US hit for Dion and The Belmonts, whose version was only a minor hit in Britain. Its success was eclipsed by covers from Marty Wilde, who reached the Top 3, and by Craig Douglas, who made the Top 20. Thus established, the pair

Doc Pomus was confined to a wheelchair for most of his life

provided more hit material for The Drifters 'Save The Last Dance For Me' as well as for Elvis Presley (notably, the chart-topping 'Surrender'), Ral Donner, Gene McDaniels and Ben E. King.

Until they lost the knack of penning hits in the mid 1960s, Pomus and Shuman were courted by all manner of major artists for their songs, and were an inspiration to Carole King, Neil Sedaka and other stars-in-embryo churning out assembly-line pop in the Brill Building, New York's famous songwriting 'factory'.

ARRIVALS

1912 – Les Brown (Lester Raymond)
1922 – Les Baxter
1931 – Phil Phillips (John Phillip Baptiste)
1933 – Quincy Jones
1945 – Walter Parazaider (Chicago)
1946 – Jim Pons (The Turtles)
1947 – Jona Lewie
1947 – Peter Skellern
1949 – Ollie Halsall (Kevin Ayers/Boxer)
1955 – Boon Gould (Level 42)
1957 – Chris Redburn (Kenny)
1963 – Steve Lambert (Roman Holliday)

★ ★ ★

DEPARTURE LOUNGE

1991 – Jerome 'Doc' Pomus

★ ★ ★

LADY' OPENS ON BROADWAY

1956

The New York premiere of the musical *My Fair Lady* took place at the Mark Hellinger Theatre with a distinguished cast headed by Rex Harrison, Stanley Holloway and comparative newcomer Julie Andrews, recent star of another Broadway hit, *The Boy Friend*. Composed by Frederick Loewe with lyricist Alan Jay Lerner, the new musical was an adaptation of George Bernard Shaw's *Pygmalion*, in which Professor Henry Higgins (played by Harrison) transforms 'gorblimey' East End flower seller Eliza Dolittle (Andrews) into a graceful society lady.

There were immediate mutterings about turning My Fair Lady into a Hollywood movie. An original-cast album was recorded, and various major artists such as Vic Damone and David Whitfield were asked to record cover versions of songs from the musical such as 'On The Street Where You Live', 'I Could Have Danced All Night' and other catchy ditties that reviewers correctly predicted would become cabaret 'standards'. The album was No. 2 in the first British LP listings, three years after its release.

RAVINGS

1957:
Frankie Lymon and The Teenagers arrived in Britain for a tour.

1972:
A Los Angeles radio station played the Donny Osmond single, 'Puppy Love', for 90 minutes non-stop.

1980:
The movie featuring The Clash, *Rude Boy*, opened in London.

1980:
Phil Lynott's third volume of poetry, *A Collected Work Of Phil Lynott*, was published.

1984:
The surviving Beatles became freemen of the city of Liverpool.

★ ★ ★

ARRIVALS

1912 – Sam 'Lightnin'' Hopkins
1916 – Harry James
1932 – Arif Mardin
1940 – Phil Lesh (Philip Chapman Lesh) (Grateful Dead)
1941 – Mike Love (Beach Boys)
1942 – Hughie Flint

1944 – Sly Stone (Sylvester Stewart)
1946 – Howard Scott (War)
1947 – Ry Cooder (Ryland Cooder)
1955 – Dee Snider (Twisted Sister)
1962 – Steve Coy (Dead Or Alive)
1962 – Terence Trent D'Arby

1964 – Rockwell (Kennedy Gordy, son of Berry Gordy Jr)
1968 Sabrina (Sabrina Salerno)

★ ★ ★

DEPARTURE LOUNGE

1959 – Lester Young

PARKER'S PACT WITH PRESLEY

1956

Parker and Presley Pact

Colonel Tom Parker officially became manager of Elvis Presley, having previously negotiated a recording contract with RCA on the singer's behalf with the agreement of the latter's father, Vernon Presley – Elvis was too young to sign contracts at the time.

Presley's recorded hybrids of country-and-western, jumped-up black R & B and sulky balladeering had made him both adored and detested throughout the Deep South. Presley had also become notorious for a wild stage act that many civic burghers found offensive, and a hoodlum image exemplified by his penchant for dressing in outrageous 'cat' clothes. A brilliantined pompadour was offset by sideburns down to his earlobes. What more did Presley need to be the rage of teenage North America?

Parker's reputation for driving a hard bargain was earned during years as a fairground huckster whose duties included palm reading. While employed as a fund-raiser for a charity organization, he discovered the financial potential of promoting country-music concerts. This led to a full-time commitment to the genre. It was while overseeing the career of Hank Snow that the Colonel – an honorary title – first noticed Elvis low on the bill of a Snow show.

TUMOUR TAKES TAMMI

1970

Following a series of eight operations, complications arising from a brain tumour claimed the life of 23-year-old soul singer Tammi Terrell, whose duets with Marvin Gaye spawned international hits in 'If I Could Build My Whole World Around You', 'Ain't Nothin' Like The Real Thing', 'You're All I Need To Get By', 'You Ain't Livin' Till You're Lovin'', 'Good Lovin' Ain't Hard To Come By' and 'The Onion Song'.

Born Tammi Montgomery in Philadelphia, her 1966 debut single, 'I Cried', was produced by James Brown who featured her in his itinerant concert troupe before she teamed up with Gaye in 1967 when his previous partner, Kim Weston, resumed her solo career. After falling unconscious in Gaye's arms during a show at Virginia's Hampden-Sydney College, Tammi underwent surgery but continued to suffer from debilitating headaches and weight loss.

Tammi Terrell – death ended a hitmaking partnership with Marvin Gaye

COSTELLO'S COCAINE COMMENTS CAUSE CLASH WITH STILLS

1979

Elvis Costello – tarred with Woodstock brush?

A scuffle broke out in a US hotel bar between Elvis Costello's Attractions and members of Stephen Stills' backing group after some offensive remarks by Costello's party referring to Stills' now discontinued cocaine habit – 'steel nose' – and to Ray Charles as 'a blind ignorant nigger'.

The bespectacled British 'New Wave' entertainer had been drinking heavily, and was believed to have been less giving voice to racist opinions than indirectly venting his annoyance at Linda Ronstadt's recent recording of five of his songs that, despite the composing royalties these

accrued, had brought Costello an unsolicited and unwelcome affinity to unfashionable 'Woodstock Generation' artists such as Ronstadt and Stills.

Intriguingly, Costello was fond of country music, a genre that most of his New Wave fans probably considered to be the corniest in pop. He was particularly keen on the music of George Jones with whom he had recorded a duet, 'Stranger In The House', for inclusion on the Texan vocalist's new album of duets *My Very Special Guests*.

RAVINGS

1957:
Fats Domino's 'I'm Walkin'' replaced his own 'Blue Monday' at the top of *Billboard's* R & B chart.

1968:
Louis Armstrong topped the UK singles chart with 'Wonderful World'.

1968:
'(Sittin' On) The Dock Of The Bay' by the late Otis Redding topped the US singles chart.

1974:
President Richard Nixon attended the first performance of the *Grand Ole Opry* at the new purpose-built (at a cost of $15 million!) Opry House.

1991:
Seven members of country star Reba McEntire's backing group perished in a plane crash.

★ ★ ★

ARRIVALS

1926 – Jerry Lewis (Joseph Levitch)
1932 – Betty Johnson
1942 – Jerry Jeff Walker (Ronald Crosby)
1943 – Jerry Goodman (Flock/Mahavishnu Orchestra)
1948 – Michael Bruce (Alice Cooper)
1951 – Ray Benson (Asleep At The Wheel)
1954 – Jimmy Nail
1954 – Nancy Wilson (Heart)
1963 – Stuart Kerr (Texas)
1965 – Byron Stingily (Ten City)

★ ★ ★

DEPARTURE LOUNGE

1970 – Tammi Terrell (Tammy Montgomery)
1975 – T. Bone Walker (Aaron Thibeaux Walker)
1976 – Arthur 'Hardrock' Gunter (writer of 'Baby Let's Play House')
1983 – Arthur Godfrey

★ ★ ★

1962

THE BLUES CAME DOWN FROM EALING

Blues in Britain grew as a bohemian cult provoked partly by scorn for the Top 10 toot-tooting of traditional jazz. Two sacked Chris Barber sidemen, harmonica player Cyril Davies and guitarist Alexis Korner, formed Blues Incorporated in 1961. In March 1962 they found a suitable venue for the band to play regularly in a downstairs room between a jeweller's premises and the ABC teashop in West London's Ealing Broadway. The Ealing Club was patronized immediately by blues enthusiasts from other London suburbs and beyond.

Alexis Korner, father of British R & B, pictured in 1964

As a hangover from trad, Blues Incorporated was primarily an instrumental unit with a rapid turnover of personnel, but featuring Charlie Watts (drums), Jack Bruce (bass), Dick Heckstall-Smith (sax) and Long John Baldry (singer) as semi-permanent fixtures.

A constant flux of other players was drawn from the audience, among them future members of such bands as The Kinks, The Yardbirds, Manfred Mann, The Rolling Stones and The Pretty Things.

ARRIVALS

1917 – Nat 'King' Cole (Nathaniel Adams Coles)
1939 – Clarence Collins (Little Anthony and The Imperials)
1939 – Lewis Mathis (The Newbeats)
1941 – Clarence Clemons (E Street Band)
1941 – John Sebastian
1941 – Paul Lorin Kantner (Jefferson Airplane /Jefferson Starship)
1944 – Bob Johnson (Steeleye Span)
1944 – Paul Pilnick (Stealers Wheel)
1946 – Harold Brown (War)
1948 – Pat Lloyd (The Equals)
1951 – Scott Gorham (Thin Lizzy)
1959 – Mike Lindup (Level 42)
1962 – Claire Grogan (Altered Images)

★ ★ ★

DEPARTURE LOUNGE

1986 – Sonny Terry (Saunders Terrell)
1990 – Ric Grech

★ ★ ★

1990

BLIND FAITH BASSMAN DIES - DRUGS TO BLAME

Ric Grech died at the age of 44 of debilities not unrelated to the drugs that had apparently been common currency when he had been a member of the Blind Faith 'supergroup' in 1969.

Born in Bordeaux, France, Richard Roman Grech was bass guitarist with the Leicester based group, Farinas, who had become Family by 1967, when they emerged as the darlings of London's 'underground' clubs.

He was invited by Steve Winwood, Ginger Baker and Eric Clapton to join Blind Faith, the supergroup who made their concert debut before thousands at a free performance in Hyde Park, and recorded a curate's egg of an eponymous album before splitting up after a US tour to promote it.

Baker, then enlisted Grech into his percussion-heavy group Air Force, after which Grech tried his luck with a short spell in Winwood's re-formed Traffic before his growing drug dependency necessitated his replacement, although he was to tread the boards with Traffic personnel again at Clapton's 'comeback' show at London's Rainbow Theatre in 1974.

Relocating to the United States, He saw out the 1970s as a temporary member of The Crickets alongside guitarist Albert Lee and as an occasional session bassist for Jim Capaldi and Ronnie Bond. He also forged a brief association with country singer Gram Parsons.

Finally, stints with KGB (another so-called 'supergroup' with Mike Bloomfield), and Grechmas (with Keith Christmas and drummer Keith Ellis). By his death, however, he had withdrawn altogether from the music business.

RAVINGS

1968:
The Bee Gees made their US television debut on *The Ed Sullivan Show*.

1978:
American Hot Wax, The film about US disc jockey Alan Freed - coiner of the 'Rock 'n' Roll' tag premiered in the US.

1990:
Prince began filming *Graffiti Bridge*, the follow-up to his *Purple Rain* movie.

★ ★ ★

1965

STONES' – STRATFORD SLASHERS

While The Beatles straightened their ties in readiness to receive their MBEs from The Queen, their belligerently unkempt rivals, The Rolling Stones, continued to make adult blood run cold with an incident that took place at a service station in Stratford's Romford Road.

It seems that a Daimler – with Mick Jagger, Bill Wyman, Brian Jones, their chauffeur and various hangers-on – had bounced on to the garage's asphalt forecourt in the late evening.

Would you let your daughter marry one of these men?

Wyman got out to ask the manager, Mr Charles Keeley, for permission to use the toilet. The public convenience was, said Keeley, out of order, and he was not prepared to let Wyman or the rest of entourage use the staff lavatory. Unabashed, Wyman, Jagger and Jones were obliged to improvise by urinating against a wall. On completing their ablutions, the visitors rendered obsequious thanks to an appalled Mr Keeley before driving off into the night.

While the police had no wish to press charges of 'insulting behaviour', Mr Keeley, abetted by Mr Eric Lavender, a local youth club organizer, brought a private prosecution against the three musicians. The case was to be heard at West Ham magistrates' court the following July.

The defence was expected to call Rolling Stones Charlie Watts and Keith Richards to testify to their colleagues' good characters. In the event they were fined £5 ($8) each.

1982

PARALYSED PENDERGRASS

32-year-old soul singer Teddy Pendergrass was paralyzed from the neck down as a result of his Rolls-Royce swerving across a street in his native Philadelphia, and going into a somersaulting skid in attempts to avoid a collision with another vehicle.

The son of a nightclub entertainer, his professional career began as drummer with The Cadillacs, a gospel combo who, in 1969, augmented Harold Melvin and The Blue Notes. The following year Teddy replaced John Atkins as lead vocalist of The Blue

Teddy Pendergrass, injured in Roller somersault

Notes, his feathery counter-tenor lacquering Melvin hits such as 'If You Don't Know Me By Now' and 1977's 'Don't Leave Me This Way'. That year, he went solo, and was soon causing Barry White nervous backward glances with the 'lurve man' burblings of 'Close The Door', 1981's 'It's Time For Love' and the like.

ARRIVALS

1936 – Robert Lee Smith (The Tams)
1939 – Kenny Lynch
1939 – Travis Pritchett (Travis and Bob)
1941 – Wilson Pickett
1943 – Dennis Linde
1947 – Barry 'BJ' Wilson (Procol Harum)
1950 – John Hartman (Doobie Brothers)
1959 – Irene Cara
1962 – Taja Sevelle
1968 – Serafina Watts (daughter of Charlie and Shirley Watts)
1986 – Charley Pride

★ ★ ★

RAVINGS

1957:
Bill Haley and The Comets arrived back in the States after a world tour during which they performed to over 500,000 fans.

1989:
Production team Stock, Aitken and Waterman had three singles in the Top 4 places of the UK chart – the hits concerned were Jason Donovan's 'Too Many Broken Hearts', Bananarama's 'Help' and Donna Summer's 'This Time I Know It's For Real'.

★ ★ ★

*1897 – Moms Mabley
(Loretta Mary Aiken)*
1919 – Lennie Tristano
1930 – Ornette Coleman
*1937 – Clarence 'Frogman'
Henry*
1938 – Walter Jackson
*1942 – Jeff Neighbour
(Joy Of Cooking)*
1942 – Robin Luke
*1946 – Paul Atkinson
(Zombies)*
*1946 – Ruth Pointer
(Pointer Sisters)*
1953 – Ricky Wilson (B52s)
*1955 – Derek Longmuir
(Bay City Rollers)*
*1959 – Terry Hall (Specials,
Fun Boy
Three, etc.)*

★ ★ ★

DEPARTURE
LOUNGE

*1976 – Gary Thain
(Uriah Heep)*
1976 – Paul Kossoff (Free)
*1982 – Randy Rhoads
(Ozzy Osbourne's
Blizzard Of Ozz)*

1957
PRESLEY'S PALACE

Former truck driver Elvis Presley purchased from Mrs Ruth Brown-Moore a stately colonial mansion on the outskirts of Memphis. 'Graceland' may have once tinkled to the sounds of Debussy and Handel during musical evenings in the last century but it would be set a-tremble by less euphonious sounds after the King of Western Bop's Cadillac sped up its gravel driveway to take up residence. Presley's parents and grandmother were expected to move in too.

1976
PAUL PASSES AWAY ON PLANE

The late Paul Kossoff

Possibly overdrawing on a misspent youth, 26-year-old UK guitarist Paul Kossoff passed away while dozing in his aeroplane seat on a flight from London to New York. The cause of death is unknown but Kossoff's heroin dependency was thought to have brought on a heart attack and associated kidney collapse that rendered him 'technically dead' for half an hour last August.

The son of celebrated Jewish comedy actor David Kossoff, he will be best remembered by pop fans as a founder member of Free. The quartet's 1973 UK Top 10 entry, 'Wishing Well', was, apparently, about Paul. Later he was to form Back Street Crawler (later, just Crawler) in hopes of filling the market void left by Free, but the group fell hirsute victim of the amateurism of the rising punk movement.

1958: Buddy Holly and The Crickets performed at The Ritz in Wigan, Lancashire, as part of their UK tour.

1970: *Rolling Stone* magazine revealed that the opening words of Lennon and McCartney's 'Come Together' were the same as lyrics in Chuck Berry's 'You Can't Catch Me': 'Here come old flat top, he come groovin' up slowly . .'

1984: Duran Duran played to a full house at New York's Madison Square Garden.

1988: Les Warner, drummer with The Cult, left the group when they decided to relocate to Los Angeles.
★ ★ ★

1982
END OF THE ROAD FOR RHOADS

Ozzy Osbourne's backing guitarist Randy Rhoads (ex-Quiet Riot) was killed while en route by light aircraft to an engagement in Florida. Travelling by tour bus, the other members of the group Blizzard Of Ozz had been 'buzzed' by the plane in which Rhoads was a passenger, which then failed to regain height before ploughing into nearby woodland. His colleagues heard the subsequent explosion.

1969

LENNON WEDS ONO

Japanese-American performance artist Yoko Ono Cox became the second Mrs John Lennon at the British Consulate building on Gibraltar. Beatle assistant Peter Brown gave the bride away, while Lennon's demeanour during the ceremony seemed casual as he stood before the registrar, smoking a cigarette. 'Intellectually, we didn't believe in getting married', he commented, 'but one doesn't love someone just intellectually.'

Within the hour, the happy couple flew to Paris, presumably for the honeymoon.

The pair first met in 1966 while both were still espoused to other partners, when a London gallery hosted one of Yoko's art exhibitions. Charmed by the all-white chess set and other puzzling creations, the Beatle funded his future wife's next event, taking a benevolent interest in her activities past and present. After Yoko and John began walking out together, they issued a trilogy of albums filled with sounds not generally regarded as pop entertainment. For the first, *Unfinished Music No. 1: Two Virgins*, it was noticed that the couple had neglected to put their clothes on for the cover photograph.

In other respects, too, their lives became an open and, to many, ludicrous book, with the planting of an acorn at Coventry Cathedral, appearances inside a kingsize white bag, and other seemingly senseless pranks.

1970

BOWIE'S BROMLEY BRIDE

David and Angela – married in Bromley

Space Oddity' hitmaker David Bowie and girlfriend Mary Angela Barnett arrived nearly 30 minutes late for their wedding at Bromley Registry 0ffice. Bowie's mother, Mrs Peggy Burns, acted as witness, having informed the local press of the nuptials. The free-thinking couple continued to live in their ground-floor flat in Southend Road's Haddon Hall, Beckenham, where members of the singer's backing group also resided. The daughter of a US army colonel, Miss Barnett ('Angie') was formerly a business and economics student at Kingston Polytechnic – an experience that would theoretically assist her with the day-to-day running of her new husband's career.

ALAN'S ARENA ANTICLIMAX

1952

Manic Cleveland radio presenter Alan Freed's *Rock 'n' Roll Stage Show* at the city's Arena stadium was cancelled after 30,000 adolescent music-lovers attempted to cram into the venue. Fire regulations decreed that there was room for only 10,000 in safety. Interestingly, a substantial minority of the disappointed audience were white. 'Rock 'n' roll', a traditional blues metaphor for sexual congress, was an expression coined by the jive-talking Freed for the black dance records he played on his show, *Moondog's Rock 'n' Roll Party*, a programme notable for its preponderance of 'sepia' sounds, and for the Philadelphia born disc jockey's habit of thumping out the beat with a telephone directory.

ARRIVALS

1902 – Son House (Eddie James House)
1930 – Otis Spann
1943 – Vivian Stanshall (Bonzo Dog Doo Dah Band)
1945 – Rose Stone (Sly and The Family Stone)
1946 – Ray Dorset (Mungo Jerry)
1950 – Roger Hodgson (Supertramp)
1954 – Wally Stocker (The Babys)
1957 – John Reddington (King Kurt)

DEPARTURE LOUNGE

1971 – Don Drummond (Skatalites)
1987 – Dean Martin Jr (Dino, Desi and Billy)

★ ★ ★

PARIS TO THE AMSTERDAM HILTON . . .

1969

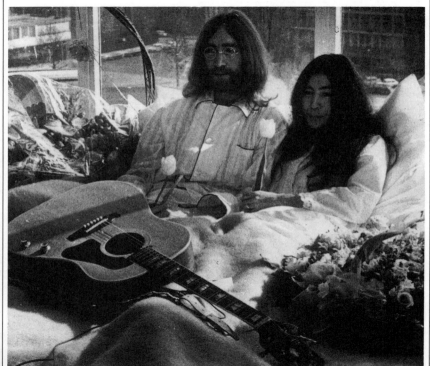

The Lennons searching for peace in a hotel room

RAVINGS

1961:
After a season at the Kaiserkeller on Hamburg's notorious Reeperbahn, The Beatles played an evening debut performance at The Cavern, a basement club in their native Liverpool.

★ ★ ★

1970:
The Guess Who's 'American Woman' single was released.

★ ★ ★

1976:
David Bowie and Iggy Pop were arrested on suspicion of marijuana possession at New York's Rochester hotel. They were released on $2,000 bail. The case was later dropped.

★ ★ ★

1976:
Rubin 'Hurricane' Carter was released from jail following publicity given to his case by Bob Dylan's song 'Hurricane'.

★ ★ ★

Newlyweds John Lennon and Yoko Ono left Paris (as Lennon later sang in 'The Ballad Of John and Yoko') to go to Amsterdam, where they spent the next eight days involved in what they called a 'bed-in for peace' at the local Hilton hotel. During this period, they only left their double bed for visits to the bathroom.

The rationale behind this prolonged sojourn between the sheets was not what most newly married couples would choose for the week immediately following their wedding day, but was to alert the attention of the world's media to the need for peace (as opposed to war). They behaved similarly two months later when they recorded 'Give Peace A Chance' while in bed together (on that occasion with Kyoko, Yoko's daughter from a previous marriage, also in the bed of Room 1742 of Montreal's La Reine Elizabeth Hotel), with help from one of the Smothers Brothers, poet Allan Ginsberg, drug guru Dr Timothy Leary, disc jockey Murray the K, Petula Clark, publicist Derek Taylor, a rabbi, a priest and members of the Radha Krishna Temple (hence the 'Hare Krishna' refrains). When released it was kept off No. 1 by the Rolling Stones.

CARL'S CRASH COULD CURTAIL CHART CLIMB

1956

Up-and-coming rock 'n' roll entertainer Carl Perkins was severely injured and his brother Jay (one of his backing musicians) killed when their car hit a pick-up truck while driving through Wilmington, Delaware, *en route* to New York for a TV appearance on the nationally networked *Perry Como Show*.

His latest single, 'Blue Suede Shoes', was prominent in *Billboard's* pop, country and western and R & B charts – record industry pundits had predicted that the disc would top all three lists within two weeks.

As Perkins was laid up for the next six months, he was close to being overtaken by a cover version sung by the younger Elvis Presley, whose bachelor status was an additional advantage in winning the support of female fans over long-married father-of-three Perkins . However, rather than becoming bitter about his ill luck, Perkins, a former farm hand, was attractive in his phlegmatic candour, reflecting that 'most kids from my background never get to drive a new car'.

RAVINGS

1958:
Buddy Holly and The Crickets played The Gaumont cinema, Salisbury, during their UK tour.

1974:
Ten Years After played a final UK concert in London. In 1978, the group's singer/guitarist, Alvin Lee, formed Ten Years Later without his ex-colleagues.

1986:
Mark Dinning died. He was the first singer to top the US singles chart with a 'death' record, 'Teen Angel'.

★ ★ ★

ARRIVALS

1937 – Johnny Ferguson
1943 – George Benson
1943 – Keith Relf (Yardbirds)
1944 – Jeremy Clyde (Chad and Jeremy)
1944 – Tony McPhee (Groundhogs)
1945 – Chuck Jackson (Independents)
1947 – Harry Vanda (Johannes Jacob Hendrickus Vandenberg) (Easybeats)
1947 – Patrick Olive (Hot Chocolate)
1948 – Andrew Lloyd Webber
1948 – Randy Hobbs (Johnny Winter Band/McCoys)
1958 – Pete Wylie (Wah!)

★ ★ ★

DEPARTURE LOUNGE

1952 – Uncle Dave Macon
1986 – Mark Dinning
1991 – Dave Guard (Kingston Trio)

★ ★ ★

POLICE BOOKED BY A & M

1978

The Police were signed by A & M, who visualized the trio as a more palatable strain of punk than The Sex Pistols who had been dropped by the label the year before. As well as providing more thoughtful copy for media hounds, The Police were also among the more musically experienced New Wave acts to emerge since 1976. Andy Summers, for instance, who replaced original guitarist Henri Padovani in 1977, had served in Zoot Money's Big Roll Band as long ago as 1964, while drummer Stewart Copeland (whose older brother, Miles Copeland II, had a financial stake in the group) was a veteran of Curved Air.

Most of The Police's teen appeal emanated from singing bass player Gordon 'Sting' Sumner, who previously played with Newcastle's jazzy Last Exit.
Released on their own Illegal Records, the unit's debut single, 'Fall Out', sold well by word of mouth but, apparently mainly at Sumner's instigation, they developed an intriguing style that owed more to reggae than punk, and it was

The Police, cleaning up the charts

this plus their instrumental competence and Sting's good looks that brought them to the Los Angeles based label's attention.

1985

BILLY MARRIES HIS UPTOWN GIRL

Soon after the granting of his first wife (and ex-manager) Elizabeth's decree absolute, Billy Joel married Christie Brinkley, the personable model and actress who played the title role in the video that promoted his 'Uptown Girl' smash in 1983, in which Joel was cast as a garage mechanic. The two had first met in November 1982, when Joel, on vacation, was playing the piano in a hotel bar in the Caribbean. The 36-year-old singing pianist was unable to match the million-plus sales of 'Uptown Girl' with any subsequent releases until the end of the decade, but he did participate in the all-star USA For Africa's chart-topping 'We Are The World', which had just entered the US Hot 100 at No. 21. On behalf of the same charity the new Mrs Joel's standing on the catwalk was such that she was conspicuous in the organization of the US contribution to Bob Geldof's Fashion Aid for Ethiopia earlier in 1985.

1992

Janet Jackson – sibling rivalry

RAVINGS

1926:
Multi-instrumentalist 'Mother' Maybelle Addington joined country music's 'royal' Carter Family by marrying Ezra Carter.

★ ★ ★

1959:
Eddie Cochran's 'C'mon Everybody' entered the UK singles chart

★ ★ ★

1964:
John Lennon's first book, *In His Own Write*, was published in Britain.

★ ★ ★

1985:
It was announced that authorities at Wembley Stadium had refused to provide free facilities for the forthcoming *Live Aid* concert. They subsequently changed their minds.

★ ★ ★

ARRIVALS

1868 – Fiddlin' John Carson
1908 – Joan Crawford
1918 – Granville H. 'Sticks' McGhee
1936 – Louisiana Red (Iverson Minter)
1940 – Alan Blaikley
1949 – Ric Ocasek (Cars)
1952 – Dave Bartram (Showaddywaddy)
1953 – Chaka Khan (Yvette Marie Stevens)
1966 – Marti Pellow (Mark McLoughlin) (Wet Wet Wet)
1968 – Damon Albran (Blur)

DEPARTURE LOUNGE

1978 – Bill Kenny (Inkspots)

★ ★ ★

JANET JACKS UP VIRGIN ADVANCE

After prolonged negotiation, Janet, the youngest of Michael Jackson's nine siblings, landed a $16,000,000 contract with Virgin Records for three albums. The 26-year-old vocalist's affinity to million-selling Michael certainly lengthened the queue of major labels submitting bids for her services when her contract with A & M expired in 1991.

At the beginning of her recording career in 1982, her surname created much more of a preconceived notion about her abilities. While this guaranteed her records a fair hearing, the public so distanced her from her more famous relation – something that could not be done with, say, Ziggy Marley or Julian Lennon – that she was able to notch up an impressive tally of hits based on commercial suitability.

This was particularly so after teaming up with top producers Jimmy Jam and Terry Lewis in 1986, when her *Control* album spawned six US chart singles hits: 'What Have You Done For Me Lately' , 'Nasty', 'When I Think Of You', the title track 'Control', 'Let's Wait Awhile' and 'The Pleasure Principle', five of which reached the US Top 5.

She ended 1986 as North America's best-selling artist, and comparable successes since have taken her even further beyond her brother's long shadow.

UNCLE SAM – HERE I AM

Two years to the day after making his final appearance on television's *Dorsey Brothers Stage Show*, Elvis Presley presented himself at Memphis Draft Board offices to enlist for a compulsory two years of national service in the US army. He was accompanied by his parents and 'Colonel' Tom Parker, his manager.

Despite a drop in pay from an estimated $10,000 to $78 per month, the King of Western Bop displayed a cheerful humility throughout the medical examination and the taking of the oath. After the induction he smiled and waved for the waiting press cameras, while accepting from his US fan club president a box containing a banana cream pie and a Bible. Enough Presley recordings had been stockpiled to maintain a regular schedule of releases until Mississippi-born Elvis resumed his singing career in 1960.

'I want to be treated no different from the other boys', Presley told journalists, as he boarded a khaki bus for Fort Chaffee, Arkansas, with twenty other new recruits. To lessen the shock of the regulation short haircut, Presley had already trimmed his brilliantined ducktail, long sideburns and gravity-defying quiff. 'Hair today, gone tomorrow', he joked, as the military barber made further adjustments. Elvis was also issued with dun-brown regimentals in marked contrast to his trademark 'cat' clothes – notably the box jackets, tapered peg trousers and the famous blue suede shoes. Fully kitted out as Private 53310761, he was transferred to Fort Hood, Texas, for basic training with the Second Armoured Division.

Elvis waves as he begins his US Army training

ARRIVALS

1922 – Dave Appell (Applejacks)
1937 – Billy Stewart
1937 – George Fenton Hollis
1938 – Holgar Czukay (Can)
1946 – Colin Peterson (Bee Gees)
1947 – Mike Kellie (Spooky Tooth)
1948 – Lee Oskar (War)
1949 – Nick Lowe
1960 – Nena (Gabriele Kerner)

★ ★ ★

RAVINGS

1973:
A crazed fan at a Lou Reed concert in Buffalo, New York, jumped on stage and bit into Reed's posterior after screaming 'Leather!'.

1986:
The soundtrack album to the movie *Absolute Beginners* was released, featuring Ray Davies, David Bowie and others.

1990:
Gloria Estefan was awarded a 'Golden Globe' by Columbia Records for selling five million albums outside the US.

★ ★ ★

SINEAD SCORES IN UK ALBUM CHART

Sinead strikes a blow for Irish women

Shaven-headed vocalist Sinead O'Connor scored a first for both her gender and her country by becoming the only Irish female solo act to top the UK album chart.

The disc that did the trick was *I Do Not Want What I Haven't Got*, which mixed her own compositions with versions of traditionals such as 'I Am Stretched On Your Grace' and the chart-topping spin-off single, Prince's 'Nothing Compares 2 U'.

Ms O'Connor's career as an entertainer had not been without controversy. She was noted for her swipes in song at the forces of law and order, and an outspoken support for the IRA that she later retracted.

1939

HILLBILLY HIT LIST

Billboard, the US record industry journal, introduced a new category of disc and sheet music sales chart. It had previously published tabulations for the 'popular' and 'sepia' (i.e. coloured) markets, but swerving off the trail and upwards into 'them thar hills', cowpoke entertainers like Fiddlin' John Carson, The Carter Family and Jimmie Rodgers ('The Singing Brakeman') had all racked up million-sellers of both 'country' and 'western' persuasion in recent years, and radio programmes such as *Louisiana Hayride*, *Ozark Jubilee* and Nashville's *Grand Ole Opry* had proved consistently popular in 'redneck' areas in the southern states of America.

Jimmie Rodgers, the Singing Brakeman

While the new 'hillbilly' chart would not include 'double-meaning records', it was now possible for a clean-minded artist to top this list without figuring at all in the parallel dimension of, say, pop – unless the record picked up enough spins on pop-orientated radio to stimulate sales in the appropriate chart-return shops.

1978

Buddy Holly – at last a Number One album

RAVINGS

1955:
British jazz trumpeter Humphrey Lyttleton enthused about American R & B star Muddy Waters in the UK pop weekly New Musical Express.

★ ★ ★

1961:
Elvis Presley made his last concert appearance for eight years at Pearl Harbour's Block Arena.

1965:
Bob Dylan and Donovan (his British 'answer') both made UK singles chart

debuts with, respectively, 'The Times They Are A Changin'' and 'Catch The Wind'.

1967:
The Turtles topped the US chart with 'Happy Together'.

★ ★ ★

ARRIVALS

1924 – Bonnie Guitar (Bonnie Buckingham)
1934 – Johnny Burnette
1938 – Hoyt Axton
1940 – Anita Bryant
1942 – Aretha Franklin
1947 – Elton John (Reginald Kenneth

Dwight)
1947 – Jack Hall (Charlie Daniels Band/Wet Wilie)
1947 – John Rowles
1948 – Michael Stanley
1951 – Maizie Williams (Boney M)
1960 – Steve 'Spiny' Norman (Spandau Ballet)
1969 – Cathy Dennis

DEPARTURE LOUNGE

1976 – Duster Bennett

★ ★ ★

HOLLY'S HITS HIT HERE

Nineteen years after his death Buddy Holly topped the UK album charts for the first time. Before the compilation album *20 Golden Greats* finally achieved this feat, the closest he and his backing group, The Crickets, had been was with 1963's *Reminiscing*, although other Holly collections had subsequently sold steadily - his first charted album, *Buddy Holly Story*, remained in the listings for over three years. It must be said, though, that at the time

of his fatal aeroplane flight in 1959, his current single, 'Heartbeat', had been a comparative flop, and he was regarded as something of a has-been. However, with bilious irony, the tragedy had so revived interest in the bespectacled Texan that his first posthumous hit, 'It Doesn't Matter Any More', had climbed rapidly to No. 1 in the UK, precipitating a schedule of posthumous releases that included the sketchiest demos, often with superimposed backing tracks.

1977

ELVIS MK II'S SINGLE DEBUT

Declan P. McManus, under his alias of Elvis Costello, released his first single, 'Less Than Zero', on Stiff Records, the pioneering independent label formed by Dave Robinson and Andre Jakwman, whose refreshingly unorthodox approach made it the envy of many A & R men working for multi-national corporations who were hampered by red tape from making similarly instant decisions.

Costello, the son of Ross McManus (who for many years had been a featured vocalist with the dance band led by Joe Loss), was a computer operator at a West London cosmetics factory, and wrote and performed songs in his spare time, playing in Flip City, a London country-rock band that never released a record in its lifetime.

Becoming bored with his day job, Costello sent a tape of his original songs to Jake Riviera, co-founder of Stiff, who was surprised that such an obviously accomplished songwriter was unsigned. Riviera immediately became Costello's guru, signing him to Stiff and acquiring a US recording contract with Columbia (CBS) by instructing Costello to sing in the street outside the London hotel where the company was holding its international annual convention.

With Nick Lowe,

Stiff's first signing, as producer, Costello's debut single, 'Less Than Zero', failed to chart, although it made him the major talking point in the British music press, due to the thinly disguised vitriol of his lyrics. With a new single released every few weeks – in May 'Alison (My Aim Is True)', in August '(The Angels Wanna Wear My) Red Shoes' – it was only a matter of time before a hit resulted, and in November his fourth single, 'Watching The Detectives', reached the UK Top 20.

1971

ELP'S LIVE EXHIBITION

For their third album, pomp-rock trio, Emerson Lake and Palmer, comprising Keith Emerson (keyboards), Greg Lake (bass) and Carl Palmer (drums), recorded their arrangement of the Mussorgsky suite 'Pictures At An Exhibition' during a concert at Newcastle City Hall, encoring with a grace-saving 'Nut Rocker', the even more radical 1962 arrangement by B. Bumble and the Stingers of another 19th-century Russian composer's 'Nut Cracker' theme. The ELP album briefly reached the UK album chart at the end of the year, peaking moment-arily in the Top 3.

Palmer, Lake and Emerson making an exhibition of themselves

ARRIVALS

1936 – Fred Parris (Five Satins)
1940 – Rod Lauren
1944 – Diana Ross
1946 – Fran Sheehan (Boston)
1948 – Richard Tandy (ELO)
1948 – Steven Tyler (Aerosmith)
1950 – Ronnie McDowell
1950 – Teddy Pendergrass
1953 – William Lyall (Pilot)
1955 – Dean Dillon
1955 – Martin Price (808 State)
1956 – Charly McClain (Charlotte Denise McClain)
1962 – Richard Coles (Communards)
1963 – Susanne Sulley (Human League)

★ ★ ★

DEPARTURE LOUNGE

1971 – Harold McNair (Ginger Baker's Airforce)

★ ★ ★

RAVINGS

1955:
Three versions of 'Let Me Go Lover' (by Dean Martin, Teresa Brewer and Ruby Murray) all featured in the Top 10 of the UK singles chart.

★ ★ ★

1980:
The Police, cureently at the height of their fame, played a one-off show in Bombay, India. They were first western pop group to do so in ten years.

★ ★ ★

BECK'S BIG BREAK

1965

Jeff Beck (left), latest Yardbirds recruit

The Yardbirds replaced departing lead guitarist Eric 'Slowhand' Clapton with Jeff Beck of London's Tridents, former backing combo to 'Singing Milkman' Craig Douglas. Recommended by Jimmy Page – The Yardbirds' first choice.

Former art student Jeff, if less committed to the blues than Eric, added a new dimension to the sound of the 'For Your Love' hitmakers via his experiments with feedback and use of extra-light strings for legato effect, as well as his fondness for incorporating Oriental-sounding riffs and snippets of show tunes into his solos.

According to Mike Vernon, editor of R & B Monthly, 'Jeff's arrival in The Yardbirds is the best thing that ever happened to them'.

To fit in with the group's corporate image, Beck agreed to sport a shorter haircut and wear Mod clothes, and was also seen in a suit of armour in a promotional film tieing in with the US release of 'For Your Love'.

His first engagement as a Yardbird was at a Radio Caroline function in Surrey on March 30. Then a 21 date, twice nightly UK package tour supporting The Kinks and Goldie and the Gingerbreads in April.

ARRIVALS

1905 – Leroy Carr
1909 – Ben Webster
1909 – Moon Mullican (Aubrey Moon Mullican)
1924 – Sarah Vaughn
1931 – John Marascalco
1935 – Ramsey Lewis
1940 – Janis Martin
1947 – Andy Bown
1950 – Tony Banks (Genesis)
1953 – Walter 'Wally' Stocker (Air Supply/Babys)
1957 – Billy McKenzie (Associates)
1959 – Andrew Farriss (INXS)
1961 – Clark Datchler (Johnny Hates Jazz)

★ ★ ★

DEPARTURE LOUNGE

1959 – Little Willie John

RAVINGS

1972: Grand Funk Railroad sacked their manager, Terry Knight.

1973: Behind bars for three hours, Grateful Dead leader Jerry Garcia was pulled over by police for speeding on the New Jersey turnpike, but the $15 ticket for speeding was nothing compared to the substantial bail he had to raise when the officers of the law found various illegal substances in his car.

1976: British ABBA clones Brotherhood Of Man topped the UK chart with their Eurovision Song Contest winner, 'Save Your Kisses For Me'.

1982: Ronnie Lane, ex-Small Faces, Faces and Slim Chance, was admitted to hospital for treatment of multiple sclerosis.

★ ★ ★

1965

CLIFF'S COVER CLIMBS CHART

Cliff, back at the top with a Nashville recording

Cliff Richard's cover of 'The Minute You've Gone', the US country hit by 'Southern Gentleman' Sonny James, crashed into the UK charts, and was destined to be the English vocalist's first No. 1 since 1963's 'Summer Holiday'.

The song was recorded during Richard's 1964 recording sessions in Nashville, under the supervision of producer Billy Sherrill, with backing musicians including the celebrated Jordanaires vocal group.

As well as 'The Minute You've Gone', Cliff also taped 'On My Word' and 'Wind Me Up (Let Me Go)', both hit singles later that year, as well as 'My Heart Is An Open Book', 'Lies And Kisses', 'Again', 'Look In My Eyes Marie' and 'Paradise Lost'.

In April, he was back at Abbey Road studios where, among other items, he recorded a German version of 'The Minute You've Gone' ('Es Konnte Schon Morgen Sein') over the Nashville backing track.

1979

ERIC INTERRUPTS TOUR TO WED PATTI

The day after the first concert of a 47-city tour of the States, guitarist Eric Clapton married Patti Boyd, ex-wife of George Harrison, in Tucson, Arizona. However, George himself was expected to attend the reception, along with Jeff Beck, Mick Jagger and other famous guests, at Clapton's Hurtwood Lodge mansion after the tour had been completed.

Patti and Eric partying in tinsel town

The romance began in 1968 when the former Yardbird was a periodic dinner guest at the Harrisons' Surrey home. While Eric was squiring former model Mrs Harrison's younger sister Paula, he and George composed 'Badge' – later, a hit for Cream – which contained the telling line 'talking about a girl that looks quite like you'. Other apparent tributes to Patti are Harrison's 'Something' and the unfinished 'Beautiful Girl', and Clapton's 'Layla'. Nevertheless, the couple's childless espousal muddled on, each partner making light of the other's infidelities.

When Eric confronted George with his feelings, the ex-Beatle defused what might have developed into an ugly showdown. Alone in a New York hotel, George had written 'So Sad' as a requiem for his life with Patti, and also included on the same 1974 album, *Dark Horse*, his revival of The Everly Brothers hit, 'Bye Bye Love', with its 'Badge' bass figure and sly lyrical digs at Patti and 'old Clapper', which were seen by some as a rebuttal to 'Layla'. The Harrisons' marriage was dissolved in 1977.

ARRIVALS

1890 – Paul Whiteman
1915 – Jay Livingston
1923 – Thad Jones (Count Basie Band)
1937 – Dean Webb (Dillards)
1941 – Charlie McCoy
1945 – Charles Portz (Crossfires/Turtles)
1948 – John Evan (Jethro Tull)
1948 – Milan Williams (Commodores)
1949 – Sally Carr (Sarah Carr) (Middle Of The Road)
1954 – Reba McEntire
1957 – Mark Spiro
1962 – Geo Grimes (Danny Wilson)
1969 – Salt (Cheryl James) (Salt 'n' Pepa)

★ ★ ★

DEPARTURE LOUNGE

1958 – W. C. Handy
1974 – Arthur 'Big Boy' Crudup

RAVINGS

1958:
Eddie Cochran recorded 'Summertime Blues'.

1964:
Radio Caroline, Britain's first 'Pirate' radio station, began broadcasting.

★ ★ ★

1982

CROSBY'S COCAINE CRASH

Portly David Crosby, former Byrd and the 'Crosby' in Crosby, Stills and Nash, slipped into a drug-induced slumber while motoring down the San Diego Highway. Uninjured after crashing into the central partition, he was arrested after police discovered a quantity of cocaine and associated freebasing 'works', plus a pistol that Crosby said he had purchased in the aftershock of John Lennon's slaying.

The 41-year-old singer was no stranger to ructions with authority. A catalogue of expulsions from school and petty crime preceded his joining The Byrds – who became vexed by his public outspokenness, embarrassing lyrics and, worse, careless use of LSD. He was fired from the group in 1967.

The death of his girlfriend, Christine Hinton, precipitated a narcotics and alcohol habit so serious that his singing voice grew unattractively hoarse, and it became necessary

David Crosby – car crash

in 1981 for friends to manhandle him into a rehabilitation clinic, where he stayed for just two days. He later entered a drug rehabilitation programme.

1957

'HILLBILLY' LONNIE'S US RETURN

Lonnie Donegan commenced his second US tour with a date at New York's prestigious Madison Square Garden. Dubiously labelled 'the Irish hillbilly' by the North American media, he was still milking his 'Rock Island Line' smash that had entered the US Hot 100 almost a year earlier to the day. Reportedly, it moved 150,000 copies in a fortnight, eventually selling over a million.

The Glasgow-born Londoner, however, received only the standard Musicians Union session fee for the recording, which was first released as an album track on *New Orleans Joys*, an album by Chris Barber's Jazz Band in which Lonnie was featured singer, guitarist and banjo player. With Barber on bass and Beryl Bryden on washboard, 'Rock Island Line' was regarded as a 'skiffle'

novelty amidst the interweaving intensity of the front-line horns that dominated other selections. There were enough BBC radio airings of 'Rock Island Line' to warrant its issue as a UK single in autumn 1955, and its rise into the Top 20 made a US release a worthwhile exercise.

Subsequent events made it expedient for Donegan to go solo – though an understanding Barber promised him his old job back when it was all over. However, more hits followed as Donegan became brand leader of the ensuing skiffle craze in Britain, which failed to grip the imagination of young America for more than a few days.

Lonnie Donegan, the king of skiffle

1964

CULTURES CLASH IN CLACTON-ON-SEA

Holidaymakers cowered as two rival youth sub-cultures – mainly male – fought their first major battle on the beaches of Clacton, Essex.

The most dandified were the motor-scooter-riding Mods whose sartorial conformity hinged largely on Cuban-heeled boots, hipster flared trousers, corduroy jackets, and either denim shirts with button-down collar and tie or roll-necked nylon pullover.

Equally uniform, The Rockers, with real or imitation black leather jackets, jeans, motorcycle boots, T-shirts and greasy coiffeur, were in direct line of descent from the 1950s' Teddy Boys.

Mods on scooters in 1964

FAB FOUR PHOTO IN FLOOD STREET

1967

The Beatles arrived at photographer Michael Cooper's studio in Flood Street, Chelsea, for a session that resulted in a most unusual front cover for their *Sgt Pepper's Lonely Hearts Club Band* album.

Dressed as pantomime militia and clutching brass and woodwind instruments, the four fronted a life-size photo collage mounted on hardboard, and consisting mostly of the images of each Beatle's all-time heroes, plus a few suggested by designer Peter Blake and London art dealer Robert Fraser.

It was possible to guess individual choices; several of George Harrison's contributions, for example, were Eastern gurus and religious leaders – though Mahatma Gandhi was vetoed by the group's record company, EMI. John Lennon was responsible principally for Oscar Wilde, Lewis Carroll, H. G. Wells, Edgar Allan Poe and other literary figures, while Paul McCartney's avant-garde preferences brought forth the likes of composer Karlheinz Stockhausen and sculptor Simon Rodia. Ringo Starr put forward fewer ideas than his colleagues. Of only a handful of icons from the world of pop, the most poignant was that of the late Stuart Sutcliffe, the group's first bass guitarist. The Beatles also acknowledged likewise the influence of Bob Dylan, The Rolling Stones (whose name was displayed on a doll's pullover) – and their earlier selves via wax models borrowed from Madame Tussaud's. Further details included a hookah, a row of nursery plants and The Beatles' name spelt out in crimson flowers.

The Beatles, 1967

ST DANIEL DOMINATES UK COUNTRY CHART

1991

Irish ballad singer Daniel O'Donnell, whose huge following among middle-aged British females was the envy of many bigger acts, reached a remarkable peak when seven of his albums occupied positions in the Top 11 places of the British country album chart. Efforts to prohibit O'Donnell's records from the chart on the basis that they were not genuinely country records caused a furore among his protesting fans, and letters were sent to the publisher of the chart, *Music Week*, from nuns complaining about the decision, which was later reversed.

Daniel O'Donnell – UK country album chart at his mercy

ARRIVALS

1913 – Frankie Laine (Frank LoVecchio)
1914 – Sonny Boy Williamson (John Lee Williamson)
1930 – Rolf Harris
1942 – Graeme Edge (Moody Blues)
1945 – Eric Clapton
1948 – Jim Dandy (Jim Mangrum) (Black Oak Arkansas)
1950 – Dave Ball (Procol Harum)
1952 – Samuel McFadin (Flash Cadillac and the Continental Kids)
1954 – Lene Lovich (Marlene Premilovich)
1955 – Randy Vanwarmer
1962 – Hammer (M. C. Hammer)
1964 – Tracy Chapman

★ ★ ★

DEPARTURE LOUNGE

1980 – Dick Haymes

★ ★ ★

RAVINGS

1957:
'Fraulein' by Bobby Helms entered the US country singles chart, where it remained for 52 weeks, making it the longest-running chart single in the 1950s.

1963:
The Chiffons topped the US singles chart with 'He's So Fine'.

1966:
Eighty five rioting fans were arrested after a Rolling Stones concert in Paris.

1976:
The Sex Pistols entertained a crowd of 50 for their first booking at London's 100 Club.

1991:
The *Greatest Hits* album by Eurythmics outsold combined sales of the next six albums in the UK chart.

1972

BEATLES FAN CLUB CLOSES

Three years after *Beatles Monthly* magazine ceased publication, falling membership led to the closure of the sundered group's official fan club a month after The Beatles Fan Club shop had gone into liquidation.

In Britain much of the blame lay with the individual images of the ex-Beatles – their vinyl output, while still commercially potent, embraced elements that were anathema to the contemporary 'glam-rock' trend. Moreover, to even the most optimistic fan, the quartet's reformation was no longer inevitable despite headlines shrieking 'Beatlemania Sweeps A City!', 'The Beatles Are Back!' after George Harrison and Ringo Starr reunited on a New York stage for Harrison's Concerts For Bangladesh in 1971.

1967

FIRE AT FINSBURY PARK

Hendrix – lighting up Finsbury Park

At London's Finsbury Park Astoria (which was later reopened as The Rainbow Theatre), the last date of a round-Britain package tour, headlined by The Walker Brothers, was enlivened by a premeditated incident while The Jimi Hendrix Experience were on stage. The act climaxed with fuzzy-haired American guitarist Hendrix squirting cigarette lighter fuel over his solid-body guitar, which he then set on fire with resulting audio and visual effect – not to mention contravention of the theatre's fire regulations. Nevertheless, the ensuing publicity assisted the continued climb up the UK Top 40 of the trio's second single, 'Purple Haze', which had been released a week before, when the Experience's debut single, 'Hey Joe', was still in the charts. Ironically, the group's debut album, *Are You Experienced*, included a Hendrix composition entitled 'Fire'.

The rest of the evening's most varied fare seemed tepid when compared to the diverting Jimi – particularly as the previous two singles by The Walker Brothers had both been comparative flops. Nevertheless, their energetic gyrations during 'Land Of 1000 Dances', one of the few uptempo items in their set, elicited the expected hysterical screaming. Audience reaction had been only fractionally less frenzied during the shorter performance of balladeer Engelbert Humperdinck, fresh from a No. 1 (and chart debut) with 'Release Me'. The bill was completed by Cat Stevens, whose new single, 'I'm Gonna Get Me A Gun', was issued the day before the Finsbury Park spectacular.

1984

MOTOWN'S MARVIN SHOT BY HOLY FATHER

After a violent argument Revd Marvin Gaye shot and killed his son, former Motown recording star Marvin Gaye. The latter, whose mental state had caused concern in the previous month after he spoke of suicide, was living at the Los Angeles house which he had purchased for his parents in the 1960s.

Ironically, a year earlier the singer had won his first ever Grammy Award for his million-selling single, '(Sexual) Healing', his first major US hit for over five years. After that 1977 triumph, his accelerating drug usage, his divorce from his wife of 16 years, Anna (the sister of Motown founder Berry Gordy Jr), and the resulting estrangement from the label for which he had made over 50 US hits since his 1962 chart debut with 'Stubborn Kind Of Fellow', left him not only at a career crossroads. His divorce

Marvin Gaye - a soul superstar who met an unlikely end

settlement with Anna Gordy, despite their having lived apart for many years, and a second failed marriage that lasted less than two years, plus an unpaid income tax bill believed to exceed $2 million, led to his moving to Hawaii (where he lived in a trailer), and by mid 1981, to Ostend in Belgium.

Having released only two albums, both commercially disappointing, since 1977, Gaye persuaded Columbia (CBS) to purchase his Motown contract for $1.5 million, signing with Columbia after protracted negotiations in which the US Internal Revenue Service (IRS) participated.

He was believed to have turned the corner towards recovery with '(Sexual) Healing' and his million-selling Midnight Love album, but a 1983 US tour had been a com-mercial failure, and he had apparently reverted to a heavy drug intake. His classic Motown hits of the previous two decades, including 'I Heard It Through The Grapevine', 'Let's Get It On' and his eleven hit duets with Tammi Terrell made him one of the most highly-rated vocalists in the world.

ARRIVALS

1942 – Alan Blakeley
(Tremeloes)
1945 – John Barbata
(Turtles/Jefferson Starship)
1946 – Arthur Conley
1946 – Ronnie 'Plonk' Lane
(Small Faces/Faces)

1948 – Jimmy Cliff
(James Chambers)
1948 – Simon Cowe
(Lindisfarne)
1950 – Billy Currie (Ultravox)
1954 – Jeff Porcaro (Toto)
1961 – Mark White (ABC)

★ ★ ★

DEPARTURE LOUNGE

1917 – Scott Joplin
1984 – Marvin Gaye

★ ★ ★

1969

SURFERS SUE CAPITOL FOR $2 MILLION

The Beach Boys, one of the most successful acts ever signed to Capitol Records, sued the label for unpaid royalties of $2 million after having launched their own Brother Records label with the rival company Reprise in 1967.

RAVINGS

1955:
George Martin took over from Oscar Preuss as the Head of A & R for EMI's Parlophone label, after five years as Preuss's assistant.

1957:
Frankie Lymon and The Teenagers opened their UK tour at London's Palladium. Having been the youngest chart topper with 'Why Do Fools Fall In Love', aged just 13, he was also the venue's youngest headliner

1976:
Over 1 million ticket applications followed the announcement of a 13 date UK tour by The Rolling Stones.

★ ★ ★

The Beach Boys

1969

SINATRA'S LONGEST RUNNING SMASH

Sinatra - doing it his way

1940s' teenage idol Frank Sinatra (who provoked screaming hysteria among wartime 'Bobby Soxers' – impressionable teenage girls whose fashion 'uniform' included ankle-length bobby socks) had been a solo star since 1942, when he left his post as vocalist with Tommy Dorsey's Orchestra. With scores of hits to his credit, Sinatra, who was well into his fifties, could hardly have expected to release his biggest ever hit as the world's charts were dominated by rock acts like his daughter, Nancy, but the first UK chart entry of his single, 'My Way', would ultimately become his new signature tune, leaving and re-entering the chart no less than eight times before the end of 1972.

'My Way' had French origins. Originally titled 'Comme D'Habitude', it was written by Gilles Thibaut (lyrics) with music by Claude Francois and Jacques Revaux. Lyrics in English were supplied by Paul Anka, no stranger to the chart as he had released his first million-seller, 'Diana', back in 1957, and by the time Sinatra's hit entered the chart, he had amassed over 30 US hit singles on his own account.

A surprisingly small hit in the USA, where it failed to reach the Top 20 when first released in 1969, it reached the UK Top 5 on its first visit to the UK singles chart, returned there on five separate occasions in 1970, re-entered for its sixth, seventh and eighth chart runs in 1971 and spent another week there at the start of 1972. With 122 chart weeks in Britain, 'My Way' has spent over a year longer on the UK singles chart than any other record.

Interestingly, the song also became a UK hit for three other acts – cabaret singer Dorothy Squires in 1970, Elvis Presley in 1977 and The Sex Pistols (with vocals by Sid Vicious) in 1978.

ARRIVALS

1939 – Marvin Gaye
1941 – Leon Russell
1942 – Phil Castrodale (Reflections)
1943 – Glen Dale (Fortunes)
1943 – Larry Coryell
1946 – Kurt Winter (Guess Who)
1947 – Emmylou Harris
1948 – Kerry Minnear (Gentle Giant)
1952 – Leon Wilkerson (Lynyrd Skynyrd)
1953 – David Robinson (Modern Lovers/Cars)
1956 – Gregory Abbott
1963 – Keren Jane Woodward (Bananarama)

★ ★ ★

DEPARTURE LOUNGE

1978 – Ray Noble
1987 – Buddy Rich

1967

WINWOOD SURVIVES PLAYING IN TRAFFIC

Steve Winwood fronting Traffic

Having become a major international star as main vocalist, guitarist and keyboard player with The Spencer Davis Group, which he joined in 1963 aged 15, Steve Winwood left that band at the height of their success to launch his own group, Traffic. Other founder members were drummer Jim Capaldi, multi-instrumentalist Chris Wood and singer-guitarist Dave Mason. Within two months Traffic were in the UK Top 10 with their debut single, 'Paper Sun'.

MADONNA LOSES PEPSI SPONSORSHIP BUT KEEPS $5M

Madonna (real name Madonna Louise Ciccone) plunged cleavage first into a major international religious row when Pepsi-Cola, with whom she had signed a $5 million sponsorship contract a month before, cancelled the deal after her promotional video for 'Like A Prayer', first screened as a TV commercial on NBC's *Bill Cosby Show*, was banned in Italy after pressure from the Vatican

Madonna - nun the poorer

because of its religious imagery, which was regarded as blasphemous.

The commercial had a different storyline than the video, for Pepsi Madonna relived a birthday party from childhood but Pepsi-Cola claimed that consumers were confused by the similarities between the ad and the video clip, although observers felt that the soft drink

company were more concerned about the potentially disastrous fall-out that might result from alienating the world's vast number of Roman Catholics following the involvement of the Church. Madonna was allowed to keep the $5 million and the furore probably contributed to the single becoming Ciccone's seventh US No. 1 single in under five years. The album, which included the song as its title track, as well as a duet with Prince, also topped the US chart.

1975

EMMYLOU UNVEILS NEW HOT BAND

Country vocalist Emmylou Harris played her first live concert with The Hot Band at the Boarding House in San Francisco.

Eddie Tickner, former manager of the Byrds, persuaded Harris to record her debut solo album *Pieces Of The Sky*, after the drug-related death of country/rock pioneer Gram Parsons, with whom she had formed a vocal partnership, recording two albums together.

The Hot Band were a group of brilliant musicians, including James Burton (lead guitar) and Glen D. Hardin (keyboards), both of whom were also in Elvis Presley's band, Emory Gordy Jr (bass), Hank DeVito (pedal steel guitar), John Ware (drums) and Rodney Crowell (guitar, vocals).

ARRIVALS

1928 – Don Gibson
1938 – Philip Wynne (Detroit Spinners)
1939 – Jeff Barry
1941 – Jan Berry (Jan and Dean)
1943 – Joe Vann (Joe Canzana) (Duprees)
1943 – Richard Manuel (The Band)
1944 – Barry Pritchard (Fortunes)
1944 – Lois Ann Wilkinson (Caravelles)
1944 – Tony Orlando (Michael Anthony Orlando Cassavitis)
1946 – Dee Murray (Elton John Band)
1951 – Mel Schacher (& The Mysterians/ Grand Funk Railroad)
1955 – Mick Mars (Bob Deal) (Motley Crue)
1960 – Nick Richards (Boys Don't Cry)
★ ★ ★

DEPARTURE LOUNGE

1950 – Kurt Weill
1990 – Sarah Vaughan
★ ★ ★

1964

FABULOUS FOUR FILL FIRST FIVE

The Beatles, virtually unknown in the USA at the start of the year, were responsible for dominating the US singles chart in a manner that seems unlikely ever to be equalled. Following their appearance on the *Ed Sullivan Show* in January (reportedly watched by an audience of over 70 million Americans!), the group's entire back catalogue instantly began selling at an incredible rate, and in the first *Billboard* Top 100 published in April, twelve singles by The Beatles were listed, including the whole Top 5.

The Beatles frolic in the American snow - it's just like the British stuff!

'Can't Buy Me Love' topped the chart, with 'Twist and Shout' at No. 2, 'She Loves You' at No. 3, 'I Want To Hold Your Hand' at No. 4 and 'Please Please Me' at No. 5. Further down the chart, 'I Saw Her Standing There' stood at 31, 'From Me To You' at 41, 'Do You Want To Know A Secret' at 46, 'All My Loving' at 58, 'You Can't Do That' at 65, 'Roll Over Beethoven' at 68 and 'Thank You Girl' at 79.

A week later, 'Love Me Do' and 'There's A Place' would enter the chart, thus establishing a record of 14 titles charting simultaneously.

They also held the top two places in the US album chart.

1987

FERRY AID SUPERSTARS RAISE MONEY FOR VICTIMS OF DROWNING DISASTER

Ferry Aid, a group of well-known British pop and rock stars, topped the UK chart with their revival of 'Let It Be', achieving a higher chart placing than the original classic hit by The Beatles from 1970. Organized and released to raise money for victims of a tragedy in the North Sea near Zeebrugge in Belgium, the single featured over 100 entertainment personalities including Paul McCartney, Boy George, Kate Bush, Bonnie Tyler the then unknown Rick Astley, model Linda Lusardi, and newsreader Anne Diamond. A Townsend Thoresen car ferry, *Herald Of Free Enterprise*, had capsized in icy water a mile offshore due to the vessel's bow doors not having been closed, thus allowing water to flood the deck where hundreds of cars were parked for the journey to Dover. 187 passengers drowned in the catastrophe.

RAVINGS

1981:
Bucks Fizz won the Eurovision Song Contest with 'Making Your Mind Up'. The group had been specially formed to enter the contest.

★ ★ ★

1987:
Starship, the group formed by ex-members of Jefferson Airplane and Jefferson Starship, scored their third US No. 1 single in 18 months when 'Nothing's Gonna Stop Us Now', from the film *Mannequin* reached the summit in the wake of 'We Built This City' (1985) and 'Sara' (1986).

1987:
U2 entered the US album chart at No. 7 with *The Joshua Tree* – this was the highest new entry in that chart since 1980.

ARRIVALS

1915 – Muddy Waters (McKinley Morganfield)
1941 – Major Lance
1942 – Christophe Franke (Tangerine Dream)
1947 – Doug Ferguson (Camel)
1948 – Berry Oakley (Allman Brothers)
1950 – Dicken (Jeff Robert Pain) (Mr Big)
1951 – Steve Gatlin (Gatlin Brothers)
1952 – Dave Hill (Slade)
1952 – Peter Haycock (Climax Blues Band/ELO Part 2)
1954 – Gary Moore
1957 – Graeme Kelling (Deacon Blue)

★ ★ ★

DEPARTURE LOUNGE

1980 – Red Sovine

★ ★ ★

1990

BROWN'S BLACK PRISON PERIOD

Godfather of Soul and the hardest working man in showbusiness James Brown finally saw light at the end of his personal tunnel when he was transferred from the Georgia jail in which he had served 15 months of a six-year sentence imposed for a variety of charges involving drugs, guns, resisting arrest etc., to Lower Savannah Work Centre, where he was paid $4 per hour for counselling drug abusers.

Brown - Godfather in trouble

Brown's problems had begun in mid 1988, when he was charged with attempted murder. Two days later, his wife, who had brought the charges, was arrested for receiving drugs; three weeks later, she dropped the attempted murder charge, but two weeks after that, set fire to a New Hampshire hotel room. Brown himself was arrested a week later and charged with assault, plus drugs and weapons charges, and these scenarios were re-enacted several more times during the summer of that year, which also saw him hospitalized for an operation on his lower jaw and involved in a high-speed car chase through two states.

It was ironic that all this non-musical activity should occur at a time when Brown's popularity was experiencing a considerable boost in Britain: his records, in particular the 'Funky Drummer' track were being sampled extensively by acts as diverse as Public Enemy and George Michael in the burgeoning British dance boom. Four of his singles, including remixed material, previously unreleased old recordings, and some brand new tracks, had reached the UK singles chart. A brand new album, *I'm Real* (which made reference to the unlawful sampling of his material), and a TV-advertised compilation had both made a major album chart impact.

1981

BEAR'S BIG HEART LOSES UNEQUAL FIGHT

Bob 'The Bear' Hite died of a heart attack at the age of 36. Hite, a founder member of highly rated Los Angeles white blues/R & B combo Canned Heat, acquired his nickname due to his bulk – his normal weight was around 300 lbs. Hite and fellow blues collector Al Wilson had founded the group in 1965, and first attracted attention when they performed at the 1967 Monterey Pop Festival. Canned Heat enjoyed several big-selling singles, including 'On The Road Again' (1968), 'Going Up The Country' (1969) and 'Let's Work Together' (1970), but the death

Hite - Heat frontman

that year of Al Wilson was a blow from which the group never totally recovered.

ARRIVALS

1928 – Tony Williams (Platters)
1929 – Joe Meek
1931 – 'Cowboy' Jack Clement
1932 – Billy Bland
1941 – Dave Swarbrick (Fairport Convention)
1941 – David LaFlamme (It's A Beautiful Day)
1941 Eric Burdon
1944 – Crispian St Peters
1944 – Nicholas Caldwell (Whispers)
1950 – Agnetha Faltskog (ABBA)
1951 – Everett Morton (The Beat)
1954 – Stan Ridgway

★ ★ ★

DEPARTURE LOUNGE

1981 – Bob 'The Bear' Hite (Canned Heat)
1983 – Danny Rapp (Danny and the Juniors)

★ ★ ★

`1979`

ROD SETTLES DOWN (?)

International superstar Rod Stewart, after a much publicized romance lasting over two years with Swedish actress Britt Ekland (ex-wife of film star and comedian Peter Sellers), finally got married – to someone else. Ekland had previously announced that she was suing her erstwhile paramour for up to $20 million, claiming half his considerable assets on the grounds that he would not have achieved super-stardom without her input and support.

Stewart, who had taken up residence in California in 1975, was renowned for his reluctance to spend money when someone else would pay the bill. Less than two months after his wedding to Alana Hamilton, ex-wife of actor 'Gorgeous' George Hamilton, in Beverly Hills, Los Angeles, British Chancellor of the Exchequer Sir Geoffrey Howe announced a cut in income tax which delighted British tax exiles all over the world. No longer could the rock star live up to the title of his big selling 1977 album *Foot Loose And Fancy Free*, of course, but at least the tax concessions would enable him to indulge in his other passion for association football (soccer). In 1978 he had recorded a single,

Rod Stewart with Alana Hamilton

'Ole Ola', with the Scottish Football World Cup squad, which quickly fell from the UK chart when Scotland were eliminated from the competition after failing to defeat Iran.

The marriage between Stewart and Hamilton ended in 1984, and in 1989, Hamilton sued her ex for increased alimony. In the interim, he had fathered a son with another girlfriend,

Kelly Emberg, who lived with him between 1985 and 1990. Emberg filed a $25 million 'palimony' lawsuit in 1991, the year he married New Zealand-born model Rachel Hunter.

`1985`

GILBERT GETS $2 MILLION

Singer/songwriter Gilbert O'Sullivan, who had been successful during the 1970s with a string of hits including two UK chart-toppers, 'Clair' (1972) and 'Get Down' (1973), won his lawsuit against his manager Gordon Mills and the latter's MAM organization for unpaid royalties. and was awarded an undisclosed sum believed to be in the vicinity of $2 million.

It was an unhappy end to a relationship that had seen O'Sullivan (real name Raymond O'Sullivan) become a close friend of the Mills family, babysitting for their daughter, about whom his 'Clair' hit was written.

O'Sullivan, winner in court

1962

FUTURE STONES IN EALING SUMMIT

The Rollin' Stones after they found their missing 'G'

The three main members of the group that would play its debut gig in July that year as The Rollin' Stones (sic) met at Alexis Korner's Ealing Club. Mick Jagger (born July 26, 1943) and Keith Richards (born December 18, 1943), who both came from Dartford in Kent, fell into conversation with Lewis Brian Hopkin-Jones (born February 28, 1942) from Cheltenham. All three were avid fans of rhythm and blues (R & B), and Hopkin-Jones was appearing at the club that night as part of a band with pianist Ian Stewart (later tour manager for The Stones), guitarist Geoff Bradford and vocalist Paul Pond (aka Paul Jones, who first emerged to stardom fronting the Manfred Mann group).

The line-up of The Rollin' Stones at their first gig was Jagger (vocals), Richard (as he now called himself, dropping the 's' as had pop star Cliff Richard) and Jones (with the Hopkin and hyphen now removed for simplicity) on guitars, Stewart on piano, Dick Taylor (later leader of The Pretty Things) on bass and Mick Avory (later a member of The Kinks) on drums.

By the end of the following January, Taylor and Avory had been replaced by Bill Wyman (bass) and Charlie Watts (drums), while Ian Stewart took more of a background role – the Rolling (with a final 'g') Stones were finally complete.

1977

CLASH UNLEASH LONG-AWAITED DEBUT

Highly rated London punk/rock band The Clash released their eponymous debut album, less than a year after their formation. Launched by singer/guitarist Mick Jones, his first recruit was Paul Simonon, who agreed to learn to play bass despite having little or no previous musical experience. They were joined by guitarist Keith Levene (who left, but later emerged as a member of John 'Rotten' Lydon's Public Image Ltd and drummer Terry Chimes, while Bernie Rhodes, an associate of Sex Pistols guru Malcolm Mclaren, became the group's manager. However, the vital spark was when singer/guitarist Joe Strummer (real name John Mellor) was persuaded to leave The 101ers. The debut album was recorded over three weekends. Chimes, who was quickly at loggerheads with the others was replaced afterwards by Nicky 'Topper' Headon.

The Clash

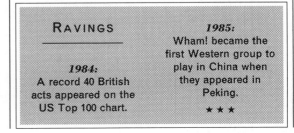

1967

BAREFOOT PUPPET TAKES EURO TITLE

Dagenham-born Sandie Shaw (real name Sandra Goodrich) became the first British performer to win the Eurovision Song Contest. Already a seasoned hitmaker with eleven UK hits to her credit since her 1964 debut, including two chart-toppers, '(There's) Always Something There To Remind Me' and 'Long Live Love', Shaw's four hits prior to her Eurovision victory had been comparatively minor, three of the four failing to reach the UK Top 30, but 'Puppet' restored her to the top after a lengthy absence of nearly two years. It was the first British victory in the Eurovision Contest since its inception in 1956, although on five previous occasions the British entry had been placed a close second.

Shaw married fashion designer Jeff Banks in 1968, a week after her 21st birthday party, which she supposedly held in the gruesome Chamber of Horrors in London's Madame Tussaud's Wax Museum. After their divorce, she married Nik Powell,

Richard Branson's original partner in Virgin Records, and in 1984 returned to the UK singles charts after a 15-year absence with her version of 'Hand In Glove', a song written by Stephen Morrissey, and the first single for his band The Smiths.

Sandie Shaw winning Eurovision

ARRIVALS

1929 – Jaques Brel
1938 – Connie Stevens (Concetta Rosalie Ann Ingolia)
1942 – Roger Chapman (Family)
1947 – Steve Howe (Yes)
1949 – Reg Isidore (Robin Trower Band)
1954 – John Schneider
1963 – Julian Lennon

★ ★ ★

DEPARTURE LOUNGE

1938 – King Oliver
1976 – Phil Ochs

★ ★ ★

RAVINGS

1966:
Saxophonist Mike Vickers left the Manfred Mann group, in which he also played guitar. Bass player Tom McGuinness moved to lead guitar, while Jack Bruce left John Mayall's Bluesbreakers to fill McGuinness's shoes.

1988:
REM left IRS Records, for whom they had recorded their first successful albums, and joined Warner Bros for an advance that Miles Copeland, the boss of IRS, recommended them to accept.

1989
Cure drummer Lawrence 'Lol' Tolhurst, a founder member of the group in 1977, left the band – leader Robert Smith reportedly felt Tolhurst was no longer making appropriate musical contributions.

★ ★ ★

1970

WOODSTOCK MOVIE PREMIERE – PEACE AND LOVE IN LONDON

The London premiere of *Woodstock*, the feature movie filmed at the celebrated Woodstock Music and Arts Festival held at Bethel, in upstate New York, during August 1969, brought many of the new sensations of popular music together on the screen, including Crosby, Stills, Nash and Young, Ten Years After, Joe Cocker, John Sebastian, Country Joe and The Fish, Sha Na Na, Santana, The Who, Joan Baez, Jefferson Airplane, Jimi Hendrix and many more.

1979

PHIL'S FINAL JOURNEY

Folk singer Phil Ochs, compared by many to Bob Dylan as a protest singer in the first half of the 1960s, when he released acclaimed albums like *All The News That's Fit To Sing* and *I Ain't Marching Anymore*, committed suicide by hanging himself while staying at his sister's house in New York. Perhaps his best-known composition was 'There But For Fortune'. Covered by Joan Baez in 1965, it was her only US Top 50 single during that decade.

1988

ARRIVALS

1898 – Paul Robeson
1932 – Carl Perkins
1937 – Dave Prater
(Sam and Dave)
1943 – Terry Knight
(Terry Knight and The Pack,
managed Grand Funk
Railroad)
1944 – Emil Stucchio
(Classics), Brooklyn

1944 – Gene Parsons (Byrds)
1946 – Les Gray (Mud)
1948 – Philip Wright
(Paper Lace)
1961 – Mark Kelly (Marillion)

★ ★ ★

DEPARTURE LOUNGE

1988 – Brook Benton

★ ★ ★

RAVINGS

1956:
Gene Vincent first recorded his timeless classic, 'Be Bop-A-Lula'.

1989:
B. B. King, who scored his first hit single when 'Three O'Clock Blues' reached the US R & B chart in the last week of 1951, finally reached the UK singles chart via his collaboration with Irish group U2, 'When Love Comes To Town'.

★ ★ ★

PET SHOP BOYS EQUAL EVERLYS AND WHAM! MARKS

Neil Tennant (left) and Chris Lowe - Pet Shop Boys

The record for chart-topping hits by a duo, previously shared between The Everly Brothers (who took 'All I Have To Do Is Dream', 'Cathy's Clown', 'Walk Right Back' and 'Temptation' to the top between 1958 and 1961) and Wham! (who did likewise with 'Wake Me Up Before You Go Go', 'Freedom', 'I'm Your Man' and 'The Edge Of Heaven' between 1984 and 1986) was equalled when vocalist Neil Tennant and keyboard player Chris Lowe, better known as Pet Shop Boys, reached the summit for the fourth time in two and a half years (slightly slower than Wham!, but faster than The Everlys).

'West End Girls' was their first No. 1 at the start of 1986, later followed by 'It's A Sin', 'Always On My Mind' and 'Heart'.

Pop journalist Tennant, who was Assistant Editor of the best-selling British teenage magazine *Smash Hits*, met Lowe in a music shop in London's Kings Road in August 1961,

and when Tennant went to New York to interview Sting for *Smash Hits* in 1983, he arranged for hit disco producer Bobby O. to produce a single for Pet Shop Boys, as he and Lowe now called themselves. Their first single, 'West End Girls', was faintly successful in continental Europe, but was a flop in the UK. Everything changed at

the end of 1985 when a re-recorded version of 'West End Girls' (produced by Stephen Hague) was released and, after three months, entered the UK Top 10, eventually reaching the top in January 1986 and repeating the feat in the US. Later that year, 'Opportunities' was reissued, this time almost reaching the UK Top 10.

1988

BROOK BENTON DIES ONE HIT SHORT OF HALF CENTURY

Brook Benton

Velvet-voiced American R & B singer/songwriter Brook Benton (real name Benjamin Franklin Peay) died of complications following spinal meningitis.

Before he embarked on his solo career in 1953, he had sung in gospel groups. His first (minor) US hit, 'A

Million Miles From Nowhere', came in 1958, and by the end of 1970 he had taken 49 singles into the US chart, including 'It's Just A Matter Of Time' and 'Endlessly' (both 1959), 'The Boll Weevil Song' (1961) and his cover of Tony Joe White's 'Rainy Night In Georgia' (1970).

1962

ORIGINAL BEATLE STUART DIES

The first bass player with The Beatles, Stuart Sutcliffe, died, aged just 21, of a brain haemorrhage in the arms of his fiancée, Astrid Kirchherr, in Hamburg, where he had lived since leaving the group he had joined in early 1960 when they were known as Johnny and The Moondogs.

Sutcliffe had become friendly with John Lennon when both attended art school, and although he was never more than an adequate musician, his obvious flair for stylish clothes and hairstyles made a considerable impact on Lennon, Paul McCartney and George Harrison.

Stuart Sutcliffe, a one-time Beatle

Sutcliffe was with the group when they failed an audition to become Billy Fury's backing band for a tour, and was still there when they worked in a similar capacity behind vocalist Johnny Gentle on a brief Scottish tour, by which time they were known as The Silver Beetles (both Sutcliffe and Paul McCartney adopted stage names for the tour – respectively Stuart de Stael and Paul Ramon). Sutcliffe was also part of the group for their first tour of Germany in the summer of 1960, but after their third German trip in mid 1961, he enrolled at Hamburg Art College, living with the family of Astrid Kirchherr, to whom he had become engaged. By this time, Paul McCartney had changed from guitar to bass. Ironically, eight years later to the day McCartney publicly announced that he was leaving The Beatles. This followed the release of his debut solo album, 'McCartney', and a growing rift between the bass player and the other members of the group, over their management.

1983

PASS THE DUTCHIE IN NEW YORK

Birmingham hitmakers Musical Youth

British teenagers Musical Youth, five schoolboys from Birmingham, played at New York's Ritz concert hall. Aged between 11 and 16, the quintet had topped the British chart six months earlier with their first single, the contagious 'Pass The Dutchie', a Jamaican song based on 'Pass The Koochie', which means the marijuana cigarette. The word was changed to avoid adverse comment to 'dutchie', which is a Jamaican cooking pot.

The single reached the US Top 10, and the group provided backing vocals on a minor hit later in the year for disco queen Donna Summer, 'Unconditional Love'.

ARRIVALS

1911 – Martin Denny
1921 – Sheb Woolley (Shelby Woolley)
1932 – Nathaniel Nelson (Flamingos)
1936 – Bobbie Smith (Detroit Spinners)
1936 – Glen Campbell
1940 – Bobby Hatfield (Righteous Brothers)
1940 – Ricky Valence
1947 – Bunny Wailer (Neville O'Reilly Livingston) (Wailers)
1950 – Dave Peverett (Savoy Brown)
1959 – Brian Setzer (Stray Cats)
1959 – Katrina Leskanich (Katrina and the Waves)

★ ★ ★

DEPARTURE LOUNGE

1958 – Cuck Willis
1962 – Stu Sutcliffe
1984 – Jimmy Kennedy

★ ★ ★

RAVINGS

1956:
Nat 'King' Cole was badly beaten up on stage while playing for an all-white audience in Birmingham, Alabama.

1967:
Paul McCartney visited a Beach Boys recording session, apparently helping them to produce 'Vegetables', a track included on the group's Smiley Smile album.

★ ★ ★

ARRIVALS

1943 – Tony Victor
(The Classics)
1945 – Robert Fripp
1949 – Lee Sheridan
(Brotherhood of Man)
1956 – Neville Staples
(Specials/Fun Boy Three)
1958 – Stuart Adamson
(Skids/Big Country)
1966 – Lisa Stansfield

1970 – Delroy Pearson
(Five Star)

★ ★ ★

DEPARTURE
LOUNGE

1988 – Dave Prater
(Sam and Dave)
1991 – Martin Hannett
(aka Martin Zero, record
producer)

RAVINGS

1956:
Elvis Presley first
used vocal backing
group The
Jordanaires on a
recording session.
The track they cut
was 'I Want You, I
Need You, I
Love You'.

1986:
Dave Clark's musical,
Time, opened at
London's Dominion
Theatre, starring
Cliff Richard in the
leading role.

★ ★ ★

1981

EUROPEAN SHOWBIZ UNION

Valerie Bertinelli, Mrs Eddie Van Halen

In Los Angeles, Eddie Van Halen, acclaimed lead guitarist with the hugely successful hard rock band Van Halen, married actress Valerie Bertinelli, one of the stars of the popular TV series *One Day At A Time*. Van Halen and his brother, Alex, were born in Nijmegen, The Netherlands, and moved to Pasadena, California, in 1965. By 1974, they had recruited vocalist David Lee Roth and bass player Michael Anthony, and formed Mammoth. By 1975 they were recognized as one of the heaviest hard rock acts in the Los Angeles area, and in that year they changed their name to Van Halen, after contemplating adopting the name Rat Salade.

1961

DYLAN DEBUT IN THE BIG APPLE

Bob Dylan, at the time almost completely unknown, gave his first solo professional public performance at Gerde's Folk City on West 4th Street, New York City, opening for bluesman John Lee Hooker.

After dropping out of the University of Minnesota in 1960, he had worked in Bobby Vee's backing band, after which the one time Robert Zimmerman adopted the name with which he became famous before travelling to New York to visit the dying Woody Guthrie.

He also got to know Guthrie's friends, including Pete Seeger, Cisco Houston, Peter LaFarge and Ramblin' Jack Elliott. Being on first-name terms with such known quantities did no harm at all to Dylan's reputation.

He began playing hoot nights (effectively talent shows) at Gerde's in Greenwich Village at the start of the month, staying on after the amateurs had gone home at midnight when the real performers, such as Dave Van Ronk and Joan Baez, would play. This led to the owner of the venue, Mike Porco, hiring him even though Dylan was under age (he was 20 on May 24, 1961) and Porco had to become his temporary guardian so that a valid contract could be issued.

Among the songs he played on that night were 'House Of The Rising Sun', the traditional song about a New Orleans brothel, which a few years later became the first No. 1 hit for The

Bob Dylan, then unknown, at a London folk club, 1962

Animals, and 'Song To Woody'. Before long, Dylan was drawing his own fans to Folk City, among them critic Robert Shelton, whose glowing review in the

New York Times first alerted Columbia Records (CBS) A & R man John Hammond Sr to his potential, and led to Dylan signing with Columbia that year.

DEAD MAN'S CURVE CLAIMS ANOTHER VICTIM

1966

Jan Berry, the leading light of surfing duo Jan and Dean, was involved in a serious car accident on Whittier Boulevard in Los Angeles, when he drove his Chevrolet Corvette into a parked truck. Berry, who had just received official notice that he was obliged to enlist in the US Army, and was also due to take an examination at medical school, may have allowed these problems to affect his concentration.

At the time of the accident, the duo were apparently contracted to appear with Elvis Presley in his *Easy Come, Easy Go* movie, and had completed negotiations to star in their own weekly TV series. They had first met while at school together, and their first hit, 'Jennie Lee', was credited to Jan and Arnie (a third member of their first group, The Barons, was Arnie Ginsburg), as Dean Torrence, who had been the lead vocalist on the song, was away in the US Army at the time it was released. On his return from serving Uncle Sam, Torrence and Berry teamed up with Herb Alpert and Lou Adler, who produced a string of minor US hits for them, the biggest of which were 'Baby Talk' (1959) and 'Heart and Soul' (1961).

In 1963, with assistance from Beach Boy Brian Wilson, their 'Surf City' topped the US singles chart, and six more US Top 40 hits followed by the end of 1964, including 'Dead Man's Curve', written about a treacherous bend on Sunset Boulevard where many major accidents occurred. Ironically, Berry's crash took place in that vicinity. He was badly injured, totally paralyzed after being in a coma and suffered brain damage that took many years to reverse.

Jan Berry (top) and Dean Torrence

DAVID ESSEX EVOKES 1950s WITH RINGO

1973

Ringo Starr (left) battles with David Essex

Actor David Essex, fresh from his rôle as Jesus in the rock musical *Godspell*, was the star of *That'll Be The Day*. The film was premiered in London's West End and received virtually unanimous critical acclaim. Others who appeared in the movie were Beatle Ringo Starr and his fellow drummer, Keith Moon of The Who, along with early sixties' teen idol Billy Fury. Essex immediately became a teenage sensation with a string of Top 10 singles

In 1974, he starred in a movie sequel, *Stardust*. Others featured in this follow-up were Adam Faith and American actor Larry Hagman.

RAVINGS

1978:
Aretha Franklin married actor Glynn Turman. Her father, the Revd C. L. Franklin officiated at the ceremony, which was attended by The Four Tops, who serenaded the bride by singing 'Isn't She Lovely'.

★ ★ ★

1982

CROSBY IN COKE CRISIS

David Crosby, a founder member of The Byrds and of Crosby, Stills and Nash, was arrested in his dressing room at Cardi's, a Dallas, Texas, nightclub when police found him preparing cocaine and in possession of a gun. Crosby had been arrested less than three weeks earlier in Los Angeles for driving while under the influence of cocaine, possessing 'drug paraphernalia' and carrying a concealed pistol.

David Crosby, a legend with a problem

Crosby (real name David Van Cortland) was a Byrd until late 1967, when he left the band after many disagreements over the group's direction, although several songs to which he contributed appeared on the group's 1968 album, *The Notorious Byrd Brothers*, whose sleeve featured group members Roger McGuinn, Chris Hillman and Michael Clarke looking out of separate doors of a stable, with a horse looking out of a fourth window – apparently the way McGuinn regarded Crosby. Crosby then became friendly with Graham Nash of The Hollies, whom he introduced to Stephen Stills, who had worked with Al Kooper on the *Super Session* album after his previous group, Buffalo Springfield, had fallen apart.

Despite their contractual commitments to rival record labels, the trio of Crosby, Stills and Nash signed with Atlantic in 1969. After three highly successful albums, two also featuring Canadian Neil Young, who had also been a member of Buffalo Springfield, Stills formed Manassas with another ex-Byrd, Chris Hillman, Crosby and Nash worked as a duo after the release of Crosby's first solo album, *If Only I Could Remember My Name*, (which featured Joni Mitchell) after which a reunion album by The Byrds, and various Crosby, Stills and Nash (and less often, Young) reunions often playing anti-nuclear benefits took up much of the rest of the 1970s.

However, many of Crosby's endeavours were less than successful, and the tragic death of his girlfriend drove him to cocaine addiction. A group of his friends cajoled him into admitting himself to hospital for a cure, but within a day he had discharged himself. After the 1982 arrests, he found further trouble in 1983 when he was sentenced to five years in prison on another drugs charge, and began to cure his addiction.

1983

WONDER'S MULTI-MILLION MOTOWN DEAL SIGNED

Stevie the superstar

Following his winning of four Grammy Awards in both 1974 and 1975, singer/songwriter/multi-instrumentalist and widely acclaimed genius Stevie Wonder re-signed with Motown Records, the company for which he had always recorded even before his first million-selling smash hit, 'Fingertips Part II', in 1963 when he was 13 years old.

Wonder (real name Stephen Judkins or Steveland Morris, depending on when he was asked), was one of the label's most consistent hitmakers during the 1960s, with such classics as 'Uptight (Everything's Alright)', 'I Was Made To Love Her', 'For Once In My Life', 'My Cherie Amour' and many others selling prodigiously. In 1971, Wonder's 21st birthday saw him receiving the royalties he had earned during the previous eight years, enabling him to launch his own production and music publishing companies, while agreeing to continue recording exclusively for Motown. In 1973/4, he had released three US No. 1 singles – 'Superstition', 'You Are The Sunshine Of My Life' and the more dance-oriented 'You Haven't Done Nothin'', the last of which featured backing vocals by The Jackson Five. His last five original albums – *Where I'm Coming From, Music Of My Mind, Talking Book, Innervisions* and *Fulfillingness' First Finale* – were all huge sellers despite their adoption of a far more serious tone than his earlier albums, which had tended to be collections of hits. The deal immediately paid off for both parties, as Wonder's next two singles, 'I Wish' and 'Sir Duke', and his *Songs In The Key Of Life* double album, all topped the US charts.

1983

SECOND PRETENDER IN DRUG-RELATED DEATH

Following the previous year's death of Pretenders guitarist James Honeyman-Scott due to cocaine and heroin addiction, the group's former bass player, Pete Farndon, overdosed while taking a bath. Farndon had been with the group since its inception in 1978 but had been fired from the group two days before Honeyman-Scott's death, reportedly because he was 'incompatible' with the other members, and at the time of his death, was reportedly in the process of forming a new group with ex-Clash drummer Nick 'Topper' Headon and ex-Bob Dylan sideman Rob Stoner.

Farndon - a sad end

ARRIVALS

1933 – Buddy Knox
1935 – Loretta Lynn
1942 – Tony Burrows
(Flowerpot Men/Edison Lighthouse/White Plains)
1945 – Ritchie Blackmore
(Deep Purple/Rainbow)
1946 – Patrick Fairley
(Marmalade)
1948 – Larry Ferguson
(Hot Chocolate)
1949 – June Millington
(Fanny)
1949 – Sonja Kristina
(Curved Air)
1952 – Jerry Knight
(Raydio)

★ ★ ★

DEPARTURE LOUNGE

1983 – Pete Farndon
(Pretenders)
1990 – Thurston Harris

1989

BIG O RETURNS TO TOP 10 FROM THE GRAVE

In one of popular music's most unexpected and universally popular comebacks ever, Texan singer/songwriter Roy Orbison returned to the US Top 10 after an absence of over 24 years with 'You Got It', a song he wrote with Jeff Lynne and Tom Petty, colleagues of Orbison in the occasional supergroup, The Traveling Wilburys.

Roy Orbison - out on a high note

Completed by George Harrison and Bob Dylan, the group was initially formed to complete a George Harrison solo album, but the participants enjoyed themselves so much that they decided to record under the Wilbury alias, pretending to be members of the same family: Harrison was Nelson Wilbury, Dylan was Lucky Wilbury, Lynne Otis Wilbury, Orbison Lefty Wilbury and Petty Charlie T. Wilbury Jr.

For Orbison, it was a comeback of remarkable proportions. Since his glory days in the mid 1960s, when his frequent smash hits, such as 'In Dreams', 'It's Over' and 'Oh Pretty Woman' (his last US Top 10 hit before 'You Got It', from 1964) had made him one of the biggest stars in the world, he had experienced a commercial decline, particularly in the US, although his international popularity continued, initially in Europe and later in other parts of the world such as Australia. Unfortunately, Orbison was unable to savour his Lazarus-like revival – he had died of a heart attack at the age of 52 a few months earlier – but he certainly went out on a high!

1989

BLACK RAP LEADS THE PACK

Loc-ed After Dark, the album by Los Angeles based rap star Tone Loc, became the first rap release by a black artist to top the US album chart. It followed his success during the year with a pair of US Top 3 singles, 'Wild Thing' and 'Funky Cold Medina', which were both certified platinum for sales of over two million copies. Tone Loc (born Anthony Smith) apparently acquired his strange stage identity from a Spanish nickname he had been given, Antonio Loco.

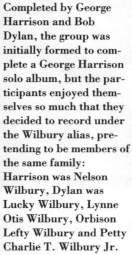

Tone Loc

1990

MANDELA CONCERT AT WEMBLEY

Tracy Chapman paying tribute to Nelson Mandela

London's Wembley Stadium hosted another massive concert, this one to celebrate the release of black South African leader Nelson Mandela. Among the artists participating in *Nelson Mandela – An International Tribute To A Free South Africa* were Peter Gabriel, Neil Young, Lou Reed, Bonnie Raitt, Simple Minds, The Neville Brothers, Tracy Chapman and Aswad.

Gabriel and Chapman had previously particpated with Sting and Bruce Springsteen in a 1989 tour in aid of Amnesty International.

Nelson Mandela, the leader of the anti-apartheid movement in South Africa, had been sentenced to life imprisonment in 1964 for sabotage and plotting to overthrow the South African government. A trained lawyer, he became involved in the fight for freedom for South Africa's black majority. From an early groundswell in Britain led by left-wing politician Anthony Wedgwood-Benn, who joined a protest outside the South African Embassy in London only months after Mandela was sentenced, the ruling white South Africans were gradually becoming isolated from the rest of the world, leading to their being banned from taking part in the 1964 Olympic Games. In early 1965 British singer Adam Faith cancelled concerts in Johannesburg after being refused permission to play to multi-racial audiences.

During the 1970s and 1980s, South Africa was further isolated, with organizations such as Artists Against Apartheid arranging benefit concerts starring many notable rock stars. In 1984 The Specials had reached the UK Top 10 with a single written by leader Jerry Dammers titled 'Nelson Mandela', and in 1988 Dammers inspired and arranged a Wembley Stadium event to celebrate the African hero's 70th birthday, starring Dire Straits, Simple Minds, Whitney Houston, Stevie Wonder and others.

RAVINGS

1964:
The first album by The Rolling Stones was released in Britain. Two weeks later, it had broken the album chart stranglehold by The Beatles, which had lasted 51 weeks.

1988:
Stock, Aitken and Waterman won the Ivor Novello Award as top songwriters of the year.

1986

QUEEN'S SOLO STUFF

After completing their new album, *A Kind Of Magic*, the title track of which went on to be their 15th UK Top 10 hit, two members of Queen contributed their talents to outside projects. Vocalist Freddie Mercury sang on three tracks of Dave Clark's *Time* musical, which starred Cliff Richard when it was staged in London, while bass player John Deacon formed an *ad hoc* group, The Immortals, to record 'No Turning Back', a track that was featured in the movie *Biggles*.

Mercury - time off from Queen

1960

COCHRAN KILLED, VINCENT INJURED – BUT ALIVE

While driving to London for a flight back to Los Angeles after a riotously successful British tour, rock 'n' roll greats Eddie Cochran and Gene Vincent were involved in a car accident on the A4 (Great West Road) near Chippenham, Wiltshire, England.

Cochran's fiancée, Sharon Sheeley, and the car's driver were injured in the crash, as was Vincent, but Cochran was thrown through the windshield when the car careered into a lamp post after a tyre blow-out. He was taken by ambulance to Bath Hospital, but died without regaining consciousness. Vincent, who was already a cripple with an iron leg support, survived. The policeman attending the accident was one David Harman (later Dave Dee of Dave Dee, Dozy, Beaky Mick and Tich).

Cochran had released four singles that reached the British chart before his death, each one a classic: 'Summertime Blues','C'mon Everybody', 'Somethin' Else' and his impressive cover of the Ray Charles classic, 'Hallelujah I Love Her So'. None of these hits had reached the UK Top 5, but the British tendency towards buying larger quantities of an artist's records after their death proved to be active, and Cochran's ironically titled 'Three Steps To Heaven', released a few weeks later, became his only UK chart-topper.

However, Cochran's British chart career was far from over, and he charted with five more hits by mid 1963. A measure of his influence is that The Sex Pistols released two covers of Cochran classics, 'Somethin' Else' and 'C'mon Everybody', which reached the UK Top 3 in 1979.

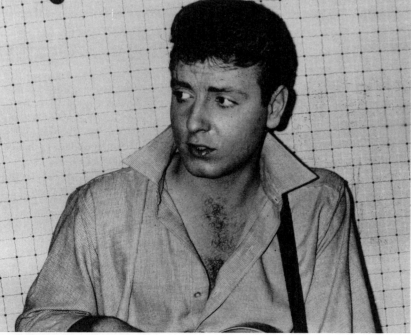

Eddie Cochrane

1986

LIBYAN BLUES TORPEDO TOUR

Stevie Ray Vaughan

Texan blues guitar phenomenon Stevie Ray Vaughan felt that it would be prudent to cancel his European tour as he feared reprisals against Americans from Libyan terrorists.

Vaughan, whose brother Jimmie played lead guitar in The Fabulous Thunderbirds, died less than five years later in a helicopter crash after leaving a festival.

1983

MOUNTAIN MAN MURDERED

Felix Pappalardi, bass player with Mountain, the high-volume quartet fronted by 'The Great Fatsby' (Leslie West), and prior to that, producer of Cream, the first supergroup, was shot dead by his wife, Gail Collins.

Pappalardi was said to have been deaf from his prolonged exposure to the elephant-stunning volume of West's guitar amplifier.

1981

YES SAY NO MORE

Bass player Chris Squire (a founder member) and drummer Alan White left Yes, the hugely successful group that had accumulated nine UK Top 10 albums since 1971, with the stated intention of forming a new supergroup with ex-Led Zeppelin members Jimmy Page and Robert Plant, which ultimately never progressed beyond the stage of rehearsing.

Yes on stage

Yes was formed in 1968 by Squire and vocalist Jon Anderson (ex-Warriors), plus acquaintances from other groups – guitarist Pete Banks (ex-The Syn, Squire's previous band), keyboard player Tony Kaye (ex-Federals) and drummer Bill Bruford (ex-Savoy Brown). Their first major exposure was as opening act for Cream's Farewell concert at London's Royal Albert Hall. Almost constantly afflicted by personnel changes in their early years – Steve Howe instead of Banks in 1970, Kaye replaced by Rick Wakeman in 1971, Bruford joining King Crimson in 1972 (whereupon White joined) – they found short-lived stability in 1973 before Wakeman left the following year and was replaced by Patrick Moraz. After taking a sabbatical when all the group members made solo albums in 1975/6, they reunited in 1977 with Wakeman back instead of Moraz before Anderson and Wakeman both departed in 1980, and were respectively replaced by Trevor Horn and Geoff Downes, both previously successful under the guise of Buggles.

By this time Anderson had another career in partnership with Greek keyboard star Vangelis Papathanassiou (as Jon and Vangelis), but when Squire (the only remaining founder member) and White embarked on their brief alliance with the ex-Zeppelin leaders, the group ceased to exist for six months. Inevitably they re-formed later in the year, this time with Squire, White, the returning Tony Kaye (who had left over ten years earlier) and newcomer Trevor Rabin (guitar, vocals). This line-up used the name Cinema, but after inviting Anderson to return, as Rabin's vocals were felt to be inappropriate, they reverted to the more familiar Yes.

ARRIVALS

1906 – Little Brother Montgomery (Eureal Wilford Montgomery)
1924 – Clarence 'Gatemouth' Brown
1928 – Ken Colyer
1936 – Lenny Baker (Sha Na Na)
1939 – Glen D.Hardin (Crickets)
1941 – Mike Vickers (Manfred Mann)
1943 – Tony Reeves (John Mayall/Colosseum)
1946 – John Kane (New World)
1946 – Skip Spence (Alexander Spence) (Jefferson Airplane/Moby Grape)
1958 – Andy Kyriacou (Modern Romance)
1958 – Les Pattinson (Echo and The Bunnymen)
1962 – Shirlie Holliman (Pepsi and Shirlie)

★ ★ ★

DEPARTURE LOUNGE

1974 – Johnny Young

★ ★ ★

1987

ARETHA'S LONG HAUL

Aretha Franklin finally reached the top of the UK singles chart 20 years after her chart debut with 'Respect' in mid 1967. In the intervening years, she had charted in Britain with 20 singles, including 1981's 'Love All The Hurt Away', a duet with George Benson, and 1985's 'Sisters Are Doin' It For Themselves' with Eurythmics, but the top slot had always eluded her until her duet with George Michael, 'I Knew You Were Waiting (For Me)', co-written by Simon Climie of pop duo Climie Fisher.

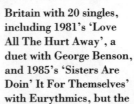

Aretha Franklin

RAVINGS

1985:
The first ever Western pop album was released in China. It was by Wham!

★ ★ ★

1986

KISS TRIPLE TOPPER FOR PRINCE

Prince (real name Prince Rogers Nelson) simultaneously topped three US charts – pop, dance and R & B – for the third time in his career. On this occasion, the single in question was 'Kiss' – Prince had previously achieved the feat twice in 1984 with 'When Doves Cry' and 'Let's Go Crazy'.

Prince - named after Prince Roger Trio

Born in Minneapolis in 1958, Prince convinced Warner Bros to allow him to produce his own debut album, *For You*, in 1978, and his eponymous follow-up album achieved platinum status in 1979. Both his first two triple chart-toppers were featured in *Purple Rain*, the first movie in which he starred, which was semi-autobiographical. He subsequently starred in other movies, including *Under The Cherry Moon* (1986, which included 'Kiss'), *Sign O' The Times* (1987) and *Graffiti Bridge* (1990), as well as topping the US singles chart in 1989 with 'Batdance', which included moments of dialogue from the movie *Batman* (starring Michael Keaton and Jack Nicholson) for which Prince wrote the score. The *Batman* soundtrack also produced two more hit singles, 'Partyman' and 'The Arms Of Orion', on which he duetted with Scottish vocalist Sheena Easton.

In 1989, veteran Welsh vocalist Tom Jones was featured on a version of 'Kiss' by British studio wizards Art Of Noise that reached the UK Top 5. Jones was just another example of the numerous (mainly female) stars who benefited from the talent of the diminutive genius – others included Chaka Khan, Martika, Sheila E., Sheena Easton, Bonnie Raitt, Sinead O'Connor, The Bangles, Wendy and Lisa, Madonna (with whom he duetted on 'Love Song', a track on her chart-topping *Like A Prayer* album), Mavis Staples and doubtless many more to follow.

1980

GEORDIE VOCALIST JOINS OUTRAGEOUS AUSSIES

AC/DC Australian hard rockers

Brian Johnson, the 32 year old singer who had previously been a member of the appropriately named group from Newcastle, Geordie, joined AC/DC, the Australian-based group, whose former vocalist, Bon Scott, had, according to the coroner who presided over his *post mortem*, 'drunk himself to death'.

While widely regarded as Australian, in fact many of AC/DC's personnel were born in the British Isles, including guitarist brothers Angus and Malcolm Young and bass player Cliff Williams – and Scott.

RAVINGS

1960:
Elvis Presley started his train journey (he had apparently developed a fear of flying) from Memphis to Los Angeles, where he would be filming *G. I. Blues*, a film which typecast him as a young US soldier in Germany.

★ ★ ★

1978:
Dead Boys drummer Johnny Blitz was stabbed in the street after a gig at New York's CBGBs club.

★ ★ ★

1980:
For the first time ever, the top five artists in the US country chart were all female: Crystal Gayle was at No. 1, followed by Dottie West, Debbie Boone, Emmylou Harris and Tammy Wynette (duetting with her ex-husband, George Jones).

★ ★ ★

ARRIVALS

1928 – Alexis Korner
1934 – Dickie Goodman (Buchanan and Goodman)
1941 – Bobby Russell
1942 – Alan Price
1942 – Mark Volman (Turtles)
1943 – Eve Graham (Evelyn May Beatson) (New Seekers)
1946 – Tim Curry

★ ★ ★

DEPARTURE LOUNGE

1952 – Steve Conway
1985 – Willie Mabon

★ ★ ★

1992

STARS PAY TRIBUTE TO FREDDIE

A royal parade of international rock stars appeared at a sold-out (72,000) tribute concert at London's Wembley Stadium in memory of Queen's late vocalist, Freddie Mercury. The emotional event helped increase AIDS awareness, and raised £10 million ($15 million) for AIDS charities.

Highlights included duets by David Bowie and Annie Lennox on 'Under Pressure', by George Michael and Lisa Stansfield on 'These Are The Days Of Our Lives' and 'Bohemian Rhapsody' fronted by Elton John and Axl Rose. Videos of Mercury and Queen linked performances by Def Leppard, Guns n'Roses, Roger Daltrey, Robert Plant, Extreme, Paul Young, Seal and Bob Geldof.

Axl Rose and Elton John at The Mercury Tribute Concert

The live show ended with Liza Minnelli leading a 90-strong choir on 'We Are The Champions'. The show, planned by the three remaining members of Queen (who were on stage throughout the show) as 'the biggest send-off in history', was seen by an estimated one billion viewers in 70 countries – a bigger audience than Live Aid.

ARRIVALS

1923 – Tito Puente
1929 – Bob Braun (Robert Earl Brown)
1939 – Johnny Tillotson
1948 – Craig Frost (Grand Funk Railroad)
1951 – Luther Vandross

DEPARTURE LOUNGE

1990 – Steve Marriott
1992 – Johnny Shines

1990

SMALL FACE MARRIOTT DIES IN HOUSE FIRE

Singer/guitarist Steve Marriott, who first achieved prominence during the 1960s as the best-known member of The Small Faces, the 'mod' group second only to The Who, perished in a fire at a cottage in Essex.

Born in the East End of London in 1947, Marriott was a child actor, he made his West End theatre debut aged 15, and made a flop single, 'Give Her My Regards', when he was 16. He then worked in a music shop in East Ham, where he encountered bass player Ronnie Lane and drummer Kenny Jones, who were playing R & B covers in local clubs with organist Jimmy Winston. The group's espousal of mod philosophies and the arrival of keyboard player Ian McLagan, who replaced Winston in late 1965, made their choice of group name apporopriate – a 'face' was a leading mod, and McLagan was as short of stature as the other three. Marriott and Lane, a fluent song-writing team, penned nine big UK hit singles, including 'All Or Nothing' (the group's only No. 1), 'Itchycoo Park', 'Tin Soldier' and 'Lazy Sunday', plus *Ogden's Nut Gone Flake*, an album that topped the UK chart for six weeks in 1968, before Marriott left the band in early 1969 to form Humble Pie with Peter Frampton.

After the band fell apart in the mid 1970s, Marriott was involved in a shortlived Small Faces reunion (without Ronnie Lane), while a Humble Pie reunion in the 1980s was no more successful.

Steve Marriott - died in fire

RAVINGS

1959:
Thirteen-year-old Dolly Parton released her first single, 'Puppy Love', in America.

1966:
Vocal tracks for 'Eleanor Rigby' were recorded for the *Sgt Pepper* album by The Beatles. Originally titled 'Daisy Hawkins', its title was changed after McCartney spotted the name Rigby on a clothes shop in Bristol.

★ ★ ★

FOLK/ROCK STAR SANDY DIES AFTER STAIR FALL

1978

Sandy Denny, who achieved international prominence as the lead vocalist of British folk/rock stars Fairport Convention, died at the age of 31 after falling down a flight of stairs at a friend's house. She had recently become a mother for the first time, when she and her husband, Australian-born singer/guitarist Trevor Lucas, became the proud parents of a daughter, Georgia.

Denny joined Fairport in mid 1968 replacing Judy Dyble, initially remaining with them for a year and a half, which produced arguably the best three albums the group ever made (*What We Did On Our Holidays*, *Unhalfbricking* and *Liege and Lief*), before leaving to launch a band with Lucas, then her boyfriend. That group, Fotheringay, had fallen apart by the start of 1971, when she embarked on a solo career that produced three excellent albums. During this period she appeared on stage several times with Fairport Convention, finally rejoining them in 1974, musically reuniting with Lucas and another ex-member of Fotheringay, Jerry Donahue. This second spell produced a live album and the excellent *Rising For The Moon*, before she left again in 1976, after a US tour, subsequently releasing a final solo album, *Rendezvous*, in 1977.

Sandy Denny, a tragic loss for music

She had fallen downstairs and seemed shaken but not seriously injured, but four days later, the twice-winner of *Melody Maker's* Female Vocalist Of The Year, who also appeared on Led Zeppelin's best-selling untitled fourth album, died of a cerebral haemorrhage.

PARTON LEAVES PORTER

1974

Vocalist Dolly Parton left the *Porter Wagoner Show* to embark on a solo career. Born in 1946, she first achieved fame as a country singer during her seven years working with Wagoner, with whom she duetted on over 20 US country hit singles. She had already scored 20 solo hit singles, including 'Coat Of Many Colors', 'Jolene' and 'My Tennessee Mountain Home', before deciding to leave Wagoner.

Her first single release after going solo was 'I Will Always Love You', a song that topped the UK singles chart in 1992 when it was revived by Whitney Houston, who performed it on the soundtrack of the Kevin Costner feature movie in which Houston co-starred, *The Bodyguard*.

Dolly - consistent and country

ARRIVALS

1924 – Ira Louvin (Lonnie Ira Loudermilk)
1939 – Ernie Maresca
1947 – Alan Wagner (Foundations)
1947 – Iggy Pop (James Jewel Osterberg)
1947 – John Weider (Animals/Family)
1948 – Paul Davis
1951 – Nicole Barclay (Fanny)
1951 – Paul Carrack (Squeeze/Ace/Mike and the Mechanics)
1958 – Mike Barson (Madness)
1959 – Robert Smith (The Cure)
1963 – Johnny McElhone (Texas)

DEPARTURE LOUNGE

1970 – Earl Hooker
1971 – Don Drummond
1978 – Sandy Denny

★ ★ ★

RAVINGS

1963:
The Beatles and The Rolling Stones met for the first time at the latter's regular Sunday evening gig at the Crawdaddy Club in Richmond, West London.

★ ★ ★

1969:
Janis Joplin played at the Royal Albert Hall, London.

★ ★ ★

1982:
Joe Strummer disappeared for three weeks, which resulted in The Clash, the group that he fronted, cancelling a scheduled tour. He was found living rough in Paris.

★ ★ ★

1990:
Amy Grant sued Marvel Comics for including her likeness in a Dr Strange comic.

★ ★ ★

ALPERT LAUNCHES VOCAL CAREER BY MISTAKE

1968

Alpert - this guy's successful!

Trumpeter Herb Alpert, owner of his own independent record company, A & M Records (the 'M' was his partner, Jerry Moss), launched a second career as a vocalist. During a TV Special screened to celebrate and promote the release of the tenth album by Herb Alpert and The Tijuana Brass, *The Beat Of The Brass* (which had advance orders of over one million copies).

Alpert felt that the audience deserved something unexpected. He sang a song written by Burt Bacharach and Hal David, 'This Guy's In Love With You', which he dedicated to his wife, Sharon. No formal plans had been made to record the track, but after CBS-TV, which had screened the Special, was inundated with calls from the public, Alpert decided to release it as a single. It reached the US No. 1 spot in six weeks and remained there for a month, qualifying for a gold record as a million-seller within three months of release. It also topped the UK chart, but only for a single week.

Surprisingly, it was later revealed that 'This Guy's In Love With You' was not Alpert's first vocal release – between 1960 and 1962 he made three unsuccessful vocal singles, the first two under the name of Dore Alpert.

ARRIVALS

1922 – Charles Mingus
1936 – Glen Campbell
1937 – Jack Nitzsche
1943 – Mel Carter
1944 – Joshua Rifkin
1950 – Peter Frampton
1969 – Craig Logan
(Bros)

★ ★ ★

DEPARTURE LOUNGE

1968 – Steve Sholes
1983 – Earl 'Fatha' Hines

SHRINE OF BRITISH ROCK 'N' ROLL CREATED IN SOHO

1956

The shrine of British rock'n'roll

In London's Old Compton Street, on the south side between Wardour Street and Dean Street, the 2I's coffee bar opened.

Many young British rock 'n' rollers performed in its small cellar during the 1950s, including Tommy Steele (Britain's first shortlived rock star, who preferred to become a 'family entertainer'), Adam Faith (as vocalist with The Worried Men, a skiffle group), Cliff Richard (Britain's biggest ever solo star, with 35 years of hits to his credit) and Terry Dene. The coffee bar got its name because it was originally owned by two Iranians, but by the rock 'n' roll era it had been bought by two Australian wrestlers, 'Rebel' Ray Hunter and Paul Lincoln (aka Dr Death), who introduced rock 'n' roll in the basement of the premises.

RAVINGS

1990:
750,000 people attended *Earth Day*, a show in New York's Central Park that starred Hall and Oates, Edie Brickell, The B-52s and Ben E. King.

1977:
The Jam released their first single, 'In The City', which peaked at No. 40 in the UK chart.

★ ★ ★

WINSTON OUT, ONO IN

1969

John Lennon, who had recently established a romantic alliance with Japanese artist Yoko Ono, changed his middle name in a ceremony that took place on the roof of 3 Savile Row, the building housing the group's Apple Corps.

From that date on, John Winston Lennon was known as John Ono Lennon.

HE DID IT SID'S WAY
1978

What could be more unlikely for Sex Pistol Sid Vicious to sing than Frank Sinatra's signature tune, 'My Way'? Yet that is precisely what occurred as filming progressed on the notorious feature film starring Britain's best-publicized punk/rock group. The film has the lovely Sid entering a small theatre in Paris where he walks on stage and begins to sing the famous ode to self-determination in an artificially deep voice, before the backing musicians speed up and, as Chuck Berry remarked 'spoil the beauty of the melody'. Sid's encore after beating the song to death is to shoot most of the audience.

This landmark in popular music was released as a single during the summer as a double B-side, coupled with an item on which the vocalist was exiled escaped criminal Ronnie Biggs, one of the Great Train Robbers, whose audacious hold-up of a mail train carrying over £2 million ($3 million) in used bank notes had resulted in a lengthy prison sentence.

Biggs was accompanied by Pistols Steve Jones and Paul Cook, who travelled to Brazil, where Biggs had lived since his escape from prison. Originally titled 'Cosh The Driver', the song's title was altered to 'No One Is Innocent'. Somewhat surprisingly (proving that bad taste can be found everywhere), the single reached the UK Top 10.

Vicious left Britain to move to New York before the end of the month, and in October of the same year was accused of murdering his girlfriend, Nancy Spungen.

ARRIVALS

1936 – Roy Orbison
1939 – Ray Peterson
1949 – John Miles
1952 – Narada Michael Walden

1960 – Steve Clark (Def Leppard)

★ ★ ★

DEPARTURE LOUNGE

1975 – Pete Ham (Badfinger)
1991 – Johnny Thunders

★ ★ ★

BADFINGER WRITER'S SAD SUICIDE
1975

Pete Ham, singer/guitarist/songwriter with Beatles protégés Badfinger, committed suicide by hanging himself. Ham, a founder member of The Iveys, who changed their name to Badfinger in September 1969, had enjoyed his biggest commercial success as co-writer with fellow group member Tommy Evans of 'Without You', a song that was memorably covered by (Harry) Nilsson, whose version topped the singles charts on both sides of the Atlantic. However, the group's business affairs were in a mess, and they split up in disarray during 1974.

The awful coda to the story is that Tommy Evans also committed suicide in 1983 under identical circumstances.

Badfinger with Pete Ham at the organ

RAVINGS

1969: The famous Ash Grove club in Los Angeles, where latterly famous acts like Canned Heat had played during their formative years, burned down.

1973: Timothy Leary received a further prison sentence following his 1970 escape.

1986: Harold Arlen, writer of 'Over The Rainbow' (recorded by Judy Garland, Gene Vincent and Jerry Lee Lewis, among others) and 'Stormy Weather', died.

1989: Kylie Minogue was seen on British TV for the first time in an Australian soap opera, *The Henderson Kids*.

FIRST AMERICAN JOINS MAC

Bob Welch

With the unexpected departure of Jeremy Spencer, the second of their three singer/guitarists, to join a religious cult known as The Children Of God – he walked out on the group during a US tour (after which they did not see him for over two years !) – Fleetwood Mac found a permanent replacement through the good offices of the wife of original Jethro Tull bass player Glenn Cornick.

Founder member Peter Green (the first of the group's singer/guitarists to jump ship) agreed to rejoin his ex-colleagues temporarily until the tour was completed, but was not interested in reclaiming his permanent position. Judy Wong, Cornick's wife, recommended Bob Welch, a singer/guitarist from Los Angeles, who joined Mick Fleetwood, John and Christine McVie and the third of the original singer/guitarists, Danny Kirwan, to record the *Future Games* album. After 1972's *Bare Trees* album, Kirwan also departed, at which point Welch became one of the group's main on-stage focal points.

Welch left Fleetwood Mac in early 1975 to form a group known as Paris with Cornick, and was replaced in Fleetwood Mac by Lindsey Buckingham and Stevie Nicks, whose arrival signalled a dramatic upturn in the group's fortunes. Welch later enjoyed some success as a solo artist with his albums *French Kiss* (1977) and *Three Hearts* (1979), but these were minor achievements compared to the world-dominating releases of the group he left only months before they hit the big time. If he had only hung on for a few more months . . .

DYLAN WITH HARRY, THE KING OF CALYPSO

Robert Zimmerman, alias young folk singer Bob Dylan guested on 'Calypso King' Harry Belafonte's album *The Midnight Special*, playing harmonica, and received a $50 session fee. The album made the Top 10 of the US chart.

RAVINGS

1958:
'I Wonder Why' became the first hit for both Bronx-based doo wop superstars Dion and The Belmonts and the label for which they recorded, Laurie Records.

1976:
Emmylou Harris scored her first country chart hit with 'Together Again'.

1987:
Stop Making Sense, the feature film made by Talking Heads, was premiered in San Francisco.

★ ★ ★

HITMAN HITS ROAD

Pete Waterman

Peter Waterman, the spokesman for and inspiration behind the incredibly successful songwriting and production team of Stock, Aitken and Waterman, launched *The Hitman Roadshow* at Wolverhampton. Headline act on the opening night was Jason Donovan, supported by Hazell Dean, Sinitta and others, all from the PWL (Peter Waterman Ltd) stable.

ARRIVALS

1933 – Freddy Scott
1942 – Barbra Streisand (Barbara Joan Streisand)
1944 – Bernard St.Clair Lee Calhoun Henderson (Hues Corporation)
1944 – Richard Sterban (Oak Ridge Boys)
1944 – Tony Visconti
1945 – Doug Clifford (Creedence Clearwater Revival)
1945 – Robert Knight
1947 – Glen Cornick (Jethro Tull)
1947 – Hubert Ann Kelly (Hues Corporation)
1948 – Steve York
1954 – Captain Sensible (Ray Burns), (Damned)
1958 – Boris Williams (Cure)

★ ★ ★

DEPARTURE LOUNGE

1970 – Otis Spann

★ ★ ★

1988

WHITNEY THE RECORD BREAKER

Whitney Houston, daughter of soul star Cissy Houston, who scored her biggest solo hit, 'Be My Baby', when Whitney was almost eight years old, and cousin of Dionne Warwick, added to the remarkable array of records she had broken since launching her solo career in 1985.

Whitney, her second album (the first album by a female artist to enter the US chart at No. 1), included Whitney duetting with her mother, Cissy Houston (ex-Sweet Inspirations), on a version of 'I Know Him So Well' written by Tim Rice and Benny and Bjorn from Abba. Sales had exceeded 10 million worldwide, and followed her eponyous debut album, which at the time had sold 13 million worldwide, making Houston the only artist whose first two albums each sold over 10 million copies.

'Where Do Broken Hearts Go' became her seventh consecutive single to top the US chart, beating the previous record of six consecutive No. 1 singles held jointly by The Beatles and The Bee Gees. Both Houston's albums had all also each sold a million copies in Britain, something never before achieved by a woman in a country where she was also the first black female artist to top the album chart.

Whitney - born to record-breaking success

1974

DEATH OF LIZARD QUEEN

With the death (via a drug overdose) of Pamela Courson, wife of the late Jim Morrison, vocalist and agent provocateur of The Doors, probably the only remaining witness of Morrison's supposed death could no longer confirm or deny the truth.

She and Morrison were living in Paris at the time of his alleged heart attack in a bath. Morrison doubtless felt more at ease in Europe than in America, where his appeal against a prison sentence for exposing himself on stage at a Miami concert in 1970 was being pursued.

He had just completed a new Doors album, *L. A. Woman* (the band's eighth) containing 'Riders On The Storm', which would became their last but also one of the group's biggest hit singles, and he had no touring obligations in America.

One theory is that Morrison simply did a vanishing act to escape the pressure of having to be The Lizard King, the mythical beast with which he supposedly identified, and was working in a bar on a small Greek island. If Pam Courson knew anything, she kept it to herself.

ARRIVALS

1918 – Ella Fitzgerald
1924 – Albert King (Albert Nelson)
1928 – Vassar Clements
1933 – Jerry Leiber
1943 – Tony Christie
(Anthony Fitzgerald)
1945 – Bjorn Ulvaeus (ABBA)
1945 – Dave Lawson (Episode Six/Greenslade)
1945 – Stu Cook (Creedence Clearwater Revival)
1949 – Michael Brown
(Michael Lukowsky) (Left Banke)
1950 – Steven Ferrone (Average White Band)
1953 – Cory Daye (Dr Buzzard's Original Savannah Band)
1958 – Fish
(Derek William Dick)
1959 – Billy Rankin (Brinsley Schwarz)
1964 – Andy Bell (Erasure)

★ ★ ★

RAVINGS

1978:
Chief Nashville outlaw Willie Nelson played the White House in Washington for President Carter, who was a great supporter of Augusta's Capricorn label, which featured The Allman Brothers.

1988:
Carolyn Franklin, younger sister of Aretha, who had a couple of small R & B hits as a soloist after working as Aretha's backing vocalist for some years, died of cancer at the age of 43.

★ ★ ★

1982

ROD ROBBED IN HOLLYWOOD

Superstar Rod Stewart was mugged and robbed while standing beside his $50,000 Porsche in Hollywood Boulevard, Los Angeles. He had just released his last hit for Riva Records in Britain, his cover of Ace's 'How Long', before embarking on a long-term deal with Warner Bros, opening his account with them in 1983 with his first UK No. 1 single for five years, 'Baby Jane'. His relationships with record companies had frequently been subject to controversy since his emergence into the big time in 1971 with 'Maggie May', when he was signed to Mercury as a solo artist, but to Warner Bros in his capacity as vocalist with The Faces.

Who would mug a man looking like this?

He had in fact made his first solo album, the snappily titled *An Old Raincoat Won't Ever Let You Down* (released in the US as *The Rod Stewart Album*) in November 1969, having simultaneously also recorded *First Step*, the debut album by The Faces, which reached the UK album chart for a single week, while *Old Raincoat* completely avoided the chart.

The second Faces album, *Long Player*, performed better than Stewart's second solo album, *Gasoline Alley*, but thereafter, Stewart's solo offerings totally eclipsed those by The Faces, especially his monumentally successful *Every Picture Tells A Story* in 1972, which topped the album charts on both sides of the Atlantic, as did the classic single it included, 'Maggie May'.

Thereafter, until the Faces' demise in 1975, Stewart's solo singles always reached the UK Top 10, while the group's singles, and particularly their albums, lacked the staying power of Stewart's solo work.

1957

BELAFONTE'S MILLION DOLLAR DEAL

Calypso hitmaker Harry Belafonte signed a $1 million deal. During 1956/7 he dominated the US charts with eight separate hit singles and five Top 3 albums, an incredible achievement by any standards.

Although the vast majority of these hits were in the West Indian calypso style – Belafonte was known as 'King Of Calypso' – he was actually born in Harlem, but spent the five years before World War II in Jamaica, where he learned local folk songs like 'Banana Boat Song', 'Mama Looka Boo Boo', 'Jamaica Farewell' and the Christmas favourite, 'Mary's Boy Child', four of his biggest hits. Between 1953 and 1974, he also appeared in eight films, and was one of the prime movers with Michael Jackson behind USA For Africa's all-star charity hit of 1985, 'We Are The World'.

RAVINGS

1978:
Ringo Starr appeared in his first TV Special, an updated version of Mark Twain's *The Prince and The Pauper.*

★ ★ ★

ARRIVALS

1886 – Ma Rainey
1938 – Duane Eddy
1938 – Maurice Williams (Gladiolas/Zodiacs)
1940 – Bobby Rydell (Robert Louis Ridarelli)
1941 – Claudine Clark
1942 – Phil Kaufman (Road Mangler Deluxe)
1944 – Giorgio Moroder
1945 – Gary Wright (Spooky Tooth)
1945 – Tony Murray (Troggs)
1946 – John Buck Wilkin (Ronny and the Daytonas)
1947 – Pete Ham (Badfinger)
1949 – Jimmy Hall (Wet Willie)
1960 – Roger Taylor (Duran Duran)

★ ★ ★

DEPARTURE LOUNGE

1984 – Count Basie
1990 – Dexter Gordon

★ ★ ★

1981

RINGO WEDS CAVEMAN CO-STAR

Former Beatle Ringo Starr met his future wife, actress Barbara Bach, in Durango, Mexico, when they both starred in the movie *Caveman*, which was not nominated for any Oscars – much of the dialogue consisted of grunting! Three months after their first meeting, they were driving to a party when their car was involved in a serious crash less than a mile from the place in Barnes, West London, where Marc Bolan had been killed, also in a car crash, in 1978. Ringo knew Bolan well – he had directed the film starring Bolan, *Born To Boogie*, in 1972.

Mr and Mrs Starr plight their troth

Although not seriously hurt themselves, the Starr car was a complete write-off. Ringo and his passenger were so relieved to have escaped death that they married in London less than a year later, with Beatles pals George Harrison and Paul McCartney in attendance.

GRAND FUNK CLAIM $8 MILLION

1972

Hard rock trio Grand Funk Railroad fired their manager, Terry Knight, who had also been the producer of their records up to that point. Drummer Don Brewer and guitarist Mark Farner had first met Knight (real name Richard Terrance Knapp) when they joined his group, Terry Knight and The Pack. With recruitment of bass player Mel Schacher, previously a member of ? and The Mysterians, the group became major stars in America, with six consecutive gold albums in three years, although they were widely reviled among rock critics – during 1971, a New York press conference drew less than a dozen of the 150 invited guests.

Immediately after splitting with Knight, whom they sued for $8 million for unpaid songwriting royalties, the group began working with Todd Rundgren as record producer, and in 1973/4 they hit paydirt with four US Top 20 hits (they had never previously reached such heights with their singles) including two that went all the way to No. 1, 'We're An American Band' and their unlikely revival of Litle Eva's 1962 chart-topper, 'The Locomotion'.

RAVINGS

1956:
Capitol Records contacted Gene Vincent, telling him they wanted him to be their Presley equivalent.

1976:
David Bowie was delayed for several hours on the border between Russia and Poland, and customs officers confiscated Nazi memorabilia.

1977:
Southside Johnny and The Asbury Jukes appeared in a movie about an underground newspaper, *Behind The Lines*.

1989:
Deacon Blue played a charity gig for the Lockerbie Air Disaster Fund.

1975

FLOYD UNWITTING BAIT FOR DRUG BUST

During five nights of Pink Floyd concerts at Los Angeles Sports Arena, no less than 511 members of the audience were arrested for smoking marijuana. The promoters involved reacted by avoiding promoting any more concerts at the auditorium, which was rarely used for rock concerts anyway.

ARRIVALS

1932 – Maxine Brown (Browns)
1944 – Herb Pedersen (Dillards, Desert Rose Band)
1947 – Ann Peebles
1948 – Kate Pierson (B52's)
1950 – Ace Frehley (Paul Frehley) (Kiss)
1958 – Keith De Nunzio (Feelies)
1959 – Marco Pirroni (Adam and the Ants)
1959 – Sheena Easton

★ ★ ★

DEPARTURE LOUNGE

1972 – Phil King (Blue Oyster Cult)
1975 – Mike Brant
1984 – Z. Z. Hill

1990

GUNS N'ROSES LINK WITH EVERLYS

Guns n'Roses leader Axl Rose married Erin Everly, daughter of Don, the older of The Everly Brothers, at Cupid's Wedding Chapel in Las Vegas, Nevada. Within a month, Rose was filing for divorce on the grounds of 'irreconcilable differences', although the couple subsequently resolved their problems before splitting up again.

Axl prepares to napalm Hollywood's China Club

It was quite a year for Rose. In a poll in *Rolling Stone* magazine in March, he was voted worst male vocalist and worst dressed male rock artist, although Guns n'Roses were winners of the Best Heavy Metal Band category. In July, over a dozen police called at Rose's apartment with batons drawn, and in October, the group sued a chain of toy shops for $2 million for apparently using their name and likeness in advertisements for a toy drum kit, claiming that they had suffered 'damage to their reputation, loss of goodwill and mental anguish'. At the end of the month, Rose was arrested for allegedly assaulting a neighbour, after she had complained to the police about the loud music coming from his home. Released on $5,000 bail, Rose lost more goodwill when he took out an injunction preventing the neighbour having any further contact with him or his wife.

After recording two double albums, *Use Your Illusion I* and *Use Your Illusion II*, both of which sold prodigiously when they were released during the following autumn, Rose and Erin Everly were finally divorced in January 1991, after an action-packed nine months of marriage.

1981

THE FINAL FLING FOR WINGS

With the departure of founder member Denny Laine (ex-Moody Blues), Paul McCartney's post-Beatles group Wings finally disbanded.

Having survived many personnel changes – original drummer Denny Seiwell (ex-Jam Factory) was replaced by Geoff Britton (ex-Wild Angels), who was replaced by Joe English (who left in 1977 to join Sea Level), who was replaced by Steve Holly in 1978. Original guitarist Henry McCullough was replaced by Jimmy McCulloch (no relation), who left to join the reformed Small Faces, and was replaced by Lawrence Juber.

Laine, after almost ten years as the only permanent feature other than McCartney and his wife, Linda, finally called it a day.

McCartney - back to solo work

ARRIVALS

1941 – Peter Anders (Anders and Poncia)
1945 – John Wolters (Dr Hook)
1947 – Brian Miller (Isotope)
1951 – Bob Robertson (Supercharge/Rumour)
1955 – Eddie Jobson (Roxy Music/Curved Air/Jethro Tull)
1960 – Andy LeGear (Rosetta Stone)
1960 – Enid Williams (Girl School)
1967 – Owen (daughter of 'Mama' Cass Elliot)
1969 – Mica Paris

★ ★ ★

DEPARTURE LOUNGE

1980 – Tommy Caldwell (Marshall Tucker Band)
1988 – B. W. Stevenson

★ ★ ★

RAVINGS

1975:
Tom Donahue, the man responsible for launching FM radio in San Francisco at station KMPX, died on the day he was due to return to the station as General Manager.

1987:
Rolling Stone Bill Wyman launched AIMS to provide promising young musicians with affordable time in recording studios.

1987:
Peter Gabriel's innovative video for 'Sledgehammer' won awards in the USA for Best Pop Video and Best Design and Art Direction.

EVERLYS LAUNCH NEW LABEL WITH CHART-TOPPING CATHY'S CLOWN

1960

Warner Bros launched its own record label in Britain with a massive hit. The first single on the label (catalogue number WB 1) was an instant success – featuring The Everly Brothers, who had previously enjoyed a string of hits on both sides of the Atlantic since mid 1957 when 'Bye Bye Love' and 'Wake Up Little Susie' became their first million-sellers.

Don (left) and Phil - The Everly Brothers

Those classics were followed in 1958 by three more that sold equally well, 'All I Have To Do Is Dream', 'Bird Dog' and 'Problems', and in 1959 by two more, 'Take A Message To Mary' and '('Til) I Kissed You'.

These massive hits were far from the complete catalogue of their recording career on orchestra leader Archie Bleyer's independent label, Cadence, as several other singles, including 'This Little Girl Of Mine', 'Let It Be Me', and even some of the B-sides of the previously mentioned million-sellers, such as 'Poor Jenny', 'Claudette' and 'Devoted To You', also achieved high chart placings in their own right.

The move to Warner Bros in February 1960, on a contract lasting ten years and guaranteeing Don and Phil $1 million, left Cadence without their most successful act. Even after their debut single on their new label, 'Cathy's Clown', which topped the US chart for five weeks and the UK chart for seven, becoming their eighth million-seller in three years, two further Cadence recordings, 'When Will I Be Loved' and 'Like Strangers', became substantial hits. Unfortunately for Warner Bros, the duo only managed one more million-seller, 1961's 'Walk Right Back', before they fell from grace in commercial terms. The Cadence recordings have been reissued ever since.

1968

HAIR - HIT ON BROADWAY

The hippie musical *Hair* opened on Broadway in New York, and caused a sensation as several of the cast removed all their clothes during each performance. Written by actors Jerome Ragni and James Rado with music by Canadian Galt McDermott, among the hit songs featured in the show were 'Aquarius - Let The Sun Shine In' an American No. 1 for the Fifth Dimension, 'Hair' by the Cowsills, 'Good Morning Starshine' by Oliver and Three Dog Night's 'Easy To Be Hard'.

Its Broadway run lasted for around 1,750 performances.

'Hair' people

1983

BLUES GREAT MUDDY DIES

AT 68 celebrated blues/R& B veteran McKinley Morganfield, better known to millions of blues fans around the world as Muddy Waters, died of a heart attack in his adopted city of Chicago, where he had moved 40 years before to work in a paper mill.

Muddy Waters in his heyday

Acquiring an electric guitar in 1944, Waters made his first commercial recordings in early 1946, before signing to the local Aristocrat label (which changed its name to Chess Records in 1948). During the 1950s many major blues artists worked with him, including Willie Dixon (who wrote many of the songs Waters made into hits), Little Walter Jacobs, Otis Spann, James Cotton, Buddy Guy, Junior Wells and more – a veritable 'Who's Who' of Chicago blues at that time. As a major inspiration behind the R & B boom of the 1960s that produced such international stars as The Rolling Stones (who took their name from one of his songs), Eric Clapton (who hired Muddy as opening act for a world tour around 1980) and Paul Butterfield.

Waters recorded many blues classics during a recording career of over 30 years, including 'Hoochie Coochie Man', 'I Just Want To Make Love To You', 'Got My Mojo Working', etc. His best records are generally agreed to have been made for Chess, the label to which he was signed until the early 1970s.

In 1976 he signed with Blue Sky Records, a label whose main stars were albino blues guitarist Johnny Winter and his multi-instrumentalist brother, Edgar. Waters made two of his most commercially successful albums, *Hard Again* (1977) and *I'm Ready* (1978), and often toured with Johnny Winter.

RAVINGS

1965:
Manchester group Herman's Hermits, led by actor Peter Noone (Ena Sharples' grandson in the long running British TV soap opera *Coronation Street*) began their first US tour, supported by The Zombies. Both groups enjoyed greater chart success in the USA than in their native Britain.

1988:
Pink Floyd's *Dark Side Of The Moon* album was absent from the US album chart for the first time in an incredible 725 weeks (three weeks short of 14 years!).

1988:
The *Dirty Dancing* soundtrack topped the UK album charts, while *More Dirty Dancing* was also in the Top 3 of the chart.

ARRIVALS

1927 – Johnny Horton
1930 – Bobby Marchan
1933 – Willie Nelson
1934 – Jerry Lordan
1941 – Johnny Farina (Santo and Johnny)
1943 – Bobby Vee (Robert Thomas Velline)
1944 – Richard Shoff (Sandpipers)
1945 – Mike Deacon (Juicy Lucy/Vinegar Joe)
1953 – Merrill Osmond
1967 – Turbo B (Snap)

★ ★ ★

DEPARTURE LOUNGE

1966 – Richard Farina
1968 – Frankie Lymon
1983 – Muddy Waters (McKinley Morganfield)

★ ★ ★

1955

KING OF THE WILD FRONTIER'S US CHART DOMINATION

The hit movie *Davy Crockett*, starring Fess Parker as 'the king of the wild frontier', featured an exceptionally catchy theme – so catchy that three different versions of the song were all in the US Top 10 at the same time by TV star Bill Hayes (the most successful, topping the chart for five weeks), 'Tennessee' Ernie Ford and Fess Parker. In Britain, Hayes and Parker both had Top 5 hits with the tune.

KING FINDS A QUEEN

Female fans of Elvis Presley who had dreamed that some day, some how, they would actually meet The King, who would be so smitten that he would whisk them off into the sunset in a pink Cadillac, had their hopes dashed when he married his sweetheart of eight years' standing, Priscilla Beaulieu.

The King weds his Queen

The rock 'n' roll wedding of the year was a remarkably modest affair, taking place in the private suite of the owner of the Aladdin Hotel in Las Vegas between 9.30 and 10 am (before most of the gambling city's residents and visitors had prepared for another day at the tables), with Nevada Supreme Court Justice David Zenoff officiating. Best man was Joe Esposito, a trusted member of Presley's so-called 'Memphis Mafia', while Priscilla's sister, Michelle, was maid of honour.

Presley had met his bride in September 1959, while in Germany during his US Army service. Priscilla, then only 14, was the daughter of USAF Major Joseph Beaulieu, who was also stationed in Bad Neuheim, Germany, with his family. When Presley was discharged by Uncle Sam, the teenage girl was allowed to live at Graceland, Presley's Memphis mansion, although she was suitably chaperoned.

After a brief reception, the newly married couple flew to Palm Springs for a one-day honeymoon – Elvis had to be in Hollywood on May 3 to complete final filming of his *Clambake* movie, after which they returned to Memphis where a second reception was held on May 29.

1977

CLASH UK TOUR TAKES PUNK TO PROVINCES

Following the debacle of the *Anarchy In The UK* tour less than six months earlier, on which they had been one of the supporting attractions to The Sex Pistols, The Clash began their own headlining tour in support of their just-released debut album.

With support acts The Jam and Manchester's Buzzcocks, the trek began at London's Roxy Club. A new single by The Clash, 'Remote Control', surprisingly failed to reach the UK chart despite the promotion opportunities offered by the tour.

(left to right) Jones, Simonon, Strummer - The Clash

ARRIVALS

1894 – Sam McGee (Uncle Dave Macon's troupe)
1907 – Kate Smith
1924 – Big Maybelle
1929 – Sonny James (Jimmie Loden)
1930 – Little Walter
(Marion Walter Jacobs)
1939 – Judy Collins
1945 – Mimi Farina (Mimi Baez)
1945 – Rita Coolidge
1954 – Ray Parker Jr
1957 – Rick Driscoll (Kenny)
1957 – Steve Farris (Mr Mister)
1959 – Phil Smith (Haircut 100)
1962 – Owen Paul

★ ★ ★

DEPARTURE LOUNGE

1964 – Spike Jones

RAVINGS

1966:
The Beatles played their last ever live show with a paying audience in Britain at London's Wembley Arena. The event was the *New Musical Express Pollwinner's* Concert, and others on the bill included The Rolling Stones and The Who.

★ ★ ★

1969:
Bob Dylan & Johnny Cash taped an ABC TV Special at Nashville's *Grand Ole Opry*.

1975:
To the surprise of journalists at a press conference, The Rolling Stones announced their forthcoming US tour by playing live on a flatbed truck moving slowly down Fifth Avenue in New York.

★ ★ ★

FILM PREMIERE INTRODUCES NEW WHO MEMBER

Mods in Brighton recreating the mid-1960s in 'Quadrophenia'

Following the death of drummer Keith Moon the previous September caused by an overdose of the drug he had been prescribed to assist his attempts to cure his alcohol addiction, The Who introduced his replacement, Kenny Jones. Few could be better qualified to replace a member of the ultimate 'Mod' group of the 1960s than a member of The Small Faces, the only other group whose 'Mod' credentials rivalled (or even exceeded) those of The Who.

At the same time, the film, *Quadrophenia*, an evocation of the 'Mod' era written by Who mastermind Pete Townshend, was premiered and created renewed interest in The Who after a seven-year period (since 1971's *Who's Next* album). *Quadrophenia* told the tale of Jimmy, a teenage 'Mod' on a search for spiritual satisfaction. Involving scooters and a trip to Brighton, it had been released as the double album follow-up to *Who's Next*, and had been compared

unfavourably with Townshend's earlier *Tommy*. Various versions of *Tommy*, including a Ken Russell directed movie starring Roger Daltrey in the title role plus Ann-Margret, Oliver Reed and Elton John, and an all-star fully orchestrated stage performance, had consumed much of Townshend's time during the mid 1970s, but the irresistible rise of The Jam, a neo-punk rock trio whose leader, Paul Weller, seemed hugely influenced by Townshend, both

philosophically and to some extent musically, restored The Who's significance. The movie added fuel to that spark, not least because a very recognizable Sting, star of another hugely popular trio, The Police, played the role of 'The Ace Face', a 'Mod' leader in terms of both clothes and lifestyle. It seemed curious that the *Quadrophenia* film premiere took place on the very same evening that Jones made his first appear-ance with The Who at London's Rainbow Theatre.

ARRIVALS

1901 – Bing Crosby
(Harry Lillis Crosby)
1933 – John Leon
(Bunk)
Gardner
(Mothers of Invention)
1943 – Hilton Valentine
(Animals)
1944 – John Verity
(Argent)
1944 – John Ware
(The Hot Band)
1945 – Goldy McJohn
(Steppenwolf)
1945 – Randy
(Rudy) Cain
(Four Gents/Delphonics)

1946 – Robert Henrit
(Argent)
1948 – Larry Gatlin
(Gatlin Brothers)
1951 – Jo Callis
(Rezillos/Human League)
1954 – Prescott Niles
(The Knack)
1961 – Dr Robert
(Robert Howard)
(Blow Monkeys)

★ ★ ★

DEPARTURE LOUNGE

1973 – June Hutton
1985 – Larry Clinton

★ ★ ★

RAVINGS

1957:
Elvis Presley recorded 'Jailhouse Rock'.

1980:
Pink Floyd's smash hit, 'Another Brick In

The Wall', was banned in South Africa as it was felt it might encourage boycotts at black schools.

★ ★ ★

ADAM GOES SOLO, ANTS DISPERSE

After a year during which Adam and The Ants released two immensely successful albums, *Kings Of The Wild Frontier* (No. 1) and *Prince Charming* (No. 2), two chart-topping singles ('Stand And Deliver' and the title track of 'Prince Charming'), plus two more Top 3 singles (the 'Kings Of The Wild Frontier' title track and 'Antrap'), registering an incredible 91 weeks on the UK singles chart in one year. Altogether nine of their singles charted in Britain, leader Adam Ant (real name Stuart Goddard) opted for a solo career.

Adam post Ants

1967

WALKERS MOVE IN DIFFERENT DIRECTIONS

Scott (left), John (with mic), Gary (drums) - The Walker Brothers

Fans of American-born, but British-based, dreamboat trio The Walker Brothers staged a protest march from Baker Street station to the Maida Vale flat of manager Barry Chapman, where John Walker was living to protest at the announcement from the stage of London's Tooting Granada that the group were splitting up due to growing personal incompatibility.

Vocalists Scott (real name Noel Scott Engel) and John (real name John Maus) Walker were playing bass and lead guitar respectively in the house band at a Hollywood club in 1964 when they got talking to Gary (real name Gary Leeds), the drummer in P. J. Proby's band at the time. Leeds, having toured Britain with Proby, felt that a group of young Americans could do well in Europe, where appearances by American acts were infrequent, and British

TV producer Jack Good supported that view. In February 1965 the trio arrived in London, soon acquired a recording contract and by the end of April, were in the UK chart with their second single, 'Love Her'. By the end of the year, they had topped the UK chart with their cover version of Jerry Butler's hit, 'Make It Easy On Yourself', by which time Scott and John had abandoned their instruments and were functioning as lead vocalists, with Gary the core of their backing group of British musicians. Five singles by the trio reached the UK charts during 1966, including 'My Ship Is

Coming In' (another cover, this time of a Jimmy Radcliffe original), which made the Top 3, and a second No. 1, 'The Sun Ain't Gonna Shine Anymore' (a Frankie Valli cover), while their first two albums, *Make It Easy* and *Portrait*, were also Top 3 successes.

1984

BACK IN THE PINK FOR DEEP PURPLE

Originally formed in 1967, rock band Deep Purple had been internationally successful during the early 1970s, but had split up in 1976 after numerous personnel changes. The group's 'Mark II' line-up of Ritchie Blackmore (guitar), Ian Gillan (vocals), Roger Glover (bass), Jon Lord (keyboards) and Ian Paice (drums) was widely regarded as the group's best. Rumours circulated that each member was offered $12 million to reunite, which they did with the release of a new album, *Perfect Strangers*, and a worldwide tour.

ARRIVALS

1919 – Pete Seeger
1924 – Joe Ames (Ames Brothers)
1928 – Dave Dudley (David Pedruska)
1928 – James Brown
1934 – Georges Moustaki (Joseph Moustacci)
1937 – Frankie Valli (Francis Castelluccio) (Four Seasons)
1944 – Pete Staples (Troggs)
1947 – John Richardson (Rubettes)

1951 – Christopher Cross (Christopher Geppert)
1955 – Steve Jones (Sex Pistols)
1959 – David Ball (Soft Cell)
1960 – Philip Cilia (Waterfront)

★ ★ ★

DEPARTURE LOUNGE

1972 – Les Harvey (Stone The Crows)
1977 – Helmut Koellen (Triumvirat)

1970

TIN SOLDIERS AND NIXON'S ARMY

Soldiers from the National Guard shot four students dead, two of them girls, when they opened fire on an unruly crowd of anti-war demonstrators at Kent State University in Ohio.

Eleven students were injured, as rioting continued for the third day. At Jackson State University in Mississippi, two black students were also shot dead in a related incident. The protests followed President Nixon's decision to mobilize

American troops in Cambodia without consulting Congress.

The reaction among rock stars was one of horror, and Neil Young, after seeing a report of the incident on television, was moved to write a protest song that he called 'Ohio', and

Neil Young

which he recorded the next day with his colleagues in the Crosby, Stills, Nash and Young supergroup.

During June 1970 'Ohio' was heading up the *Billboard* singles chart, jockeying for position with 'Teach Your Children', another track by CSN and Y, but this time from their latest album, *Déjà Vu*. Eventually, both singles reached the US Top 20, but both similarly peaked just outside the Top 10.

1968

TWIGGY RECOMMENDS MARY HOPKIN TO MACCA

Famed model and film star Twiggy (real name Lesley Hornby) was watching a long-running TV Talent Show, *Opportunity Knocks*, when she was captivated by the performance of a Welsh teenage singer, Mary Hopkin, whose voice was remarkably mellifluous and tuneful. Twiggy immediately telephoned Paul McCartney, recommending that he investigate this unknown teenager with a view to her recording for Apple Records, the label about to be launched by The Beatles.

Hopkin's *Opportunity Knocks* win was an excellent birthday present – she had celebrated her 18th birthday the day before. Three months later, Hopkin's debut single for Apple, 'Those Were The Days', which was

Mary Hopkin – innocence personified

produced by McCartney, was released, and by the end of September was ensconsed at the top of the UK chart, where it remained for six weeks.

It was a perfect start for the fledgling label, as Hopkin's single replaced the first Apple Records release, 'Hey Jude' by The Beatles, at No. 1 .

ROCK MARRIAGE OF THE YEAR

Chrissie Hynde, leader/vocalist/ songwriter of The Pretenders, married Jim Kerr, her counterpart in Scottish band Simple Minds in New York's Central Park, following a whirlwind romance. Just over a year before, in February 1984, Hynde had given birth to a daughter, Natalie, whose father was Ray Davies, leader of The Kinks.

from Hereford: James Honeyman-Scott (lead guitar), Pete Farndon (bass) and Martin Chambers (drums). Named The Pretenders (apparently after the 1950s hit by The Platters, 'The Great Pretender'), the group's first single was a cover version of a relatively obscure song by The Kinks, 'Stop Your Sobbing', produced by Nick Lowe, which was a UK Top 40 hit. During January 1980 they became the first act to enter the UK album chart at No. 1 with a debut album (the eponymously titled Pretenders), simultaneously topping the UK singles chart with 'Brass In Pocket'. That year also saw Hynde meeting Ray Davies for the first time. In April 1982 a registrar refused to marry them because they argued incessantly.

Chrissie and Jim - a Central Park union

ARRIVALS

1901 – Blind Willie McTell (Willie Samuel McTell)
1934 – Ace Cannon
1942 – Jim King (Family)
1942 – Tammy Wynette (Virginia Wynette Pugh)
1948 – Bill Ward (Black Sabbath)
1950 – Eddy Amoo (Real Thing)
1950 – Maggie McNeal (Sjoukje van Spijker) (Mouth and McNeal)
1957 – Thereza Bazar (Dollar)
1959 – Ian McCulloch (Echo and the Bunnymen)
1961 – Sean McLuskey (JoBoxers)
1962 – Gary Daly (China Crisis)
1962 – Kevin Paul Mooney (Adam and the Ants)
1964 – Kevin Saunderson (Inner City)
1964 – Lorraine McIntosh (Deacon Blue)

★ ★ ★

DEPARTURE LOUNGE

1972 – 'Reverend' Gary Davis

Hynde was born in 1951, in Akron, Ohio (where Hynde and Devo keyboard player Mark Mothersbaugh played together in a teenage group). After studying art at Kent State University (where four students were shot by the US National Guard in 1970, Hynde moved to London in 1973. A meeting with *New Musical Express* writer Nick Kent led to her writing for the rock weekly, augmenting her income by modelling at London's St Martin's Art College and working in Malcolm McLaren's Kings Road clothes shop, before moving to Paris to join a short-lived group in 1974 and returning to the US in 1975 to join a band in Cleveland.

1976 found her back in London, where attempts to form groups with members of Johnny Moped (The Berk Brothers) and with Steve Strange (the Moors Murderers) bore little fruit. After linking up with Dave Hill, who was about to launch a new label, Real Records, she assembled a group composed of musicians

RAVINGS

1968:
Buffalo Springfield disbanded. Stephen Stills teamed up with David Crosby and Graham Nash in Crosby, Stills and Nash (which also sometimes featured Neil Young, another ex-Springfield member), while Ritchie Furay formed Poco with Jim Messina.

1987:
135 girls fainted at a gig in Liverpool by Curiosity Killed The Cat.

1990:
A John Lennon tribute concert took place in Liverpool, with Daryl Hall and John Oates, Kylie Minogue, Terence Trent D'Arby and Dave Edmunds among the performers.

★ ★ ★

LED ZEP BREAK THEIR OWN RECORD

The record breaking Led Zeppelin

Led Zeppelin played a concert at the Silverdome in Pontiac, Michigan, attended by an audience that exceeded 76,000 people. This broke the group's own record for the biggest ever attendance at a concert with a single headlining attraction, set almost exactly four years before by one of their concerts in Tampa, Florida, where nearly 57,000 attended, which in its turn took the record from the 1965 Shea Stadium Concert featuring The Beatles. During the 1970s, Led Zeppelin were a consistently huge live attraction - selling out whole tours in just a few hours.

Their manager, the larger-than-life ex-wrestler Peter Grant, is credited with completely reversing the usual relationship between artists and promoters by apparently telling one promoter who wanted to present a Led Zeppelin concert, 'We don't work for you – if you want to do business, you'll be working for us for a percentage of the profits'. In July 1973 the group's concert at New York's Madison Square Garden was filmed and formed part of the footage in the group's 1976 feature film, *The Song Remains The Same*, although the day of the concert was marred when the group found they were robbed of $180,000, which was removed from a safety deposit box at a New York hotel, and was never recovered.

ARRIVALS

1895 – Rudolph Valentino
1904 – Cliff Carlisle (Carlisle Brothers)
1913 – Carmen Cavallaro
1915 – Orson Welles
1939 – Herbie Cox (Cleftones)
1942 – Colin Earl (Mungo Jerry/Foghat)
1945 – Bob Seger
1948 – Mary McGregor
1951 – Davey 'Shaggis' Johnstone
1960 – Larry Steinbachek (Bronski Beat)

★ ★ ★

DEPARTURE LOUNGE

1971 – Dickie Valentine
1983 – Kai Winding

1973

SIMON GOES IT ALONE

Singer/songwriter Paul Simon launched his first solo tour since splitting with his friend of 20 years and musical partner for much of that time, Art Garfunkel, with a concert at the Music Hall in Boston, Massachusetts. Seven albums by the duo had reached the US Top 30 in the previous seven years, all of them being certified gold, and three of them, the soundtrack to the film *The Graduate*, *Bookends* and *Bridge Over Troubled Water*, reaching the No. 1 position. However, the two had apparently grown apart during the 800-plus hours taken to complete the recording of the last of those chart-topping albums.

Garfunkel's film commitments (he was making his debut as an actor in the movie of Joseph Heller's black comedy, *Catch 22*, at the time) and his objection to a song by Simon, 'Cuba Si, Yankee No', made the album sessions fraught with tension.

Nevertheless, both the album and its title track topped the US charts during the same week as they also topped the UK charts. Simon's solo career was immensely successful, and recordings from this first solo tour were used in his live album *Live Rhymin'*, released in 1974.

Simon goes solo

1969

KING OF THE ROAD LAUNCHES BOBBY MCGEE

Country hitmaker Roger Miller, notable for such smash hits as 'Dang Me', 'Chug-A-Lug', 'King Of The Road' and 'England Swings' earlier in the 1960s entered the US country singles chart with his version of a song written by Kris Kristofferson, 'Me and Bobby McGee'.

Kristofferson, a Texan who had won a Rhodes scholarship to England's Oxford University in 1958 before teaching at West Point military academy, had moved to Nashville in 1965 to become a songwriter after being inspired by a meeting with Johnny Cash. The only job Kristofferson could find in Music City was as a janitor at Columbia Studios – he was emptying ashtrays as Bob Dylan recorded his *Blonde On Blonde* double album. Johnny Cash recommended 'Me and Bobby McGee' to Miller, who thus became the first notable artist to cover a Kristofferson song. Its composer, who by then was a staff writer at Combine Music, recalled that the title was suggested by his boss as 'Me and Bobby McKee'.

The lady in question was a secretary in the office of songwriter Boudleaux Bryant, who wrote numerous classics with his wife, Felice, for The Everly Brothers in the 1950s, such as 'Bye Bye Love' and 'All I Have To Do Is Dream'. Kristofferson misheard the name, thinking it was McGee, and recalled it as he reacted to the rhythm of the windscreen wipers while driving in the rain. Including the names of places he had been ('Busted flat in Baton Rouge', etc.), he wrote a song about an old girl-friend and remembering the title he had been given some time before, called her Bobby McGee.

The song topped the chart in 1971 by Kristofferson's one-time girlfriend, Janis Joplin.

Kristofferson - first hit about old flame

1972

STONES MAIN STREET DOUBLE

Having launched their own label, Rolling Stones Records, in 1971 with the chart-topping *Sticky Fingers* album, so-called 'bad boys of rock' followed it up with their first original double album, *Exile On Main Street*. At the start of the year their old label, London, had released a

The Stones strut their stuff at Wembley

compilation double album, *Hot Rocks 1964–1971*, which had reached the US Top 5 and was resident in the US album chart for over four years. *Exile* peaked higher, topping the US album chart for a month, but remained in that chart for only a little over one year.

1976

ABBA AVOID OBLIVION

Proving that not every non-British act that wins the Eurovision Song Contest is destined to be quickly forgotten, Swedish quartet ABBA achieved their second UK chart-topper of the year, and their third in all, when 'Fernando' reached No. 1.

The song, which was first recorded by Frida on her album *Frida Alone*, also topped the chart in Australia where they had a total of five singles in the Top 30. The group, whose name came from the initial letters of their

(left to right) Bjorn, Agnetha, Anni-Frid and Benny - back from the dead

first names, comprised Anni-Frid ('Frida') Lyngstad, Bjorn Ulvaeus, Benny Andersson and Agnetha Faltskog. They emerged in 1974 when 'Waterloo' not only won the Eurovision title, but also brushed aside all opposition to top the UK singles chart. No previous non-British winner of the Song Contest had ever survived the stigma

attached to the annual gala designed to produce a song that would have commercial appeal throughout Europe. ABBA, who had entered the contest hoping to widen their audience beyond Sweden, proved that their talent could conquer the world marketplace by scoring

hits in Australasia (it is estimated that one in four Australians own a copy of their *Greatest Hits* album), the Far East, both North and South America and Britain. During the 1970s, they were certainly one of the most consistently successful acts in the world.

ARRIVALS

1905 – Red Nichols (Ernest Loring)
1911 – Robert Johnson
1940 – Gary Glitter (Paul Gadd)
1940 – Ricky Nelson (Eric Hilliard Nelson)
1941 – John Fred (John Fred Gourrier) (John Fred and his Playboy Band)
1942 – Euclid James Motorhead' Sherwood (Mothers of Invention)
1943 – Paul Samwell-Smith (Yardbirds)
1943 – Toni Tennille

(Captain and Tennille)
1945 – Keith Jarrett
1951 – Chris Frantz (Talking Heads)
1951 – Philip Bailey (Earth Wind and Fire)
1953 – Billy Burnette (Fleetwood Mac)
1955 – Alex Van Halen (Van Halen)

★ ★ ★

DEPARTURE LOUNGE

1974 – Graham Bond
1982 – Neil Bogart

★ ★ ★

RAVINGS

1954:
Johnnie Ray's 'Such A Night' was banned by the BBC, even though it had already topped the UK chart. Listeners complained that it was 'suggestive'.

★ ★ ★

1970:
Let It Be, the last original album by The Beatles, was released.

★ ★ ★

1977:
Olivia Newton-John made her New York concert debut at the Metropolitan Opera House.

★ ★ ★

1978:
Donny Osmond got married at the age of 21, doubtless breaking the hearts of many fans.

★ ★ ★

1965

BRITANNIA RULES THE COLONIES

Before The Beatles, The Stones, the Dave Clark Five and all the rest captivated the USA in

1964, few British-made singles had reached the US chart, but for one week in 1965 it became

Freddie Garrity (centre) surrounded by his Dreamers

clear just how the tide had turned when nine of the singles in the US Top 10 were British.

Herman's Hermits were clearly the flavour of the moment with both the No. 1, 'Mrs Brown, You've Got A Lovely Daughter', and a second single, 'Silhouettes', in the Top 10. Both The Beatles and The Stones were listed, as were Wayne Fontana and Freddie and The Dreamers, as well as The Seekers (actually Australian), Petula Clark (unrelated to Dave) and Sounds Orchestral. The only US record in the Top 10 was 'Count Me In' by Gary Lewis and The Playboys.

1974

BREAKTHROUGH FOR THE BOSS WITH 'BORN TO RUN'

With two albums already released, *Greetings From Asbury Park, N. J.* in early 1973, and *The Wild, The Innocent and The E Street Shuffle* at the end of that year, neither of which had even approached the US chart, it was beginning to look as though Springsteen, the latest discovery of famed talent scout John Hammond, might have been misjudged by the man who had signed Bob Dylan.

Bruce - born to run and succeed

Bonnie Raitt was the headliner of the show at Harvard Square Theatre in Cambridge, Massachusetts, she agreed to allow Springsteen, who was booked as the opening act, to play his full two-hour set. He went down a storm. One member of the audience was rock critic Jon Landau who was later widely misquoted when he wrote in a review 'I saw rock and roll's future and its name is Bruce Springsteen'.

Springsteen invited Landau to assist in the recording of his new project. His involvement resulted in an old friend of Springsteen, singer/guitarist Steve Van Zandt, also helping out, but no one could argue with the results, as *Born To Run*, the album that resulted, became the breakthrough record for Springsteen, going gold and reaching the Top 3 of the US chart.

1964

BERRY BOUNCES BACK TO ROCK IN LONDON

Having served a three-year prison sentence for an offence involving an under-age Indian prostitute, Norine Janice Escalanti, who worked in a nightclub he owned, Chuck Berry opened his first UK tour with a show at Finsbury Park Astoria (later The Rainbow Theatre). During his enforced absence Berry had become a major star due to such notables as The Beatles and The Rolling Stones recording cover versions of his songs. The first single by The Stones was Berry's 'Come On', and their first EP included Berry's 'Bye Bye Johnny', while their debut album opened with their version of Bobby Troup's 'Route 66', which Berry had included on his *Juke Box Hits* album.

Chuck Berry - rollin' and rockin'

1963

STONES START TO ROLL

Back in January 1963 The Rolling Stones had recorded five tracks in a three-hour session engineered by Glyn Johns, but despite their growing fan following around London, nobody wanted to give the group a record deal. Then the group were 'discovered' by ex-Beatles publicist Andrew Loog Oldham, who became their manager with his boss, Eric Easton. Oldham very cleverly frightened Decca A & R man Dick Rowe (immortalized as 'the man who turned down The Beatles') into signing them in case he missed the boat a second time.

Rock rebels get deal

He obviously did not, of course, and whether or not Oldham believed what he told Rowe, he had indeed discovered a phenomenon...

Three days after signing with Oldham's Impact Sound production company on May 6, the group had been leased to Decca, and were in the studio the next day, with Oldham, who knew virtually nothing about making records, as their producer. The decision had been made to avoid all the well-known Chuck Berry material that dominated their riotous live shows (and were played by many other R & B bands in Britain), so 'Roll Over Beethoven', 'Sweet Little Sixteen', 'Around and Around' and 'Memphis Tennessee' were among the songs they discarded, choosing instead a much less familiar Berry song, 'Come On', which was particularly obscure, as it had never been released in Britain.

Decca rejected the original recording as 'dreadful' and requested the group re-record the track, a month later it was this version that

broke the Stones. For the follow-up, Oldham asked his ex-clients from Liverpool for a song. They gave him 'I Wanna Be Your Man', which almost made the Top 10, and the rest is history.

RAVINGS

1964:
Bob Dylan arrived in Britain for his first tour.

★ ★ ★

1967:
Mick Jagger and Keith Richard were prosecuted on drug charges, and Brian Jones was charged with possession of marijuana.

★ ★ ★

1969:
Both The Turtles and The Temptations are believed to have snorted cocaine in The White House after performing there.

★ ★ ★

1974:
The Who sold out Madison Square Gardens, New York, for four nights – all 80,000 tickets were sold in eight hours.

★ ★ ★

1954

HALEY CUTS HISTORIC SMASH

Bill Haley recorded 'Rock Around The Clock', and popular music would never be the same again. However, there was nothing instant about its success, and it was not until it was played over the opening titles of the film *Blackboard Jungle* that anyone realized how exciting and contagious it was. By July 1955 it was topping the US charts, where it remained for eight weeks.

CANCER CLAIMS REGGAE SUPERSTAR

Although his cancer-related illness had been known to have worsened over the previous six months, Bob Marley's death at Miami's Cedars Of Lebanon hospital still stunned the music world. Reggae music's only true ambassador and superstar was only 36 years old.

The son of a British Army Captain and a Jamaican mother, Marley had been the major inspiration for a generation of his contemporaries and had seen his songs covered by international stars like Johnny Nash and Eric Clapton (who recorded Marley's 'I Shot The Sheriff' on his 1974 album, *461 Ocean Boulevard*), while becoming the artistic voice of the Jamaican Rastafarian movement.

He cut his first record in 1961, but his first success came in 1962 with 'One More Cup Of Coffee' after Jimmy Cliff had introduced him to local producer Leslie Kong. Two years later, he had formed The Wailers, which also included Peter Tosh and Bunny Livingstone. In 1966 American singer Johnny Nash discovered

Bob Marley, reggae's biggest star

Marley while looking for songs in Jamaica, but it was not until the 1970s that Nash started having hits with Marley compositions like 'Stir It Up' and 'Guava Jelly'.

Marley continued to score hits in Jamaica during t he late 1960s, but found a far wider constituency after Island Records boss Chris Blackwell signed him. The seminal *Catch A Fire* was his first internationally acclaimed album in 1972, but his first chart breakthrough in the UK and US came with 1975's *Natty Dread* album and perhaps his most familiar song, 'No Woman, No Cry'. Having made the breakthrough, Marley's fame accelerated with 'Exodus', 'Jamming', 'Could You Be Loved', 'Rastaman Vibration', 'One Love' and many others, and hugely successful tours of Europe and the USA, as well as appearances in Africa, made him an international superstar.

LENNON CLAIMS OF FBI PHONE TAPS

Resident in New York since 1970, ex-Beatle John Lennon appeared on the highly rated *Dick Cavett TV Show* claiming that he was under constant surveillance by the FBI, and that his telephone had been tapped – part of a plot to

Lennon - phone complaint

have him deported from the US as an undesirable alien, due to his political involvement.

MEAT SHORT OF BREAD

Meat Loaf - not yet a starvation victim

1983

Economy-sized hard rock vocalist Meat Loaf (real name Marvin Lee Aday) filed for bankruptcy with debts of over $1 million. His rise to prominence came in 1977/8 with *Bat Out Of Hell*, an album on which he interpreted the often literally fantastic songs of Jim Steinman. By the end of 1992 this album had spent over eight years on and off in the UK album listings. It achieved platinum status in the USA during an 18-month chart residency during which it peaked outside the Top 10, while in Britain it briefly reached the Top 10, although its remarkable achievement was its incredible staying power.

Meat Loaf, who earned his living as a vocalist in the theatre after an apprenticeship as vocalist in groups like Popcorn Blizzard, had first encountered Steinman in 1974 in New York, where he played two roles during each performance of an off-Broadway musical written by Steinman, *More than You Deserve*.

Bat Out Of Hell, which was produced by Todd Rundgren, was partly composed of songs written by Steinman for *Neverland*, a futuristic version of *Peter Pan*. The project was finally backed by Cleveland International Records, who licensed it to Columbia/CBS.

The album took off in Britain after a video clip of the title track had been screened on BBC 2's *Old Grey Whistle Test* TV show, when it swiftly entered the UK album chart. Among the musicians who played on the album were Roy Bittan and Max Weinberg (both from Bruce Springsteen's E Street Band) and Edgar Winter. While Meat Loaf's 1981 follow-up album, *Dead Ringer*, was initially far more successful in Britain, where it topped the album chart, it was only a minor triumph in the USA, briefly reaching the Top 50.

RAVINGS

1960:
Elvis Presley made his TV comeback after two years in the US Army on a *'Welcome Back' Special* hosted by well-known rock 'n' roll fan Frank Sinatra.

1971:
Mick Jagger married Bianca Perez Morena De Macias in the Town Hall at St Tropez in France.

1986:
Joe Strummer of The Clash was banned from the road for drunken driving.

EDDIE DROPS DEBBIE AND LIFTS LIZ

1959

Crooner Eddie Fisher, who accumulated 18 US hit singles during the 1950s, married film star Elizabeth Taylor. Fisher had previously been married to film star Debbie Reynolds, who topped the US chart in 1957 with 'Tammy', the theme song from the movie *Tammy And The Bachelor*. Fisher and Reynolds produced a daughter, Carrie, who starred in the *Star Wars* movies and later married Paul Simon.

Debbie Reynolds - a scene from a 'Tammy' film

ARRIVALS

1901 – Whitey Ford 'The Duke of Paducah' (Benjamin Francis Ford)
1928 – Burt Bacharach
1941 – Jay Otis Washington (Persuasions)
1942 – Billy Swan
1942 – Ian Dury
1944 – James Purify
1945 – Bob Rigg (Frost)
1946 – Ian McLagan (Small Faces)
1946 – Robert MacVitte (Sugarloaf)
1948 – Steve Winwood
1950 – Billy Squier
1957 – Shannon (Brenda Shannon Greene)
1960 – Terry McKee (Rosetta Stone)
1961 – Billy Duffy (Cult)

May

1977

BEATLES – A TALE OF TWO LIVE ALBUMS

Seven years after the group's dissolution in a mass of lawsuits, two live albums by The Beatles appeared on the market within two weeks. The more 'official' of

The unexpected appearance of a double album of much earlier live recordings of the band was not, apparently, the reason for the re-emergence of the 'Hollywood Bowl' tapes, however, which had been discovered in the vaults of Capitol Records in Los Angeles after having been forgotten for over ten years. In fact, it was more likely that the announcement of the impending release of the 'Hollywood Bowl' material had reminded the owners of the existence of a tape recorded at Hamburg's Star Club in late 1962 by Adrian Barber via a hand-held microphone at the instigation of fellow Liverpool musician Ted 'Kingsize' Taylor. The tape had been offered to Brian Epstein, who considered it to have no commercial value, and offered £20 ($30) for it, which Taylor rejected as being too little, whereupon it was left in a derelict building in Liverpool until 1972 when Alan Williams, who had managed The Beatles for a few months prior to Epstein's involvement, learned of its existence and retrieved it.

Williams later offered the tape to George Harrison and Ringo Starr for £5000 ($8000), but since Apple was experiencing financial difficulties at the time, the offer was declined. Williams eventually sold the tape to BUK Records, a small label, and it was eventually licensed to the German Bellaphon label.

The Beatles attempted to take out an injunction to prevent it being released, but British courts ruled that the double album of the Hamburg live recordings was of historical interest, and their objections were overruled. *Live At The Hollywood Bowl* triumphed, becoming the group's 12th No. 1 album in the UK and No. 2 in the US. *Live At The Star Club In Hamburg*, stalled at No. 111 in America and completely failed in Britain.

The Beatles light up Hollywood

the two, *The Beatles Live At The Hollywood Bowl*, had been recorded under the supervision of George Martin at two concerts at that venue on August 23, 1964, and August 30, 1965 – interestingly, only three songs were common to both sets: 'Twist and Shout', 'Can't Buy Me Love' and 'A Hard Day's Night'.

1976

DEATH OF A YARDBIRD

Keith Relf (at mic) with (left to right) Yardbirds Samwell-Smith, Dreja (partly obscured), McCarty and Clapton

Former Yardbirds vocalist Keith Relf was electrocuted while tuning his guitar at his home. Since the dissolution in 1968 of the group that had spawned three world-class lead guitarists, Relf had worked with Renaissance (which also included his sister, Jane Relf, and ex-Yardbirds colleague Jim McCarty), before playing with Medicine Head and forming the shortlived Armageddon in 1975. He was on the verge of forming a new group to be called Illusion with his sister and McCarty when the fatal accident occurred.

The Yardbirds formed in mid 1963, and during their five-year existence, went through five line-ups, each new formation resulting from a change of guitarist. This ability to attract a succession of exciting and charismatic lead players resulted in the group becoming legendary, particularly in the USA, where the adjective most frequently used to describe them was 'seminal'. All the attention paid to their guitarists sometimes deflected attention from the other members of the group, drummer McCarty, bass player Paul Samwell-Smith, rhythm guitarist Chris Dreja and vocalist Relf, who also played harmonica.

The group's original lead guitarist, who remained with the band for less than six months, was Anthony 'Top' Topham, who was actually still at school when the band was launched, but was eventually persuaded to complete his studies when the band invited Eric Clapton to leave the band he had joined only the month before, Casey Jones and The Engineers. That was in October 1963, and Clapton stayed for around 18 months, playing on the group's first singles and their debut album, *Five Live Yardbirds*, before leaving to join John Mayall's Bluesbreakers when he felt the Yardbirds had moved too far away from the blues. Clapton was replaced by Jeff Beck, during whose tenure the band scored a string of hit singles including 'Heart Full Of Soul', 'Over Under Sideways Down', 'Evil Hearted You' and 'Shape Of Things'. Samwell-Smith left in mid 1966, and was replaced by Jimmy Page.

When Beck left and Page moved to lead guitar, Relf was growing tired of the group, and when Page wanted the Yardbirds name when the band broke up in the summer of 1968, Relf agreed. Led Zeppelin played several early gigs as The New Yardbirds, but Relf was long gone.

ARRIVALS

1934 – Mike Preston
1936 – Bobby Darin (Walden Robert Cassotto)
1936 – Charlie Gracie
1943 – Derek Leckenby (Herman's Hermits)
1943 – Jack Bruce
1944 – Gene Cornish (Young Rascals)
1947 – Al Ciner (American Breed/Three Dog Night/Rufus)
1947 – Art Grant (Edgar Broughton Band)
1951 – Jay Beckenstein (Spyro Gyra)
1952 – David Byrne (Talking Heads)
1953 – Tom Cochrane (Red Rider)
1962 – C. C. Denville (Poison)
1962 – Ian Astbury (Cult)
1966 – Fabrice Morvan (Milli Vanilli)

★ ★ ★

DEPARTURE LOUNGE

1976 – Keith Relf

★ ★ ★

RAVINGS

1959:
Cliff Richard's first movie, *Serious Charge*, was premiered.

★ ★ ★

1988:
Led Zeppelin re-formed for Atlantic's 40th Birthday Celebrations, with Jason Bonham on drums replacing his late father.

★ ★ ★

HERMITS HITSVILLE HEIGHTS

Two singles simultaneously in the US Top 5 is a considerable achievement that few can boast, even in a year when the USA was temporarily British shaped. One of the less likely sensations of the US charts was a group from Manchester with the gimmicky name of Herman's Hermits, masterminded by Mickie Most and fronted by a child actor he had seen on *Coronation Street*.

1965

By September 1964 the group had reached the top of the UK singles chart with 'I'm Into Something Good', which also reached the US Top 20 and became their first million-seller. A follow-up in Britain, 'Show Me Girl' was a lesser hit at the end of the year, but after the group made a cameo appearance in the Connie Francis movie vehicle, *Where The Boys Meet The Girls*, the floodgates opened for the group. During 1965 six of their singles reached the US Top 10, including two No. 1s, 'Mrs Brown, You've Got A Lovely Daughter' and 'I'm Henry VIII, I Am'.

While Herman and Co. remained popular in Britain with cover versions of 'Silhouettes' by The Rays and Sam Cooke's 'Wonderful World', their UK fame was slight compared with the adulation they received in the States, where they accumulated 18 hit singles, including a dozen that reached the Top 10, and eight chart albums, three of which made the Top 5, in a mere three years. Even more remarkably, by mid 1968 the group was commercially finished in the USA.

Herman - a dentist's dream

1982

UNKNOWN PERFORMS 500TH BRITISH CHART-TOPPER

Nicole - fleeting fame

A major milestone in UK chart history, the 500th No. 1 was not by contemporary megastars like The Jam or The Police or even Bucks Fizz, but was 'A Little Peace', a plea for tolerance by a young German girl, Nicole, who had become her country's first ever winner of the Eurovision Song Contest. 'Ein Bisschen Frieden' had destroyed the opposition, but the stigma of non-British Eurovision winners remained – her follow-up, 'Give Me More Time' charted for a single week at No. 75.

1985

SIX MILLION DOLLAR HIT

Columbia Records Senior Vice President Al Teller presented a cheque for $6.5 million to Ken Kragen, President of the United Support Of Artists for Africa foundation (USA for Africa) as the first royalty payment on a single that had reached the record stores of the USA only two months before, on March 7.

A galaxy of stars raising money for African famine relief

The single, 'We Are The World', was the American response to 'Do They Know It's Christmas?', a British charity recording released in late 1984 to benefit the starving people in Africa. The latter single had been organized by ex-Boomtown Rats leader Bob Geldof with an all-star cast of the biggest British rock stars, including Phil Collins, Sting, Boy George, George Michael, Duran Duran, Spandau Ballet and many more, and had sold over three million copies in Britain alone.

It topped the UK chart for five weeks over Christmas 1984, raising a very large amount of money, but hardly enough to scratch the surface of the problem. On January 28, 1985, an all-star group of the biggest contemporary stars of American popular music assembled at A & M Studios in Hollywood, to record a similar tribute. Kragen credited Harry Belafonte with the original idea of a concert by black performers to raise money for Africa, but when it was felt this too would be only a drop in the ocean, the idea of 'We Are The World' was suggested. Kragen called Lionel Richie, whom he managed, to participate and also invited producer Quincy Jones, who involved Michael Jackson. When Stevie Wonder and Bruce Springsteen also joined in, it was clear that this had every chance of being a major success. Eventually, no less than 45 artists took part, other notables including Ray Charles, Bob Dylan, Daryl Hall, Billy Joel, Cyndi Lauper, Bette Midler, Willie Nelson, Smokey Robinson, Kenny Rogers, Diana Ross, Paul Simon, Tina Turner and Dionne Warwick.

ARRIVALS

1913 – Woody Herman
1919 – Liberace (Lee Liberace)
1932 – Isaak Holt (Ramsey Lewis Trio)
1946 – Robert Fripp (King Crimson)
1946 – Roger Earl (Savoy Brown)
1947 – Barbara Lee (Chiffons)
1947 – Derrell Sweet (Nazareth)
1949 – William 'Sputnik' Spooner (Tubes/Grateful Dead)
1953 – Richard Page (Mr Mister)
1955 – Hazel O'Connor
1958 – Glenn Gregory (Heaven 17)
1959 – Jock Bartley (Fallen Angels/Firefall)
1966 – Janet Jackson

★ ★ ★

DEPARTURE LOUNGE

1953 – Django Reinhardt
1990 – Sammy Davis Jr

★ ★ ★

1986

HERE COMES THE BRIDE —

King Crimson guitarist and leader Robert Fripp, who came from the town of Wimborne in Dorset, married actress and ex-punk hitmaker Toyah Willcox from Birmingham and whose hits included 'It's A Mystery' and 'I Want To Be Free'.

1987

HERE COMES THE BRIDE – 2

David Crosby married Jan Dance, his longtime girlfriend, in Los Angeles, while his friend and colleague, Graham Nash, and his wife Susan renewed their wedding vows at the same ceremony held at the Nash's home. Crosby celebrated by signing a deal with A&M Records.

1975

ROLLER TOO OLD FOR TARTAN

The British teenybop sensation of the year, Edinburgh's tartan-clad Bay City Rollers, suffered an unwanted personnel change when founder member and bass player Alan Longmuir announced that he would be leaving, despite the group being at the height of their fame.

Longmuir had formed the band in 1967 as The Saxons, with his younger brother, Derek, as drummer and vocalist Gordon 'Nobby' Clark. With encouragement from dance band leader Tam Paton, who became their manager, they apparently selected a new name via a random glance at a map of the USA. After numerous personnel changes, one of which produced guitarist Eric Faulkner, the group's first UK Top 10 single, a revival of 'Keep On Dancing', the US hit by The Gentrys, came in 1971.

After hitless years in 1972/3, which brought Les McKeown into the band instead of vocalist Clark, and added second guitarist Stuart Wood, the band adopted a uniform of white clothes with tartan edging, which quickly became a major fashion craze among adolescent girls.

The band produced a string of insubstantial but immensely successful UK hit singles with titles like 'Remember (Sha La La)', 'Shang-A-Lang', 'Summerlove Sensation' and 'All Of Me Loves All Of You', all of which made the UK Top 10 in 1974. Two No. 1s followed in 1975, 'Bye Bye Baby' and 'Give A Little Love', as well as two chart-topping albums, *Rollin'* and *Once Upon A Star*, but Alan Longmuir, well into his twenties, began to feel that there was more to life. In fact, he did not leave until the following year, by which time they had scored a US No. 1 single with 'Saturday Night' and two more major hits.

His replacement was Ian Mitchell, who played rhythm guitar while Wood moved to bass. Mitchell himself left in 1977, and was replaced by Pat McGlynn, but by then, punk rock had largely obliterated interest in tartan-clad Bay City Rollers.

Bay City Rollers - tartan to the core

1986

SELF AID FROM IRISH ROCKERS

Taking their cue from Bob Geldof's organization of the fantastically successful Live Aid (it went on to raise £50 million) during the previous summer, virtually all Ireland's best known musicians (and many of Irish extraction), including Van Morrison, U2, The Pogues, Elvis Costello and Geldof himself, played a benefit concert in Dublin to raise money to support initiatives to improve prospects for the young in Ireland.

NEW ORDER FROM JOY DIVISON DEATH

Joy Division go mainstream

ARRIVALS

1911 – 'Big' Joe Turner
1922 – Kai Winding
1942 – Albert Hammond
1942 – Rodney Dillard
1944 – Joe Bonsall
(Oak Ridge Boys)
1946 – George Alexander
(Flaming Groovies)
1948 – Feliciano 'Butch'
Tavares (Tavares)
1949 – George Weyman
1949 – Rick Wakeman
1949 – William Wallace
(Guess Who)

1954 – Wreckless Eric
(Eric Goulden)
1958 – Toyah
(Victoria Wilcox)
1961 – Simon Ellis
(Ellis Beggs and Howard)

★ ★ ★

DEPARTURE LOUNGE

1975 – Leroy Anderson
1980 – Ian Curtis
(Joy Division)

★ ★ ★

1963

BEATLES LAUNCH THIRD UK TOUR IN SIX MONTHS

Gerry and the Pacemakers

Having dominated the British charts with their 'Please Please Me' single followed to the top by 'From Me To You', and the debut *Please Please Me* album also topping the chart, The Beatles embarked on their third British tour of the year, this time co-headlining with Roy Orbison and with fellow Liverpudlians Gerry and The Pacemakers. The 21-date tour closed on 9 June.

Ian Curtis, vocalist and inspiration behind Joy Division, the Manchester band that had built a growing cult following for its music, which non-believers saw as doom-laden, hanged himself in his Manchester home. Once again, the curious British tendency to heap retrospective commercial praise on artists whose career has ended came into play – 'Love Will Tear Us Apart', their critically acclaimed single, had reached the UK independent chart but had remained absent from the 'real' chart before Curtis died, but a month later it began a residency of several months in the lists, peaking strongly in the UK Top 20, while the group's second LP, *Closer*, reached the Top 10 of the UK album chart.

Curtis, who suffered from epilepsy, had formed the group almost exactly three years before with Bernard Dicken (guitar, who later called himself Bernard Sumner and Bernhardt Albrecht), Peter Hook (bass) and Steven Morris (drums). They originally called themselves The Stiff Kittens, then Warsaw (after a track on *Low*, an album by David Bowie, who was a major influence on the band), and by the end of 1977, became Joy Division (a name inspired by a novel about prostitution in Nazi concentration camps). The group were seen and appreciated during a talent contest at a Manchester club by Tony Wilson, who later signed them to his Factory label, and Rob Gretton, who became their manager.

The death of Curtis

RAVINGS

1956:
Black British pianist Winifred Atwell was presented with two gold singles for sales of her hit medleys, 'Let's Have A Party' and 'Let's Have Another Party'.

1968:
The bill for the Northern California Rock Festival in Santa Clara included The Doors, Jefferson Airplane, Grateful Dead, Big Brother and The Holding Company and The Steve Miller Band.

★ ★ ★

ironically became the trigger for the growth of Joy Division from an underground cult to almost a mainstream act – as well as 'Love Will Tear Us Apart' becoming a hit, it was even covered by pop star Paul Young.

The remaining group members recruited keyboard player Gillian Gilbert and renamed themselves New Order.

1978

SULTANS SWING INTO ACTION

At the height of British fascination with punk rock, a group based in South London known as Dire Straits released their first major label single, 'Sultans Of Swing'. The quartet had been formed in 1977 in South London, by singer and lead guitarist Mark Knopfler.

Mark Knopfler

Together with his younger brother and fellow guitarist David Knopfler, bass player John Illsley and Welsh drummer Pick Withers, they had scraped together £120 ($175) to record a five-song demo tape at Pathway Studios in Islington, which they sent to disc jockey and rock historian Charlie Gillett, who played several tracks on his *Honky Tonk* radio show. The station switchboard lit up within seconds of

'Sultans Of Swing' being played, as numerous A & R men asked Gillett how to contact these highly impressive unknowns.

Eventually, the group, who had taken their name because an acquaintance had commented that it accurately described their financial circumstances, were signed by John Stainze to Phonogram Records in the UK, and recorded their first album at Island Studios under the watchful eye of producer Mervyn 'Muff' Winwood,

brother of Steve and veteran with Steve of the Spencer Davis Group – Muff had played bass. The album cost £12,500 to complete. 'Sultans Of Swing' was a Mark Knopfler composition inspired by a group of

middle-aged semi-professional jazz musicians whom he had seen performing in a London hostelry. The single received appreciative reviews, but was not an immediate hit. Not until the group

had signed with Warner Brothers in the US and the single had begun to climb the chart – it eventually peaked within the Top 5 – did Britain belatedly accept its excellence, when it reached the Top 10.

1979

FAB THREE AND FRIENDS PLAY AT WEDDING OF ERIC AND PATTI

Three erstwhile Beatles, Paul McCartney, Ringo Starr and George Harrison, all performed together for the first time

since the break-up of the band at the wedding reception following the marriage of Eric Clapton and Harrison's ex-wife,

Patti (née Boyd).

Clapton joined the trio on stage along with Mick Jagger, while other members of rock's aris-

tocracy who also strutted their stuff were Denny Laine, Ginger Baker and skiffle-king Lonnie Donegan.

ARRIVALS

1941 – Eddie Raynor (Split Enz)	Sweat and Tears)	Showaddywaddy)	(Curiosity Killed The Cat)
1945 – Pete Townshend (Peter Dennis Blandford Townshend)	1947 Jerry Hyman (Blood, Sweat and Tears)	1952 – Grace Jones	★ ★ ★
1946 – Philip Rudd (AC/DC)	1949 – Dusty Hill (Z.Z.Top)	1952 – Joey Ramone	**DEPARTURE LOUNGE**
1947 – Greg Herbert (Blood,	1950 – Mike Wedgwood (Curved Air/Caravan)	1956 – Martyn Ware (Human League/ Heaven 17)	
	1950 – Romeo Challenger (Black Widow/	1960 – Yazz (Yasmin Evans)	1969 – Coleman Hawkins
		1963 – Ben Volpeliere-Pierrot	★ ★ ★

1970

LET IT BE THE END

The final feature film involving The Beatles, *Let It Be*, was premiered in Britain simultaneously in London and Liverpool a week after it was unveiled in the USA. None of the members of the group attended either premiere, further fuelling the growing belief that the quartet had to all intents and purposes called it a day and disbanded.

The Beatles contemplate solo careers

Paul McCartney had insisted on releasing his debut solo album, McCartney, on the same day chosen for the release of the *Let It Be* album a few weeks before, and it was generally felt that the group were hardly interested in either the film, which clearly shows the discontent among the Beatles at the time, or the album.

In fact, the original title for both film and album had been *Get Back*, but delays in editing the film apparently organised by Allen Klein, who was trying to take over the group's management, initially put it on hold and even at one point led the group to abandon the project entirely. When it became clear that the group was unlikely to work together ever again, the audio tapes were retrieved and given to American record producer Phil Spector, who had become friendly with John Lennon and George Harrison after producing solo records for them, to remix and re-sequence into the *Let It Be* album. Paul McCartney was reported to be most unhappy with some of Spector's work, particularly Spector's addition of an orchestra to 'The Long And Winding Road'. When the latter was released as a single in the USA – it was not released as a single in Britain at the time – it swiftly ascended to the No. 1 position, selling over one million copies within two days of its release.

1971

CHICAGO'S CETERA SET UPON

Pete Cetera, vocalist and bass player with Chicago, underwent emergency surgery lasting five hours after losing four teeth while attending a baseball game between the Brooklyn Dodgers and the Chicago Cubs. A gang of rednecks objected to the length of Cetera's rock star hair, and clarified their feelings with their fists in a somewhat cowardly manner. Cetera, it would seem, made a complete recovery – in 1986, his solo single, 'Glory Of Love', topped the US chart for two weeks.

Cetera - long hair victim

ARRIVALS

1940 – Shorty Long
1942 – Paula (Jill Jackson)
1943 – Terry Smith
1944 – Joe Cocker
1946 – Cher (Cherilyn Sarkasian LaPierre)
1950 – Steve Broughton (Edgar Broughton Band)
1951 – Warren Cann (Ultravox)
1954 – Jimmy Henderson (Black Oak Arkansas)
1955 – Steve George (Mr Mister)
1958 – Jane Wiedlin (Go-Gos)
1960 – John and Susan Cowsill (Cowsills)
1961 – Nick Heyward (Haircut 100)
1963 – Brian Nash (Frankie Goes To Hollywood)
1967 – Kit Clark (Danny Wilson)

RAVINGS

1955:
Ruth Brown's US hit, 'Mama He Treats Your Daughter Mean' was banned in Britain by the BBC as it was felt to suggest wife-beating.

1967:
Jimi Hendrix signed to Reprise Records in the USA – he was already signed to Track/Polydor in Britain.

1978:
The Buddy Holly Story film, the 'biopic' with Holly played by Garey Busey, was premiered in Holly's home town of Lubbock, Texas.

★ ★ ★

1955

BERRY BEGINS TO MOTIVATE

Singer/guitarist Chuck Berry recorded 'Ida Red', a song he had written that had resulted in his being signed by Chess Records. He had been recommended to the label by Muddy Waters, and this was his first studio session for the Chicago-based company. During the recording, it was decided to rework the song and give it a new title, 'Maybellene', in which guise it became Berry's first hit, reaching No. 1 in the US R & B charts, which it dominated for eleven weeks, and also became his first Top 3 single in the US pop chart.

A young Chuck Berry

1979

ELTON TAKES ROCK TO RUSSIA

Superstar Elton John played the first of eight concerts in Leningrad (now St Petersburg), becoming the first solo Western rock artist to undertake a tour of the USSR (as it was then known). The concerts in Russia were an

Elton John - Russia rocks!

extension of his first tour of any sort since 1976, when he had announced his retirement from road work after an exhausting six years of almost constant concerts. The show from the Rossya Hall in Moscow was broadcast live on BBC Radio One back in Britain, and a film documentary, *To Russia With Elton*, was made about the trip, which was arranged by Harvey Goldsmith, the international concert promoter.

Elton later recalled that Goldsmith had sent an official letter asking if concerts by Elton in Russia would be permitted by the Soviet authorities. A reply agreeing to the proposal came after a week, and soon afterwards Russian officials travelled to Britain to watch a performance by Elton accompanied by Percussionist Ray Cooper in Oxford. It transpired later that very few of the tickets for the concerts were available to the general populace of Russia, and that most had been reserved for Communist Party members. Elton was most upset about this aspect of his pioneering visit, although he had been in no position to change the distribution of tickets. However, he had given the Eastern bloc a flavour of Western pop music and begun to break down barriers that had seemed unassailable.

RAVINGS

1963:
'Little' Stevie Wonder, who had celebrated his thirteenth birthday only eight days before, recorded his first million-selling single, 'Fingertips'.

★ ★ ★

1968:
Pete Townshend of The Who married dress designer Karen Astley, whose brother Jon Astley was a record producer, and whose sister, Virginia Astley, was a recording artist and member of all-female group The Ravishing Beauties.

1988:
Wet Wet Wet's charity single, their version of 'With A Little Help From My Friends', written by John Lennon and Paul McCartney, topped the UK singles chart.

★ ★ ★

ARRIVALS

1904 – Fats Waller (Thomas Waller)
1917 – Dennis Day (Eugene Patrick McNulty)
1923 – Hilton Valentine (Animals)
1928 – Tom Donahue (US disc jockey)
1940 – Tony Sheridan (Anthony Esmond Sheridan McGinnity)
1941 – Ronald Isley (Isley Brothers)
1943 – Vince Crane (Vincent Rodney Chessman)
1948 – Leo Sayer (Gerald Sayer)
1961 – Tim Lever (Dead Or Alive)

★ ★ ★

DEPARTURE LOUNGE

1957 – Juan Llossas (tango king)
1973 – Vaughn Monroe (US bandleader)

1982

NUTTY BOYS TOP UK ALBUM CHART

Madness, the seven-piece group from North London's Camden Town district, topped the UK album chart with a 'best of' compilation entitled *Complete Madness*. They had emerged in 1979 as Madness, taking their name from a song by the ska/bluebeat star Prince Buster. While they were beginning to play their chosen style of music in London, coincidentally 100 miles north, in Coventry, The Specials (originally known as The Special AKA), were pursuing an almost identical musical course.

Madness - making a meal of it?

Keyboard player Mike Barson, guitarist Chris Foreman and saxophonist Lee Thompson had formed The Invaders in 1976, and vocalists Cathal Smyth (aka Chas. Smash) and Graham 'Suggs' McPherson had joined in 1977 and 1978. The group's line-up was completed by Mark Bedford (bass) and 'Woody' Woodgate (drums). They changed the group name to Madness in March 1979, after which Suggs made contact with The Specials when the latter band played at London's Hope and Anchor hostelry, and Madness made their first recording for 2-Tone, the label launched by The Specials. That first single, 'The Prince', a tribute to Prince Buster written by Lee Thompson, was also the first Madness hit.

During the month in which it was released, Madness played at the wedding reception of Dave Robinson, boss of Stiff Records, and as a result swiftly signed to the highly regarded independent label. In under five years, between November 1979 and June 1984, the group released 18 UK hit singles, all but three reaching the UK Top 10 and including 'House Of Fun', the group's only No. 1. In addition, they released three albums that reached the UK Top 5, *One Step Beyond*, *Absolutely* and *Madness Seven*, before *Complete Madness*, which included all their hits, took them to the top of the album chart. In 1992 they turned the trick again when another greatest hits compilation, *Divine Madness* with a similar tracklisting to that of *Complete Madness* topped the UK chart.

1958

CHILD BRIDE SCANDAL HITS PIANO PUMPER

Piano-pumping rock 'n' roll star Jerry Lee Lewis arrived in Britain for his first UK tour, having topped the British singles chart over the previous Christmas period with 'Great Balls Of Fire'.

Everything was fine until a reporter discovered that Lewis was married to his 14-year-old cousin, whereupon he returned to the USA when the tour was abandoned after 34 of the scheduled 37 dates were cancelled.

Jerry Lee Lewis

1981

Jaap Eggermont, drummer with Golden Earring

ARRIVALS

1910 – Artie Shaw
1918 – Bumps Blackwell
1918 – Robert Blackwell
1920 – Helen O'Connell
(Dorsey Band)
1921 – Humphrey Lyttleton
1925 – Mac Wiseman
(Malcolm Wiseman)
1928 – Rosemary Clooney
1943 – 'General' Norman
Johnson
(Chairman of the Board)
1946 – Daniel Klein
(J Geils Band)

1947 – Bill Hunt
(ELO/Wizzard)
1953 – Rick Fenn
(10CC)
1957 – Therese Bazaar
(Dollar)
1967 – Junior Waite (Musical
Youth)

★ ★ ★

DEPARTURE
LOUNGE

1963 – Eddy Howard
1975 – Moms Mabley

★ ★ ★

STARS ON 45 DOMINATE THE CHARTS EVERYWHERE

They sounded, if the listener was not over-familiar with the original. Clearly armies of record-buyers thought so, as a single by Starsound, 'Stars On 45', careered up the charts on both sides of the Atlantic.

In retrospect, for a medley of hits by The Beatles performed by a faceless group of Dutch session musicians with a tight disco beat to top the US singles chart was pretty remarkable.

Starsound was the brainchild of Jaap Eggermont, a Dutch musician who had been Golden Earring's drummer for a while. He was commissioned by the man who owned the copyright on 'Venus', the 1970 US chart-topping single by Dutch group Shocking Blue, who had discovered that a 12 inch single that featured an illegally bootlegged medley of old hits was selling in large quantities and was very popular in discotheques.

'Venus' was the opening song of the medley, but it was being used without copyright payments, and he asked Eggermont to create a similar medley, but legally. Eggermont decided to feature more Beatle songs than had appeared on the bootleg, and using top Dutch session musicians to sing like the individual Beatles – Bas Muys was a perfect John Lennon clone vocally, while Okkie Huysdens took the Paul McCartney parts and Hans Vermeulen was the George Harrison soundalike – created a medley that lasted eleven and a half minutes.

For American release, publishers insisted that the titles of the songs in the medley be included in its title, resulting in a 41 word title, the longest of any single to make the chart.

Later Eggermount scored similar success with Abba and Stevie Wonder soundalikes.

1957

TEENAGER LYMON RECORDS IN LONDON

Frankie Lymon

Frankie Lymon, lead vocalist with The Teenagers, the black vocal quintet who actually were teenagers, recorded in London with British producer Norrie Paramor, who would become the producer of dozens of hits by Cliff Richard in the following year. Lymon was 13 years old when 'Why Do Fools Fall In Love' became a British No. 1 and his group's only US Top 10 hit.

He tragically died of a drug overdose in 1968, when he was still only 25.

RAVINGS

1977:
Jefferson Starship were prevented from playing a free concert in Golden Gate Park, San Francisco, due to a ban on electronic instruments. They later said that one of their biggest hits, 'We Built This City', had been inspired by the ban.

1979:
The film biography of The Who, *The Kids Are Alright*, was premiered in New York.

1987:
The Beastie Boys and Run-DMC opened their UK tour in London.

1991

BYRD GENE FLYS NO MORE

Byrds - (l to r) Gene Clark, Roger McGuinn, Chris Hillman, David Crosby, Michael Clarke

Gene Clark, a founder member of The Byrds, died of a heart attack after undergoing considerable dental work that was causing him great pain, and for which he was taking prescribed medication.

Harold Eugene Clark joined the New Christy Minstrels in the early 1960s after forming his own band, The Sharks, and then joining The Surf Riders, a folk trio. Eventually tiring of the cheerful Minstrels fare, epitomized by their 1963 Top 20 hit, 'Green Green', he teamed up with fellow singer-guitarists Jim McGuinn and David Crosby. With encouragement from independent producer Jim Dickson, they became The Jet Set, and recorded demos, although they released their first single, 'Please Let Me Love You', as The Beefeaters, a name chosen because of its supposed Englishness – The Beatles had conquered America at the start of the year, and anything with even vague British connotations was likely to excite interest among young American pop and rock fans. The single was a flop, at which point the trio became a quintet, with the recruitment of drummer Michael Clarke and mandolin star Chris Hillman as bass player. Crosby had been playing bass, but instead played rhythm guitar, leaving Clark to concentrate on vocals.

Clark was part of The Byrds for their first two albums, *Mr Tambourine Man* and *Turn Turn Turn*, which were their most commercially successful, not least because the title track of each album was a US No. 1 single. He left the band in 1966, briefly returned in 1967, but then teamed up with banjo maestro Doug Dillard as Dillard and Clark, while also making a series of critically acclaimed but rarely commercial solo albums. He participated in a 1973 reunion album by the original line-up of The Byrds, from time to time thereafter working with one or more of his former colleagues, but generally adopted a low profile, although his songwriting ability remained highly regarded.

1970

GREEN QUITS MAC

Singer/guitarist Peter Green, the founder of and inspiration behind Fleetwood Mac, left the group agig with them at Bath Festival.
He had apparently felt mentally tortured by the pressures of fame as witnessed in the lyrics of his last single with the group, 'The Green Manalishi (With The Two Prong Crown)', and opted for a solo career, which produced an album, *The End Of The Game*, before he effectively retired, although he briefly returned to recording at the end of the 1970s.

M a y

STRAITS NO LONGER DIRE

Brothers In Arms, the long-awaited fifth studio album by Dire Straits, entered the UK chart at No. 1, equalling the achievement of their previous studio album, *Love Over Gold*, in 1982.

The title of the album initially might have been presumed to refer in some way to the fact that Dire Straits originally included two brothers, Mark and David Knopfler, although in fact David had left the group in 1980, during the recording of the third album, *Making Movies*. He was replaced later that year by American Hal Lindes, while keyboard player Alan Clark was recruited at the same series of auditions. By late 1982

original drummer Pick Withers had also left, and was replaced by Welshman Terry Williams, previously a member of Man and later of Rockpile, the group formed by Dave Edmunds and Nick Lowe, leaving Mark Knopfler and bass player John Illsley as the only remaining original members.

The first single from the album released in Britain was 'So Far Away', which was a reasonable success, just

Dire Straits with John Illsley (left) and Mark Knopfler (with headband)

creeping into the Top 20, but it was already on the slide when the album was released. After two weeks at the top, the album fell away, but returned to No. 1 for two more weeks

in August, when 'Money For Nothing' (their only American chart-topper) was released as a single.

The album regained the No. 1 position in the UK chart in early 1986

for a further ten weeks and by the end of 1987 it had sold over three million copies in the UK alone, making it the biggest-selling album ever in Britain.

1956

TOP BANDLEADER PREDICTS SHORT LIFE FOR ROCK 'N' ROLL

56 year old Ted Heath, leader of one of Britain's most popular dance bands, whose singles included 'Hot Toddy', 'Skin Deep', 'The Faithful Hussar' and the theme to 'Dragnet' became the first British

dance band to tour America. Returning from the tour, he noted: 'Rock 'n' roll is mainly performed by coloured artists for coloured people, and is therefore unlikely to ever prove popular in Britain'.

Ted Heath (front) surveys his musicians

1974

TRAGEDY AT CASSIDY CONCERT

David Cassidy provoking teenage hysteria

During an open-air concert at London's White City stadium starring American teenybop idol David Cassidy, over one thousand people had to be treated by first aid workers due to the frenzied excitement among the crowd at seeing the star of the TV series *The Partridge Family* in person. Most of the casualties soon recovered, but 14-year-old Bernadette Whelan was less fortunate and died from heart failure four days later.

Cassidy was extremely shaken by the sad news. He had become an immense star in Britain (mainly among female adolescents) as a result of the TV series. Between 1972 and 1975, Cassidy took nine singles into the UK Top 20, reaching No. 1 twice, with 'How Can I Be Sure' in 1972 and with 'Daydreamer' in 1973, while also taking lead vocal on five separate Top 20 singles by The Partridge Family. His biggest album success in Britain came in late 1973, when *Dreams Are Nothin' More Than Wishes* topped the chart following two albums in the previous 18 months, *Cherish* and *Rock Me Baby*, which had peaked at No.2. In the US, his biggest single came in his Partridge Family guise, when 'I Think I Love You' reached No. 1 in 1970, and three Partridge Family albums reached the US Top 10.

RAVINGS

1953:
Elvis Presley was placed second in a talent contest held at a Jimmie Rodgers Memorial Show.

1989:
The estate of Roy Orbison, who died in December, 1988, was sued by the music publishing company to which he had been signed because he had failed to complete his commitments under a contract signed in 1985.

1990:
David Bowie was sued by his ex-wife Angela for $56 million.

★ ★ ★

1990

WOMEN ROOL OK?

For the first time ever, the top five positions in the US singles chart were held by female artists. Madonna was at No. 1 with 'Vogue', followed by Heart (led by sisters Ann and Nancy Wilson) with 'All I Wanna Do Is Make Love To You' at No. 2, Sinead O'Connor at No. 3 with 'Nothing Compares 2 U' (the previous chart-topper), Wilson Phillips at No. 4 with 'Hold On' (which became the next chart-topper) and Michael Jackson's sister Janet, with 'Alright' at No. 5.

ARRIVALS

1942 – Ray Ennis (Swinging Blue Jeans)
1943 – Levon Helm (The Band)
1944 – Verden Allen (Mott The Hoople)
1945 – Garry Peterson (Guess Who)
1948 – Stevie Nicks (Stephanie Nicks)
1949 – Hank Williams Jr
1949 – Mick Ronson
1949 – Phillip-Michael Thomas
1958 – Marian Gold (Alphaville)
1959 – Wayne Hussey (Sisters of Mercy/Mission)
1960 – Chris Duffy (Waterfront)
1964 – Lenny Kravitz

★ ★ ★

DEPARTURE LOUNGE

1933 – Jimmie Rodgers
1968 – Little Willie John
1977 – Billy Powell (O'Jays)

★ ★ ★

CLIFF'S 100TH SINGLE

Cliff Richard, without any doubt Britain's ultimate pop star, released his one hundredth single, 'The Best Of Me', which became his 26th to reach the UK Top 3 over a period of just over 30 years.

Richard (real name Harry Rodger Webb) was one of the very few British artists (although he was born in Lucknow, India) to produce authentic rock 'n' roll records in the 1950s, starting with 'Move It', widely regarded as the very first homegrown single to capture the uninhibited excitement of American rock stars such as Elvis Presley, whom he rivalled in popularity until the early 1960s. While the watershed in Presley's career came when he joined the US Army in 1958 (only weeks before 'Move It' was released), Richard began making moves towards becoming what was sneeringly referred to by British rock 'n' roll fans as 'an all-round entertainer' after playing the role of Bongo Herbert in his second feature film, *Expresso Bongo*. After that, most of his hits favoured the melodic ballad style that has been the predominant feature of his work ever since. His least successful period was during the early 1970s, when he managed only two UK Top 10 singles in six years.

Richard, who has been one of the UK's best-known Christian spokespeople since the mid 1960s, returned in style in 1976 with his first ever US Top 10 hit, 'Devil Woman', during a two-year period when his singles were released in the USA by Elton John's Rocket Records. In 1979 he scored his tenth UK No. 1 with 'We Don't Talk Anymore', his first chart-topper for over ten years, and his best selling single in the UK to date.

He continued to accumulate hits in Britain through the 1980s (although his US success had tailed off by then), and added two more UK chart-toppers over the Christmas periods of 1988, with 'Mistletoe and Wine', and 1990, with 'Saviour's Day', the latter single following his hit with 'From A Distance', which wiped the floor in Britain with a version by Bette Midler.

Britain's most enduring pop star, Cliff Richard

ARRIVALS

1935 – Ramsey Lewis
1939 – Don Williams (Donald Ray Williams)
1943 – Cilla Black (Priscilla White)
1945 – Bruce Cockburn
1947 – Marty Kristian (New Seekers)
1948 – Pete Sears (Jefferson Starship)
1949 – James Mitchell (Detroit Emeralds)
1957 – Siouxsie Sioux (Susan Dallion) (Siouxsie and the Banshees)
1958 – Neil Finn (Split Enz/Crowded House)

★ ★ ★

DEPARTURE LOUNGE

1984 – Onie Wheeler

★ ★ ★

1969

PROUD MARY MARKS CREEDENCE DEBUT

Creedence - (l to r) Stu Cook, Doug Clifford, John Fogerty

On the 24th birthday of the group's mastermind, John Fogerty, San Francisco based quartet Creedence Clearwater Revival made their first appearance on the UK singles chart with 'Proud Mary', which eventually reached the Top 10, and was the first of ten UK hit singles in just over two years.

Originally formed in 1959 by singer/guitarist Fogerty with schoolfriends Stu Cook (bass) and Doug Clifford (drums), the trio expanded to a quartet in the early 1960s with the addition of Fogerty's older brother, Tom, also a singer/guitarist. Originally known as Tommy Fogerty and The Blue Velvets, they first recorded as The Golliwogs in 1964, although none of the group was happy with that name, which had been chosen by the label to which they were signed, Fantasy Records. The group also suffered when Clifford and John Fogerty were drafted into the forces during 1966/7, but on their return they adopted the name with which they achieved fame, allegedly taking 'Creedence' from the name of a friend, 'Clearwater' from an advertisement for beer and 'Revival' as a statement of their musical aims.

In 1968 their first US hit single was a cover version of the Dale Hawkins hit from 1957, 'Susie-Q', which they followed with another cover, 'I Put A Spell On You', after which came seven US Top 5 hits in 1969/70 with original songs by John Fogerty, including 'Proud Mary', 'Bad Moon Rising' (their only UK chart-topper), 'Green River', 'Travelin' Band' and 'Lookin' Out My Back Door', all five singles stalled just one place short of the No. 1 position.

In the same two-year period both *Green River* and *Cosmo's Factory* topped the US album chart.

1983

SCHOOLKIDS TOP UK CHART

New Edition - doing a Jackson Five

New Edition, a teenage black vocal quintet from Boston, Massachusetts, reached No. 1 in Britain with 'Candy Girl'. The group had been groomed by producer and manager Maurice Starr to fill the gap left by The Jackson Five.

Later group members Bobby Brown (who married Whitney Houston in 1991) and Ralph Tresvant went on to solo success while Ricky Bell, Michael Bivins and Ronald DeVoe scored under the Bell Biv Devoe moniker.

1981

BOSS RETURNS TO BRITAIN

Bruce Springsteen returned to Britain in triumph for his first tour in five years. His first concert appearance in Britain had been in late 1975, when his British record label had embarrassed the emergent star with a poster proclaiming, 'At last London is ready for Bruce Springsteen'.

Soon after that, a protracted battle began between Springsteen and his manager, Mike Appel, over what the former saw as an inequitable contract in which he received only 20 per cent of royalties on record sales of his first two albums *Greetings From Asbury Park N.J.* and *The Wild, The Innocent and The E Street shuffle*, while Appel took 80 per cent. This led to Appel barring Springsteen from using journalist Jon Landau as co-producer of his next album – Landau's involvement with *Born To Run*, the third album by Springsteen, had helped the artist to achieve the commercial breakthrough that had previously eluded him.

Legal problems with Appel were finally resolved with an out of court settlement, with Appel receiving substantial monies, but Springsteen was now free to seek new management and make his own decisions.

All this had delayed the recording of *Darkness On The Edge Of Town*, but it was finally released in mid 1978. Landau, who by then had become Springsteen's manager, had also produced that album, which many Springsteen fans regarded as somewhat downbeat. During his enforced absence from the studio, Springsteen had achieved considerable fame as a live attraction, often playing three-hour sets with his backing group, The E Street Band, which were frequently bootlegged and sold in prodigious quantities, and the *Darkness* album seemed to lack the spark of the illegal recordings.

In late 1980 Springsteen released his first double album, *The River*, his first to top the US album chart and also his first to make the Top 3 of the UK album chart. It included his first two UK hit singles, 'Hungry Heart' (his first to reach the US Top 10) and the title track, although neither reached the Top 30 in Britain.

After the disappointment of his first visit (when a noted British rock commen-tator expressed the feelings of many when he remarked, 'They promised us Jesus Christ but sent us Billy Graham'), the 1981 tour was a triumph.

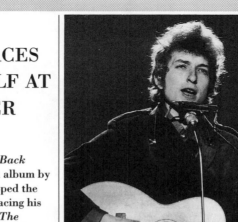
Bruce Springsteen (left) shares a smile with 'Miami' Steve Van Zandt

1965

DYLAN DISPLACES HIMSELF AT NUMBER ONE

Bringing It All Back Home, the fifth album by Bob Dylan, topped the UK chart, replacing his second album, *The Freewheelin' Bob Dylan*, in the top spot. Remarkably, Dylan did not top the US album chart until 1974, when *Planet Waves*, his first album on a label other than Columbia, finally found him looking down on the competition from the summit.

Dylan - hogging the top spot

1980

DOOMED EX-DOMINO CONTINUES SAD SAGA

The death of Carl Radle, erstwhile bass player with Derek and The Dominos, was the second premature departure to affect the personnel of that group, and would not be the final tragedy afflicting the musicians who played on the *Layla - and Other Assorted Love Songs* album.

Duane Allman, who had guested on the album's title track, was killed in a motorcycle accident in October 1971, while Eric Clapton, the group's leader, had spent two years during the early 1970s heavily addicted to heroin (from which he happily recovered).

Radle, who died of kidney failure said to have been caused by his chronic drug abuse during the early 1970s, was less than three weeks short of his 35th birthday. From Oklahoma, he had played on dozens of celebrated records, including George Harrison's 'All Things Must Pass', Joe Cocker's 'Mad Dogs and Englishmen', and albums by Leon Russell, J. J. Cale and Delaney and Bonnie, and was the only member of The Dominos who continued working with Clapton throughout the 1970s, until the forma-tion of Clapton's all-British band in 1979.

Five years later, another ex-Domino, drummer Jim Gordon (who had also been responsible for the unforgettable piano passage that brings the 'Layla' track to a climax), bludgeoned his 72-year-old mother to death. He was diagnosed as an acute paranoid schizophrenic and received a prison sentence of 16 years to life. He claimed to have been hearing 'voices' that instructed him to kill his mother, who wanted him to commit the deed. It was a very sad end to the musical career of a man who was regarded as one of the most reliable and inspired musicians in rock, who had worked with The Everly Brothers, George Harrison, John Lennon, Steely Dan, Frank Zappa, Traffic, Carly Simon, Maria Muldaur and, like Radle, had been part of Joe Cocker's 'Mad Dogs & Englishmen' extravaganza.

1953

SAM PLAYS IT FOR THE LAST TIME

Dooley Wilson, the actor who played the pianist in the classic movie *Casablanca* starring Humphrey Bogart and Ingrid Bergman, died.

He had become famous as the Sam who was instructed by Bogart to 'Play it again', and what he was being told to play was 'As Time Goes By', which reached the UK Top 20 in 1978, nearly a quarter of a century after his death.

Dooley Wilson with Humphrey Bogart in 'that' scene from Casablanca

GABRIEL ADOPTS NOVEL APPROACH

Peter Gabriel's fifth studio album, *So*, entered the UK chart at No. 1, eventually spending almost 18 months in the lists, by far the most successful of his seven solo albums released since he left Genesis in 1975.

Marketing men had been given the unenviable task of selling four consecutive albums by Gabriel that all shared the same title – Peter Gabriel.

Not that they had been stiffs in sales terms in the US where the first three had all charted, peaking respectively in the Top 40, Top 50 and Top 30, while all four had reached the UK Top 10.

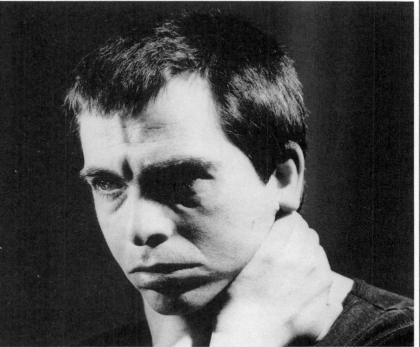

Gabriel - imaginative album titles

In fact, the fourth album was released in the US with a sticker on the sleeve that read 'Security', to give it a different identity. Once again, it made the US Top 30. Then came a double live album, *Peter Gabriel Plays Live* and after that, a soundtrack album titled *Birdy – Music From The Film*, which was a much lesser hit in chart terms. *So* was an immense success in the UK, while it made the Top 3 in the US, fuelled by the inclusion of a million-selling single, 'Sledgehammer', which topped the US singles chart.

The single's success was assured when the remarkable video clip made for the track was screened, as it used an extremely innovative and expensive technique known as 'clamation'. Even so, the album sold exceptionally well, provoking the thought in some areas of the record industry that had it been the fifth album titled *Peter Gabriel*, results might not have been so impressive.

1989

YES SAY MAYBE NOT

After 20 years of coming and going, a dispute finally began over who had the right to the group name Yes. 1984's *90125* album (that included their only US No. 1 hit 'Owner Of A Lonely Heart') had featured Geoff Downes, Alan White, Chris Squire, Trevor Horn, Tony Kaye and Trevor Rabin, with vocals by Jon Anderson, and the same line-up minus Horn) had played on 1987's *Big Generator*.

By 1989, Anderson had joined three more ex-members of Yes, (Bill) Bruford, (Rick) Wakeman and (Steve) Howe in a group democratically named Anderson Bruford Wakeman Howe. Either band had reasonable claims to the name Yes, and it took over a year, but common sense prevailed, and an expanded group of Anderson, Squire, White, Howe and both Kaye and Wakeman on keyboards performed a world tour under the title of Yesshows before making a new album, *Union*.

RAVINGS

1961:
Chuck Berry opened Berry Park, an amusement complex near St Louis.

1969:
Plastic Ono Band recorded 'Give Peace A Chance' in a hotel room in Canada.

★ ★ ★

ARRIVALS

1930 – Clint Eastwood
1938 – Peter Yarrow (Peter Paul and Mary)
1939 – Charles Miller (War)
1940 – Augie Meyers (Texas Tornados)
1941 – Johnny Paycheck (Donald Lytle)
1944 – Mick Ralphs (Mott The Hoople/Bad Company)
1947 – Junior Campbell (William Campbell) (Marmalade)
1948 – John 'Bonzo' Bonham

1954 – David Sterry
1962 – Corey Hart
1963 – Wendy Smith (Prefab Sprout)
1966 – Johnny Diesel

★ ★ ★

DEPARTURE LOUNGE

1967 – Billy Strayhorn (US composer/pianist)

★ ★ ★

STONES INVADE STATES

1964

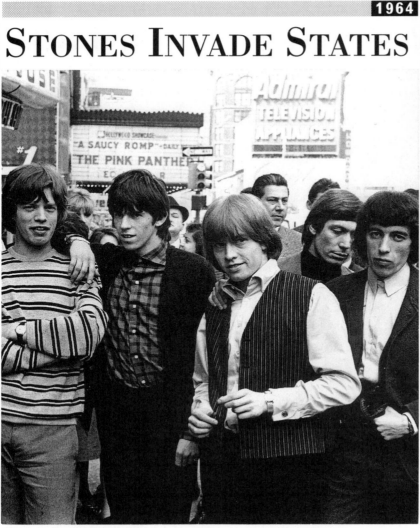

Stones in the Big Apple - (l to r) Jagger, Richards, Jones, Watts, Wyman

ARRIVALS

1921 – Nelson Riddle
1926 – Marilyn Monroe
1934 – Pat Boone
(Charles Eugene Boone)
1945 – Linda Scott
(Linda Joy Sampson)
1947 – Ron Wood
1949 – Mike Levine
(Triumph)
1950 – Charlene (Charlene
D'Angelo Duncan)
1950 – Graham Russell
(Air Supply)
1959 – Alan Wilder
(Depeche Mode)
1960 – Simon Gallup (Cure)
1963 – Mike Joyce
(Smiths/Adult Net)
1968 – Jason Donovan

DEPARTURE LOUNGE

1948 – Sonny Boy
Williamson
1984 – Nate Nelson
(Flamingos)
1991 – David Ruffin

The Rolling Stones arrived at John F. Kennedy airport in New York on a British Airways flight numbered 505 (later immortalized as the title of a song on their 1966 album *Aftermath*) for their first US tour. While the group were already rivalling the popularity of The Beatles in Britain, they were much less celebrated in the USA, where their first fully released single, 'Not Fade Away', had only crept into the Top 50. Even so, a minor riot ensued as waiting fans stampeded through a police cordon.

During their brief tour they made their US TV debut on *The Les Crane Show*. One other particular highlight when the group fulfilled an ambition by recording at the famous Chess studio in Chicago, working with engineer Ron Malo and meeting idols like Muddy Waters, Willie Dixon and Chuck Berry. Apart from an EP, 'Five By Five', which included a track titled '2120 South Michigan Avenue' (the address of the studio), the major result of the sessions was the group's classic cover version of 'It's All Over Now', previously recorded by The Valentinos, whose lead vocalist, Bobby Womack, had co-written the song. The single by the Stones was the first of five consecutive UK No. 1s in 18 months.

PEPPER UNVEILED

1967

The album by The Beatles that is widely regarded as their finest moment, *Sergeant Pepper's Lonely Hearts Club Band*, was released. With a sleeve photograph that featured a montage of pictures of a crowd of over 50 personalities surrounding The Beatles, it was lampooned by Frank Zappa on the sleeve of his 1968 album *We're Only In It For The Money*.

Beatle manager Brian Epstein was sufficiently concerned about the problems raised by the *Pepper* sleeve – everyone whose likeness appeared in the picture had to give their approval, and film star Shirley Temple initially said she wanted to hear the album before she would agree – that he seriously considered packaging the album in a plain brown wrapper.

RAVINGS

1956:
Doris Day signed a five-year recording contract with Columbia (CBS) Records worth $1 million.

★ ★ ★

1959:
Juke Box Jury started its long run on BBC television.

★ ★ ★

1964:
Dolly Parton spent her first day in Nashville in search of a record deal.

1971:
The two-room shack in Tupelo, Mississippi, where Elvis Presley was born on January 8, 1935, was opened to the public as a tourist attraction.

★ ★ ★

1975:
The Rolling Stones played their first US concert with new member Ron Wood, who was also celebrating his 28th birthday.

★ ★ ★

1973

ELO ATTACK SAN DIEGO WITH CELLOS

Electric Light Orchestra, the group originally formed by Roy Wood, Bev Bevan and Jeff Lynne, who were also playing in The Move at the time, began their first US tour, a 40-date trek, in San Diego, California.

By this time the group had undergone several major personnel changes, notably Wood, who preferred to launch his own band, Wizzard, shortly after the group's eponymous debut album was released in the summer of 1972. While that album had spent a month in the UK chart, peaking just outside the Top 30 fuelled by a Top 10 single, '10538 Overture', it had performed less well in the US, where it was titled No Answer – a secretary at United Artists, the group's US label, had been asked to telephone Harvest Records in London to ask the title of the album, but was unable to get a response, and had left a message to that effect!

After Wood, keyboard player Bill Hunt and cellist Hugh McDowell's departure, Lynne and Bevan had recruited a new line-up featuring cellists Mike Edwards and Colin Walker, as one of the group's unique features was its use of cellos – Lynne wanted the group to start at the point where The Beatles had stopped with their 1968 hit, 'I Am The Walrus', which featured the unusual sound (for rock music) of cellos. The first recording by the new line-up was Chuck Berry's 'Roll Over Beethoven', which began with cellos playing the familiar riff from Beethoven's Fifth Symphony before plunging into a rocking version of Berry's anthem.

Co-founders of ELO, Jeff Lynne and Bev Bevan (playing drums)

RAVINGS

1953:
Elvis Presley left L. C. Humes High School in Memphis, Tennessee.

1972:
Dion and The Belmonts, who had split up in 1960 when Dion DiMucci opted for a solo career, reunited for a special concert at New York's Madison Square Garden. Their performance was recorded and released as a live album in 1973.

★ ★ ★

ARRIVALS

1927 – Carl Butler
1932 – Sammy Turner (Samuel Black)
1936 – Otis Williams (Charms)
1939 – Charles Miller (War)
1941 – Charlie Watts
1941 – William Guest

(Gladys Knight and The Pips)
1944 – Marvin Hamlisch
1947 – Antone 'Chubby' Tavares (Tavares)
1948 – Jerry Mathers (Beaver)
1959 – Michael Steele (Bangles)
1960 – Tony Hadley

(Spandau Ballet)
1965 – David White (Brother Beyond)

★ ★ ★

DEPARTURE LOUNGE

1987 – Sammy Kaye

1967

BOWIE DEBUT ALBUM

David Bowie released his first album, simply titled *David Bowie*. Produced by Mike Vernon, previously better known for his production of the John Mayall/Eric Clapton *Bluesbreakers* album in 1966, it was later described by a Bowie biographer as, 'mostly put together with a "musical production" in mind', and it was indeed somewhat theatrical, quite unlike most of Bowie's earlier recordings with The King Bees, The Manish Boys and The Lower Third.

What an innocent face....

1964

SORE THROAT GROUNDS STARR

Ringo Starr collapsed during a recording session in London, and was rushed to hospital, necessitating the temporary recruitment of a stand-in for scheduled concerts in Europe and the Far East.

The Beatles with Ringo's temporary stand-in, drummer Jimmy Nicol

The first three days of June were spent recording at Olympic Studios in Barnes, south west London, cutting tracks to complete the group's third album, *A Hard Day's Night*, but Ringo's collapse, which was diagnosed at University College Hospital, where he was rushed by ambulance, as resulting from exhaustion, necessitated finding a replacement very quickly. The man who got the job, becoming a Beatle for ten days, was Jimmy Nicol, drummer with a little-known group known as The Shubdubs (and later with Georgie Fame and The Blue Flames), who played shows with The Beatles in Denmark, Holland, Hong Kong and Australia. Ringo was well enough by mid June, flying out to join the group in Melbourne

At the end of the year, after an unbelievably frantic and successful period that included making a feature film,

two albums and touring in Europe, Asia and North America, Ringo's recurring tonsilitis and pharyngitis and resulting poor health led to his having his tonsils removed, again at London's University

College Hospital. Such was the interest from Beatles fans enquiring about their hero that the hospital, whose switchboard had been jammed since his arrival, installed a 24 hours-a-day 'Ringo-line', giving

details of his progress. On December 10, nine days after the operation, Ringo was discharged, and when asked how he was, took the opportunity to plug the group's new single by replying, 'I feel fine'.

1975

RICKY'S DADDY DIES

Ozzie Nelson, father of US pop star Ricky Nelson, died at the age of 68. The weekly show that featured the Nelson family, *The Adventures of Ozzie and Harriet*, began on radio in 1944, and graduated to the small screen in 1952. It also featured the Nelson children, David and Eric (Ricky), who launched a successful solo career when he sang Fats Domino's 'I'm Walking' on the show.

Harriet (left) and Ozzie - Ricky's parents

FATHER OF BEACH BOYS DIES

1973

Murry Wilson, the father of the three brothers who were the backbone of The Beach Boys, died of a heart attack at the age of 55. Wilson and his wife, Audree, produced three sons, Brian (born 1942), Dennis (born 1944) and Carl (born 1946), and encouraged their musical ambitions when they formed a vocal quintet with their cousin, Mike Love (the son of Murry Wilson's sister) and school friend Al Jardine.

First briefly known as Carl and The Passions, then as The Pendletones, the group recorded a single for a small independent label of a song written by Brian Wilson and Mike Love, 'Surfin' – Dennis Wilson was an enthusiastic lover of the nautical sport that was widely practised in California, where the Wilson family lived.

When the label (which had supplied the new name of The Beach Boys) went out of business in 1962, Murry Wilson became the group's manager and found them a contract with Capitol Records, for whom they recorded the vast majority of their hits.

However, the Wilson brothers soon found that having their father as their manager was an impossible strain. In 1964 Brian, by then 21 years old and acknowledged as the major talent in the group because he wrote most of their hits, which he was also heavily involved in producing, dismissed Murry from his management post after a major disagreement in the studio during the recording of their first US No. 1 hit, 'I Get Around'. By then, Murry controlled the music publishing interests of the group, which were administered by a company he established called Sea Of Tunes. This would later become a bigger bone of contention than his apparently officious management technique after he sold the publishing company for what was felt to be a fraction of its worth at a time when Brian was experiencing mental instability due to a variety of problems.

UNDERTONES AND BIRTHDAY PARTY FOLD SIMULTANEOUSLY

1983

The Undertones, Derry's finest, with lead vocalist Feargal Sharkey (left)

Irish punk/rock hitmakers The Undertones and Australian rock group Birthday Party both decided to disband on the same day. Respective lead vocalists Feargal Sharkey and Nick Cave both went on to solo careers. Sharkey topped the UK singles chart in late 1985 with 'A Good Heart', a song written by Maria McKee, the remainder of the Undertones formed That Petrol Emotion.

ARRIVALS		DEPARTURE LOUNGE
1903 – Charlie Monroe (elder brother of Bill)	1945 – Gordon Waller (Peter and Gordon)	1973 – Murry Wilson
1932 – Oliver Nelson	1950 – Peter Van Hooke	1991 – Stiv Bators (Dead Boys)
1937 – Freddy Fender (Baldemar Huerta)	1952 – Jimmy McCulloch (Thunderclap Newman/Wings)	★ ★ ★
1940 – Cliff Bennett	1961 – Colin McKee (Rosetta Stone)	
1944 – Roger Ball (Average White Band)	1962 – El DeBarge (DeBarge)	

1977

RATBITE KILLS ROCK STAR

To many, the pet boa constrictor belonging to rock star Alice Cooper, which had been a significant part of Cooper's live show for several years, was one of the stars of the Cooper experience. When it unfortunately died after being bitten by a rat that was about to become its midday meal, Cooper was upset by the loss of a trusted colleague, and held a public audition to find a suitable replacement.

Absurd though all the above may appear, it was a fairly routine day in the bizarre life of Cooper (born Vincent Furnier) who was brought up in Phoenix, Arizona, and was the son of a clergyman. Still calling himself by his real name, he recruited other teenagers to form backing groups, two early bands he fronted being The Earwigs and The Spiders. In 1968, he and the other Spiders moved to Los Angeles, where Furnier began to call himself

Alice Cooper (supposedly after the spirit of a 17th-century witch, which manifested itself during a seance). Soon afterwards, the group as a whole also became Alice Cooper, and signed to Frank Zappa's Straight Records.

Their first two albums were unremarkably average and eventually the group relocated to Detroit, where they acquired a new record deal and introduced numerous theatrical stage gimmicks (including the boa constrictor), They became immensely popular, particularly after their anthem of teenage rebellion, 'School's Out', reached the US Top 10 and topped the UK singles chart in 1972, and was followed by another big hit, 'Elected'. Their 1973 album, *Billion Dollar Babies*, topped the charts on both sides of the Atlantic, but during 1974 Cooper fired the band and hired a group of experienced hard rock session players. Cooper's popularity was sustained initially, but the death of the reptile was followed in 1978 by his committing himself to hospital for treatment of his chronic drinking habit. He wrote a concept album, *From The Inside*, about his experiences.

Alice with a friend - ratbite causes search for a new star

RAVINGS

1965:
Joan Baez and Donovan performed at a rally in London's Trafalgar Square organized by the Campaign For Nuclear Disarmament.

★ ★ ★

1971:
As their *Survival* album became their biggest hit to date, entering the US Top 10 at No. 6, Grand Funk Railroad sold out Shea Stadium in 72 hours, even faster than The Beatles at the height of their fame.

★ ★ ★

1974

SLY STONE PLIGHTS TROTH AT MADISON SQUARE GARDEN

Sylvester 'Sly Stone' Stewart married Kathy Silva on the stage of New York's Madison Square Garden before a performance by the group he led, Sly and The Family Stone. At the end of October, Silva filed for divorce, and in 1976, Stone filed for bankruptcy.

ARRIVALS

1926 – Bill Hayes
1926 – Floyd Butler (Friends of Distinction)
1945 – Don Reid (Statler Brothers)
1946 – Freddy Stone (Fred Stewart) (Sly and The Family Stone)
1947 – Tom Evans (Badfinger)
1950 – Laurie Anderson
1950 – Ronnie Dyson
1956 – Keith Marshall
(Hello)
1956 – Richard Butler (Psychedelic Furs)
1964 – Mags (Fuzzbox)

★ ★ ★

DEPARTURE LOUNGE

1977 – Sleepy John Estes

★ ★ ★

1971

ZAPPA'S MOTHERS JAM WITH LENNONS

During a concert at New York's Fillmore East auditorium by Frank Zappa's Mothers Of Invention, John Lennon and Yoko Ono joined the group on stage for what can only be described as an undisciplined jam session, it was Lennon's first stage appearance in nearly two years. Zappa's band also recorded a live album at the same venue during the same month, and although there appears to be no confirmation that this was recorded on the same occasion as the tracks featuring Zappa and Co. with John and Yoko, it seems a safe assumption.

The latter recordings were included on a double album by Lennon and Ono entitled *Some Time In New York City* released in 1972, which also included an album's worth of studio recordings on which the Lennons (credited as The Plastic Ono Band, whose only other member on this occasion was drummer Jim Keltner) were backed by New York rock band Elephant's Memory. The album featuring the live tracks with Zappa was supposedly a bonus album, and its first side included two tracks recorded by an all-star Plastic Ono Band (with Derek and The Dominos led by Eric Clapton, George Harrison, Keith Moon of The Who and others) in London in December 1969 at a charity concert for UNICEF staged at the Lyceum Ballroom. The tracks with Zappa began with a real song, 'Well (Baby Please Don't Go)', a cover of a track recorded in 1958 by The Olympics, and released as the B-side of their 'Western Movies' hit. This recognizable item was followed by three tracks that were virtually a continuous passage of free-form extemporization, and which were given the titles on the album of 'Jamrag', 'Scumbag' and 'Au'.

1966

ORBISONS'S MISFORTUNES

Roy Orbison's first wife, Claudette, was killed in Gallatin, Texas, aged only 25, when she and her rock star husband were riding back to their home on motorcycles after attending a drag-racing event in Tennessee. She collided with a truck that pulled out of a side road. Orbison had written 'Claudette', a song about her, in 1958, which became an international hit for The Everly Brothers, hitting No. 1 in the UK coupled with 'All I Have To Do Is Dream'.

Mr and Mrs Orbison

1969

SUPERGROUP'S HYDE PARK DEBUT

Blind Faith, the so-called 'super-group' formed by guitarist and vocalist Eric Clapton and drummer Peter 'Ginger' Baker (both from Cream) with vocalist and keyboard player Steve Winwood (ex-Traffic) played their first and last British live show, a free concert in London's Hyde Park before a large crowd, variously estimated at between 30,000 and 120,000 people. With Ric Grech recruited from Family as bass player, the group, which had formed in February 1969, completed its debut album, simply titled *Blind Faith* and produced by Jimmy Miller.

The album swiftly topped the charts on both sides of the Atlantic with two different sleeves as the original UK cover featuring a nude 11 year old girl was though too controversial for America. Released during the group's US tour, on which the support act was Delaney and Bonnie And Friends with additional guest guitarists George Harrison and Dave Mason (Winwood's ex-colleague in Traffic), it was widely felt to be little more than adequate considering the reputation of those involved, and after the US tour ended in September, the group split up.

During the 1980s the *Blind Faith* album was reissued as a CD, and included three previously unheard tracks that had been discovered several years after they had been recorded, but clearly these were previously unreleased because they were unfinished. Apart from the fact that Ric Grech died in 1990, making a reunion impossible, all those involved felt that the project was misguided.

ARRIVALS

1924 – Dolores Gray
1934 – Wynn Stewart
1940 – Tom Jones
1944 – Clarence White
1944 – Miguel Rios
1946 – Bill Kreutzman (Grateful Dead)
1946 – Mickey Jones (Man)
1955 – Joey Scarbury
1957 – Paddy McAloon (Prefab Sprout)
1958 – Prince (Prince Rogers Nelson)

★ ★ ★

DEPARTURE LOUNGE

1964 – Meade Lux Lewis
1976 – Bobby Hackett

RAVINGS

1963:
The Rolling Stones made their British TV debut on *Thank Your Lucky Stars*.

1967:
Three members of Moby Grape were arrested in San Francisco for 'contributing to the delinquency of minors' by having schoolgirls in the back seat of their car.

1970:
The Who performed the rock opera *Tommy* at the Metropolitan Opera House in New York.

1975:
Elton John's *Captain Fantastic and The Brown Dirt Cowboy* album became the first album ever to enter the US chart at No. 1. He was to turn the trick again later in the year when *Rock Of The Westies* did likewise.

★ ★ ★

1957, 63, 79

BERRY BITS

June 7 must be a date that causes Chuck Berry to hesitate whenever it comes round, as important events that affect him have occurred over three decades. In 1957 two of his classic singles were released by different record companies in the UK, 'Roll Over Beethoven' on London and 'School Day' on EMI's Columbia label. The latter gave him his first taste of British chart action, climbing to No. 24 and becoming his first single to sell a million copies worldwide.

In 1963 the debut single by The Rolling Stones was a cover version of Berry's 'Come On' which went on to be their first chart entry.

In 1979 he not only played at The White House for President Jimmy Carter, but was also charged with income tax evasion relating to offences in 1973 and sentenced to five months imprisonment.

Berry - a day to remember?

THE INEVITABLE DEPARTURE OF JONES THE STONE

Brian Jones, a founder member of The Rolling Stones (and its original leader, according to some sources), announced that he was leaving the group on the grounds that he no longer saw 'eye to eye' with the rest of the band over the music they were recording. It was widely rumoured that the truth behind his departure was somewhat less straightforward, and had more to do with his becoming a liability to his colleagues through his drug abuse, general unreliability and the fact that he had become a target for police harassment.

1969

Brian Jones - the first Stone to fall

At the end of 1967 Jones had been sentenced to nine months' imprisonment (later reduced to a heavy fine) for drug offences, after psychiatrists had called him 'an extremely frightened young man', and a similar scenario, drug offences and a fine, also occurred during 1968. Jones was perhaps understandably frustrated that the prolific and successful songwriting team of Mick Jagger and Keith Richards provided very few opportunities for the other members of the group to contribute original material, even though he himself had rarely written anything of note. Jones also lived the life of a rock star to the ultimate degree, and in fact had fathered illegitimate children (two of whom he somewhat perversely named Julian) by different women several years earlier. His drug intake was apparently of Olympian proportions, and unlike his colleagues in the Stones, his poor health – he suffered from asthma, which was not improved by his substance abuse – made him less capable of withstanding the pressures of fame and the scrutiny of the law.

1974

WAKEMAN LEAVES COSMIC CRUSADERS

Keyboard star Rick Wakeman announced that he was leaving Yes, the immensely successful group he had joined in 1971. He had already released two big-selling solo albums, *The Six Wives Of Henry VIII*, which had reached the Top 10 of the UK chart, and *Journey To The Centre Of The Earth*, which had reached No.

1, and unsurprisingly was convinced that a successful solo career was perfectly feasible. His snappily titled 1975 album, *The Myths And Legends Of King Arthur And The Knights Of The Round Table*, also reached the Top 3, but thereafter his albums were increasingly smaller hits, and he rejoined Yes at the end of 1976.

Rick Wakeman (right) at a recording session in 1975

1958

MATHIS' GREATEST JUMPS TO THE TOP

The new album at the top of the US charts was *Johnny's Greatest Hits* by Johnny Mathis, which set a record ten years later as the album that had spent the most weeks in the *Billboard* long player listings.

Mathis was a classy pop ballad vocalist, whose youth and stylishness gave him a quality that did not totally alienate teenagers. Many of his contemporaries would have killed to equal his 36 US hit singles in eight years after his first hit in 1957, 'Wonderful! Wonderful!'. But Mathis was no ordinary person – born in San Francisco in 1935, he was an outstanding athlete at school, and was chosen to compete in the trials for the US Olympic team in 1956, his particular skill being the high jump. However, he turned down the invitation, and

with encouragement from his father, who had worked in vaudeville, and had started teaching Johnny to sing when the child was ten years old, he decided on a music career.

Strangely, while his first hit album bore the same title as his previously mentioned first hit single, the song was not included on the album. However, it was included on *Johnny's Greatest Hits*, as were several songs that were familiar to British teenagers like 'Teacher Teacher' and 'The Twelfth Of Never'.

Since the mid 1970s,

Mathis has been periodically successful in chart terms, reaching the UK Top 10 in 1975 with 'I'm Stone In Love With You', topping the UK chart with a Christmas single in 1976, and recording hit duets with Deneice Williams, Gladys Knight and Dionne Warwick. The record set by *Johnny's Greatest Hits* of 490 weeks in the US album chart was beaten as the longest charted album of all time in the US by Pink Floyd's *Dark Side Of The Moon*, which by mid 1985 had been listed in the US chart for over 550 weeks.

Five Star - repossesion problem

1990

FAMILY HITMAKERS HIT TROUBLE

The Sunningdale mansion owned by the Pearson family, the five children of which were the hit group Five Star, was repossessed by bailiffs after non-payment of the mortgage on the property. With 20

UK hit singles to their credit including six Top 10 hits in the previous five years, plus a chart-topping album, *Silk and Steel* in 1986, many found the group's financial plight hard to credit.

ARRIVALS

1891 – Cole Porter
1902 – Skip James
1916 – Les Paul (Lester William Polfus)
1929 – Johnny Ace (John Marshall Alexander Jr)
1934 – Jackie Wilson
1941 – Billy Hatton (Fourmost)
1941 – Jon Lord (Deep Purple)
1946 – Stuart Edwards (Edison Lighthouse)
1947 – John 'Mitch' Mitchell

(Jimi Hendrix Experience)
1949 – Francis Monkman (Curved Air)
1950 – Trevor Bolder (Spiders From Mars/Uriah Heep)
1951 – Terry Uttley (Smokie)
1953 – Errol Kennedy (Imagination)
1954 – Peter Byrne (Climie Fisher)
1962 – Eddie Lundon (China Crisis)

★ ★ ★

Johnny Mathis, who preferred showbiz to Olympic competition

RAVINGS

1989:
The re-formed Doobie Brothers played their first US concert.

★ ★ ★

1990:
Michael Jackson was admitted to hospital with a mystery illness. It was later diagnosed as costochondritis – an inflamed cartilage in his rib cage.

★ ★ ★

1972

EP ROCKS MSG IN NY

The King adresses his courtiers

Elvis Presley played his first ever concert in New York, and the shows were recorded for a live album entitled *Elvis As Recorded At Madison Square Garden*.

Over 80,000 tickets were sold at great speed for the four concerts, and an album by Presley that was scheduled for imminent release was shelved in favour of the publicity-conscious gimmick of making a live album that would be in the stores within two weeks of being recorded.

This feat was achieved with time to spare, but commentators later noted that the album had been assembled ignoring the earlier matinée show that included performances that were somewhat superior to the tracks that appeared.

Presley's backing group for this album included several star sidemen, such as guitarist James Burton (ex-Ricky Nelson's band) and Glen D. Hardin (an ex-member of The Crickets) as well as the excellent rhythm section of Jerry Scheff (bass) and Ronnie Tutt (drums).

The songs Presley chose to perform included examples from his classic Sun Records days ('That's All Right (Mama)'), his pre-Army days ('Hound Dog', 'Heartbreak Hotel', 'All Shook Up', 'Love Me Tender' and '(Let Me Be Your) Teddy Bear') and some of the best of his later hits, like 'Suspicious Minds', 'For The Good Times' and 'American Trilogy'. The album went gold for sales of 500,000 copies almost immediately, and it has almost certainly become a million-seller in the two decades since it was released.

1989

CHART-TOPPING HAT TRICK FOR PWL LABEL

With Jason Donovan's revival of Brian Hyland's 1962 hit, 'Sealed With A Kiss', reaching the top of the UK singles chart, the PWL record label and its prolific hitmaking songwriting and production team of Mike Stock, Matt Aitken and Peter Waterman had released three consecutive No. 1 singles in the UK chart, the first label to achieve this feat for 24 years. In 1965 three Decca singles – 'It's Not Unusual' by Tom Jones, 'The Last Time' by The Rolling Stones and 'Concrete And Clay' by Unit Four Plus Two – had achieved the hat trick, and in 1989 PWL's record-equalling trio were Kylie Minogue's 'Hand On Your Heart', Ferry Aid's 'Ferry Cross The Mersey' and 'Sealed With A Kiss'.

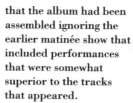

Kylie (left) and Jason (right) with a young fan

ARRIVALS

1910 – Howlin' Wolf (Chester Burnett)

1922 – Judy Garland (Frances Gumm)

1925 – Don Costa

1941 – Shirley Alston (Shirley Owens) (Shirelles)

1942 – Janet Vogel (Skyliners)

1944 – Rick Price (Move/Wizzard)

1949 – Perry Kibble (Taste Of Honey)

1961 – Mark Shaw (Then Jericho)

1967 – Human Breathbox (Darren Robinson) (Fat Boys)

★ ★ ★

DEPARTURE LOUNGE

1982 – Adie Harris (Shirelles)

★ ★ ★

RAVINGS

1989:
Madonna's 'Express Yourself' became her 18th UK Top 5 hit, a record for a female vocalist.

★ ★ ★

1991:
David Ruffin (ex-Temptations) was buried. Aretha Franklin and Stevie Wonder sang in the congregation and the bill for the funeral was paid by Michael Jackson.

★ ★ ★

1988

NELSON MANDELA BIRTHDAY BASH

Jerry Dammers, leader of The Specials (or The Special AKA, as they were known at various points in their career), was the prime mover behind a concert at London's Wembley Stadium staged to celebrate the 70th birthday of African National Congress leader Nelson Mandela, who had been imprisoned in South Africa since 1962.

The Nelson Mandela Tribute Concert

Dammers had been a leading light in various anti-apartheid movements in Britain, and in 1983 The Special AKA had released a single titled 'Racist Friend', which was a minor UK hit. The following year, the group released 'Nelson Mandela', a single that reached the UK Top 10, and that became a global anthem at gatherings for anti-racist causes. In 1986 Dammers had launched Artists Against Apartheid, an organization that staged an anti-apartheid concert on London's Clapham Common, at which stars such as Elvis Costello, Sting, Boy George and Peter Gabriel were among the performers who entertained a crowd estimated at 250,000 people.

With public support for Mandela's release growing internationally, the 70th Birthday Party (which he was unable to attend as he was still incarcerated) was a very popular event, and was seen on television in many countries live via satellite. Among the performers were Whitney Houston, Stevie Wonder, Dire Straits, Simple Minds and Tracy Chapman, who was virtually unknown before the concert, but made a huge impression when she played an extended set filling in for Wonder, whose synthesizer was malfunctioning.

1977, 88

A GOOD DAY FOR THE MARLEYS

In 1977, *Exodus* by Bob Marley and The Wailers entered the UK album chart, eventually becoming the group's first Top 10 LP. A decade later, the group fronted by his son, Ziggy Marley and The Melody Makers, scored their first UK hit single with 'Tomorrow People'. Sadly Ziggy's father was unable to see his son's triumph, as Bob had died of cancer in 1981.

Bob Marley

ARRIVALS

1934 – James 'Pookie' Hudson (Spaniels)
1939 – Wilma Burgess
1940 – Joey Dee (Joseph DiNicola)
1946 – John Lawton (Uriah Heep)
1947 – Glenn Leonard (Temptations)
1949 – Frank Beard (Z. Z. Top)
1950 – Lynsey De Paul (Lynsey Rubin)
1952 – Donnie Van Zandt (.38 Special)

★ ★ ★

RAVINGS

1966:
Janis Joplin played her first date as vocalist of Big Brother and The Holding Company.

★ ★ ★

1976:
Australian hard rock band AC/DC started their first headline tour of Britain in Scotland, where several members of the band were born.

★ ★ ★

1983:
British group Naked Eyes peaked in the US Top 10 with their single, 'Always Something There To Remind Me', which had failed to reach the UK Top 40. Group member Rob Fisher later joined Simon Climie as Climie Fisher, who had four UK Top 40 singles in 1988, only one of which made the Top 20.

★ ★ ★

1987

U2 FILL WEMBLEY

Leading Irish rock quartet U2 filled Wembley during their world tour promoting *The Joshua Tree*, which had entered the UK album chart at No. 1 and earned platinum status in just two days, becoming the fastest-selling album ever at the time. It was also their first album to top the US album chart, where it remained at No. 1 for a total of nine weeks.

Bono Vox, U2's spearhead

Formed in 1976 in Dublin as neo-punks who called themselves Feedback, they then became The Hype (until original member Dick Evans, brother of Dave 'Edge' Evans, left to launch The Virgin Prunes), and finally U2. Signed to CBS Records (Ireland), the group released an EP titled 'U2 – 3' in 1979, which topped the domestic

chart, whereupon they signed with Island Records worldwide.

In early 1981, *Boy* reached the US chart, and in the middle of that year, 'Fire' became their first UK hit single, after which *Boy* finally began selling fast enough to make the UK album chart. That year saw increasing success in Britain, with their second hit single,

'Gloria', and their *October* album just failing to make the Top 10. By 1983, the group were solidly established as international stars, with their albums, *War*, and a live offering *Under A Blood Red Sky*, going platinum in America and topping the UK chart. *War* included a powerful song written by guitarist The Edge, 'Sunday Bloody Sunday', about

the day in January 1972, when British para-troopers opened fire on participants in a civil rights march that turned into a riot. The song became the first US hit single for the group whose charismatic vocalist, Paul Hewson, apparently assumed the stage name of Bono Vox after seeing the phrase on a poster advertising a hearing aid.

ARRIVALS

1932 – Charlie Feathers
1941 – Chick Corea (Armando Anthony Corea)
1941 – Roy Harper
1942 – Len Barry
1943 – Reg Presley (Reginald Ball) (Troggs)
1948 – Barry Bailey (Atlanta Rhythm Section)
1948 – Lyn Collins (James Brown Revue)
1951 – Brad Delp (Boston)
1951 – Bun E. Carlos (Brad Carlson) (Cheap Trick)
1952 – Dale Krantz (.38 Special/Rossington Collins Band)
1952 – Pete Farndon (Pretenders)
1953 – Rocky Burnette

★ ★ ★

DEPARTURE LOUNGE

1957 – Jimmy Dorsey
1971 – Ambrose (Bert Ambrose)
1978 – Johnny Bond

★ ★ ★

1966

DC5 SET SULLIVAN RECORD

The Dave Clark Five, whose popularity in America far outstripped their fame in Britain, made a record twelfth appearance on the *Ed*

Sullivan Show on US television. While they accumulated 24 US hit singles between 1964 and 1967, the same period only brought 13 entries

in the UK singles chart, although the group managed to sustain their success in Britain until the start of the next decade.

RAVINGS

1957:
'Whole Lotta Shakin' Goin' On' by Jerry Lee Lewis entered the US chart. It eventually sold six million copies and as a result, Lewis

supposedly raised his price for playing concerts from $50 to $10,000.

1982:
An estimated half a million people attended a peace rally in New York's Central

Park to watch performances by Bruce Springsteen, Jackson Browne, Linda Ronstadt, Gary 'U. S. ' Bonds and others.

★ ★ ★

Dave Clark (right) and his four colleagues

1969

NEW STONE STARTS ROLLING IN PARK

Ex-God turns to Stone - Mick Taylor

Mick Taylor, the new guitarist in The Rolling Stones, who was recruited to replace the departing Brian Jones, was introduced to the media at a photo call by a bandstand in London's Hyde Park. The choice of this location was significant as within a few days, it was announced that the group would be playing a free concert in Hyde Park on July 5.

Taylor was 21 years old at the time, considerably younger than his new colleagues. He had, however, established his reputation working with John Mayall's Bluesbreakers, where he followed in the footsteps of two extremely popular guitarists, Eric Clapton, who was in the Mayall band from April 1965 to July 1966, when he left to form Cream, and then Peter Green, who was a Bluesbreaker from Clapton's departure until June 1967, when he formed Fleetwood Mac with another ex-Bluesbreaker, drummer Mick Fleetwood, later that year recruiting to the new band another Bluesbreaker, bass player John McVie. At that point, Mayall had to form a completely new band, and Taylor was one of the first to join, along with drummer Keef Hartley, two sax players and a succession of bass players, one of whom was Andy Fraser, who later was a founder member of Free.

Taylor had been working with The Gods, a group that achieved little success with their two original albums, but at various times also included Ken Hensley and Lee Kerslake, who were both later members of Uriah Heep, and Greg Lake, who joined King Crimson before forming ELP with Keith Emerson and Carl Palmer. Taylor played on several notable Mayall albums including *Diary Of A Band*, *Bare Wires* and *Blues From Laurel Canyon*, and when he was invited to become a Rolling Stone, Mayall finally disbanded The Bluesbreakers, forming a more acoustic band without need of a drummer.

RAVINGS

1970:
'The Long And Winding Road' by The Beatles reached the Top of the US singles chart.

1972:
Clyde McPhatter, original lead vocalist of The Drifters, died. Elvis Presley often said that he wished his voice were the equal of McPhatter's.

1980

ALL STAR 'ROADIE' MOVIE OPENS

A galaxy of stars from various musical genres featured in *Roadie*, the film starring Meat Loaf, which opened in the USA. The 'Bat Out Of Hell' hitmaker starred as Travis W.Redfish, a fictional road manager for rock groups who can fix any problem that presents itself. The soundtrack double album also featured Deborah Harry and Blondie, Pat Benatar, Cheap Trick, Joe Ely, Alice Cooper, Styx, Teddy Pendergrass, Roy Orbison and Emmylou Harris (duetting on 'That Lovin' You Feelin' Again'), Jerry Lee Lewis and Asleep At the Wheel.

Meat is Redfish

ARRIVALS

1927 – Slim Dusty (David Gordon Kirkpatrick)
1940 – Bobby Freeman
1941 – Esther Ofarim (Esther Zaied)
1942 – James Carr
1949 – Dennis Locorriere (Dr Hook)
1951 – Howard Leese (Spirit/Heart)
1954 – Bo Donaldson (Robert Donaldson)
1954 – Jorge Santana (Malo)
1957 – Rolf Brendel (Nena)
1968 – Deniece Lisa Maria Pearson (Five Star)

★ ★ ★

DEPARTURE LOUNGE

1972 – Clyde McPhatter
1986 – Benny Goodman

★ ★ ★

BOY GEORGE WAXED AND READY

A model of George O'Dowd, better known to millions as Boy George, was unveiled at Madame Tussaud's waxworks in London on the singer's 23rd birthday. Boy George became world-famous as lead vocalist with Culture Club, a group he formed with Jon Moss, a drummer who had worked with several punk rock bands during the latter years of the 1970s, black London-born ex-disc jockey Mikey Craig, who played bass, and eventually guitarist and keyboard player Roy Hay.

Boy George and dummy

However, while the group's music was both interesting, and, by the end of 1982, extremely successful (their third single, 'Do You Really Want To Hurt Me', topped the UK charts and made the Top 3 of the US chart in early 1983), O'Dowd became a media personality. His penchant for dressing in outrageous (and often female) clothes, made him prime fodder for press photographers and stories of decadence in the twilight world of London's night-club circuit. At the end of 1983, by which time the name of Boy George was known throughout the western world, both 'Karma Chameleon' and *Colour By Numbers*, the album on which the song was included were at the top of the UK charts. The single, which also topped the US chart, became a million-seller, and won a BRIT Award as Best British single. The group won the title of Best British Group at the same award ceremony, and later that month won a Grammy Award as Best New Artist of 1983.

QUEEN'S 'MAGIC' IS FIFTH NUMBER ONE ALBUM

Queen had first topped the UK album chart in 1975, with *A Night At The Opera*, and had repeated the achievement in early 1977 with *A Day At The Races*, a second album whose title was inspired by a classic Marx Brothers movie. 1980 brought their third chart-topping album with *The Game*, and the following year's *Greatest Hits* was their fourth to reach the summit. The group had produced fewer original albums during the first half of the 1980s, but *A Kind Of Magic*, which included tracks written for the feature film *Highlander*, confirmed that the group's appeal remained intact, as it restored them to the No. 1 spot.

Queen reign supreme

ARRIVALS

1909 – Burl Ives (Burle Icle Ivanhoe Ives)
1941 – Julie Felix
1943 – Muff Winwood (Mervyn Winwood) (Spencer Davis Group)
1945 – Rod Argent (Zombies/Argent)
1949 – Alan White (Plastic Ono Band/Yes)
1952 – Jimmy Lea (Slade)
1959 – Nick van Eede (Cutting Crew)
1961 – Boy George (George O'Dowd)
1963 – Chris DeGarmo (Queensryche)

★ ★ ★

DEPARTURE LOUNGE

1968 – Ernest 'Pop' Stoneman
1969 – Wynonie Harris
1973 – Clarence White (Byrds)

★ ★ ★

RAVINGS

1969:
R & B star Wynonie Harris, who claimed that Elvis Presley 'stole my hip shake and sneer', died.

★ ★ ★

1979:
The 'No Nukes' benefit concert starring Bruce Springsteen, Bonnie Raitt, Stephen Stills and others attracted a large crowd at the Hollywood Bowl in Los Angeles. Recordings of the event were later released as a triple album and a feature film.

★ ★ ★

EASTERN PROMISE?

1963

Kyu Sakamoto, Japanese pop star of the 1960s

When 'Sukiyaki' replaced Lesley Gore's 'It's My Party' at the top of the *Billboard* singles chart, Kyu Sakamoto became the first Japanese artist to chart let alone reach No. 1 in the USA.

When an English record company boss heard this song while on a trip to Tokyo, he took a copy of Sakamoto's record back to London because he felt it would be a suitable tune for jazzman Kenny Ball to record. Ball had scored a big hit in 1961 with 'Midnight In Moscow', and repeated the success in 1962 with 'March Of The Siamese Children', so a Japanese tune would be equally exotic. The record executive realized that most British disc jockeys would find difficulty in pronouncing its Japanese title, 'Ueo Muite Arako' which translates as 'I Look Up When I Walk', so he made an executive decision to change it to an oriental word that would be familiar to most people. Kenny Ball recorded it and it was a UK Top 10 hit.

Then Rich Osborne, a disc jockey in Washington state acquired a copy of Sakamoto's original version, and played it. Despite the language barrier it was an immediate smash hit. It was swiftly licensed for American release, and rushed up the chart, making the 21-year-old Sakamoto the most unlikely star of the year.

In 1981 American disco quartet A Taste Of Honey recorded a version of the song with English lyrics. Released as a single, it went gold and reached the Top 3 in the US. Five years later, Sakamoto, who had charted with a follow-up single, 'China Nights (Shina No Yu ro)', which peaked outside the US Top 50, was killed in an air disaster when a Japan Airlines 747 crashed near Tokyo.

ARRIVALS

1917 – Leon Payne (Texas Playboys)
1921 – Erroll Garner
1941 – Harry Nilsson
1943 – Johnny Hallyday
1949 – Michael Lutz (Brownsville Station)
1949 – Noddy Holder (Neville John Holder) (Slade)1950
1949 – Russell Hitchcock (Air Supply)
1951 – Steve Walsh (Kansas)
1953 – Richie Puente (Foxy)

1954 – Terri Gibbs (Sound Dimension)
1957 – Brett Gillis (Rubicon)
1958 – Neil Arthur (Blancmange)

★ ★ ★

DEPARTURE LOUNGE

1968 – Wes Montgomery
1980 – Bob Nolan
1989 – Pete de Freitas (Echo and the Bunnymen)

★ ★ ★

1991

CHANGING PLACES

In one of the more bizarre coincidences to occur in popular music, Paula Abdul changed places at the top of the US album chart with her erstwhile babysitter, Michael Bolton. What made this even more unlikely was that Abdul's 'Opposites Attract' had replaced Bolton's 'How Am I Supposed To Live Without You' at the top of the US singles chart in the previous year.

Paula Abdul - who's babysitting now?

RAVINGS

1985:
Bruce Springsteen had all seven of his albums released up to that time in the UK chart simultaneously, as his first two albums, *Greetings From Asbury Park, N.J.* and *The Wild, The Innocent And The E Street Shuffle* finally entered the chart more than a decade after release in the wake of the immense success of *Born In The USA*.

1986:
Sting and U2 headlined a concert in New Jersey celebrating 25 years of the Amnesty International organization.

★ ★ ★

1967

THE POP FESTIVAL AS PIONEERED BY MONTEREY

Some would say that its organizers had a lot to answer for, but the Monterey International Pop Festival was the first legendary festival of rock and pop music. It was an immense success, and made world-famous stars of a number of performers, at least six of whom subsequently died of unnatural causes.

Heat leader Hite

Jimi Hendrix, who set light to his guitar at Monterey and became an overnight sensation, died in 1970, while Otis Redding died in an air crash only six months after his Monterey breakthrough. Cass Elliott (of the Mamas and Papas) choked on a sandwich in 1974, and Keith Moon of The Who overdosed in 1978. Grateful Dead keyboard player Ron 'Pigpen' McKernan died of a liver complaint in 1973, and two members of Canned Heat, Al Wilson (a drug-related suicide, 1970) and Bob Hite (a drug-related heart attack in 1981) died well before their 40th birthdays. Janis Joplin, memorably fronting Big Brother and The Holding Company, overdosed in 1970 and Brian Jones of The Rolling Stones, who was in the audience, drowned in 1969.

Janis at Monterey

1955

UNCHAINED DOMINANCE

No less than four different versions of the same song, 'Unchained Melody', simultaneously jostled for position in the UK Top 20. Latterday disc jockey Jimmy Young was the first to reach the chart, but was quickly overtaken by Al Hibbler's American version. Hibbler could not overtake the four versions of 'Stranger In Paradise' which were also in the Top 20 (by Tony Bennett, Tony Martin, The Four Aces and trumpeter Eddie Calvert (the only British reprsentative in the 'Paradise' contest). Then orchestra leader Les Baxter arrived with a third version of 'Unchained Melody', and that was followed by a fourth, by American pianist Liberace. A week later, the Jimmy Young version finally took the song to No. 1, displacing another single by Eddie Calvert, his version of 'Cherry Pink and Apple Blossom White', which had fought its own battle with the American version of the tune by Perez Prado. Got that?

RAVINGS

1980:
The feature film The *Blues Brothers*, starring John Belushi and Dan Aykroyd as Jake and Elwood Blues, was premiered in Chicago.

★ ★ ★

1982:
James Honeyman-Scott, guitarist with The Pretenders, overdosed the day after his colleague, bass player Pete Farndon, had left the band.

1990:
'Paint It Black' by The Rolling Stones topped the charts in the Netherlands for a second time – after a 24-year gap.

1990:
British pop duo Bros (the Goss brothers), paid just over £40,000 ($60,000) in settlement of a legal dispute over management.

★ ★ ★

DEF HEADBANGERS CATCH UP WITH BOSS

1989

Hysteria, the album by Def Leppard, the heavy metal band from Sheffield (England), equalled the remarkable achievement of Bruce Springsteen's *Born In The USA* in 1984/5 by accumulating 96 consecutive weeks in the Top 40 of the US album chart.

Def Leppard formed in 1977 as Atomic Mass, then became Deaf Leopard, before settling on the name with which they found fame. In 1978 they rehearsed for the first time with guitarist Steve Clark, and when he accurately copied the guitar solo from Lynyrd Skynyrd's epic 'Free Bird', he was immediately invited to join the band, which at the time also included vocalist Joe Elliott and bass player Rick Savage. At the end of that year, the band recorded a three-track EP, which they released on their own Bludgeon Riffola label in early 1979, creating considerable interest in the media, where their musical style was dubbed 'New Wave Of British Heavy Metal'.

By the end of 1979 they were signed by Phonogram, and acquired new management who aimed the band primarily at the American market, although both their early albums, *On Through The Night* (1980) and *High 'N' Dry* (1981) reached higher chart positions in the UK than in the US. After extended periods of touring in the US, their third album, *Pyromania*, spent nearly a year in the US Top 40, peaking at No. 2 behind Michael Jackson's *Thriller*.

At the end of 1984, after several months spent recording a follow-up album supervised by Jim Steinman (who had been largely responsible for Meat Loaf's record-breaking *Bat Out Of Hell* album), they decided to dismiss Steinman and produce the album themselves, but on New Year's Eve of that year, tragedy struck when drummer Rick Allen was involved in a car accident that resulted in his left arm being torn off. It was stitched back to his body as quickly as possible, but almost inevitably, infection occurred, and the arm had to be amputated. This further delayed recording of the album, as Allen was keen to rejoin the group, using computerized and synthesized drums.

During the summer of 1986 the group returned to live work at various festivals like The Monsters Of Rock, and a year later *Hysteria* was finally released, three years after recording started on the project.

Joe Elliott, Def Leppard vocalist

J u n e

RAVINGS

1955:
Hit vocalist Eddie Fisher married Hollywood star Debbie Reynolds. Their union produced film star and novelist Carrie Fisher.

1966:
Peter Green joined John Mayall's Bluesbreakers.

1976:
Ian Dury played his last date with Kilburn and The High Roads.

1989:
Marillion announced that their new vocalist would be Steve Hogarth (ex-Europeans), who replaced the departed Fish.

★ ★ ★

ARRIVALS

1910 – Red Foley (Clyde Julian Foley)
1915 – Stringbean (David Akeman)
1917 – Dean Martin (Dino Crocetti)
1939 – Dickey Doo (Dave Allred) (Dickey Doo and the Donts)
1942 – Norman Kuhlke (Swinging Blue Jeans)
1944 – Chris Spedding
1946 – Barry Manilow (Barry Allan Pinkus)
1947 – Eric Lewis (Middle Of The Road)
1951 – Lenny LeBlanc

★ ★ ★

DEPARTURE LOUNGE

1986 – Kate Smith

1977

ROTTEN IN PUNK ROCK RAZOR RUCK

Rotten (with light jacket) - razor victim

As he was leaving a public house in North London to return to nearby Wessex Studios with record producer Chris Thomas and engineer Bill Price, protestors wielding razors attacked Johnny Rotten, vocalist with punk rock pioneers The Sex Pistols. It was the latest in a series of apparently unprovoked attacks suffered by members of the group.

Three weeks earlier, the group had released a single called 'God Save The Queen', which shared its title, but not its lyrics or its tune, with the British National Anthem. Released in a picture sleeve that portrayed Queen Elizabeth II with a safety pin through her lips, it had clearly shocked many people, who regarded it as an affront to Her Majesty, and wanted to make their feelings forcibly known to The Sex Pistols. The single had been launched by a boat trip on the River Thames that ended in considerable confusion as the police arrested several of the passengers on the ironically named Queen Elizabeth when it returned to its berth.

It seemed that the establishment were determined to suppress the group, who they possibly felt presented a threat to law and order, and BBC Radio One did not play the single at the time. When its chart position was announced in chart programmes, it was referred to as 'the record by The Sex Pistols', leading to great interest among record-buyers who were most interested to hear a record the title of which the national pop station could not bring itself to read on the air. It was the biggest hit single the group ever released, although the only album they released while Johnny Rotten was a member of the group, *Never Mind The Bollocks*, entered the chart at the top and remained there for a second week.

1976

MAY MOVES OUT

The vocalist and only remaining original member of The Pretty Things, Phil May, left the group after eleven years. At the time of their emergence in 1965, the R & B group were promoted as a dirtier version of The Rolling Stones, in an early version of which guitarist Dick Taylor had played.

RAVINGS

1915:
A. P. Carter married Sara Dougherty in Virginia, USA, starting the country music dynasty that produced June Carter, Carlene Carter and Rosanne Cash.

★ ★ ★

1960:
Tommy Steele, one of Britain's earliest rock 'n' rollers (and one of the first to move into less controversial music), was married. He has never subsequently reached the Top 20 of the UK singles chart.

★ ★ ★

1983:
The release of the world's first three-dimensional picture disc was announced. Swiss electronic group Yello's 'I Love You' came complete with glasses that gave a 3-D effect.

★ ★ ★

Pretty Things - ironically named?

1926

OPRY COLOUR BLIND?

The first black musician appeared on Nashville's *Grand Ole Opry* show when DeFord Bailey, a harmonica player, made his debut. Forty years later, the most successful black country performer ever, Charley Pride, achieved a similar feat.

Charley Pride - in Bailey's footsteps

1971

TOOMORROW TOO MANUFACTURED

Olivia - Toomorrow a turkey, later a star

Mastermind music mogul Don Kirshner, who had been responsible for the immense success of The Monkees, assembled another group using the same blueprint.

Unfortunately, Toomorrow, who were unveiled via a musical comedy science fiction feature film called Toomorrow, were considerably less successful than the chartbusting Monkees, and quietly disbanded.

No one would probably remember them at all were it not for the fact that one of the members of Toomorrow was Olivia Newton-John.

Born in Cambridge in 1948, Olivia moved with her parents to Australia when she was five years old. By her mid teens, she was working with girl friend Pat Carroll as a duo, Pat and Olivia, and they won a trip to England in a talent contest in 1965. When Pat Carroll's work permit expired after a year, Newton-John remained in Britain and picked up the threads of her abandoned solo recording career. Her first hit single came in 1971 with a cover version of Bob Dylan's 'If Not For You', which was produced by Australian John Farrar, who was not only married to her old partner, Pat Carroll, but was also a member of Marvin, Welch and Farrar, the trio formed by the two guitarists when The Shadows were inactive.

By 1972 Newton-John had discovered a new and extremely lucrative career as a star of the US country chart, winning a Grammy Award in 1975 for 'I Honestly Love You', a single that sold a million and topped the US chart, but failed to reach the UK Top 20. Becoming a massive star in the US with 23 hit singles during the 1970s, she released three Top 5 singles during 1978, two of them duets with John Travolta that were featured in the film *Grease*, 'You're The One That I Want' and 'Summer Nights', both of which topped the UK chart and are among the Top 10 best selling singles of all time in the UK.

In 1980 she appeared in another musical feature film, the critically slated *Xanadu*, which produced three more hits, including her fourth US No. 1, 'Magic'.

1969

MAJOR TOM TAKES OFF

David Bowie signed with Mercury Records, who released his first hit single, 'Space Oddity'. Dropping out of the UK chart after a single week in the Top 50, it returned to the chart in the following week, this time climbing into the Top 5. Bowie would not release another hit until mid 1972.

During this period, Bowie and his girlfriend (later wife), Angela Barnett, lived with Tony Visconti and his girlfriend, Liz, in the ground-floor flat of Haddon Hall, a Victorian town house in Southend Road, Beckenham, Kent (about 15 miles south-east of London).

Later, Mick Ronson and the other members of Bowie's group, The Spiders From Mars, also shared the flat, and it was where the Ziggy Stardust concept was obviously initially conceived.

Although Visconti has been inextricably linked with Bowie as producer of many of his albums, he turned down the chance to produce 'Space Oddity' on the grounds that it could prove impossible to follow up, although he was fairly sure it would become a hit. Visconti later recalled, 'Gus Dudgeon was dying to work with David, so he did that track using the whole band that I was already using for the rest of the album.' The album in question was *David Bowie*, which failed to reach the chart when it was initially released, but reached the Top 20 when it was reissued in 1972 and retitled *Space Oddity* in the wake of Bowie's first great success with *The Rise And Fall Of Ziggy Stardust and The Spiders From Mars*.

David Bowie with gold disc

1980

BOB DYLAN PRAISES GOD

The release of the album *Saved* by Bob Dylan, added to the confusion felt by many of his fans, who had been surprised at the similar style of his previous album, *Slow Train Coming*, in 1979. An obviously religious offering, *Saved* further reflected Dylan's recent conversion from Judaism to Christianity, and became the singer/songwriter's first album since 1964 to peak outside the US Top 20 (in the UK, it made the Top 3). Although its songs were booed when Dylan performed them in concert, *Slow Train Coming* had become only Dylan's second album to sell a million copies, and included the Grammy-winning single, 'Gotta Serve Somebody'.

Bob Dylan

RAVINGS

1981:
Guitarists Gerry Cott and Bernie Torme left their respective bands, The Boomtown Rats and Gillan.

1981:
Vocalist Pauline Black left The Selecter.

1983:
Duane Eddy opened his first US tour in 15 years in San Francisco.

1986:
The Prince's Trust concert at Wembley starred Paul McCartney, Elton John, Tina Turner, Paul Young and Phil Collins.

★ ★ ★

PRISMATIC PURPLE

1975

Guitarist and prime mover behind Deep Purple, Ritchie Blackmore, announced that he was quitting the group to form Rainbow. Replacing him was guitarist Tommy Bolin.

Blackmore (left) with the second Deep Purple line-up

Blackmore, a veteran of early 1960s groups, was one of the original members of Roundabout, the group led by Chris Curtis, ex-drummer with The Searchers, which formed in early 1968, and after two months had metamorphosed into Deep Purple. Also in the short-lived Roundabout was organist Jon Lord, and the other original Deep Purple members were vocalist Rod Evans, Nick Simper on bass and Ian Paice (drums). The line-up stayed together for less than 18 months, but during that time released three albums, none of which reached the UK chart, although all three were fairly successful in the US, particularly their debut, *Shades Of Deep Purple*.

In July 1969 the group's personnel radically altered when Evans and Simper were respectively replaced by Ian Gillan and Roger Glover. The chemistry in the new line-up was immediate, and in four years together the group released six hit albums, including *Fireball* (1971) and *Machine Head* (1972), which both topped the UK chart, while two singles, ' Black Night' and 'Strange Kind Of Woman', were UK Top 10 hits. However, internal friction (largely, it appeared, between Blackmore and Gillan) forced the band to recruit new vocalist David Coverdale and bass player Glenn Hughes, but while the two albums by this line-up, *Burn* and *Stormbringer* were commercially successful, Blackmore remained restive. He recruited four members from Elf, a band based in New York state, to form his own group, Rainbow.

1981

DAN DISBANDS IN DISARRAY

Steely Dan, the uniquely sophisticated rock group that took its name from a steam-powered dildo in William Burroughs' novel, *The Naked Lunch*, called it a day. Formed by vocalist/keyboard player Donald Fagen and bass player Walter Becker, who met in 1967 as college students, the group's constantly shifting personnel did not prevent them consistently releasing superior hit singles like 'Do It Again', 'Reeling In The Years', 'Rikki Don't Lose That Number' and others, as well as five gold albums followed by three that went platinum.

Dan co-leader Donald Fagen

ARRIVALS

1932 – Lalo Schifrin
1932 – O. C. Smith (Ocie Lee Smith)
1942 – Deodato (Eumir Deodato Almeida)
1944 – Jon Hiseman (Colosseum)
1944 – Ray Davies (Kinks)
1945 – Chris Britton (Troggs)
1946 – Brenda Holloway
1947 – Joey Molland (Badfinger)
1950 – Joey Kramer (Aerosmith)
1951 – Alan Silson (Smokie)
1953 – Nils Lofgren
1957 – Mark Brzezicki (Big Country)
1967 – Tim Simenon (Bomb The Bass)

★ ★ ★

DEPARTURE LOUNGE

1980 – Bert Kaempfert
1990 – June Christy

★ ★ ★

LITTLE STEVIE WONDER STORMS US CHART AT 13

1963

Stevie Wonder (known at the time as Little Stevie Wonder) first entered the US pop chart with his frenetic single, 'Fingertips Parts One and Two'. Wonder had celebrated his thirteenth birthday the previous month, and when the single topped the US chart in August, he became one of the youngest ever chart-toppers. Born Steveland Morris (or Hardway or Judkins, depending on his mother's current companion) on May 13, 1950, in Saginaw, a town in north Michigan, Wonder was blind from birth, and was first captivated by music in a Baptist church.

Teaching himself to play drums and later keyboards, he formed a duo with a friend whose uncle was a member of The Miracles, the group fronted by Smokey Robinson, and this led to an introduction to Motown Records in 1960, who signed him when the infant prodigy was only ten years old.

His first single, 'I Call It Pretty Music (But The Old People Call It The Blues)', was released in the summer of 1962, but failed to chart – among the musicians on the single was Marvin Gaye, at the time a session drummer. A week after his thirteenth birthday, a concert by Wonder was recorded in Detroit, and from these tracks, 'Fingertips Part Two' was selected as a single. It became the first live single to top the US chart and sold a million copies, while the album, *Recorded Live – The 12 Year Old Genius* (which was untrue by eight days), also reached No. 1 in the US.

However, follow-up singles and albums were considerably less successful in 1964/5, and it was not until early 1966 that Wonder returned to the upper reaches of the chart with 'Uptight (Everything's Alright)', which was also his first UK hit single. He remained successful, albeit with occasional gaps, next hitting the number one slot with his 23rd charted single 'Superstition' in 1973.

Stevie - Number One at 13!

1985

POLICE GO TO LAW

Police - still together

Highly successful British-based trio The Police issued a writ against a newspaper that had suggested that the group were breaking up. Doubtless misled by the news that both bass player Sting and drummer Stewart Copeland were involved in solo projects, the group performed at a concert in aid of Amnesty International in Atlanta, Georgia, in 1986.

COURT OF CRIMSON KING RE-OPENS

Seven years after founder and leader Robert Fripp had found himself the only member of King Crimson, the group he launched in 1969, he announced he was renaming his latest band, Discipline, as King Crimson. The only other member of the new King Crimson who

Robert Fripp - resurrecting the monarchy

had previously played in the group was former Yes drummer Bill Bruford, and the new line-up was completed by two Americans, guitarist Adrian Belew (ex-David Bowie) and in-demand session bass player Tony Levin. Personnel changes had been a continuing feature of the original band, and this tradition would be continued.

While it may seem hard to believe in view of the perceived seriousness of King Crimson's approach, the first album on which guitar genius Fripp featured was entitled *The Cheerful Insanity of Giles, Giles and Fripp*. This was a group comprising Pete Giles (bass) and his brother Mike (drums), along with saxophonist Ian McDonald and eventually lyricist Pete Sinfield. The commercial failure of the album in 1968 led to Pete Giles leaving, and he was replaced by Greg Lake (bass, vocals) from The Gods. Soon afterwards,

G.,G. and F became King Crimson, and one of their earliest gigs was in front of an immense audience in Hyde Park on the same bill as The Rolling Stones. Their debut album, *In The Court Of The Crimson King*, reached the Top 5 in the UK chart and the Top 30 in the USA, but soon after it was released two members of the band left to form the logically named McDonald and Giles. Lake also departed to join Keith Emerson and Carl Palmer in ELP.

A second King Crimson album, *In The Wake Of Poseidon*, featured Fripp with Gordon Haskell

(bass, vocals), Mel Collins (saxophone) and guest appearances from the Giles brothers. Subsequent recruits included Andy McCullough and Ian Wallace (drums) and bass player/vocalist Boz Burrell (later in Bad Company), but by 1972, everyone else bar Fripp had left the band, after which Bill Bruford joined for two years.

The 1981 reincarnation of the band was no longer-lived – by 1982, Fripp had fallen out with his erstwhile colleagues, and in 1984 was once again the only member of the band.

ARRIVALS

1915 – Zeb Turner
(William Edward Grisham)
1923 – Dotty Todd
1929 – June Carter
1940 – Adam Faith
(Terence Nelhams)
1944 – Rosetta Hightower
(Orlons)
1945 – Paul Goddard
(Atlanta Rhythm Section)
1952 – Betty Dragstra
(Pussycat)
1957 – Leee John
(Imagination)
1962 – Richard Coles
(Communards)

★ ★ ★

DEPARTURE LOUNGE

1972 – Elton Britt

RAVINGS

1984:
An auction of items connected with John Lennon was held at Sotheby's in London.

1989:
George Michael

received the Silver Clef Award for outstanding achievements relating to British music.

1990:
American producer/songwriter Maurice Starr had seven acts with whom

he had been or still was associated in the Top 100 of the US chart: Perfect Gentlemen, Ana, New Kids On The Block, Seiko and Donnie, Bell Biv Devoe, Johnny Gill and Bobby Brown.

★ ★ ★

LENNON GOES LITERARY AGAIN

Bart and Lennon

John Lennon's second book of poetry and drawings, *A Spaniard In The Works*, was published in Britain by Jonathan Cape.

It followed his triumph the previous year with *In His Own Write*, a similarly anarchic collection of original works. This first book was an instant bestseller on both sides of the Atlantic. It was published in the US by Simon and Schuster, and the same publishing house was also responsible for a French edition with the title *En Flagrante Delire*. The huge success of *In His Own Write* made the publication of *A Spaniard In The Works* one of the highlights of the book world in 1965.

The story that gave the book its title featured a Spaniard with the unlikely name of Jesus El Pifco, who went to work in Scotland, where he had a romantic tryst with a girl with the equally unlikely name of Spastic Sporran. There was talk of a third book in the series, but apparently Lennon lost interest in the idea, probably due to pressure of work.

It had been announced a few days before that The Beatles had been awarded the honour of being named Members Of The British Empire (MBE), and would be presented with their medals by Queen Elizabeth II at Buckingham Palace (they later admitted to smoking marijuana in the toilets), whereupon numerous holders of the MBE wrote letters of protest, and a number of recipients returned their MBE medals, one, a Canadian Member Of Parliament complaining that he had been put in the same category as 'a bunch of vulgar numbskulls'.

In August, the group visited one of their early heroes, Elvis Presley, in California at one of his homes, a few days after the celebrated Beatle concerts at Shea Stadium that grossed over $300,000 (£200,000), a record for a pop show.

RAVINGS

1955:
Successful ballad singer Ray Burns left his position singing in front of the very popular Cyril Stapleton Orchestra to embark on a solo career after reaching the UK Top 10 with 'Mobile'.

★ ★ ★

1989:
The Who started their highly successful US tour in Toronto, at the same venue where they had played their farewell performance in 1982.

★ ★ ★

1990:
Donnie Wahlberg of New Kids On The Block was badly hurt when he fell through a trap door on stage during a New York concert.

★ ★ ★

ANOTHER BEATLE RECORD?

Rosanne's chart-topping Beatle cover

Several years after Lennon's death, a song by John Lennon and Paul McCartney topped the US country chart for the first time ever when 34 year old Rosanne Cash, daughter of Johnny Cash, topped that chart with her version of 'I Don't Want To Spoil The Party'.

ARRIVALS

1900 – Gene Austin (Eugene Lucas)
1929 – Connie Hall
1942 – Mick Fleetwood
1944 – Arthur Brown (Arthur Wilson)
1944 – Chris Wood (Traffic)
1944 – Jeff Beck
1944 – John 'Charlie' Whitney (Family)
1945 – Colin Blunstone (Zombies)
1948 – Patrick Moraz (Refugee/Yes/Moody Blues)
1957 – Astro (Terence Wilson) (UB40)
1959 – Andy McClusky (Orchestral Manoeuvres In The Dark)
1961 – Curt Smith (Tears For Fears)
1970 – Glenn Allan Medeiros

★ ★ ★

1967

ALL YOU NEED IS SATELLITE

Abbey Road Studios in London was the setting for the worldwide television spectacular, *Our World*, in which 26 countries and five continents were linked via satellite, with an estimated audience of around 400 million people.

Our world - *around the world*

The Beatles were filmed recording a live version of a brand new song, 'All You Need Is Love', in the large recording studio within the Abbey Road complex. Mindful of the need for an international feel to the song, it began with an introductory passage from the French National Anthem, 'The Marseillaise', and included a riff from the theme tune of America's Glenn Miller Orchestra, 'In The Mood' (George Martin was later successfully sued for royalty payments by Miller's publishers). It also included a passage from 'Greensleeves' (supposedly written by King Henry VIII, the English king who founded the Church of England because The Pope of the time would not sanction his impending divorce), and a brief 'Yeah, Yeah, Yeah' chorus from the group's earlier hit, 'She Loves You'.

The marketing men could hardly believe their luck – a brand new anthem from the biggest group in the world promoted live around the world as part of a historic TV show to an audience of hundreds of millions, with a backing choir of superstars including Mick Jagger and Keith Richards, Eric Clapton, Keith Moon, one of The Walker Brothers and one of The Hollies. It came as no great surprise that when 'All You Need Is Love' was released as a single two weeks later, it topped the charts in Britain and America.

1988

BOSS AND BAND BRING TUNNEL TOUR TO LONDON

Bruce Springsteen and The E Street Band played London's Wembley Stadium on the European leg of their *Tunnel Of Love* tour. The album of the same name had been released during the previous October, and had topped the charts on both sides of the Atlantic, although many obviously regarded it as less impressive than Springsteen's previous album, *Born In The USA* (which spawned seven US Top 10 singles), as can be judged from the fact that the latter remained in the UK album chart for nearly two and a half years, while *Tunnel Of Love* said its chart farewell after eight months.

Bruce The Boss

RED LETTER DAY FOR ELVIS

1977

Elvis Presley - a day to remember

Although he could never have known that June 26 would turn out to be a crucial date from several different aspects. The King would have known that it was 'Colonel' Tom Parker's 68th birthday as he walked on stage at the Market Square Arena in Indianapolis, Indiana, but he could hardly have known that this would be his final performance, and he clearly could have had no idea that he would be dead less than two months later. Two years later, another tragedy afflicted the Presley family on June 26 – Elvis's father, Vernon , died of a heart attack at the age of 63. His mother, Gladys had passed away on August 14, 1960, almost 17 years to the day before her son.

Vernon Presley and Tom Parker were undoubtedly major influences on Elvis at various points in his life, despite the fact that both had secrets in their past involving illegal acts. Vernon had been in prison for forging a cheque, although he was obviously not a habitual criminal.

Parker, on the other hand, was an opportunist. Born Andreas Cornelis Van Kuijk in Breda. The Netherlands, he apparently arrived in the USA in 1927, stayed for a year and then returned home but left again in the summer of 1929, and never returned. It has been widely suggested that a major reason for Presley's failure to perform in Europe was that Parker was concerned that if he left the US he would not be allowed to return as he did not have a visa.

Elvis's final concert followed the pattern of many of his latterday concerts. Introduced to the strains of 'Also Sprach Zarathustra' (the theme music from the film *2001 – A Space Odyssey*), he sang oldies like 'Jailhouse Rock' and 'Hound Dog', as well as more recent additions to his repertoire like 'Bridge Over Troubled Water', ending the concert with 'Can't Help Falling In Love'.

RAVINGS

1973:
Marsha Hunt brought a paternity suit against Mick Jagger.

★ ★ ★

1982:
Bryan Ferry, erstwhile leader of Roxy Music, married Lucy Helmore. One of Ferry's previous girlfriends, Texan model Jerry Hall, later married Mick Jagger.

1974

I NOT GOT YOU BABE – SONNY AND CHER SPLIT

One of pop music's apparently perfect couples, Sonny and Cher, were divorced. Married in 1963, their first and biggest hit was 'I Got You Babe', a No. 1 hit all over the world in 1965, selling a million copies. Cher remained a highly rated pop/rock star and won an Oscar in 1987 as an actress in the film *Moonstruck*.

Sonny and Cher - split

ARRIVALS

1893 – Big Bill Broonzy
1910 – Colonel Tom Parker
1940 – Billy Davis Jr (Fifth Dimension)
1942 – Larry Taylor (Canned Heat)
1943 – Georgie Fame (Clive Powell)
1943 – Jean Knight
1948 – Richard McCracken (Taste)
1949 – John Illsley (Dire Straits)
1950 – Junior Daye (Sweet Sensation)

1951 – Rindy Ross (Quarterflash)
1955 – Mick Jones (Clash/Big Audio Dynamite)
1956 – Chris Isaak (Christopher Joseph Isaak)
1957 – Patti Smyth (Scandal)
1960 – Chris Duffy (Waterfront)
1961 – Terri Nunn (Berlin)

★ ★ ★

1968

BACK FROM THE DEAD

Regarded by many of his fans as artistically defunct, Elvis Presley finally showed the world that there was more to him. He began making a TV Special at NBC Studios in Burbank, California.

which reminded his declining following that he could still rock. The highlight of the show for many was a section in which he appeared on a stage in the centre of the studio, surrounded by his audience.

Elvis jamming live

With minimal backing from his original backing musicians, guitarist Scotty Moore and drummer D. J. Fontana, plus Charlie Hodge, a member of the so-called Memphis Mafia (Presley's constant companions during the 1970s), and Alan Fortas on tambourine, he ran through many of his early classics, including 'That's All Right (Mama)', 'Heartbreak Hotel', 'Lawdy Miss Clawdy', 'Blue Suede Shoes' and many more. When the show was screened later that year, it demonstrated just how impressive Presley had been at the start of his career in the mid 1950s, and that in the right circumstances he was quite capable of recreating those halcyon days.

His renaissance was recognized – the soundtrack album of the TV Special, simply called *Elvis*, was his first to reach the Top 10 in the USA for three years, and his first Top 3 album in Britain since 1962. The King was not dead, he had just been asleep.

1987

WHITNEY WINS FIRST LADY TITLE

When her second album, *Whitney*, entered the US chart at No. 1, Whitney Houston became the first woman in chart history to achieve the considerable feat of simultaneously entering and topping the *Billboard* album chart. On the same day she also became the first female artist to top the chart with four consecutive singles. The track in question was 'I Wanna Dance With Somebody (Who Loves Me)'. She would beat this latter record three more times in the next ten months.

1964

STONES SET UNIQUE PRECEDENT ON TV

During the 1960s one of the most popular shows on British television was *Juke Box Jury*, on which a panel of four personalities passed judgement on new single releases, predicting whether or not they would become hits. When The Rolling Stones were the panel, a new system of voting on the 'hit' or 'miss' questions had to be evolved, as the studio set that was normally used only contained four panels on which votes could be registered, and there were five members of the group. The Stones, as expected, were critical of some of the records they heard, but the show passed with little controversy.

1992

ELTON, ERIC AND BONNIE WIN AT WEMBLEY

Wembley Stadium was packed for concerts starring two of Britain's most popular and enduring rock stars, Eric Clapton and Elton John. Also appearing on the bill was Bonnie Raitt (said to be the only act whom both the superstars specified as a preference to open the show for them).

Bonnie Raitt - subject of superstar approval

Elton John premiered his new crowning glory – the unfortunate singer/songwriter had been sensitive about his thinning hair, and several painful hair transplants later appeared with a highly hirsute look and a brand new album, *The One*. Rapturously received by capacity crowds, he neither upstaged Clapton, nor was he overshadowed by the guitar star, who was given a great reception, especially when he played 'Tears In Heaven', the song he wrote after the tragic death of his son Conor.

It seemed that many members of the audience were previously unaware of Bonnie Raitt, the vocalist and slide guitarist from California who had enjoyed belated success in 1990 when her *Nick Of Time* album won three Grammy Awards. Raitt, the daughter of Broadway musicals star John Raitt, who had starred in shows such as *Oklahoma* and *Carousel*, had been releasing excellent albums throughout the 1970s that rarely sold in the quantities her fans believed they deserved.

Between 1979 and 1988, Raitt had only released three albums, none of which had approached the excellence of her previous half dozen, but a collaboration with producer Don Was on tracks for two compilation albums led to *Nick Of Time*, which eventually sold over two million copies. Apart from the three Grammies (for Album Of The Year, Best Pop Vocal Performance (Female) and Best Rock Vocal Performance (Female), Raitt also took a fourth Grammy, for Best Traditional Blues Recording for 'I'm In The Mood', her duet with John Lee Hooker on the veteran bluesman's album, *The Healer*.

1986

WHAM! WAVE GOODBYE

The hugely successful duo Wham! (vocalist George Michael and guitarist Andrew Ridgeley) played their farewell concert at a sold-out Wembley Stadium after five years of consistent success that produced four UK No. 1 singles, two chart-topping albums, another Top 3 album and six more Top 10 singles including the million-selling 'Last Christmas', the biggest selling record not to top the chart.

ARRIVALS

1902 – Richard Rodgers
1914 – Lester Flatt
1925 – George Morgan
1943 – Bobby Harrison (Procol Harum/ Freedom/Snafu)
1945 – Dave Knights (Procol Harum)
1946 – John Martyn
1963 – Andy Coulson (All About Eve)

DEPARTURE LOUNGE

1965 Red Nichols
1982 Harry Mills (Mills Brothers)

★ ★ ★

★ ★ ★

RAVINGS

1973:
British groups from the 1960s replayed the British Invasion when The Searchers, Gerry and The Pacemakers, Herman's Hermits and Wayne Fontana played a revival concert at New York's Madison Square Garden.

1989:
The Pet Shop Boys began their first ever tour in Hong Kong.

They also played dates in Japan before making their live debut in Britain.

1989:
UK rapper Merlin was released from a youth custody centre where he had been serving a sentence for burglary. His biggest hit had been the ironically entitled 'Who's In The House' with Beatmasters earlier in the year.

★ ★ ★

1979

LITTLE FEAT MAESTRO'S FATAL HEART ATTACK

Lowell George - willing to be movin'

The day after a sell-out solo performance in Washington, Lowell George, leading light of Little Feat, the critically acclaimed 1970s Californian rock group, died in a motel in Arlington, Virginia, of a heart attack induced, according to a post mortem, by drug abuse. George was 34 years old.

The sad news came only two months after the group's keyboard player, Bill Payne, had announced that the group had disbanded. Both Payne and Paul Barrère, the group's other guitarist, had just completed a tour on which they had backed singer/songwriter Nicolette Larson, while George had been on the road in the US promoting his first solo album, *Thanks, I'll Eat It Here*, on which Payne and

Little Feat's drummer, Richie Hayward, had participated, although the group's other three members, Barrère, bass player Kenny Gradney and percussionist Sam Clayton, were not involved.

Little Feat was formed in late 1969 by Lowell George at the instigation of Frank Zappa. Zappa had heard George's truck driver's anthem, 'Willin'', and suggested that George should form his own band. George recruited Zappa's bass player, Roy Estrada, and Payne, who had failed an audition for Zappa's Mothers Of Invention (in which George was playing at the time), while the final member of the original quartet was Hayward, with whom George had played in The Factory, a Hollywood group of the mid 1960s. Little Feat's eponymous debut album was released in 1971 after having been completed for some time, and Estrada left to join Captain Beefheart's Magic Band after the release of their second album, *Sailin' Shoes*, in early 1972, whereupon Gradney (ex of Delaney Bramlett's Band), Clayton (who had been fired from Bramlett's

group) and Barrère (ex-Lead Enema), were recruited. This line-up released *Dixie Chicken* in 1973, but after it was no more commercially successful than the first two albums, the group split up for six months. They then re-formed, making five more albums before their 1979 break-up. All these albums were substantial hits in the USA, the biggest of them 1978's live double, *Waiting For Columbus*, which reached the Top 20 and was certified gold. The group is believed to have got its name from Jimmy Carl Black, another member of The Mothers Of Invention, who was amazed at how small George's shoes were.

RAVINGS

1953:
The first single by famed R & B group The Drifters, 'Lucille', was recorded.

1973:
Deep Purple played a concert in Osaka, Japan, which was their final gig before the departure of vocalist Ian Gillan and bass player Roger Glover.

1983:
Harlem's Apollo Theatre was designated a New York landmark.

ARRIVALS

1908 – Leroy Anderson
1935 – Leonard Lee (Shirley and Lee)
1938 – Billy Storm (Valiants)
1943 – Little Eva (Eva Narcissus Boyd)
1943 – Roger Ruskin Spear (Bonzo Dog Doo Dah Band)
1945 – Johnnie Richardson (Johnnie and Joe/Jaynettes)
1947 – Carlo Santanna (Paper Lace)
1948 – Dervin & Lincoln Gordon (Equals)
1948 – Ian Paice (Deep Purple/Whitesnake)
1953 – Colin Hay (Men At Work)
1964 – Stedman Pearson (Five Star)

★ ★ ★

DEPARTURE LOUNGE

1964 – Eric Dolphy
1969 – Shorty Long
1975 – Tim Buckley
1979 – Lowell George

1983

EVERLY BROS TO REUNITE AFTER A DECADE APART

After splitting up in 1973 during a show in Hollywood when Phil smashed his guitar and angrily stormed off stage, The Everly Brothers announced that they had settled their differences, and would reunite for a concert at London's Royal Albert Hall in September. Phil was quoted as saying: 'We settled it in a family kind of way - a big hug did it'.

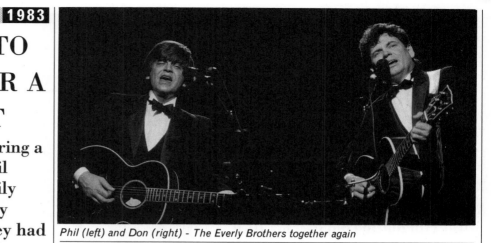

Phil (left) and Don (right) - The Everly Brothers together again

During the 1950s and early 1960s, The Everly Brothers were among the most successful pop/rock acts in the world. With their distinctive country-based sibling harmonies (which owed more to their bluegrass roots in Kentucky than to rock 'n' roll), and a seemingly inexhaustible supply of classic teen anthems, they had scores of international pop hits. Their break-up in 1973 had been acrimonious and was not unexpected, as it was well known that their relationship had been stormy for some years.

The sons of Ike and Margaret Everly, who hosted their own radio show, Don (born in 1937) and Phil (born 1939) first appeared on the air around 1950, and in 1955 they went to Nashville in search of a recording deal. Signed to Columbia (CBS) in 1956, they released a single that was unsuccessful. Their father contacted Chet Atkins about his sons, and Atkins assisted them in acquiring a music publishing contract with major Nashville publishing house Acuff-Rose. Managed by Wesley Rose, the son of the founder of that company, they were introduced to Archie Bleyer of Cadence Records.

Between 1957 and 1960, the duo took 18 hit singles into the US chart, including 'Wake Up Little Susie', 'All I Have To Do Is Dream' and 'Bird Dog', all of which topped the chart, and 'Bye Bye Love', 'Problems' and '('Til) I Kissed You', which made the Top 5. A move to Warner Bros in 1960 in a $1 million deal brought an immediate dividend when 'Cathy's Clown' became their fourth No. 1 and their all-time biggest seller, but after 1962 they were permanently absent from the US Top 10.

ARRIVALS

1930 – June Valli
1936 – Dave Van Ronk
1939 – Tony Hatch
1941 – Larry Hall
1941 – Larry Henley (Newbeats)
1943 – Eddie Rambeau (Edward Flurie)
1943 – Florence Ballard (Supremes)
1944 – Gene Cotton
1946 – Billy Brown
1949 – Andy Scott (Sweet)
1951 Stanley Clarke
1952 – Stefan Zauner
1956 – Adrian Wright (Human League)
1962 – Julianne Regan (All About Eve)

★ ★ ★

DEPARTURE LOUNGE

1983 – Bo Gentry

★ ★ ★

1975

ROCK STARS TIE THE KNOT

Cher, who had been divorced from her husband/duet partner and svengali Sonny Bono for four days, married Gregg Allman. Within ten days of their marriage, Cher and Allman announced that they were splitting. They were reconciled, then they split up again. Eventually, their marriage lasted three years, long enough for them to become parents to Elijah Blue Allman.

Gregg and Cher - on the rebound?

RAVINGS

1981:
Jerry Lee Lewis was rushed to hospital and was not expected to survive. He lived.

1987:
Beastie Boy Ad-Rock became engaged to Molly Ringwald, star of the *Pretty In Pink* movie.

1990:
Eric Clapton and other stars played a concert at Knebworth for the Nordoff-Robbins Music Therapy charity.

1990:
Notorious US rappers 2 Live Crew were arrested and charged with profanity during their US tour.

★ ★ ★

1975

BOWIE FALLS TO EARTH IN ALBUQUERQUE

David Bowie began work for his first cinematic rôle in *The Man Who Fell To Earth*, an adaptation of the science fiction novel by Walter Trevis. Bowie travelled by rail on the Santa Fe Superchief to Albuquerque, New Mexico, where shooting began on the film.

He had just released his *Young Americans* album, featuring Luther Vandross on backing vocals, marking his temporary move into disco music. Much of the album had been recorded at Sigma Sound in Philadelphia, where producers Kenny Gamble and Leon Huff presided over the roster of hitmakers on their Philadelphia

International record label.

Bowie's starring role in the movie (about an alien) seemed out of context, as did his adoption for the film of a new hairstyle and spectacles (previewed later in the year on the picture sleeve of the reissue of his 'Space Oddity' single that topped the UK chart). Bowie played the title

role of Thomas Jerome Newton, while other notables in the film (regarded as Bowie's best), directed by Nicholas Roeg, were Rip Torn, Candy Clark, Buck Henry and Captain James Lovell, the Commander of Apollo 13, who played himself.

Bowie - from another planet?

1956

ELEVEN YEAR OLD SIGNS RECORDING CONTRACT

Little Miss Dynamite - Brenda Lee

Brenda Lee (born Brenda Mae Tarpley in Lithonia, Georgia), signed a record deal with Decca Records (later MCA) in the USA. Not yet twelve years old, she had won her first talent contest at the age of six, and earlier in 1956, had been invited by country star Red Foley to appear on his TV show *Ozark Jubilee*. Although her first release, 'Jambalaya', was not a hit, 'One Step At A Time', released in 1957 not only reached the Top 20 of the US country

chart, but also made the Top 50 in the US pop chart, and before long, she became known as 'Little Miss Dynamite' – not only was her voice striking, but she never grew taller than four feet eleven inches.

Between 1960, when 'Sweet Nothin's' became her first US Top 5 hit, and 1969, she released 48 US pop chart hits, including that made it right to the top, 'I'm Sorry' and 'I Want To Be Wanted', in 1960, and 'All Alone Am I', a Top 3 hit in 1962

SINATRA – NO STRANGER TO THE CHART

Sinatra's Kaempfert Konnection

His first appearance at the US No. 1 spot was in 1940 as vocalist with The Tommy Dorsey Band, but after an absence of over eleven years – from 1955 with 'Learnin' The Blues' – Frank Sinatra returned to the summit with 'Strangers In The Night'.

In his fiftieth year, Sinatra had been somewhat dismissive of rock 'n' roll when it first emerged around the time he had last reached No. 1, and in retrospect his somewhat derogatory remarks could be seen as self-serving. Perhaps he realized that upstarts like Elvis Presley (who appeared with him on ABC television in America in 1960, when Presley returned from his stint in the US Army) presented a threat to his popularity.

'Strangers In The Night' was brought to Sinatra as an instrumental by his record producer, Jimmy Bowen, who had been given several themes written by

1966

German orchestra leader Bert Kaempfert, written for the soundtrack of *A Man Could Get Killed*. Kaempfert had an enviable track record – he had recorded an international No. 1, 'Wonderland By Night', which topped the US chart in early 1961, and had written the music for 'Wooden Heart', a US No. 1 for Joe Dowell also in 1961 and a UK No. 1 for Elvis Presley in the same year – and his music publisher was asked to get English lyrics written, after which Sinatra would record it. In fact, both Bobby Darin and Jack Jones were also about to record the song, but Bowen quickly arranged a recording session with a full orchestra for Sinatra, and the latter's record was on American radio 24 hours after he had taped his vocal.

RAVINGS

1964
Cliff Richard attended the London premiere of *Wonderful Life*, the film in which he starred featuring the UK Top 10 hit 'On The Beach'.

★ ★ ★

1967
Cream, Jeff Beck and John Mayall played a concert at London's Saville Theatre.

★ ★ ★

1988
'Theme From S-Express', the chart-topping UK single by S-Express, topped the US club chart, despite failing in the US pop chart.

★ ★ ★

ARRIVALS

1925 – Marvin Rainwater (Marvin Karlton Percy)
1926 – Lee Allen
1930 – Ahmad Jamal
1930 – Randy Starr (Warren Nadel)
1934 – Tom Springfield (Dion O'Brien) (Springfields)
1939 – Paul Williams (Temptations)
1942 – Leapy Lee (Lee Graham)
1945 – Peter Cruickshank (Groundhogs)
1950 – Hans Bathelt (Triumvirat)
1951 – Joe Puerta (Ambrosia)
1954 – Pete Briquette (Boomtown Rats)
1957 – Mike Anger (Blow Monkeys)
1964 – Dave Parsons (Transvision Vamp)

★ ★ ★

DEPARTURE LOUNGE

1982 – Deford Bailey

1973

ENO QUITS AFTER FERRY CLASH

Roxy Music's synthesizer wizard, Eno (full name Brian Peter George St John Le Baptiste De La Salle Eno), left the band after personality clashes with the group's vocalist and main songwriter, Bryan Ferry. Eno had joined the band in 1971 after an introduction from saxophonist Andy Mackay, and appeared on their first two albums, *Roxy Music* (1972) and *For Your Pleasure* (1973), and on their first two hit singles, 'Virginia Plain' and 'Pyjamarama'.

Bye Bye Brian

1969

STONE FAILS TO FLOAT

Rolling Stones founder member Brian Jones died in the swimming pool of his home, Cotchford Manor, near Hartfield, Sussex, when the combined effects of alcohol and barbiturates heightened a probable asthma attack as he took a midnight swim. Friends tried to revive him, but failed. He was 27 years old.

Brian Jones

Born in Cheltenham, Gloucestershire, he had been fired only a month before from the group he helped to found in the early 1960s, and had been working with R & B veteran Alexis Korner in attempts to rediscover his musical direction. Korner had acted as the original catalyst for the formation of the Stones, and had often given Jones a bed when he was too late to return to Cheltenham, also teaching Jones about their mutual passion for the blues, which had also been the initial inspiration for Mick Jagger and Keith Richards. Jones had helped to broaden the sound of the Stones by playing exotic instruments like the sitar.

In the group's early days, Jones's boyish good looks had made him as much the group's focal point as Jagger, but his determination to experiment with mind-expanding substances had led to a ravaged appearance, not to mention a string of court appearances that had eventually led to his dismissal from the band. This initially threw him into despair, but he rallied with help from Korner and others, and close friends dismiss suggestions that he committed suicide. He was apparently determined to prove that his back-to-basics R &B could be as successful as the more commercial pop-oriented direction he perceived that his old group were following.

1971

DOOR DIES IN BATH

Jim Morrison, lead singer with The Doors, died in Paris, of a heart attack while in the bath.

Morrison had moved to Paris earlier in the year, claiming that he wished to concentrate on writing, and possibly recording, poetry he had written. At the time he was also under pressure due to the appeal that his lawyers were preparing against his conviction for exposing himself on stage during a Doors concert in Miami in 1969.

Morrison was supposedly buried in Père Lachaise cemetery in Paris, although the unexpected circumstances surrounding his death fuelled speculation that he did not die, and that the coffin is either empty or contains the corpse of someone else.

Jim Morrison

RAVINGS

1964
The Beach Boys, Jan and Dean, The Kingsmen and Peter and Gordon starred in *The Million Dollar Party*, which took place in Hawaii.

1973
David Bowie announced his retirement from live work from the stage of London's Hammersmith Odeon at the end of the *Ziggy Stardust* tour.

★ ★ ★

ARRIVALS

1940 – Fontella Bass
1940 – Maureen Kennedy (Vernons Girls)
1943 – Judith Durham (Seekers)
1945 – Johnny Lee (John Lee Ham)
1948 – Paul Barrerre (Little Feat)
1949 – Johnnie Wilder (Heatwave)
1950 – Damon Harris (Delfonics)
1955 – Mike Corby (Babys)
1957 – Laura Branigan
1959 – Stephen Pearcy (Ratt)
1960 – Stephen Morgan (Icehouse)
1962 – Taylor Dayne

★ ★ ★

DEPARTURE LOUNGE

1969 – Brian Jones
1971 – Jim Morrison

1977

BLONDIE BLOW AS BASSMAN BAILS OUT

Gary Valentine, bass player with New York New Wave group Blondie, quit the band citing 'artistic integrity' as the cause of his departure.

Deborah Harry, Blondie's focal point

Formed in 1974, the group took its name from its extremely photogenic vocalist Deborah Harry, who was in fact by far its most experienced member, having recorded an album as part of Californian hippie group Wind In The Willows back in 1968. That album was a failure, and Harry had earned her living in many ways in the intervening years, at one point working as a secretary at the BBC office in New York, before teaming up with two other aficionados of the 'girl group' sound, as epitomized by The Ronettes, The Crystals and others in the mid-1960s, as The Stillettos. The latter's backing band included guitarist Chris Stein and bass player Fred Smith. When the other two vocalists departed, Clem Burke was recruited as drummer, Smith left to join Television, and Burke recommended his friend Valentine. After keyboard player Jimmy Destri joined, the group was ready to record, and they signed with the independent Private Stock label, for whom they made the *Blondie* album.

While this album did not make the group overnight stars, it was well received in Britain, and they toured in Europe as opening act for Television. It was after this tour that Valentine departed to form his own group, The Know, and Blondie were signed by Chrysalis Records, who bought their previous album from Private Stock.

1980

BEACH BOYS CELEBRATE INDEPENDENCE

Beach Boys vocalist Mike Love

The Beach Boys gave a free concert in Miami attended by 500,000 people. This became a regular annual attraction during the 1980s, as the group, who were dubbed the quintessential American band, recycled their 1960s hits for a huge audience each year.

They were able to demonstrate that even though they had experienced more than their fair share of problems in the past – drummer Dennis Wilson drowned in 1983, producer and main songwriter Brian Wilson became self-indulgently eccentric, and internal quarrels became a regular feature – their chart-toppers like 'I Get Around', 'Help Me Rhonda' and 'Good Vibrations', retained a place in the hearts of pop fans.

JAGGER'S HYDE PARK TRIBUTE TO LATE COLLEAGUE

The Stones in Hyde Park - butterfly ball?

The free concert given by The Rolling Stones in London's Hyde Park was scheduled as a celebration of a new line-up of the group, the first public outing of Mick Taylor, the replacement for founder member Brian Jones, and the unveiling of new songs from the band's forthcoming album, *Let It Bleed*.

No official estimate of the size of the crowd that packed into the area known as the cockpit has ever been given, but somewhere between 250,000 and half a million people seems a reasonable guess.

Inevitably, it turned into a tribute to Brian Jones, the lamb who had strayed from the group's fold a month earlier, and who had drowned only two days before. After discussing the pros and cons of going ahead with the concert, the Stones decided to to press on.

Before starting what was a fairly shambolic set, Jagger, dressed in a white smock (as worn by Greek peasants) read lines from Shelley's *Adonais*, written to commemorate the death of poet John Keats. Hundreds of white butterflies were released from cardboard boxes in what was meant to be a symbolic liberation of a free spirit, and some flew into the sky, but many more, weak from the heat inside the boxes, flopped on to the front of the stage and died.

However, the Hyde Park concert achieved its principal objectives – of laying Jones to rest, and of launching a new chapter in the story of one of the world's greatest rock 'n' roll bands.

ARRIVALS

1913 – Smiley Lewis (Overton Lemons)
1938 – Thomas 'Snuff' Garrett
1944 – Robbie Robertson (The Band)
1945 – Dick Scoppettone (Harpers Bizarre)
1946 – Michael Monarch (Steppenwolf)
1946 – Victor Unitt (Pretty Things/Edgar Broughton Band)
1950 – Andy Ellison (John's Children)
1950 – Huey Lewis (Hugh Anthony Gregg)
1954 – Michael Sadler (Saga)

★ ★ ★

DEPARTURE LOUNGE

1983 – Harry James

RAVINGS

1954
Elvis Presley recorded with Scotty Moore and Bill Black for the first time on the country ballad 'I Love You Beacause'.

★ ★ ★

1964
The Four Seasons were invited by President Lyndon Johnson to perform at The White House.

★ ★ ★

1978
Staff at EMI's pressing plant halted production of the new albums by The Rolling Stones, *Some Girls*, after complaints from celebrities (including Lucille Ball) who were featured in mock advertisements on the album sleeve.

★ ★ ★

1983
British gothic rock group Bauhaus split up.

CHARLES NUKES NEWPORT

Despite protests from hard-core stuffed shirt so-called purists who considered him a rock 'n' roller with minimal connections to jazz, Ray Charles (born Ray Charles Robinson) made his first appearance at Newport Jazz Festival, Rhode Island, and received a well-deserved standing ovation from the many who found his mixture of soul, R & B, gospel and big band jazz uplifting.

The 27 year old blind vocalist/pianist's debut at Newport forced many reviewers to search for new superlatives – just as well, then, that Atlantic Records had arranged in advance for his performance to be recorded for a live album, *Ray Charles At Newport*.

Ray Charles at Newport

1990

MADONNA FINALLY CLICKS WITH DICK

Critical reaction to Madonna's movies had been indifferent – until she played the part of Breathless Mahoney in *Dick Tracy*, opposite her then current lover, Warren Beatty, and the press in London, where the film had its European premiere in Leicester Square, were generally positive.

Beatty and 'Breathless' - Beautiful People?

RAVINGS

1957
John Lennon met Paul McCartney for the first time at a church fete in Woolton, Liverpool.

1964
Premiere of Beatle film *A Hard Day's Night* in the presence of Princess Margaret and Lord Snowdon.

1978
Tammy Wynette married George Richey.

★ ★ ★

Although this movie had a soundtrack album packed with big names – k.d.lang (duetting with brilliant accapella sextet Take Six), Jerry Lee Lewis, Brenda Lee, Erasure, Kid Creole (aka August Darnell), Al Jarreau – the album included nothing by Madonna, although she did sing three songs in the movie, written by Stephen Sondheim including the Oscar winning 'Sooner Or Later' which were included on her album, *I'm Breathless*. It surprisingly failed to reach No. 1 in the US, unable to shift the record-breaking *Please Hammer, Don't Hurt*

Em by rapper MC Hammer, which topped that chart for 21 weeks, a record for a debut album. And that wasn't the only bad news for Madonna at that time . . The week before the premiere she had been sued for $500,000 by a 13 year old who claimed to suffer from nightmares and bed-wetting after he tried to take a photograph of her and she snatched his camera, knocked him down and tried to strangle him. Madonna in turn sued the older sister of the 13 year old, calling her obsessive and accusing her of 'threatening, abusive, vexatious and obscene' statements.

1964

BEATLES ON BIG SCREEN

The first Beatles feature film, *A Hard Day's Night*, was premiered at the London Pavilion cinema in Piccadilly Circus. Thousands of fans caused traffic chaos in London's West End. The movie, shot in black and white no doubt because financial backers were apparently unconvinced that it would become a success, became immensely popular, not least because it included two

No. 1 singles, the title track and 'Can't Buy Me Love'.

Directed by American Richard Lester (previously responsible for the celebrated *Running, Jumping and Standing Still Film*, starring Spike Milligan and Peter Sellers), *A Hard Day's Night* was a comedy that delighted its audiences all over the world. Coincidentally, Peter Sellers later recorded an extremely different version of 'A Hard Day's Night', as performed by a Shakespearean actor, which made the UK Top 20 in 1965.

Penguin impersonations - Beatles and Brian Epstein

1971

SWEDISH STARS MARRY AMID CROWDS CHAOS

26-year-old pop star Bjorn Ulvaeus and his 21-year-old fiancée, fellow star Agnetha Faltskog, were married in a Gothic church in the village of Verum, near Skane in the south of their native Sweden. Faltskog had been a star in

Bjorn and Agnetha plighting their troth

Scandanavia since she first topped the local chart in 1968 with 'I Was So In Love', and had also attracted favourable reviews for her portrayal of Mary Magdalene in a Swedish production of the Tim Rice and Andrew Lloyd Webber rock opera *Jesus Christ Superstar*, scoring a major hit with her version of 'I Don't Know How To Love Him'.

Ulvaeus had led a successful folk/rock group, The Hootenanny Singers, but had also formed a songwriting partnership with Benny Andersson, the keyboard player from The Hep Stars (known as 'The Swedish Beatles').

The church had been selected for its romantic atmosphere, but 3,000 fans of both the participants in the wedding arrived to watch, causing mounted police to be called to control the crowds. A police horse stepped on the bride's foot, and she was slightly injured, but other than that, the day went fairly well, as Benny Andersson played the 'Wedding March' on the church organ. Two years later Ulvaeus, Andersson and Faltskog formed ABBA with Andersson's fiancée, Anni-Frid Lyngstad.

1968

BYE BYE 'BIRDS

The Yardbirds called it a day after a US tour on which a New York concert had been recorded. However, the group, by this time largely controlled by guitarist Jimmy Page, reserved the right of approval, and unhappy with the quality of the album, *Live Yardbirds Featuring Jimmy Page*, they refused to sanction its release, although copies briefly appeared in shops on at least two occasions.

After a few gigs as The New Yardbirds, Page, along with new recruits Robert Plant (vocals), John Paul Jones (bass, keyboards) and drummer John Bonham formed Led Zeppelin.

1980

BYE BYE ZEP

Exactly twelve years after The Yardbirds split up, Led Zeppelin played its final gig, at the Eissporthalle (ice rink) in West Berlin. Three months later, after a rehearsal at Page's mansion in Windsor, Berkshire, Bonham went to bed but never awoke, choking to death after drinking heavily for much of the previous evening.

A statement was issued in December announcing the group's decision not to continue after 'the loss of our dear friend'.

RAVINGS

1954
Dewey Phillips, a disc jockey at WHBG, a Memphis radio station, played Elvis Presley's 'That's All Right (Mama)' on the air. It was the first time a Presley record had been played on the radio anywhere.

★ ★ ★

1989
It was announced that, for the first time, compact discs were outselling vinyl albums.

★ ★ ★

ARRIVALS

1906 – Anton Karas
1916 – Lloyd 'Tiny' Grimes
1917 – Elton Britt (James Britt Baker)
1927 – Charlie Louvin
1928 – Mary Ford
1930 – Doyle Wilburn (Wilburn Brothers)
1932 – Joe Zawinul (Josef Erich Zawinul) (Weather Report)
1940 – Ringo Starr (Richard Starkey)
1944 – Warren Entner (Grass Roots)
1945 – Jim Rodford (Argent/Kinks)
1947 – Rob Townsend (Family)
1948 – Larry Reinhardt (Iron Butterfly)
1950 – David Hodo (Village People)*1950*
1962 – Clive Jackson (Dr and The Medics)

★ ★ ★

DEPARTURE LOUNGE

1975 – George Morgan

July

1980

BIAFRA RUNS FOR MAYOR

Regarded by some as the American equivalent of Britain's own cuddly spiky-headed agents provocateurs, The Dead Kennedys were not the first of San Francisco's punk groups but they quickly became the most successful. As their name suggests, the group were formed and famed for outrage, and so were the stage names chosen by the group members – Klaus Fluoride, Ray Valium and especially lead vocalist Jello Biafra, whose real name was Eric Boucher. The group also enjoyed an interesting line in song titles – 'Kill The Poor' was a UK Top 50 hit during 1980 on their own Alternative Tentacles label, and the next year brought their biggest single, 'Too Drunk To Fuck' which climbed as high as No. 36. Their fans preferred earlier diatribes with such titles as 'California Uber Alles', 'Holidays In Cambodia', 'Nazi Punks Fuck Off' and the *Fresh Fruit For Rotting Vegetables* album.

Jello Biafra testifies

Biafra was no stranger to courting political controversy - the single 'California Uber Alles' had been a thinly disguised, vitriolic attack on state governor Jerry Brown -but it was widely believed that when Biafra ran for the post of Mayor of San Francisco, it was little more than another publicity stunt.

However, the citizens of the Californian city apparently felt that some aspects of his manifesto were worthy of being taken seriously because although he did not win he was certainly not placed last in the poll

1965

DC5 MOVIE OPENS

Catch Us If You Can, the feature film starring the Dave Clark Five, was premiered at London's Rialto cinema. The group's starring role was a reflection of their considerable popularity in the USA, where they were regarded as major rivals of The Beatles and The Rolling Stones. The movie was retitled as *Having A Wild Weekend* when it was released in the US, presumably to tie in with the group's album released three months earlier, *Weekend In London*. The end of 1965 saw the group achieve its sole US chart-topping single, 'Over And Over', although their next six singles in the USA all failed to reach the Top 10.

1978

SCOTSMAN TOPS US ALBUM CHART

Gerry Rafferty, the singer/songwriter from Scotland, found himself in the US album chart with his *City To City* album, which included the hit single, 'Baker Street'. Prior to his solo career, Rafferty had been one half of The Humblebums, a duo he formed with comedian Billy Connolly. After he was the leading light of Stealer's Wheel, who hit the US and UK Top 10 in 1973 with 'Stuck In The Middle With You'.

ARRIVALS

1914 – Billy Eckstein
1932 – Jerry Vale (Genaro Louis Vitaliano)
1935 – Steve Lawrence
1941 – 'Papa' Link Davis
1944 – Jai Johanny Johanson (Allman Brothers)
1945 – Ricky Wolff
1947 – Willie Wilson (John Wilson) (Quiver)
1956 – Russell Christian (Christians)
1961 – Andy Fletcher (Depeche Mode)

★ ★ ★

1968

NEW TEMPTATION MAKES ON-STAGE DEBUT

Motown's Temptations live on British television

With the departure of David Ruffin, The Temptations played their first live concert with new group member Dennis Edwards.

The Temptations had originally formed in 1960 as a merger between two Detroit-based vocal groups, The Primes and The Distants. The Primes included Eddie Kendricks and Paul Williams, and The Distants Melvin Franklin and Otis Williams, all of whom were original members of The Temptations, whose classic line-up was completed in early 1962 when David Ruffin replaced Eldridge Bryant (another original member, previously of The Distants) following the commercial failure of the first two singles by The Temptations.

The group achieved their first hits working with songwriter/producer Smokey Robinson, including 'The Way You Do The Things You Do' (1964, with lead vocal by Eddie Kendricks), 'My Girl' (1965, the group's first US chart-topper, with lead vocal by Ruffin), 'It's Growing' (also 1965), and 'Get Ready' (1966), before starting to work with Norman Whitfield. The hits continued, but by 1968 Ruffin was becoming increasingly unhappy with sharing the lead vocalist spot with Kendricks, and left for a solo career.

The brother of fellow Motown star Jimmy Ruffin (of 'What Becomes Of The Broken Hearted' fame), David Ruffin started well with a US Top 10 hit, 'My Whole World Ended (The Moment You Left Me)', in 1969, and followed it with two further hits during the same year, but apart from a minor 1970 hit duet with his brother, Jimmy, he was absent from the US singles chart until 1975/76.

Nine years later he and Kendricks were reunited, appearing with Daryl Hall and John Oates at the reopening of the Apollo Theatre in New York's Harlem district, and recording a Top 20 single called 'A Nite At The Apollo Live!'. In June 1991 Ruffin died of a drug overdose in Philadelphia.

ARRIVALS

1907 – Eddie Dean
1916 – Joe Liggins
1923 – Molly O'Day (LaVerne Williamson)
1927 – Ed Ames (Ames Brothers)
1929 – Jesse McReynolds (Jim and Jesse)
1929 – Lee Hazlewood
1941 – Donald McPherson (Main Ingredient)
1946 – Bon Scott (Ronald Scott) (AC/DC)
1946 – Mitch Mitchell (Jimi Hendrix Experience)
1953 – Kate Garner (Haysi Fantayzee)
1954 – Debbie Sledge \(Sister Sledge)
1959 – Jim Kerr (Simple Minds)
1959 – Peter Marc Almond (Soft Cell)
1971 – Kelvin Grant (Musical Youth)

1972

WINGS TAKE FLIGHT OFFICIALLY

Wings, the group led by Paul McCartney and featuring his wife, Linda, ex-Moody Blue Denny Laine, American drummer Denny Seiwell and guitarist Henry McCullough (ex-Grease Band) started their first scheduled tour with a concert in the small French town of Châteauvillon.

Earlier in the year, the group had performed several ad hoc gigs at colleges and universities, where they simply arrived and asked if they could play that evening.

Mr. and Mrs. Macca winging it

ULTIMATE TALENT SCOUT DIES

1987

John Henry Hammond, the man who signed a galaxy of brilliant musicians during a career lasting over 50 years, died at the age of 76. His most recent discovery had been Texan guitarist Stevie Ray Vaughan, but he was probably best known for nurturing the talents of Bob Dylan and Bruce Springsteen, although in both cases he was heavily criticized among his colleagues at Columbia (CBS) Records when they failed to hit an instant seam of gold.

Hammond's first sessions as a producer in the 1930s involved work with Bessie Smith and Billie Holiday, as well as Benny Goodman, Count Basie, Lester Young and other notable jazz stars. His other achievements included organizing the celebrated *Spirituals To Swing* concerts at New York's Carnegie Hall in 1938 and 1939 and casting the all-black *Carmen Jones* musical. Returning to Columbia after spells with other labels, he signed Pete Seeger, Aretha Franklin, George Benson and Leonard Cohen.

His son John Hammond Jr remains a highly rated and successful country performer.

The ultimate talent scout John Hammond

ARRIVALS

1937 – Sandy Stewart
(Sandra Ester Galitz)
1941 – Ian Whitcomb
1943 – Jerry Miller
(Moby Grape)
1944 – Beaky
(John Dymond)
(Dave Dee, Dozy,
Beaky, Mick and Tich)
1947 – Arlo Guthrie
1948 – Ronnie James Dio
(Rainbow/Black Sabbath)
1949 – Dave Smalley
(Raspberries)
1953 – Rik Emmett
(Triumph)
1954 – Neil Tennant
(Pet Shop Boys)
1957 – Derry Grehan
(Honeymoon Suite)

★ ★ ★

DEPARTURE LOUNGE

1941 – Jelly Roll Morton
1987 – John Hammond Snr

RAVINGS

1964
200,000 people packed the route taken by The Beatles to a civic reception in Liverpool.

★ ★ ★

1968
The Nice were banned from playing at London's Royal Albert Hall after burning an American flag on stage.

★ ★ ★

1977
Elijah Blue Allman was born. His parents were Gregg Allman and Cher.

★ ★ ★

1983
Bon Jovi signed to Mercury and The Smiths to Rough Trade.

★ ★ ★

DAVID'S DIAMOND DOGS – LIVE IN PHILADELPHIA

1974

David Bowie played a week of live dates at the Tower Theatre in Philadelphia promoting his first American Top 10 album, *Diamond Dogs*. The album included the tracks 'Big Brother' and '1984' (inspired by the George Orwell novel) and the single 'Rebel Rebel'. Several of the highly choreographed and theatrical shows were recorded and resulted in his *David Live* album released later in the year.

The album peaked at No. 2 in Britain behind The Bay City Rollers' *Rollin'*, a significant achievement - as live albums rarely repeat the successes of their studio counterparts, and it became his second Top 10 hit in America.

There had been plans to release a live album of Bowie's earlier equally theatrical *Ziggy Stardust* shows, but it was felt that the recordings made in New York and California in 1972 and at Hammersmith in July 1973 (where he announced his decision to retire the stage persona of Ziggy) would need considerable studio polishing before they were considered worthy of release by his record company.

With a new band, including guitarist Earl Slick, keyboard players Mike Garson and Michael Kamen, David Sanborn (saxophone), Herbie Flowers (bass), Aynsley Dunbar (drums) and others, and with Tony Visconti producing, two shows from this season in Philapdelphia were recorded, although the backing band refused to play unless their fees were increased to reflect the fact that an album was being recorded rather than simply playing a straightforward concert.

1962

PICTURES OVER THE POND

With the first transatlantic satellite broadcast having taken place, British record producer Joe Meek, who made many hits from a recording studio above a shop in North London's Holloway Road, was inspired to write a tune commemorating the achievement. To record it he recruited a group of session musicians who he had used to back artists such as John Leyton and Michael Cox on record, and who also worked on stage with Billy Fury.

Christened The Tornados, the group were seen by Meek as rivals to The Shadows, but with an organ-based sound played by Roger LaVern rather than the Hank Marvin-dominated guitar attack of Cliff Richard's backing group.

Heinz Burt - bass player for Tornados

'Telstar', Meek's tune, was an instant hit, topping the UK singles chart for five weeks in the autumn of 1962, and at the end of the year also topping the US singles chart for three weeks. The Tornados thus became the first British group to reach No. 1 in the USA. They failed to approach that success again, however, although Meek produced other chart-toppers, such as John Leyton's 'Johnny Remember Me' in 1961 and 'Have I The Right' by The Honeycombs in 1964.

Meek, who was an avid fan of Buddy Holly, committed suicide on the eighth anniversary of Holly's death – February 3, 1967. He is remembered as the first successful independent record producer in Britain.

1962

RUST NEVER SLEEPS EVEN IN HOLLYWOOD

Neil Young's feature film *Rust Never Sleeps* was premiered in Los Angeles. Directed by Young himself under the name of Bernard Shakey, it featured Young's longtime backing group, Crazy Horse, and included a song titled 'Hey Hey My My (Into The Black)', which was released as a single and whose lyrics reflected the *Rust Never Sleeps* title – it was also the title of a simultaneously released album. With a stage set composed of giant speaker cabinets and a mysterious group of 'road-eyes' (whose eyes shone through the all-pervading gloom of the hardly illuminated stage), the film became something of a cult item.

Among the musicians who formed this version of Crazy Horse were Nils Lofgren on guitar and bass player Bruce Palmer, a fellow Canadian who had also worked with Young in Buffalo Springfield during the 1960s.

RAVINGS

1959
Joan Baez made her first recording, a duet with Bob Gibson at Newport Folk Festival.

★ ★ ★

1966
The Spencer Davis Group and Dave Berry began filming the non-Oscar winning movie *The Ghost Goes Gear*.

1967
Kenny Rogers formed his group, The First Edition.

1969
David Bowie first released 'Space Oddity', which excited little interest.

★ ★ ★

ARRIVALS

1916 – Bill Snyder
1931 – Tab Hunter
(Arthur Gellen)
1931 – Thurston Harris
1938 – Terry Garthwaite
(Joy Of Cooking)
1944 – Commander Cody
(George Frayne)

1947 – Jeff Hanna
(Nitty Gritty Dirt Band)
1951 – Bonnie Pointer
(Pointer Sisters)
1953 – Peter Brown
1957 – Pete Murphy
(Bauhaus)
1959 – Suzanne Vega
1960 – Richie Sambora
(Bon Jovi)

1966 – Mel Appleby
(Mel and Kim)

★ ★ ★

DEPARTURE LOUNGE

1937 George Gershwin

★ ★ ★

SUN SIGNS TRUCK DRIVER

1954

Sam Phillips, owner of the Memphis Recording Service, 706 Union Avenue, Memphis, Tennessee, signed a 19-year-old employee of the Crown Electric Company, truck driver Elvis Presley, to a recording contract.

Almost exactly a year earlier, Presley had gone to the Union Avenue studio to make a private recording, for which he paid $4 (£2). Marion Keisker, who worked for Sam Phillips and had been operating the recording equipment when Presley came to the studio, felt that there was something unique about the young man's voice, and had taped part of his recordings of 'My Happiness' and 'That's When Your Heartaches Begin' to play to her boss.

Phillips apparently showed little interest at the time, but when Presley returned to the studio in early January 1954, Keisker made sure that she took his address and telephone number, so that he could be contacted if an opportunity arose for a formal recording session. From time to time Phillips would be sent songs that needed a vocalist to make test recordings, after which they could be sent to established stars who might record them, and this is exactly what happened. Phillips was sent a song and needed a vocalist, whereupon Keisker reminded him of the young truck driver. After a few practice sessions with guitarist Scotty Moore and bass player Bill Black, Phillips felt that he could risk trying a proper recording. The trio ran through a ballad, 'I Love You Because', but it was fairly routine. Then the recording equipment needed reloading, and Presley began an uptempo version of a song by bluesman Arthur 'Big Boy' Crudup, and Moore and Black joined in. It was exactly what Phillips had been searching for – a white man who sounded black. The world would reverberate to his discovery, and a week later he signed Presley to his label, Sun Records.

Just A Boy - Elvis Presley

RAVINGS

1964
The Rollin' Stones (sic) played their first gig at London's Marquee Club with a line-up of Mick Jagger, Keith Richards, Elno Lewis (aka Brian Jones), Dick Taylor and Mick Avory.

1968
Mickey Dolenz of the Monkees married Samantha Juste, the English girl whom he had met when she appeared on a British TV show, at the house they shared in Laurel Canyon, Los Angeles.

1977
Thin Lizzy topped the bill at Reading Rock Festival in England.

★ ★ ★

ARRIVALS

1895 – Oscar Hammerstein
1938 – Bill Cosby
1942 – Steve Young
1942 – Swamp Dogg (Jerry Williams Jr)
1943 – Christine McVie (Christine Perfect) (Chicken Shack/Fleetwood Mac)
1945 – Butch Hancock
1946 – Jeff Christie (Christie)
1949 – John Wetton (Family/King Crimson/Uriah Heep/Roxy Music)
1950 – Eric Carr (Kiss)
1952 – Liz Mitchell (Boney M)

★ ★ ★

DEPARTURE LOUNGE

1979 – Minnie Ripperton
1983 – Chris Wood (Traffic)

WORLD TUNES INTO GELDOF'S GLOBAL JUKEBOX

1985

Fighting famine - Geldof's miracle

The statistics alone made *Live Aid* – the international music festival staged to raise relief funds for the starving people of Ethiopia – an absolutely incrdible concept. Two massive open-air arenas, Wembley Stadium in London and JFK Stadium in Philadelphia, had to be transformed almost overnight into concert auditoria containing enough state-of-the-art equipment to ensure a trouble-free worldwide link-up via satellite for 18 consecutive hours.

International superstars who would normally charge a king's ransom merely for appearing (let alone playing) contributed their time, their talent, their support team and pieces of equipment for free. Stage crews, limousine rental firms, trucking companies and others did the same, working until they dropped to ensure it all worked.

Credit for the whole miracle has to go to Bob Geldof, leader of the then fast-fading Boomtown Rats. His dream, born out of a BBC TV newscast from Ethiopia, galvanized him into action, first with the chart-topping Band Aid single, 'Do They Know It's Christmas' in 1984. Starring a host of big names, it sold well over three million copies in Britain alone becoming the biggest selling single in British pop history and raising several million dollars. It inspired Harry Belafonte to lobby American stars for a similar project, 'We Are The World', by USA For Africa, which further swelled the coffers by selling over four million copies in America.

When Geldof tabled the notion of a live event and indicated the scale he envisaged, many felt he had exceeded the bounds of possibility. Fortunately, they were wrong, and with the help of British promoters Harvey Goldsmith and Maurice Jones, and with assistance in the USA from Bill Graham and Larry Magid, *Live Aid* became reality. The London line-up included a re-formed Who, David Bowie (who also recorded a special duet with Mick Jagger of 'Dancing In The Street', which was shown on video), George Michael, Paul McCartney, Queen, Status Quo, U2 and many more big names. In Philadelphia, Lionel Richie rubbed shoulders with Madonna, Prince, Michael Jackson, Tina Turner, Mick Jagger, Hall and Oates and Dionne Warwick to create an unforgettable day. Phil Collins played at both Wembley and Philadelphia thanks to Concorde, and millions of pounds were raised by pledges from the billions watching on television all over the world.

Geldof later received a well deserved honorary knighthood.

BYRD KILLED BY DRUNK DRIVER

1973

Clarence White, lead guitarist with The Byrds, was killed when he was hit by a car while loading equipment into a van after playing a date in California with The Kentucky Colonels, the band he led with his brother, Roland, after Roger McGuinn had disbanded The Byrds earlier in the year. The driver who killed White was inebriated.

After his funeral, attended by other erstwhile members of The Byrds, Gram Parsons and his tour manager, Phil Kaufman, spent the evening drowning their sorrows, and it was on this occasion, according to several sources, that Parsons and Kaufman made a pact that whichever of them died would be cremated by the survivor in the desert.

This would be Kaufman's defence later in the year when Gram Parsons died in mysterious circumstances, Kaufman diverted the coffin containing Parsons's body and attempted to incinerate it near the Joshua Tree National Monument. As his story could not be proved false, he was fined for making the coffin unusable.

Clarence - victim of alcohol

ARRIVALS	
1912 – Woody Guthrie (Woodrow Wilson Guthrie)	1954 – Chris Cross (Chris Allen) (Ultravox)
1933 – Del Reeves	★ ★ ★
1938 – Bob Scholl (Mellow Kings)	DEPARTURE LOUNGE
1939 – Vince Taylor	1973 – Clarence White

END OF EVERLY ERA

1973

Don (left) and Phil - a duo dead for a decade?

At John Wayne Theatre, Bueno Park, California, Phil Everly threw his guitar on the ground and walked off stage. His brother Don continued with a solo set and told the audience, 'The Everly Brothers have already been dead for ten years'. It was the almost inevitable culmination of sibling rivalry from brothers who had been forced together for most of their lives. Now in their mid-thirties and without a hit in America for six years, the stresses of drugs, divorce and impending obscurity had finally boiled over into open warfare.

The solo careers that ensued were, if anything, even less of a success, though both brothers released albums that were artistically excellent. Phil's *Star Spangled Springer* included a song entitled 'The Air That I Breathe', written by Englishman Albert Hammond; the song was covered by The Hollies, whose version reached the Top 10 on both sides of the Atlantic. Don's *Sunset Towers* featured backing by British group Heads, Hands and Feet (with guitarist Albert Lee). Phil's 1983 duet with Cliff Richard, 'She Means Nothing To Me' (with Mark Knopfler playing guitar) briefly restored him to the UK Top 10, but the real event was the statement in mid 1983 that the duo would reform.

ELVIS DEBUTS ATTRACTIONS

1977

Penzance in Cornwall was the unlikely choice for the first live show by Elvis Costello and his recently recruited band, The Attractions. With a rhythm section of two unrelated musicians named Thomas – Bruce Thomas (ex- Sutherland Brothers, Quiver) on bass and drummer Pete Thomas (ex-Chilli Willi and The Red Hot Peppers) – and an ex-music student known as Steve Naive on keyboards, The Attractions were swiftly acclaimed as a highly reliable combo.

> ### RAVINGS
>
> ***1980***
> Allen Klein, who managed both The Beatles and The Rolling Stones, began serving a two-month prison sentence for falsifying an income tax return.

1952

GOLD FOR GLADYS

Eight-year-old Gladys Knight from Atlanta, Georgia, won a $2000 (£1000) prize and a gold cup for her inspired rendition of the appropriately titled 'Too Young' on US TV's *Ted Mack's Amateur Hour*. It would be the first of many awards and tributes that Knight would accumulate in a career that began in 1961, and shows little sign of ending at the time of writing 32 years later.

RAVINGS

1955
Alma Cogan, 'the girl with the giggle in her voice', reached the top of the UK chart for the first and only time with 'Dreamboat'.

★ ★ ★

1958
The Ash Grove, a noted folk venue, opened on Melrose Avenue, Los Angeles.

★ ★ ★

1969
Folk singer Judy Collins appeared in a production of *Peer Gynt* at New York's Shakespeare Festival.

★ ★ ★

1988
Simply Red's 'If You Don't Know Me By Now' became their second single to top the US chart.

★ ★ ★

Even before her television triumph, Knight had sung all over America's Deep South with the Morris Brown Choir, following in the footsteps of her parents, who were members of the Wings Over Jordan gospel group. At her brother Merald's tenth birthday party in 1952, he, Gladys and their sister Brenda began singing with their cousins William and Eleanor Guest. They continued working together, and took the name The Pips, making their first record in 1957, when Gladys was 13. It was not a hit, and by the end of the decade, Brenda and Eleanor had left the group, and been replaced by two male singers, including Edward Patten.

In 1960 the group recorded a song written by Johnny Otis, 'Every Beat Of My Heart', and although it was not an instant hit, it created enough interest for it to be sold to a bigger label,

Soul stylist supreme, Gladys Knight - a long and successful career

while the group also signed to a third label, for whom they re-recorded the song. Both the original and the re-recorded versions reached the US chart, and eventually the first version reached the Top 10 of the US pop chart and topped the US R & B chart just after Gladys celebrated her 17th birthday.

A follow-up single, 'Letter Full Of Tears', also reached the Top 20 of the US pop chart, but little of note occurred for the group, now known as Gladys Knight and The Pips, until 1967, when they signed with Soul Records, a Motown subsidiary, for whom they recorded the original version of 'I Heard It Through The Grapevine', which sold a million copies in reaching No. 2 in the US. The song was also recorded in 1968 by Marvin Gaye, whose version topped both the British and American charts.

ARRIVALS

1915 – Guy James Willis (Willis Brothers)
1940 – Johnny Sea (John Seay)
1940 – Tommy Dee
1944 – Millie Jackson
1945 – Peter Lewis (Moby Grape)

1946 – Linda Ronstadt
1948 – Artimus Pyle (Lynyrd Skynyrd/Atlanta Rhythm Section)
1948 – Ian Campbell (Middle Of The Road)
1949 – Trevor Horn
1950 – Geoffrey Richardson (Caravan/Penguin Cafe Orchestra)
1952 – David Pack

(Ambrosia)
1953 – Alicia Bridges
1956 – Ian Curtis (Joy Division)

★ ★ ★

DEPARTURE LOUNGE

1982 – Bill Justis
1990 – Bobby Day

1981

'W-O-L-D' CHAPIN IN DEATH CRASH

Harry Chapin - much missed by fans

Singer/songwriter Harry Chapin died when a tractor ran into his car on a freeway in New York, exploding the petrol tank. An autopsy found that Chapin, who was 38, had suffered a heart attack, although it was not able to say whether it was as a result of the collision or had been its cause.

After a successful early career in film, he returned to music in the early 1970s. He and his brothers with Carly and Lucy Simon had worked briefly during the Sixties as an informal folk group called The Brothers and Sisters, but he had not embarked on a full-time career as a singer until he formed a group that included cellist Tim Scott. Chapin's first album, *Heads and Tales* included the semi-autobiographical 'Taxi', a US Top 30 single, but his biggest successes came with 1974's 'W-O-L-D', the story of a washed-up disc jockey, a Top 40 single on both sides of the Atlantic, and his US chart-topping 'Cat's In The Cradle', also from 1974, which was based on a poem written by his wife about the young never having time to spend with their parents.

1972

SMOKEY SPLITS

Smokey - going solo

William 'Smokey' Robinson, founder and leader of The Miracles, played the final date of a six-month farewell tour, after which he left the group to embark on a solo career. Formed as The Matadors in 1954 by Robinson and teenage school friends, the group became The Miracles in the mid-1950s when Claudette Rogers, sister of group member Bobby Rogers, joined. Claudette and Smokey married in 1959.

The Miracles scored their first minor US hit in 1959 with 'Bad Girl' (leased by Gordy to the Chess label, as Motown had yet to become a fully fledged record company), and their first million-seller, 'Shop Around', followed in 1961. Another major success came with 'You've Really Got A Hold On Me', a US Top 5 hit that was covered by The Beatles on their second album, *With The Beatles*, but perhaps the group's best-loved song is the 1965 classic, 'The Tracks Of My Tears'.

In 1970, 'The Tears Of A Clown' was an international No. 1 hit but Robinson had to wait another 11 years until he was able to top the UK chart again in 1981 with 'Being With You'.

1946

CLARK TV DEBUT AT 13

Child star Petula Clark made her first appearance on British television in a series called *Cabaret*. Aged 13, she was already a star on radio, having sung on well over 100 shows, and was also contracted to the Rank Organisation to make films, her first, *Murder In Reverse*, when she was only ten years old.

Her first single, 'Put Your Shoes On Lucy', was released in 1949 (three years before the first British chart), and her first hit, 'The Little Shoemaker', made the UK Top 10 in 1954. Hit singles followed with some consistency until 1958, when she spent almost three years establishing herself in the French entertainment industry, meeting her husband, Claude Wolff, at a recording session in Paris. 1961 brought her first UK No.1, 'Sailor', while the same year also brought her her first million-seller, 'Romeo', which reached the UK

Top 3. In 1962 came two more million-sellers, 'Monsieur' (which failed to reach the UK chart) and 'Chariot' (only released as a B-side in Britain).

By this time living in France, she was known as Petu LaClark, and her biggest international success came with 1964's 'Downtown', written by Tony Hatch, which topped the US singles chart and became her fourth million-seller and won a Grammy Award for Best Rock 'n' Roll recording. In 1965, she returned to the top of the US chart with 'My Love', and in 1967 released her

Petula Clark, child star becomes grown-up pop star

second UK No.1, 'This Is My Song'.

Clark continued to appear in the charts on both sides of the Atlantic until 1972, when she began to devote more time to her family (having been a star for

three-quarters of her life). In 1983 she returned to the US chart with 'Natural Love', and in 1988 an updated dance version of her 1964 hit, released as 'Downtown '88', saw her back in the UK Top 10.

1968

LONDON SUBMARINE CARTOON LAUNCH

His colleagues inspect cardboard John Lennon

Yellow Submarine, the animated feature film that starred cartoons of The Beatles, was premiered at the London Pavilion cinema in Piccadilly Circus (where the group's first film, *A Hard Day's Night*, had also premiered four years earlier). The Beatles made a cameo appearance at the film's end but did not supply their own voices for the characters.

MARLEY LIVELIES UP LYCEUM

1975

Bob Marley and The Wailers recorded *Live!*, an in-concert album, at the Lyceum Ballroom in London. It was the prelude to the group's swift rise to prominence and Marley's own personal superstardom in the latter half of the decade.

Live! followed Marley's UK chart breakthrough, *Natty Dread*, which made its debut after the media explosion resulting from the Lyceum show. The Wailers by this time included the solidly reliable rhythm section of the Barrett brothers, Aston (nicknamed 'Family Man', as he had fathered many children) on bass, and Carlton on drums. At this point American/Jamaican lead guitarist Al Anderson was also a Wailer, as was keyboard player Bernard 'Touter' Harvey, while the always appropriate I-Threes (Marcia Griffiths, Rita Marley – Bob's wife – and Judy Mowatt) added perfect backing vocals as well as providing visual contrast with the dreadlocked instrumentalists, who were augmented by percussionist Alvin 'Seeco' Patterson.

The album was preceded by the single 'No Woman, No Cry', which became Marley's first UK hit. When it was reissued in 1981, two months after Marley's death, it reached the Top 10 of the singles chart, while the live album also returned to the chart at the same time. Marley's next album, *Rastaman Vibration*, released in 1976, was his first to reach the Top 20, and its successor, *Exodus*, was his Top 10 debut in 1977. His greatest album success, however, came in 1984 with the million-selling *Legend*, a greatest hits compilation.

Bob Marley, reggae's first and only superstar

STARSHIP CREW RETURN TO 'PLANE

1989

Paul Kantner, one of the founder members of San Franciscan psychedelic pioneers Jefferson Airplane, re-formed the original band with other early members, including Marty Balin, Jorma Kaukonen and Jack Casady, as well as vocalist Grace Slick.

This was the culmination of a 'musical chairs' act of alarming proportions. Kaukonen and Casady had worked as Hot Tuna since 1970 and, unlike the others, had not been involved in Jefferson Starship, the splinter group that effectively ended Jefferson Airplane in 1974. Balin, Kantner and Slick had all left Jefferson Starship, but Slick had rejoined, and was a member when the band abbreviated its name to simply Starship in 1985, when Kantner left. It was this line up that had been most successful, scoring a trio of American No. 1s with 'We Built This City', 'Sara' and 'Nothing's Gonna Stop Us Now'.

BIRMINGHAM BEATSTERS CALL IT A DAY

1969

The Spencer Davis Group, which first brought Steve Winwood to fame, played hits like 'Keep On Running' for the last time as Davis decided to split up the band and continue as a solo artist.

Spencer Davis (fourth from left) pictured with a late line-up of his group

The band was formed in 1963 by Welsh-born singer/guitarist Davis, a student at Birmingham University, with the Winwood brothers (singer/guitarist and keyboard player Steve, who was then only 15 years old, and bass player Mervyn, nicknamed 'Muff') and drummer Pete York, who all worked at a local pub, The Golden Eagle.

In 1964 the group was spotted by Island Records founder Chris Blackwell, who signed them, and their first hit, 'I Can't Stand It', came at the end of that year.

The group's major breakthrough came in 1966, when 'Keep On Running' topped the UK chart. The song was written by Jamaican Jackie Edwaards, another Blackwell discovery, who also wrote the group's follow-up hit, 'Somebody Help Me', which was their second chart-topper. The end of that year saw a third US Top 3 single (in just over a year), 'Gimme Some Loving', written by Steve Winwood. After one more UK Top 10 hit, 'I'm A Man' (written by the younger Winwood and producer Jimmy Miller), in 1967, the Winwoods left the band, Muff to become a record producer – he produced the first album by Dire Straits – and Steve to form Traffic.

York remained with Davis, who recruited keyboard player Eddie Hardin and guitarist Phil Sawyer, but the magic had left with Steve Winwood whose vocals led the group to success.

Davis eventually went to work for Island Records, Muff Winwood joined Columbia (CBS) as A & R executive while Steve's solo career flourished with two US No. 1 singles: 'Higher Love' in 1986 and 'Roll With It' in 1988.

ROGERS TAKES RUBY TO THE COUNTRY

1969

Kenny Rogers and The First Edition first appeared in the US country chart with their international hit, 'Ruby, Don't Take Your Love To Town'. Although the group had scored US hits in 1968 – with 'Just Dropped In (To See What Condition My Condition Was In)' and in early 1969 with 'But You Know I Love You' – 'Ruby' not only became their biggest pop hit up to that point, but was also their first hit under the name of Kenny Rogers and The First Edition.

Kenny Rogers (second from left) with The First Edition

ARRIVALS

1926 – Sue Thompson (Eva Sue McKee)
1937 – George Hamilton IV
1938 – Vikki Carr (Florencia Bisenta de Castillas Martinez Cordona)
1944 – Clarence White
1946 – Allan Gorrie (Average White Band)
1947 – Bernie Leadon
1947 – Brian May
1948 – Keith Godchaux (Grateful Dead)
1952 – Allen Collins (Lynyrd Skynyrd)
1953 – Silver Pozzoli (Club House)

★ ★ ★

DEPARTURE LOUNGE

1975 – Lefty Frizzell

RAVINGS

1958
The manager of The Drifters, George Treadwell, sacked the entire group and hired the then hardly known Ben E. King and his group, The Five Crowns, as their replacements.

1976
Deep Purple announced they were finally splitting up.

1989
James Brown was moved from a minimum security prison to a medium security jail after large amounts of money were found in his cell.

★ ★ ★

1986

HAPPY BIRTHDAY, CARLOS

Noted guitarist Carlos Santana presided over a double celebration in San Francisco. On his 39th birthday he was the main attraction at a concert in which ex-members of Santana, the band he founded 20 years before, reunited on stage.

Santana himself was born in Mexico, growing up in Tijuana before moving to San Francisco, where he formed the Santana Blues Band in 1966 with keyboard player Gregg Rolie, bass player David Brown and others. In 1968 the band became simply Santana, and new recruits included Mike Shrieve (drums) and percussionists José 'Chepito' Areas and Mike Carabello. This sextet was the basic line-up for the group's eponymous debut album in 1969, although Santana himself first appeared on record earlier in that year.

Carlos Santana - a celebration

Following the success of the gold *Super Session* album featuring Al Kooper, Mike Bloomfield and Stephen Stills, Kooper and Bloomfield played for two nights in San Francisco with the intention of making a live album along the same lines. The first night's recording was straight-forward, but before the second show, the erratic Bloomfield had vanished, and Kooper invited Santana, a fast-rising local star, to guest. Thus the first album on which he played was *The Live Adventures Of Mike Bloomfield and Al Kooper*.

Later in 1969 the Santana group played the Woodstock Festival, becoming one of the event's unexpected sensations, the percussive attack of 'Soul Sacrifice' being one of the festival's highlights. The band had just signed with Columbia (CBS), and when their debut album was released, it went gold.

In 1971 Schon and Rolie left to form Journey, and well over fifty musicians played on Santana albums during the next two decades, while Carlos himself also made solo albums and recorded special projects with John McLaughlin, Alice Coltrane and Buddy Miles.

1968

GOLD BUTTERFLY IN GARDEN

Iron Butterfly, one of the first heavy metal bands, entered the US chart with their second album, *In-A-Gadda-Da-Vida*, which peaked in the Top 5 of that chart, selling over three million copies. The second side of the album was the 17-minute title track, which was the band's interpretation of 'In The Garden Of Eden', although some felt that this essentially peaceful place was a most inappropriate for a very loud band whose previous album was titled *Heavy*.

Iron Butterfly - heavy, hard and long

1959

BOBBY VEE DEBUTS WITH SUZY BABY

'Suzy Baby', the first single by Bobby Vee and The Shadows, a group from Fargo, North Dakota, fronted by Robert Velline, was released on the independent Soma label. Better known as Bobby Vee, Velline was starting a recording career that would blossom during the 1960s.

Bobby Vee - Holly replacement

The diminutive 15 year old's group played mainly instrumentals, but with a few covers of Buddy Holly songs, and when it was announced over a local radio station on February 3, 1959, that local musicians were needed to fill out the bill of the Winter Dance Party tour due to the plane crash that killed Buddy Holly, Richie Valens and The Big Bopper, The Shadows offered their services.

Later that year, the group travelled to Minneapolis in the neighbouring state of Minnesota to cut their first single, 'Suzy Baby', which was a local hit and interested Hollywood-based Liberty Records enough for them to purchase the recording and also sign Vee.

The summer of 1960 brought Vee his first US Top 10 hit, 'Devil Or Angel', a cover of the 1956 hit by black R & B group The Clovers, by which time the group had hired, and fired, a piano player named Bob Zimmerman. Calling himself Elston Gunn at the time, he left after two shows and moved to New York during the following year, where he renamed himself Bob Dylan. In retrospect, it seems unlikely that Dylan and Vee would have much in common musically.

Vee eventually accumulated over 30 hits during the 1960s, including such classic pop singles as 'Rubber Ball' (1960), 'Take Good Care Of My Baby' (US No. 1, 1961), 'Run To Him' (also 1961), 'The Night Has A Thousand Eyes' (1962) and 'Come Back When You Grow Up' (1967).

1977

RONSTADT TUMBLES WITH STONE

Linda Ronstadt joined Mick Jagger and the rest of The Rolling Stones on stage at a concert in Tucson, Arizona, where they duetted on 'Tumbling Dice', a 1972 hit for The Stones that Ronstadt had recorded on her platinum album *Simple Dreams* released the previous year. Her version of the song was no doubt designed to continue the purple patch that she had enjoyed since 1974 with revivals of oldies like 'You're No Good', 'When Will I Be Loved' and 'Heatwave' (all US Top 10 hits in 1975), 'That'll Be The Day' (in 1976) and 'Blue Bayou', 'It's So Easy' (in 1977), but her cover of 'Tumbling Dice' peaked outside the US Top 30.

Linda Ronstadt

ARRIVALS

1895 – Ken Maynard
1898 – Sara Carter (Sara Dougherty) (Carter Family)
1922 – Kay Starr
1942 – Kim Fowley
1946 – Barry Whitham (Herman's Hermits)
1947 – Cat Stephens (Stephen Demetri Georgiou)
1950 – Larry Tolbert (Raydio)
1958 – Henry Priestman (Christians)
1962 – Lee Aaron

★ ★ ★

DEPARTURE LOUNGE

1992 – Champion Jack Dupree

★ ★ ★

HAT-TRICK FOR CLIFF

1960

Not yet 20 years old, British pop sensation Cliff Richard took 'Please Don't Tease' to the top of the UK singles chart. It was his third No. 1 within a year, following 'Living Doll' in July 1959, and 'Travellin' Light' in October that year.

'Please Don't Tease', written by Bruce Welch, rhythm guitarist of The Shadows, Richard's backing band, with Peter Chester, son of comedian Charlie Chester, was the singer's twelfth hit single in less than two years since he first charted in the autumn of 1958 with 'Move It', a Top 3 hit.

That was followed at the end of that year by 'High Class Baby' (Top 10), and in 1959 came 'Livin' Lovin' Doll', 'Mean Streak' (Top 10) and 'Never Mind' before his first No. 1, 'Living Doll', which was written by songwriter Lionel Bart (who was responsible for the hugely successful musical *Oliver*) for

inclusion in *Serious Charge*, the first film in which Cliff appeared. Next came 'Travellin' Light', whose B-side, 'Dynamite', also reached the Top 20 in its own right. 1960 brought Richard's second movie, *Expresso Bongo*, from which an EP reached the Top 20, after which one of the tracks from the soundtrack EP, *A Voice In The Wilderness*, was released as a single and raeched the Top 3. Next came another Top 3 hit, 'Fall In Love With You', and that was followed by 'Please Don't Tease'.

Cliff - three Number Ones in a year

ARRIVALS

1874 – Obed 'Dad' Pickard (Pickard Family)
1924 – Margaret Whiting
1937 – Chuck Jackson
1940 – George Clinton (Parliament/Funkadelic)
1940 – Thomas Wayne (Thomas Perkins)
1944 – Estelle Bennett (Ronettes)
1944 – Richard Davies (Supertramp)
1945 – Bobby Sherman
1947 – Don Henley
1954 – Al DiMeola

★ ★ ★

BEATLE DRUG BUST

1972

As the second hit single by Wings, 'Mary Had A Little Lamb', left the UK Top 20, group leader Paul McCartney suffered another mishap when he and his wife, Linda, were arrested in Sweden for possession of drugs. This was not the last time McCartney would fall foul of the law in this respect – two months later he was arrested for the same offence at his farmhouse in Scotland (near the Mull Of Kintyre, which he immortalized in a 1977 single that topped the UK singles chart for nine weeks, but completely failed in the US, where it did not reach the Top 100). In March 1973 he was again arrested in Scotland, this time for growing marijuana.

Paul - three times loser

RAVINGS

1969
Aretha Franklin was arrested for causing a disturbance in a Detroit car park. After paying a $50 fine, she apparently ran over a road sign on her way back to the street.

1977
The independent label Stiff Records released *My Aim Is True*, the debut album by Elvis Costello.

1977
Tony Orlando announced his retirement from performing during a show by Dawn, the group he fronted. Other members of Dawn were surprised as he had not warned them of his intentions.

1984
Madonna's support act on a US tour was The Beastie Boys.

★ ★ ★

1979

DEAD KEYBOARD STIGMA?

The death of Grateful Dead keyboard player Keith Godchaux four days after his 32nd birthday as a result of injuries sustained in a car accident was the second chapter in a three part (so far) series of disasters afflicting those who played piano for the band.

Original ivory-tinkler Ron 'Pigpen' McKernan died in March 1973 of a stomach haemorrhage, reportedly caused by a surfeit of alcohol. He had been forced to rest and abandon live work during 1972 after serious liver damage was detected, and Godchaux was introduced, along with his vocalist wife, Donna, as his replacement. The Godchaux couple remained with the band until April 1979, when they were asked to leave due to differences of musical philosophy, and while Donna was not replaced, a new keyboard player was obviously necessary. The position was taken by Brent Mydland, who was also part of Bobby and The Midnights, the group led by Grateful Dead rhythm guitarist Bob Weir when he was free of commitments with the main group. Mydland had also played in Silver, a group that included Tom Leadon, brother of Eagles founder Bernie Leadon.

Mydland managed to survive until 1991, but died on July 26 that year from a drug overdose. He was temporarily replaced by singer/songwriter Bruce Hornsby, but the latter had a successful career of his own, and so in September 1991 Vince Welnick (ex-Tubes) joined the band.

1966

WHICH ONE'S DOZY?

Dave Dee (in driving seat) and Dozy, Beaky, Mick and Tich

Hitmaking group Dave Dee, Dozy, Beaky, Mick and Tich breakfasted with British Prime Minister Harold Wilson and his wife Mary, when they found themselves together on a train to Liverpool (where Wilson's Huyton constituency was located).

Wilson was not going to Merseyside only to meet his constituents, but to perform the re-opening ceremony at The Cavern Club, where The Beatles had played innumerable gigs before their breakthrough.

1977

ZEP DRUMMER CHARGED WITH ASSAULT

Led Zeppelin drummer John Bonham and the group's manager, Peter Grant, were charged with assault after a backstage fracas at Oakland Coliseum in California. Three employees of promoter Bill Graham brought the charges of battery and received an out-of-court settlement of around $2 million. It was a difficult time for the famous group – three days later, while on the same American tour, vocalist Robert Plant's son, Zarac, died of a respiratory ailment, after which the tour was abandoned and rumours of a break-up spread.

ARRIVALS

1935 – Cleveland Duncan (Penguins)
1942 – Madeline Bell
1943 – Tony Joe White
1945 – Dino Danelli (Young Rascals)
1946 – Andy Mackay (Roxy Music)
1947 – David Essex
1950 – Blair Thornton (Bachman Turner Overdrive)
1957 – Dennis Greaves (Nine Below Zero)
1961 – Martin Gore (Depeche Mode)
1964 – Tim Kellett (Simply Red)

★ ★ ★

DEPARTURE LOUNGE

1980 – Keith Godchaux
1985 – Kay Kyser

ELTON EVENTUALLY TAKES THE TOP SPOT IN BRITAIN

1976

Kiki Dee sings her chart-topping hit solo, cardboard Elton is silent

ARRIVALS

1917 – Robert Farnon
1935 – Les Reed
1941 – Barbara Jean Love
(Friends Of Distinction)
1942 – Heinz Burt
(Tornados)
1946 – Alan Whitehead
(Marmalade)
1950 – Chris Townson
(John's Children)
1951 – Lynval Golding
(Specials)
1958 – Mick Karn
(Anthony Michaelides)
(Japan)

★ ★ ★

DEPARTURE LOUNGE

1972 – Bobby Ramirez
(Edgar Winter's
White Trash)
1980 – Peter Sellers

★ ★ ★

Despite having been arguably the biggest solo artist in the world during the previous several years, Elton John had never succeeded in taking a single to the top of the UK charts. When his name did appear in that highly desirable No. 1 spot at last he had to share the limelight, with Kiki Dee (real name Pauline Matthews), with whom he duetted on a contagious love song, 'Don't Go Breaking My Heart', which topped the UK chart for six weeks, repeating the process in the US chart, although for only four weeks.

Like most of Elton's biggest hits (and all his earlier classics), the song was written by Elton with lyricist Bernie Taupin, using the pseudonyms Ann Orson and Carte Blanche (which might be pronounced as 'horse and cart' by unwary radio announcers). The hit was probably never performed live by the duo, although Elton sang it with Miss Piggy when he appeared on the televised *Muppet Show*, and Kiki sang it solo during a free concert in London's Hyde Park, with a mounted lifesize picture of Elton standing on stage beside her.

Kiki Dee had been highly regarded in British music circles since her emergence in the mid 1960s, but she had never reached the UK chart with a single until 1973, when she signed with Rocket Records, the label launched by Elton and his manager, John Reid. She quickly scored with a fine version of 'Amoureuse', a song written by French singer Veronique Sanson (who at one point was married to Stephen Stills). That single reached the Top 20, as did the raunchy 'I Got The Music In Me' in 1974, while a cover version of Nancy Wilson's 1964 US hit, '(You Don't Know) How Glad I Am' reached the Top 40 in 1975. The next year brought the release of the title track of her *Loving and Free* album as a single, with 'Amoureuse' as its flip side, and with the undoubted assistance of the chart-topping duet that was still in the UK chart at the time. 1977 brought a minor hit with 'First Thing In The Morning', after which came a Top 30 entry with 'Chicago', which was released as a double A-side with Elton John's 'Bite Your Lip (Get Up And Dance)'. After that, Dee moved to another label and did not chart again until 1981.

RAVINGS

1965
The Lovin' Spoonful played in Greenwich Village, New York, to an audience that included Phil Spector and Bob Dylan.

1967
All The Beatles, Brian Epstein and many others signed a petition in *The Times* calling for the legalization of marijuana.

★ ★ ★

DOWNEY DUO TOP US CHART

1970

Richard and Karen Carpenter, the brother and sister from the Los Angeles suburb of Downey, topped the US singles chart with their version of the Burt Bacharach and Hal David song '(They Long To Be) Close To You', which became their first disc to sell a million copies.

The Carpenters

Richard Carpenter, a talented pianist and student of popular music, formed a jazz trio with fellow student Wes Jacobs on bass and 17-year-old Karen on drums in 1967. When Jacobs left to go to college, Richard and Karen joined a sextet called Spectrum, which played for visitors at Disneyland, and when the group broke up, the siblings worked on creating multi-layered harmonies. A tape of their demos found its way to Herb Alpert at A & M Records, who signed them in 1969.

Their first album, *Offering*, was commercially ignored, but their inspired revival of 'Close To You', a little-known song that had been recorded by Dionne Warwick but ignored by the public, was a smash hit, launching a career that produced two dozen hit singles by the end of the 1970s. Among their biggest hits were 'We've Only Just Begun' (1970), 'For All We Know', 'Rainy Days And Mondays' and 'Superstar' (all Top 3 hits in 1971), 'Hurting Each Other' and 'Goodbye To Love' (1972), 'Sing', 'Yesterday Once More' and their second No. 1, 'Top Of The World' (1973), 'Please Mr Postman' (their third No. 1, 1974) and 'Only

Yesterday' (1975).

At that point The Carpenters entered a slump they found difficult to overcome and seemingly lost their appeal to American audiences. Their hits became smaller and they took a self-imposed rest until 1980 when they released the *Made In America* album, this coincided with Karen's growing obsession with her weight. Although she was far from fat, she developed anorexia nervosa, which eventually killed her in 1983 when she was only 32 years old. Her death was a tragedy that might have been avoided had her disease been taken more seriously.

1965

DYLAN SCORNED BY FOLKIES

Bob Dylan, the noted protest singer of the first half of the 1960s, was booed by the large audience at the Newport Folk Festival in Rhode Island. His desire to change, as evidenced by his use of Paul Butterfield's Blues Band as a backing group, was not appreciated by the traditionalists among the festival audience, who displayed their displeasure. One noted folk singer referred to Dylan as Judas.

Dylan - electric backing brings boos

1968

STONES IN RELIEF BOTHER – AGAIN

July seemed to be the month for The Rolling Stones to experience problems related to the exercise of bodily functions. July 1965 found them fined and headlined for answering the call of nature against a garage wall, and July 1968 brought another lavatorial landmark, this time relating to the sleeve of their *Beggar's Banquet* album. The group wanted to use a photograph of a toilet with graffiti on its walls, the graffiti featuring the track titles and credits, but both Decca (the group's British label) and London (their US counterpart) refused to countenance the idea, removing the album from its scheduled release date.

In retrospect, it is difficult to disagree with the decision – the album is widely regarded as one of the group's masterpieces, and the sleeve appeared to bear little relation to its contents. Eventually released at the end of the year in a sleeve that resembled an invitation to a function, the banquet of the title. The press launch in London at the Queensgate hotel was an actual banquet which degenerated into a custard pie fight between all those present.

The album included several notable songs, in particular 'Street Fighting Man', a song about rioting in public, and 'Sympathy For The Devil', which was presumed to be about racial prejudice. The controversy over the sleeve is also believed to have been the final straw that destroyed the already tense relationship between the group and Decca, the band's label since the start of their recording career, but whose traditionally minded chief executive, Sir Edward Lewis, saw eye to eye with Jagger and Co. increasingly rarely. In 1970, the group were on their way out to form their own label, but Decca reminded them that another track was contractually necessary before they could legally depart. The Stones delivered 'Cocksucker Blues', the tale of a rent boy, which Decca declined to release.

The Stones give a banquet for the press

ARRIVALS

1914 – Erskine Hawkins
1937 – Al Banks (Turbans)
1941 – Bobby Hebb
1941 – Neil Landon (Ivy League/Flowerpot Men/Fat Mattress)
1941 – Brenton Wood (Alfred Wood)
1942 – Dobie Gray
(Leonard Victor Ainsworth)
1943 – Mick Jagger
1949 – Roger Taylor
1950 – Duncan Mackay
1960 – Danny Stagg (Kingdom Come)
1961 – Andy Connell (Swing Out Sister)
1962 – Miranda Joyce (Belle Stars)

1968

GABRIEL'S HAMMER

Peter Gabriel's 'Sledgehammer' became his first US chart-topping single, there was no doubt that the success was aided by an inventive video clip, an alarmingly expensive and totally original concept that saw Gabriel's facial features changing into vegetables using a technique known as 'claymation' – all synchronized to the rhythm of the track. At the BRIT Awards in early 1987, Gabriel was voted Best British Male Artist, while the video clip inevitably won in its class.

LENNON'S GREEN GO-AHEAD

1976

John Lennon at Palm Beach

Three years and four months after he was ordered to leave the United States by Immigration Department officials, erstwhile Beatle John Lennon was finally granted a 'Green Card' allowing him to reside in the USA, where he had been living illegally since he and his second wife, Yoko Ono, were served with a deportation order in March 1972 and his appeal failed. This effectively prevented Lennon from leaving the States, as he would be unable to return (a similar problem apparently prevented Elvis Presley ever performing in Britain, as his manager, 'Colonel' Tom Parker, might be unable to return to the USA if he ever left).

Lennon had waged a campaign to acquire an alien residential permit, accusing the US Government of tapping his phone, and in late 1975 a New York court quashed the deportation order. Public sympathy favoured Lennon's case, as he was no longer involved in political upheaval as he had been when the deportation order was served. The grounds for his deportation were a conviction for using cannabis in 1978, but this was clearly not the over-riding reason for US authorities wishing to ban him from his New York home.

Among the witnesses who spoke on his behalf in court were noted novelist Norman Mailer and screen legend Gloria Swanson, both of whom testified to his excellent character. Had the evidence of such famous names been rejected, there could have been hell to pay from the media, and a judge approved Lennon's application for Green Card No. A17-597-321. As matters transpired, Lennon was no problem for four years, spending all his time overseeing the infancy of his second son, Sean.

Three months after he returned to public life, he was murdered – conspiracy theories have been suggested, but none proved.

1985

YOUNG HAPPY ABOUT DEPARTURE

British white soul vocalist Paul Young topped the US singles chart with his cover version of 'Every Time You Go Away', a song written by Daryl Hall (of Hall and Oates). Young had first emerged in Streetband, who scored a hit with 'Toast' in 1978 – the song was originally released as a B-side, but its unique novelty appeal forced it into the UK Top 20. In 1980, he began fronting a British soul band, Q-Tips, who were a major live attraction, but whose records were unfairly seen as ersatz. After the band fell apart in late 1982, Young went solo, topping the UK chart for three weeks in 1983 with a cover of an obscure Marvin Gaye track, 'Wherever I Lay My Hat (That's My Home)' and following it up with five consecutive Top 10 hits

Paul Young - US Number One

RAVINGS

1967
Britain's pirate radio stations were declared illegal, and BBC Radio One was launched

1976
In response to his manager, Mike Appel, informing Bruce Springsteen that he must not use erstwhile rock writer Jon Landau to produce his next album, Springsteen's lawyers issued counter writs on Appel alleging fraud and breach of trust

MASSIVE WATKINS GLEN CONCERT

1973

Organizers called it the biggest rock audience ever – 600,000 people turned up to an open air show at Watkins Glen racetrack in upstate New York for a *Summer Jam*, featuring The Allman Brothers Band, The Band and The Grateful Dead. Presumably most of the crowd were there due to the atmosphere of this gathering of the clans – it is difficult to believe that many of them could see the performers.

ARRIVALS

1938 – George Cummings (Dr Hook)
1940 – Phil Proctor (Firesign Theatre)
1943 – Michael Bloomfield
1945 – Rick Wright (Pink Floyd)
1946 – Jonathan Edwards
1949 – Peter Doyle (New Seekers)
1949 – Simon Kirke (Free/Bad Company)
1949 – Steve Peregrine Took (Tyrannosaurus Rex)
1951 – Gregg Guiffria (Angel)
1962 – Rachel Sweet
1965 – Tex Axile (Transvision Vamp)

★ ★ ★

MILLER'S GOLDEN EAGLE

1976

Fly Like An Eagle, the long-awaited follow-up to his gold 1973 album *The Joker*, gave Texan guitar star Steve Miller another gold record. Miller, who emerged to international fame from a base in San Francisco (where he had moved from Chicago), had been regaining his strength after touring for many months with *The Joker*, his eighth original album and his biggest by far. The title track, which topped the US chart in 1973 and the UK chart in 1990, was one of several songs that appeared to portray Miller in such roles as the 'Space Cowboy', the 'Gangster Of Love', and someone called Maurice. *The Joker* had captured the public imagination, as would several tracks on *Fly Like An Eagle*, including the spacey title track, the raunchy 'Rock'n Me' and the Bonnie and Clyde story told in 'Take The Money And Run' of Billie Joe and Bobbie Sue, two young lovers who did nothing but take drugs and watch television.

Steve 'Guitar' Miller

ELVIS – NOTHING DIRTY

1954

The first press interview by overnight sensation Elvis Presley was published. The *Memphis Press-Scimitar* attempted without much success to get the 19 year old to say something other than 'yes' or 'no'.

Fortunately, Sun Records employee Marion Keisker was more effusive in her answers. Presley's diffidence was probably explained by what took place a few days before, when Presley was requested to appear on *Red Hot And Blue*, the radio show hosted by Dewey Phillips on station WHBQ, Memphis. When Presley confided to the disc jockey that he knew nothing of interviews, Dewey Phillips warned him, 'Just don't say nothing dirty'.

Elvis Presley in the 1950s, a clean boy?

RAVINGS

1956
Gene Vincent appeared on the *Perry Como Show*, his first national exposure on American TV.

1965
Rolling Stone Charlie Watts purchased a 16th-century manor house in Sussex.

★ ★ ★

1970
Jimi Hendrix played his final gig in his home town of Seattle.

1980
The Dalmount Festival in Dublin featured headliners The Police and Squeeze. Further down the bill was a local group, U2. Their first single had been released in Britain several weeks earlier, but had failed to chart.

1974

MAMA'S FATAL LONDON TRIP

'Mama' Cass Elliot died in a London flat she was renting, from a heart attack apparently induced by choking on a ham sandwich, after which she inhaled her own vomit. (A similar accident apparently caused the death of Jimi Hendrix in 1970.)

Elliot, who could be said to have been built for comfort rather than for speed, had embarked on a solo career after The Mamas and Papas, the group that she helped to launch in 1965, had fallen apart when the personal relationship between 'Papa' John Phillips and his wife, 'Mama' Michelle, ended in 1968 (their daughter Chynna Phillips later became one-third of Wilson Phillips with Beach Boy Brian Wilson's daughters Carnie and Wendy).

Elliot avoided legal action instituted by Dunhill Records, the group's label, against John and Michelle Phillips and Denny Doherty by immediately signing a solo recording deal, releasing her first album at the end of 1968, quickly reaching the Top 20 on both sides of the Atlantic with 'Dream A Little Dream Of Me', which was in fact a recording by the group on which she sang lead. Her biggest subsequent hit came in August, 1969, with 'It's Getting Better',

which was her only UK Top 10 hit and her final single to reach the US Top 30. While five of her albums made the US chart between 1968 and 1971, none was a major success, the biggest being the shortlived collaboration with Dave Mason, ex-Traffic, in 1971. At the end of that year, in order to avoid further legal problems, the original quartet re-formed The Mamas and Papas for *People Like Us*, which was clearly an album made to fulfil contractual obligations.

Mama Cass - sandwich tragedy

1966

DYLAN'S BAD BIKE CRASH

Bob Dylan suffered neck injuries in a serious motorcycle accident that took place near his home in Woodstock, New York state. This followed a British tour on which Dylan was backed by The Band – their concert at London's Royal Albert Hall was later released as a bootleg known as *Great White Wonder*.

Dylan did very little work until he had completely recovered from his injuries, eventually starting to record new tracks with The Band in their Woodstock house, Big Pink. The Band's first album, released in 1968,

Bob Dylan - neck injuries

was titled *Music From Big Pink*, and included several previously unreleased Dylan songs. In 1975, eight years after

they were recorded, the recordings made by Dylan and The Band were finally released as *The Basement Tapes*.

1968

BEATLE BOUTIQUE CLOSES

The Apple boutique opened by Apple Corps, the company formed by The Beatles in the wake of the death of their manager, Brian Epstein, closed its doors and gave away all its remaining stock.

The boutique had opened in December 1967 at 94 Baker Street, in London's West End.

The Apple boutique

A huge mural decorated one of its outside walls, and was the work of three members of a Dutch artists' co-operative known as The Fool, who had previously applied their talents to John Lennon's Rolls Royce. The trio were also involved in creating designs for merchandise that could be sold in the boutique.

Unfortunately, too little attention was paid to security and much of the merchandise that was on sale was stolen, while whatever did reach the till was also severely depleted to the point where the shop had become a bottomless pit that was consuming Apple's money at a much faster rate than it was being accumulated. The Beatles had no real alternative but to close it down only seven months after it had opened.

1986

DENVER DUMPED

Multi-million selling singer/songwriter John Denver's contract with RCA Records was not renewed. Since 1971, Denver (real name John Deutschendorf) had been one of the most profitable acts on the company's artist roster, but after RCA's sale to General Electric, a major producer of military equipment, the new management were believed to have taken exception to a single by Denver titled 'Let Us Begin (What Are We Making Weapons For?)', an anti-war duet with Russian singer Alexander Gradsky.

Denver's previous career had been an almost continuous catalogue of success, with four singles that topped the US chart: 'Sunshine On My Shoulders' and 'Annie's Song' (both 1974) and 'Thank God I'm A Country Boy' and 'I'm Sorry' (both 1975), plus three No. 1 albums: *Greatest Hits* (1973), *Back Home Again* (1974) and *Windsong* (1975), among twelve gold and four platinum LPs. However, Denver had ambitions in other fields and gave the impression of being too successful, which explained the media sniggers in 1983 when he and his wife Ann (the subject of 'Annie's Song') began divorce proceedings.

John Denver

1981

BLONDIE SOLO SURPRISE

Debbie Harry, lead singer and focal point with Blondie, the New York New Wave group that had been among the most popular acts in the world at the end of the 1970s, released a solo album, *Koo Koo*, produced by Nile Rodgers and Bernard Edwards (of Chic).

Generally viewed as somewhat disappointing compared to notable Blondie albums such as 1978's *Parallel Lines* or 1979's *Eat To The Beat*, it also featured a sleeve picture of Harry with long needles penetrating her cheeks, which many found upsetting and unpleasant. After *Koo Koo*, Blondie re-formed for a final album, *The Hunter*, which was considerably less successful than its immediate predecessor, *Autoamerican*, which topped the album charts of both Britain and the USA. After the comparative failure of *The Hunter*, the group broke up – rhythm guitarist Frank 'The Freak' Infante had sued the rest of the group at the start of 1982, claiming he was not included in decision-

Harry - solo with needles

making meetings. He won his case and out-of-court damages, but the writing was on the wall.

Harry's paramour, guitarist Chris Stein, launched his own label, Animal Records, signing such acts as Iggy Pop, but became seriously ill

and was nursed back to health by Harry. In 1983, she played the part of a female wrestler in *Teaneck Tanzi* in a New York theatre, but it closed ignominiously after a single performance (in contrast to the British stage

version, *Trafford Tanzi*, in which Toyah starred), after which she virtually retired for two years before returning with a second solo album, *Rockbird*, which included a UK Top 10 single, 'French Kissin' (In The USA)'.

1980

PAPA JOHN BUSTED FOR DEALING

John Phillips, erstwhile leader of the highly successful Mamas and Papas in the 1960s, had fallen into drug addiction, and was finally apprehended by FBI narcotics agents in possession of cocaine. He was sentenced to five years in prison, but this sentence was latter commuted to 250 hours community service – giving anti-drug lectures.

John Phillips

ARRIVALS

1932 – Morey Carr (Playmates)
1937 – Bonnie Brown (The Browns)
1942 – Daniel Boone (Peter Lee Sterling)
1943 – Lobo (Kent Lavoie)
1946 – Gary Lewis
1946 – Bob Welch, (Fleetwood Mac)
1947 – Karl Green (Herman's Hermits)
1951 – Carlo Karges (Nena)
1953 – Hugh MacDowell (Wizzard/ELO)
1957 – Daniel Ash (Bauhaus)
1958 – Bill Perry (REM)
1960 – Malcolm Ross (Aztec Camera)
1963 – Norman Cook (Housemartins)

★ ★ ★

DEPARTURE LOUNGE

1964 – Jim Reeves

★ ★ ★

1971

DYLAN AND CLAPTON HELP GEORGE'S BANGLADESH SHOWS

(left to right) George Harrison, Bob Dylan, Leon Russell

Bob Dylan and Eric Clapton were two of the numerous friends who donated their time and talent for two shows at New York's Madison Square Garden that had been organized by George Harrison and his one-time sitar teacher, Ravi Shankar, to raise money for the drought-stricken country of Bangladesh, formerly East Pakistan.

Also appearing in the shows, simply billed as *The Concert For Bangladesh*, were Ringo Starr, Billy Preston, Leon Russell and ex-Manfred Mann bass player Klaus Voorman. Apple Records group Badfinger were also in attendance along with a host of American session-playing luminaries, including Jesse Ed Davis, Don Nix, Jim Horn, Chuck Findley. Don Preston, Claudia Lennear and Carl Radle.

The shows began with Harrison and Shankar explaining why they had organized the event. Shankar, himself a Bengali, had outlined the tragic situation in his homeland to his former pupil while asking about fund-raising ideas. Stunned by what he heard, Harrison set the wheels in motion himself and put the event together in only five weeks.

After an opening set by Shankar and other Indian musicians, Harrison, Clapton, Starr and others took the stage for a set that included 'My Sweet Lord', 'That's The Way God Planned It', 'While My Guitar Gently Weeps', 'Jumpin' Jack Flash' and 'Here Comes The Sun'.

Bob Dylan's much-rumoured, but unconfirmed, arrival was greeted with a standing ovation, which he repaid with a fine set including classics like 'A Hard Rain's Gonna Fall', 'Blowin' In The Wind', 'Mr Tambourine Man' and 'Just Like A Woman'.

It was left to George Harrison to close proceedings (which raised $250,000 in ticket sales alone) with the haunting 'Bangladesh'. The shows were recorded and a triple-album boxed set, produced by Harrison and Phil Spector, was rush released by Apple Records to add further much-needed revenue to the relief fund.

1960

ARETHA GOES POP

Having previously recorded only gospel music, starting when she was 14 years old, Aretha Franklin made her first recordings of secular material under the guidance of Columbia (CBS) Records A & R man John Hammond. This new direction would not prove commercially successful, but opened the door for her to sign with Atlantic Records in the mid 1960s, where she became the queen of soul for several years.

Lady Soul - Aretha Franklin

PAPA JOHN DEMANDS $9 MILLION

1973

'Mama' Michelle Phillips

John Phillips, leader and founder of The Mamas and The Papas, filed a lawsuit on behalf of the group in the USA against Dunhill Records, the group's label during their glory days of the 1960s.

Asking for damages of $9 million, Phillips charged the label with 'systematic, cold-blooded theft of perhaps up to $60 million, stolen from each and every artist who recorded for it during a seven year period'. The label, unsurprisingly, denied the charges, which related to unpaid royalties.

It was a sad (although not untypical) sign-off for the group that broke up in 1968 after only four years together – a brief career that nevertheless was notable for a series of huge hits, including the US No. 1 'Monday Monday', that swiftly became rock standards and remain firm favourites on 'Gold' (oldie) radio.

Apart from their numerous hit singles and albums, John Phillips was also one of the guiding lights behind the Monterey Pop Festival in 1967, which saw the emergence of a number of major stars to the international stage, including Jimi Hendrix, Janis Joplin, Otis Redding, Canned Heat and others.

RAVINGS		
	Searchers their first UK No. 1 hit. ★ ★ ★	had played a pre-fame apprenticeship. ★ ★ ★
1963 'Sweets For My Sweet', a cover of the 1961 US Top 20 hit by The Drifters, gave Merseybeat group The	**1964** Ray Charles performed at Hamburg's Star Club, where The Beatles	**1977** The Who purchased Shepperton Film Studios for £350,000 ($500,000).

HORNSBY LIFT-OFF

1986

The Way It Is', the first UK single released by Bruce Hornsby and The Range, entered the UK chart. It was the culmination of several years of dues-paying by keyboard playing singer/songwriter Hornsby, an erstwhile student at Boston's Berklee School of Music, who also spent three years signed as a songwriter to the music publishing arm of 20th Century Records, and had worked as a member of Sheena Easton's backing band.

Bruce Hornsby

ARRIVALS		
	(Doris Coley) (Shirelles)	(Patty Kotero)
1935 – Hank Cochran	1948 – Hank DeVito	1961 – Pete de Freitas
(Garland Perry)	1949 – Fat Larry	(Echo and The Bunnymen)
1937 – Garth Hudson	(Larry James)	★ ★ ★
(The Band)	(Fat Larry's Band)	
1939 – Edward Patten	1950 – Andy Fairweather-Low	DEPARTURE LOUNGE
(Gladys Knight and The Pips)	1951 – Andrew Gold	
1940 – Dave Govan	1951 – Steve Hillage	1953 – Betty Jack Davis
(Jayhawks/Vibrations)	1953 – Clive Wright	(Davis Sisters)
1941 – Doris Kenner	(Cock Robin)	1972 – Brian Cole
	1961 – Apollonia	(Association)

ASSOCIATION STAR COLE'S DRUG DEATH

1972

Brian Cole, bass player and one of the five vocalists in The Association, died of a heroin overdose. Formed in 1965, the group enjoyed success between 1966 and 1968, when they released two US No. 1 singles, 'Cherish' and 'Windy', as well as other international hits such as 'Along Comes Mary' (which was regarded by some as a glorification of marijuana), 'Never My Love', 'Everything That Touches You' and 'Time For Living', plus three gold albums, *...Along Comes The Association*, *Insight Out* and *Greatest Hits*, that all reached the US Top 5.

The Association on stage

1971

WINGS IN LIFT OFF

Denny Laine - wings recruit

Having announced that The Beatles was a thing of the past in April 1970, Paul McCartney proclaimed the formation of a new group, Wings, comprising himself, his wife Linda and drummer Denny Seiwell, who had played on *Ram*, the album by Paul and Linda McCartney released earlier in the year.

Deciding he needed a guitarist to complete the group – Paul would play bass and Linda keyboards – he contacted Denny Laine, who had first emerged into the big time as vocalist on 'Go Now', the 1965 UK No. 1 by The Moody Blues, who were formed by notable musicians of several Birmingham-based groups. After leaving The Moody Blues at the end of 1966, Laine attempted to form an ambitious group known as Denny Laine's Electric String Band, but despite releasing two excellent singles, the first of which was 'Say You Don't Mind', which later became a hit for Colin Blunstone in the early 1970s, he found it impossible to sustain the group and since early 1969 had been a member of Balls, a group that also included Steve Gibbons. Balls, like the Electric String Band, fell apart, and Laine was thus ready and willing to join Wings.

1974

DAN DEPARTURES

The exits of guitarist Jeff 'Skunk' Baxter and drummer Jim Hodder, founder members of Steely Dan, signalled the end of the group as a live concert attraction, although the group continued to produce new albums until 1980.

Formed in 1972 by vocalist/keyboard player Donald Fagen and vocalist/bass player Walter Becker, who met at college in New York state in the late 1960s, the group was named after a steam-powered dildo featured in William Burroughs' novel *The Naked Lunch*. The group produced a series of impeccable albums in terms of music and production, although their lyrics (written by Becker and Fagen) were somewhat cryptic. This made little difference to fans of the band (which was ulti-mately composed of Becker and Fagen plus session players), as their first five albums – *Can't Buy A Thrill, Countdown To Ecstasy, Pretzel Logic, Katy Lied* and *The Royal Scam* – were all certified gold, and their final three – *Aja, Greatest Hits* and *Gaucho* – all went platinum.

Steely Dan - no more live work

1979

BENEFIT FOR LOWELL

Lowell George in full flight

A galaxy of stars mainly from the Los Angeles area played at a benefit concert to raise money for Lowell George's widow. The genius who had been the major inspiration behind Little Feat had died of a heart attack linked to a drug overdose a few weeks before after a concert in Washington DC to promote his first solo album,

Thanks, I'll Eat It Here. The benefit concert, held at The Forum in Los Angeles, featured the surviving members of Little Feat – Payne, Barrere, Kenny Gradney, Sam Clayton and Richie Hayward – plus Jackson Browne, Bonnie Raitt, Emmylou Harris, Linda Ronstadt, Michael McDonald and Nicolette Larson.

California governor Jerry Brown was among the 20,000 audience that raised over $200,000.

The group had split up earlier in the year after keyboard player Bill Payne and George's fellow guitarist, Paul Barrere, had joined Nicolette Larson's band after touring with her. It was an ignominious end to the career of one of the best bands of the 1970s, whose first three albums, *Little Feat* (1971), *Sailin' Shoes* (1972) and *Dixie*

Chicken (1973), had failed to chart in the USA, despite critical acclaim. After three commercial failures, the group split up, but were persuaded to re-form at the end of 1974, after which their next five albums all reached the Top 40 of the US chart, the biggest success coming in 1978 with a double live album, *Waiting For Columbus*, which peaked inside the Top 20 and became their first to achieve gold status.

1980

FLOYD BUILD WALL

After their immense success in 1979, when 'Another Brick In The Wall (Part II)' became the group's biggest ever UK single, topping the chart for five weeks over the Christmas period, while the album on which it was included, *The Wall*, made the UK Top 3 and topped the US album chart for 15 weeks, Pink Floyd began a five-night season at London's Earls Court Arena, after playing a number of US dates. The concerts were unique in that during the first half of the show a wall was built across the front of the stage (to represent the separation of the group from its audience), and the latter half of the show saw it destroyed.

OSMONDS LOSE DONNY AFTER SPLIT

Formed in 1959 by brothers Alan, Wayne, Merrill and Jay Osmond, all of whom were under eleven years old, The Osmonds announced they were breaking up after 21 years. It would not be long before the original quartet re-formed, but without younger brother Donny, who had joined the family group in 1963, when he was six years old, and had been the major star during their most commercially successful era in the first half of the 1970s.

After singing in the local church in their birthplace of Ogden, Utah, the original four, who performed as The Osmond Brothers, a barber shop quartet, joined in with a professional quartet at Disneyland, and this led to appearances on TV's *Andy Williams Show* over the next five years, during which Donny was incorporated into the group.

After abbreviating the group name to The Osmonds, the big breakthrough came in 1971, after they were signed by Mike Curb to MGM Records. Curb saw them as a white version of The Jackson Five, and their first single, 'One Bad Apple', sounded very like a Jackson Five track, topping the US singles chart for five weeks and becoming a million-seller. Immediately, Donny was launched as a solo singer alongside his work with The Osmonds, and by the end of the year, had also topped the US singles chart with 'Go Away Little Girl', a cover of Steve Lawrence's 1963 US No. 1. This was the 13-year-old Donny's second million-seller in six months, following his cover of Roy Orbison's 1958 flop, 'Sweet and Innocent', which was his first to reach the US Top 10.

The group's US chart success effectively ended in the mid 1970s, although Donny and sister Marie maintained their chart popularity a little longer, starring in their own variety series on American television from 1976 to 1978 and Marie becoming a country star in the 1980s.

In 1989 Donny returned to the Top 3 of the US singles chart after a 17-year absence with 'Soldier Of Love', which is regarded by commentators as one of the most remarkable comebacks in the history of popular music.

The Osmonds with Donny (centre)

SYMPHONIC PROCOL IN CANADA

British rock group Procol Harum played a concert in Edmonton, Alberta, Canada, accompanied by the Edmonton Symphony Orchestra and a singing group. The concert was recorded and released in May 1972 under the logical title of *Procol Harum In Concert With The Edmonton Symphony Orchestra*.

While the album reached the Top 50 in Britain for a single week before dropping out of the chart for ever, it was their most commercially successful album in the USA by a considerable margin, becoming their only gold Top 5 success – none of the group's other ten US chart albums even reached the Top 20. The live album also included a hit single,

'Conquistador', a studio version of which had previously been included on the group's debut album in 1967.

The group were never able to equal the international success of their first single, 'A Whiter Shade Of Pale', whose melody was based according to various sources either on the J. S. Bach cantata, 'Sleeper's Wake', or the same

composer's 'Air On A G String'. Released at the start of the 'Summer Of Love' in 1967, it topped the UK singles chart, remaining at No. 1 for six weeks, although it only reached the Top 5 in the USA. Surprisingly, it also topped the singles chart in France for an incredible eleven weeks, and global sales were estimated at over six million copies.

GELDOF PLAYS PINK

Geldof thinks pink

The $10 million feature film based on Pink Floyd's 1979 album *The Wall* opened in New York to mixed reactions. Starring Bob Geldof as a rock star named Pink (an in-joke dating from the group's first visit to the USA, when a PR at the group's American record company enquired, 'Which one of you is Pink?'), it was directed by Alan Parker and featured live action mixed with animation that was the conception of British avant-garde artist and political cartoonist Gerald Scarfe.

RAVINGS

1960
Chubby Checker performed 'The Twist' on American television for the first time on Dick Clark's *American Bandstand*.

1981
Fleetwood Mac vocalist Stevie Nicks released her first solo album, *Bella Donna*, which included two US Top 10 singles that were both duets. 'Stop Draggin' My Heart Around' teamed Nicks with Tom Petty and The Heartbreakers, while 'Leather & Lace' featured her with Don Henley of The Eagles.

★ ★ ★

BEACH 'BOYS' RETURN TO TOP OF CHART

A compilation album comprising tracks from the 1960s, *The Very Best Of The Beach Boys*, topped the UK album chart. The youngest of these 'boys', Carl Wilson, was 36 years old, while vocalist Mike Love was 42.

ARRIVALS

1938 – Isaac Hayes
1939 – Mike Elliott (Foundations)
1939 – Mike Sarne
1948 – Allan Holdsworth (Soft Machine)
1949 – Carol Pope (Rough Trade)
1952 – Pat McDonald (Timbuk 3)
1958 – Randy DeBarge (DeBarge)
1959 – Joyce Sims
1963 – Jamie Kensit (Eighth Wonder)

★ ★ ★

DEPARTURE LOUNGE

1931 – Bix Beiderbecke

★ ★ ★

1974

WOLFMAN MARRIES BONNIE

Peter Wolf, charismatic frontman of the J. Geils Band, married film star Faye Dunaway in a ceremony in Beverly Hills, Los Angeles. A union of two such high-profile people seemed to many unlikely to survive, and indeed ended in divorce in 1979.

Dunaway was internationally famous largely due to her role as Bonnie Parker, the girlfriend of Clyde Barrow (played by Warren Beatty) in *Bonnie and Clyde*, the 1967 feature film about teenage gangsters.

Wolf had been a member of The Hallucinations, a Boston, Massachusetts, R & B group that guitarist Jerome Geils joined in 1967. Wolf (real name Peter Blankenfield) had worked as a radio disc jockey and was an expert on R & B. The group were signed to Atlantic Records in 1969, and each of their nine albums for the label by 1977 reached the US chart, the biggest being 1973's 'Bloodshot', the only one of the nine to make the Top 10.

In 1978 the group

Peter Wolf in supercharged action

signed with EMI-America, and in 1981 achieved their biggest success by far with *Freeze-Frame*, an album that topped the US chart for a month and included their only two million-selling singles, 'Centerfold', which topped the US chart for six weeks in early 1982 and was their only substantial UK hit single, and the title track, which reached the US Top 5. In early 1983 Wolf left the band, some members of which claimed he had been sacked. He embarked on a solo career which began promisingly when 'Lights Out' was a Top 20 US single in 1984, but three years elapsed before he returned with 'Come As You Are'. Sadly, the profile of the J. Geils Band was even less glorious.

RAVINGS

1965
Mike Smith, vocalist of the Dave Clark Five, broke two ribs when he was pulled offstage by fans in Chicago.

1970
Opening of the Armadillo World Headquarters, Austin, Texas.

1982
Kids From 'Fame', an album featuring cast members of the American TV show, topped the UK album chart, although it was a comparative flop in the US, peaking far outside the Top 100.

★ ★ ★

ARRIVALS

1910 – Freddie Slack
1925 – Felice Bryant
1926 – Stan Freberg
1936 – Roland Kirk
1936 – Charles Pope (Tams)
1939 – Ron Holden
1949 – Tim Renwick (Quiver)
1950 – Rodney Crowell
1952 – Andy Fraser (Free)
1952 – Alexei Sayle
1958 – Bruce Dickinson (Iron Maiden)
1960 – Jacqui O'Sullivan (Bananarama)

★ ★ ★

DEPARTURE LOUNGE

1971 – Homer (Henry Haynes) (Homer and Jethro)
1978 – Eddie Calvert
1984 – Esther Phillips

★ ★ ★

1954

JOHNNY SUCKS IT TO 'EM

22-year-old Johnny Cash, just discharged from the US Air Force, married Vivian Liberto in San Antonio, Texas. After the ceremony they moved to Memphis, Tennessee, where Johnny intended to train as a salesman for household appliances such as vacuum cleaners. While in Memphis he formed a trio with guitarist Luther Perkins and bass player Marshall Grant, and in 1955 they were signed to Sun Records.

1981

MTV SCREENS REO

REO Speedwagon - named after a fire engine

The recently launched MTV, a TV station launched with the intention of screening music-related material, broadcast its first live concert in stereo sound, a show by REO Speedwagon from Denver, Colorado.

REO Speedwagon apparently took its name from a pre-First World War make of fire engine when it formed in Champaign, Illinois, in 1968. After a four year apprenticeship 'paying their dues' by playing locally and building a significant following, the group made several major strides in 1972, recruiting a new lead singer, Kevin Cronin, and signing to Epic Records. However, their eponymous debut album failed to chart, and Cronin left for a solo career after arguments with guitarist/main songwriter Gary Richrath.

After three moderately successful albums, Cronin rejoined in 1976, and the group's first platinum album, a live double album entitled *You Get What You Play For*, came in 1977. For the next five years, the group was immensely successful, a series of gold and/or platinum albums and a seemingly endless touring schedule (almost exclusively in the USA) making them a household name, despite the cringeworthy title of their 1978 platinum album *You Can Tune A Piano But You Can't Tuna Fish*.

Their major breakthrough arrived in late 1980 with the release of their tenth original album, *Hi-Infidelity*, which topped the US album chart for 15 weeks and included their first chart-topping single, 'Keep On Loving You', which was written by Kevin Cronin and was also their only single to reach the UK Top 10. After further platinum albums, *Good Trouble* (1982) and *Wheels Are Turnin'* (1984, with another US Number One single, 'Can't Fight This Feeling', included), the group enjoyed a well-earned two-year rest before returning with a new album, *Life As We Know It*, which peaked somewhat lower in the US chart than its predecessors.

ARRIVALS

1923 – Jimmy Witherspoon
1926 – Webb Pierce
1933 – Joe Tex
1938 – Don Jacobucci
(Regents/Runarounds)
1939 – Philip Balsley
(Kingsmen/Statler Brothers)
1942 – Jay David
(John David) (Dr Hook)
1944 – Michael Johnson
1955 – Chris Foreman
(Madness)
1956 – David Grant
1956 – Ali Score
(A Flock Of Seagulls)
1959 – Ricki Rocket
(Poison)
1961 – The Edge
(David Evans) (U2)
1967 – Lorraine Pearson
(Five Star)

★ ★ ★

DEPARTURE
LOUNGE

1969 – Russ Morgan
(US bandleader)
1975 – Julian 'Cannonball'
Adderley

1975

HANK JUNIOR'S WINGLESS FLIGHT

Hank Williams Jr, son of the legendary country singer, fell 152 m (500 ft) down a mountain while hiking in Montana. He later recalled, 'It was just like falling out of an airplane – straight down'. He hit a boulder headfirst and suffered terrible injuries, but after being airlifted to hospital, where he spent several hours in the operating theatre, he survived, and after two years of surgery to rebuild his body, returned to music as a legend.

Hank Junior - famous son of a famous father

MANSON 'FAMILY' MASSACRE SHARON TATE AND FRIENDS

The citizens of Beverly Hills double-checked their security systems and shivered with horror as news spread of the multiple murder of actress Sharon Tate and four friends at a mansion at 10050 Cielo Drive. Their assailants had used blood from the bodies of their victims to scrawl messages on the walls of the house, and even more appalling was the fact that Tate was only weeks away from giving birth to her first child, fathered by her film director husband Roman Polanski.

Charles Manson faces murder charges

Although he was not at Cielo Drive that night, Charles Manson was held to be responsible for the murders, as it was on his instructions that the killers acted – he was later charged with the Tate murders as well as a number of others.

Manson had spent most of his life in youth custody or prison for various offences, and had been in prison until early 1967 in Los Angeles. On his release, after studying black magic and scientology and learning to play guitar, he decided on a career in music on the advice of fellow inmate Phil Kaufman – who made the headlines on his own account in 1973 when he stole the body of Gram Parsons. Undoubtedly charismatic, he also continued with a life of crime, gathering around him a 'family' of drop-outs and acid heads and abusing everyone with whom he came into contact. According to a 'family' member, Manson's motive was apparently to precipitate a black versus white war, following which he would take command of the black victors and become king of the world. This Armageddon, called 'Helter' Skelter' was supposedly predicted in the Beatles' song of that name.

Manson was also encouraged in his musical ambitions by Beach Boy Dennis Wilson and Terry Melcher, the record producer son of 1950s superstar Doris Day, and with their help, recorded several demos. The Beach Boys recorded a song he wrote, 'Cease To Exist' (which they re-titled 'Never Learn Not To Love').

BRITISH ELVIS GETS RECORD DEAL

1958

17-year-old vocalist Cliff Richard signed with Columbia (EMI) Records in Britain. He had already recorded two tracks produced by Norrie Paramor, 'Schoolboy Crush' (a cover of a US single by Bobby Helms) and 'Move It', an original song written by Ian Samwell, a member of The Drifters, the singer's backing group. The single was released at the end of August 1958, but caused little interest until Jack Good, producer of the teenage TV show *Oh Boy!*, heard 'Move It', which he

greatly preferred. Swiftly, EMI began promoting what had originally been the B-side of the single and before long Cliff was in the UK Top 3 for the first time.

Cliff Richard

DIRT BAND ASSEMBLE COUNTY GREATS

1971

A summit meeting of past and present stars of country music took place at Woodland Studios in Nashville when recording began of *Will The Circle Be Unbroken*. This would turn out to be a triple album by the Nitty Gritty Dirt Band, a group formed in California in the mid 1960s, but one which revered the country stars of the past, and whose members were more than happy to work as the backing band to a procession of legends who recreated many of their old classics for the edification of a new generation.

Among the legends were 'Mother' Maybelle Carter, the mother of June Carter (Mrs Johnny Cash), banjo virtuoso Earl Scruggs, blind singer/guitarist Arthel 'Doc' Watson, veteran hitmaker Roy Acuff (the first living artist elected to the Country Music Hall Of Fame), influential singer/guitarist Merle Travis and bluegrass star Jimmy Martin.

The album was the idea of Dirt Band manager William E. McEuen (whose brother, John McEuen, played banjo and fiddle in the band), to assemble all the country performers he most admired in a studio and record them performing material from their classic repertoire. When the triple album was released in 1972 it became the group's first to achieve gold status.

In 1989 the group repeated the process, but this time using a later generation of country stars, including Chet Atkins, Bernie Leadon (ex-Eagles), Roger McGuinn and Chris Hillman (ex-Byrds), Emmylou Harris and others, while Roy Acuff returned at the age of 86!

LYON FINDS MATE

1982

'Southside' Johnny Lyon

'Southside' Johnny Lyon, leader of The Asbury Jukes, a group from Asbury Park, New Jersey, which emerged in the wake of the great success of Bruce Springsteen and The E Street Band, married Jill Glassner.
At the reception afterwards Johnny's old chum Bruce was one of the musicians who played to celebrate the nuptials.

1966

BEATLES APOLOGIZE FOR 'BIGGER THAN JESUS' REMARK

At a televised press conference at the Astor Towers Hotel in Chicago, held shortly after The Beatles arrived at the start of a US tour, John Lennon apologized for remarks he had made in a British newspaper interview several months earlier. It was the kind of quote any journalist would kill for when he said, 'Christianity will go, it will shrink and vanish – we're more popular than Jesus now. I don't know which will go first, rock 'n' roll or Christianity.'

John Lennon - apology

Lennon was being interviewed by Maureen Cleave of London's *Evening Standard* in March 1966. Few in Britain took any notice – in the USA, however, the reaction was quite different. Teen magazine *Datebook* ran the interview as a cover story, lifting the contentious quote as a front page headline . A bonfire party was held in Memphis with Beatle records as fuel, and similar events took place in Alabama and Oklahoma, as local radio stations, often encouraged by, or in cahoots with, local chapters of the Ku Klux Klan, showed their disgust at this blasphemy.

Beatles manager Brian Epstein flew to the States to decide whether or not the group's imminent tour should be cancelled, and was persuaded by promoter Nat Weiss that security would not be a problem, but the story was still front-page news when the group arrived at the press conference to find three network TV crews in attendance. Shaken by the flood of hate mail and death threats, Lennon made a public apology: 'I'm sorry I opened my mouth. I'm not anti-God, anti-Christ or anti-religion. I wouldn't knock it. I didn't mean we were greater or better.' It was a very different way to launch a US tour that would turn out to be the last one by The Beatles.

RAVINGS

1952
Hank Williams was fired from the *Grand Ole Opry* for unreliability caused by alcoholism.

1972
The mayor of San Antonio declared this as Cheech and Chong

day. *Big Bambu*, the new album by the drug comedians, was near the top of the US chart.

1973
Guitarist Henry McCullough and drummer Denny Seiwell left Wings, the group led by Paul McCartney.

★ ★ ★

1969

ROSS LAUNCHES JACKSON FIVE

Diana Ross invited 350 special guests to the super-trendy Daisy club in Beverly Hills to see new Motown signings The Jackson Five. Ross had seen the group of brothers earlier in the year at a campaign benefit for the Richard Hatcher, the mayor of Gary, Indiana (the quintet's home town), which she attended with Motown founder Berry Gordy Jr.

ARRIVALS

1942 – Mike Hugg (Manfred Mann)
1942 – Guy Villari (Desires)
1943 – Michael James Kale (Guess Who)
1946 – John Conlee
1947 – Jeff Hanna (Nitty Gritty Dirt Band)
1948 – Bill Hurd (Rubettes)
1949 – Eric Carmen (Raspberries)
1950 – Erik Braunn (Iron Butterfly)
1954 – Bryan Bassett (Wild Cherry)
1957 – Richie Ramone (Richie Beau) (Ramones)
1959 – Alan Frew (Glass Tiger)
1960 – Paul Gendler (Modern Romance)
1964 – Hamish Seeloghan (Pasadenas)
1968 – Charlie Sexton

★ ★ ★

DEPARTURE LOUNGE

1984 – Percy Mayfield

1967

FLEETWOOD MAC DEBUT AT WINDSOR

The first appearance of Fleetwood Mac was at the National Jazz and Blues Festival, held at Windsor, where they shared the bill with John Mayall, Cream, Jeff Beck, Chicken Shack and others.

They had been working for Blue Horizon label boss Mike Vernon as a backing band for touring American bluesman Eddie Boyd, and hoped that Vernon, who was also producer of Mayall's records, would sign them to his label, especially as Vernon had introduced founders Peter Green (vocals, lead guitar) and Mick Fleetwood (drums) to a third member of the group, singer/guitarist Jeremy Spencer, after Spencer's previous group, The Levi Set, had auditioned unsuccessfully for Blue Horizon.

The original group was completed by bass player Bob Brunning, although he was not the first choice of either Green or Fleetwood, who had tried without success to persuade John McVie to leave John Mayall's Bluebreakers, in which they had worked with the bass player for some time before planning a new group when Mayall fired Fleetwood. McVie felt that the security offered by Mayall was more attractive than a doubtful future in a brand new group.

Fleetwood Mac made a positive impression at Windsor, enough perhaps to persuade McVie that he had possibly been unadventurous in turning down the offer after all. By September, he had left John Mayall (who subsequently used three bass players, Paul Williams, Keith Tillman and Andy Fraser, in the next six months). McVie joined, Brunning went off to join Savoy Brown, and Fleetwood Mac (whose name made more sense: it came from the title of an unreleased instrumental track recorded by The Bluesbreakers – Green, McVie and Fleetwood – without Mayall) were finally offered a recording contract by Mike Vernon.

Fleetwood Mac - the first incarnation

1960

BEST JOINS BEETLES

Liverpool quintet The Silver Beetles, just returned from a short tour of Scotland backing vocalist Johnny Gentle, recruited a new drummer, Pete Best, to replace temporary incumbent Tommy Moore, who found it difficult to take time away from work for bookings that often left him without sleep (he was a fork-lift truck driver). Best joined John Lennon, Paul McCartney, George Harrison and Stuart Sutcliffe for the group's first tour of Germany, which began five days after Best was recruited.

Pete Best

1973

MOORE THE DRIFTER

Two years after the formation of black R & B vocal group The Drifters, 21-year-old Johnny Moore was recruited by George Treadwell, who legally owned the rights to the group name although he was not an actual performer.

Johnny Moore, longstanding Drifter

Exactly 18 years later, Moore was the leader of the group when they signed to Bell Records in Britain and began one of the most remarkable comebacks in the history of popular music.

No one could accuse The Drifters of keeping a stable line-up – up to 30 members of the group had been accumulated by the early 1980s, although Moore was undoubtedly the longest serving. The first Drifters hit on which he sang lead was 'Adorable' in 1955, and he was also lead vocalist on 1956's 'Ruby Baby'. In 1957, he was drafted into the US Armed Forces. Soon

after that, Treadwell fired the entire group, replacing them with The Five Crowns, a group whose lead singer was Ben E. King, who largely sang lead on Drifters hits like 'There Goes My Baby', 'Save The Last Dance For Me' and others until 1961, when he left for a solo career, at which point Rudy Lewis piloted the group through the next three years of hits, including 'Sweets For My Sweet', 'Up On The Roof' and 'On Broadway'. When Lewis unexpectedly died of a heart attack in 1964

Moore rejoined the group, and was featured vocalist on 'One Way Love', 'Under The Boardwalk' and 'Saturday Night At The Movies'.

After that, the group went into gradual decline with Moore the only constant group member, but after two reissued hits from the previous decade made the UK Top 10 ('At The Club' and 'Come On Over To My Place'), the group signed to Bell Records and charted nine new recordings in three years, six of them reaching the UK Top 10.

ARRIVALS

1921 – Jimmy McCracklin
1938 – Dave 'Baby' Cortez
1939 – Joel Scott Hill
(Canned Heat/Flying Burrito Brothers)
1940 – Sean James Stokes (Bachelors)
1941 – Craig Douglas (Terry Perkins)
1948 – Tony Santini (Sha Na Na)
1949 – Cliff Fish (Paper Lace)
1950 – Pluto Shervington
1951 – Dan Fogelberg
1958 – Feargal Sharkey (Undertones)
1959 – Mark Nevin (Fairground Attraction)

★ ★ ★

DEPARTURE LOUNGE

1971 – King Curtis
1974 – Bill Chase
1982 – Joe Tex

1990

MAYFIELD PARALYZED AFTER ON-STAGE ACCIDENT

Curtis Mayfield was performing at an outdoor concert in New York during a storm when a gust of wind blew a heavy lighting rig over. It fell on him, paralyzing him from the neck down.

Mayfield was born in 1942 in Chicago and emerged in the late 1950s with The Impressions, singing lead on over two dozen US hit singles such as 'It's All Right', 'Keep On Pushing' and 'Amen', before leaving for a solo career in 1970.

Curtis Mayfield

RAVINGS

1965
Jefferson Airplane made their debut at San Francisco's Matrix Club.

★ ★ ★

1976
The Clash made their unofficial live debut at a London rehearsal room.

1977
Runaways vocalist Cherie Currie left the

group to embark on a solo career.

1981
Echo and The Bunnymen's 32-minute film *Shine So Hard* was premiered.

★ ★ ★

1976

LOWE'S STIFF START

Nick Lowe, previously vocalist and bass player with the group Brinsley Schwarz, released his first solo single, 'So It Goes'/'Heart Of The City', which was also the first release on Stiff Records, the label launched by ex-Brinsley Schwarz manager Dave Robinson and Andrew Jakeman (aka Jake Riviera), ex-manager of Chilli Willi and The Red Hot Peppers. Since both groups had split up, Lowe had embarked on a solo career, but when he had recorded the two solo tracks the decision was made to release them via a brand new independent label.

Nick Lowe - solo debut for stiff

Using the ironic name of Stiff Records – in music industry parlance, a stiff is a non-hit – the label's early releases featured artists from the London 'pub rock' era, including The Pink Fairies, Roogalator and The Tyla Gang, but Stiff was also open to the rapidly emerging punk rock phenomenon, releasing the first British punk single of the era, 'New Rose' by The Damned, a month before 'Anarchy In The UK' by The Sex Pistols was released by EMI. Stiff also released the classic New York punk EP by Richard Hell and The Voidoids, *Blank Generation*, but is probably most celebrated for Riviera's discovery of Elvis Costello, whose first four singles, 'Less Than Zero', 'Alison', 'Red Shoes' and 'Watching The Detectives', plus his first album, *My Aim Is True*, were released by Stiff.

Many of the early Stiff releases were produced by Nick Lowe, including all the Costello releases, the first two singles and first album by The Damned, and early releases by Wreckless Eric, etc

1992

PLATTERS STAR DIES

Tony Williams, original lead singer with The Platters, the black vocal group whose commercial success virtually ended when he was replaced by Sonny Turner after leaving the group in 1961, died at the age of 64 of emphysema, a condition complicated by diabetes.

With his soaring tenor to the fore, the group accumulated a series of early classics of the rock era, including four US No. 1 hits – 'The Great Pretender' and 'My Prayer' (both 1956), 'Twilight Time' (1958) and 'Smoke Gets In Your Eyes' (1959).

The Platters

ARRIVALS

1926 – Buddy Greco (Armando Greco)
1940 – Dash Crofts (Seals and Crofts)
1941 – David Crosby (David van Cortland) (Byrds/CSN and Y)
1941 – Connie Smith
1942 – Gil Bridges (Rare Earth)
1944 – Tim Bogert (Vanilla Fudge/Cactus)
1946 – Larry Graham (Sly and The Family Stone/Graham Central Station)
1947 – George Newsome (Climax Blues Band)
1956 – Sharon Bryant (Atlantic Starr)
1961 – Sarah Brightman

★ ★ ★

DEPARTURE LOUNGE

1956 – Berthold Brecht
1958 – Big Bill Broonzy
1978 – Joe Venuti
1988 – Roy Buchanan

★ ★ ★

RAVINGS

1956
Eddie Cochran was signed by producer Boris Petroff to appear in the movie *The Girl Can't Help It*, starring Jayne Mansfield, Tom Ewell and Edmond O'Brien alongside a galaxy of early rock 'n' roll stars, also including Little Richard, Fats Domino and Gene Vincent.

1970
Stephen Stills was arrested at a motel in La Jolla near San Diego on drug charges.

1988
John Cougar Mellencamp became a grandfather at the age of 37.

★ ★ ★

1967

MARINE OFFENCES BILL SINKS PIRATES

For the previous two years, so-called 'pirate' radio stations broadcasting from ships in the sea had ruled the airwaves in Britain, feeding their combined audience of millions with a diet they could not find anywhere else – a non-stop feast of pop and rock. These unlicensed and unregulated broadcasters were sentenced to a watery grave by the passing in to law of the Marine Offences Bill.

It was not the music to which the British government objected; it was the fact that the pirate stations were outside British territorial limits, paying no taxes and doing more or less what they liked because the ships were moored outside British jurisdiction. Some of them, notably Radio London and Radio Caroline, were making large profits from advertising revenue, and because of the musical diet they transmitted, they were extremely popular among those under 30 years old.

Pirate disc jockeys were household names, stars even. Although the audience for 24 hours a day popular music could not be measured, the BBC was forced to launch its own pop station, and as the various pirate stations were silenced, the most popular disc jockeys were hired to work on the new BBC Network, Radio One when it started broadcasting on September 30, 1967.

Disc Jockey Keith Skues (front) with members of Radio Caroline's Crew

---

RAVINGS

1958
Buddy Holly married Maria Elena Santiago.

★ ★ ★

1959
The first British single by Scott Engel (aka Scott Walker of The Walker Brothers), 'The Livin' End', was released but sold only a handful of copies.

1969
The start of the Woodstock Festival.

1991
Paul Simon played a free concert in New York's Central Park before an audience of three quarters of a million people.

★ ★ ★

1965

BEATLES PLAY SHEA

The Beatles started their third North American tour with a concert at Shea Stadium on Long Island, New York. With an audience of over 55,000 screaming fans, the gross receipts from the concert exceeded $300,000 (a world record), and a security army of over 2,000 tried to maintain order. The support acts were the King Curtis Band – Curtis was a celebrated saxophone player who worked with The Coasters, Buddy Holly, The Allman Brothers, Aretha Franklin and many more – Cannibal and The Headhunters, whose only US hit came in that year (1965) with 'Land Of 1000 Dances', Motown star Brenda Holloway (whose biggest hit was 'Every Little Bit Hurts', covered by the Spencer Davis Group with vocals by Steve Winwood), and British instrumental combo Sounds Incorporated. After being introduced by Ed Sullivan, The Beatles hit the stage and played a dozen songs in 30 minutes.

ARRIVALS

1925 – Oscar Peterson
1933 – Floyd Ashton (Tams)
1933 – Bill Pinkney (Drifters)
1934 – Bobby Byrd (JBs)
1938 – 'Stix' Nesbert Hooper (Crusaders)
1939 – Jim Dale
1942 – Pete York (Spencer Davis Group)
1944 – Frederick Knight
1946 – Jimmy Webb
1949 – Kate Taylor
1950 – Thomas Aldridge (Black Oak Arkansas)
1961 – Matt Johnson (The The)
1962 – Marshall Schofield (The Fall)
1967 – MCA (Adam Yauch) (Beastie Boys)

★ ★ ★

DEPARTURE LOUNGE

1984 – Norman Petty

★ ★ ★

1977

THE KING IS DEAD

Elvis Presley, the original and undisputed King of Rock 'n' Roll, was found dead in his bathroom at Graceland, his Memphis mansion. His body was discovered by girlfriend Ginger Alden, who called for help. Although attempts were made to resuscitate the singer, doctors at a Memphis hospital pronounced him dead.

Unprecedented tributes were paid to him by public figures and the media, and radio stations abandoned their regular formats to play non-stop Elvis.

Long live the King!

A multitude of fans from all over the world set out for Memphis, where the funeral would be held two days later, and florists reported record business as wreaths and floral tributes descended on Tennessee. Even President Jimmy Carter was moved to say, 'Elvis Presley's death deprives our country of a part of itself. He was unique and ireplaceable. His music and personality . . .

permanently changed the face of American popular culture.'

While there is little doubt that although he was selling millions of records around the globe, Presley's career had deteriorated into a shadow of former glories and that he had allowed himself to be steered into a succession of pathetic (but lucrative) movies and an increasingly pitiful (but lucrative) series of live shows at Las Vegas, longtime fans could console themselves with memories of a feisty lean and mean young truck driver who had transformed their lives 20 years earlier.

1962

BEST NO LONGER

Beatles manager Brian Epstein informed drummer Pete Best that he was being replaced by Richard Starkey (better known as Ringo Starr), previously with Rory Storm and The Hurricanes. Best's fans demonstrated their disapproval of his departure outside The Cavern, the Liverpool cellar where The Beatles frequently played, although the group was in fact playing in Chester that night without Best or Ringo, who had to work out his notice before leaving The

Hurricanes. Johnny 'Hutch' Hutchinson of The Big Three was temporarily hired to play Beatles shows until Ringo was available.

Pete Best

ARRIVALS

1927 – Fess Parker
1929 – Bill Evans
1931 – Eydie Gorme
1934 – Ketty Lester
1942 – Barbara George
1944 – Kevin Ayers
1945 – Gordon Fleet

(Easybeats)
1945 – Gary Loizzo
(American Breed)
1948 – Barry Hay
(Golden Earring)
1948 – Danny Flowers
1953 – James 'J.T.' Taylor
(Kool and The Gang)
1958 – Madonna (Madonna

Louise Ciccone)
1967 – M. C. Remedee
(Cookie Crew)

★ ★ ★

DEPARTURE LOUNGE

1977 – Elvis Presley

RAVINGS

1962
(Little) Stevie Wonder released his debut single, 'I Call It Pretty Music But The Old Folks Call It The Blues (Parts 1 and 2)'. It was not a hit.

1975
Peter Gabriel announced that he was leaving Genesis.

1976
Cliff Richard embarked on a sold-out tour of Russia, starting with a concert at Leningrad's Hall Of The October Revolution.

1983
Paul Simon married actress Carrie Fisher, the daughter of 1950s hitmakers Eddie Fisher and Debbie Reynolds. Also at the ceremony was another chart star from the past, her stepmother Connie 'Sixteen Reasons' Stevens.

1969

PEACE, LOVE AND DOPE

The Woodstock Music and Arts Festival, held in Bethel, upstate New York, ended after three days. Up to half a million people migrated to a 600 acre farm owned by Max Yasgur. Such an immense crowd quickly rendered all security irrelevant, and the festival eventually became a free event. All roads near the site were subject to gridlocked traffic jams, some with queues of up to 20 miles, a situation that was not improved by torrential rain that turned what had been fields into swamps.

Janis Joplin

The crowd did not care, because the array of talent on stage was arguably more impressive than at any festival before or since, a who's who of the biggest and newest names in rock, many of whom became overnight stars as a result of their performances. Among these were John Sebastian, whose happy-go-lucky style as the tie-dye clad hippy was perfectly in serendipity with half a million stoned kids who were far from worldly restrictions, Ten Years After, with guitarist Alvin Lee's express picking on the epic 'Goin' Home', Joe Cocker as the hoarse-voiced king of white R & B, Sha Na Na with their energetic pastiche of vintage rock 'n' roll, the magnificent Crosby, Stills, Nash and Young, Country Joe McDonald's slightly adapted 'Fish Cheer' ('Gimme an "F", gimme a "U", gimme a "C", etc. – what's that spell?'). Three people died, two were born and there were six miscarriages, as announcements from the stage warned of 'bad acid'. Food and drink were quickly consumed, clothes were discarded and it was all filmed and recorded.

A 1970 triple album topped the US chart for a month, and a 1971 double album with more of the stars of the show made the US Top 10.

1969

SOUL SUPERSTARS BID CURTIS FAREWELL

The funeral of saxophone genius Curtis Ousley (aka King Curtis) in New York was conducted by the Revd Jesse Jackson, who preached a sermon to a congregation including Cissy Houston (Whitney's mother), Stevie Wonder, Aretha Franklin, Delaney and Bonnie, Duane Allman (who himself had less than three months to live), Brook Benton and others. Curtis had been murdered outside his New York apartment.

Fans at Woodstock

1977

POLICE GET SMALLER THEN BIGGER

Andy Summers, Sting, Stewart Copeland – The Police

The Police played Rebecca's in Birmingham, their first gig in the form in which they would achieve immense fame, with founder members Stewart Copeland on drums and vocalist/bassist Sting plus later recruit Andy Summers on guitar.

Copeland had been drummer with Curved Air, the progressive rock group that was on its last legs by early 1977. He met bass player Sting (real name Gordon Sumner), a teacher from Newcastle who was playing in Last Exit, a local jazz/rock group, and they began to rehearse with guitarist Henri Padovani, recording their debut single, 'Fall Out', during that spring. Calling themselves The Police, they mainly worked initially as backing group to New York singer Cherry Vanilla, a one-time associate of David Bowie.

During May that year, Copeland and Sting met Summers (previously a member of Zoot Money's Big Roll Band, Eric Burdon and The Animals, the bands of Kevin Ayers and Kevin Coyne, etc.) at a session by Strontium 90, a spin-off of space/rock combo Gong. Summers (real name Andrew Somers) was then invited to join The Police, but after two months as a quartet, Padovani left the band. The trio then began to establish themselves on the UK pub and club circuit.

In early 1978 The Police began recording their own first album at a small studio in Surrey, with the recording costs being paid partly by their manager, Copeland's older brother, Miles Copeland III. The trio also appeared in a TV commercial for Wrigley's chewing gum, which necessitated them dying their hair blond – this eventually became the basis of their visual image when they began having hits after signing with A & M Records in the spring of 1978.

1966

EX-ANGEL REPLACES POND

After a string of hit singles in the previous two and a half years, including two No. 1s with 'Do Wah Diddy Diddy' and 'Pretty Flamingo', Manfred Mann vocalist/harmonica player Paul Jones (real name Paul Pond) left the group for a solo career.

After the group considered Rod Stewart and Wayne Fontana, he was replaced by Mike D'Abo, previously singer/keyboard player of A Band Of Angels, a group formed at Harrow School, which also included singer/guitarist John Gayden, who later founded EG management, a company that represented T. Rex, Roxy Music, Emerson, Lake and Palmer and King Crimson.

Mike D'Abo (left) and his colleagues

1967

FLOYD AT GATES OF CHART

Pink Floyd entered the UK album chart for the first time with their debut LP *Piper At The Gates Of Dawn*. This followed two hit singles earlier in the year, 'Arnold Layne', which reached the Top 20 and 'See Emily Play', their first UK Top 10 hit.

Apparently named after two obscure American bluesmen, Pink Anderson and Floyd Council, Pink Floyd first formed in Cambridge in late 1964 as a six-piece group of Syd Barrett (guitar, vocals), Nick Mason (drums), Roger

Waters (bass, vocals) and Rick Wright (keyboards) plus guitarist Bob Klose and vocalist Chris Dennis. Dennis had left in early 1965 and Klose followed him that summer, which left the quartet who made the hits mentioned above.

Not long after *Piper At The Gates Of Dawn* was released, Syd Barrett began to show increasing signs of damage caused, so it was believed, by over-indulgence in the psychedelic drug LSD. He became totally unpredictable and somewhat unreliable to the point where Waters invited guitarist Dave Gilmour to join the Floyd. The idea was to allow Barrett to concentrate on writing songs while Gilmour assumed his role on stage, but after about three months it became clear that this arrangement was unworkable and Barrett was finally fired just before the group's second album, *A Saucerful Of Secrets*, released in June 1968.

Pink Floyd (left to right) Wright, Waters, Mason, Barrett

ARRIVALS		
1913 – Harry Mills (Mills Brothers)	1943 – Don Fardon (Donald Maughn)	(Europe)
1939 – Ginger Baker (Peter Baker) (Cream/Blind Faith/Airforce)	1943 – Billy J. Kramer (William Howard Ashton)	1970 – MC Eric (Technotronic)
1940 – Roger Cook (David and Jonathan/ Blue Mink)	1944 – Eddy Raven	★ ★ ★
	1945 – Ian Gillan (Deep Purple)	DEPARTURE LOUNGE
	1948 – Elliott Lurie (Looking Glass)	1895 – John Wesley Hardin
1940 – Johnny Nash	1951 – John Deacon (Queen)	1959 – Blind Willie McTell
	1963 – Joey Tempest	1979 – Dorsey Burnette

RAVINGS

1962
Ex-Shadow Jet Harris made his solo debut in Torquay on a bill with Mark Wynter and Craig Douglas.

1967
On the day 'All You Need Is Love' moved to the top of the US singles chart, Maureen Starkey gave birth to Ringo's second son, Jason.

1988
US jukebox operators named their All Time Most Played records as Elvis Presley's 'Hound Dog', followed by Patsy Cline's 'Crazy'.

★ ★ ★

1972

SUPREMES CHART FAREWELL

The Supremes were regular entrants to the Top 20 of the UK singles chart between 1964, when 'Where Did Our Love Go' was their first big hit, until 'Automatically Sunshine' became the final original single by the group to reach those heights.

The group had changed considerably in those years. Original member Florence Ballard left in 1967 and was replaced by Cindy Birdsong. Lead vocalist Diana Ross launched a solo career in 1969 and Jean Terrell was recruited in her place.

The Supremes in the 1970s

Linda Lawrence replaced Cindy Birdsong in 1972, just before 'Automatically Sunshine' became the group's 21st original release (as opposed to reissues) to reach the UK Top 20 (including hit duets with other groups such as The Four Tops and The Temptations).

STONES BOSS STARTS IMMEDIATE

Rolling Stones manager Andrew Loog Oldham announced the formation of his own record company, Immediate Records. Along with his partner Tony Calder, Oldham launched a label that would burst on the British record scene with formidable force, flare brilliantly for three years and end its days bankrupt.

Small Faces (left to right) Kenny Jones, Ian McLagen, Ronnie Lane, Steve Marriott

Whether or not Oldham's new 'hobby' diverted his attention from The Stones (as many believed) or not, his relationship with the group soured over the next year, and by the time they started recording 1967's misconceived *Their Satanic Majesties Request* album, Oldham was in the out tray.

Still, Immediate was keeping him busy with hits hot enough to keep anyone on the boil. At its zenith, Immediate boasted a roster that included The Small Faces, Chris Farlowe, Amen Corner, P. P. Arnold and The Nice. Commercially, The Small Faces were the jewel in Immediate's belly, blending psychedelia with the dress sense and spark of Mods from London's East End (which was exactly what they were). Ex-child actor Steve Marriott's soulful voice gave the songs he wrote with bass player Ronnie 'Plonk' Lane a novel quality that brought them huge hits like 'Itchycoo Park', 'Lazy Sunday' and 'Tin Soldier' on which label-mate Pat Arnold (previously a member of The Ikettes, the vocal trio behind Ike and Tina Turner) wailed soulfully. She had her own hits as well, especially a cover of the Cat Stevens song, 'The First Cut Is The Deepest' and 'Angel Of The Morning'. She briefly worked with The Nice as her backing group, a quartet featuring keyboard showman Keith Emerson and eccentric Davy O'List on guitar who scored one hit, 'America' in 1968.

Chris Farlowe, a white singer with a black voice, topped the chart with his version of a Rolling Stones song, 'Out Of Time', with producer Mick Jagger helping him promote it on TV, while Welsh septet Amen Corner also topped the chart for two weeks with '(If Paradise Is) Half As Nice'. The only problem was that Immediate spent more money than it earned.

DARIN SELLS MILLION-DOLLAR SONGS

Hitmaking vocalist Bobby Darin sold his music publishing company for a cool $1 million. In the previous month he had started his own label, Direction, launching it with his own latest album, *Born Walden Robert Cassotto*, which also boasted 'written, arranged, produced, designed and photographed by Bobby Darin' and included protest songs and some of his poetry.

Bobby Darin

ARRIVALS

1924 – Jim Reeves (James Travis Reeves)
1940 – John Lantree (Honeycombs)
1942 – Isaac Hayes
1947 – James Pankow (Chicago)
1948 – Robert Plant (Led Zeppelin)
1951 – Phil Lynott (Thin Lizzy)
1952 – Rudy Gatlin (Gatlin Brothers)
1952 – Doug Fieger (Knack)
1955 – Gary Lalonde (Honeymoon Suite)
1955 – Mike McKenzie (Child)
1957 – Richard Zatorski (Real Life)

★ ★ ★

DEPARTURE LOUNGE

1986 – Thad Jones
1988 – Leon McAuliffe

RAVINGS

1955
Bo Diddley made his first appearance at New York's Apollo Theatre.

1969
The Mothers Of Invention was disbanded by Frank Zappa, reported as being tired of 'people who clap for all the wrong reasons'.

★ ★ ★

DOOBIE BROS HIT GOLD STANDARD

The Doobie Brothers

CHARTERHOUSE REUNION

Both producer Jonathan King and new group Genesis had attended the same top-drawer school, Charterhouse, so there was a certain logic about the 'Everyone's Gone To The Moon' hitmaker giving his younger schoolmates the benefit of his experience. After several singles that failed to chart, King produced their debut album, *From Genesis To Revelation*, which was also a flop.

The group, which included vocalist/lyricist Peter Gabriel, Tony Banks (keyboards) and Mike Rutherford (guitar, bass), then rethought their approach and released a second album, *Trespass*, in 1970. Before it was released, a new drummer had been recruited who had not been to Charterhouse School, Phil Collins, who later also became the group's vocalist after Gabriel left in 1975 for a solo career.

Genesis - Rutherford, Banks, Gabriel, Collins

Toulouse Street, the second album by The Doobie Brothers, achieved gold status during a US chart residency of over two years. Formed under the name Pud by drummer John Hartman and singer/ guitarist Tom Johnston, the group changed its name at the end of that year to The Doobie Brothers (a doobie is supposedly slang for a joint or marijuana cigarette).

The introduction of another singer/guitarist, Pat Simmons, new bass player Tiran Porter and a second drummer, Michael Hossack, produced the sound they wanted and made them major stars for the rest of the decade.

Starting with songs written by Johnston like 'Listen To The Music', 'Long Train Runnin'' and their first US chart-topper, 'Black Water', the group maintained gold album status with *The Captain and Me* (1973), *What Were Once Vices Are Now Habits* (1974) and *Stampede* (1975), but the constant touring led to Johnston collapsing on the fifth day of a 50-date tour. Recent recruit lead guitarist Jeff 'Skunk' Baxter recommended an ex-colleague from Steely Dan (who had just decided never to tour again), Michael McDonald, an exceptionally talented vocalist, and even when Johnston returned, the new boy remained as lead singer, writing all their hits including another No. 1, 'What A Fool Believes', in 1979. The album that included the chart-topper 'Minute By Minute' also topped the US chart and was a third platinum album following the first one featuring McDonald, *Takin' It To The Streets*, and a *Best Of* compilation.

ARRIVALS

1904 – Count Basie (William Basie)
1924 – Clara Ward
1930 – Christiane Legrand (Blue Stars)
1938 – Kenny Rogers
1939 – James Burton
1939 – Harold Reid (Statler Brothers)
1941 – Tom Coster (Santana)
1944 – Jackie De Shannon (Sharon Myers)
1952 – Glenn Hughes (Trapeze/Deep Purple)
1952 – Joe Strummer (John Mellors) (Clash)
1957 – Budgie (Siouxsie and The Banshees)
1957 – Kim Sledge (Sister Sledge)

★ ★ ★

DEPARTURE LOUNGE

1977 – Tarheel Slim
1980 – Joe Dassin

RAVINGS

1963
Cliff Richard won the award in America's top teen magazine 16 as 'Most promising male singer'.

1971
Diana Ross topped the UK chart for the first time as a solo artist with 'I'm Still Waiting'. She had to wait 15 years before 'Chain Reaction' returned her to the top.

★ ★ ★

1987

DUSTY BACK AFTER LONG ABSENCE

After being absent from the Top 10 of the UK singles chart for around 18 years, Dusty Springfield, widely regarded as Britain's finest female pop star, returned to where many felt she had always belonged.

Duetting with hotshot hitmakers Pet Shop Boys, 'What Have I Done To Deserve This' ultimately peaked inside the UK Top 3 (a height to which she had not aspired since 1966!) and also became her first US Top 3 hit.

Born Mary O'Brien in 1939, Dusty had worked as part of The Lana Sisters, a vocal trio, before joining her brother, Dion O'Brien (aka Tom Springfield) and Tim Field in folk/country trio The Springfields, who released two UK Top 10 singles, 'Island Of Dreams' (1962) and 'Say I Won't Be There' (1973), as well as a US Top 20 hit, 'Silver Threads and Golden Needles'. In late 1963 Dusty embarked on a solo career, releasing regular UK Top 10 hits such as 'I Only Want To Be With You' (1963), 'I Just Don't Know What To Do With Myself' (1964), 'In The Middle Of Nowhere' and 'Some Of Your Lovin'' (both 1965), 'You Don't Have To Say You Love Me' (her only No. 1) and 'Goin' Back' (both 1966) and 'Son Of A Preacher Man' (1968), plus a number of critically acclaimed albums.

Dusty - still a star

1981

CHEAP TRICK SEEK EXPENSIVE PAY-OFF

Hard rock group Cheap Trick sued the company to which they were signed, Columbia (CBS) Records, for $28 million, following a lawsuit launched by CBS against the group a few weeks earlier. Group members Robin Zander (vocals, guitar), Rick Nielsen (guitar, vocals) and Bun E. Carlos (real name Brad Carlson, drums) were also attempting to end their contract with CBS's Epic label, to which they had been signed since the mid 1970s.

The group's commercial peak was in 1979, when two albums, *Cheap Trick At Budokan* (a live album recorded in Japan, where the group were regarded as superstars) and *Dream Police*, both achieved platinum status and reached the Top 10 of the US chart.

Cheap Trick - out of love with label

RAVINGS

1956
Elvis Presley started work on his first movie, *Love Me Tender*.

1979
Led Zeppelin released their final original album, *In Through The Out Door*. John Bonham's death in 1980 led to the group's disbanding.

1981
Anglo American hard rock combo Foreigner topped the US album chart with their fourth album, appropriately entitled *4*.

★ ★ ★

ARRIVALS

1917 – John Lee Hooker
1923 – Sonny Thompson
1926 – Bob Flanigan (Four Freshmen)
1938 – Dale Hawkins (Delmar Allen Hawkins)
1939 – Fred Milano (Belmonts)
1945 – Ron Dante (Archies/Cufflinks)
1947 – Donna Godchaux (Grateful Dead)
1948 – Sam Neely
1954 – Frank Marino (Mahogany Rush)
1958 – Ian Mitchell (Bay City Rollers)
1961 – Roland Orzabal (Tears For Fears)
1961 – Debbie Peterson (Bangles)
1963 – James DeBarge (DeBarge)

★ ★ ★

VELVETS LOSE LOU

After a gig at Max's Kansas City, the celebrated New York club, Lou Reed left The Velvet Underground, the group he had formed in 1964 with John Cale. The group's performance was later released as an album, appropriately called *Live At Max's Kansas City*.

Reed (real name Louis Firbank), a singer/guitarist, had been working as a songwriter before he met Cale, a Welsh music student who played viola and other instruments, who was in New York after winning a scholarship. They decided to form a group, Reed introducing guitarist Sterling Morrison and Cale percussionist Angus Maclise. In 1965, they came to the attention of media Messiah Andy Warhol, who became the group's patron and recruited an additional vocalist, German chanteuse Nico (real name Christa Paffgen). This apparently upset Maclise, who left the band as a result (and starved to death in Nepal in 1979), whereupon the group hired female drummer Mo (Maureen) Tucker. This was the line-up that recorded the group's first album, *The Velvet Underground and Nico*, which was produced by Warhol and released in 1967. At this juncture, Reed, the main songwriter, began to call the shots, distancing the band from Warhol and Nico, who went on to a solo career and achieved cult status before her death in 1988 from a brain haemorrhage.

The remaining quartet recorded their second album, *White Light, White Heat*, in a single day and it was released in early 1968. It included a bizarre track featuring Cale recounting the story of a man who wrapped himself up and had himself delivered to his girlfriend, who killed him by sticking a carving knife into the parcel without opening it. The story was only audible if the listener heard only one side of the stereo mix, as the other side featured a loud freeform psychedelic instrumental! After that album Cale left the band to be replaced by Doug Yule. They released a third album, eponymously titled in 1969, after which their record company, who clearly totally failed to understand how extremely original the group were, did not renew their recording contract. They moved to a new label for *Loaded*, whereupon Reed left the band after the album was remixed without his knowledge. Yule continued with the Velvet Underground monicker until 1973.

Velvet Underground with Lou Reed (second from left)

SINEAD BANS BANNER

1990

Irish singer Sinead O'Connor caused considerable controversy by her refusal to allow the American national anthem, 'The Star Spangled Banner', to be played at a New Jersey concert. O'Connor, whose shaven head had made her one of the most instantly recognizable stars in rock history, had earlier in the year achieved an international hit of Olympian proportions with her cover of an old Prince song, 'Nothing Compares 2 U', topping the charts of 18 countries including the US and UK.

Sinead O'Connor - no anthem

Sinead O'Connor's first notable appearance on record was in 1986 when she was the vocalist on 'Heroine', a track on the soundtrack album of the film *The Captive* with music by Dave Evans (aka The Edge) of U2. Even before it was released, she was signed by the pioneering British independent label, Ensign Records, and given a job in the Ensign office while preparing to start her own recording career. In 1987, she appeared on *Private Revolution*, the debut album by World Party, another Ensign act, and at the end of that year, her own debut single, 'Troy', was released, but failed to chart, although the following year's 'Mandinka' became her first UK Top 20 single. Her first album, *The Lion and The Cobra* featured fellow Irish recording artist, Enya, and made the UK Top 30 and US Top 40.

At the end of 1989 she split with her manager, Fachtna O'Ceallaigh, just before shooting the video for 'Nothing Compares 2 U', the first single from her second album. The song was written by Prince and originally recorded by his protegés, Family, in 1985. When the video was screened and showed O'Connor crying with deep emotion, it only served to increase sales of what swiftly became one of the fastest-selling singles in chart history. That second album, *I Do Not Want What I Haven't Got*, also topped the charts all over the world, quickly achieving triple platinum status.

RAVINGS

1967
17-year-old Bruce Springsteen joined a trio called Earth, which quickly became dust.

1977
Waylon Jennings, recently named an honorary police chief in Nashville, was arrested on cocaine charges.

1979
B. B. King celebrated 30 years as an entertainer with a show at Sunset Strip's Roxy Club in Los Angeles.

★ ★ ★

1981
Mark Chapman, who killed John Lennon, was sentenced to 20 years in prison.

★ ★ ★

ARRIVALS

1905 – Arthur Crudup
1915 – Wynonie Harris
1938 – David Freiberg (Quicksilver Messenger Service)
1939 – Ernie Wright (Little Anthony and The Imperials)
1942 – Fontella Bass
1943 – John Cipollina (Quicksilver Messenger Service)
1944 – James Brady (Sandpipers)
1944 – Jim Capaldi (Traffic)
1945 – Malcolm Duncan (Average White Band)
1945 – Ken Hensley (Uriah Heep)
1948 – Jean Michel Jarre
1951 – Mike Derosier (Heart)
1955 – Jeffrey Daniel (Shalamar)
1961 – Mark Bedford (Madness)

★ ★ ★

DEPARTURE LOUNGE

1978 – Louis Prima

★ ★ ★

1983

RIP MRS JERRY LEE (NUMBER 5)

Shawn Stevens, the fifth wife of Jerry Lee Lewis (after Dorothy Barton, Jane Mitcham, Myra Brown and Jaren Pate), died of a methadone overdose after less than three months of marriage. Marriage was clearly a state Lewis should have avoided, but in 1984 he married for the sixth time - 22-year-old Kerrie McCaver.

The Killer - Jerry Lee

THREE AND A HALF YEAR RUN ENDS

Kylie - 'Neighbours' to Number One

The prominent songwriting and production team of Mike Stock, Matt Aitken and Peter Waterman were not represented in the UK singles listings for the first time since February 1987.

Waterman had worked for the independent Magnet label running the A & R department, and in the early 1980s was signing and producing hitmakers for MCA, launching his hugely successful songwriting/production team with Stock and Aitken around 1983. Stock had a small home studio where he and Aitken wrote and produced demo recordings. Their first UK Top 20 hit as producers came with 1984's 'You Think You're A Man' by outrageous transvestite Divine, and it was soon followed by 'Whatever I Do (Wherever I Go)' by Hazell Dean, the first UK Top 10 hit which

they both wrote and produced. The first chart-topping hit they produced was Dead Or Alive's 1985 hit, 'You Spin Me Round (Like A Record)'. The first US act they worked with was The Three Degrees in 1985, while the first established UK act to use them was Bananarama in 1986, whose revival of Shocking Blue's 'Venus' not only made the UK Top 10, but also was the first Stock, Aitken and Waterman production to top the US chart. 1986 brought another dozen hits, and 1987 included 14 UK Top 20 productions, featuring the chart-topping debut from Rick Astley, 'Never Gonna Give You Up' (also an American No.

1), and another No. 1, 'Let It Be', by the all-star Ferry Aid charity ensemble. The same year brought the launch of the PWL label – an early signing was Kylie Minogue, a young Australian actress whose image as one of the stars of the popular TV soap opera *Neighbours* was perfect. She launched her pop career in early 1988 with 'I Should Be So Lucky', which topped the UK chart for five weeks, and went on to a run of 13 successive UK Top 10 singles, while her TV 'husband', Jason Donovan, also benefited, racking up a string of big Stock/Aitken/Waterman-produced hits (including two No. 1s) that has rarely been matched.

Bananarama

RAVINGS

singer/songwriter David Ackles.

1970
Elton John made his first live appearance in the US at The Troubadour in Los Angeles, opening for

1984
Michael Jackson's video for *Thriller* was shown on TV in Britain for the first time.

ARRIVALS

1918 – Leonard Bernstein
1933 – Wayne Shorter (Weather Report)
1942 – Walter Williams (O'Jays)
1949 – Gene Simmons (Chaim Witz) (Kiss)
1951 – Rob Halford (Judas Priest)
1951 – James Warren

(Korgis)
1954 – Elvis Costello (Declan Patrick McManus)
1958 – Damian McKee (Rosetta Stone)
1965 – Nigel Durham (Saxon)

★ ★ ★

DEPARTURE LOUNGE

1979 – Stan Kenton

1967

WILSON BACK ON WAVES

Brian Wilson, the songwriter and guiding genius behind the Beach Boys, made his first on-stage appearance with

them for two years at a show in Honolulu, Hawaii. It was an isolated return, and although he occasionally

appeared with them subsequently, the rare sightings were much valued by Wilson watchers because they were usually totally unexpected.

1973

10CC'S MANX DEBUT

Hitmaking quartet 10cc, comprising Graham Gouldman, Eric Stewart, Kevin Godley and Lawrence Creme, played their first live gig at the Palace Lido in Douglas, Isle Of Man.

Formed in 1971 by the four Manchester-based musicians, the group had enjoyed a Top 3 hit with 'Donna' in 1972. A follow-up, 'Johnny Don't Do It', was a total flop at the end of that year, but a third single, 'Rubber Bullets', in early 1973, became the group's first of three No. 1 hits from 1973 to 1978, the second, in 1975, was the seminal love song 'I'm Not In Love'

10cc (left to right) Graham Gouldman, Lol Creme, Eric Stewart, Kevin Godley

Each of the four members of the group had previously achieved success, the best known being Graham Gouldman, who had written a number of hits for The Yardbirds, Herman's Hermits and The Hollies. His 10cc colleague Eric Stewart had been a member of The Mindbenders, the group who backed Wayne Fontana on his biggest hits, and remained with the group when they left Fontana, singing on their major hit, 'A Groovy Kind Of Love'. Drummer Kevin Godley and Lawrence 'Lol' Creme had worked with Stewart and Gouldman in 1970 on a project released under the name Hotlegs.

1967

PURPLE LETTER DAY FOR HENDRIX

Jimi Hendrix first appeared in the US singles chart, with 'Purple Haze', his second UK hit – the first, 'Hey Joe', did not reach the US chart. Exactly three years later the Isle Of Wight Festival began, where the unique guitarist played his final major gig.

In the three intervening years Hendrix had progressed from a little-known cult figure to an international superstar. After ex-Animal Chas Chandler had become his manager in 1966, Hendrix burst onto the UK scene like a shooting star, releasing four hit singles in nine months: after 'Hey Joe' reached the Top 10 at the start of 1967, 'Purple Haze' made the Top 3 in the spring and 'The Wind Cries Mary' was his summer Top 10 hit, while 'Burning Of The Midnight Lamp' kept him in the Top 20 during the latter part of the year. His albums were even greater successes. *Are You Experienced* and *Axis: Bold As Love* (both 1967) were Top 5 items, and 1968's *Smash Hits* compilation did equally well, while the epic double album, *Electric Ladyland*, was an immense international success, topping the US album chart.

Jimi Hendrix, 1967

BEATLES MANAGER BRIAN DIES

1967

Brian Epstein, manager of The Beatles, was found dead at his London home, having overdosed. According to friends, he had been suffering from severe depression for some time, although theories that he may have commited suicide have never been proven. He was only 32-years-old.

Epstein - Beatles guru

Epstein had declined the invitation to accompany the group and their wives to Bangor in North Wales, where they were attending a conference given by an organization known as the Spiritual Regeneration League that involved the study of transcendental meditation, as taught by the Maharishi Mahesh Yogi, an Indian philosopher. A few days earlier, George Harrison's wife, Patti, had heard that the Maharishi was giving a lecture in London, and convinced George to attend with her. The 'guru' then invited the group to Bangor, and other pop stars also took the trip to Bangor, including Mick Jagger and his then girlfriend, Marianne Faithfull, film star Mia Farrow, Donovan and others.

Several of The Beatles, led by Ringo and his wife Maureen, who had given birth to her second son, Jason, only a few days earlier, soon left to return to London. These included even John Lennon, who had a confrontation with the Maharishi (and apparently wrote the song 'Sexy Sadie' about the Maharishi, who showed a somewhat un-guru like interest in some of the young female attendees at the conference) and left with his wife, Cynthia.

The news about Epstein had also shocked The Beatles, who would realize in the coming months just how much they missed his steady hand guiding them.

CONNIE'S RETURN TO THE TOP

1977

The chart heyday of American singer Connie Francis had been between 1958 and 1962, when she had 16 US Top 10 hits, including three No. 1s: 'Everybody's Somebody's Fool' and 'My Heart Has A Mind Of Its Own' (both 1960) and 'Don't Break The Heart That Loves You' (1962). All these golden oldies and many more were included in her *20 All-Time Greats* album, which became the first album by a female solo vocalist to top the UK chart. It was a significant achievement, especially as less than three years before Francis had been raped at knife-point in a New York motel after a concert.

Connie Francis returns with a smile

1959

Here Comes a One-Hit Wonder

Jerry Keller, from Fort Smith, Arkansas, entered the UK singles chart for the first time with his classic seasonal hit, 'Here Comes Summer', which eventually reached No. 1 (in an autumnal October), selling over a milion copies worldwide.

Keller never reached the charts again after this one memorable hit. Very little information is available on Keller other than the fact that he both wrote and recorded one of the most popular seasonal singles of the rock era. He apparently joined a religious vocal group, The Tulsa Boy Singers, when he was 13 years old, and got his chance for a recording contract after winning a TV talent show and getting advice from Pat Boone, who attended the same church as Keller, on who to approach for a deal.

Ravings

1965
The audience at Forest Hill, New York, booed Bob Dylan because he was playing an electric guitar.

1969
Paul and Linda McCartney became the parents of a daughter, Mary, named after Paul's mother, whom he also mentioned in the chart-topping song, 'Let It Be'.

★ ★ ★

1973

Smoke Turns Purple Gold

Deep Purple

British hard rock stars Deep Purple were awarded a gold disc for half a million sales of their celebrated 'Smoke On The Water', a song whose lyrics, written by vocalist Ian Gillan, were based on an actual event.

In 1971, the group had been recording their *Machine Head* album in Montreux, Switzerland, when the building in which they were working, Montreux Casino, burnt down during a concert by Frank Zappa. With the casino being situated on the shore of Lake Geneva, Gillan wrote what he had seen, and with an unforgettable guitar riff coined by Ritchie Blackmore, a classic was born. Surprisingly not released as a single in Britain, although the chart-toping achievement of the *Machine Head* album, which included the track, perhaps made it unnecessary, it became the group's second US Top 5 single, the first being their debut hit, 'Hush', back in 1968.

Arrivals

1925 – Billy Grammer
1931 – John Perkins (Crew Cuts)
1938 – Clem Cattini (Tornados)
1943 – Honey Lantree (Ann Lantree) (Honeycombs)
1943 – David Soul (David Solberg)
1946 – Ken Andrews (Middle Of The Road)
1948 – Daniel Seraphine (Chicago)
1949 – Hugh Cornwell (Stranglers)
1951 – Wayne Osmond (Osmonds)
1961 – Kim Appleby (Mel and Kim)

★ ★ ★

1988

Kylie Bonanza

20-year-old Kylie Minogue, the Australian soap opera star whom Stock, Aitken and Waterman had transformed into a teenybop sensation in Britain, broke a record as her debut album, *Kylie*, approached the two million sales mark to become the biggest selling first album by a female in Britain. This came as no real surprise, as each of her first four singles, 'I Should Be So Lucky' (No. 1), 'Got To Be Certain', 'The Loco-Motion', 'Je Ne Sais Pas Pourquoi' and 'Especially For You' all reached either the top or the second position in the UK chart. She began 1989 with another No. 1, 'Hand On Your Heart', and her next single, 'Wouldn't Change A Thing', made No. 2.

'Lucky' Kylie

1976

SPIRIT REUNITES AFTER FIVE YEARS

Randy California, ever-present Spirit star

The original line-up of Spirit, the Los Angeles based group formed as Spirits Rebellious in 1966, re-formed for a concert in Santa Monica with Neil Young joining them on stage for an encore of Bob Dylan's 'Like A Rolling Stone'. Spirit consisted of drummer Ed Cassidy, whose shaven head made him visually distinctive in the rock genre, singer/guitarist Randy California (real name Randy Craig Wolfe), keyboard player John Locke, lead vocalist Jay Ferguson and bass player Mark Andes.

Signed to Lou Adler's newly launched Ode label in 1968, their eponymous debut album reached the Top 40 of the US chart, and 1969's *The Family That Plays Together* achieved the group's highest chart position, stopping just short of the US Top 20, no doubt assisted by the Top 30 status of a single excerpted from the album, 'I Got A Line On You'. Also in 1969 came a third album, *Clear Spirit*, which peaked just outside the Top 50. At that point the group signed with Epic Records, and their fourth album, *The 12 Dreams Of Dr Sardonicus*, became the only one of their early LPs to achieve gold status.

The group then disintegrated, with California going solo and Andes and Ferguson forming Jo Jo Gunne with guitarist Matt Andes (Mark's brother) and drummer Curly Smith. Where Spirit had always failed to release chart-friendly singles, Jo Jo Gunne immediately scored with 'Run Run Run', which reached the UK Top 10 and the US Top 30. Spirit meanwhile continued, with Cassidy and Locke recruiting guitarist Chris Staehely and his bass-playing brother Al. The one album by this line-up, *Feedback*, in 1972, made the US chart, but Cassidy and Locke then left. In the same year California's first solo album, *Captain Kopter and The Fabulous Twirlybirds*, was released, and in 1974 he and Cassidy reformed Spirit with a new bass player. The reunion of the original quintet in 1976 also produced a new album, *Son Of Spirit*.

ARRIVALS

1920 – Charlie Parker
1924 – Dinah Washington
(Ruth Lee Jones)
1943 – Dick Halligan
(Blood, Sweat and Tears)
1945 – Chris Copping
(Procol Harum)
1947 – Tony Eyers
1947 – Dave Jenkins
(Pablo Cruise)

1953 – Rick Downey
(Blue Oyster Cult)
1958 – Michael Jackson
1958 – Lenny Henry
1959 – Eddi Reader
(Fairground Attraction)

★ ★ ★

DEPARTURE LOUNGE

1976 – Jimmy Reed

RAVINGS

1958
The Quarrymen played their first live show with 15-year-old guitarist George Harrison joining John Lennon, Paul McCartney and drummer Ken Brown.

1966
The Beatles played their final live concert at Candlestick Park, San Francisco.

★ ★ ★

1977

BODYSNATCHERS TARGET ELVIS

Three people were arrested by police in Memphis, charged with attempting to steal the body of Elvis Presley, who had been buried at the local Forest Hill cemetery a week and a half earlier. One theory was that they were hoping to hold Presley's corpse for ransom. As a result of this incident Vernon Presley, Elvis's father, arranged for the bodies of both his son and his wife Gladys to be removed and re-buried side-by-side in the in the grounds of his Graceland mansion. A trip to the site has since become a pilgrimage for many Presley fans.

1970

HENDRIX FAREWELL

Jimi Hendrix played his final gig in Britain, the country where his unique qualities were first appreciated, on the final day of the Isle Of Wight festival. He was working with Mitch Mitchell, who had been a member of the Jimi Hendrix Experience, but had left Hendrix when that band split up. Mitchell continued to work with Hendrix sporadically, but with a fairly new bass player, Billy Cox, whom Hendrix had met during his days in the US Army.

Cox had appeared on the most recently released Hendrix album, 1970's live *Band Of Gypsys*, which reached the Top 10 on both sides of the Atlantic, with drummer Buddy Miles as his rhythm section partner, but in early 1970, Mitchell returned to the fold. The *Band Of*

Gypsys album was recorded to fulfil contractual obligations.

Before he achieved fame in Britain, Hendrix had signed a highly disadavatageous recording contract that gave one Ed Chalpin the right to a percentage of royalties. Chalpin had gone to court to enforce

Jimi Hendrix - last show at the Isle of Wight

that contract, the settlement being a new Hendrix live album in which Chalpin would have a continuing financial interest.

Unfortunately Hendrix's set at the Isle Of Wight festival was some way from being his finest ever show. Three weeks later, he was dead.

1972

JOHN AND YOKO'S CHARITY SHOW

John Lennon and his second wife, Yoko Ono, appeared at New York's Madison Square Garden in a concert staged for the benefit of the One To One charity. This was Lennon's first publicized solo show, staged to benefit the Willowbrook Hospital in New York, and also on the bill were Stevie Wonder, Sha Na Na and Roberta Flack, all of whom performed

for free. Wonder and Flack joined the Lennons on stage for a rousing encore of 'Give Peace A Chance', and the concert raised in excess of $250,000. John and Yoko were backed by Elephant's Memory, the New York group who also appeared on 'Some Time In New York City', the double album by the Lennons released during the previous month.

John and Yoko

1963

RONETTES HIT THE CHARTS

'Be My Baby', the single by The Ronettes produced by Phil Spector, entered the US chart, giving Spector his third US Top 3 single in under twelve months and his second US Top 3 act.

The Ronettes - Peppermint Lounge to the top of the chart

The Ronettes were sisters Veronica and Estelle Bennett and their cousin Nedra Talley, a trio of teenage girls from New York, who had launched a show business career as dancers at New York's Peppermint Lounge (where the resident band was twist star Joey Dee and his group, The Starliters). They had made some unsuccessful recordings in 1962 as Ronnie and The Relatives (also highlighting the name of lead singer Veronica 'Ronnie' Bennett), but were recommended to Spector, who was already enjoying considerable success with another girl group, The Crystals, by a magazine writer. The group signed to Spector's Philles label (deriving its name from the first names of its founders, Phil Spector and Les (Lester) Sill) and spent weeks perfecting the recording of their first two singles, 'Be My Baby' and 'Baby I Love You'. Spector's pursuit of perfection paid dividends with the earlier release, although unaccountably, 'Baby I Love You' peaked outside the US Top 20 at the end of the year, and while it almost reached the UK Top 10, The Ramones (!) scored a bigger hit with their 1980 Spector-produced cover version.

Both songs were written by the peerless songwriting team of Spector with Jeff Barry and Ellie Greenwich, who also collaborated in 1966 on the composition of the Ike and Tina Turner classic, 'River Deep – Mountain High'.

In 1964 Ronnie married Spector, which effectively ended her recording career until they were divorced in 1973. Her first solo album, *Siren*, was released in 1981.

1986

GELDOF MARRIES TV PERSONALITY

Former Boomtown Rat and Live Aid inspiration Bob Geldof, who had received an honorary knighthood two months earlier, married his longtime girlfriend, Paula Yates, daughter of the unlikely union between religious TV personality Jess Yates and Scandinavian showgirl Heller Torren.

Yates had followed her father into television, although she concentrated on a diametrically opposite type of programme, presenting a highly rated pop show, *The Tube*, and 'authoring' a ludicrously opportunist book entitled *Rock Stars In Their Underpants*. She and Geldof had already produced a child, Fifi Trixiebelle (their second, born in 1989, was named Peaches). The witnesses at the wedding, which took place in Las Vegas, were Dave Stewart and Annie Lennox, better known as Eurythmics.

Bob and Paula - rock royalty

SCAGGS REJOINS MILLER

Singer/guitarist William 'Boz' Scaggs joined The Steve Miller Band, reuniting with the group's leader, with whom he had previously worked six years before in Madison, Wisconsin, where both had been at university, having also been together in a band during their teenage years in Dallas, Texas.

Miller had been given his first guitar lesson by Mary Ford, who, with her husband, Les Paul, had been regular visitors to the Miller household. When Miller dropped out of university in the USA, he spent a year studying at the University of Copenhagen, Denmark, before returning to the US and moving to Chicago in 1964. Here, the pioneers of white blues (Paul Butterfield, Mike Bloomfield, Harvey Mandel, Charlie Musselwhite, etc.) were starting to play with their black counterparts. Miller formed the World War Three Blues Band with keyboard player Barry Goldberg, but it was a shortlived undertaking, whereupon he moved to San Francisco, forming a band with local musicians that became one of the most popular live attractions in the Bay Area.

At the end of 1967 the group were Chuck Berry's backing band on an album recorded in concert, *Live At The Fillmore*, by which time Scaggs had come back to the States from Sweden, where he had recorded his first album, *Boz*, and rejoined the band replacing guitarist James Cooke.

Soon afterwards, the Steve Miller Band signed to Capitol Records, making their debut album, *Children Of The Future*, in England with British record producer Glyn Johns. When released in mid 1968 it reached the US album chart, but a second album, *Sailor*, again recorded in England with Johns producing, was a far greater success, peaking just outside the Top 20 of the US album chart. Even before it was released, however, Scaggs had left Miller for a solo career.

CLASH FIRE JONES

Mick Jones, lead guitarist with The Clash, was fired by the group's other members, bass player Paul Simonon and singer/guitarist Joe Strummer, who claimed that he had 'drifted apart from the original idea of The Clash'. This followed the group's greatest success, which occurred earlier in the year when 'Rock The Casbah' had made the US Top 10 and their fifth album, *Combat Rock*, had become their only platinum release and their only album to reach the Top 10 on both sides of the Atlantic.

The Clash - Paul Simonon (left) and Joe Strummer (centre)

ARRIVALS

1904 – Joe Venuti
1931 – Boxcar Willie (Cecil/Lecil Travis Martin)
1933 – Conway Twitty (Harold Lloyd Jenkins)
1941 – Diane Ray
1944 – Archie Bell (Archie Bell and The Drells)
1947 – Barry Gibb
1949 – Greg Errico (Sly and The Family Stone)
1949 – Russ Field (Showaddywaddy)
1950 – Steve Goetzman (Exile)
1950 – Peter Hewson (Chicory Tip)
1955 – Bruce Foxton (Jam)
1957 – Gloria Estefan

★ ★ ★

RAVINGS

1977
Blondie signed to Chrysalis Records, which purchased the group's previous recordings (and their recording contract) from the Private Stock label.

★ ★ ★

1979
U2 released their first record. An EP entitled *U2–3*, it was released in their native Eire.

★ ★ ★

1980
Founder member Ken Hensley left Uriah Heep, leaving guitarist Mick Box as the only remaining original group member.

★ ★ ★

ROE TAKES SHEILA TO THE TOP

19-year-old Tommy Roe topped the US chart for the first time with his own composition, 'Sheila', which was later described as 'a bald rewrite of Buddy Holly's 'Peggy Sue''.

Roe, born in Atlanta (and sharing his birthday with the author of this book), formed a rock group, The Satins, while at school in the late 1950s. Apparently heavily influenced by Holly, they were offered the chance to make a record by Judd Phillips, brother of Sam Phillips, founder of Sun Records (where Presley, Cash, Lewis, Perkins, Orbison,

etc. made early recordings), and cut 'Sheila', which was a local hit in 1960, but was not promoted nationally.

In 1961 Roe was recommended to producer Felton Jarvis (who later produced many latterday Elvis Presley records). Jarvis, who worked for ABC-Paramount Records, produced a track with Roe singing titled 'Save

Tommy Roe

Your Kisses', and a re-recorded version of 'Sheila' was used as the B-side of the single. While 'Save Your Kisses' was a flop, disc jockeys began playing 'Sheila', and when it began to climb the charts, the label reportedly offered him $5,000 to leave his day job and become a full time recording artist.

By 1973 he had accumulated a total of 22 US hit singles, six of which reached the US Top 20, including 'Everybody' (1963, his third UK Top 10 single), 'Sweet Pea' (1966) and 'Dizzy' (1969, his second US chart-topper and his only UK No. 1).

1965

STONES STUFF

This was a period of intense activity for The Rolling Stones. Their latest single, '(I Can't Get No) Satisfaction', had just been released in Britain, and was proceeding to the top of the chart, having become the group's first US No. 1. They had also topped the US album chart for the first time with *Out Of*

Our Heads, which included 'Satisfaction' and their previous hit, 'The Last Time'. Neither track was included on the British version of *Out Of Our Heads*, which was released later, and was unable to overtake either *Help!* by The Beatles or *The Sound Of Music* soundtrack album in the chart.

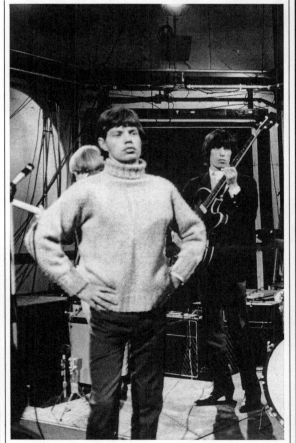
The Rolling Stones on TV's Ready Steady Go

RAVINGS

1982
The house in Surrey owned by Rolling Stone Keith Richards was badly damaged by fire for the second time in nine years.

★ ★ ★

1988
A worldwide charity tour to raise funds for Amnesty International was launched with a concert at London's Wembley Stadium featuring Bruce Springsteen, Sting, Peter Gabriel, Tracy Chapman and Youssou N'Dour.

ARRIVALS

1912 – Johnnie Lee Wills
1927 – Russ Conway
(Trevor Stanford)
1928 – Horace Silver
1939 – Bobby Purify
(Robert Lee Dickey)
(James and Bobby Purify)
1940 – Jimmy Clanton
1943 – Rosalind Ashford
(Martha and The Vandellas)
1943 – Joe Simon
1944 – Jack White
(Horst Nussbaum)
1947 – Richard Coughlan
(Caravan)
1951 – Mik Kaminski
(ELO/Violinski)
1957 – Steve Porcaro
(Toto)
1958 – Fritz McIntyre
(Simply Red)

★ ★ ★

1982

US MAKES BIG LOSSES AND HUGE STEPS FORWARD

Financed by the founder of Apple Computers, the US Festival (as in 'we', not as in 'America') was an unprofitable undertaking by all accounts, despite an estimated audience of 400,000 over three days that should have produced a gross income of $10 million.

Fleetwood Mac

year-plus residency), Jackson Browne, Talking Heads, The Cars, Tom Petty and The Heartbreakers, The Grateful Dead and many more, the show, which took place at San Bernardino, California, was inevitably an artistic success. Those who attended had little to complain about – it was one of the first times huge video screens were used (later a normal feature of outdoor

concerts) which allowed the vast crowd to follow the action despite their distance from the stage.

Eight months later the same financier presented the US Festival '83. Despite a considerably increased audience (approaching three quarters of a million), the festival again lost money, apparently because the stars on the bill – David Bowie and Van Halen – were each paid $1 million.

With an all-star bill, including Fleetwood Mac (whose *Mirage* album was at the top of the US chart at the time), The Police (very hot with their platinum *Ghost In The Machine* album still in the US chart, almost halfway through a two -

RAVINGS

1977
Elvis Presley had 27 albums and nine singles in the Top 100 of the UK chart. He was top of the singles listings with 'Way Down' and he presided over the albums chart with *40 Greatest Hits*.

1985
Johnny Marks, who composed the perennial Christmas classic, 'Rudolph The Red-Nosed Reindeer', died at the age of 75.

★ ★ ★

1966

SUPERMAN LEITCH TOPS US CHART

Scottish-born folk singer Donovan (real name Donovan Leitch) topped the US singles chart for the first and only time with 'Sunshine Superman'.

It was a change of direction for the so-called 'British Bob Dylan'. Having previously specialized in acoustic material and performances, the introduction of hitmaking record producer Mickie Most provided a much more adventurous approach to his music, in particular, electric instruments. All Donovan's biggest US hits, such as 'Mellow Yellow', 'Hurdy Gurdy Man' and 'Atlantis' (all produced by Most), concentrated on this aspect of Donovan's talent at the expense of gentler material, like 'Jennifer Juniper' from 1968, written by Patti Boyd's sister, Jenny, who operated a stall in London's Portobello Road street market (Patti herself was later to have 'Layla' written about her by her beau, Eric Clapton)

Donovan's last US Top 30 hit was an item titled 'Goo Goo Barabajagal (Love Is Hot)', on which he was backed by the Jeff Beck Group.

Donovan, the British Bob Dylan

ARRIVALS

1915 – Memphis Slim (Peter Chatman)
1925 – Hank Thompson (Henry William Thompson)
1933 – Tompall Glaser
1934 – Freddie King (Freddie Christian)
1942 – Al Jardine (Beach Boys)
1944 – Gary Walker (Gary Leeds) (Walker Brothers)
1945 – Mike Harrison (Spooky Tooth)
1945 – George Biondo (Steppenwolf)
1947 – Eric Bell (Thin Lizzy)
1948 – Don Brewer (Grand Funk Railroad)
1952 – Leroy Smith (Sweet Sensation)
1957 – Suzanne Freitag (Propaganda)
1962 – Lester Noel (Beats International)

★ ★ ★

DEPARTURE LOUNGE

1970 – Al Wilson (Canned Heat)
1985 – Johnny Marks

★ ★ ★

1962

BEATLES ABBEY ROAD DEBUT

The Beatles completed their first recording session at EMI's Abbey Road Studio complex in St John's Wood, north west London. Producer George Martin wanted them to record a song written by professional songsmith Mitch Murray, 'How Do You Do It', which they did, although with some reluctance, making it clear to Martin that they would prefer to record a song they had written themselves, and also recorded 'Love Me Do', one of the songs they had included on the audition tape that convinced Martin to sign them in the first place.

A week later the group returned to Abbey Road to re-record 'Love Me Do', this time with Ringo Starr, who had joined the group less than a month before, playing percussion and session man Andy White playing drums. Although there is actually little difference between the two versions, the earlier version with Ringo on drums was released as a single initially, but after the Andy White version was included on the group's debut album, *Please Please Me*, the White version was also used on later pressings of the 'Love Me Do' single when it was repressed in 1963, seven months after its original release.

In 1982, when EMI Records began reissuing each of the singles by The Beatles on the 20th Anniversary of its release, a 12 inch single included both versions of 'Love Me Do'.

Madness

1986

MADNESS SPLIT

North London group Madness, one of the most successful groups of the past seven years, during which they had accumulated 23 UK hit singles including the No. 1 'House Of Fun', announced that the group was splitting up. Six years later the group re-formed after a compilation album of their hits topped the UK album chart.

RAVINGS

1957
Frankie Lymon dropped out of the UK chart for the last time while still not having reached his 15th birthday.

1976
The Sex Pistols made their first television appearance on British TV show *So It Goes*.

1968

BEATLES FILM CLIP WITH FANS

Having recorded their international chart-topper, 'All You Need Is Love', in front of an audience of millions in 1967, it was decided to shoot a film that could also premiere their second single of 1968 on television with, it was hoped, a similar result.

Fifty fans were invited to Twickenham Film Studios (where the group would also record much of the *Let It Be* album). The 1968 single was 'Hey Jude', the longest single the group ever released, lasting over seven minutes (although four minutes were taken up by a long repetitive singalong of the chorus).

BANANAS MISS CHART, BUT NEW DEAL RESULTS

1981

Bananarama

Vocal trio Bananarama released their debut single, 'Ai A Mwana', on the London independent label, Demon Records, but it failed to reach the Top 75 of the UK singles chart. However, the single attracted enough attention to reach the independent chart, as a result of which these latterday revivalists of the celebrated 'girl group' sound of the mid 1960s signed to London Records.

Formed by two ex-school friends from Bristol, Keren Woodward and Sarah Dallin. with their flatmate, Siobhan Fahey,

Bananarama began by performing as an unaccompanied vocal trio in pubs and clubs, but after encouragement from a

local disc jockey, they recorded the first single, which was reissued by London immediately after the group was

signed. At the end of 1981 Fun Boy Three, an all-male trio, invited Bananarama to back them on 'It Ain't What

You Do It's The Way That You Do It', which reached the UK Top 5. Two months later roles were reversed as Fun Boy Three provided vocal backing for Bananarama's revival of 'He Was Really Sayin' Somethin'', originally a 1965 US hit for The Velvelettes. The Bananarama version again reached the UK Top 5, as did their next single, 'Shy Boy'. Their biggest 1983 hit was another revival, this time of Steam's 'Na Na Hey Hey Kiss Him Goodbye', and in 1983 'Robert De Niro's Waiting' was their first UK Top 3 hit.

This was followed by less successful years, until the trio began working with hitmaking production team Stock, Aitken and Waterman in 1986. Their first collaboration, a remake of 'Venus', the 1970 US No. 1 by Dutch group Shocking Blue, also reached the top of the US chart and restored the trio to the US Top 10 in 1986.

In 1987 Siobhan Fahey married Dave Stewart of Eurythmics, and in early 1988 she left the group and was replaced by Jacqui Sullivan.

SKYNYRD STAR BATTERED IN CAR CRASH

1976

Gary Rossington, one of the three guitarists in the 'Southern Boogie' band Lynyrd Skynyrd, was seriously injured in a car crash in Jacksonville, Florida, leaving him with a broken kneecap and minus several teeth. He

got off lightly compared to three of his colleagues who were killed in a plane crash just over a year later, when Rossington sustained further injuries, although again he made a full recovery.

ARRIVALS

1907 – Sunnyland Slim (Albert Luandrew)
1939 – John Stewart
1941 – Walt Ford (Rays)
1943 – Joe 'Speedo' Frazier (Impalas)
1945 – Al Stewart
1946 – Dean Ford (Thomas McAleese) (Marmalade)
1946 – Freddie Mercury (Frederick Bulsara) (Queen)
1946 – Buddy Miles

1946 – Loudon Wainwright III
1949 – Dave 'Clem' Clempson (Humble Pie)
1958 – Sal Solo (Classix Nouveaux)
1969 – Dweezil Zappa

★ ★ ★

DEPARTURE LOUNGE

1969 – Josh White
1978 – Joe Negroni (Teenagers)

1976

MAC BACK AT TOP OF STACK

Fleetwood Mac topped the US album chart for the first time when their eponymous album, which had been released well over a year earlier and had first entered the US album chart in August 1975, finally reached No. 1. It was a remarkable comeback for the group, which had been very big in Britain in the late 1960s, but had relocated to the USA in the early 1970s and had spent five years altering and consolidating its line-up.

The departure of founder member Peter Green in 1970 brought vocalist and keyboard player Christine McVie into the band. Already well known in Britain as Christine Perfect, the vocalist on Chicken Shack's hit single, 'I'd Rather Go Blind', she was also married to Fleetwood Mac bass player John McVie, and Green's departure was a perfect cue for her to work with her husband. During her first six months in the band another of its original members, singer/guitarist Jeremy Spencer, also left, at which point singer/guitarist Bob Welch became the first American to join the group. This line-up – Welch, Mr and Mrs McVie, drummer Mick Fleetwood and yet another singer/guitarist, Danny Kirwan – stayed together for nearly 18 months, releasing two albums, *Future Games* and *Bare Trees*, both of which reached the Top 100 of the US album chart, but in the summer of 1972, Kirwan left. He was replaced by two English musicians, vocalist Dave Walker (ex-Savoy Brown) and singer/guitarist Bob Weston (ex-Long John Baldry), but Walker did not stay long and Weston was fired in 1974 after an illicit affair with the wife of another group member.

This made Fleetwood Mac a quartet of Welch, Fleetwood and the McVies, who recorded two albums in 1974, *Mystery To Me* and *Heroes Are Hard To Find*, but at that point Welch left to form a new group, Paris, with ex-Jethro Tull bass player Glenn Cornick and ex-Sparks drummer, Hunt Sales. Welch was replaced in Fleetwood Mac by singer/guitarist Lindsey Buckingham and vocalist Stevie Nicks, who had cut an album entitled *Buckingham Nicks*, before they were invited to join. The first album by Fleetwood Mac on which they appeared was the one that topped the US chart.

Christine McVie

ARRIVALS

1925 – Jimmy Reed (James Mathis)
1939 – David Allan Coe
1942 – Dave Bargeron (Blood, Sweat and Tears)
1944 – Mel McDaniels
1944 – Mickey Waller
1944 – Roger Waters (Pink Floyd)
1947 – Sylvester James
1949 – James Litherland (Bandit/Colosseum)
1954 – Stella Barker (Belle Stars)
1954 – Louis Molino (Cock Robin)
1954 – Banner Thomas (Molly Hatchet)
1958 – Buster Bloodvessel (Douglas Trendle) (Bad Manners)
1961 – Pal Gamst Waaktaar (A-Ha)

★ ★ ★

DEPARTURE LOUNGE

1984 – Ernest Tubb
1990 – Tom Fogerty

★ ★ ★

RAVINGS

1956
The first rock 'n' roll club opened in Britain at Studio 51 in London's Great Newport Street.

★ ★ ★

1956
Little Richard recorded 'Rip It Up'.

★ ★ ★

1989
Madonna's *Like A Prayer* was voted top video of the year by MTV viewers.

★ ★ ★

1991

GLORIA GETS $5 MILLION

Gloria Estefan was awarded damages of $5 million for the injuries she sustained in a traffic accident in March 1990 when she suffered fractures and dislocated spinal vertebrae.

Gloria Estefan - a Queen's ransom?

Gloria Fajardo was born in Havana, Cuba, in 1957, but moved to Miami, Florida, as an infant. She met fellow Cuban Emilio Estefan when he lectured to the music class at her school, and he encouraged her to sing, offering her the position of vocalist with his band, The Miami Latin Boys. Gloria at first turned down the job, preferring to complete her studies – she was taking a degree in psychology at the University of Miami – but her mother persuaded her to study during the week and sing with the band at weekends. She and Estefan also became romantically involved.

The group's name was changed to Miami Sound Machine, and the couple married on Gloria's 21st birthday in 1978.

The group recorded a series of albums aimed at the Hispanic market. but in 1984 they released a track sung in English, which became a UK Top 10 hit. In 1985 a further track in English was released, 'Conga', which became the group's first US Top 10 hit (and their first million-seller). After two more US Top 10 hits in 1986, the group recognized Gloria's importance to their success and the billing on their records became Gloria Estefan and Miami Sound Machine. Major hits followed, such

as the chart-topping 'Anything For You' (1987) and 'Don't Wanna Lose You' (1989), before the tragic accident: the group's tour bus was rammed by a tractor and trailer on a road in Pennsylvania covered in snow on March 20, 1990. Gloria was air-lifted to a hospital in Manhattan, where her injuries were repaired in a four-hour operation. She returned to the stage, her popularity umimpaired, and scored another US No. 1 with 'Coming Out Of The Dark', in 1991.

1984

JACKSON – THE SEVEN-MONTH ITCH

Janet Jackson, the youngest child of the Jackson family, announced that she had married James DeBarge. The couple had eloped during the previous month, but by the spring of 1985 the marriage was over and she was back at the Jackson family home in California with her mother and two of her brothers.

Janet - eloped

ARRIVALS

1920 – Al Caiola (Alexander Emil Caiola)
1929 – Sonny Rollins (Theodore Walter Rollins)
1931 – Johnny Duncan
1934 – Little Milton (James Campbell)
1936 – Buddy Holly (Charles Hardin Holley)
1940 – Ronnie Dove
1946 – Alfa Anderson (Chic)
1949 – Gloria Gaynor
1951 – Chrissie Hynde (Pretenders)
1953 – Dave King
1957 – Margot Chapman (Starland Vocal Band)
1956 – Robin Beck
1962 – Jermaine Stewart
1966 – Calvin Williams (B.V.S.M.P.)

★ ★ ★

DEPARTURE LOUNGE

1978 – Keith Moon

★ ★ ★

1972

SPANN REMEMBERED AT ALL-STAR FESTIVAL

Otis Spann on stage at Ronnie Scott's Jazz Club in the 1960s

Otis Spann, a highly regarded R & B pianist, had died in 1970, after doctors had diagnosed that he had cancer of the liver – he had apparently failed to reduce his significant intake of alcohol, even after a heart attack, and died a month after his thirtieth birthday. The Ann Arbor Blues and Jazz Festival in 1972 was held in his memory.

The site of the festival was formally dedicated to the legendary bluesman as Otis Spann Memorial Field by Muddy Waters, Spann's widow, Lucille, and festival organizer John Sinclair, and an all-star bill entertained an audience of 15,000 people over three days.

Waters himself performed, as did another of Spann's colleagues who was signed to Chess Records, Howlin' Wolf. Junior Walker and The All Stars represented the R & B of the local Motown label, and noted blues guitarists Freddie King, Otis Rush and Johnny Shines performed as did Dr John and vocalist Bobby 'Blue' Bland. Slide guitarist Bonnie Raitt performed a tribute to another great bluesman, 'Mississippi' John Hurt, and also performed with her elderly role model, Sippie Wallace. The somewhat left-field Sun Ra and His Solar-Myth Arkestra played something titled 'Life Is Splendid' from their 'Space Is The Place' suite, and apparently everyone had a fine time, to judge from the evidence to be heard on the double album that was released of the festival's highlights.

1977

McCULLOCH FLIES AWAY

Glasgow-born guitarist Jimmy McCulloch left Wings, Paul McCartney's group in which he had played for three years, appearing on the albums *Venus and Mars*, *Wings At The Speed Of Sound* and *Wings Over America*. He left to join the re-formed Small Faces on a tour to promote their *Playmates* album, but it was generally felt that the reunion had not been a great success, and after a second album, *78 In The Shade*, the group swiftly fell apart.

McCulloch died in September 1979, at the age of 26. In his short life he had worked with a remarkable number of notable bands – apart from Wings and The Small Faces, he had been a founder member of Thunderclap Newman, playing on their 1969 UK chart-topper, 'Something In The Air', and also played in Stone The Crows, Blue, One In A Million and others.

Jimmy McCulloch

ELVIS BACK ON THE ROAD AFTER FILM FIASCOS

Although he had performed some triumphant live shows in Las Vegas, during the entire decade of the 1960s, Elvis Presley had not undertaken a US tour, concentrating on a series of increasingly pathetic films.

By 1970 he was bored with storylines that would embarrass the intelligence of a halfwit, and later in the year he embarked on what was for him an intrepid undertaking – he played a short US live tour.

Starting in Oakland, California, he played St Louis, Missouri, on September 10, Detroit, Michigan, on September 11, Miami, Florida, on September 12, two shows at Tampa, Florida, on September 13 and

Elvis - escape from Hollywood

Mobile, Alabama, on September 14. Six one-night stands in a row – something Presley had not attempted since 1958, before he went into the US Army.

For the rest of his life (the next seven years), Presley undertook tours in the autumn, visiting parts of the States from which he had been absent for many years, his final gig (in Indianapolis) being less than two months before his premature death.

BOWIE AND BOLAN IN TV DUET

In the late 1960s David Bowie and Marc Bolan were (usually) friendly rivals, as both worked with Tony Visconti, and frequently socialized with their American record producer friend.

Bolan was the more successful at the start of the 1970s, with a string of big-selling singles, including four UK No. 1s, 'Hot Love', 'Get It On', 'Telegram Sam' and 'Metal Guru', plus six more Top 10 hits in two and a half years, but he was no longer flavour of the month by 1977, and his later records (now made without

Visconti) were much less successful.

Bowie, on the other hand, had become a superstar with classic albums like *The Rise And Fall Of Ziggy Stardust and The Spiders From Mars* (1972), *Aladdin Sane, Pin-Ups* (both 1973), *Diamond Dogs* (1974) and *Young Americans* (1975), the latter earning

him his first US No. 1 single with 'Fame'. He was now in-ternationally celebrated (something that Bolan was never able to claim).

When Bolan was chosen to host an afternoon TV series, *Marc*, he invited his old rival to be a guest, and they sang a duet, 'Standing Next To You'. A week later, Bolan was dead.

ARRIVALS

1926 – Bob Luman
1941 – Otis Redding
1942 – Luther Simmons Jr. (Main Ingredient)
1942 – Inez Foxx
1945 – Dee Dee Sharp (Dione LaRue)
1946 – Doug Ingle (Iron Butterfly)
1946 – Trevor Leslie Oaks (Showaddywaddy)
1946 – Billy Preston
1947 Freddy Weller
1949 – Larry Stabbins (Working Week)
1952 – Dave Stewart (Tourists/Eurythmics)
1963 – Peter Noone (Cross)
1966 – Greg Kane (Hue and Cry)

★ ★ ★

DEPARTURE LOUNGE

1979 – Norrie Paramor

★ ★ ★

RAVINGS

1956
Elvis Presley's first appearance on TV's *Ed Sullivan Show* attracted an estimated audience of over 50 million people, one third of the population of the United States.

★ ★ ★

1979
Cat Stevens, born Stephen Georgiou, but known since his conversion to the Muslim faith as Yusuf Islam, married Fouzia Ali at Kensington Mosque in west London.

★ ★ ★

1973

STONES IN STAR STAR SCANDAL

The final track on *Goat's Head Soup*, the album by The Rolling Stones released a few days earlier, was the subject of a ban by the British national radio network, BBC Radio One.

The Stones and (below left) their 'Goat's Head Soup' album sleeve

It hardly came as a surprise to anyone who played the track, whose title was listed as 'Star Star' – it was obvious to even anyone with less than perfect hearing that the chorus was predominantly composed of the word 'starfucker' It was the third album released by the group on their Rolling Stones Records label, formed in 1971 and licensed to Atlantic Records, and Atlantic boss Ahmet Ertegun was less than impressed – not with the track in general, but with the use of 'that word'. The song was about a groupie (a person – usually female – who craves sex with a rock star) and, as Jagger pointed out, it was the group's own label, on which they could release whatever they liked. Ertegun felt that Atlantic, as distributors of the album, might be sued over the track's title, but compromised on a change to 'Star Star' when Steve McQueen, mentioned in the song, confirmed he would not sue.

1975

'HAMMOND'S FOLLY' PAYS TRIBUTE TO TALENT SCOUT

A TV Special made for a Chicago educational channel about the life of John Hammond, the legendary talent scout who had worked with Fletcher Henderson, Bessie Smith, Billie Holiday and Benny Goodman in the 1930s and later signed stars like Ray Bryant, Pete Seeger, Aretha Franklin and Carolyn Hester, featured a number of Hammond's discoveries, but the most surprising aspect of the show was the appearance of Bob Dylan, known to the staff of Columbia (CBS) Records in the early 1960s as 'Hammond's folly'.

Dylan had hardly played live since his tour with The Band that produced the *Before The Flood* album 18 months before, so his appearance, backed by a trio of Howie Wyeth (drums), Rob Stoner (bass) and Scarlet Rivera (violin), was somewhat of a coup for the TV station, especially as he played the previously unheard 'Oh Sister', which would appear three months later on his *Desire* album, 'Simple Twist Of Fate' from his chart-topping *Blood On The Tracks* album, and two versions of 'Hurricane', his protest song about ex-boxer and convicted murderer Rubin 'Hurricane' Carter.

ARRIVALS

1922 – Yma Sumac (Zoila Imperatriz Charrari Sumac del Castillo)
1925 – Roy Brown
1937 – Tommy Overstreet
1940 – Roy Ayers
1942 – Danny Hutton (Three Dog Night)
1945 – Jose Feliciano
1949 – Barriemore Barlow (Jethro Tull)
1950 – Vic Collins (Kursaal Flyers)
1950 – Joe Perry (Aerosmith)
1950 – Don Powell (Slade)
1956 – Johnnie Fingers (John Moylett) (Boomtown Rats)
1955 – Pat Mastelotto (Mr Mister)
1957 – Carol Decker (T'Pau)
1960 – Siobhan Fahey (Bananarama)

★ ★ ★

RAVINGS

1989
Scottish hitmakers Wet Wet Wet starred in a free concert held in Glasgow, attended by 60,000 people.

1990
Jason Donovan began a ten-day UK tour which climaxed with three nights at London's Hammersmith Odeon.

★ ★ ★

1987

'LEGALIZE IT' TOSH DIES

Peter Tosh - murder victim

Peter Tosh, guitarist and founder member of the seminal reggae group, The Wailers, was murdered by burglars at his home in Jamaica, just over a month before his 43rd birthday.

Tosh (born Winston Hubert McIntosh), Bunny Wailer (born Neville Livingston) and Bob Marley formed The Wailin' Wailers in 1964, making numerous local hits. In 1972 the group was signed by Island Records' founder Chris Blackwell, who recognized that they could become international stars if their music were presented and recorded in a more polished style.

The group's first two albums for Island, *Catch A Fire* and *Burnin'* (both 1972), were acclaimed without quite reaching the UK album chart, after which internal power struggles resulted in both Tosh and Wailer departing for solo careers, leaving Marley as the sole star of the group.

Tosh's first subsequent solo album, *Legalize It*, was a plea for the unrestricted use of marijuana, after which he signed to Rolling Stones Records, releasing two albums, *Bush Doctor* (1978) and *Mystic Man* (1979), which both made significant dents in the US chart. In 1983 his *Mama Africa* album peaked just outside the US Top 50. Tosh's constant brushes with authority led to several confrontations with the Jamaican police and several spells (usually brief) in prison.

RAVINGS

1963
Bob Dylan's *Great White Wonder*, the world's first significant rock music bootleg album, appeared in Los Angeles record stores.

1982
John Cougar Mellencamp's *American Fool* topped the US album chart.

★ ★ ★

1960

SANDS/SINATRA IN CHART MARRIAGE

The wedding took place between American teenage idol Tommy Sands and Nancy Sinatra, daughter of the famous Frank.

Sands, born in 1937 in Chicago, was from a musical family. He scored his first (and biggest) US hit in 1957 with 'Teenage Crush'. Although he charted with ten more singles by 1960, none of them came close to approaching the Top 3 status of that debut hit. Sands was also a noted movie star, appearing in such films as *Sing Boy Sing*, *Babes In Toyland* and in a dramatic role in the all-star movie about the Second World War, *The Longest Day*.

Nancy Sinatra was three years his junior. She had appeared with her father and Elvis Presley on television, but only began making hits after she and Sands were divorced in 1965. She had 21 US hit singles in the second half of the 1960s all on her father's Reprise label, including two international No. 1s, 'These Boots Are Made For Walkin'' (1966) and a charming duet with her father, 'Somethin' Stupid', in 1967.

ARRIVALS

1935 – Ben Hewitt
1938 – Charles Patrick (Monotones)
1944 – Phil May (Pretty Things)
1945 – Leo Kottke
1947 – Bob Cately (Magnum)
1948 – John Martyn
1948 – Dennis Tufano (Buckinghams)
1953 – Tommy Shaw (Styx)
1957 – Jon Moss (Culture Club)
1958 – Mick Talbot (Merton Parkas/Style Council)
1959 – Rory Lyons (King Kurt)
1967 – Harry Connick Jr

★ ★ ★

DEPARTURE LOUNGE

1969 – Leon Payne (Bob Wills Band)
1987 – Peter Tosh

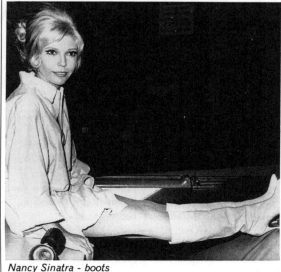

Nancy Sinatra - boots

1987

MORRISSEY SPLITS SMITHS

After vocalist/songwriter and pontificator Stephen Morrissey had appeared without the rest of The Smiths, the group he had founded with guitarist Johnny Marr in 1982, on the video for the group's Top 20 single, the typically cheerful 'Girlfriend In A Coma', rumours of the band's imminent dissolution seemed to be confirmed. It was an inopportune moment for the relationship between Morrissey and Marr to fall apart, as the group were due to sign with EMI Records after having achieved considerable fame via the independent Rough Trade label.

Morrissey

The Smiths had first reached the UK singles chart in late 1983 with 'This Charming Man', after which they had released regular hits, the biggest of which were 'Heaven Knows I'm Miserable Now' in 1984, and 'Sheila Take A Bow' in 1987, both of which reached the Top 10, while five of their albums had reached the UK Top 3: *The Smiths* and *Hatful Of Hollow* in 1984, *Meat Is Murder*, which topped the chart in early 1985, *The Queen Is Dead* (1986) and *The World Won't Listen* in 1987, at the end of which year *Strangeways Here We Come* was also in the Top 3. 1987 saw a third Smiths album in the UK chart, a compilation titled *Louder Than Bombs* that was assembled for release in the US (where it became the group's fourth chart album) and was imported into Britain, peaking just inside the Top 40.

Eventually it transpired that Morrissey and Marr had seriously fallen out, which spelt the end for the group. While Marr worked with Talking Heads, Ferry and Paul McCartney, as well as brief liaisons with The Pretenders, The The and playing in the house band at the Wembley Stadium concert staged for Nelson Mandela's Birthday Party, Morrissey signed with EMI as a solo artist, achieving four UK Top 10 hits within 18 months.

ARRIVALS

1914 – Eddy Howard
1924 – Ella Mae Morse
1931 – George Jones
1937 – Gus Backus (Donald Edgar Backus) (Del-Vikings)
1940 – Tony Bellamy (Redbone)
1943 – Maria Muldaur
1944 – Barry White
1944 – Colin Young (Foundations)
1945 – Andrea Simpson (Caravelles)
1948 – Will Birch (Martin Birch) (Kursaal Flyers/Records)
1952 – Gerry Beckley (America)
1952 – Neil Peart (Rush)
1956 – Barry Andrews (King Crimson/XTC)
1956 – Brian Robertson (Thin Lizzy/Motorhead)
1968 – Kenny Thomas

★ ★ ★

RAVINGS

1948
The Presley family – parents Vernon and Gladys and 13-year-old Elvis – moved from Tupelo, Mississippi, to Memphis, Tennessee.

1970
Bob Dylan, Joan Baez and Arlo Guthrie were among a galaxy of stars who appeared at the *Woody Guthrie Memorial Concert* at Hollywood Bowl.

★ ★ ★

1987

LA BAMBA GIVES WOLVES DOUBLE TOP

Los Lobos - Spanish for 'The Wolves' - were a chicano (Mexican-American) group from East Los Angeles. They topped both the albums and singles charts in the USA with their revival of 'La Bamba', the song that was originally a hit nearly 30 years before for Ritchie Valens.

The song, taken from the soundtrack of the film (also called *La Bamba*) starring Lou Diamond Phillips about the short life of Valens, was over 200-years-old and means wedding march. It had been a part of Los Lobos' repertoire since their formation in 1974

Los Lobos

LIVE PEACE IN TORONTO

1969

John and Yoko 'bed-in'

ARRIVALS

1911 – Bill Monroe (William Smith Monroe)
1916 – Dick Haymes
1924 – Maurice Jarre
1925 – Mel Torme
1939 – James Johnson (Jayhawks)
1939 – Dave Quincy (Jet Blacks/Manfred Mann's Earthband)
1941 – David Clayton-Thomas (David Thomsett) (Blood, Sweat and Tears)
1944 – Peter Cetera (Chicago)
1952 – Randy Jones (Village People)
1954 – Dan Hegarty (Darts)
1956 – Joni Sledge (Sister Sledge)
1965 – Zak Starkey

★ ★ ★

The Plastic Ono Band performed a concert in Toronto, Canada, which was later released as an album titled *Live Peace In Toronto*. The group had been hastily added to the bill for a *Rock 'n' Roll Revival Concert* that also starred Chuck Berry, Gene Vincent, Bo Diddley, The Doors and Alice Cooper.

The involvement of The Plastic Ono Band, the group formed (with ever-changing personnel) by John Lennon and Yoko Ono, who had married six months earlier, resulted from an invitation they had received when they were in Montreal, Canada, three months before. There, they had been publicizing their call for world peace by a 'bed-in' at the Hotel La Reine Elizabeth during which they recorded 'Give Peace A Chance'.

Lennon and his wife telephoned anyone they could think of who might be free to dash across the Atlantic for a single concert, and in fact assembled a trio of notable musicians at short notice. Guitarist Eric Clapton had just completed the only tour undertaken by the shortlived supergroup Blind Faith. Bass player Klaus Voorman was an old friend of Lennon's, having met The Beatles in Hamburg before they were famous. Subsequently, he had moved to Britain and played with Manfred Mann, replacing Jack Bruce in that group, which had broken up a few months earlier. Drummer Alan White was the least famous member of the ad hoc group – he had mainly worked as a session musician, but would later become a longtime member of Yes.

The group flew to Toronto on a Boeing 707 on which they rehearsed their set. What appeared three months later on the live album recorded in Toronto was a performance that seemed to be in three sections. The first consisted of three cover versions of oldies, 'Blue Suede Shoes', 'Money', and 'Dizzy Miss Lizzy'. Next came three Lennon compositions, 'Yer Blues', 'Cold Turkey', and 'Give Peace A Chance'. Side two of the album consisted of two songs written by Ono, one of which lasted twelve minutes.

1979

ABBA LIVE IN AMERICA

Although Swedish quartet ABBA, with seven UK No. 1 singles to their credit in the previous five years, had toured in Europe and Australasia, they had never previously played in North America before the opening concert of their 1979 world tour, which began in

Edmonton, Canada and ended in Toronto. During the 18-date North American leg of the tour, it was estimated that the group played to a total audience of 140,000 people.

They were extremely popular in America, racking up a total of 14 Top 30 hits including four Top 10s: 'Waterloo' (in 1974), 'Dancing Queen' (which topped the chart in 1977), 'Take A Chance On Me' (1978) and 'The Winner Takes It All' (1981) and five Top 40 albums with *Abba - The Album* selling over a million copies. Despite this, ABBA consider America to be their one failure with their sales there paling beside those in other territories.

RAVINGS

1969
Santana's eponymous debut album entered the US chart, where it remained for over two years.

★ ★ ★

September

1955

RICHARD ROCKS WITH TUTTI FRUTTI

Little Richard rocks

Richard Penniman, better known as Little Richard, completed his first two-day recording session for Hollywood-based Specialty Records. He had auditioned for the label six months earlier, and was booked into Cosimo Matassa's studio in New Orleans, where he was backed by a group of well-known local session musicians, including drummer Earl Palmer and pianist Huey 'Piano' Smith.

The first day of recording produced four tracks, none of which sounded spectacular, and the first four tracks taped on the next day seemed similarly uninspiring, until the musicians went for a meal break in a restaurant known as The Dew Drop Inn, where Richard, at the restaurant's piano, played producer 'Bumps' Blackwell an uptempo nonsense song he had written enitled 'Tutti Frutti'. He apparently normally only played the song to white audiences.

He had coined the hook line of 'A-wop-bop-a-loo-bop-a-lop-bam-boom' while working washing dishes, a job he was forced to take in order to support his family following the death of his father. When acquaintants would joke at his oft-expressed desire to be a professional musician, he would say 'A-wop-bop', etc., which was meaningless but conveyed his disdain.

'Tutti Frutti' was released at the end of the year, and immediately entered the US R & B chart, where it reached the Top 3, also becoming Little Richard's first pop chart Top 20 item. It was somewhat less successful in Britain, where it was only released as the B-side to 'Long Tall Sally', his biggest American hit and Richard's first UK Top 3 hit. 'Tutti Frutti' did, however, creep into the Top 30 for a single week in its own right.

ARRIVALS

1946 – Pete Agnew (Nazareth)
1947 – John 'Bowser' Baumann (Sha-Na-Na)
1949 – Steve Gaines (Lynyrd Skynyrd)
1950 – Paul Kossoff (Free/Back Street Crawler)
1955 – Barry Cowsill (Cowsills)
1959 – Morten Harket (A-Ha)

★ ★ ★

DEPARTURE LOUNGE

1948 – Vernon Dalhart
1981 – Furry Lewis
1989 – Perez Prado

1976

GOLD 'WIRED' FOR BECK

Jeff Beck's instrumental jazz/rock album *Wired* was certified gold. It was his second gold album in succession, following the previous year's *Blow By Blow* album (produced by George Martin), his only release to reach the Top 5 of the US chart. Guitarist Beck's antipathy towards vocalists seemed to date from his having been forced by producer Mickie Most to sing on his first two hits, 'Hi Ho Silver Lining' and 'Tallyman', in preference to the then little-known Rod Stewart, who was a member of The Jeff Beck Group. Stewart sang on Beck's first two albums, *Truth* and *Beck-Ola*, but then left with bass player Ron Wood to join The Faces, where Wood played lead guitar.

Jeff Beck - guitar great

RAVINGS

1968
The Archies, the cartoon group whose 1970 single, 'Sugar Sugar', sold over six million copies, first appeared on American TV screens.

1968
Pete Townshend, in an interview in *Rolling Stone* magazine, spoke about a rock opera he was writing about a boy who is deaf, dumb and blind and 'sure played a mean pinball'.

★ ★ ★

1962

'SHERRY' LAUNCHES SEASONS

The Four Seasons, the vocal group from New Jersey led by Frankie Valli, topped the US singles chart for the first time with their unforgettable hit, 'Sherry', which remained at the top of the tree for five weeks.

The Four Seasons with Frankie Valli (third from left)

Formed as The Variatones in 1955 by lead vocalist Frankie Valli (born Francis Castelluccio), Tommy De Vito and two others who had both left the group by 1959, they changed their name in 1956 to The Four Lovers, scoring a minor US hit single that year with 'You're The Apple Of My Eye', and adopted the name with which they achieved international fame in early 1962 – it was the name of a famous New York restaurant. By then, the other two longterm members of the group, Bob Gaudio (ex-Royal Teens, of 'Short Shorts' fame) and Nick Massi, had been recruited, and this line-up remained constant until 1965, by which time the group had accumulated nine US Top 10 hits in less than three years, including three more No. 1s – Big Girls Don't Cry' (1962), 'Walk Like A Man' (1963) and 'Rag Doll' (1964), as well as over a dozen other chart singles.

The group's main selling point was Valli's remarkable ability to sing in a loud and very accurate falsetto voice. When Nick Massi left in 1965 the group's success continued unabated and, unlike most American acts, The Four Seasons were virtually unaffected by the so-called 'British Invasion'. They

increased their tally of US hit singles to 40 by the end of the decade, although the second half of the decade only produced four more Top 10 successes.

In 1966 Valli also embarked on a solo career alongside his work with the group, his biggest early success on his own account being the gold single, 'Can't Take My Eyes Off You', in 1967 (a US No. 2).

ARRIVALS

1903 – Roy Acuff
1921 – Snooky Pryor (James Edward Pryor)
1928 – Cannonball Adderley (Julian Edwin Adderley)
1940 – Jimmy Gilmer (Fireballs)
1941 – Les Braid (Swinging Blue Jeans)
1942 – Lee Dorman (Iron Butterfly/Captain Beyond)
1956 – Jaki Graham
1971 – Frederick Eugene Byrd (B.V.S.M.P.)

★ ★ ★

DEPARTURE LOUNGE

1980 – Bill Evans
1983 – Willie Bobo

1979

DYLAN TURNS TO GOD

Protest singer Bob Dylan, who had been making acclaimed albums since 1962, released Slow Train Coming, an album of religious songs. This provoked rumours that Dylan, who had been brought up in the Jewish faith, had become a 'born again' Christian. Mark Knopfler of British group Dire Straits played on the album, which nevertheless became only Dylan's second ever platinum-certified release.

Although the tour promoting the album received a distinctly cool reception, the album reached the Top 3 of the US chart, and a track from it, 'Gotta Serve Somebody', won Dylan a Grammy Award in early 1980 for Best Male Rock Vocal Performance.

Dylan - converted to Christianity

RAVINGS

1971
Donny Osmond topped the US chart as a solo artist with 'Go Away Little Girl'.

1980
David Bowie opened on Broadway in the title role of the play *The Elephant Man*.

★ ★ ★

September

1977

BOLAN LOSES ARGUMENT WITH TREE

Marc Bolan, the performer who more than any other epitomized the 'Glam Rock' movement that dominated the British charts during the mid 1970s, was killed when the car in which he was a passenger collided with a tree on Barnes Common in south west London.

Born Mark Feld in London in 1947, Bolan joined John's Children as lead guitarist in 1967. Later that year he launched Tyrannosaurus Rex, an acoustic duo in which he was vocalist, guitarist and songwriter, with percussionist Steve Peregrine Took.

The object of T.Rextasy

At the instigation of producer Tony Visconti, the group changed its name to the more acceptable T. Rex, and with the more outgoing Mickey Finn replacing

Took as bongo basher, the music became more electric. Starting in late 1970 with their first Top 3 hit, 'Ride A White Swan', which opened the floodgates for a string of

23 hit singles to 1977, although his greatest success came between 1970 and 1973 when he topped the chart four times: 'Hot Love' and 'Get It On' (both 1971),

and 'Telegram Sam' and 'Metal Guru' (both 1972).

In 1972 he reached the US Top 10 for the first and only time with 'Get It On'. Even then, the

song's title had to be changed, to.'(Bang A Gong) Get It On', to avoid confusion with another hit entitled 'Get It On', recorded by jazz/rock group Chase.

ARRIVALS

1925 – B. B. King
(Riley B. King)
1931 – Little Willie Littlefield
1934 – Richard Brandon (Dubs)
1943 – Joe Butler (Lovin' Spoonful)
1944 – Bernie Calvert (Hollies)
1944 – Betty Kelley (Martha and The Vandellas)
1947 – Russ Abbott
1947 – Sonny Lemaire

(Exile)
1948 – Kenny Jones (Small Faces/Faces/Who)
1950 – David Bellamy (Bellamy Brothers)
1953 – Earl Klugh
1956 – Charles Fearing (Raydio)
1958 – Rodney Franklin
1963 – Richard Marx

★ ★ ★

DEPARTURE LOUNGE

1977 – Marc Bolan

1963

AMERICA SHUNS BEATLE NUMBER ONE

As The Beatles were signed to EMI Records worldwide, their early British hits were automatically available to EMI's flagship label in the US, Capitol. However, Capitol decided not to exercise their option on 'Please Please Me', 'From Me To You' and the first Beatles album, which were then licensed to independent American labels. When Capitol put their weight behind the group's

fourth single, 'I Want To Hold Your Hand', which topped the US chart in early 1964, all the previously released Beatles singles suddenly entered the US chart. 'She Loves You', the group's third hit in Britain, had been released by Swan Records, a small independent label, in September 1963, but had hardly sold at all. After the group's US breakthrough, it burst into the

US chart, climbing to No. 1 in March 1964.

RAVINGS

1970
Led Zeppelin won the Best Group category in the *Melody Maker* poll, the first time in years any other act had threatened the predominance of The Beatles.

1977

SUPREMES TOP UK CHART WITH OLDIES ALBUM

Diana Ross and The Supremes, the trio who became one of the Motown label's most successful acts during the 1960s and had been defunct since 1970, when Ross left for a solo career, topped the UK album chart with *20 Golden Greats*, a compilation album of their hits.

The Supremes - still a No. 1 act

The album remained at the top of the UK chart for seven weeks – no surprise, as it included an incredible 12 US No. 1 hits: 'Where Did Our Love Go', 'Baby Love' and 'Come See About Me' (all from 1964), 'Stop! In The Name Of Love', 'Back In My Arms Again' and 'I Hear A Symphony' (all from 1965), 'You Can't Hurry Love' and 'You Keep Me Hangin' On' (both from 1966), 'Love Is Here And Now You're Gone' and 'The Happening' (both from 1967) and the controversial song, 'Love Child' from 1968, by which time the group name had changed from simply The Supremes to Diana Ross and The Supremes, and the final single featuring Ross, 'Someday We'll Be Together'.

1977

RICH PICKINGS FOR RIVERS

'Poor Side Of Town' became the eleventh US hit single by Johnny Rivers, one of America's most consistent hitmakers of the mid 1960s. In the following November it became his only US No. 1.

Rivers, born John Ramistella in New York City, grew up in Baton Rouge, Louisiana, where he was exposed to the area's early rock'n'roll stars like Fats Domino, Frankie Ford and Huey 'Piano' Smith. He began writing songs as a teenager, and on a trip to New York to visit a relative waited outside WINS, the radio station that employed Alan Freed, until he met the disc jockey. He played some of his work to Freed, who arranged a recording deal and also renamed Ramistella as Johnny Rivers.

In the late 1950s Rivers moved to Los Angeles, and began playing as a singer/guitarist in Hollywood clubs, building up a strong following that convinced a local business man, Elmer Valentine, to open a new club, the Whisky-a-Go-Go, where Rivers was the main attraction.

In 1964 Rivers scored his first US Top 3 hit with a cover version of Chuck Berry's 'Memphis', and he continued to chart with cover versions of oldies like Berry's 'Maybelline', Harold Dorman's 'Mountain Of Love' and bluesman Willie Dixon's 'Seventh Son'. However, it was not until he was confident enough to record his own songs that he reached the elusive No. 1 spot with 'Poor Side Of Town'.

Hitmaker Johnny Rivers

RAVINGS

1987
Bad, the long-awaited follow-up to Michael Jackson's hugely successful *Thriller* (which topped the US album chart for 37 weeks!), spent its first week at the top of the UK album chart.

1990
Natalie Cole married record producer Andre Fisher.

★ ★ ★

ARRIVALS

1923 – Hank Williams (Hiram King Williams)
1926 – Bill Black
1929 – 'Sil' Sylvester Austin
1934 – Little Milton (Milton Campbell)
1937 – Phil Cracolici (Mystics)
1940 – Lamonte McLemore (Fifth Dimension)
1950 – Fee Waybill (John Waldo) (Tubes)

★ ★ ★

DEPARTURE LOUNGE

1951 – Jimmy Yancey
1973 – Hugo Winterhalter

★ ★ ★

1970

HENDRIX DEATH STUNS ROCK WORLD

Hailed as a genius, fêted as a hero and scarred by the inevitable ravages wrought by those who achieve overnight success, Jimi Hendrix died in London. The official cause of his death was that he inhaled his own vomit at a time when it was widely presumed that he was under the influence of drugs or alcohol or both.

Born in Seattle, he taught himself guitar as a child, and enlisted in the US paratroop division, from which he was medically discharged after an accident during training, whereupon he made a career as a guitarist for hire, working with Little Richard and The Isley Brothers among others. In 1965 he moved to New York, where he played in a band backing soul singer Curtis Knight before forming his own band, Jimmy James and The Blue Flames. In

The late Jimi Hendrix

1966, Chas Chandler, ex-bass player with The Animals, saw Hendrix/James playing at the Cafe Wha?, and signed him to a management contract, taking him to London at the end of the year, where Hendrix became a sensation.

Working with the English rhythm section of Noel Redding (bass) and Mitch Mitchell (drums), he made magnificent recordings for the next two years, but the acclaim he received, both for hit singles like 'Purple Haze' and albums such as *Axis: Bold As Love*, and for his amazing live performances at Monterey in 1967 and at

Woodstock, where he gave a show-stopping version of the American national anthem, confirmed his brilliance.

Disenchanted with the limitations of the original trio, Hendrix recruited a replacement American rhythm section, but he was already careering headlong down the path of excess, the only possible end to which was death. Drug busts and management problems did not assist his plight, and his messy set at the 1970 Isle Of Wight festival was disappointing. Back in London after the festival, he visited his German girlfriend, Monika Danneman, in whose flat he died.

1990

NEW KIDS MAKE IT NINE IN A ROW

When 'Tonight' entered the US Top 10, it gave Boston, Massachusetts, quintet New Kids On The Block an enviable start to their career of nine consecutive Top 10 hits. Before 'Tonight', the titles that turned the trick for them (all between 1988 and 1990) were 'Please Don't Go Girl', 'You Got It (The Right Stuff)', 'I'll Be Loving You (Forever)', 'Hangin' Tough', (Didn't I) Blow Your Mind', 'Cover Girl', 'This One's For The Children' and 'Step By Step'. Their next single, 'Let's Try It Again' stalled at 53.

Short trousers - New Kids

1981

SIMON AND GARFUNKEL REUNITE ON RECORD

1970's *Bridge Over Troubled Water* had been an incredibly successful album for Paul Simon and Art Garfunkel, the folk-based duo, topping the charts on both sides of the Atlantic, but it had been their final original album together. Both had embarked upon successful solo careers after *Bridge* had dominated the 1971 Grammy Awards. Their reunion concert in New York's Central Park was something not to be missed, and an audience of around 400,000 saw them recreate their musical magic.

Garfunkel (left) and Simon on stage in Central Park

Personal differences were the reason for their split in 1970, but they reunited for a one-off concert in aid of presidential candidate George McGovern in 1972 and collaborated on 'My Little Town', a track that appeared on both their 1975 albums – Simon's *Still Crazy After All These Years* and Garfunkel's *Breakaway*. In 1977 they had appeared at an Awards Ceremony in London commemorating Queen Elizabeth II's Silver Jubilee, where *Bridge Over Troubled Water* was judged Best non-British Album released during the Queen's 25-year reign, while the title track was similarly honoured as Best Single.

Simon had also guested on a track of Garfunkel's 1978 album *Watermark*, and had repeated the gesture on a track of his ex-partner's 1981 album *Scissors Cut*, but to have this immensely popular duo performing a complete concert together, and more significantly for those unable to attend the show, to have it preserved for posterity on both record and video, made the Central Park show a Red Letter occasion for their numerous fans around the world.

1960

TOP 100 TRIO BY TWISTER

Hank Ballard and The Midnighters became the first group with three singles in the US Top 100 simultaneously, when 'Let's Go, Let's Go, Let's Go', which eventually achieved his highest ever US chart position, joined 'Finger Poppin' Time', his first Top 10 hit, and 'The Twist'.

The latter, which was written by Ballard, became an international hit for Chubby Checker after Ballard reportedly refused to promote it on a highly rated US TV show, after which the then little-known Checker (real name Ernest Evans) became the King Of The Twist. 'The Twist' was originally released by Ballard as the B-side of his first US hit in 1969, 'Teardrops On Your Letter', and was apparently based on 'Whatcha Gonna Do?', a 1953 B-side by The Drifters.

Hank Ballard

RAVINGS

1955
Top Canadian vocal group The Crew Cuts started a UK tour.

1990
Stock, Aitken and Waterman scored their 100th UK chart entry. The record in question was 'Better The Devil You Know' by Kylie Minogue.

★ ★ ★

ARRIVALS

1921 – Billy Ward (Dominoes)
1926 – Nini Rosso (Celeste Rosso)
1931 – Brook Benton (Benjamin Franklin Peay)
1935 – Nick Massi (Four Seasons)
1940 – Bill Medley (Righteous Brothers)
1943 – Cass Elliott (Ellen Naomi Cohen) (Mamas and Papas)
1945 – David Bromberg
1945 – Freda Payne
1946 – John Coghlan (Status Quo)
1947 – Lol Creme (Lawrence Creme) (10cc)
1952 – Nile Rodgers (Chic)
1955 – Rex Smith
1957 – Rusty Egan (Rich Kids/Visage)
1958 – Lita Ford (Runaways)

★ ★ ★

DEPARTURE LOUNGE

1973 – Gram Parsons

1973

BROWN TAKES CROCE TO TOP TOO LATE

Singer/songwriter Jim Croce was one of the select few who had topped the US singles chart, although he was only able to enjoy his exalted status for two months before he and his friend and lead guitarist, Maury Muehleisen, were killed. The light plane Croce had hired to take them to play a second concert in one day hit a tree on take-off from Natchitoches, Louisiana, where they had played a concert at a local university.

Croce had been a songwriter and performer with his wife Ingrid for ten years before his US chart debut with 'You Don't Mess Around With Jim', which reached the US Top 10 in September 1972.

During the next twelve months he released another US Top 20 hit, 'Operator (That's Not The Way It Feels)', a third hit single, 'One Less Set Of Footsteps', which made the US Top 40, an album, also entitled *You Don't Mess Around With Jim*, which was listed in the *Billboard* chart for over 18 months before it reached No. 1, where it remained for five weeks, and a second album, *Life And Times*, which reached the US Top 10.

A track from that album, 'Bad, Bad Leroy Brown', had given Croce his first No. 1 single, and he was on the crest of a wave of success at the time of his death, as was proved the following month when 'I Got A Name' became his third Top 10 single and was swiftly overtaken by 'Time In A Bottle', a track from the earlier *You Don't Mess Around With Jim* album, which shot straight to No. 1.

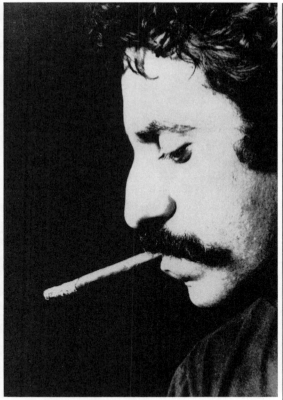
Jim Croce - cut off in his prime

1976

PUNK ROCK COMES TO OXFORD STREET

The original Sex Pistols

The 100 Club in London's Oxford Street was the venue for the first punk rock festival in Britain. Once a traditional jazz club run by noted British jazz trumpeter Humphrey Lyttleton, by 1976 it featured jazz along with many other styles of music.

Ron Watts, an entrepreneur who had been the leader of Brewer's Droop, a pub rock combo that briefly included Mark Knopfler as a member (pre-Dire Straits), had promoted several punk shows at the 100 Club, and decided to showcase as many punk acts as could be found in his festival. This eventually included The Sex Pistols, The Clash, The Damned, The Buzzcocks, The Vibrators, Subway Sect featuring Vic Goddard and Siouxsie and The Banshees featuring Sid Vicious on drums.

ARRIVALS

1890 – Jelly Roll Morton (Ferdinand Joseph Lamenthe)
1895 – Bob Miller
1924 – Gogi Grant (Audrey Brown)
1934 – Sophia Loren
1940 – Richard Stephens (String-A-Longs)
1946 – Mick Rogers (Manfred Mann's Earthband)
1949 – Chuck and John Panozzo (Styx)
1959 – Alannah Currie (Thompson Twins)
1960 – David Hemmingway (Housemartins/Beautiful South)

★ ★ ★

DEPARTURE LOUNGE

1973 – Jim Croce
1973 – Ben Webster
1984 – Steve Goodman

RAVINGS

1958
Tommy Steele became the first rock 'n' roller immortalized in wax at London's world famous Madame Tussaud's Waxworks.

1975
The Bay City Rollers made their US TV debut on *Saturday Night Variety Show*, on which they performed – appropriately enough – 'Saturday Night', their first (and only) US No. 1 single.

★ ★ ★

1974

BENDER QUITS MOTT

Mott The Hoople (left to right) Overend, Buffin, Hunter, Ronson and Morgan Fisher

British rock group Mott The Hoople lost their second lead guitarist in just over a year when Ariel Bender left the band.

Founded in 1968 by Pete 'Overend' Watts (bass), Dale 'Buffin' Griffin (drums), Mick 'Ralpher' Ralphs (lead guitar) and Verden 'Phally' Allen (keyboards), the group were joined by vocalist Stan Tippins and adopted the highly inappropriate name Silence. After sending a demo tape to Island Records, the label's A & R boss, Guy Stevens, became the group's manager. Tippins left the band, later becoming their personal manager, and Stevens advertised in *Melody Maker* for a replacement. The successful applicant was Ian Hunter (Ian Hunter Patterson), and with his recruitment came another name change, to Mott The Hoople (inspired by the Willard Manus novel of the same name).

While quickly accumulating a large and avid following on the live circuit, the group's albums sold in disappointingly small quantities, and a single produced by the legendary George 'Shadow' Morton (creator of The Shangri'Las hits), 'Midnight Lady', failed to chart at all. 1n 1972 they decided to split up during a tour, but David Bowie offered them one of his songs if they would continue recording. The group left Island and signed with Columbia (CBS), their first single on the new label being 'All The Young Dudes', which was also produced by Bowie and became a Top 3 hit in Britain. The UK Top 10 hits continued with 'All The Way From Memphis' and 'Roll Away The Stone' (both 1973), but between those singles a discontented Ralphs left to become a founder member of Bad Company and was replaced by Bender (better known as Luther Grosvenor when he was in Spooky Tooth). He had allegedly acquired his name due to his habit of bending the radio aerials of parked cars he came accross.

1956

HALEY HAS FIVE HITS IN TOP 30

Rock 'n' roll's John The Baptist, Bill Haley, was regarded as the King in the UK before the arrival of young whippersnapper Elvis Presley. A few months after the hillbilly cat from Memphis crashed into the UK chart with 'Heartbreak Hotel', Haley had five singles in the UK Top 30. Both 'See You Later Alligator' and 'Rock Around The Clock' had returned to the chart, which also included three other Haley hits, 'The Saints Rock 'n' Roll', 'Rockin' Through The Rye' and 'Razzle Dazzle'.

Bill Haley (centre) and his Comets

ADAMS BEATS 36-YEAR-OLD RECORD

1991

When '(Everything I Do) I Do It For You' by Bryan Adams began its twelfth consecutive week at the top of the UK singles chart, it shattered a record that had seemed unassailable.

Country-and-western yodeller Slim Whitman had established an apparently unbeatable mark in 1955, when his version of 'Rose Marie' had remained at No. 1 in the UK singles chart for eleven consecutive weeks, topping David Whitfield's achievement in 1954, when 'Cara Mia' had spent ten consecutive weeks at the top.

Bryan Adams

RAVINGS

1962
'Silver Threads and Golden Needles' by The Springfields became the first single by a British vocal group to reach the US Top 20.

★ ★ ★

1989
Irving Berlin, one of the USA's most famous composers of popular songs, died aged 101.

★ ★ ★

Whitfield's ballad had taken the title from three singles that had each spent nine weeks at No. 1. The record was established by the very first No. 1 in a published chart in Britain, Al Martino's 'Here In My Heart', the only No. 1 single of 1952. Martino's mark had been equalled in 1953 by Frankie Laine's neo-religious ballad of redemption, 'I Believe', although when the facts are considered, it becomes fairly clear that Laine's record should really have held the title.

Not only did 'I Believe' enjoy a run of nine consecutive weeks before it was toppled by

Eddie Fisher's slushy 'I'm Walking Behind You', it allowed Fisher a single week at No. 1 before returning to the top for six more consecutive weeks (making 15 out of 16). To cap it, when 'Moulin Rouge', an orchestral version of a film theme by Mantovani, knocked 'I Believe' down the chart for another single week,

the recalcitrant single by Laine returned to No. 1 for another three consecutive weeks, making an unbelievable 18 weeks out of 20! At the end of that year Laine and Whitfield had a nine-week fight with rival versions of the same song, 'Answer Me'. Whitfield got to the top first for a single week, then Laine took over for

the next five, after which Whitfield's sales rallied and for the seventh week with 'Answer Me' at the top, his single and Laine's tied. For the next three weeks, Laine held pole position by himself, making a ten-week No. 1 song. It was replaced by another nine week chart-topper, Eddie Calvert's trumpet solo of 'Oh Mein Papa'.

ARRIVALS

1913 – Leroy Holmes (Alvin Holmes)
1930 – Joni James (Joan Carmella Babbo)
1942 – Mike Patto (Mike McCarthy)
(Timebox/Patto)
1951 – David Coverdale (Deep Purple/Whitesnake)
1956 – Debbie Boone (Deborah Ann Boone)
1960 – Joan Jett (Joan Larkin) (Runaways)

★ ★ ★

DEPARTURE LOUNGE

1989 – Irving Berlin
1990 – Tom Fogerty (Creedence Clearwater Revival)

★ ★ ★

THE PAUL IS DEAD FIASCO

1969

The USA was shaken by the widely broadcast rumour that Paul McCartney had died in a car accident in 1966. To support this preposterous suggestion, many so-called 'clues' were cited from Beatle records and from the group's album sleeves.

The theory suggested that a contest was held to discover a McCartney lookalike, and the winner was one William Campbell, who was under strict instructions never to discuss the contest.

Many of the 'clues', which were supposedly pre-planned by the surviving Beatles to break the sad news gently to their fans, were listed. A voice can be heard on 'Strawberry Fields Forever' saying 'I buried Paul', a part of the largely unlistenable 'Revolution 9' was said to reveal the words 'Turn me on, dead man' when played backwards (!), while the sleeve of the *Sergeant Pepper* album includes a picture of McCartney wearing a pin badge with 'O.P.D.' on

Paul, alive and well

it. 'Officially pronounced dead', the rumours suggested, although the genuine explanation was less prosaic – the badge had been acquired by McCartney in Canada, and the initials were those of the Ontario Police Department. The clincher was supposedly the sleeve of the *Abbey Road* album, with all four Beatles in single file on a pedestrian crossing. This, it was said, was a funeral procession, with John Lennon as the preacher, George Harrison as the grave digger and Ringo Starr a mourner, while

McCartney is both barefoot (who puts shoes on the mangled victim of a car crash?) and out of step with his erstwhile colleagues.

McCartney attempted to convince the world that he was alive and

well, but by then the conspiracy was so widely believed that he decided to retreat to his Scottish farm, thereby vanishing from circulation and giving the rumour even greater credibility.

1967

MOTHERS AT ALBERT

The Mothers Of Invention led by Frank Zappa played their first British concert at London's Royal Albert Hall, backed by an orchestra. The group had released two albums, *Freak Out* (a double album) and *Absolutely*

Free, both of which reached the US album chart but seemed so incomprehensible to mainstream record-buyers that the group, and particularly Zappa, instantly gained a reputation as 'weird'and off the wall.

FISH SWIMS TO FREEDOM

Vocalist and songwriter Fish, widely regarded as the group's most charismatic member, left British rock band Marillion for a solo career. It was widely predicted that his departure would herald the group's swift fall from commercial grace, but the prophets of doom proved inaccurate.

Marillion with Fish (left)

The group was formed in 1978 as Silmarillion (the title of a children's novel by J. R. R. Tolkien), but made little progress until ex-Forestry Commission worker Derek Dick auditioned as vocalist in early 1981, having written lyrics to one of the group's existing instrumental compositions, 'The Web'. (Dick was

reportedly known as Fish due to his tendency to take overlong baths.) Immediately stamping his personality on the band, which by then had abbreviated its name to Marillion, he was frequently compared to Peter Gabriel during the latter's years as focal point of Genesis, and the band developed a fanatical following for its

live appearances, although its personnel seemed to be in a frequent state of flux, with regular changes.

However, Marillion had become a major attraction, with a string of UK Top 10 albums, including *Script For A Jester's Tear*, *Fugazi* and 1985's chart-topping *Misplaced Childhood*, and major hit singles like

'Kayleigh' and 'Lavender' (both 1985) and 1987's 'Incommunicado'.

In early 1988 the band held a summit meeting to discuss the increasing distance that had developed between Fish and his colleagues, mainly about Marillion's future musical direction, and by the autumn he had departed for a solo

career. It took six months before the group officially announced that Steve Hogarth (ex lead singer of The Europeans) would replace him, but while the group's subsequent albums spent briefer periods in the UK Top 10, by 1993 they had scored a creditable eight Top 50 hits while their ex-leader could only manage five.

1977
At the first Elvis Presley Convention in Cincinatti, Ohio, original copies of some early Presley singles sold for $300 (£200).

★ ★ ★

1988
After a gap of over 23 years The Hollies returned to the top of the UK singles chart at a time when 'He Ain't Heavy, He's My Brother' was being used in a TV commercial.

★ ★ ★

JAILBAIT ANNABELLA LEAVES BOW WOW WOW

Annabella - Burmese born punkette

With the departure of teenage vocalist Annabella Lwin, another

chapter was added to the already bizarre story of Bow Wow Wow, the

group whose short history involved Adam Ant, Boy George and Malcolm McLaren.

Drummer Dave Barbarossa and guitarist Matthew Ashman had been members of The Ants (Adam's group) until late 1979, when the latter invited McLaren, fresh from his success with the by then defunct Sex Pistols, to act as his Svengali. Within weeks McLaren had convinced the other Ants to ditch Adam and to change their name to Bow Wow Wow, after recruiting 14-year-old Burmese schoolgirl Annabella, whom he met in a launderette. The group went on to have ten UK hits between 1980 and 1983.

1931 – Anthony Newley
1940 – Barbara Allbut (Angels)
1942 – Phyllis Allbut (Angels)
1941 – Linda McCartney
1942 – Gerry Marsden (Gerry and The Pacemakers)
1946 – Kjell Asperud (Titanic)
1946 – Jerry Donahue (Fotheringay/Fairport Convention)
1967 – M.C. Miker G.

★ ★ ★

1991 – Peter Bellamy

September (273)

1980

VODKA BINGE LEAVES LED ZEP A MAN SHORT

John Bonham - 40 measures of vodka

ARRIVALS

1933 – Ian Tyson
1933 – Erik Darling
(Rooftop Singers)
1934 – Royce Kendall
(Kendalls)
1943 – John Locke (Spirit)
1943 – Onnie McIntyre
(Average White Band)
1947 – John Fiddler
(Medicine Head/Box Of
Frogs)
1951 – Burleigh
Drummond (Ambrosia)
1955 – Steve Severin
(Siouxsie and The
Banshees)

★ ★ ★

DEPARTURE
LOUNGE

1980 – John Bonham (Led
Zeppelin)
1982 – Jimmy Wakely
1991 – Miles Davis

★ ★ ★

John 'Bonzo' Bonham, drummer of Led Zeppelin, died after a drinking bout during which it was estimated that he drank 40 measures of vodka. He spent his last hours alive at the Windsor mansion of the group's founder and leader, guitarist Jimmy Page.

Bonham had joined the group after a recommendation by vocalist Robert Plant, who himself had been suggested by Terry Reid, one of the candidates for the job of singer in the band. Upon the dissolution of The Yardbirds in mid 1968 Page had been approached by session musician John Paul Jones (real name John Baldwin), who knew Page from the latter's days as a session player. After a few live shows as The New Yardbirds, the group adopted the name Led Zeppelin, which was coined by either Keith Moon or John Entwistle of The Who – both have claimed credit for suggesting that the new band would 'go down like a lead balloon', although whichever of them it was could hardly have been more incorrect.

The group's eponymous debut album in 1969 was an instant success, especially in the USA, where it entered the chart almost two months before it was similarly listed in Britain. Thereafter, their next eight albums all topped the UK chart, six of them also reaching No. 1 in the US and the other two peaking one place short at No. 2.

Led Zeppelin were noted for their pursuit of excess, not only in their music, which was more powerful and exciting than that of their contemporaries and rivals, but also in their offstage activities – Bonham and the group's manager, Peter Grant, were arrested after seriously injuring members of the stage crew during a 1977 US tour – but Bonham should be remembered for his magnificent work during the group's heyday than for his sad departure.

1976

WINGS LET WATER IN

When Paul McCartney agreed to perform a UNESCO charity concert in St Mark's Square in Venice, Italy to raise money to reinforce the city against the ravages wrought by the water on which it stands, he cannot have realized that the weight of the temporarily installed seating and staging equipment would further weaken the city's already cracked fabric. However, perhaps the $500,000 plus raised by the event was some consolation.

RAVINGS

1954
Elvis Presley released his second single on Sun Records, 'Good Rockin' Tonight', a cover of a 1948 R & B hit by Wynonie Harris.

1979
The Tim Rice/Andrew Lloyd Webber musical *Evita*, about the wife of Argentinian dictator Juan Peron, opened on Broadway.

1990
A street was named Little Richard Boulevard in the legendary rock star's home town of Macon, Georgia.

★ ★ ★

1937

EMPRESS BESSIE DIES

The untimely death of incomparable blues singer Bessie Smith in a car accident robbed the world of a rare and exceptional talent that would not merely survive via a large catalogue of classic recordings, but would also influence many latterday female vocalists, most notably Janis Joplin.

Born in Chattanooga at the end of the 19th century, her style was originally based on the gospel singing she heard in church, but she was discovered by blues belter Ma Rainey and became part of Rainey's Rabbit Foot Minstrels touring show. Even in those early days, it was clear that Smith was quite different from her contemporaries, bending notes and using dramatic pauses and key changes to increase the impact of her performance – some called her the first singer to combine rural blues with instrumental jazz.

Unsurprisingly, her style was considered too adventurous by major record labels, and she did not record until 1923, when she was nearly 30 years old. Between 1923 and 1933, she cut the substantial part of her recorded work for Columbia (CBS), her most successful single, 'Down Hearted Blues', coming at the start of that period. Among the musicians who backed her were such famous names as Louis Armstrong, Fletcher Henderson, Benny Goodman and many other jazz greats. Unfortunately, she fell out of favour during the depression of the early 1930s – perhaps the audience favoured light and cheerful music rather than Smith's tortured laments. She turned to alcohol for solace, and became increasingly unreliable.

The Empress Of The Blues died from loss of blood in the car accident – the rumour that she was refused admission to a hospital because she was black was denied.

Bessie Smith, the Empress of The Blues

RAVINGS

1957
Buddy Holly and The Crickets scored their only US No. 1 hit with 'That'll Be The Day'.

★ ★ ★

1971
Deep Purple were at No. 1 in the UK album chart for the first time with *Fireball*. They repeated the success seven months later with *Medicine Head*.

★ ★ ★

1980
A show by San Francisco punk group The Dead Kennedys was banned because of the group's name.

★ ★ ★

1981

SAMSON SINGER JOINS METAL MAIDEN

Bruce Dickinson, previously vocalist with heavy metal group Samson, joined the similarly styled Iron Maiden, replacing Paul Di'Anno. Dickinson was from an academic background, and had studied history at university. His invitation to join Iron Maiden (named after a medieval cage used in torture chambers) arrived shortly before the release of the group's first No. 1 album *The Number Of The Beast*. By the end of 1992 the group had

Bruce Dickinson

accumulated a total of 24 UK chart singles and 10 albums, including a second chart-topper, *Seventh Son Of A Seventh Son*, in 1988.

ARRIVALS

1905 – Ernie Fields
1925 – Marty Robbins
1926 – Julie London (Julie Peck)
1931 – George Chambers (Chambers Brothers)
1934 – Dick Heckstall-Smith
1941 – David Frizzell
1941 – Joe Bauer (Youngbloods)
1945 – Bryan Ferry
1947 – Lynn Anderson
1948 – Olivia Newton-John
1951 – Stuart Tosh (Pilot/10cc)
1954 – Craig Chaquico (Jefferson Starship/Starship)
1955 – Carlene Carter Tennessee
1962 – Tracey Thorn (Everything But The Girl)

★ ★ ★

DEPARTURE LOUNGE

1937 – Bessie Smith

★ ★ ★

1963

CILLA MAKES TV DEBUT

Cilla Black (born Priscilla White) made her first appearance on TV on the day her first single, 'Love Of The Loved', was released.

The single's peak just within the UK Top 40 (promoted by her *Ready Steady Go* performance) was a very modest debut (despite being written by Lennon and McCartney, who never recorded it legally as The Beatles) compared with her next two hits, both in 1964. 'Anyone Who Had A Heart' was a cover version of a Dionne Warwick hit written by Burt Bacharach and Hal David, and Black's version topped the UK chart for a month, while her follow-up, 'You're My World' (another cover, this time of an Italian song entitled 'Il Mondo', but with English lyrics) also reached No. 1, this time for three weeks.

A chart battle she seemed to be winning, but eventually lost, came in 1965, when she covered 'You've Lost That Lovin' Feelin'', the Phil Spector-produced Righteous Brothers classic. The Black version reached No. 2 in the UK charts, but was then overhauled by the Righteous Brothers' now classic original.

The ex-cloakroom attendant at Liverpool's Cavern, where The Beatles were discovered by Brian Epstein (who also managed Black), seemed to lose her

Priscilla White as Cilla Black

interest in being a pop star when her hits dried up around 1970, but was already the successful host of her own TV variety show. In the 1990s she was a regular TV chat show hostess, her days as teenage hairdresser to Ringo Starr's mother long behind her.

ARRIVALS

1941 – Don Nix
1942 – Alvin Stardust/Shane Fenton (Bernard William Jewry)
1943 – Randy Bachman (Guess Who, Bachman-Turner Overdrive)
1947 – Barbara Dickson
1947 – Meat Loaf (Marvin Lee Aday)
1953 – Greg Ham (Men At Work)
1953 – Robbie Shakespeare (Sly and Robbie)
1958 – Shaun Cassidy

★ ★ ★

DEPARTURE LOUNGE

1972 – Rory Storm (Alan Caldwell)
1976 – Hondo Crouch
1979 – Gracie Fields
1979 – Jimmy McCulloch

★ ★ ★

RAVINGS

1980
Martha Ladley, one of two members named Martha in the Canadian group Martha and The Muffins, left the 'Echo Beach' hitmakers.

1990
Marvin Gaye's name was added to the 'Walkway Of The Stars' on Hollywood Boulevard, Los Angeles, six years after his death.

★ ★ ★

1979

GRACIE FIELDS DIES AT 81

Arguably the most popular British female singer of the 20th century, Gracie Fields died on the Isle Of Capri, where she had lived for much of the previous 20 years. Also a comedienne who appeared in numerous films during the 1930s, she came from Rochdale in Lancashire and was instantly recognizable for her broad Northern England accent. Her real surname was Stansfield, and in the late 1980s another female vocalist from Rochdale became an international star – quite coincidentally her name was Lisa Stansfield.

1980

100 K CATS

Virtually unknown New York rockabilly trio The Stray Cats were signed by Arista Records in the UK for £100,000.

Comprising the quiffed Brian Setzer on guitar, Lee Rocker on double bass and Slim Jim Phantom on drums, they swiftly repaid the label's faith by releasing two UK Top 10 singles in the next four months, 'Runaway Boys' and 'Rock This Town', both taken from their eponymously titled Top 10 debut album.

MILES GOES TO BLOW WITH GABRIEL

1991

Miles Davis was given a trumpet by his father on his 13th birthday in May 1939, neither father nor son could have known that his gift would set Miles on the road to becoming one of the giants figures of Jazz.

Miles Davis - Jazz trumpet immortal

Few musicians are fortunate enough to be recognized as the founder of a new musical genre. Even fewer could claim to have heavily influenced two new musical styles, but one man who is in that category was trumpeter Miles Davis, who died in New York, aged 65.

During the mid 1940s, Davis played alongside alto sax giant Charlie Parker, helping to create Bebop, the revolutionary freewheeling jazz style also played by such as Dizzy Gillespie and Dexter Gordon. Over the next 20 years he straddled the jazz scene like a colossus, spawning dozens of classic albums with other notable jazzmen such as pianist Red Garland, saxophonist John Coltrane, etc., also working with pioneers of similar status like Milt Jackson, Thelonius Monk and 'Cannonball' Adderley.

During the 1960s he was inspired by the burgeoning acid rock movement and formed a quintet that included pianist Herbie Hancock and drummer Tony Williams. Later groups he formed featured players like Chick Corea, Joe Zawinul and English guitarist John McLaughlin. His most successful era in commercial terms was between 1969, when *Bitches Brew* became his only US Top 40 album, and 1971 with *Live – Evil*, but his name appeared regularly in the chart – rarely as high as his influence deserved, but nevertheless present.

ARRIVALS

1926 – Jerry Clower
1930 – Tommy Collins
1935 – Koko Taylor
(Cora Watson)
1946 – Helen Shapiro
1947 – Peter Hope-Evans
(Medicine Head)
1948 – Finbar Furey
(Fureys)
1949 – Jimmy Bo Horne

1950 – Paul Burgess (10cc)
1952 – Andy Ward
(Camel/Marillion)
1953 – Jim Diamond
1955 – Annabel Lamb
1960 – Jennifer Rush

★ ★ ★

DEPARTURE LOUNGE

1991 – Miles Davis

1956

RCA CLAIM PRESLEY WAS A GOOD INVESTMENT

RCA Records boasted that Elvis Presley had sold over 10 million records in his first year with the label. That year included four US No. 1 singles, 'Heartbreak Hotel' (eight weeks at the top), 'I Want You, I Need You, I Love You' (just one week) and the double A-sided 'Don't Be Cruel'/ 'Hound Dog' (both listed at No. 1 for eleven weeks eventually!). RCA also announced that 'Love Me Tender' (the next Presley release) had become the first single for which advance orders exceeded one million. In the next twelve months, Presley would take four more singles to the very top.

Elvis Presley - 10 million in first year

RAVINGS

1928
The first recording session in Nashville took place at the YMCA. Among the acts who were recorded were Warmack's Gully Jumpers.

1963
The Springfields, who had been voted Britain's Top Group, announced that they were splitting up and that female singer Dusty Springfield would be embarking on a solo career.

★ ★ ★

1968
Albert Grossman, Janis Joplin's manager, announced that she would be leaving Big Brother and The Holding Company, the group with which she came to fame, at the end of the year.

★ ★ ★

1990

THREE GENERATIONS TOP US CHART

The Nelson family created a record when three generations of the dynasty topped the US chart, an achievement that certainly seems unique. The 1990 Nelsons were Gunnar (bass, vocals) and Matthew (rhythm guitar, vocals), who simply called themselves Nelson. Their No. 1 was a million seller, '(Can't Live Without Your) Love and Affection'.

Their father Rick (or Ricky, as he was known when he started recording) had released 54 US hits between 1957 and 1973, including no less than 19 that reached the Top 10, although only two of them reached No. 1, 'Poor Little Fool' in 1958 and 'Travelin'

Man' in 1961. Rick's father was Oswald 'Ozzie' Nelson, whose 38 hits between 1930 and 1940 included 'And Then Some', a No. 1 in 1935.

Ozzie and his wife Harriet (née Hilliard) were the stars of a radio show, *Ozzie and Harriet*, from 1944 to

1952, when it moved to television where it remained popular until 1966. Ricky and his brother David were featured in the show from 1949 onwards.

The story goes that when Ricky was 17, he dated a girlfriend who expressed her admiration for Elvis Presley. This made Ricky boast that he could do equally well, and when it was made clear that his becoming a pop star would be reflected in the TV show, it did not take long before he was offered a recording contract. Both sides of his debut single, 'I'm Walkin'' and 'A Teenager's Romance', reached the Top 5 of the US singles chart.

Rick Nelson in 1964

1963

STONES ROLLING NATIONWIDE

The Rolling Stones began their first British tour, a 32 date package with them as the opening act on a bill headlined by The Everly Brothers, Bo Diddley and Little Richard below Mickie

Most. Dressed in matching leather waistcoats and wearing ties, they had released their debut single, 'Come On', some two months before, and it was still in the chart, although it

Jones, Wyman, Richards, Watts, Jagger - The Stones

eventually just failed to reach the Top 20.

Prior to the tour, the group had mainly played around Greater London, especially at the Crawdaddy club in Richmond, west London,

where they had built a massive following on Sunday evenings at the clubhouse of Richmond Athletic Ground, before that they had played a few hundred yards away at the Railway Hotel.

ARRIVALS

1907 – Gene Autry
1935 – Jerry Lee Lewis
1942 – Jean-Luc Ponty
1944 – Tommy Boyce
1946 – Timi Donald (Quiver/Cody/Blue)
1946 – Nick Taylor (Bloodrock)

1948 – Mark Farner (Grand Funk Railroad)
1948 – Mike Pinera (Blues Image/Iron Butterfly)
1950 – Alvin Crow
1957 – Mari Wilson
1968 – Matt and Luke Goss (Bros)

★ ★ ★

RAVINGS

1957
Buddy Holly and The Crickets released their second single, 'Oh Boy !'/'Not Fade Away'.

1975
Jackie Wilson fell into a coma from which he never recovered. When he died in 1984 he had spent nine years as a virtual vegetable, and in 1986 topped the UK singles chart with the 29-year-old 'Reet Petite'.

1976
Boy George was expelled from school.

★ ★ ★

1955

REBEL LIVED FAST, DIED YOUNG

James Dean was not a rock 'n' roller, not even really a musician – yet his influence on the era during which rock 'n' roll first became a sensation was incalculable. The mean, moody and magnificent Hollywood film star, whose portrayal of mixed-up and misunderstood teenagers in *Rebel Without A Cause* and *East Of Eden* rocketed him to international stardom, died when his Porsche collided with another vehicle near Los Angeles, California.

James Dean - gone but not forgotten

Dean was only 26 years old, but the attitude he portrayed in those two movies made him a role model for the attitude that early rock 'n' roll stars were supposed to convey. He was a figure with whom disaffected youth could identify. His ability to translate the tribulations of teendom into acting that seemed too natural to be anything but genuine proved his talent to be extraordinary.

James Byron Dean was born in a small town near Indianapolis in February 1931 and moved with his dental mechanic father to Santa Monica in southern California when he was six years old. His mother's death three years later devastated him, and he returned to Indiana to be raised by his father's family. He was a promising athlete, and after graduation returned to the Los Angeles area, working as a PE instructor at a military academy and also enrolling as a drama student at UCLA. After his memorable *Macbeth* he was soon appearing on TV. In early 1954 film director Elia Kazan saw him on stage in New York, and signed him to play a leading role in his screen version of John Steinbeck's novel, *East Of Eden*.

In the 18 months before his untimely death Dean made three films, dying before the last of the three, *Giant*, was released. Some say that Andy Warhol best explained his appeal: 'He is not our hero because he was perfect, but because he perfectly represented the damaged but beautiful soul of our time'.

ARRIVALS

1934 – Freddie King
1935 – Z. Z. Hill (Arzel Hill)
1935 – Johnny Mathis
1942 – Gus Dudgeon
1942 – Frankie Lymon
1942 – Dewey Martin (Buffalo Springfield)
1943 – Marilyn McCoo (Fifth Dimension)
1945 – Mike Harrison (Spooky Tooth)
1946 – Sylvia Peterson (Chiffons)
1947 – Marc Bolan (Marc Feld)
1953 – Deborah Allen
1954 – Patrice Rushen
1956 – Basia (Basia Trzetrzelewska)
1957 – Dave Betts (Honeymoon Suite)

★ ★ ★

DEPARTURE LOUNGE

1977 – Mary Ford

★ ★ ★

1985

KATE WALKS DOGS TO THE SUMMIT

Kate Bush took her fifth album, *Hounds Of Love*, to the top of the UK chart five years (to the week) after first achieving the feat with her third album, *Never For Ever*. Six of Bush's first seven albums reached the Top 3 of the UK album chart.

Kate Bush - second Number One album

1975

MG DRUMMER MURDERED

Al Jackson, drummer with the seminal house band at Stax Records, Booket T. and The MGs ('MG' stood for Memphis Group), and thus the rock-steady rhythm behind hits by Otis Redding, Sam and Dave and other great soul stars of the 1960s, was shot and killed when he confronted an intruder at his Memphis home. Jackson was 39 years old.

While Memphis had been regarded in the 1950s as a 'white' music city, as it was most readily identified with the rock 'n' roll of Elvis Presley, Jerry Lee Lewis, Carl Perkins, etc., the steady rise in crossover popularity of soul and R & B helped make it also one of the most influential centres for 'black' popular music in the 1960s.

The heart of Memphis soul was located in a converted cinema on McLemore Avenue that contained the recording studio used by Stax/Volt Records. The quartet who were almost invariably used as the rhythm section behind the tracks that were recorded were two young black musicians, keyboard player Booker T. Jones and drummer Al Jackson, and two similarly young whites, guitarist Steve Cropper and bass player Donald 'Duck' Dunn (who replaced Lewis Steinberg, apparently due to the latter's unpunctuality) – Booker T. and The MGs. Jackson and Dunn were a perfectly synchronized super-tight funk machine, laying a rock-solid foundation on which Cropper and/or Booker T. could overlay anything they wished, from melodic chords to percussive riffs, also allowing vocalists to float and sting above the instrumental carpet.

As well as providing seamless studio backings to many classic soul hits, Booker T & The MGs toured Europe as part of the legendary Stax/Volt European tour in 1967, when they backed Redding, Sam and Dave, Eddie Floyd and others, also playing both as Booker T. and The MGs and as part of The Mar-Keys. They also scored US and UK Top 10 hits with 'Green Onions' and 'Time Is Tight'.

Booker T. Jones (front) and the MGs (l t r) Duck Dunn, Al Jackson, Steve Cropper

1977

FRENCH CHART TOPPERS

To the end of 1992 only 90 records by French artists have charted, 26 of them making the Top 10. For the only time to date, three singles made in France by French artists were together in the UK Top 10. 'Magic Fly', a novelty instrumental by a group called Space, was at No. 3, immediately followed by another instrumental, Jean-Michel Jarre's 'Oxygene', while at No. 8 was female vocal duo La Belle Epoque with their disco-flavoured remake of the 1966 smash hit 'Black Is Black' by Los Bravos.

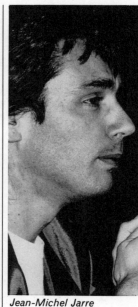

Jean-Michel Jarre

1961

HITMAKER SPECTOR DEBUTS ON OWN LABEL

Noted record producer Phil Spector, who had been responsible for three US Top 10 singles during the previous twelve months, released the first single on his own label, Philles. It was also the debut single by black girl group The Crystals, coupling 'Oh Yeah, Maybe Baby' with 'There's No Other (Like My Baby)'.

At first, disc jockeys in the USA were suspicious, hardly programming 'Oh Yeah', which was designated as the A-side, but by the end of November, the single had been 'flipped', and 'There's No Other' had entered the US chart, eventually peaking just within the Top 20. It was somewhat less of a hit than previous Spector-produced hits such as 'Corinne Corinna' by Ray Peterson, 'Pretty Little Angel Eyes' by Curtis Lee and 'I Love How You Love Me' by The Paris Sisters, but was nevertheless a winning start for the new label launched by Spector and his music publisher partner, Lester Sill – the label's name was a combination of their first names, Phil and Les.

Of course, none of these hits approached the chart-topping success of Spector's first single, released when he was 17 in 1958. That was 'To Know Him Is To Love Him' by The Teddy Bears, a trio of which he was a member. That single, which was also written by Spector, topped the US chart and sold a reputed two and a half million copies. The

The Teddy Bears, with Phil Spector (left)

song was inspired by the inscription on Spector's father's gravestone in Beth David cemetery – 'To know him was to love him'. Phil took the words on Ben Spector's grave and put them in a romantic rather than neo-religious context.

1980

BEE GEES SUE BENEFACTOR FOR SEVERAL KING'S RANSOMS

Maurice, Barry and Robin Gibb - The Bee Gees

Barry, Robin and Maurice Gibb, the brothers better known as The Bee Gees, started a lawsuit against Robert Stigwood, claiming $2 million and alleging misrepresentation and fraud. Commentators noted that the trio had been very fortunate when Stigwood had retained his faith in them during the early 1970s when they were absent from the US Top 10 for over three years. He had financed the *Saturday Night Fever* movie that restored their popularity in 1977, when their domination of the American charts came close to matching that of The Beatles in 1964: for three consecutive weeks they were responsible for writing/producing five records in the Top 10.

ARRIVALS

1927 – Leon Rausch (Bob Wills and Texas Playboys)
1939 – Jimmy Torres (String-A-Longs)
1939 – Lolly Vegas (Redbone)
1941 – Ronald Meagher (Beau Brummels)
1945 – Don McLean
1949 – Richard Hell (Richard Meyers) (Television/Voidoids)
1950 – Michael Rutherford (Genesis)
1951 – Sting (Gordon Sumner)
1952 – Ish Ledesma (Foxy)
1952 – John Otway
1955 – Philip Oakey (Human League)
1956 – Freddie Jackson
1961 – Robbie Nevil
1971 – Tiffany (Tiffany Renee Darwisch)

★ ★ ★

DEPARTURE LOUNGE

1985 – Rock Hudson

1967

WOODY, VOICE OF THE AMERICAN RADICAL, SILENCED

If any performer could claim to be the artistic voice of the American left, it would be Woody Guthrie, the singer/songwriter who died in New Jersey after many years of suffering from Huntington's Chorea, a wasting disease that first struck him in the 1950s.

Woody Guthrie - inspiration for Bob Dylan

Born of pioneer stock in Oklahoma in 1912, Guthrie was surrounded by music from birth. Everyone in the family played or sang, and as a child he was influenced by folk and black and white church music, as well as work songs and North American Indian music. Teaching himself guitar and harmonica, he began travelling round the USA at the age of 16, and by his early twenties was in California where he was writing songs, often highlighting the plight of immigrant workers who were being exploited. He thus became involved in the early fight for the creation of trade unions.

After starting to write for the communist newspaper, *Daily Worker*, he was invited to Washington DC, where folklorist Alan Lomax was building an archive of American folk music.

Among the songs Guthrie wrote (or collected) were 'This Land Is Your Land' (a socialist alternative to 'The Star Spangled Banner'), 'Do Re Mi', 'Pastures Of Plenty' and 'So Long, It's Been Good To Know You', and he also formed The Almanac Singers, a folk group with Pete Seeger, Lee Hays and others, in New York in the early 1940s.

As his illness became more debilitating, he was forced to give up travelling, but a younger generation of singers whom he inspired kept his name alive. These included his son, Arlo Guthrie, Bob Dylan, Phil Ochs, Ry Cooder and Peter LaFarge.

1977

BUNCH OF STIFFS ON THE ROAD

Stiff Records, the pioneering British independent record label founded by Dave Robinson and Jake Riviera, launched a package tour featuring several of the major acts signed to Stiff, including Elvis Costello and The Attractions, Ian Dury and The Blockheads, Nick Lowe's Last Chicken In The Shop (which included Lowe's great friend and co-hort in Rockpile Dave Edmunds), Larry Wallis' Psychedelic Rowdies and Wreckless Eric and The New Rockets. The personnel of many of these shortlived groups was somewhat interchangeable – for example, Pete Thomas, drummer with The Attractions, also played in the groups fronted by Lowe and Wallis.

Elvis Costello, 1977

JOPLIN'S FATAL OVERDOSE

Janis Joplin's flirtation with syringes ended in a Hollywood hotel rooom when she took an overdose of heroin. She was 27 years old and had been an international star for less than three years, but had spent most of that period living her life to the limits expected of a rock celebrity.

Janis Joplin - posthumous 'Pearl' LP

Born in Port Arthur, Texas, Janis was inspired by blues greats like Bessie Smith and Leadbelly, but sang in country and bluegrass bands before deciding to concentrate on folk/blues when she enrolled at the University of Texas in Austin. In 1966, she left Texas for San Francisco, where she became vocalist with acid rock band Big Brother and The Holding Company.

Their local reputation became international after their appearance at the 1967 Monterey Festival, where Janis, along with Jimi Hendrix, Otis Redding, Canned Heat and many more, had the audience screaming their approval.

Signed to a management contract with Bob Dylan's then mentor, Albert Grossman, the group's

1970

Cheap Thrills album, released in 1968, sold over a million copies, and a few months later she left the group for a solo career. In 1969 her debut solo album, *I Got Dem Ol' Kozmic Blues Again, Mama*, was well received, but soon after its release she formed a new backing group, The Full Tilt Boogie Band, and was in the middle of recording a follow-up album when she died. The tracks she had completed were the basis of her posthumous *Pearl* album, which topped the US chart and was the greatest success of her career.

A mass of contradictions, Janis Joplin was a sensitive woman who possessed tragically little self-esteem, and her unfortunate death came as no real surprise to those who knew her.

ARRIVALS

1929 – Leroy Van Dyke
1937 – Lloyd Green
1944 Larry Collins
(Collins Kids)
1944 – Marlena Davies
1944 – Patti LaBelle
(Patricia Louise Holt)
(LaBelle)
1947 – Jim Fielder
(Blood, Sweat and Tears)
1952 – Jody Stevens
(Big Star)
1957 – Barbara Kooyman
(Timbuk 3)
1959 – Chris Lowe
(Pet Shop Boys)
1963 – Lena Zavaroni

★ ★ ★

DEPARTURE LOUNGE

1970 – Janis Joplin

★ ★ ★

RAVINGS

1956
Johnny Cash was jailed for one night for possession of pills.

★ ★ ★

1962
Bob Dylan played a showcase concert at New York's Carnegie Chapter Hall, attracting an audience of 53 people.

★ ★ ★

1974

NEW LOOK LIZZY DEBUTS IN WALES

Thin Lizzy with Phil Lynott (second left)

Thin Lizzy, up to this point an Irish trio, became an international quartet with the introduction of two lead guitarists, Californian Scott Gorham and Glaswegian Brian Robertson. The first concert by the new line-up, at Aberystwyth University in Wales, coincided with the group's debut single and album on a new label, Vertigo, after their first three albums, *Thin Lizzy* (1971), *Tales From A Blue Orphanage* (1972) and *Vagabonds Of The Western World* (1973) had all been released by Decca, but had failed to reach the UK chart. Along with founder members Phil Lynott (vocals, bass, songwriting) and drummer Brian Downey, this line-up of Thin Lizzy is generally regarded as the group's best.

1968

GOODBYE CREAM

(left to right) Baker, Clapton, Bruce - Cream curdled

After a brief but incredibly successful life lasting less than two and a half years, but with three gold albums (out of three), the last of which topped the US chart, Cream began their farewell tour. The group was formed by three well-known musicians – Eric Clapton, the guitar star of The Yardbirds and then of John Mayall's Bluesbreakers, bass player and vocalist Jack Bruce, who had worked with Clapton in The Bluesbreakers, and with drummer Ginger Baker, the third member of the trio, in Alexis Korner's Blues Incorporated and in The Graham Bond Organization.

Dubbed a 'supergroup' by the media, their first album, *Fresh Cream*, seemed disappointing to those who expected something earth-shattering, but their second album of 1967, *Disraeli Gears*, was a big seller on both sides of the Atlantic. 1968 brought *Wheels Of Fire*, a double album that topped the US chart for four weeks and was half studio recordings and half concert material. This was what the world had been expecting, but unfortunately, internal pressures began to cause divisions within the band, and before the end of what was a successful year for Cream, the band fell apart.

ARRIVALS	
1936 – George Jones Jr (Edsels)	(Geordie/AC/DC)
1938 – Johnny Duncan	1949 – B. W. Stephenson
1938 – Carlos Mastrangelo (Belmonts)	1950 – Eddie Clarke (Motorhead/Fastway)
1941 – Arlene Smith (Chantels)	1952 – Harold Faltermeyer
1942 – Richard Street (Temptations)	1953 – Russell Mael (Dwight Russell Day) (Sparks)
1943 – Steve Miller	1954 – Bob Geldof
1945 – Brian Connolly (Sweet)	1955 – Leo Barnes (Hothouse Flowers)
1947 – Brian Johnson	1961 – Lee Thompson (Madness)
	★ ★ ★

1969

HELLO MONTY PYTHON

The first show of *Monty Python's Flying Circus* was screened on British television. 'The Pythons' were a group of university graduates who had begun to make their name both as writers and performers of comedy – John Cleese (real name John Cheese), for example, had appeared in such shows as *The Frost Report* (with David Frost, Ronnie Barker and Ronnie Corbett) and *At Last The 1948 Show* (with Graham Chapman, another member of the Python team), while Michael Palin and Terry Jones had featured in *Do Not Adjust Your Set*, a show that also featured David Jason and The Bonzo Dog Doo Dah Band. Another major contributor was Terry Gilliam, a highly original cartoonist and animator from the USA, and the show was an instant artistic success.

Less than twenty Monty Python shows were screened, but their impact was such that many of the sextet have enjoyed huge success with subsequent endeavours, including John Cleese's *Fawlty Towers* and *The Rutles*, the spoof documentary about a group not unlike The Beatles, which starred Eric Idle (the sixth member of the team), plus numerous other cinematic and/or televisual comedy entertainments.

Monty and the Pythons

1973

ART'S SOLO CHART START

Art Garfunkel's first solo single reached the US Top 40. The immensely successful partnership of songwriter/guitarist/harmony vocalist Paul Simon and Art Garfunkel, he of the choirboy voice, ended in 1970, although their records continued to sell prodigiously. Garfunkel wanted to move into acting, following his debut in the Mike Nichols movie *Catch 22*, based on Joseph Heller's novel. 1971 found him appearing alongside Jack Nicholson and Ann-Margret in another 'progressive' movie, *Carnal Knowledge*, but after that he was prepared to re-enter the popular music arena as a ballad singer.

Still charting without Paul Simon - Art Garfunkel

His first US Top 40 success as a soloist came with his cover version of 'All I Know', a song written by Jimmy Webb. It was also included on his debut solo album, *Angel Clare*, released the previous month and which was eventually certified gold, reaching the Top 5 of the US chart. Two years later, he released a follow-up album, *Breakaway*, the title song of which was written by Scottish singer/songwriters Benny Gallagher and Graham Lyle. The album again reached the US Top 10 and went gold, its biggest included US single hit being a duet with Simon, 'My Little Town', which was also included on Simon's *Still Crazy After All These Years*, an album that topped the US chart.

However, at the end of the year Garfunkel scored an unexpected No. 1 in Britain, when his mellifluous cover version of 'I Only Have Eyes For You', which had been the 106th US hit single by Ben Selvin and His Orchestra in 1934, and in 1959 had become a US Top 20 doo-wop classic for The Flamingos, topped the UK singles chart. Not having reached the UK singles chart subsequently, Garfunkel was then invited to sing 'Bright Eyes', a song written by Mike Batt for the animated film of *Watership Down*, based on Richard Adams's popular novel, and in 1979 that single also topped the UK chart.

RAVINGS

1927
The first full length 'talkie' (a film with sound), *The Jazz Singer*, starring Al Jolson, was premiered.

1990
Notorious American rap artist Luther Campbell of 2 Live Crew paid Lucas Films, owners of the copyrights to Star Wars, $300,000 for his unauthorized choice of Luke Skywalker as the name of his label.

★ ★ ★

ARRIVALS

1917 – Bob Neal (ex-Presley manager)
1928 – Ennio Morricone
1945 – Robin Shaw (White Plains/Flowerpot Men)
1947 – Millie Small (Millicent Smith)
1949 – Thomas McClary (Commodores)
1949 – Bobby Farrell (Boney M)
1951 – Kevin Cronin (REO Speedwagon)
1951 – Gavin Sutherland (Quiver)
1960 – Richard Jobson (Skids)
1962 – Danny Simcic (Real Life)

★ ★ ★

DEPARTURE LOUNGE

1978 – Johnny O'Keefe
1985 – Nelson Riddle

1978

ABBA DUO PLIGHT TROTH – AT LAST

Benny Andersson and Anni-Frid Lyngstad, two members of the successful Swedish quartet ABBA, married in an unpublicized ceremony at their local church, the witnesses being a churchwarden and the couple's housekeeper. They had been living together for nine years, but had preferred to remain single up to this point.

Frida and Benny - legalised at last

1966

PIRATE CAPTAIN DIES IN CAR CRASH

Johnny Kidd, one of Britain's most inventive and influential rock singers before The Beatles, died in a car crash near Manchester. He was only 27 years old.

Born Frederick Heath in Willesden, north London, his importance as a stylist and trendsetter at a time when British rock music was searching for direction can hardly be exaggerated, although his comparatively small collection of hit singles and his minimal, not to say non-existent, profile in the USA suggest that he was an also-ran.

His major importance was as a pioneer, leading numerous British musicians to an interest in black music some time before such behaviour was regarded as normal. Kidd's covers of hits by

Johnny Kidd - crash victim

American black acts made them commercially acceptable. His records were tough and muscular and he stayed true to his chosen direction, which reached its commercial peak in 1960, when he and his group, The Pirates, scored with three hits, the biggest his only UK No. 1, 'Shakin' All Over'. He also charted with covers of Marv Johnson's 'You Got What It Takes' and Ray Sharpe's 'Linda Lu' as well as originals like 'I'll Never Get Over You' (his other Top 10 hit).

1977

GENESIS GUITAR MAN GOES SOLO

After playing on the group's first seven hit albums, Genesis guitarist Steve Hackett left the group for a solo career. He had been recruited to replace original guitarist Anthony Phillips, who left the group to both study classical guitar and make occasional solo albums.

Hackett had stayed with Genesis after Peter Gabriel's departure and the inexorable rise of Phil Collins, joining from a number of unknown groups. At the end of 1975, he had released a solo album, *Voyage Of The Acolyte*, and after leaving Genesis released a second, *Please Don't Touch*. With eight solo albums that briefly charted in the UK, the only one to make the Top 10 being *Defector* in 1980, Hackett's, er, defection may have been justified.

Steve Hackett - defector from Genesis

DRUMMER DISPLAYS VOCAL CONSISTENCY

Phil Collins - doubly talented

Phil Collins notched up his eighth US Top 10 single in under three years with his inspired revival of the 1966 UK Top 3 hit for The Mindbenders, 'A Groovy Kind Of Love' from the film Buster in which he starred. It became his fifth US chart-topper, after 'Against All Odds (Take A Look At Me Now)', a movie theme (1984), and three No. 1s in 1985, 'One More Night', 'Sussudio' and his duet with Marilyn Martin, 'Separate Lives', also a film theme.

Collins first achieved fame in rock music as drummer with Genesis, joining the group in 1970 around the same time as Steve Hackett. Collins answered an advertisement in *Melody Maker*, and had been a child actor, appearing in the London West End production of *Oliver*. He had also played drums in Flaming Youth, a progressive rock group of the late 1960s (of which John Mayall's son is also alleged to have been a member).

His arrival in Genesis coincided with the group's rise to chart action, and when vocalist Peter Gabriel left for a solo career in 1975, he assumed the role of vocalist and front man, confounding the many doubters who reasoned that the post-Gabriel band would soon fall apart by leading them to even greater success. After he had undertaken a double role on the 1976 Genesis album *A Trick Of The Tail*, another drummer; Bill Bruford, joined for six months for a US tour, but thereafter Collins drummed on record while Chester Thompson, an American who had worked with Weather Report, played drums on the group's increasingly successful tours.

Collins, who had topped the UK album chart with his solo album *Face Value*, in 1981, returned to duty with Genesis periodically, but by 1989, when three of his first four albums had topped the UK chart, there was inevitably some doubt about whether Genesis or his solo career would eventually take precedence.

ARRIVALS	
1932 – Pete Drake	(Redbone)
1934 – Doc Green (Drifters)	1945 – Ray Royer (Procul Harum)
1940 – George Bellamy (Tornados)	1947 – Tony Wilson (Hot Chocolate)
1941 – Dave Arbus (East Of Eden)	1948 – Johnny Ramone (John Cummings) (Ramones)
1942 – Buzz Clifford (Reese Francis Clifford)	1949 – Hamish Stuart (Average White Band)
1944 – Susan Raye	1950 – Robert 'Kool' Bell (Kool and The Gang)
1945 – Butch Rillera	★ ★ ★

EMI SIGNS THE PISTOLS

EMI Records signed Britain's most newsworthy punk rock band, The Sex Pistols outbidding Chrysalis, RAK and Polydor.

However, unlike the long and mutually rewarding relationships that the company enjoyed with earlier stars, their liaison with The Pistols was brief and expensive – two and a half months at a cost of £40,000 ($60,000) and a protest strike at the company's pressing plant.

RAVINGS	1969	1980
1957 Jerry Lee Lewis recorded the rock 'n' roll classic, 'Great Balls Of Fire'.	*Abbey Road*, the final studio album recorded by The Beatles, entered the UK chart at No. 1. ★ ★ ★	Bob Marley collapsed on stage during a concert in Pittsburgh. He would never appear on stage again. ★ ★ ★

1973

KING AND CILLA DIVORCE

It was almost inevitable that the unthinkable would happen – that one of the world's most envied women, Priscilla Presley, should grow tired of being neglected by her husband, and would request (and be granted) a divorce.

The Presley family: (l to r) Priscilla, Elvis, Lisa Marie

The King and his Queen had been married for less than six and a half years, although Priscilla Beaulieu had lived at Graceland, Elvis's Memphis mansion, for several years before.

They had met in September 1959, while Presley was in the US Army stationed in Germany and was introduced to the then 14-year-old stepdaughter of a Captain in the US Air Force. With her parents' consent, she was allowed to spend Christmas 1960 with Presley and his parents in Memphis, and before long she was living permanently in Presley's home, theoretically under the eye of a chaperone who was a

relative of Elvis.

After twelve years of the fairytale life of Presley's woman, she understandably grew bored. Their daughter, Lisa Marie, had been born on February 1, 1968 , and while Priscilla may reasonably have been concerned about the welfare of her child growing up in the artificial world that Elvis had created, she was also feeling the need for love and affection that her husband seemed incapable of providing.

It would take an exceptionally audacious man to risk the censure of millions of Elvis fans by romancing the wife of The King Of Rock. However, Priscilla found such a man in Mike Stone, whom she met because he was Elvis's karate instructor. Even so, there were rumblings of Presley's desire to have Stone assassinated. Priscilla and Stone lived together for three years after the divorce, but never married.

1980

GLITTER BANKRUPT

Glam Rock superstar Gary Glitter was officially declared bankrupt. This was particularly untimely as an EP featuring his first four UK Top 3 singles was about to leave the UK chart after a three-week stay during which it failed to reach the Top 50. Nevertheless, the EP with 'Rock and Roll (Part 2)', 'I'm The Leader Of The Gang (I Am)', 'Hello Hello I'm Back Again' and 'Do You Wanna Touch Me (Oh Yeah)', had been Glitter's only singles chart entry since 1977, when 'A Little Boogie Woogie In The Back Of My Mind' just failed to penetrate the UK Top 30. In the interim, Glitter had been working away from Britain, notably in an Australian production of *The Rocky Horror Show*.

Gary Glitter, The Leader of the Gang

AEROSMITH CHERRY-BOMBED IN PHILLY

1978

Vocalist Steven Tyler and guitarist Joe Perry of Aerosmith were injured during a concert by the group in Philadelphia when an over-excited fan threw a powerful firework (known as a cherry bomb) on stage.

Aerosmith was formed in New England by Tyler (real name Steven Talarico), Perry and bass player Tom

The Jimi Hendrix Experience, and Tyler was initially to be the group's drummer, but before long opted to be

After signing to Columbia (CBS) Records in 1972, their eponymous debut album, which included a US Top 10 single, 'Dream On', was a qualified success in 1973, while a 1974 follow-up album, *Get Your Wings*, peaked only just in the Top 75 of the US chart. 1975's *Toys In The Attic* was Aerosmith's break-through album, just failing to reach the US

hit for rap stars Run-DMC, with Tyler and Perry guesting on the revival.

1976 brought Aerosmith's first platinum album, *Rocks*, which made the US Top 3, and both 1977's *Draw The Line* and 1978's *Live! Bootleg* also achieved platinum status. Also in 1978, the group appeared as villains in Robert Stigwood's film version of *Sergeant Pepper's Lonely Hearts Club Band*, becoming one of the few participants to profit from the disappointing film when their version of 'Come Together' reached the US Top 30.

Steven Tyler of Aerosmith

Hamilton. The original idea was that the group should be based on the blueprint of Cream or

vocalist as a second guitarist, Brad Whitford, and drummer Joey Kramer were recruited.

Top 10 and including a second US Top 10 single, 'Walk This Way' – in 1986 this song became a

1978

STIFF STARS RETURN TO ROAD ACTION

Following the previous year's successful package tour featuring the top acts signed to Stiff Records (including Elvis Costello, Nick Lowe, Ian Dury, Dave Edmunds and others), the label repeated the scheme, although by this time several of the stars of the previous tour had left the label. One survivor of the 1977 tour, Wreckless Eric (real name Eric Goulden), was still with Stiff, and he was joined on the tour by Jona Lewie (real name John Lewis), who had previously been a member of Brett Marvin and The Thunderbolts, a London-based jug band who, under the pseudonym Terry Dactyl and The Dinosaurs, had scored a novelty UK Top 3 hit in 1972 with 'Seaside Shuffle'.

ARRIVALS

1917 – Thelonius Monk
1943 – Denis D'Ell (Denis Dalziel) (Honeycombs)
1945 – Alan Cartwright (Procol Harum)
1945 – Jerry LaCroix (White Trash/Blood, Sweat and Tears)
1946 – Keith Reid (Procol Harum)
1946 – John Prine
1953 – Midge Ure

(James Ure) (Ultravox)
1955 – David Lee Roth (Van Halen)
1958 – Tanya Tucker
1959 – Kirsty MacColl
1960 – Al Connelly (Glass Tiger)
1961 – Martin Kemp (Spandau Ballet)
1968 – Michael Bivins (New Edition/Bell Biv Devoe)

★ ★ ★

1976 1978

RED-LETTER DAYS FOR PISTOLS

ARRIVALS

1919 – Art Blakey
1932 – Dottie West
(Dorothy Marie West)
1943 – Gene Watson
1948 – Daryl Hall
(Daryl Hohl)
(Hall and Oates)
1950 – Andrew Woolfolk
(Earth, Wind and Fire)

★ ★ ★

DEPARTURE LOUNGE

1963 – Edith Piaf

★ ★ ★

On October 11, 1978, Sid Vicious, ex-bass player of The Sex Pistols, was living at New York's Chelsea Hotel with his American girl friend, Nancy Spungen (known to acquaintances of Vicious as 'nauseating Nancy'). Both were seriously addicted to heroin, and

Sid and Nancy, a non-dynamic duo

RAVINGS

1962
The Beatles first appeared in the UK chart with their debut single, 'Love Me Do', which was placed at Number 49.

1975
The USA's highly rated TV show *Saturday Night Live* was screened for the first time. Among the stars it showcased were Dan Ackroyd, John Belushi, Chevy Chase and Gilda Radner.

Vicious, who could have been charitably described as dangerously unstable (a condition almost certainly aggravated by his heroin habit), woke up after a night that he claimed to remember nothing about, to find Spungen dead from multiple stab wounds.

He was charged with murder and placed in the detoxification unit of a New York prison, eventually being released on bail after Malcolm McLaren, the manager of and mastermind behind the group, had convinced Virgin Records, the label to which the group were signed, to provide the necessary bail. Soon after his release Vicious was again in trouble, causing a fracas and becoming involved in a knife fight, but he never faced the murder charge as he was already dead – on February 2, 1979, he overdosed on heroin that had been acquired for him by his mother.

Having completed the detoxification, he unthinkingly prepared a 'fix' of the same strength he had been using at the time of Spungen's death, and his weakened tolerance for the drug allowed him a reunion with Nancy rather more quickly than he had expected.

What a contrast to the same day exactly two years earlier, when the group, which did not include Vicious, who joined in February 1977, recorded their first single, 'Anarchy In The UK', it sold 55,000 copies in just four weeks before an alarmed EMI pulled the single, worried about the resultant controversy. Arguably the only classic track to emerge from the British punk rock movement of the late 1970s, it remains a magnificent example of the essence of rock music – loud, fast, obnoxious and everything parents hated their children enjoying.

1986

JANET JACKO HELPS BIG BROTHER TO CREATE A RECORD

'When I Think Of You' became the first single by Janet Jackson to top the US chart. The US No. 1 single exactly 14 years before – to the day – had been the first US No. 1 for another member of the Jackson family, Janet's brother, Michael.

Janet Jackson's career had been slow to take off and it was only when she began working with the writing and production team of Jimmy Jam and Terry Lewis that she became a chart regular. 'When I Think of You' was the biggest of her four US Top 5 singles released in 1986.

Janet Jackson, a chip off the old block

ROCK HERO VINCENT FINALLY SUCCUMBS

Gene Vincent, the rock 'n' roll pioneer who had remained a firm favourite with black-leather rebels (especially in Europe) even when his hits had stopped, died of a perforated ulcer in California, where he had returned apparently in an attempt to bolster his flagging finances.

Gene Vincent, a black leather rebel

No one could say that Vincent's life had been easy. When he left the US Navy in mid 1955, it was due to a serious leg injury caused by an accident that occurred during his work as a despatch rider. His impatience to return to normal life had not allowed the broken bones to heal, and he spent the rest of 1955 in hospital.

Returning to his home town of Norfolk, Virginia, Vincent sang with a local group, The Virginians, and a local disc jockey, 'Sheriff' Tex Davis, heard him perform 'Be-Bop-A-Lula', which he then arranged for Vincent to record, also signing the 20 year old to Capitol Records in exchange for a co-writing credit on the song (which Vincent had purchased from a friend in the Navy).

The single reached the US Top 10, eventually selling a million worldwide, but Vincent never returned to such heights in his native land. He was in the car in which Eddie Cochran was killed, surviving that crash but further aggravating his bad leg, on which he permanently wore metal supports. He had first been seen in Europe performing a wild version of his big hit in the classic rock 'n' roll movie *The Girl Can't Help It*. The image he portayed – mean, moody and too down at heel to be magnificent – appealed strongly to teddy boys in Britain and France, and he spent much of the final part of his life on tour in Europe.

He was later fondly remembered by Ian Dury in his song 'Sweet Gene Vincent'.

FINAL FACES FLING AS ROD REVOLTS

The Faces played their final live concert at Nassau Coliseum, Long Island, New York. Vocalist Rod Stewart, who was far more successful on record as a solo artist than as the group's frontman, was reportedly displeased that guitarist Ron Wood, the man who had introduced him to The Faces in the first place, was working with The Rolling Stones. Stewart later claimed in interviews that the departure of Ronnie Lane had removed the heart from the group, and that it would always lack a vital ingredient.

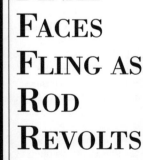
The Faces with Rod Stewart (fifth from left)

1971

ESSEX TO PLAY CHRIST

David Essex, drummer in an East London group known as The Everons, was 'discovered' by journalist Derek Bowman, who became his manager in 1964.

However, it was as a singer, actor and film star that Essex (real name David Cook) made his name, and his first major success came when he was chosen to play the part of Jesus Christ in the neo-religious stage musical *Godspell*. After a highly successful year in London's West End, Essex was approached to play a leading part in *That'll Be The Day*, a feature film also starring Ringo Starr, Billy Fury and others, and the acclaim that greeted the film led to Essex signing to CBS Records. In 1973, he scored UK Top 10 hits with 'Rock On' and 'Lamplight', after a number of flop singles earlier in his career had led to the belief that pop stardom was unlikely.

Frank Ifield

'Godspell' star David Essex

1962

IFIELD'S US PEAK

Frank Ifield, the yodelling vocalist born in Coventry, England, but who found fame in Britain after returning from Australia, where he had emigrated as a child, scored his biggest US hit single with his revival of Jimmy Dorsey's 1942 hit, 'I Remember You', which reached the Top 5 in the US singles chart.

It had been Ifield's first UK No. 1 in the summer of 1962, and he followed it with further successful cover versions that he also took to the top of the British singles chart: 'Lovesick Blues', 'The Wayward Wind', and 'Confessin'', thereby becoming the first artist to score three consecutive UK No. 1s.

1977

ORLON MURDERED

Shirley Brickley, a founder member of The Orlons, the group who scored three US Top 5 hits in under a year, died of gunshot wounds. She was 32 years old. The Orlons were a vocal quartet, part of the Cameo Parkway label's stable of stars in the late 1950s and early 1960s that included Chubby Checker and Bobby Rydell. Their third single, 'The Wah-Watusi', was a million seller in the autumn of 1962, while its follow-up, 'Don't Hang Up', was another big hit, also charting briefly in Britain. Weeks later came 'South Street', another big hit, but their subsequent hits during the rest of 1963 and 1964 were increasingly minor.

ARRIVALS

1940 – Chris Farlowe (John Henry Deighton)
1941 – Art Garfunkel
1944 – Robert Lamm (Chicago)
1947 – Sammy Hagar (Montrose/Van Halen)
1948 – Peter David Spencer (Smokie)
1949 – Craig McGregor (Foghat)
1950 – Simon Nicol (Fairport Convention)
1959 – Marie Osmond
1960 – Joey Belladonna (Anthrax)
1965 – Cherelle

★ ★ ★

DEPARTURE LOUNGE

1977 – Shirley Brickley (Orlons)

RAVINGS

1958
Gene Vincent recorded his classic 'Say Mama' single.

★ ★ ★

1963
The Beatles headlined the British TV Variety Show *Sunday Night At The London Palladium*, the resulting chaos leading to the coining of the term 'Beatlemania'.

★ ★ ★

1986
Australian rock star Nick Cave was jailed for two days in New York on suspicion of being a potential vagrant.

★ ★ ★

1966

GREAT SOCIETY SINGER JOINS JEFFERSON

Having lost Signe Toly Anderson in the very month the group released its debut album, San Francisco folk/R&B group Jefferson Airplane had to quickly find a replacement for the departed singer who had just become a mother.

One of the group's singer/guitarists, Paul Kantner, suggested Grace Slick, who fronted a rival Bay Area band, The Great Society.

Married to film-maker Jerry Slick, she had been a model before she, Jerry, his brother Darby, and others had formed The Great Society in 1965. When Grace left, the rest of that group decided not to continue. The Great Society had never been signed by a record label before they split up, but after Grace found fame with the Airplane, two live albums by her first band were released, which had been recorded at San Francisco's Matrix club. These were regarded as especially important because included were two songs that Grace had brought with her to her new group, 'Somebody To Love' and 'White Rabbit', which were recorded by Jefferson Airplane and became their first two US Top 10 hit singles.

1977

OLD GROANER SILENCED

Bing Crosby - Bolan/Bowie connection

The death at the age of 76 of Harry Lillis Crosby was the end of the career of by far the most popular entertainer of the first half of the 20th century. Bing, as he was known, scored his first US hit single in 1931 with 'I Surrender Dear', and by 1955, when rock 'n' roll started, he had accumulated no less than 340 hit singles, an average of around 14 per year – more than one every month for almost a quarter of a century.

The pace had obviously slowed as he grew older, but one strange aspect of his death was that both he and Marc Bolan had (separately) appeared on television with David Bowie in the weeks before their death.

ARRIVALS

1927 – Kenny Roberts
1930 – Robert Parker
1938 – Melba Montgomery
1940 – Cliff Richard
(Harry Webb)
1945 – Marcia Barrett
(Boney M)
1945 – Colin Hodgkinson
(Back Door/Whitesnake)
1946 – Justin Hayward
(Moody Blues)
1946 – Dan McCafferty
(Nazareth)

1948 – Ivory Tilmon
(Detroit Emeralds)
1952 – Chris Amoo
(Real Thing)
1958 – Thomas Dolby
(Thomas Morgan
Robertson)
1965 – Karyn White

★ ★ ★

DEPARTURE LOUNGE

1977 – Bing Crosby
1990 – Leonard Bernstein

1955

HOLLY OPENS HALEY SHOW

The Lubbock-based duo of Buddy Holly and his schoolfriend, Bob Montgomery, found themselves in great demand as an opening act for nationally known rock 'n' roll stars. On consecutive days in October 1955 Buddy and Bob (as they were known professionally), appeared as support act to Bill Haley and The Comets (at a show promoted by KDAV, the Lubbock radio station) and on October 15 opened at Lubbock's Cotton Club for Elvis Presley.

RAVINGS

1964
Charlie Watts of The Rolling Stones and Shirley Shepherd were married in Bradford, Yorkshire.

1989
The name of Roy Orbison was added to the West Texas Walk Of Fame.

PROBLEMATIC DEBUT FOR FAMILY QUINTET

Five Star, the black R & B quintet who were all members of the Pearson family and who lived in the east London suburb of Romford, released their debut single, 'Problematic', on their own Tent Records.

The label was launched by their father, Buster Pearson, who had worked as a guitarist behind such visiting stars as Wilson Pickett, Jimmy Cliff, Lee Dorsey, etc. The single was not a hit, but a few months later, the Tent label (and its major asset, Five Star), were acquired by RCA Records. By the end of 1985 the group had released four hit singles, two of which reached the UK Top 20.

1986 was the group's big year, when five of their singles reached the UK chart, four of them – 'System Addict', 'Can't Wait Another Minute', 'Find The Time' and 'Rain Or Shine' (their biggest, a No. 2 hit) – making the Top 10.

The Five Star family

RAVINGS

1960
Loretta Lynn, the subject of the successful bio-pic *Coal Miner's Daughter*, made her debut at Nashville's *Grand Ole Opry*. She was warmly received, paid $15 and invited to return.

1964
Screaming Lord Sutch, noted British rock 'n' roll revivalist, was a candidate in a British parliamentary election, standing against Prime Minister Harold Wilson. He did not win.

1966
Pink Floyd and Soft Machine played at the launch party for 'underground' newspaper *International Times*.

DISAPPROVAL INSPIRES NELSON COMEBACK HIT

Ricky (or Rick, as he later became – his name was Eric) had been absent from the Top 10 of the US singles chart since early 1964. When he appeared at the seventh Annual Rock 'n' Roll Revival show at New York's Madison Square Garden he was perturbed when his performances of the material he used with his newly recruited Stone Canyon Band were booed by an audience who seemingly only wanted to hear him revive his old hits.

Nelson, however, had reached the US chart with two new recordings in the previous year, a version of Bob Dylan's 'She Belongs To Me' and his own composition, 'Easy To Be Free', and refused to regard himself as a relic from the past.

The crowd reaction incensed him to the point where he wrote a new song, 'Garden Party', expressing his disgust at their refusal to give his new work a chance. As he sang, 'If you gotta play at Garden Parties, I which you a lot of luck, But if memories were all I sang, I'd rather drive a truck'. 'Garden Party' was released as a single in 1972. It returned Nelson to the US Top 10 for the first time in eight years and became only his second gold single. Unfortunately it was also his last chart hit.

ARRIVALS

1925 – Mickey Baker (McHouston Baker) (Mickey and Sylvia)
1935 – Barry McGuire
1938 – Marv Johnson
1938 – Fela Anikulapo Kuti
1942 – Chris Andrews
1942 – Don Stevenson (Moby Grape)
1946 – Richard Carpenter
1947 – Chris de Burgh (Christopher Davidson)
1951 – Frank DiMino (Angel)
1953 – Tito Jackson (Toriano Adaryll Jackson) (Jackson 5)
1966 – Douglas Vipond (Deacon Blue)

★ ★ ★

DEPARTURE LOUNGE

1964 – Cole Porter
1980 – Bobby Lester (Moonglows)
1981 – Jud Strunk
1984 – Tasha Thomas

★ ★ ★

Rick Nelson

FOLK STAR BAEZ JAILED

Folk singer Joan Baez, one of the USA's most consistent album sellers of the first half of the 1960s, was arrested along with over 100 other anti-draft demonstrators (who disagreed with compulsory military training) at the Armed Forces Induction Center in Oakland, California. Baez was sentenced to ten days in prison.

Joan Baez (born to a Mexican father and Scottish mother) began performing as a folk singer while she was a drama student at university in Boston, Massachusetts, and performed at Newport Folk Festival while still a

Joan Baez - ten days inside

teenager. Signing to Vanguard Records in 1960, her eponymous debut album eventually spent nearly three years in the US chart, reaching the Top 20, although it only entered that chart in the wake of the success of Baez's second album, the intriguingly titled *Joan Baez Vol. 2*.

Baez was Bob Dylan's greatest supporter during his early years in New York's Greenwich Village, after she first met him at Gerde's Folk City in 1962. Her third album for Vanguard, *Joan Baez In Concert*, became her third consecutive release to be certified gold, reaching the US Top 10 in early 1963, a year which also saw an album of her early recordings with the inaccurate title *The Best Of Joan Baez*, reaching the Top 50 of the US chart. The end of that year brought another US Top 10 album, *Joan Baez In Concert Part 2*. In 1964 she refused to pay the percentage of her income tax that would be spent on armament, and also became a protester against racial discrimination in employment, refusing to appear on a popular TV show because it would not book certain acts.

RAVINGS

1954
Elvis Presley appeared on the *Louisiana Hayride* radio show in Shreveport, and was given a year's contract to appear on the programme.

1987
Dave Robinson resigned as Managing Director of Stiff Records, the maverick independent label he launched in 1976 with Jake Riviera, manager of Elvis Costello.

★ ★ ★

1986

BERRY WELCOMES SEVENTH DECADE

Chuck Berry's 60th birthday was celebrated by an all-star concert in St Louis that was filmed and released as part of a TV biography of the rock 'n' roll giant called *Hail! Hail! Rock 'n' Roll*. Rolling Stone Keith Richards was musical director and among those who made guest appearances in the live show were Eric Clapton, Robert Cray, Linda Ronstadt, Etta James and Julian Lennon (whose father had once said, 'If you ever tried to give rock 'n' roll another name, you might call it Chuck Berry'). Earlier that year Berry had been inducted by Richards into the first annual Rock 'n' Roll Hall of Fame in New York.

Chuck Berry - another name for rock 'n' roll

ARRIVALS

1923 – Bert Kaempfert
1935 – Sugar Pie DeSanto (Umpeylia Marsema Balinton)
1937 – Emile Ford
1938 – Nico (Christa Paffgen) (Velvet Underground)
1942 – Dave Lovelady (Fourmost)
1943 – Fred Turner (Bachman-Turner Overdrive)
1947 – Bob 'Ace' Weir (Grateful Dead)
1953 – Tony Carey (Rainbow)
1954 – Danny McIntosh Jr (Hazard/Bandit)
1956 – Kelly Marie
1959 – Gary Kemp (Spandau Ballet)
1969 – Wendy Wilson (Wilson Phillips)

★ ★ ★

DEPARTURE LOUNGE

1969 – Leonard Chess (founder of Chess Records)
1973 – Gene Krupa

★ ★ ★

1979

TUSK LAUNCHES 'RUMOURS' FOLLOW-UP

Following the record-beating success of *Rumours*, the Fleetwood Mac album that topped the US chart for an astounding 31 weeks in 1977/8, the Anglo - American quintet released the first single from their much-anticipated next album, 'Tusk'.

That single was the title track, a percussive and largely instrumental piece recorded live at Dodger Stadium in Los Angeles with the University of Southern California's Trojan Marching Band comprising 260 people. This was the largest act ever to reach the UK chart, although surprisingly was well beaten in the US by the 1958 Top 20 'Battle Hymn Of The Republic' by The Mormon Tabernacle Choir (with 375 members) directed by Richard Condon plus the Philadelphia Orchestra conducted by Eugene Ormandy, probably adding up to around 400. Even that giant group pales into insignificance compared to the audience of Lanchester Arts Festival in 1972 who can be heard stridently joining in with Chuck Berry on the chorus of his UK No. 1 single, 'My Ding-A-Ling'. Who knows how many people were in the hall when they switched on the tape recorder, and how many actually participated?

1990

BYE BYE VINYL

Vanilla Ice - a pioneer?

For the first time the album at No. 1 in the US chart was only available on compact disc (CD) or cassette, and could not be found on vinyl.

While some may feel that as the album in question was *To The Extreme* by Vanilla Ice, it may not be so important that a vinyl version was not released, they may be missing the point. If major labels no longer feel that a chart-topping album should be available in the format that was the midwife to rock music's 1970s breakthrough as a 'megabucks' industry, then an era that influenced the entire civilized world is clearly in its death throes.

The compact disc is undoubtedly the perfect medium for recordings made digitally, but much of the finest music made in the rock era was recorded in the traditional analogue format, and many feel that the vinyl album is the sound-carrier that best displays the quality of that music. It is also true that the CD is far less prone to careless damage than the easily scratchable vinyl album, although the size of a traditional album sleeve is a far superior medium for information than the much smaller CD booklet.

1967

LENNON MOVIE PREMIERES

With The Beatles in attendance, the premiere of the feature film *How I Won The War*, took place at the London Pavilion, the Piccadilly Circus cinema where many other Beatle-connected films were shown.

The Beatle connection in this case was that John Lennon was one of the movie's stars, although his was a totally non-

Roy Kinnear (left) and John Lennon in the trenches

musical role in the anti-war satire directed by Richard Lester, who had also worked on the two fully realized Beatles films, *A Hard Day's Night* and *Help!*. However, *How I Won*

The War was a very different proposition. Lennon played the part of Private Gripweed, a member of the third troop of the (fictional) Fourth Musketeers in World War II, who were

commanded by Lieutenant Goodbody (played by Michael Crawford). Other well-known actors appeared in the movie, but it received only moderate reviews.

1969

ROD 'THE MOD' MAKES SMALL FACES BIGGER

Ronnie Lane (left) with Rod Stewart

Having played their final show earlier in the year, after which vocalist and guitarist Steve Marriott joined Peter Frampton (ex-The Herd) in a neo-supergroup Humble Pie, The Small Faces first recruited guitarist Ron Wood, who had been playing bass in the Jeff Beck Group, but after rehearsals it became clear that the group really needed a strong vocalist. New recruit Wood suggested his ex-colleague fron the Beck band, Rod Stewart join, although he was also contracted as a solo artist to a different label from the one that was interested in The Faces.

In view of the remarkable success that later greeted Rod 'The Mod' (as he was known in the early 1960s), it is interesting to reflect that the first two singles by The Faces (the name that the group adopted when Stewart and Wood joined – Marriott, like Ronnie Lane, Ian MacLagan and Kenny Jones, had been short in stature, but the two newcomers were of medium height) both failed to reach the UK chart. 'Flying'/'Three Button Hand Me Down' was released in February 1970, a month before the group's debut album, *First Step*, which charted for a single week. In early 1971 their second single, 'Had Me A Real Good Time'/'Rear Wheel Skid', again flopped, but thereafter the group were more successful.

YARDBIRDS SHED STAR ON US TOUR

1966

The Yardbirds, one of Britain's most innovative groups, flew to the USA to participate in a tour under the banner of Dick Clark's *American Bandstand*. Travelling by bus, just two days into the trek lead guitarist Jeff Beck left the tour and the band with an acute case of tonsilitis and formed a new group with Rod Stewart and Ronnie Wood. Also on the tour were Brian Hyland (of 'Itsy Bitsy Teeny Weeny Yellow Polka Dot Bikini' fame) and Sam The Sham and The Pharaohs ('Wooly Bully').This marked the end of the very brief life of what is widely seen as the most interesting Yardbirds line-up.

Founder members Keith Relf (vocals), Chris Dreja (rhythm guitar) and Jim McCarty (drums) were ever-present, Beck had not appeared on the Yardbirds' first Top 3 hit, 'For Your Love' but had been with the group for 18 months during which the group had released three UK Top 3 hits, 'Heartful Of Soul', 'Evil Hearted You'/'Still I'm Sad' (a double A-side) and 'Shapes Of Things', within nine months, after which came another Top 10 hit, 'Over Under Sideways Down'.

Soon after that, bass player Paul Samwell-Smith opted to leave the band he had helped to form, becoming a successful record producer, whose clients included Carly Simon, Cat Stevens and Jethro Tull. His replacement in June 1966 was Jimmy Page, a session player who had actually been in the frame with Beck as Clapton's replacement. For the second time of asking he was invited to become the group's bass player, but apparently joined on the under-standing that he and Chris Dreja would swap instruments when Dreja had mastered the bass.

Rod Stewart adjusts his dress

ROD'S FOURTH NUMBER ONE ALBUM ON THE TROT

1974

When *Smiler* topped the UK album chart, it became Rod Stewart's fourth consecutive No. 1 album, following 1971's *Every Picture Tells A Story*, *Never A Dull Moment* (1972) and *Sing It Again Rod* (1974).

Stewart's first two solo albums, *An Old Raincoat Won't Ever Let You Down* and *Gasoline Alley* (both released in 1970), had been less successful. The earlier of the two (which was retitled *The Rod Stewart Album* for American release) was never listed in the UK chart, while its successor spent a mere week on the chart. However, each of Stewart's first six albums reached the US chart, although only *Every Picture Tells A Story* made No. 1. His greatest UK commercial success was to come the following year with *Atlantic Crossing* and in the US, in 1976, *A Night On The Town* was the first of six consecutive million selling albums.

1977

SKYNYRD TRIO KILLED IN PLANE CRASH

Three members of Lynyrd Skynyrd, the 'Southern Rock' band from Jacksonville, Florida, that had released its sixth album, *Street Survivors*, three days earlier, were killed when the rented small plane in which they were travelling from South Carolina to Baton Rouge, Louisiana, crashed into a swamp near Gillsburg, Mississippi.

The group's tour manager Dean Kilpatrick, also died along with vocalist and front man Ronnie Van Zant, guitarist Steven Gaines and his sister, backing singer Cassie Gaines. Other members of the group, including guitarists Gary Rossington and Allen Collins, keyboard player Billy Powell and bass man Leon Wilkerson, were seriously injured, but survived to play another day.

The group had emerged in late 1973 with an album curiously titled *(pronounced leh-nerd skin-nerd)* which reached the Top 30 of the US chart and was eventually certified gold. The album included 'Free Bird', which became the group's anthem, featuring expert work from three lead guitarists.

1974 brought another gold album, *Second Helping*, which included a US Top 10 single, 'Sweet Home Alabama', while further gold albums, *Nuthin' Fancy* (1975) and *Gimme Back My Bullets*, expanded the group's reputation so they were regarded as one of the USA's most popular live acts, as was proved when the double live album *One More From The Road* achieved platinum status.

1969

LENNON RELEASES THIRD NON-BEATLE ALBUM IN 12 MONTHS

John and Yoko disembark at Geneva airport, 1969

John Lennon and Yoko Ono released *The Wedding Album* in the US. Supposedly a souvenir of their marriage earlier in 1969, and was sold as a boxed set containing not only the album (as unlistenable, generally speaking, as its two predecessors) but also a poster of wedding pictures, a photograph of a piece of wedding cake inside a plastic bag, and several other artefacts of minimal commercial value.

Like their two previous experimental releases, *The Wedding Album* only briefly appeared in the US album chart.

1958

BUDDY'S LAST STUDIO DATE

Buddy Holly embarked on what would turn out to be his final formal session in a recording studio. During the evening he cut four tracks, three of which later became major hits, although not necessarily as recorded by Holly himself.

Buddy Holly with The Tanner Sisters - who? - in 1958

Having moved to New York earlier in the month with his new wife, Maria Elena, whom he had married two months before, Holly had split from The Crickets, with whom he had enjoyed considerable success in the previous two years, and from Norman Petty, who had been his mentor, but whom he now felt might not have

been totally honest in their business dealings.

On the previous trip to New York during which he had met Maria Elena, Holly had recorded two songs produced by Dick Jacobs of Coral Records, the label to which he was signed at Coral's New York studios on 80th Street, which were known as The Pythian Temple. Jacobs was

again the producer when Buddy went back to Pythian Temple, although this time, Jacobs also booked a 12-piece string section to sweeten the four tracks Holly recorded, which were 'It Doesn't Matter Anymore' (written by Canadian Paul Anka, who also wrote the lyrics to 'My Way'), 'Raining In My Heart' (by Felice

and Boudleaux Bryant, who wrote many hits for The Everly Brothers), 'True Love Ways' (co-written by Holly and Petty) and 'Moondreams' (another Petty-penned song).

'It Doesn't Matter Anymore' was Holly's latest release when he died in February 1959, and became a No. 1 single in Britain.

ARRIVALS

1937 – Norman Wright (Del-Vikings)

1940 – Jimmy Beaumont (Skyliners)

1940 – Manfred Mann (Michael Lubowitz)

1941 – Steve Cropper

1943 – Ron Elliott (Beau Brummels)

1946 – Lee Loughnane (Chicago)

1947 – Tetsu Yamauchi (Free/Faces)

1948 – John 'Rabbit' Bundrick (Free/Back Street Crawler)

1953 – Charlotte Caffey (Go-Go's)

1954 – Phillip Chen (Keef Hartley Band/Butts Band)

1954 – Eric Faulkner (Bay City Rollers)

1957 – Julian Cope (Teardrop Explodes)

1957 – Steve Lukather (Toto)

1959 – Rose McDowell (Strawberry Switchblade)

★ ★ ★

DEPARTURE LOUNGE

1965 – Bill Black

★ ★ ★

1965

BRAIN TUMOUR CLAIMS PRESLEY SIDEMAN

Bill Black, the latter half of Scotty and Bill, the original musicians who backed Elvis Presley

during his dynamic rise to fame, died of a brain tumour a month after his 39th birthday. After leaving Presley in the late 1950s, bass player

Black formed his own group, Bill Black's Combo, and scored 19 hits before his death, the biggest of which were 'White Silver Sands',

'Josephine', 'Blue Tango' and 'Don't Be Cruel' (an instrumental version of the Presley hit on which he had played), all in 1960.

RAVINGS

1985
Carl Perkins was honoured in a concert in London taped for television to commemorate the 30th

Anniversary of his 'Blue Suede Shoes' classic. Among those appearing with him were George Harrison, Ringo Starr and Dave Edmunds.

★ ★ ★

1989
Polygram Inc. purchased A & M Records from founders Herb Alpert and Jerry Moss for between $400 and $500 million.

★ ★ ★

Waiting for the bus?

PUNK ROCK BORN TO DAMNED QUARTET

The Damned (l to r) Sensible, Vanian, Scabies, James

Formed earlier in the year, The Damned released what is generally regarded as the first punk rock single, 'New Rose'/'Help' (the latter a cover version of the hit by The Beatles). It was not a hit, but pre-dated the first genuine British punk rock hit, 'Anarchy In The UK' by The Sex Pistols, released five weeks later.

The Damned formed originally as a trio of Brian James (real name Brian Robertson, guitar), Captain Sensible (real name Ray Burns, bass) and Rat Scabies (real name Chris Miller, drums), and were completed when ex-gravedigger Dave Vanian (real name David Letts) joined as vocalist. They played their first gig opening for The Sex Pistols at London's 100 Club, and met Nick Lowe when travelling to France for the Mont De Marsan punk festival, where both were on the bill. Signing to Stiff Records four months after their formation, the group's debut single was produced by Lowe.

In 1977 the group also became the first British punk act to play in the USA, also releasing their debut album, *Damned, Damned Damned*, which was again produced by Lowe and spent ten weeks in the UK chart, peaking inside the Top 40. Their second album, Music For Pleasure, was released seven months later, and was produced by Pink Floyd drummer Nick Mason, whom many regarded as a bizarre choice. It failed to equal its predecessor's achievement in charting, and before it was released, Scabies left and was replaced by Jon Moss, who later founded Culture Club with Boy George.

Probably the most surprising achievement by any member of The Damned occurred in 1982, when Captain Sensible's revival of 'Happy Talk', a song from the musical *South Pacific*, topped the UK singles chart for two weeks and outsold every previous Damned record. In 1986 The Damned themselves, without Captain Sensible reached the Top 3 of the UK chart with their revival of 'Eloise', the 1968 UK Top 3 hit by Barry Ryan.

BEACH BOYS MASTERPIECE HITS US CHART

Brian Wilson

Good Vibrations', the breathtaking single by The Beach Boys, entered the US chart on its way to becoming the group's third US chart-topper and their second million-selling '45'. This was the peak of their success. The track reputedly took Beach Boys founder and resident genius Brian Wilson six months to complete, involving 17 separate sessions at four different studios. It also topped the UK chart. At the 1967 Grammy Awards 'Good Vibrations' was beaten to the award for Best Contemporary Recording by the New Vaudeville Band's 'Winchester Cathedral' - a decision as intelligent as that of the famed Decca Records in preferring Brian Poole and The Tremeloes to The Beatles.

ARRIVALS

1921 – Georges Brassens
1942 – Annette Funicello
1943 – Robert Fuller (Bobby Fuller Four)
1945 – Leslie West (Leslie Weinstein) (Mountain)
1946 – Eddie Brigati (Young Rascals)

★ ★ ★

RAVINGS

1956
Britain's first rock 'n' roll stage show was launched featuring Ronnie Harris and Kenny Flame and The Rockets.

★ ★ ★

1950

DEATH OF WORLD'S GREATEST ENTERTAINER

Al Jolson, who called himself – quite justifiably, some might say – 'The World's Greatest Entertainer', died in San Francisco six months before his 65th birthday.

Born Asa Yoelson in Russia, Jolson migrated to the USA as a child, and worked in vaudeville as a teenager, later performing with his brother Harry as a duo. When Al was 16, his brother wore black make-up on his face and hands, which later became one of Al's major innovations. Al Jolson first recorded when in his mid-twenties, but it was when he appeared in the title role of the first 'talkie', *The Jazz Singer*, in 1927, that Jolson became world-famous, even though he was never regarded as a jazz singer.

Interestingly, when the film was remade in 1980, with Neil Diamond in the title role, the latter was again not associated with jazz, and while the later film included three US hit singles, it was critically slated, whereas the earlier version starring Jolson was a huge box office triumph.

Between 1912 and 1948 Jolson released nearly 100 hit singles, including 23 that were rated as chart-toppers, among them 'You Made Me Love You', 'Rock-A-Bye Your Baby With A Dixie Melody', 'Swanee', 'Toot Toot Tootsie (Goo'bye)', 'California

Al Jolson, born in Russia, a star in America

Here I Come!' and many more, all promoted by Jolson in black make-up. This would later lead to the bizarre phenomenon known as 'Black and White Minstrels', in which a group of white men with black greasepaint would sing songs in the style of Jolson accompanied by white females.

An album in this style by The George Mitchell Minstrels, *The Black and White Minstrel Show*, first topped the UK chart eight months after it was first listed, eventually logging seven weeks at No. 1 in four spells at the top spot during 1961.

1964

PLANE CRASH TAKES SECOND CRICKET

Thanks to Don McLean's 'American Pie', the date of February 3, 1959, is widely known as 'The day the music died' (when Buddy Holly was killed along with Ritchie Valens and The Big Bopper), fewer people realize that just over five and a half years later, one of Holly's successors as lead vocalist with The Crickets, David Box, was also killed in a plane crash.

ARRIVALS

1939 – Charlie Foxx
1940 – Ellie Greenwich
1947 – Greg Ridley (Spooky Tooth/Humble Pie)
1948 – Richie Bull (Kursaal Flyers)
1949 – Wurzel (Michael Burston) (Motorhead)
1953 – Pauline Black (The Selecter)
1954 – Dwight Yoakam
1957 – Kelly Marie

★ ★ ★

DEPARTURE LOUNGE

1950 – Al Jolson
1963 – Michael Holliday
1969 – Tommy Edwards
1976 – Leonard Lee (Shirley and Lee)
1978 – Mother Maybelle Carter

★ ★ ★

'RUMOURS' SETS NEW LONGEVITY MARK

When Fleetwood Mac's record-breaking album *Rumours* chalked up its 397th week on the UK chart, it became the holder of the record for most weeks on that chart, overtaking Meat Loaf's similarly revered *Bat Out Of Hell*.

The trials and tribulations of Fleetwood Mac's three singer/ guitarists between May 1972 and April 1974 was a hammer blow few groups could withstand, and between 1970's *Kiln House* (which briefly reached the Top 40 in Britain) and 1976's *Fleetwood Mac* (their first album to feature Lindsey Buckingham and Stevie Nicks), the group's original new albums (as opposed to compilations of old material from the Peter Green era) failed to chart in Britain, although all five of them (which featured American singer/guitarist Bob Welch) reached the US album chart. 1975's *Heroes Are Hard To Find*, became the group's first album to reach those heights in the USA.

Fleetwood Mac (an intriguing title for a group's eleventh original album?) totally outperformed all their previous albums in the USA by topping the chart, and also became their comeback album in Britain. It was followed by *Rumours*, which topped the US chart for 31 weeks (a record for a non-soundtrack album until it was beaten by Michael Jackson's *Thriller* in 1983) and also topped the UK chart for a single week, but refused to leave the listings. By the end of 1991 *Rumours* had accumulated 443 weeks on the chart, over six month's worth more than Meat Loaf's mere 416.

Their comeback album

RAVINGS

1962
James Brown recorded his legendary *Live At The Apollo* album.

★ ★ ★

1978
Keith Richards of The Rolling Stones was convicted in Canada of heroin possession, for which he received a one-year suspended sentence and was ordered to play a charity concert for the blind, also in Canada.

★ ★ ★

1983
Yoko Ono announced that she planned to give part of her vast fortune to charity, as she believed her late husband would have wished.

★ ★ ★

McCARTNEY GOES RHODIUM

Paul McCartney was presented with a medallion made of rhodium, an extremely precious metal, by the Arts Minister of the British government as the best-selling songwriter and recording artist in history, according to the *Guinness Book Of Records*. Between 1962 and 1978 he had been involved (either alone or with collaborators, notably John Lennon) in 43 songs that had each sold a million copies. His sales were estimated to be over 100 million units each of singles and albums.

ARRIVALS

1911 – Sonny Terry (Saunders Terrell)
1920 – Steve Conway (Walter James Groom)
1927 – Gilbert Becaud (François Silly)
1930 – Big Bopper (Jilles Perry Richardson)
1936 – Bill Wyman
1937 – Santo Farina (Santo and Johnny)
1940 – Ricky Brook (Brook Brothers)
1944 – Taffy Danoff (Starland Vocal Band)
1944 – Ted Templeman (Harper's Bizarre)
1946 – Edgar Broughton
1946 – Jerry Edmonton (Steppenwolf)
1946 – Rob van Leeuwen (Shocking Blue)
1948 – Paul and Barry Ryan
1950 – Dale Griffin (Mott The Hoople)
1958 – Alan Jackman (Outfield)

★ ★ ★

1974

AL GREEN SCALDED BY GIRLFRIEND'S GRITS

28-year-old soul star Al Green was taking a shower at his home in Memphis when his ex-girlfriend, Mary Woodson, burst in and threw a pan of boiling hot grits over him, before shooting herself with his gun. She may well have been miffed by the title of one of his current hits, 'Let's Get Married', which she perhaps felt might have been addressed to her.

Green, who was originally a gospel singer, moved into secular music in much the same way as Sam Cooke, releasing his first US hit in late 1967 as the leader of Al Greene (sic) and The Soul Mates, on their own label, Hot Line Music. He left the group to go solo in 1968, and in 1969 he met Willie Mitchell of the Memphis-based independent label, Hi Records. In three years from mid 1971, he scored a series of classic hits on Hi, including 'Tired Of Being Alone', 'Let's Stay Together' (his only US pop chart No. 1 to date), 'Look What You Done For Me', 'I'm Still In Love With You' and 'You Ought To Be With Me'.

He claimed to have experienced a religious rebirth in 1973, and after the grits attack he reverted to sacred music, buying a Memphis church and becoming its minister. He was ordained as a pastor of the Full Gospel Tabernacle.

Green, soul star turned preacher

1961

ALL THE THRILLS OF HAYLEY MILLS

Hayley, film star with a hit

Hayley Mills became the first British female vocalist to reach the US Top 10 since ballad singer Vera Lynn, who had achieved this distinction twice in 1952, first with 'Auf Wiederseh'n Sweetheart' (a million selling chart-topper) and also with 'Yours (Quierme Mucho)'.

Hayley, who was born in 1946, appeared in a number of movies as a juvenile Disney starlet, such as *Tiger Bay* (co-starring with her father, John Mills), *Pollyanna* and *Whistle Down The Wind*. She was featured singing 'Let's Get Together' in her dual role in *The Parent Trap*, and it was released as a single in the US on the Disney-related Vista label, peaking within the Top 10 of the singles chart and also reaching the UK Top 20. In the US, she also charted in 1962 with 'Johnny Jingo', which all but reached the Top 20.

JOINTS IN BUCK HOUSE
1965

The Beatles were presented with MBE (Member Of The British Empire) medals by Queen Elizabeth II in a formal ceremony that took place at London's Buckingham Palace, the residence of the reigning monarch.

This decoration is regarded as royal recognition of an extremely significant achievement, and few other pop stars have ever been granted such an accolade.

Subsequent interviews with the group revealed that they had been incredibly nervous before meeting Her Majesty The Queen, and to bolster their confidence some members of the group had retreated to the Palace rest room for a swift smoke on a 'joint' (or marijuana cigarette). This may have been the first occasion on which ban-ned drugs were con-sumed on royal property.

CANCER TAKES GIRL WITH LAUGHING VOICE
1966

Alma Cogan, one of Britain's most popular and consistent vocalists during the second half of the 1950s, died of cancer at the tragically early age of 34. Known as 'the girl with the laugh in her voice', she accumulated 21 hit singles (a record for a female vocalist at the time) between 1954, when 'Bell Bottom Blues' became her first UK Top 5 hit, and 1961 when 'Cowboy Jimmy' dropped out of the charts. She was famous for her bubbly light-weight songs such as 'Never Do A Tango With An Eskimo' and 'I Can't Tell A Waltz From A Tango'. Her biggest hit was 1955's 'Dreamboat', which topped the UK chart for two weeks before it was overtaken by Slim Whitman's record-setting 'Rose Marie', whose eleven weeks at No. 1 remained unbeaten until Bryan Adams surpassed it in 1991 with '(Everything I Do) I Do It For You'.

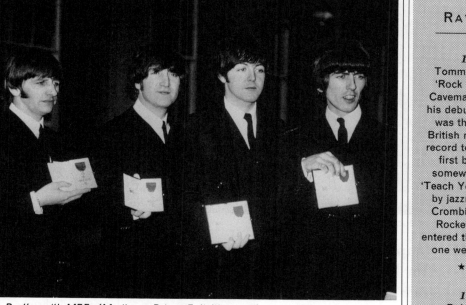
The Beatles with MBEs (Marijuana Brings Enlightenment)

PRESSURIZED SUPERSTAR SUMMIT MEETING
1981

David Bowie and British superstar quartet Queen both maintained properties near Montreux in Switzerland, and according to Queen guitarist Brian May, Bowie would occasionally visit Queen's Mountain Studio, where the group recorded many of their hits. On one such visit it was suggested that the two hitmaking acts should attempt a recording collaboration.

May revealed, 'The next night, we listened to the tapes of what we'd done, and picked out a couple of pieces which seemed to be promising, and then we just worked on one particular idea, which became 'Under Pressure', for a whole night – an extremely long night'. 'Under Pressure' topped the UK singles chart in late 1981 and also reached the US Top 30, but it looks unlikely there will be a follow-up.

ARRIVALS
1911 – Mahalia Jackson
1913 – Charlie Barnet
1940 – Keith Hopwood (Herman's Hermits)
1944 – Michael Piano (Sandpipers)
1949 – Wes McGhee
1951 – William 'Bootsy' Collins (Funkadelic, Bootsy's Rubber Band)
1953 – Keith Strickland (B-52s)
1963 – Daniel John Ohm

★ ★ ★

DEPARTURE LOUNGE
1966 – Alma Cogan

★ ★ ★

RAVINGS

1956
Tommy Steele's 'Rock With The Caveman' became his debut UK hit. It was the second British rock 'n' roll record to chart, the first being the somewhat ersatz 'Teach You To Rock' by jazzman Tony Crombie and His Rockets, which entered the UK chart one week earlier.

★ ★ ★

1963
Bob Dylan played a sell-out concert at New York's Carnegie Hall.

★ ★ ★

1980
Paul Kantner of Jefferson Starship suffered a stroke and became seriously ill during recording sessions for the group's *Modern Times* album, but recovered completely after some time in hospital.

★ ★ ★

1960

BEN E. KING CUTS FIRST SOLO SIDES

King - fired from Drifters, back in the chart

Ben E. King completed his first recording session as a solo artist after leaving The Drifters, the group he had fronted since July 1958. After singing lead on such magnificent classics as 'There Goes My Baby' (US Top 3), 'Dance With Me', 'This Magic Moment', 'Save The Last Dance For Me' (a US No. 1) and 'I Count The Tears', all of which made the US Top 20, King had been fired from The Drifters by George Treadwell, who owned the rights to the group's name, after King had protested that the group's wages ought to be increased to reflect their growing commercial success.

As many of those hits had been produced by Jerry Leiber and Mike Stoller, they also supervised King's initial solo recordings. Four tracks were cut in three hours, including 'Spanish Harlem' (King's first solo hit, which reached the US Top 10 and was written by Leiber and Phil Spector), its flip side, 'First Taste Of Love' (a minor US hit in its own right written by Spector and Doc Pomus), 'Stand By Me' (written by King, Leiber and Stoller, a Top 5 US hit in 1961 and a UK chart-topper in 1987, when it was used in a Levi Jeans commercial and as the title song to a hit feature film), and 'Young Boy Blues' (again written by Spector and Pomus, and a minor US hit in late 1961).

ARRIVALS

1926 – Kai Warner (Werner Last) (brother of James Last)
1933 – Floyd Cramer
1939 – Dallas Frazier
1942 – Philip Catherine
1942 – Lee Greenwood
1956 – Hazell Dean (Hazell Dean Poole)
1958 – Simon Le Bon (Duran Duran)
1961 – Eddie Hind (Picnic At The Whitehouse)

★ ★ ★

DEPARTURE LOUNGE

1938 – Alma Gluck
1975 – Oliver Nelson
1980 – Steve Peregrine Took (Tyrannosaurus Rex)

★ ★ ★

RAVINGS

1963
Peter, Paul and Mary occupied the top two positions in the US album chart, with *Peter, Paul and Mary* and *In The Wind*.

1973
'Midnight Train To Georgia' by Gladys Knight and The Pips was at No. 1 in the US singles chart.

1990
Michael Waite of 'Pass The Dutchie' hitmakers Musical Youth, was jailed for four years for robbery.

★ ★ ★

1975

BOSS ON BOTH COVERS

Bruce Springsteen's emergence as a star was confirmed when he was featured on the cover of *Time* and *Newsweek*. This was an event which had rarely occurred before, and never featuring a pop star, as the two magazines were rivals appealing to the same audience. The excitement over Springsteen resulted from the release of his first hit album, *Born To Run*, and its title track, which was a US Top 30 hit. As a result of the publicity for *Born To Run*, Springsteen's first two albums, *Greetings From Asbury Park, N.J.* and *The Wild, The Innocent and The E Street Shuffle*, both entered the US chart for the first time in 1975, having been released earlier in 1973.

Bruce Springsteen

JANET JACKSON'S STAR SPANGLED ALBUM

Rhythm Nation 1814, Janet Jackson's follow-up to her chart-topping 1987 album *Control*, also reached No. 1 in the USA. '1814' was a reference to the year when Francis Scott Key composed the American national anthem, 'The Star-Spangled Banner'.

In early 1991, when 'Love Will Never Do (Without You)' reached the US Top 5, Jackson became the first artist to extract seven US Top 5 singles from the same album. The earlier hits were 'Miss You Much', 'Rhythm Nation', 'Escapade', 'Alright', 'Come Back To Me', and 'Black Cat', the only track on the album on which she did not collaborate as a songwriter with producers Jimmy Jam and Terry Lewis.

Perhaps fortuitously for Michael Jackson's younger sister, her contractual commitments to A & M Records were completed by *Rhythm Nation 1814*, and she was swiftly signed by Richard Branson to Virgin Records for what was the biggest advance ever paid – $50 million. Branson commented: 'A Rembrandt rarely becomes available. When it does, there are many people determined to get

Janet Jackson - to Virgin for $50 million

it. I was determined.' During the following year, Branson sold Virgin Records to EMI.

Janet's biggest ever advance record stood for about one month.

Michael, her brother, beat it when he re-signed with Sony for what was called the first billion-dollar deal for an entertainer, and dwarfed that of Janet.

NEVER MIND THE CONTROVERSY . . .

NEVER MIND THE BOLLOCKS

HERE'S THE

Sex Pistols

The offending album sleeve

Two weeks before the long-awaited debut album by The Sex Pistols, *Never Mind The Bollocks, Here's The Sex Pistols*, was released in Britain, a bootleg appeared in numerous record shops entitled *Spunk*, which was quite obviously something very similar to the forthcoming album. Containing the group's first three hit singles, 'Anarchy In The UK' (re-titled 'Nookie'), 'God Save The Queen' ('No Future') and 'Pretty Vacant' ('Lots Of Fun'), it also included six other songs from the official album (although not the group's fourth hit single, 'Holidays In The Sun').

Never Mind entered the UK album chart two weeks later at No. 1 displacing Cliff Richard's *40 Golden Greats*, where it remained for two weeks.

A policewoman saw the album in a shop window and unsuccessfully sued the retailer, claiming it controvened the Indecent Advertising Act.

ARRIVALS

1927 – Cleo Laine (Clementina Dinah Campbell)
1929 – Mitchell Torok
1936 – Charlie Daniels
1937 – Graham Bond
1941 – Curtis Lee
1941 – Hank B. Marvin (Brian Rankin) (Shadows)
1945 – Wayne Fontana (Glynn Ellis)
1948 – Thelma Hopkins (Dawn)
1948 – Ricky Lee Reynolds (Black Oak Arkansas)
1957 – Stephen Morris (New Order)
1959 – Neville Henry (Blow Monkeys)

★ ★ ★

DEPARTURE LOUNGE

1965 – Earl Bostic
1970 – Baby Huey (James Ramey)
1987 – Woody Herman
1991 – Bill Graham

RAVINGS

1958
Buddy Holly made his last major TV appearance, on *American Bandstand*.

★ ★ ★

1972
The US Council For World Affairs adopted 'Join Together' by The Who as its anthem.

★ ★ ★

1989
It was proudly announced that 'Lambada' by the French group, Kaoma, had sold 1.7 million copies in France. Described as a multi-national group of singers, musicians and dancers, Kaoma was far less successful in Britain, where it reached the Top 5, and especially in the US, where it peaked outside the Top 40.

1971

DOCTORS CANNOT SAVE DUANE ALLMAN

Surgeons in Macon, Georgia, fought unsuccessfully for three hours to save Duane Allman's life after he was involved in a motorcycle accident. Allman was three weeks short of his 25th birthday, but had established an enviable reputation as one of the most influential blues/rock guitarists of the rock era.

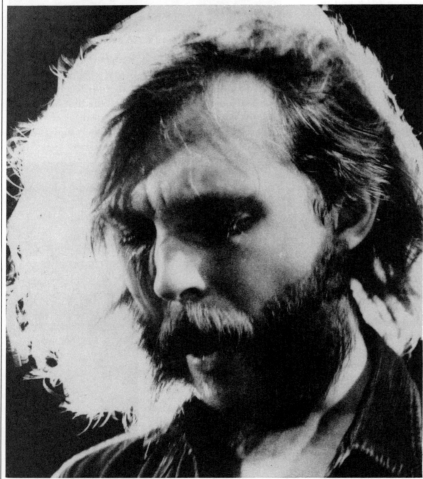

Tragic end for a talented musician

He was returning from the house of Berry Oakley, a fellow member of The Allman Brothers Band, after delivering a birthday present to Oakley's wife, Linda, when he swerved to avoid an oncoming truck.

Born in Nashville but raised in Florida, Allman and his brother, singer and keyboard player Gregg, had moved to Los Angeles in 1967 where they formed Hour Glass, a group that released two albums in six months and recorded a third that was rejected by the group's record company. In mid 1968 Duane and Gregg returned to Jacksonville, where Duane became a much in-demand session musician, playing on records by Wilson Pickett, Aretha Franklin, King Curtis and others. This led to Duane and Gregg forming The Allman Brothers band with bass player Oakley, second guitarist and vocalist Dickey Betts, and two drummers, Butch Trucks and Jai Johanny 'Jaimoe' Johanson (real name John Lee Johnson). The group made two excellent albums, 1969's eponymous debut and 1970's *Idlewild South*, which reached the Top 40 of the US chart.

Duane continued with his session work, in particular providing a chapter in rock history when he guested on *Layla And Other Assorted Love Songs* by Derek and The Dominoes, duelling with group leader Eric Clapton on the album's classic title track. Duane also featured strongly on *At Fillmore East*, a stunning double live album.

1971

HAIR TODAY, BROADWAY TOMORROW

The so-called 'American tribal love-rock musical' *Hair*, opened in New York's Public Theater. Arguably the first true youth culture stage show, it included considerable nudity and a number of hit songs, such as 'Aquarius', 'Let The Sunshine In', 'Good Morning Starshine' and 'Ain't Got No – I Got Life', while the original cast album of the show topped the US album chart for three months in 1968.

RAVINGS

1966
'96 Tears' by ? (Question Mark) and The Mysterians topped the US singles chart.

1983
Pink Floyd's *Dark Side Of The Moon* became the longest listed album in the history of the US chart when its total reached 491 weeks.

1988
R.E.M.'s album amusingly entitled *Eponymous* entered the UK album chart, but left again after three weeks.

★ ★ ★

'SHE'S GONE' STARTS RECORD-BREAKING

Daryl Hall and John Oates entered the Top 10 of the US singles chart with 'She's Gone'. In early 1988 'Everything Your Heart Desires' became their 16th US Top 10 hit, more than any duo had ever achieved during the rock era – The Everly Brothers had previously been the holders of this title, with 15 US Top 10 hits between 1957 and 1962.

Daryl Hall (real name Daryl Hohl) and John Oates met at university in 1967, having both been raised in Philadelphia (and thus having absorbed the sound of Philly Soul in its formative years). In 1969 they were colleagues in Gulliver, a group that recorded an album for Elektra, and when that band folded they began to work together as a duo, signing to Atlantic in 1972. They recorded three albums, the most successful of which was 1974's *Abandoned Luncheonette*, which included 'She's Gone', which became a minor hit when it was released as a single in 1974.

After the duo's third album, *War Babies*, their contract with Atlantic ended, and they signed with RCA Records, releasing an eponymous album in late 1975. This album included 'Sara Smile', a song written about Hall's girlfriend, which was released as a single in early 1976. This was their breakthrough, and Atlantic quickly reissued 'She's Gone', hoping to capitalize on the duo's newfound stardom.

The duo topped the US chart with six singles before 1985: 'Rich Girl' (1977), 'Kiss On My List' and 'Private Eyes' (both 1981), 'I Can't Go For That (No Can Do)' and 'Maneater' (both 1982) and 'Out Of Touch' (1984). In 1985 they appeared at Live Aid and in 1986 they split when Hall embarked upon a solo career. Reuniting in 1988 and signing to Arista Records, the hits - although smaller - continued.

John Oates (left) and Daryl Hall

ARRIVALS

1914 – Patsy Montana (Rubye Blevins)
1934 – Hamilton Camp
1939 – Eddie Holland (Holland/Dozier/Holland)
1939 – Grace Slick (Grace Wing)
1941 – Otis Williams (Otis Miles)
1945 – Henry 'Fonz' Winkler
1946 – Chris Slade (Manfred Mann's Earthband)
1947 – Timothy B.Schmit (Poco/Eagles)
1960 – Byron Burke (Ten City)
1962 – Geoff Beauchamp (Eighth Wonder)

★ ★ ★

DEPARTURE LOUNGE

1981 – Georges Brassens

★ ★ ★

RAVINGS

1971
John Lennon's *Imagine* became his first album to top the charts on both sides of the Atlantic.

1982
Elton John appeared at a Royal Command Performance in Britain.

★ ★ ★

FANS MOURN DISINTEGRATING JAM

Paul Weller, vocalist, guitarist and major songwriter with The Jam, announced that the group were splitting up. Of all the British punk rock acts of the late 1970s, this trio were arguably the most popular and successful.

Formed during schooldays by singer/guitarist Paul Weller, drummer Rick Buckler and bass player Bruce Foxton (who was the last to join in 1975), The Jam (as they called themselves, apparently because Weller and Buckler had met while informally playing together – jamming) accumulated 18 UK hit singles in under six years, including four No. 1s: 'Going Underground'/'Dreams Of Children' and 'Start' (both 1980), and 'Town Called Malice'/'Precious' and 'Beat Surrender' (both 1982). Five of the seven albums they released during that period also reached the top of the UK chart.

(left to right) Weller, Buckler, Foxton - The Jam

QUEEN FREDDIE, BOHEMIAN DIVA

1975

Queen's 'Bohemian Rhapsody', a remarkable technical masterpiece of popular music featuring a passage clearly inspired by opera, was released in the UK.

Lasting seven minutes, it was originally felt by EMI Records, the group's label, to be far too long for release as a single, as many radio stations would refuse to programme it.

However, the group and Roy Thomas Baker, who had produced the track, played it to an influential London disc jockey who played it on the air 14 times in two days. Record shops were deluged with requests for the single, which was soon made available by public demand, a rare instance when such a claim was genuine. By the end of the next month, 'Bohemian Rhapsody' was at No. 1 in the UK chart, where it remained for nine weeks.

It was re-issued 17 years later after the death of lead singer Freddie Mercury and became the only song to top the chart on two separate occasions.

(left to right) Brian May, John Deacon, Freddie Mercury, Roger Taylor

1983

FRANKIE ADVISES RELAXATION

Liverpool group Frankie Goes To Hollywood released their debut single, 'Relax', which was the first release on ZTT Records, the label launched by record producer Trevor Horn.

The group was formed in Liverpool in 1980 by vocalists Holly Johnson (real name William Johnson, ex-Big In Japan) and Paul Rutherford (ex-Spitfire Boys) with three other members of smalltime local Merseyside groups. Taking their memorable group name from a newspaper headline above an article about either British vocalist Frankie Vaughan or Frank Sinatra making films – sources differ as to which Frank it may have been – the group recorded a session for BBC Radio One. Soon afterwards, at the end of 1982, they appeared on the trendy British TV show *The Tube*, which was apparently where Horn became aware of them.

The release of 'Relax' was promoted by widely distributed T-shirts bearing the legend 'Frankie Says', and before long the single began to attract attention after a video clip of the song was banned. However, the single went into orbit when BBC Radio One disc jockey Mike Read announced on the air that he would not be playing the record as he considered it obscene. The controversy this caused was enough to propel it to No. 1 in Britain, for five weeks, astonishingly remaining on the chart for a whole year.

Frankie Goes To Hollywood

1983

WHAM! INJUNCTED BY LABEL

Innervision Records, the neo-independent label that was the only record company interested enough in George Michael and Andrew Ridgeley (better known collectively as Wham!) to sign them at the start of their career, took out an injunction to prevent the duo recording.

George (left) and Andrew - a double Whammy

Ridgeley and Michael (real name Georgiou Panayiotou) met at school in a London suburb, and formed their first band together in 1979. In 1981 they became Wham!, and after being turned down by all the major labels in London, signed to Innervision, the dance label financed by CBS and launched by Paul Dean. Although their first single release, 'Wham Rap', failed to chart, its follow-up, 'Young Guns (Go For It)', slowly climbed the chart, taking eight weeks to reach the UK Top 3, after which 'Wham Rap' was reissued and this time made the Top 10 in early 1983. Three months later came 'Bad Boys', which again reached the UK Top 3, despite a promotional video that worsened the already deteriorating relationship between label and act.

During the summer of that year, as 'Club Tropicana' became the duo's fourth Top 10 single in nine months, and their debut album, *Fantastic*, entered the UK chart at No. 1, they engaged veteran pop entrepreneur Simon Napier-Bell, erstwhile manager of Marc Bolan, The Yardbirds, Japan and others, and owner of the highly successful Nomis rehearsal studio complex, as their manager. Napier-Bell was given ammunition to fight the injunction preventing Wham! from further recording when Innervision released a medley of remixed album cuts as a single called 'Club Fantastic Megamix', which became Wham!'s first comparative failure since their debut single, peaking outside the Top 10 after Wham! requested fans not to buy the single. By April, 1984 Michael and Ridgeley had signed with Epic.

1986

WATERS TRIES TO FINISH FLOYD

Roger Waters, a founder member of Pink Floyd, and widely regarded as its driving force since the departure of Syd Barrett in 1968, asked a court to dissolve the group's partnership. He had been the major contributor to *The Final Cut*, the group's 1983 album, since when all three remaining group members had worked on solo projects – keyboard player Rick Wright had left the band in 1980, after major disagreements with Waters.

Both guitarist Dave Gilmour and drummer Nick Mason had completed their solo projects and wanted to revive Pink Floyd, but Waters felt that as he was no longer interested in rejoining his colleagues, they should not be able to call themselves Pink Floyd.

Pink Floyd pre-lawsuit

RAVINGS

1979
Bob Dylan began a US tour in San Francisco, promoting his first religious album, *Slow Train Coming*.

1986
Virgin Records was floated on the British stock market.
★ ★ ★

ARRIVALS

1937 – Bill Anderson
1944 – Mike Burney (Wizzard)
1944 – Keith Emerson
1946 – Ric Grech (Family/Blind Faith)
1946 – Robert Yeazel (Beast/Sugarloaf)
1950 – Dan Peek (America)
1951 – Ronald Bell (Kool and The Gang)
1954 – Chris Morris (Paper Lace)
1957 – Lyle Lovett
1959 – Eddie MacDonald (Alarm)
1962 – Mags Kuruholmen (A-Ha)
1963 – Rick Allen (Def Leppard)

1967

MOVE LOSE IN COURT BATTLE WITH PM

The Move, the quintet from Birmingham that had formed in 1966 and had scored two Top 5 singles, 'Night Of Fear' and 'I Can Hear The Grass Grow', in the first half of 1967, were sued by Prime Minister Harold Wilson over a postcard caricaturing him (and showing him naked) promoting the group's third single, 'Flowers In The Rain'.

The suitably psychedelic Move

The single became a very big hit, reaching the UK Top 3, and is especially remembered as being the first single played on BBC Radio One when it began broadcasting on the last day of September 1967, but The Move hardly profited from its success. Wilson inevitably won the case, and as a result, all the royalties the group would have earned went to charity.

The Move was formed by members of Birmingham's most popular acts – lead vocalist Carl Wayne, bass player Chris 'Ace' Kefford and drummer Bev Bevan had been in Carl Wayne and The Vikings, lead guitarist Trevor Burton came from Danny King and The Mayfair Set, while singer, guitarist and songwriter Roy Wood was from Mike Sheridan and The Nightriders. The group was afflicted by numerous personnel changes, but still accumulated ten UK hit singles by mid 1972, seven of which reached the Top 10.

ARRIVALS

1926 – Charlie Walker
1937 – Earl 'Speedo' Carroll (Cadillacs/Coasters)
1938 – David 'Jay' Black (Jay and The Americans)
1941 – Bruce Welch (Shadows)
1945 – John David Souther
1946 – Len 'Chip' Hawkes (Tremeloes)
1947 – Dave Pegg (Uglys/Fairport Convention/Jethro Tull)
1952 – Maxine Nightingale

★ ★ ★

DEPARTURE LOUNGE

1966 – Mississippi John Hurt

RAVINGS

1966
Blues legend Mississippi John Hurt, who wrote 'Coffee Blues', the song that included the phrase 'Lovin' Spoonful', died at the age of 74.

1986
Billy Bragg was arrested for cutting through wire fences surrounding a US Air Force base in Norfolk, England.

★ ★ ★

1981

SPECIALS FRAGMENT

After a highly successful two and a half years that had provided seven UK Top 10 singles, including two No. 1s, 'Ghost Town' and a live EP with 'Too Much Too Young' as its featured track, The Specials fell apart.

Vocalists Terry Hall and Neville Staples and guitarist Lynval Golding left to form Fun Boy Three, while guitarist Roddy Radiation formed his own group, The Tearjerkers, and bass player Sir Horace Gentleman joined a religious sect. This left only keyboard player and group leader Jerry Dammers and drummer John Bradbury, who re-formed the group with vocalists Rhoda Dakar (from The Bodysnatchers) and Stan Campbell (from The Selecter), who were also attached to the group's 2 Tone label. However the new line-up managed only one hit, 'Nelson Mandela' in 1984.

Fun Boy Three

1974

BEATLE GEORGE'S SOLO TOUR

George Harrison became the first member of The Beatles to embark on a solo tour of the USA, playing his opening concert in Vancouver, Canada. Supporting him on the tour were Harrison's sitar teacher, Ravi Shankar, and black organ player Billy Preston, but audiences were not amused by the non-inclusion of Beatles material, and the tour apparently played to half-full houses.

JAMES AND CARLY MARRY

Singer/songwriters James Taylor and Carly Simon married in the latter's New York home. Taylor announced the happy event to the audience at Radio City Music Hall, where he was performing that same evening.

Taylor had emerged into the big time in 1970 with a US Top 3 single, 'Fire and Rain', topping the chart the following year with 'You've Got A Friend', while Simon first reached the US Top 10 in 1971 with 'That's The Way I've Always Heard It Should Be'. Taylor had moved away from the USA in 1968 in an unsuccessful attempt to cure his heroin addiction, and while living in Notting Hill, west London, had been signed by Peter Asher (of Peter and Gordon) to Apple Records, the label launched by The Beatles, for whom he recorded his eponymous debut album. Asher then became his manager and producer, and his second album, *Sweet Baby James*, achieved gold status. Simon had first recorded with her older sister, Lucy, in the mid 1960s, when they recorded two albums that were minor successes.

In 1968 Simon formed a songwriting partnership with Jacob Brackman, film critic of *Esquire* magazine, and was signed by Elektra Records during the following year. Her eponymous debut album, released in 1971, reached the US Top 40, and after she had performed at the Troubadour, the Los Angeles club, Taylor came backstage to meet her. Her second album, *Anticipation*, was recorded in London and produced by ex-Yardbird Paul Samwell-Smith, and the title track was a US Top 20 hit. However, it was her third album, *No Secrets*, which topped the US album chart for five weeks, and included the US chart-topping single, 'You're So Vain', that elevated her to superstardom, not least because it featured backing vocals by Mick Jagger of The Rolling Stones.

Mr and Mrs Taylor testifying on stage

COUNTRY MUSIC HALL OF FAME ELECTS FIRST MEMBERS

Nashville's Country Music Hall Of Fame, established to honour those who had made a significant contribution to country music, elected its first members – Jimmie Rodgers, the legendary 'Singing Brakeman', Hank Williams, and Fred Rose, co-founder with Roy Acuff of Acuff Rose, the music publishing company to which The Everly Brothers and many notables of country music were signed.

1989

ELTON JOINS EXCLUSIVE CLUB

Elton John in the late 1980s

ARRIVALS

1868 – Scott Joplin
1899 – Kirk McGee (McGee
Brothers/Dixieliners)
1929 – Dickie Valentine
1938 – Harry Elston
(Friends Of Distinction)
1940 – Delbert McClinton
1954 – Chris Difford
(Squeeze)
1957 – James Honeyman-
Scott (Pretenders)
1960 – Mark Jefferis
(T.X.T.)
1966 – Kool Rock (Damon
Wimbley) (Fat Boys)

★ ★ ★

DEPARTURE LOUNGE

1942 – George M. Cohen

1988

LOCOMOTION THIRD TIME AROUND

Kylie Minogue's cover version of 'The Loco-Motion' reached the Top 5 in the US singles chart, providing a third major success for the song written by Carole King and her then husband, Gerry Goffin.

In 1962 the song was a US No. 1 hit for Little Eva (real name Eva Narcissus Boyd), a black 16 year old who met Goffin and King when she was employed as their babysitter. Eva followed it with 'Keep Your Hands Off My Baby', which reached the US Top 20, but was far less memorable than her million-selling debut.

In 1974 Michigan hard rock quartet Grand Funk (previously known as Grand Funk Railroad) had revived the song with record producer Todd Rundgren, and once again it had topped the US chart and sold a million copies.

When 'Sacrifice' entered the UK singles chart, it gave Elton John his 50th chart hit in Britain, enabling him to join an exclusive elite club, with just two previous members, Elvis Presley and Cliff Richard. With at least one chart hit every year, it had taken him 18 years to achieve the half century.

Elton's first hit was 'Your Song' in 1971, and as well as solo hits he also charted in partnership with Kiki Dee (on 'Don't Go Breaking My Heart', his first UK chart-topping single), John Lennon (on 'I Saw Her Standing There'), Millie Jackson (on 'Act Of War') and Cliff Richard (on 'Slow Rivers').

RAVINGS

1977
The Last Waltz, the feature movie by Martin Scorsese of the final concert by The Band, premiered in New York and was acclaimed as one of the finest concert films ever made.

1978
Bass player Greg Reeves sued his ex-colleagues in Crosby, Stills, Nash and Young for $1 million that he claimed were due to him from the hugely successful *Deja Vu* album.

★ ★ ★

1978

TRAVOLTA HAS TOP TWO

Singing actor John Travolta occupied the top two positions on the UK singles chart – not bad at a time when punk rock was making the headlines in the British music weeklies. At No. 1 was his duet with Olivia Newton-John, 'Summer Nights', which was included in the movie musical *Grease*. This was the duo's second duet to reach the top of the chart in six months, their previous hit being 'You're The One That I Want', which was also featured in *Grease*. Travolta was also at No. 2 in the chart with another hit from the same film, 'Sandy', and would chart again with a fourth song from the film, 'Greased Lightning', at Christmas.

In a vintage year that saw more singles sold than ever before or since, Travolta chalked up more sales than any other artist.

BEACH 'BOYS' TOP CHART AFTER LONG ABSENCE

The last time The Beach Boys had topped the US singles chart was in 1966, when the magnificent 'Good Vibrations' became their 13th US Top 10 single in less than four years. Since then they had only once reached the US Top 10 again, in 1976.

Erstwhile Beach Boy Brian Wilson (left) with psychiatrist Dr. Eugene Landy

That resurrection was dwarfed by 'Kokomo', a song from the soundtrack of the feature movie *Cocktail*, which went all the way to No. 1. At the same time, former Beach Boy Brian Wilson released his own solo single: 'Love and Mercy', it failed to chart.

Those who inspected the songwriting credits to 'Kokomo' were surprised to find no less than four names listed as composers: Beach Boys frontman Mike Love, ex-leader of The Mamas and Papas John Phillips, 'San Francisco' hitmaker Scott McKenzie, and Terry Melcher (son of Doris Day and noted record producer of hits for The Byrds and for Paul Revere and The Raiders).

As the final decade of the 20th century approached, The Beach Boys had changed considerably since their glory days of the 1960s. Mike Love was still there, as were Al Jardine and guitarist Carl Wilson, but neither of the latter's older brothers, both founder members of the band back in 1961, were involved. Brian Wilson, the writer of nearly all their early hits, had effectively left the band in the early 1980s when he was increasingly under the influence of a psychiatrist, and drummer Dennis Wilson had drowned in an accident at the end of 1983. However, Bruce Johnston, who had been a member of the group between 1965 and 1972, had rejoined in 1979.

GREEN BERET MAN'S FINAL BATTLE

Staff Sergeant Barry Sadler, the US Army veteran who had topped the US singles chart for five weeks in 1966 with 'The Ballad Of The Green Berets', died at the age of 51.

Sadler had enrolled in the US Army Special Forces (known as 'The Green Berets'). He was posted to Vietnam, where on patrol he fell into a booby trap, impaling his leg on a poisoned spear made of bamboo. He was honourably discharged from the US Army, and returned to the USA, where RCA Records signed him to record the somewhat jingoistic 'Ballad Of The Green Berets', which topped the US singles chart, selling a million records in two weeks, and eventually exceeding five million

Proud to be Green Beret...

sales.

In September 1988 Sadler was shot in the head in Guatemala, he was hospitalized for 14 months before he died.

1989

ARRIVALS

1931 – Ike Turner (Izear Turner)
1936 – Billy Sherrill
1941 – Paul Simon
1946 – Gram Parsons (Cecil Ingram Connor)
1947 – Peter Noone (Herman's Hermits)
1948 – Rock Cobb (Bloodrock)
1948 – Peter Hammill (Van Der Graaf Generator)
1957 – Mike Score (A Flock Of Seagulls)

1959 – Bryan Adams
1959 – Rob Fisher (Climie Fisher)
1965 – Paris Grey (Inner City)

★ ★ ★

DEPARTURE LOUNGE

1989 – Barry Sadler
1977 – Guy Lombardo
1954 – Oran 'Hot Lips' Page (Kansas City Jazz Band)
1956 – Art Tatum

★ ★ ★

RAVINGS

1956
Tommy Steele made his stage debut at the Empire Theatre, Sunderland, in the north east of England.

1979
The Executives, a group that included future Wham! duo George Michael and Andrew Ridgeley, played their first gig.

★ ★ ★

CLIFF'S LUCKY DAY

Cliff Richard's hits compilation *40 Golden Greats* topped the UK album chart 16 years to the week since his first chart-topping album, *21 Today*. Inevitably, much had changed in the interim, but it was a measure of how well loved Britain's ultimate pop star had remained despite the arrival (and departure) of The Beatles and the numerous other notable groups who had assumed control of the charts from 1963 onwards.

Cliff performing at London's Royal Albert Hall, 1978

Benefiting from being advertised on TV (a style of promotion that was comparatively new in Britain for albums featuring a single artist, as opposed to collections of hits by a number of acts on the same album), the album might have been expected to inevitably include Richard's nine UK No. 1s (a figure he would subsequently increase to a dozen by the end of 1990) as well as dozens more of his notable hits. Surprisingly, the reality was different. He first topped the UK singles chart with 'Living Doll', which was followed by 'Travellin' Light', a similar mid-tempo ballad with simple backing by The Shadows. During 1960 he released two more No. 1 singles, 'Please Don't Tease', which was included on the compilation, and 'I Love You', which was not. Neither was 'Voice In The Wilderness', the major hit from the first movie in which took a starring role, *Expresso Bongo*. 'The Twelfth Of Never', a 1964 Top 10 hit, was omitted, while 'Blue Turns To Grey', a 1966 hit which did not make the UK Top 10, but was written by Mick Jagger and Keith Richard of The Rolling Stones, was included.

RAVINGS

1965
The Grateful Dead and Jefferson Airplane were the attractions at the opening night of San Francisco's celebrated Fillmore West venue.

1975
The Sex Pistols played their first live gig at London's St Martin's School Of Art. Their set apparently lasted ten minutes before organizers switched off the electricity.

1984
The Revd Marvin Gaye Sr was sentenced to five years in prison for the manslaughter of his soul star son.

DEATH OF A DOLL

New York Dolls drummer Billy Murcia died of a heroin overdose while the pioneering punk rock quintet were in London to play a live show supporting The Faces. The group thereupon retreated to the city from which they took their name, and regrouped with Jerry Nolan as drummer. The group subsequently released two albums, *New York Dolls* (1973) and *Too Much Too Soon* (1974). Intriguingly, one Stephen Morrissey, who later formed the Smiths, was the UK president of their fan club.

New York Dolls - too much too soon

ARRIVALS

1932 – Stonewall Jackson
1933 – Joseph Pope (Tams)
1937 – Eugene Pitt (Jive Five)
1938 – Jim Pike (Lettermen)
1938 – P. J. Proby (James Marcus Smith)
1941 – Doug Sahm (Sir Douglas Quintet)
1941 – Guy Clark
1943 – Mike Clifford
1947 – George Young (Easybeats)
1948 – Glenn Frey (Eagles)
1949 – Frankie Miller
1950 – Chris Glen (Alex Harvey Band/Michael Schenker Group)
1961 – Ricky Wilde

★ ★ ★

DEPARTURE LOUNGE

1972 – Billy Murcia (New York Dolls)
1989 – Dickie Goodman

★ ★ ★

FOGERTY CLEARED OF PLAGIARISM

1988

The great John Fogerty

John Fogerty, the vocalist, lead guitarist and predominant songwriter of the hugely successful Creedence Clearwater Revival spent a reported $400,000 (£250,000) on legal fees, but was found not guilty of plagiarism in a case brought to the US legal system by Fantasy Records, the label for which Creedence Clearwater Revival (and mainly Fogerty) had made a fortune between 1968 and 1971.

Fogerty had left his erstwhile colleagues in 1972, when the band split up, and continued as a solo recording artist, releasing *The Blue Ridge Rangers*, a country/rock album on which he was the only musician involved in early 1973. By 1975 he was no longer hiding behind a group alias, and released an excellent eponymous album that included 'Rockin' All Over The World' and 'Almost Saturday Night', which were both released as John Fogerty singles. They became minor US hits, but were rather more successful by others – Status Quo's version of the former song was a Top 3 UK hit in 1977. 'Almost Saturday Night' was covered by artists such as Rick Nelson and Dave Edmunds.

By 1976 Fogerty was in conflict with Fantasy Records, who refused to release his follow-up album, *Hoodoo*. Fogerty then went to ground until 1985, when he signed to a new label and released *Centerfield*, a million-selling album that topped the US chart. It included a US Top 10 single, 'The Old Man Down The Road', which was the subject of the bizarre lawsuit brought by Fantasy, who claimed that it plagiarized 'Run Through The Jungle', a song that appeared on Creedence's 1970 album, *Cosmo's Factory*.

1987

TEENAGE TIFF TOPS US CHART

16-year-old Tiffany (real name Tiffany Darwisch) topped the world's charts with revival of a song that was a hit four years before she was born, the 1967 US Top 5 hit by Tommy James and The Shondells, 'I Think We're Alone Now'. She became the youngest solo artist to top the US singles chart since 1972, when Michael Jackson, then just 14 years old, reached the summit with 'Ben', a song about a rat featured in a movie.

Tiffany, teenage chart-topper

ARRIVALS

1914 – Archie Campbell
1922 – Al Hirt
1937 – Mary Travers (Peter, Paul and Mary)
1938 – Dee Clark (Delectus Clark)
1942 – Johnny Rivers (John Ramistella)
1943 – Joni Mitchell (Roberta Joan Anderson)
1951 – Nick Gilder
1951 – Kevin Scott MacMichael (Cutting Crew)
1957 – Jellybean (John Benitez)
1964 – Liam O'Maonlai (Hothouse Flowers)
1967 – Sharleen Spiteri (Texas)

★ ★ ★

DEPARTURE LOUNGE

1960 – A. P. Carter (Alvin Pleasant Carter) (Carter Family)

1958

FIRST CHART-TOPPING ALBUM IN BRITAIN

The first British album chart was published in *Melody Maker*, and the very first No. 1 album was the film soundtrack to *South Pacific*, the musical by Richard Rodgers and Oscar Hammerstein. The album remained at No. 1 in Britain until March 1960, when *The Explosive Freddy Cannon* overtook it for a single week, after which *South Pacific* returned to the top for another 19 weeks until the end of July, when *Elvis Is Back* overtook it for a single week, after which it was back at No. 1. It continued periodically to top the chart until September 1961, and remains the album that has spent most weeks at the top of the UK chart. Its incredible total of 115 weeks (or over two years) is 45 more than the next longest resident at the top, the film soundtrack to *The Sound Of Music* (also by Rodgers and Hammerstein).

South Pacific graphically illustrates how long the Great British public in general needed before a rock record topped the album chart. That it was by Freddy Cannon rather than by Elvis Presley or Cliff Richard or even Frank Sinatra, all of whom had released several albums that failed to outsell *South Pacific* is also interesting. The film's success seems to be largely due to its record-breaking run at London's Dominion Theatre, where it was screened for 231 consecutive weeks encompassing over 2,500 showings between 1958 and 1962. The soundtrack album was also the first to sell a million copies in Britain alone (a mark it reached in 1963).

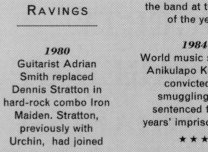

RAVINGS

1980
Guitarist Adrian Smith replaced Dennis Stratton in hard-rock combo Iron Maiden. Stratton, previously with Urchin, had joined the band at the start of the year.

1984
World music star Fela Anikulapo Kuti was convicted of smuggling and sentenced to five years' imprisonment.

★ ★ ★

1980

EX-HUMAN LEAGUE DUO LAUNCH NEW GROUP

Glenn Gregory, Heaven 17 vocalist

Sheffield-born ex-computer operators Martyn Ware and Ian Craig Marsh had been founder members of The Human League in 1977, and had appeared on the latter group's early singles and debut album, but after disagreements with vocalist Phil Oakey, the two synthesizer players left the band to form a new group, Heaven 17, with vocalist Glenn Gregory. Oakey and remaining Human League member Adrian Wright then recruited two more synthesizer players and two teenage girls, Susanne Sulley and Joanne Catherall, whom Oakey spotted dancing in a Sheffield club. Both Heaven 17 and The Human League enjoyed chart success thereafter.

ARRIVALS

1927 – Chris Connor
1927 – Patti Page (Clara Ann Fowler)
1942 – Gerald Alston (Manhattans)
1944 – Bonnie Bramlett (Bonnie Lynn) (Delaney and Bonnie)
1944 – Robert Nix (Atlanta Rhythm Section)
1946 – Roy Wood (Move/ELO/Wizzard)
1947 – Minnie Riperton
1949 – Alan Berger (Southside Johnny and The Asbury Jukes)
1949 – Bonnie Raitt
1951 – Larry Burnett (Firefall)
1954 – Rickie Lee Jones
1958 – Terry Lee Miall (Adam and The Ants)
1959 – Alan Graham Frew (Glass Tiger)
1961 – Leif Garrett

★ ★ ★

DEPARTURE LOUNGE

1974 – Ivory Joe Hunter

★ ★ ★

1966

BEATLE MEETS SECOND WIFE

John Lennon met Yoko Ono, who would become his second wife, for the first time. It was at London's Indica Art Gallery, where Lennon had attended a preview of her exhibition, which she titled *Unfinished Paintings And Objects*.

John and Yoko - clothed (and just as well)

Lennon was instantly captivated by the Japanese avant garde artist, and thereafter the two were inseparable, to the point where Lennon's first recording project without his Beatle colleagues was an album released in late 1968, *Unfinished Music No. 1 – Two Virgins*, by Lennon and Ono. Many felt that while the first word of the title was accurate, to refer to the contents of the album as 'music' was stretching the truth. It was recorded in May 1968,

while Lennon's first wife, Cynthia, was on holiday in Italy with their son, Julian. While Cynthia was away, John invited Yoko to his Weybridge mansion where they recorded just under half an hour's worth of material, theoretically comprising a dozen tracks, eleven of which were called 'Two Virgins 1', 'Two Virgins 2', etc. The odd one out was a version of 'Together', a 1928 chart-topper for Paul Whiteman and His Orchestra, which was successfully revived by

several artists, and was a UK Top 10 hit for P. J. Proby in 1964. The version by Lennon and Ono was not a hit, nor was the album on which it was included, which bore a sleeve photograph of the duo, naked in full frontal glory.

This unsurprisingly led to considerable conflict, including between Lennon and his fellow Beatles, who initially were reluctant to allow the photo to appear on the sleeve of one of the first releases on their Apple label (the first Apple album released was George

Harrison's *Wonderwall Music*, which Harrison had written to accompany *Wonderwall*, an avant garde film). Eventually, the other Beatles agreed to let the photograph appear on the cover, although EMI Records refused to distribute the album.

ARRIVALS

1895 – George Dewey Hay
1937 – Roger McGough (Scaffold)
1941 – Tom Fogerty (Creedence Clearwater Revival)
1943 – Lee Anthony Graziano (American

Breed)
1943 – James Talley Oklahoma
1944 – Phil May (Pretty Things)
1948 – Joe Bouchard (Blue Oyster Cult)
1969 – Pepa (Sandra Denton) (Salt-n-Pepa)

★ ★ ★

RAVINGS

1958
Elvis Presley's 'Hound Dog' exceeded three million sales in the USA, a figure only previously achieved by Bing Crosby's 'White Christmas' and Gene Autry's 'Rudolph The Red-Nosed Reindeer'.

1961
Brian Epstein first saw The Beatles perform at a lunchtime show at Liverpool's famed Cavern Club.

1967
The first issue of *Rolling Stone* magazine was published.

1985

OLIVIER, OLDEST TOP 40 HITMAKER

Actor Sir Laurence Olivier became the oldest performer to appear on a UK Top 40 hit when Paul Hardcastle's 'Just For

Money' reached the requisite height in the UK chart. 78-year-old Olivier and fellow thespian Bob Hoskins can be heard on

the single, which was Hardcastle's official follow-up to his five week chart-topper, 'Nineteen'. Ironically, 'Just For Money' peaked at 19 in the UK chart and was resident there for five weeks.

Hardcastle - '19' follow up gets to No. 19

1967

MOODIES RETURN WITH NIGHTS

After a two-year absence from the UK chart, The Moody Blues released the single that would become their most requested song during the next 25 years, 'Nights In White Satin'. The single was a track excerpted from their *Days Of Future Passed* album, which remained in the US chart for nearly two years, going gold and peaking within the Top 3, and also became their first album to reach the UK chart.

Justin Hayward debuts with a hit

The group had undergone a major transformation since their 1965 incarnation as a beat group who topped the UK chart with 'Go Now'. Both vocalist Denny Laine and bass player Clint Warwick had left the band, who had recruited bass player John Lodge from El Riot and The Rebels in which he had played with Moody Blues keyboard player Mike Pinder and harmonica/flute player-cum-singer Ray Thomas. Drummer Graeme Edge had played in Gerry Levene and The Avengers (aka Gerry Latrine and The Four Flushers!) with Roy Wood, later of The Move. For the crucial role of singer and lead guitarist, they chose Justin Hayward, who had played with Marty Wilde.

They were not doing too well until their label, Decca, needed a group to make a demonstration album to display the qualities of the company's hi-fi equipment, and The Moodies were given two days in the studio. The result was *Days Of Future Passed*, which included both 'Nights In White Satin' and 'Tuesday Afternoon', restoring the group to the US chart. Backed on the album by the London Festival Orchestra and produced by Tony Clark, in order to perform the album in concert the group acquired a mellotron, a keyboard instrument that produced the sound of an orchestra. Thus began a movement of bands that similarly utilized the sound of the mellotron, including Gracious and Barclay James Harvest – the latter recorded a track called 'Poor Man's Moody Blues' in response to a critical album review.

1967

PARISIAN LOVE-IN

A two night all-night festival, the Paris Love-In, began in France with concerts by several leading British psyche-delic bands, including The Spencer Davis Group (without Steve Winwood, who had left to form Traffic), Soft Machine (with Robert Wyatt and Kevin Ayers), Dantalion's Chariot (with Zoot Money and Andy Summers, later of Police) and Tomorrow (with Keith West and Steve Howe).

Soft Machine

ARRIVALS

1939 – Tommy Facenda
1939 – Hubert Laws
1940 – Screamin' Lord Sutch (David Edward Sutch)
1942 – Pete Frame
1943 – Mel Noonan (New World)
1944 – Tim Rice
1947 – Greg Lake (King Crimson/ELP)
1947 – Dave Loggins
1949 – Bram Tchaikovsky (Peter Bramall) (Motors)
1949 – Donna Fargo (Yvonne Vaughan)
1950 – Ronnie Hammond (Atlanta Rhythm Section)
1951 – Ritchie Cole (Stray)
1958 – Frank Maudsley (A Flock Of Seagulls)
1961 – Junior Giscombe

DEPARTURE LOUNGE

1973 – David 'Stringbean' Akeman

★ ★ ★

RAVINGS

1978
The Clash released their second album, *Give 'Em Enough Rope*, produced by Blue Oyster Cult manager, Sandy Pearlman.

★ ★ ★

1990
It was announced that Madonna's total worldwide sales to date were 54 million albums and 26 million singles.

★ ★ ★

1972

SECOND ALLMAN KILLED ON BIKE

In a tragic example of history repeating itself, Berry Oakley, bass player with The Allman Brothers Band, was killed in a motorcycle accident one year and 13 days after Duane Allman also perished in a similar manner. Oakley's collision with a bus also occurred in Macon, Georgia, only three blocks away from where Allman's motorcycle had crashed.

In the year between the two tragedies, the group had released *Eat A Peach*, the double album that gave them their first Top 10 placing. Containing the final three tracks recorded by Duane with the band, it propelled them into the big time. Despite this second body blow, the group, now led by Duane's brother, Gregg Allman, and by guitarist Dickey Betts, recruited a replacement for Oakley, Lamar Williams, added keyboard player Chuck Leavell, and carried on. The success of *Eat A Peach* was consolidated soon afterwards when their first two albums, *The Allman Brothers Band* and *Idlewild South*, were reissued as a double album, *Beginnings*, which became their third gold album in less than two years, and was followed by their next original release, *Brothers and Sisters*, which became their biggest success, topping the US chart for five weeks in the autumn of 1973.

The Allman Brothers - happier days

1970

DYLAN PUBLISHES NOVEL

Bob Dylan's novel *Tarantula* was published. Earlier in the year, the acclaimed singer/songwriter had released a double album, *Self Portrait*, which included several cover versions, such as Gordon Lightfoot's 'Early Morning Rain', Paul Simon's 'The Boxer' and two songs connected with The Everly Brothers, 'Let It Be Me' and 'Take A Message To Mary', as well as the Rodgers and Hart standard, 'Blue Moon', plus several unlikely live versions of his own classics. The album confused critics, who generally disapproved of what they saw as a loss of integrity. *Tarantula*, described by one Dylan biographer as 'surreal' was swiftly followed by *New Morning*, a more accessible Dylan album.

1979

LIZZY'S NEW AXEMAN

After a long period during which Thin Lizzy guitarists seemed to join, leave, rejoin and come and go on a regular basis, the group finally achieved a stability that would last for two years, something that they had failed to achieve since the start of 1977, when Brian Robertson injured his hand in a fight, and was replaced temporarily by Gary Moore, who had been in the band for several months during 1974.

Lizzy (left to right) Downey, Lynott, Gorham, White

Robertson had returned in mid 1977, and left again in the summer of 1978 to launch his own group, Wild Horses, whereupon Moore returned for another spell, until he was fired by the band's management in July 1979. His replacement was 'Midge' Ure, previously of The Rich Kids and subsequently of Ultravox, who was recruited on a temporary basis to work with the other three members of the band, leader/vocalist/bass player Phil Lynott, guitarist Scott Gorham and drummer Brian Downey.

Ure worked on tours of Japan and the USA before joining Ultravox, and was then replaced by 'Snowy' White, who had played on Peter Green's latterday solo albums and as part of Pink Floyd's on-stage band. During White's tenure with the band, Lynott released his first solo album, *Solo In Soho*, which included two hit singles, 'Dear Miss Lonely Hearts' and 'King's Call', the latter a tribute to Elvis Presley. Lynott's album featured many Thin Lizzy alumni, including Ure, White, Moore, Gorham and Downey, as well as Gorham's cousin, drummer Bob C. Benberg (from Supertramp), Mark Knopfler (of Dire Straits) and Huey Lewis.

1970

DOORS PLAY LAST SHOW WITH LIZARD KING

The Doors played in New Orleans what would be their last concert with Jim Morrison as lead vocalist. This was obviously a highly significant occasion, although none of those either on stage or watching in the audience could have been aware that it marked the end of an era.

During the next four months, the group recorded a new album, *L.A. Woman*, on which Morrison participated as normal, and it was released during the summer of 1971, becoming the group's eighth consecutive gold LP, also including their sixth (and last) US Top 20 single, 'Riders On The Storm'.

Having finished work on the album, Morrison left America to live in Paris, where was said to have died from a heart attack in a bathtub in July 1971.

Morrison - gone but not forgotten

1982

CURE MAN JOINS BANSHEES

Robert Smith, leader and founder of The Cure, rejoined Siouxsie and The Banshees, with whom he had worked in 1979. On this latter occasion he was asked to substitute for guitarist John McGeoch, who was suffering from nervous exhaustion, and remained a Banshee when other commitments allowed until mid 1984, when he too had to throw in the towel due to exhaustion.

Smith had first met Steve Severin, bass player of The Banshees, in 1979, and as a result The Cure were the opening act on a tour by Siouxsie and Co. That might have been Smith's only connection with the latter, had not two members of The Banshees, guitarist John McKay and drummer Kenny Morris, decided to leave suddenly in the middle of the tour. Smith was asked to fill in on guitar until the end of the tour. In 1980 Smith decided that his major priority was The Cure, at which point McGeoch joined from Magazine, the group formed by ex-Buzzcock Howard DeVoto.

When McGeoch fell ill, Smith was the obvious replacement, and during this spell with The Banshees, he and Severin formed a separate recording group, The Glove. This was possibly in answer to the other extra-mural recording group launched by Siouxsie and Banshees drummer, Budgie, who were known as The Creatures.

Robert Smith of The Cure

ARRIVALS

1918 – Perez Prado
1940 – Baby Washington (Jeanette Washington)
1942 – John Hammond Jr (John Paul Hammond)
1944 – Timmy Thomas
1949 – Terry Reid (Peter Jay and The Jaywalkers)
1954 – Jeannie Kendall (Kendalls)
1960 – Wayne Parker (Glass Tiger)

★ ★ ★

DEPARTURE LOUNGE

1973 – Jerry Lee Lewis Jr

★ ★ ★

RAVINGS

1964
A supposedly official biography of The Rolling Stones, *Our Own Story*, was published as a paperback book.

1973
Jerry Lee Lewis Jr, the son of the self-styled 'Killer', died in a car accident at the age of 19. The drummer in his father's band, he was the second of Lewis's children to die young in an accident.

★ ★ ★

1959

MATHIS TAKES SECOND ALBUM TO TOP OF CHART

With rock 'n' roll no longer regarded as merely a shortlived novelty at the end of the 1950s, the US album chart was nevertheless still dominated by music from an earlier era. By the end of 1959 the only rock-associated albums to have reached the top of that chart were four by Elvis Presley (*Elvis Presley* and *Elvis*, both in 1956, and the *Loving You* soundtrack and *Elvis' Christmas Album*, both in 1957, after which The King went to work for Uncle Sam), one by Ricky Nelson (*Ricky* in 1958) and two by The Kingston Trio (*The Kingston Trio* in 1958 and *The Kingston Trio At Large* in 1959).

Otherwise, the major albums of the era included numerous soundtrack albums: *South Pacific* (which topped the chart for 31 weeks in 1958), *Around The World in 80 Days* and *Gigi*, Harry Belafonte's *Calypso* (a 31 week topper in 1956), *Tchaikovsky's Piano Concerto No. 1* and the hugely successful *Johnny's Greatest Hits* by Johnny Mathis. His second No. 1 album was *Heavenly*, a collection of show tunes and standards, which was listed on the chart for 295 weeks.

A young Johnny Mathis

1981

AUSTRALIANS IN CHART TAKE-OVER

Rick Springfield - from Zoot to the top

While most acts whose hits reach the US Top 10 tended to come from the USA, Britain or Canada, Australia was enjoying a period of pre-eminence such as had never previously occurred, with three singles in the US Top 10 (and a fourth if Olivia Newton-John, whose career began down under, is considered as an Aussie). The singles concerned were Little River Band's 'The Night Owls', Air Supply's 'Here I Am (Just When I Thought I Was Over You)' and Rick Springfield's 'I've Done Everything For You', while Olivia was at No. 1 for the start of a 10-week run with 'Physical'.

Several of these acts enjoyed considerable international popularity at the end of the 1970s and the start of the 1980s. Little River Band was formed in 1975 and named after a holiday resort near Melbourne in the state of Victoria, and enjoyed five US Top 10 hits between 1978 and 1981. John Farnham, who had a UK Top 10 hit in 1987 with 'You're The Voice', was a Little River Band member shortly before his solo hit. Air Supply were even more successful, with eight US Top 10 hits between 1980 and 1983, including 'Lost In Love', 'All Out Of Love', 'The One That You Love' (a No. 1) and 'Making Love Out Of Nothing At All', all of which reached the Top 3. Rick Springfield had been in Zoot, a noted Australian teenybop act, before moving to the USA where he became a star of the popular TV soap opera *General Hospital*. He accumulated five US Top 10 singles between 1981 and 1984, including 'Jessie's Girl', a 1981 chart-topper, and 'Don't Talk To Strangers', which reached the Top 3 in the following year.

RAVINGS

1954
Bill Haley's first US Top 10 hit, 'Shake, Rattle and Roll' peaked at No. 7 in the US chart.

1986
Amnesty International released its all-star album *Conspiracy Of Hope*.

★ ★ ★

1952

FIRST BRITISH CHART PUBLISHED

The first British pop chart was published in *New Musical Express*, dated November 15, 1952. The top six positions were occupied by American acts, headed by Al Martino, whose 'Here In My Heart' also topped the US singles chart. Others in the Top 6 were Jo Stafford, who scored over 90 US hits between 1944 and 1957, Nat 'King' Cole, Bing Crosby, Guy Mitchell and Rosemary Clooney. Frankie Laine was listed twice, once as a solo artist for 'High Noon' and again duetting with Doris Day on 'Sugarbush'. British vocalist Vera Lynn was represented three times in the chart, while Max Bygraves was also a chart debutant with 'Cowpuncher's Cantata'.

ARRIVALS

1938 – Cornelius Gunter (Flairs/Coasters)
1939 – James Gilreath
1939 – Walter/Wendy Carlos
1940 – Freddie Garritty (Freddie and The Dreamers)
1947 – Marvyn Harris (Proudfoot)
1949 – James Young (Styx)
1950 – Colleen Peterson
1951 – Stephen Bishop
1951 – Barry Brandt (Angel)
1953 – Alexander O'Neal
1955 – Frankie Banali (Quiet Riot)
1955 – Alec John Such (Bon Jovi)
1964 – John Andrew Banfield (Pasadenas)
1964 – Joseph 'Run' Simmons (Run DMC)

★ ★ ★

WOMEN RULE OK?

For the first time in the British pop singles chart, the top five positions were held by female vocalists. In descending order, these feminine role models were Terri Nunn, Kim Wilde, Susannah Hoffs, Mel and Kim Appleby and Corinne Drewery.

Terri Nunn was the vocalist with Berlin, a Los Angeles-based electropop duo. Berlin's No. 1 hit was 'Take My Breath Away', the theme From from the Tom Cruise film *Top Gun*. Nunn left the group in 1987. At No. 2 was Kim Wilde, daughter of early British rock 'n' roller Marty Wilde, and Kim's hit was her revival of 'You Keep Me Hangin' On', previously a hit for both The Supremes and

Vanilla Fudge during the 1960s. Susannah Hoffs was the vocalist of The Bangles, the all-female quartet from Los Angeles, whose No. 3 hit at the time was 'Walk Like An Egyptian', which topped the US singles chart and sold a million copies. The other members of the group were sisters Vicki and Debbi Peterson, who respectively played lead guitar and drums, while despite her name,

Terri Nunn of Berlin takes our breath away

Michael Steele played bass, and had been a member of an earlier all-female group, The Runaways. Mel and Kim Appleby were sisters from Britain, whose first hit, 'Showing Out (Get Fresh At The Weekend)' was at No. 4. In 1990, Mel Appleby died of cancer while still in her 20s. Corinne Drewery of Swing Out Sister's hit was 'Breakout'.

RAVINGS

1958
Tommy Steele split with his backing group, The Steelemen.

★ ★ ★

1986
Freddie Jackson replaced his own No. 1 in the US R & B chart when 'A Little Bit More', his duet with Melba Moore, was supplanted by his solo single, 'Tasty Love'.

ARRIVALS

1928 – C. W. McCall (William Fries)
1932 – Petula Clark
1942 – Clyde McPhatter (Drifters)
1937 – Little Willy John (John Davenport)
1940 – Hank Wangford (Sam Hutt)

1945 – Anni-Frid Lyngstad (ABBA)
1949 – Steve Fossen (Army/White Heart/Heart)
1952 – Michael Cooper (ConFunkShun)
1954 – Tony Thompson (Chic)
1957 – Joe Leeway (Thompson Twins)

★ ★ ★

1987

THREE-MILLIONTH BROTHER

The remarkably successful Dire Straits album *Brothers In Arms* became the first to sell over three million copies in Britain, and the UK's second biggest-selling record of any sort, following Band Aid's all-star charity single, 'Do They Know It's Christmas'.

Many critics regarded *Brothers In Arms* as a good but unexceptional album, whose success was partly due to the fast-growing popularity of the compact disc (CD), whose qualities were perfectly displayed by *Brothers In Arms*. Conceivably this did increase the album's sales, but its 14 chart-topping weeks, and its ten-week residency at No. 1 during its third spell at the top eight months after release suggest that the audience for the album expanded for a long time. It was further kept in the public's attention by five UK hit singles: 'So Far Away' (Top 20), 'Money For Nothing' (with Sting as guest vocalist, Top 5), 'Brothers In Arms' (Top 20), 'Walk Of Life' (Top 3) and 'Your Latest Trick' (Top 30).

Dire Straits - brothers in the record book

1974

BACKING VOCALIST ELTON BOOSTS LENNON

John Lennon topped the US singles chart for the only time during his life with 'Whatever Gets You Thru The Night', a track from his *Walls and Bridges* album. Guest star Elton John played piano and organ on the track, as well as providing backing vocals. Thus Elton was a member of The Plastic Ono Nuclear Band for one day, joining such notable session musicians as Jim Keltner (drums), Klaus Voorman (bass), Jesse Ed Davis (lead guitar), Bobby Keyes (saxophone) and others. Lennon himself is credited as Hon. John St John Johnson.

Elton John had been convinced when he heard the completed track that it would be a big hit, and told Lennon so. Lennon was dismissive, Elton persisted and bargained with the erstwhile Beatle that if the song reached the top of the chart Lennon would make an on-stage appearance at one of Elton's concerts. He did so and together they sang 'I Saw Her Standing There'. Lennon rarely played in front of an audience during the 1970s, and for him to work with Elton was a milestone in the lives of them both.

1979

INFINITY BELLY UP

The recently launched Infinity Records label went out of business due to parent company MCA's withdrawal of its financial support. The label was launched in Britain with a magnificent party at London Zoo attended by hundreds of guests, but its artist roster produced too few hit albums. As MCA President Sidney Sheinberg remarked, the label's demise was duo to 'present day economic realities'.

However, the label was not completely without hits. Jazz/rock group Spyro Gyra's *Morning Dance* album went gold, while the title track was a US Top 30 single, and British group Hot Chocolate enjoyed a Top 10 single with 'Every 1's A Winner', while the album that shared its title became the group's only Top 40 entry. American rock group Orleans made the US

Rupert Holmes, Infinity's major success

Top 20 with their 'Love Takes Time' single, and producer/arranger/songwriter Rupert Holmes, who was born in England, but moved to

New York at the age of six, achieved Infinity's biggest success, when his million-selling 'Escape (The Pina Colada Song)' became the last No. 1 of

the 70s by topping the US chart at Christmas 1979, just five weeks too late to save the label, whose catalogue was absorbed by MCA.

1960

GEORGIA ON RAY'S MIND

Ray Charles, the innovative blind R & B singer and keyboard player, topped the US singles chart for the first time with his revival of Hoagy Carmichael's classic 'Georgia On My Mind'. Charles (real name Ray Charles Robinson) apparently only recorded the song because his chauffeur, Tommy Brown, used to sing it incessantly while driving Charles around.

The Legendary Ray Charles

Charles, who was born, appropriately enough, in Georgia, went blind at the age of 7 due to glaucoma. He studied music at a school for the blind in Orlando, Florida, and started playing professionally at the age of 17, using the Nat 'King' Cole Trio as his role model. Having worked under his real name, he began using his two first names to avoid confusion with the champion boxer 'Sugar' Ray Robinson, and released his first record in 1949. His first US R & B hits came in 1951, and in the following year he signed to Atlantic Records, where he first achieved success, cutting a series of R & B classics including '(Night Time Is) The Right Time', 'Let The Good Times Roll' and his first US Top 10 pop hit, 'What'd I Say'.

In mid 1960 he moved to ABC-Paramount Records, where he achieved his greatest commercial successes, starting with 'Sticks and Stones' and continuing with his biggest hit, 'I Can't Stop Loving You'.

RAVINGS

1967
Pink Floyd released their third single, 'Apples and Oranges'. Although their first two singles, 'Arnold Layne' and 'See Emily Play', had both been significant UK hits, the third '45' failed to chart.

1979
Jethro Tull bass player John Glascock died, aged 26, after open heart surgery. His replacement in the long-running group was Dave Pegg, who was also concurrently a member of Fairport Convention.

★ ★ ★

1970

ELTON'S LIVE SHOW

Elton in mid-flight

Elton John recorded a live album in New York, which was recorded and also broadcast live by a local FM radio station. When it was released as a live album in 1971 it was entitled '11–17–70' in the USA, where the numerical month is the first number in a date, but in Britain, where the numerical day comes first, it was known as '17–11–70'. This difference between the USA and UK is also the reason why many birthdates appear to differ – 9/10/63 is September 10 in the US, and October 9 in the UK.

1968

FEATHERS DEBUT

The Country Club in Belsize Park, Hampstead, was the venue for the first gig by Feathers, a small mime troupe led by David Bowie. Also featuring Bowie's then girlfriend, Hermione Farthingale and bass player John 'Hutch' Hutchinson, the group also played at London's Middle Earth club but did not record commercially, and lasted only into early 1969.

ARRIVALS

1938 – Gordon Lightfoot
1941 – Gene Clark (Byrds/Dillard and Clark)
1942 – Bob Gaudio (Four Seasons)
1946 – Martin Barre (Jethro Tull)
1947 – Rod Clements (Lindisfarne)
1948 – Iain Sutherland
1952 – Dean Martin Jr (Dino, Desi and Billy)
1955 – Peter Cox (Go West)
1967 – Ronald DeVoe (New Edition/Bell Biv DeVoe)

★ ★ ★

DEPARTURE LOUNGE

1979 – John Grascock (Jethro Tull)

1972

CRAZY HORSE'S DANNY DIES

Guitarist Danny Whitten, a member of Crazy Horse, the group who backed Neil Young on his acclaimed *Everybody Knows This Is Nowhere* album, died of a heroin overdose at the age of 29.

Whitten had been a founder member of The Rockets, a Los Angeles-based group of the 1960s, along with bass player Billy Talbot, drummer Ralph Molina and others. They apparently encountered Neil Young for the first time around 1966, when the latter was a member of Buffalo Springfield, who were making their debut album at the time. The Rockets made only one album, eponymously titled and released in 1968.

Neil Young, meanwhile, made his first solo album, which was released in early 1969 and at which point he felt the need to form a band. The trio from The Rockets thus became Crazy Horse and worked on Young's second solo album, *Everybody Knows This Is Nowhere*, which was released in mid 1969 and which many regard as his finest work, as it included such timeless classics as 'Down By The River', 'Cowgirl In The Sand' and 'Cinnamon Girl'. In 1970 Young recorded *After The Goldrush*, again using Crazy Horse, but this time also with guitarist Nils Lofgren. By this time, however,

Whitten's heroin addiction was getting difficult to handle, and for his fourth album, *Harvest*, he used a group of studio musicians whom he named The Stray Gators.

Crazy Horse then made an eponymous album of its own, released in 1971, which included Danny Whitten's finest song, 'I Don't Want To Talk About It', later covered by Rod Stewart, whose version was a UK No. 1 in 1977 and Everything But The Girl who took it into the Top 3 in 1988.

1975

LONDON IS FINALLY READY...

Bruce Springsteen and The E Street Band played their first concert in Britain at London's Hammersmith Odeon. CBS Records had attempted to publicize the long-awaited event with a widespread poster

RAVINGS

1965
Marc Bolan (previously known as Toby Tyler, although his real name was Mark Feld) released his first single, 'The Wizard'.

★ ★ ★

1979
The eponymous debut album by Athens, Georgia, quintet The B-52s was certified gold.

★ ★ ★

Bruce Springsteen

campaign proclaiming 'London Is Finally Ready For Bruce Springsteen', but the artist himself was unimpressed and boycotted the after-show party that had been prepared at great cost.

ARRIVALS

1909 – Johnny Mercer
1936 – Don Cherry
1941 – Con Clusky (Bachelors)
1946 – Dave Irving (Supercharge)
1949 – Herman Rarebell (Scorpions)
1950 – Graham Parker
1954 – John Parr
1957 – Jenny Burton (C-Bank)
1960 – Kim Wilde
1962 – Kirk Hammett (Metallica)

★ ★ ★

DEPARTURE LOUNGE

1969 – Ted Heath
1971 – Junior Parker
1972 – Danny Whitten (Crazy Horse)
1978 – Lennie Tristano
1983 – Tom Evans (Badfinger)

★ ★ ★

1989

SHANGRI'LAS WIN, THREE DEGREES LOSE

Two all-female groups who had gone to court in disputes over who owned the rights to their group names came away with different results. The Three Degrees were told that their group name belonged to their former manager Richard Barrett, while The Shangri'Las were told that they had the right to license their group name to whoever they wanted.

TINA RETURNS TO UK CHART

Tina - back where she belongs

Tina Turner's 'Let's Stay Together' entered the UK singles chart. She had been absent from the chart for ten years, her previous hit being 'Nutbush City Limits', on which she shared billing with her then husband, Ike Turner.

Her relationship with Ike was fast deteriorating – she later claimed he had frequently beaten her during their 18-year marriage, which ended in 1976. Tina, who had become a Buddhist, found sufficient strength in her faith to dare to leave her husband, with whom she had recorded and performed on stage since 1957, when she was 18 years old. The years between 1976 and 1979 were difficult for her – she had four children to support, and she was forced to accept money for food from the US Government.

Her first stroke of good fortune came when she met Roger Davies, a young Australian who became her manager and helped her to recover from the depths she had reached by booking her on to the R & B circuit rather than the cabaret clubs where she had been scraping a living.

In 1981 she was contacted by Ian Craig Marsh and Martyn Ware (aka Heaven 17), who wanted her to contribute to an album entitled *Music Of Quality and Distinction* they were making under their alter ego of British Electric Foundation. The track in question, a cover of 'Ball Of Confusion', the 1970 hit by The Temptations, was praised by critics, and in 1983 she worked again with Marsh and Ware, this time on her own first single for Capitol Records, with whom she had signed after some years in the wilderness.

The track chosen was another cover, of Al Green's 1972 hit, 'Let's Stay Together', which restored her to the UK chart and eventually peaked within the UK Top 10. During the 1980s she was a frequent visitor to the charts all over the world, and deservedly ended the decade as a superstar.

ARRIVALS

1905 – Tommy Dorsey
1934 – Dave Guard (Kingston Trio)
1937 – Ray Collins (Mothers Of Invention)
1938 – Hank Medress (Tokens)
1935 – Jerry Foster
1944 – Fred Lipsius (Blood, Sweat and Tears)
1945 – Andrew McCulloch (King Crimson/Greenslade)
1946 – Joe Correro Jr (Paul Revere and The Raiders)
1954 – Annette Guest (First Choice)

★ ★ ★

DEPARTURE LOUNGE

1966 – Francis Craig

ROYAL TOLERANCE PLEA BY ROSS

Diana Ross and The Supremes appeared before Queen Elizabeth II at the annual Royal Variety Performance held at London's Palladium Theatre, where Ross made a considerable impact with an unrehearsed speech between songs urging racial tolerance. This followed the group's million-selling 'Love Child', a song about social tolerance, which became their eleventh US No. 1 in under five years.

RAVINGS

1966
Orchestra leader Francis Craig, the first artist to top the US chart with a record on an independent label, died. On the Bullet label, the 1947 single was 'Near You', which became comedian Milton Berle's signature tune.

1979
Chuck Berry was released from prison after serving a short sentence for tax evasion.

1970

KINK RAY IN TRANSATLANTIC DASH

Ray Davies, leader of The Kinks, had a controversial year, having to cross the Atlantic twice to amend a lyric he had recorded. During the summer he had to drop in the words 'cherry cola' to replace 'Coca Cola', as the BBC refused to play 'Lola', not because it dealt with transvestism but because it mentioned a product name, a matter about which the corporation was highly sensitive. 'Lola' became the group's first US Top 10 single since 1965 and their first UK Top 3 single since 1967.

Ray Davies - change the Coke for a cherry

The group's follow-up single, 'Apeman', was the reason for the second transatlantic dash by Davies. It included the line, 'The air pollution is a-foggin' up', which many felt, not unreasonably, might be misheard as a less acceptable word. On this second occasion, the change did not result in such spectacular success – 'Apeman' made the UK Top 5, but peaked outside the US Top 40, after which the group were absent from the US singles chart for six years. However, this was nothing compared to their fall from commercial grace in their own country. 'Supersonic Rocket Ship' reached the UK Top 20 in 1972, after which the group's next UK hit single was 'Better Things', which briefly reached the Top 50 11 years later in 1981.

1973

WHO SUBSTITUTE FOR MOON

Pete Townshend of The Who

During the first date of a US tour by The Who, drummer Keith Moon collapsed during the group's set at San Francisco's Cow Palace, suffering from jet lag. Guitarist Pete Townshend asked whether anyone in the audience would sit in with the band to complete the concert, and Scott Halpin, a 19 year old from Iowa, volunteered. He later said he was impressed by the band's stamina, as he was exhausted after playing only three songs.

While mentioning The Who, it is interesting to note that the group only reached the Top 10 of the US singles chart once during the period 1965–1990. Their only big hit came in 1967 with 'I Can See For Miles'.

MRS MITCHELL BECOMES MRS KLEIN

1982

Canadian singer/songwriter Joni Mitchell (born Roberta Joan Anderson in 1943 in Alberta) married her bass player, Larry Klein, in Malibu, California.

She had previously been married to fellow folk singer Chuck Mitchell, whose surname she retained when they were divorced in the second half of the 1960s.

Joni Mitchell built a reputation as a promising young songwriter in the 1960s, when both Tom Rush and Judy Collins recorded her songs. Her first album was produced by erstwhile Byrd David Crosby. Called simply *Joni Mitchell* (although it is often referred to as 'Song For A Seagull'), it also featured Stephen Stills.

In 1969 she did not attend the celebrated Woodstock Festival due to a prior commitment to appear on a TV chat show, but was sufficiently inspired by the importance of the event to write a song about it. 'Woodstock' was a No. 1 hit in the UK for Matthews Southern Comfort and was a US Top 20 hit for Crosby, Stills, Nash and Young. Having won a Grammy Award for her second album, *Clouds*, released in 1970 and including her versions of her own notable compositions, 'Both Sides Now' and 'Chelsea Morning', she recorded her third album, *Ladies Of The Canyon*, while living with C, S, N and Y member Graham Nash in Laurel Canyon, Los Angeles, and it became her first gold album, also including her only UK hit single, 'Big Yellow Taxi', a song that protested in a light-hearted manner about the lack of attention being paid to what are known internationally today as 'green' issues.

Joni Mitchell, back in 1969

GOODBYE MUDDAH, GOODBYE FADDAH

1963

Allan Sherman, the comedian who took 'Hello Muddah, Hello Faddah' to the top of the US singles chart in 1963 (and won a Grammy Award for Best Comedy Performance) died of respiratory failure a few days before his 49th birthday. He was born Allen Copelon on November 30, 1924 and began his career as a professional comedy writer for American comedian Jackie Gleason. The song, which was more or less a monologue set above Poncielli's 'Dance Of The Hours', a well-known classical music theme, was a letter from a child to his parents on his first day at summer camp.

Surprisingly, it was not Sherman's first million-selling record release. The previous year had seen the release of *My Son The Folk Singer*, an album of familiar songs with re-written lyrics that highlighted Sherman's Jewish humour.

Allan Sherman

RAVINGS

1983
Michael Jackson's award-winning 14-minute video for *Thriller*, which cost over $1 million to make, was premiered in Los Angeles.

1984
It was announced that all six brothers in the Jackson family (Jackie, Tito, Jermaine, Marlon, Michael and Randy) would be appearing on stage for the first time on the *Victory* tour, promoting the album of the same name by The Jacksons.

★ ★ ★

ARRIVALS

1904 – Coleman Hawkins
1933 – Jean Shepard
1940 – Paul (Paul and Paula) (Ray Hildebrand)
1941 – Dr John (Malcolm John Rebennack)
1941 – David Porter
1948 – Lonnie Jordan (Leroy Jordan) (War)
1948 – Alphonse Mouzon
1949 – Randy Z (Randy Zehringer) (McCoys)
1950 – Livingston Taylor
1965 – Fiachna O'Braonain (Hothouse Flowers)

★ ★ ★

DEPARTURE LOUNGE

1973 – Allan Sherman

★ ★ ★

KENNEDY ASSASSINATION SPOILS SPECTOR'S XMAS

1963

Producer Phil Spector intended *A Christmas Gift For You*, his album of yuletide favourites, to be the perfect end to a year that had seen the singles he produced for such artists as The Crystals, The Ronettes, Bob B. Soxx and The Blue Jeans and Darlene Love all becoming major hits. Unfortunately, he did not consider the name of Lee Harvey Oswald in his calculations.

killed in Dallas, Texas, purportedly by Oswald, and the USA instantly went into deep mourning to the extent that pop records were forgotten and Spector's masterpiece suffered along with everyone else's, totally failing to chart.

What brought the US back to life was the arrival of The Beatles in America in February 1964, after which things were never the same again. Ironically, The Beatles were great fans of Phil Spector.

Spector - stymied by JFK's death

A breathtaking album (despite being recorded in the summer), it featured all the artists named above who were signed to Spector's Philles label. Its contents included The Ronettes singing 'Frosty The Snowman', 'Sleigh Ride' and 'I Saw Mommy Kissing Santa Claus', The Crystals with 'Rudolph The Red-Nosed Reindeer' and 'Santa Claus Is Coming To Town' and Bob B. Soxx and Co's 'Here Comes Santa Claus', while Darlene Love sang 'White Christmas', 'Winter Wonderland' and the one original song on the album, 'Christmas (Baby Please Come Home)'.

It had just been released when President John F. Kennedy was

RAVINGS

1965
Singer/songwriter Bob Dylan married Sara Lowndes, a divorcée with a child who had been a model. He would not acknowledge that he was married until the following year.

1980
Actress and occasional vocalist Mae West died at the age of 87. In 1966 her rock 'n' roll album, *Way Out West*, charted for five weeks in the USA.

ARRIVALS

1899 – Hoagy Carmichael
1941 – Ron McClure
1942 – Steve Caldwell (Orlons)
1942 – Jamie Troy (Classics)
1946 – Aston 'Family Man' Barrett (Upsetters/Wailers)
1948 – Dennis Larden (Every Mother's Son)
1949 – Will Danford (Proudfoot)
1950 – Little Steven/Miami Steve (Steven Van Zandt) (E Street Band)
1950 – Tina Weymouth (Talking Heads)
1957 – Sharon Bailey (Amazulu)

★ ★ ★

DEPARTURE LOUNGE

1943 – Lorenz Hart
1980 – Mae West

JAPAN GOES WEST

1982

After five years of varying fortunes, South London group Japan played their final concert at London's Hammersmith Odeon. Formed by schoolfriends in south London and basing themselves on Roxy Music, the group achieved little until they changed record labels.

Their early work for Ariola-Hansa was largely ignored in chart terms, but as soon as Virgin Records signed them in 1980, the hits began, and ironically five of their Hansa tracks, including their first major breakthough hit 'Quiet Life' became hit singles as reissues.

Japan

1974

SPOOKY TOOTH FINALLY FINISHES

Respected but rarely commercially successful progressive rock group Spooky Tooth finally threw in the towel after seven years, six different line-ups, fourteen musicians and seven original albums. None of the group's albums or singles ever appeared in the UK chart, although all seven albums charted in America – surprising for a totally British band.

The first line-up of the group, most of whom were previously members of The VIPs (a band formed in Carlisle in the north east of England, who later changed their name to Art), included guitarist Luther Grosvenor, bass player Greg Ridley and drummer Mike Kellie. The group was completed by two vocalists who played keyboards, Mike Harrison (another ex-VIP) and Gary Wright. Ridley joined Humble Pie, the supergroup formed by Steve Marriott and Peter Frampton, in 1969, and when Wright left the band to make a solo album in 1970, the remaining trio made a fourth album, *The Last Puff*, before effectively falling apart.

In late 1972 three members of Wonderwheel, the group formed by Gary Wright, joined Harrison in a third Spooky Tooth line-up that lasted six months, at which point Kellie rejoined Wright and Harrison along with guitarist Mick Jones for the final 18 months.

While this may all seem fairly routine, it is worth remembering how various members of Spooky Tooth earned their livings after leaving the group. Mick Jones was arguably the most successful, founding and leading the highly successful Foreigner (with 9 US Top 10 singles), Grosvenor (aka Ariel Bender) joined Mott The Hoople, Kellie was a founder member of acclaimed New Wave group The Only Ones, while Gary Wright's 1973 solo album *The Dream Weaver* was certified gold and reached the US Top 10. Seminal seems to be the appropriate word for Spooky Tooth.

1976

SILLY KILLER!

The self-styled 'Killer', Jerry Lee Lewis, was arrested for the second time in two days. As Lady Bracknell in *The Importance Of Being Earnest* might have remarked, getting arrested once might be considered unlucky, but to be arrested two days running seems like carelessness.

The two incidents were preceeded on September 29 by Lewis accidentally shooting his bass player Norman Owens in the chest while blasting holes in his own office door. Owens was lucky to survive and later sued his boss. On November 22, he drove his Rolls Royce into a ditch and was accused of driving while drunk, and on November 23, he was arrested outside Graceland, Elvis Presley's Memphis mansion, for backing up his demands to see his former Sun Records colleague with a Derringer pistol.

Elvis died less than a year later in 1977, when 42-year-old Lewis scored his first Top 5 US country hit in five years with the aptly-titled 'Middle Age Crazy'.

ARRIVALS
1916 – Perez Prado
1939 – Betty Everett
1940 – Freddie Marsden (Gerry and The Pacemakers)
1948 – Anthony Bourge (Budgie)
1949 – Sandra Stevens (Brotherhood Of Man)
1954 – Bruce Hornsby
★ ★ ★

DEPARTURE LOUNGE
1985 – Joe Turner
1969 – Spade Cooley
★ ★ ★

Jerry Lee - careless?

RAVINGS

1899
The world's first jukebox was installed at San Francisco's Palais Royal Hotel.

1964
The Rolling Stones were banned from recording sessions for BBC radio for their unpunctuality.
★ ★ ★

1974
Billy Swan, who had worked at Columbia Studios in Nashville as a janitor, topped the US singles chart with 'I Can Help'.
★ ★ ★

DEATH OF A SUPERSTAR

Freddie Mercury, lead vocalist and sometimes pianist of Queen, died of AIDS. He had announced only days before that he was suffering from the disease, and his death had been widely predicted for some time as rumours spread of his being seriously ill.

Freddie salutes his subjects

Born in Zanzibar, Mercury was one of rock music's most flamboyant figures, the ultimate camp showman. He was a founder member of Queen in 1970, and quickly became its best-known figure, seeming to epitomize the group's confrontational name. He was an inspired singer and contributed strongly to the group's repertoire, writing Queen's best-known song, 'Bohemian Rhapsody', which topped the UK singles chart for two months in 1975/6, 'We Are The Champions', 'Killer Queen' (the group's first UK Top 3 single), 'Somebody To Love' and 'Love Of My Life', all strong favourites among Queen fans, among many other songs recorded by the group. Of their 19 charted albums (including 8 No. 1s), their two Greatest Hits collections have combined UK sales of nearly 5 million.

Mercury was also the most successful member of Queen in his solo projects outside the group. His first solo single, 1984's 'Love Kills' (which was featured on the new soundtrack produced by Giorgio Moroder for the 1926 Fritz Lang movie *Metropolis* was a UK Top 10 hit, and his 1985 follow-up, 'I Was Born To Love You', almost equalled its success. In 1987 his revival of the 1950s hit by The Platters, 'The Great Pretender', made the UK Top 5, and later that year, he duetted with Spanish opera diva Monserrat Caballe on the truly excessive 'Barcelona', which also reached the Top 10 of the UK chart, and was used in 1992 as the theme music to the Barcelona Olympic Games. This incongruous couple also recorded an album called after their hit, which reached the Top 30 of the UK album chart.

ARRIVALS

1868 – Scott Joplin
1940 – Johnny Carver
1941 – Pete Best
(Randolph Peter Best)
(Beatles)
1941 – Donald 'Duck' Dunn
1942 – Billy Connolly
1943 – Robin Williamson
(Incredible
String Band)
1945 – Lee Michaels
1946 – Bev Bevan
(The Move/ELO)
1946 – Tony Clarkin
(Magnum)
1947 – Dave Sinclair
(Caravan)
1953 – Gary Cooper
(Sly Fox)
1958 – Carmel
(Carmel McCourt)
1962 – Derrick Murphy
(Chalk Circle)

★ ★ ★

DEPARTURE LOUNGE

1991 – Eric Carr
(Kiss)
1991 – Freddie Mercury
(Frederick Bulsara)

★ ★ ★

SILVER FOX TOPS THE CHART

1973 became 41-year-old grey-haired singer/piano player, Charlie Rich's red-letter year when 'Behind Closed Doors' topped the US country chart, selling a million and becoming his first US Top 20 pop chart hit. Five months later it was followed by 'The Most Beautiful Girl', which not only topped the US country chart but also its pop equivalent, again selling a million copies.

Charlie Rich

RAVINGS

1972
The first show in Don Kirshner's very popular *In Concert* TV series was screened. Among the attractions were The Allman Brothers Band, Chuck Berry, Blood, Sweat and Tears, Alice Cooper and Poco.

1990
The Righteous Brothers had three different *Greatest Hits* compilations on different labels in the US album chart.

1976

BAND'S LAST WALTZ EXTRAVAGANZA

Canadian rock quintet, The Band, made their farewells to the world at a concert at San Francisco's Winterland ballroom where they acted as the backing group to a veritable 'who's who' of the world's greatest contemporary rock stars.

Promoter Bill Graham had transformed the venue into a room fit for a palace to allow one of the greatest American rock bands to commemorate its dissolution in a style that would be remembered.

Friends, associates and fellow rock stars who appeared on stage with the much-admired quintet included Bob Dylan, Van Morrison, Eric Clapton, Joni Mitchell, Neil Young, Stephen Stills, Ringo Starr, Emmylou Harris,

Muddy Waters, Ronnie Hawkins (under whose patronage the group had formed), Bobby Charles and an unlikely star in this company, Neil Diamond, whose *Beautiful Noise* album had just been produced by Band guitarist and vocalist Robbie Robertson.

Fortunately, the show was recorded (and later released as a triple album called, like the event, *The Last Waltz*), and was also filmed by noted director Martin Scorsese.

RAVINGS

1961
The Everly Brothers joined the US Marine Corps Reserve.

1984
The biggest-ever selling record in Britain, 'Do They Know It's Christmas', was recorded at London's Island Studios.

★ ★ ★

The Band - waltzing into the sunset

ARRIVALS

1924 – Paul Desmond (Paul Breitenfield) (Dave Brubeck Quartet)
1926 – Biff Collie (Hiram Abiff Collie)
1940 – Percy Sledge
1943 – Roy Lynes (Spectres/Status Quo)
1944 – Bev Bevan (Move/ELO)
1944 – Bob Lind
1947 – Val Fuentes (It's A Beautiful Day)
1951 – Del Bromham (Stray)
1959 – Steve Rothery (Marillion)
1960 – Amy Grant
1966 – Stacy Lattislaw

★ ★ ★

DEPARTURE LOUNGE

1974 – Nick Drake

1972

BIGGEST HIT, DUMBEST SONG

Chuck Berry remains one of the foremost heroes of rock 'n' roll, largely due to his seamlessly brilliant output between 1955 and 1964. He subsequently became a bigger attraction as a live performer than as a recording artist, but scored his biggest hit in 1972, when 'My Ding-A-Ling', a novelty song that scarcely deserves the description 'smutty' ('pathetic' seems a better word), topped the charts on both sides of the Atlantic and became his first officially certified million seller.

1969

LENNON RETURNS QUEEN'S GIFT

And you can have this flower as well, your majesty

John Lennon, who had controversially received the award of an MBE from Queen Elizabeth II in 1965 together with the rest of The Beatles, returned his medal to Buckingham Palace with a note that read, 'Your Majesty, I am returning this MBE in protest against Britain's involvement in the Nigeria–Biafra thing, against our support of America in Vietnam, and against "Cold Turkey" slipping down the charts. With love, John Lennon of Bag.'

Lennon's humourous but rather childish outburst seemed to do little more than confirm that the disgusted old soldiers who had returned their decorations when The Beatles were awarded theirs may have had a point. The chart decline of 'Cold Turkey' was not reversed, and Lennon's involvement in politics probably made little difference to the conflict in Africa, although he was not alone in his disapproval of the Vietnam war.

1955

CASH DEBUTS ON COUNTRY CHART

23-year-old Johnny Cash made his very first chart appearance when 'Cry! Cry! Cry!' spent a single week in the Top 10 of the US country chart together. With his back-

No tears for Johnny

ing musicians, Luther Perkins (guitar) and Marshall Grant (bass) (aka The Tennessee Two), Cash was beginning a career that would involve over 130 US country chart hits. Around 30 of his early hits were recorded for Sun Records in Memphis, before he signed with Columbia (CBS) in 1958, where he remained for 30 years.

1976

PISTOLS DEBUT WITH 'ANARCHY'

The most notorious act in rock music, the Sex Pistols, released their debut single, 'Anarchy In The UK'. It swiftly entered the UK chart, but on January 6, 1977, the group's contract was terminated, they were paid a reported £40,000 ($60,000), being the balance of the advance EMI had agreed to pay to them. The single spent four weeks in the UK singles chart, peaking within the Top 40 before it was withdrawn.

1976

5CC LEAVE 10CC

Manchester quartet 10cc, who had enjoyed considerable success with hit singles and albums during the first half of the 1970s, split in half when singer/guitarist Lol Creme and singing drummer Kevin Godley announced to their colleagues Graham Gouldman and Eric Stewart that they were leaving the group to concentrate on marketing and exploiting an instrument they had invented known as the gizmo, a device used with the guitar to produce neo-orchestral sounds.

Gouldman and Stewart continued as

10cc, increasing the group's already impressive string of hits, recruiting a new band that included two drummers, Paul Burgess and Stuart Tosh, bass player Rick Fenn and ex-Kokomo keyboard player Tony O'Malley, but they were only able to rack up a further two hits.

Godley and Creme launched their own career, logically enough as Godley and Creme, scoring three hits between 1981 and 1985, by which time they were better known as video producers than chart stars.

ARRIVALS

1933 – Garnet Mimms
1938 – Tina Turner (Annie Mae Bullock)
1945 – John McVie (Fleetwood Mac)
1945 – Jim Mullen (Kokomo)
1946 – Bert Ruiter (Focus)
1948 – John Rossall (Glitter Band)
1949 – Martin Lee (Brotherhood Of Man)
1966 – Mark Gillespie (Big Fun)

★ ★ ★

DEPARTURE LOUNGE

1956 – Tommy Dorsey
1973 – John Rostill (Shadows)

1958

FOLKIES ARE FIRST GROUP TO TOP US ALBUM CHART

During the 1960s more groups than solo artists topped the US album chart, but in the 1950s the first (and only) group to ascend to that summit was The Kingston Trio, a folk-based group who took five albums to the top of the US chart in two years, between 1958 and 1960.

The Kingston Trio

RAVINGS

1973
John Rostill, bass guitarist with The Shadows from late 1963 until the group disbanded in 1968, died when he was electrocuted while playing guitar in the studio in his home.

★ ★ ★

1980
The concert movie starring Paul

McCartney and Wings, *Rockshow*, was premiered in New York. The film documented a show from the group's 1976 US tour.

★ ★ ★

1983
An audience numbering a reputed 80,000 people watched a David Bowie concert in Auckland, New Zealand.

★ ★ ★

1964

JAGGER'S SECOND DRIVING FINE IN THREE MONTHS

Rolling Stone Mick Jagger was convicted of a second driving offence within three months. On August 10 he was fined £32 ($50) in Liverpool for exceeding the speed limit and driving without insurance, and on November 27 he was fined £12 ($20) in Staffordshire for further offences. His erudite brief advised the court to ignore Jagger's long hair, noting that The Duke Of Marlborough's long hair had not prevented him becoming a national hero for winning wars, and added that The Duke used powder in his hair to prevent fleas, something of which Jagger had no need. He also noted that the dollar-earning capacity of The Rolling Stones was important to Britain, and asked the court not to deprive Jagger of his driving licence lest his earning capability were adversely affected.

1959

CLIFF'S BONGO MOVIE

The second film of the year featuring British teenage pop star Cliff Richard was premiered in London. Where his earlier movie, *Serious Charge*, portrayed Richard in a largely dramatic role in a story about a preacher accused of being too devoted to some young members of his flock, *Expresso Bongo* was a more light-hearted item written by Wolf Mankowitz and many felt it mirrored Richard's own mercurial rise to stardom. He played the part of Bongo Herbert, a teenager who was discovered performing in a coffee bar and whose career was manipulated by a double-dealing manager (played by Laurence Harvey). This latter aspect was not an accurate reflection of Cliff's career, it should be emphasized, but the character played by Harvey seemed to be authentic.

A four-track EP of the music from the film featuring both Richard and his backing group (renamed The Shadows only a short time before as their previous name of The Drifters was already being used by the black American vocal group formed in 1953), reached the Top 20 of the UK singles chart. It was also the first disc to top the newly formed EP chart, inaugurated on March 10, 1960, it ran alongside the singles listings until November 30, 1967. The most popular track from *Expresso Bongo* was 'A Voice In The Wilderness', which was released as a single and reached the UK Top 3, although another ballad that was included, a song called 'The Shrine On The Second Floor', also had its supporters.

Cliff (right) in a still from 'Expresso Bongo'

ARRIVALS

1924 – Bonnie Lou
1935 – Al Jackson
(Booker T. and The MGs)
1942 – Jimi Hendrix
1944 – Dozy
(Trevor Leonard Davies)
(DD,D,B,M and T)
1944 – Eddie Rabbitt
(Edward Thomas Rabbitt)
1948 – Barry Devlin
(Horslips)
1951 – Kevin Kavanaugh
(Southside Johnny and The Asbury Jukes)
1959 – Charlie Burchill
(Simple Minds)
1960 – Ashley Ingram
(Imagination)

★ ★ ★

DEPARTURE LOUNGE

1973 – John Wildener
1981 – Lotte Lenya

★ ★ ★

RAVINGS

1974
Elton John's *Greatest Hits* album became his fourth consecutive UK No. 1 album. Surprisingly, he did not add to his total of chart-topping albums until 1989's *Sleeping With The Past*.

★ ★ ★

1976
20 Golden Greats became Glen Campbell's only album to date to top the UK chart. It hung on to the No. 1 spot fot six weeks.

★ ★ ★

1987

FIRST UK HIT FROM ATHENS BAND

R.E.M., the quartet from Athens, Georgia, first entered the UK singles chart with 'The One I Love'. It was not only their first British hit single but also their first US Top 10 hit.

Originally launched informally in 1978 by vocalist and songwriter Michael Stipe and guitarist Peter Buck, the group was completed in early 1980 when the duo met bass player Mike Mills and drummer Bill Berry at a party, soon after which the group really began, naming themselves after the initials of the technique supposedly used by US soldiers in combat, rapid eye movement. After independently releasing their debut single, 'Radio Free Europe', in 1981, the group were signed by Miles Copeland's IRS label in 1982, and in 1983 released their debut album, *Murmur*, which reached the Top 40 of the US chart. 1984's *Reckoning* continued the group's climb to fame, reaching the Top 30 in the US during a chart residency of a year and briefly entering the UK

R.E.M. vocalist Michael Stipe, pictured in 1987

album chart. 1985's *Fables Of The Reconstruction* again reached the Top 30 in the US and became the group's first substantial UK hit. 1987's *Document* reached the US Top 10 and the UK Top 30, after which the group were wooed away from IRS by Warner Bros., and after *Rolling Stone* magazine had called them 'America's Best Rock 'n' Roll Band', their first album for the new label, *Green*, was a major success. 1991's *Out Of Time* and 1992's *Automatic For The People* topped the album charts on both sides of the Atlantic.

ARRIVALS

1929 – Berry Gordy Jr
1933 – Agato Barbieri
(Leandro Barbieri)
1939 – Gary Troxel
(Fleetwoods)
1940 – Bruce Channel
1940 – Clem Curtis
(Foundations)
1943 – Randy Newman
1944 – R. B. Greaves
(Ronald Bertram Aloysius Greaves)
1948 – Beeb Burtles
(Zoot/Little River Band)

1949 – Hugh McKenna
(Alex Harvey Band)
1954 – David Jaymes
(Modern Romance)
1955 – John Spinks
(Outfield)
1958 – David Van Day
(Dollar)
1962 – Princess
(Desiree Heslop)

★ ★ ★

DEPARTURE LOUNGE

1971 – Papa Lightfoot

RAVINGS

1964
Willie Nelson made his debut performance at the *Grand Ole Opry* in Nashville.

★ ★ ★

1977
The stage musical *Elvis*, starring P. J. Proby, Shakin' Stevens and Timothy Whitnall playing The King at three different stages of his life, opened in London.

★ ★ ★

1974

THE PAYBACK

Unpredictable and an ex-Beatle he might have been, but John Lennon was not about to break a promise to a friend, and he had promised Elton John, who played and sang on the track, that if 'Whatever Gets You Thru The Night' reached the top of the US chart, he would appear on stage with Elton.

Lennon joined Elton at Madison Square Garden on Thanksgiving Day, and they played 'I Saw Her Standing There'. The song was from the first Beatles album and was introduced by Lennon as 'a number by an estranged fiancé', by which he meant Paul McCartney. It was belatedly released as a single in 1981 following Lennon's death). They also played 'Whatever Gets You Thru The Night' and 'Lucy In The Sky With Diamonds'.

1979

DOUBLE LIVE AT LE PAVILLON

Supertramp's concerts at the Paris arena, Le Pavillon, were recorded and highlights were released as a double live album at the end of 1980. The live album, *Paris*, was recorded at the height of Supertramp's fame – earlier in 1979 their *Breakfast In America* album had achieved platinum status and topped the US chart for six weeks.

Formed in 1969 by singer and keyboard player Richard Davies, the band adopted its more familiar name at the suggestion of saxophonist Dave Winthrop from the celebrated book *The Autobiography Of A Supertramp* by W. H. Davies.

Signed to A & M Records in 1970, the group changed personnel after two albums, *Supertramp* and *Indelibly Stamped*, both failed to reach the UK chart, leaving Davies and lead guitarist Roger

Hodgson as the only original members remaining. In 1973 the most successful line-up of the band assembled, with saxophonist John Helliwell (ex-Alan Bown Set), and a rhythm section of Dougie Thomson (bass) and Bob

C. Benberg (drums, a cousin of Thin Lizzy guitarist Scott Gorham).

Their first gold album, *Crime Of The Century*, was a US Top 40 hit at the end of 1974, and a year later came *Crisis? What Crisis?*, which consolidated the group's position. 1977 brought a second gold album, *Even In The Quietest Moments*, which reached the Top 20 in the USA, but the group's biggest success was certainly *Breakfast In America*, which not only achieved the No. 1 spot in the US but also became the group's only album to make the Top 3 in their native Britain. The double live album reached the Top 10 on both sides of the Atlantic.

Supertramp

1986

BOSS STARTS AT THE TOP

Following the staggering success of his 1984 album *Born In The USA*, which included seven US Top 10 single hits, Bruce Springsteen released a live anthology covering ten years of live work. The album entered the US album chart at No. 1 and remained at the top for seven weeks, making it the first boxed set ever to enter the chart in pole position. Containing five albums (or three CDs or cassettes), *Bruce Springsteen and The E Street Band Live 1975–1985* was the most expensive record ever to top the chart. It included 40 tracks and a 36-page full-colour booklet. As with all Springsteen releases, its success in the UK was less marked. It entered the chart at No. 4 but charted for a mere nine weeks.

BOONE BOWS OUT WITH 21ST UK HIT

1962

Pat Boone, a big star in the 1950s

Pat Boone's final UK hit single, 'The Main Attraction', entered the Top 20, becoming his 21st single to reach such heights.

Born Charles Eugene Boone, he was a direct descendant of pioneering American frontiersman Daniel Boone, and married the daughter of country music star Red Foley in 1953, the year before he won a talent contest and made his first record.

White, smartly dressed and well educated, Boone was the acceptable face of popular music at a time when racial prejudice was rife, and the majority of his early hits were somewhat sanitized versions of black R & B originals. His first US chart-topper in 1955 was his version of Fats Domino's 'Ain't That A Shame'. Domino's original topped the US R & B chart, but Boone clearly won the battle in the US pop chart, where Domino's version just reached the Top 10. In 1956 again Boone won the pop chart battle when 'I'll Be Home' reached the US Top 5 and topped the UK singles chart for five weeks, while a version by The Flamingos was a Top 5 R & B hit. In 1956 his covers of 'Long Tall Sally' and 'Tutti Frutti', both originally by Little Richard, were just bettered by Richard Penniman's versions. Boone's second US No. 1 was 'I Almost Lost My Mind' in 1958.

His final US Top 10 hit with a whitened cover of a black hit came at the end of 1956, when his revival of Joe Turner's 'Chains Of Love' was released as a double A-side with 'Don't Forbid Me', which became Boone's seventh million-seller. 1957 found him recording chart-topping film themes like 'Love Letters In The Sand' and 'April Love', after which he had no real reason to further plunder the black chart.

RAVINGS

1980
Elvis Costello and Squeeze jointly headlined a benefit concert in Swansea, South Wales, for the family of boxer Johnny Owen, who died from injuries received during a fight in the USA.

1985
The Dead Kennedys released their *Frankenchrist* album, which included a poster deemed to be obscene.

★ ★ ★

ARRIVALS

1929 – Dick Clark (American Bandstand)
1937 – Jimmy Bowen
1937 – Noel Paul Stookey (Peter, Paul and Mary)
1943 – J. J. Barnes
1943 – Leo Lyons (Ten Years After)
1944 – Luther Ingram
1944 – Robert Grill (Grass Roots)
1945 – Roger Glover (Deep Purple/Rainbow)
1953 – Shuggie Otis
1957 – John Ashton (Psychedelic Furs)
1957 – Richard Barbieri (Japan)
1955 – Billy Idol (William Broad)
1958 – David McClymont (Orange Juice)
1958 – Stacey Q (Stacey Swain)
1965 – Paul Wheeler (Icehouse)

★ ★ ★

1963

CHUCK AND BO, THE CHART RIVALS

Chess Records labelmates Chuck Berry and Bo Diddley were among the black R & B stars whose hits were substantial parts of the repertoire of white British groups like The Rolling Stones, The Yardbirds and Manfred Mann. Both Bo (real name Ellas McDaniel) and Chuck found themselves in the British album chart, Berry with *Chuck Berry* and *More Chuck Berry* and Diddley with *Bo Diddley* and *Bo Diddley Rides Again*.

Chuck Berry

CLARKE LEAVES TO JOIN ALF

Depeche Mode founder member and songwriter Vince Clarke, who preferred working in the recording studio to performing live, announced that he was leaving the band to form Yazoo with vocalist Alison Moyet.

Clarke had formed Depeche Mode in 1980 with Martin Gore and Andy Fletcher, although the group, whose members all came from Basildon, Essex, had not adopted the name with which they became famous at the time. Their first success came when they were seen by entrepreneur Stevo, who was assembling an album by new acts for a project that he called *The Some Bizzare Album*. Depeche Mode contributed 'Photographic', though Stevo did not sign the group to his label.

By this time a quartet (as Clarke was not happy singing, Dave Gahan had been recruited), the group signed with Daniel Miller's Mute label, releasing their first single, 'Dreaming Of Me', in April 1981, which was a minor UK hit.

During the summer of that year, a follow-up single, 'New Life', became their first Top 20 hit. 'Just Can't Get Enough', which highlighted the group's almost totally synthesized sound, reached the Top 10 later in the year, as their debut album, *Speak And Spell*, also reached the UK Top 10.

At that point Clarke chose to leave, teaming up with vocalist Alison Moyet (familiarly known as 'Alf') in Yazoo, a duo who were instantly successful. Their debut single, 'Only You', was a UK Top 3 hit, its follow-up, 'Don't Go', was similarly successful, and their debut album, *Upstairs At Eric's* (referring to producer Eric Radcliffe), was also a Top 3 hit.

Clarke split with Moyet in mid 1983 after yet another Top 3 single, 'Nobody's Diary', and a No. 1 album, *You And Me Both*, whereupon he launched the successful Erasure and she embarked on a solo career.

1983

YOUNG SUED BY LABEL

Neil Young – pink and shocked!

Geffen Records, the label to which Neil Young was signed, sued the artist for $3 million, claiming that his records were 'not commercial in nature and musically uncharacteristic of his previous albums'. This followed the poor response that greeted *Everybody's Rockin'*, an album of undistinguished rockabilly items credited to Neil Young and The Shocking Pinks, which was his least successful album since 1969.

RAVINGS

1976
The Sex Pistols first attracted nationwide notoriety with their appearance on early evening television during which they used the 'F' word.

1987
Brothers Boon and Phil Gould both left Level 42, Boon with an ulcer and Phil with nervous exhaustion.

ARRIVALS

1934 – Billy Paul (Paul Williams)
1935 – Lou Rawls
1944 – Eric Bloom (Blue Oyster Cult)
1944 – John Densmore (Doors)
1944 – Charlie Grima (Mongrel/Wizzard)
1945 – Bette Midler
1946 – Gilbert O'Sullivan (Raymond Edward O'Sullivan)
1949 – Klaaseje Van Der Wal (Shocking Blue)
1951 – Jaco Pastorius (John Francis Pastorius) (Weather Report)
1959 – Steve Janson (Steve Batt) (Japan)
1963 – Sam Reid (Glass Tiger)

★ ★ ★

DEPARTURE LOUNGE

1954 – Fred Rose
1966 – Carter Stanley
1969 – Magic Sam
1986 – Lee Dorsey

★ ★ ★

STARS DIVORCE

The end of a professional as well as personal partnership occurred when the marriage between chart stars Kris Kristofferson and Rita Coolidge came to an end after six years.

Kristofferson had attended Oxford University in England as a Rhodes scholar before working as a military helicopter pilot in Germany. In 1965, rather than accepting a job teaching English literature at West Point military academy, he decided to develop a career as a songwriter after meeting Johnny Cash. Moving to Nashville, he took a job as a night janitor at CBS (Columbia) Studios while attempting to interest Music City publishers in his songs by day. He was working at the studio when Bob Dylan recorded *Blonde On Blonde* in 1966, but failed to achieve a breakthrough until the late 1960s, when Cash recommended Kristofferson's 'Me and Bobby McGee' to Roger Miller. The song became his 16th US country chart Top 20 hit in 1969.

Numerous other covers of Kristofferson songs swiftly followed, includ-ing 'Sunday Morning Coming Down', a US country No. 1 for Johnny Cash ,and 'Help Me Make It Through The Night', a country chart-topper for Sammi Smith in 1971, the year when Janis Joplin recorded 'Me and Bobby McGee' on her final album and it topped the US pop chart after her death.

Rita Coolidge, the daughter of a Baptist Minister father and a Cherokee Indian mother, first emerged as a member of Delaney and Bonnie and Friends in 1969. Both she and her former husband enjoyed chart success as vocal-ists, separately and as duet partners, before the divorce.

Kris Kristofferson

MONKEES MAKE IT FOUR IN A YEAR

With four US No. 1 albums in the same year, The Monkees created a record that has not been beaten at the time of writing. The group's eponymous debut album was at No. 1 from mid-November 1966, until it was replaced by their follow-up, *More Of The Monkees*, in February 1967. In June of that year *Headquarters* became the group's third consecutive No. 1 album, and *Pisces, Aquarius, Capricorn and Jones Ltd.* made it four in a row. The group occupied the coveted No. 1 position for 30 weeks of the year when *Sergeant Pepper* by The Beatles was No. 1 for 15 of the remaining weeks.

RAVINGS

1959
Marty Wilde, one of Britain's biggest rock stars, married Joyce Baker, a member of hitmaking vocal group The Vernons Girls. In 1960 their first offspring was a daughter named Kim, who scored her own debut hit in 1980.

★ ★ ★

1972
'Oh Carol' by Neil Sedaka re-entered the Top 20 of the UK singles chart, having previously been there almost 13 years before.

★ ★ ★

ARRIVALS

1906 – Peter Carl Goldmark (inventor of the LP)
1915 – Roebuck 'Pops' Staples
1915 – Adolf Green
1941 – Tom McGuinness (Manfred Mann/Blues Band)
1943 – Dave Munden (Tremeloes)
1950 – John Wesley Ryles
1952 – Peter Kingsbery (Cock Robin)
1960 – Sydney Youngblood
1960 – Rick Savage (Def Leppard)

★ ★ ★

DEPARTURE LOUNGE

1949 – Albert Ammons
1982 – David Blue

★ ★ ★

(left to right) Mickey Dolenz, Peter Tork, Mike Nesmith, Davy Jones - The Monkees

ELEVEN DIE AT WHO CONCERT

At a concert headlined by The Who at River Front Coliseum, Cincinatti, Ohio, eleven members of the audience were trampled to death in the rush to reach unreserved seats as near as possible to the stage. Dozens more were injured and a subsequent investigation laid the blame both on the auditorium having too few access doors and on the concept of unreserved seating (known as 'Festival seating').

Jones, who had been recruited to fill the shoes of the late Keith Moon, who had died only three months before. Jones had first achieved fame in the mid 1960s as a 'Mod' groups, the other being The Who. Jones's first public performance with The Who was at London's Rainbow Theatre in May 1979 on the same night as the

The new Who (l to r) Pete Townshend, Kenny Jones, Roger Daltrey, John Entwistle

It was the first tour with The Who for the group's new drummer, Kenny member of The Small Faces, regarded by many as one of the two main premiere of the movie based on The Who's *Quadrophenia* album.

WINGS TAKE BAGPIPE LAMENT TO NO. 1

Wings' million-selling success

'Mull Of Kintyre' by Wings, the group fronted and led by Paul McCartney, became the latter's first post-Beatles No. 1 single in Britain, and making up for lost time refused to vacate the top spot for nine weeks. It swiftly became Britain's best selling single, eclipsing The Beatles' 'I Want To Hold Your Hand'.

Surprisingly, it was a flop in the USA, where its UK B-side, 'Girls' School', was regarded as the A-side. Perhaps the view of McCartney's US label was that the bagpipes providing the main instrumental backing would not be to the taste of American record-buyers.

BEATLES START FINAL UK TOUR

Although no one knew it at the time, the concerts by The Beatles at the Odeon Cinema, Glasgow, were the start of the last tour of Britain by the group, who headlined the short tour (nine venues in 10 days) with a supporting line-up that included The Moody Blues, The Paramounts (who later metamorphosed into Procol Harum), Beryl Marsden and others. The new album by The Beatles, *Rubber Soul*, had been released two days before, while their new single, a double 'A' side, 'Day Tripper' coupled with 'We Can Work It Out', had been released that very day.

RAVINGS

1968
The celebrated *Elvis TV Special* was screened, proving that Presley was not artistically bankrupt. It drew rave critical reactions and also the year's largest viewing figures for a musical special

★ ★ ★

1971
Montreux Casino in Switzerland burnt down during a gig by Frank Zappa. Ian Gillan, vocalist of Deep Purple, who were recording in close proximity, was inspired to write the classic 'Smoke On The Water' about the incident.

★ ★ ★

ARRIVALS

1910 – Rabon Delmore (Delmore Brothers)
1928 – Andy Williams (Howard Andrew Williams)
1940 – John Cale (Velvet Underground)
1944 – Ralph McTell (Ralph May)
1946 – Vic Malcolm (Geordie)
1948 – Ozzy Osbourne (John Michael Osbourne) (Black Sabbath)
1949 – Mickey Thomas (Elvin Bishop Band/Starship)
1949 – John Wilson (Them/Taste)
1951 – Nicky Stevens (Brotherhood Of Man)
1951 – Mike Stock (Stock Aitken Waterman)
1967 – Adamski (Adam Tinley)

★ ★ ★

MILLION-DOLLAR QUARTET CONVENE

1956

The Million Dollar Quartet

Elvis Presley, who had recorded his first (and arguably best) tracks for Sun Records of Memphis, was back in that city to spend Christmas with his family. Presley had signed with RCA Records at the end of 1955, but dropped in to the Sun Records studios at 706 Union Street to see his friends and ex-colleagues who worked there.

Carl Perkins was recording that night, with Jerry Lee Lewis guesting on piano. Johnny Cash was also in the building, although he is hardly noticeable, if indeed he was actually in the studio, on the recordings that resulted.

The main photographic evidence of this occasion shows Cash watching with Lewis while Presley sits at the piano and Perkins strums his guitar, so the meeting of this quartet of young stars was dubbed 'The Million Dollar Quartet Session'. The three backing musicians were all members of Carl Perkins's group.

ARRIVALS

1915 – Hondo Crouch
1915 – Eddie Heywood
1940 – Freddy Cannon (Frederick Anthony Picariello)
1942 – Chris Hillman (Byrds/Flying Burrito Brothers/Desert Rose Band)
1942 – Bob Mosley (Moby Grape)
1944 – Dennis Wilson (Beach Boys)
1948 – Southside Johnny (Johnny Lyon)
1951 – Gary Rossington (Lynyrd Skynyrd/Rossington-Collins Band)

★ ★ ★

DEPARTURE LOUNGE

1976 – Tommy Bolin
1983 – Perez Prado

★ ★ ★

PURPLE AXEMAN'S OD

1976

Tommy Bolin, the lead guitarist with Deep Purple for the last 14 months of the group's life before it finally fell apart in 1976, died of an overdose of heroin at a hotel in Miami, Florida. Bolin, who had previously been a member of The James Gang (some time after Joe Walsh) had replaced Ritchie Blackmore on guitar, widely regarded as the group's major musical force, in April 1975 when the latter left to form his own group, Rainbow.

RAVINGS

1986
Fans of A-Ha, the Norwegian trio, stopped the traffic in London's Oxford Street when they made a personal appearance at a record store.

1988
Roy Orbison played his final gig, which took place in Cleveland, Ohio, appropriately the future home of the Rock 'n' Roll Hall Of Fame.

★ ★ ★

BOB MARLEY ESCAPES ASSASSINATION

1976

Seven gunmen burst into Bob Marley's house in Kingston, Jamaica, and Marley, his wife Rita and his manager, Don Taylor, were all injured. Marley was regarded as a potent force in local politics and as a major spokesman for the neo-religious Rastafarian movement, which believed that Haile Selassie, the ex-Emperor of Ethiopia, who had died in 1975, was the reincarnation of Christ, that marijuana was a holy sacrament, and that hair should be worn as dreadlocks. Fortunately, Marley was not badly injured and was able to appear at the Smile Jamaica concert that took place a few days after the incident, although caution led him to record his next album, *Exodus*, in the USA.

In 1978 Marley made the ultimate non-political gesture when he presided over an on-stage handshake between Jamaican Prime Minister Michael Manley and the leader of the main Jamaican opposition party, Edward Seaga.

'Smile' - Bob Marley

1968

NASH LEAVES HOLLIES TO FORM SUPERGROUP

Graham Nash announced that he was leaving The Hollies, the group he had formed in 1961 with fellow vocalist Allan Clarke. He was unhappy with the band's musical direction and angry at the decision to record an album of covers of songs by Bob Dylan, and the inclusion in live shows of versions of the Peter, Paul and Mary song 'Puff The Magic Dragon' and Roger Miller's 'Dang Me'.

Nash had also met David Crosby (ex-The Byrds) on a trip to Los Angeles in 1967, and the two had discussed joining forces. When Buffalo Springfield founder Stephen Stills had sung along with the duo at a party, their three-part harmonies had convinced all three that they should work together, the result being Crosby, Stills and Nash, one of the earliest supergroups.

A track on the group's eponymous debut album was Nash's 'Marrakesh Express', which became C, S and N's first US Top 20 hit single. *The Crosby, Stills and Nash* album sold over two million copies in two years, but surprisingly failed to top the US chart. For their first US tour, the trio recruited a fourth superstar member, Stills's ex-Buffalo Springfield colleague Neil Young, not only to add to their vocal line-up but also to bolster their limited instrumental capabilities – neither Crosby nor Nash were much more than rhythm guitarists, leaving Stills and drummer Dallas Taylor (ex-Clear Light) to bear most of the instrumental burden.

Young played with the group at the Woodstock Festival in August 1969 and was part of the group for their follow-up album, *Déjà Vu*, which was thus credited to Crosby, Stills, Nash and Young, but thereafter was an occasional

(left to right, foreground) Stills, Crosby, Nash, Young

member, also working with his own group Crazy Horse, although he did appear on *Four Way Street*, the double live album released as by C, S, N andY in 1971.

1970

COLLINS BEGINS AMAZING RUN

'Amazing Grace', the accapella single by folk singer Judy Collins, entered the UK singles chart for the first time. It left and re-entered the chart seven more times in the next two years, eventually accumulating 67 chart weeks, which made it the single that spent the greatest

number of weeks on the chart of all hits bar one – 'My Way' by Frank Sinatra, which managed 122 chart weeks between 1969 and 1972.

Despite her long run, Judy Collins was eclipsed in sales by The Royal Scots Dragoon Guards, whose version hit No. 1 and sold a million copies.

Judy Collins - 67 weeks!

1969

Altamont – The End of Peace and Love

When The Rolling Stones played their free concert in London's Hyde Park earlier in 1969, security had been provided by Hell's Angels, motorcycle-riding leather-clad contemporary outlaws. As a result of such an aggro-free event, the group were happy to hire Californian Hell's Angels as security at the free concert they staged at Altamont Raceway, Livermore, California, but the American bikers were considerably less gentle than their British so-called equivalents.

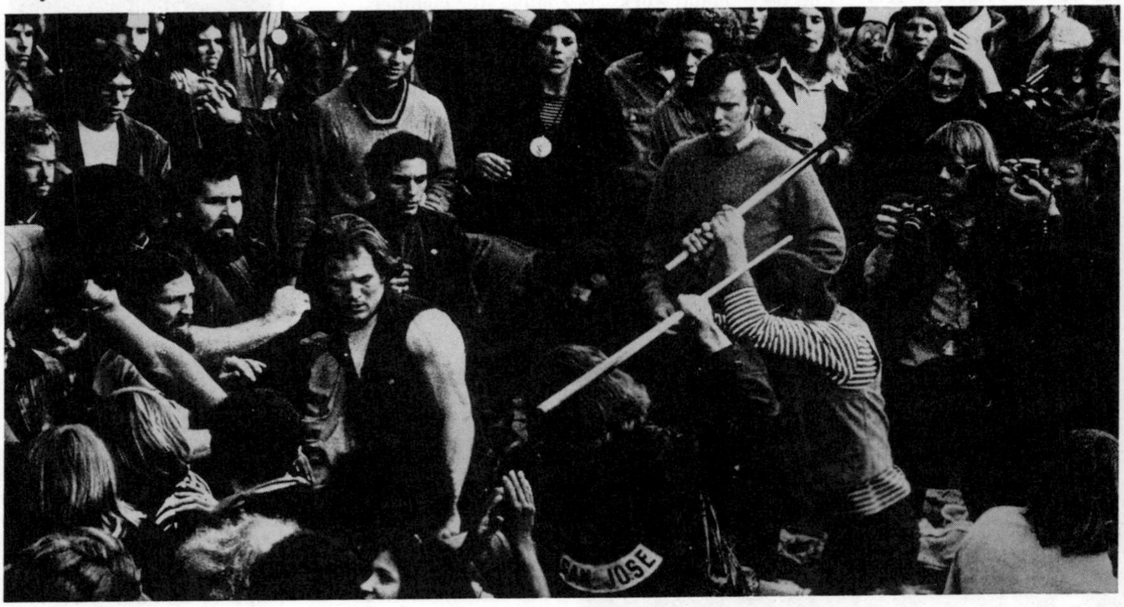

Peace love and ...?

The trouble started long before The Stones hit the stage. The huge crowd pressed forward to watch the star-studded opening acts – Santana, Jefferson Airplane, Flying Burrito Brothers and Crosby, Stills, Nash and Young, and as the multitude approached the stage they were met with stony glares from the Angels, who wielded pool cues to enforce their authority. By the time The Stones took the stage for the climax of the show, which was being filmed by New York cinematographers Albert and David Maysles, the atmosphere was deathly, as if something terrible were going to happen. Mick Jagger played the title role of *Sympathy For The Devil*, inciting the audience with new songs like 'Midnight Rambler' in which he quoted The Boston Strangler, Albert De Salvo. Meredith Hunter, an 18-year-old boy, was beaten to death by the Angels who said they had seen a gun in his hand that was pointed at Mick Jagger. It was the end of a decade that had been utterly memorable.

1969

Twenty Million See Asia In Asia

Supergroup Asia, whose members had played in Roxy Music, Yes, King Crimson, Atomic Rooster and Emerson, Lake and Palmer, played a concert at Tokyo's Budokan Theatre that was transmitted live to an estimated television audience of 20 million people in the USA under the title *Asia In Asia*. The show marked the debut of bass player Greg Lake, who had been recruited to replace founder member John Wetton. Lake thus teamed up with his ex-colleague in ELP, drummer Carl Palmer, while ex-Yes members Steve Howe (guitar) and Geoff Downes (keyboards, vocals) completed the group's line up.

Arrivals

1920 – Dave Brubeck (David Warren Brubeck)
1940 – Steve Alaimo
1941 – Helen Cornelius
1942 – Len Barry (Leonard Borisoff)
1944 – Jonathan King (Kenneth King)
1947 – Kim Simmonds (Savoy Brown)
1947 – Miroslav Vitous (Weather Report)
1950 – Joe X. Dube (Starz)
1950 – Jeff Grobe (Looking Glass)
1955 – Rick Buckler (Jam/Time U.K.)
1955 – Eddie Tudorpole (Tenpole Tudor)
1956 – Peter Buck (REM)
1961 – Eugene Wilde
1962 – Ben Watt (Everything But The Girl)

★ ★ ★

Departure Lounge

1949 – Leadbelly (Huddie Ledbetter)

★ ★ ★

Ravings

1968
US President-elect Richard Nixon supposedly sent a letter to Elvis Presley asking for the King's support in his first four-year term at the White House.

1986
'Hey Luciani', the first play written by Mark E. Smith, leader of The Fall, premiered at London's Riverside Theatre.

★ ★ ★

1988

BIG O LOSES FINAL BATTLE

Roy Orbison died during the first minutes of the new day in Hendersonville Hospital near Nashville, where he had been taken after being afflicted by a heart attack while at his mother's house. He was 52 years old, and was enjoying a considerable comeback to popularity at the time of his death.

A black day for popular music

In his early heyday during the first half of the 1960s Orbison had enjoyed eleven UK Top 20 hits, including three No. 1s, and had been one of the few American acts to be seemingly unaffected by the predominance of British beat groups, led by The Beatles and The Rolling Stones, who had forced a number of American stars to move to the cabaret circuit in order to survive. Between August 1963 and December 1964 the only American act to top the British singles chart was Orbison, who achieved the feat twice, first with the ballad 'It's Over' and again with the more uptempo 'Oh Pretty Woman'. During the rest of the 1960s he continued to have hits, but they gradually decreased in size, and he was absent from the UK singles chart for the entire 1970s and the first nine years of the 1980s, although compilation albums of his early hits sporadically sold in large quantities.

In 1987 he had signed a new recording contract with Virgin Records after Bruce Springsteen had inducted him into the Rock 'n' Roll Hall Of Fame, and was also part of the informal supergroup, The Traveling Wilburys, along with Bob Dylan, George Harrison, Tom Petty and Jeff Lynne. In that year as well he had been the star of a concert in Los Angeles during which he was backed by an all-star band of rock luminaries including Springsteen, Elvis Costello, Jackson Browne, Tom Waits, James Burton and k.d.lang, with whom he had duetted in early 1988 on a revival of his 1961 million seller, 'Crying', which was featured on the soundtrack of the movie *Hiding Out*.

1978

SID LIVES UP TO HIS ASSUMED NAME

Erstwhile Sex Pistol Sid Vicious, out of prison on bail after being charged with murdering his girlfriend, Nancy Spungen, at New York's Chelsea Hotel, was arrested for assaulting Patti Smith's brother, Todd, with a beer glass at a Manhattan night club.

Sid looks lovable

ARRIVALS

1924 – Bent Fabric (Bent Fabricius-Bjerre)
1931 – Bob Osborne (Osborne Brothers)
1942 – Harry Chapin
1942 – Johnny Mars
1949 – Tom Waits
1954 – Mike Nolan (Bucks Fizz)
1958 – Timothy Butler (Psychedelic Furs)
1959 – Nicole McCloud (Nicole McCranie)
1963 – Claudia Brucken (Propaganda)
1963 – Barbara Weathers (Atlantic Starr)
1964 – Duncan Miller (Blue Mercedes)
1970 – Lindy Layton

★ ★ ★

DEPARTURE LOUNGE

1987 – Abdul Rashid Talhah (Richard Taylor) (Manhattans)
1988 – Roy Orbison
1990 – Dee Clark

RAVINGS

1956
Tommy Steele made his British concert debut at London's Finsbury Park Astoria, later renamed the Rainbow Theatre.

★ ★ ★

1963
The Beatles recorded their appearance as the panel of judges for *Juke Box Jury*, a TV show on which personalities gave their opinions on new record releases.

★ ★ ★

STARTING OVER? ALL OVER

The death of John Lennon, the ex-Beatle who was murdered outside the Dakota Building, the New York apartment block in which he lived with his wife, Yoko Ono, was doubly tragic as Lennon had emerged from five years of self-imposed retirement only weeks before. His assassin was Mark Chapman, who had sought (and received) Lennon's autograph earlier that day.

Lennon's first new album since 1975, *Double Fantasy*, had been released in the previous month, along with an excerpted single, '(Just Like) Starting Over'. After initial excitement over the return of the prodigal star, the single was actually dropping in the British chart until Lennon's death, whereupon many of his records started to sell prodigiously. 'Starting Over's decline reversed, dramatically jumping from No. 21 to the top spot of it the UK chart. During January 1981 a reissued 'Imagine' (arguably Lennon's finest soló record) topped the UK chart for a month, 'Happy Xmas (War Is Over)' re-entered behind it at No. 2, followed by 'Woman', a track from the *Double Fantasy* album, which dethroned 'Imagine'.

COUNTRY STAR MARTY'S FATAL HEART ATTACK

Country star Marty Robbins, who had accumulated 90 US country chart hits since his chart debut almost exactly 30 years before, died of a heart attack at the age of 57.

The 90 hits included 16 No. 1s, and between 1956 and 1970, 21 of those hits also reached the US pop chart, including 'Singing The Blues' (Top 20, 1956), 'A White Sport Coat (And A Pink Carnation)' (Top 3) and 'The Story Of My Life' (Top 20, both 1957), 'El Paso' (No. 1, 1960) and 'Don't Worry' (Top 3, 1961). Other well-known Robbins hits included 'Knee Deep In The Blues', 'Devil Woman' and 'Ruby Ann', but he was regarded by many as one of the great cowboy singers for his hugely

Marty Robbins - 90 country hits

successful albums of the early 1960s, *Gunfighter Ballads and Trail Songs* and *More Gunfighter Ballads and Trail Songs*. Robbins had at least one hit on the US country singles chart every year for 27 years between 1956 and 1982.

RAVINGS

1956
Eleven-year-old Brenda Lee released her first single in Britain, 'I'm Gonna Lasso Santa Claus'. It was not a hit.

★ ★ ★

1984
'The Power Of Love' became the third consecutive UK No. 1 single for Liverpool group Frankie Goes To Hollywood, equalling the achievement of fellow Scousers Gerry and The Pacemakers, whose first three singles had also topped the UK chart in 1963.

★ ★ ★

1990
MCA Records was sold to the Japanese corporation Matsushita for $3.1 billion.

★ ★ ★

ARRIVALS

1914 – Floyd Tillman
1921 – Johnny Otis
1925 – Jimmy Smith (James Oscar Smith)
1942 – Bobby Elliott (Hollies)
1943 – Jim Morrison (Doors)
1943 – Lee Pickens (Bloodrock)
1944 – George Baker (Johannes Bouwens),(George Baker Selection)
1946 – Graham Knight (Marmalade)
1947 – Gregg Allman (Gregory Lenoir Allman) (Allman Brothers)
1949 – Ray Shulman (Simon Dupree and The Big Sound/Gentle Giant)
1956 – Warren Cuccurullo (Frank Zappa/Missing Persons)
1959 – Paul Rutherford (Frankie Goes To Hollywood)

★ ★ ★

DEPARTURE LOUNGE

1980 – John Lennon
1982 – Marty Robbins
1982 – Big Walter 'Shakey' Horton

1972

HELEN REDDY TOPS US CHART WITH FEMINIST ANTHEM

Helen Reddy became the first Australian female to top the US chart when her song from the film *Stand Up And Be Counted*, 'I Am Woman' became an anthem for the feminist movement.

Born in Australia in 1941, Reddy had moved to the USA in 1966 after winning a talent contest, but had not found New York's streets paved with gold. She decided to return to Australia and threw a farewell party that was gatecrashed by Jeff Wald from the William Morris Agency, who proposed marriage a few days later.

The couple eventually moved to California, and she signed with Capitol Records in 1970, making her first record in 1971, a cover of the Tim Rice/Andrew Lloyd Webber song, 'I Don't Know How To Love Him', which reached the US Top 20. Two follow-up singles in the same year were much smaller hits, but Reddy strongly believed in 'I Am Woman', a song whose lyrics she had written and that had been included on her debut album. She subsequently changed some of the words, adding an extra verse and re-recorded the song, which won a Grammy Award.

Her acceptance speech remains legendary: 'I want to thank everyone

Helen Reddy - God is a girl?

at Capitol Records, my husband and manager, Jeff Wald, because he makes my success possible, and God because She makes everything possible.' Reddy went on to release two more US chart-topping singles, 'Delta Dawn' in 1973 and 'Angie Baby' in 1974.

ARRIVALS

1932 Jesse Hill
1934 Junior Wells (Amos Blackmore)
1938 David Houston
1940 Sam Strain (Little Anthony and The Imperials/O'Jays)
1941 Dan Hicks (Hot Licks)
1943 Rick Danko (The Band)
1943 Kenny Vance (Jay and The Americans)
1944 Shirley Brickley (Orlons)
1944 Neil Innes (Bonzo Dog Band/Rutles)
1948 Dennis Dunaway (Alice Cooper)
1950 Joan Armatrading
1953 Jill Saward (Shakatak)
1956 Sylvia (Sylvia Kirby Allen)
1957 Donny Osmond

★ ★ ★

DEPARTURE LOUNGE

1981 Sonny Til (Earlington Carl Tilghman) (Orioles)

★ ★ ★

RAVINGS

1981
Sonny Til, who had been the lead vocalist with doo-wop stars The Orioles, died of a heart attack at the age of 51. The group is best remembered for their 1953 original version of 'Crying In The Chapel', which was revived by Elvis Presley in 1965 and whose version sold a million copies.

★ ★ ★

1989
Rodney Crowell, husband of Johnny Cash's daughter, Roseanne, became the first artist to release an album that included five US country No. 1 singles.

★ ★ ★

1972

ALL-STAR TOMMY OPENS IN LONDON

A stage version of Pete Townshend's celebrated rock opera *Tommy*, with an all-star cast including the London Symphony Orchestra, was staged at London's Rainbow Theatre. Among those taking part were all four members of The Who, along with Rod Stewart, Steve Winwood, Maggie Bell, Sandy Denny, Richie Havens, Ringo Starr and Richard Harris. Two shows were staged as charity performances to raise funds for the Stars Organisation For Spastics, and £10,000 ($15,000) was donated, while a live album recorded at the Rainbow was released soon afterwards achieving gold status.

SOUL STAR OTIS DIES IN PLANE CRASH

1967

An aeroplane carrying Otis Redding crashed into Lake Monona in Madison, Wisconsin, killing the soul star and four members of his backing group, The Bar-Kays.

Otis Redding had become an international pop/rock star largely as a result of his stunning performance six months before in the Monterey Pop Festival, but even before that he had established himself as a soul star with a series of classic US R & B hits including 'Pain In My Heart' (1964), 'Mr Pitiful', 'I've Been Loving You Too Long' and 'Respect' (all 1965), 'Satisfaction' (a cover of the Rolling Stones hit) and 'Fa-Fa-Fa-Fa-Fa (Sad Song)' (both 1966) and 'Try A Little Tenderness' (early 1967). Only three days before his death he had recorded what would become his biggest hit, '(Sittin' On) The Dock Of The Bay', which he co-wrote with guitarist Steve Cropper. When it was released it topped the US singles chart for a month, selling over a million copies.

Redding was only 26 years old when he died.

In the mid 1960s he had been one of the great soul stars whose work appeared on the very popular 1966 compilation album *Solid Gold Soul*, sharing the billing with Solomon Burke, Don Covay, Ben E. King, Wilson Pickett and Joe Tex. No party without this album was worth attending in the second half of the 1960s.

Otis Redding - unequalled before or since

RAVINGS

1949
21-year-old Antoine 'Fats' Domino recorded his first million seller, 'The Fat Man', at Cosimo Matassa's J & M Studio in New Orleans.

★ ★ ★

1984
'Do They Know It's Christmas', the charity single by the all-star group Band Aid (recruited by Bob Geldof, leader of The Boomtown Rats), was released. It entered the UK chart at No. 1, becoming the biggest-selling record of all time in Britain.

★ ★ ★

1971

ZAPPA INJURED BY JEALOUS FAN

During a concert at London's Rainbow Theatre by Frank Zappa and The Mothers Of Invention, 24-year-old Trevor Howell, the jealous companion of an avid female Zappa fan, pushed the group leader off the stage into the orchestra pit, resulting in Zappa sustaining a broken leg and ankle and a fractured skull, from which it took him almost a year to fully recuperate.

It had been a week to remember for Zappa. Only seven days before, he and The Mothers had been playing a concert in Switzerland at Montreux Casino, which was completely destroyed that night by fire.

Zappa - a difficult week

ARRIVALS

1910 – John Hammond Sr.
1926 – Guitar Slim (Eddie Jones)
1942 – Peter Sarstedt
1943 – Chad Stuart (Chad and Jeremy)
1945 – Ralph Tavares (Tavares)
1946 – Chris 'Ace' Kefford (Move)
1946 – Walter Orange (Commodores)
1946 – Keith Smart (Mongrel/Wizzard/Rockin' Berries)
1948 – Jessica Cleaves (Friends Of Distinction)
1948 – Brenden Harkin (Starz/Kool and The Gang)
1952 – Johnny Rodriguez (Juan Raul Davis Rodriguez)
1954 – Geoff Deane (Leyton Buzzards/Modern Romance)
1957 – Paul Hardcastle
1958 – Pepsi Demacque (Pepsi and Shirlie)

★ ★ ★

DEPARTURE LOUNGE

1967 – Otis Redding

SAM COOKE SHOT IN LOS ANGELES MOTEL

Soul/R & B star Sam Cooke was shot and killed at a Los Angeles motel, The Hacienda, by its manageress Bertha Franklin, who claimed that Cooke had attempted to rape a young woman named Elisa Boyer and had assaulted Franklin when she tried to help

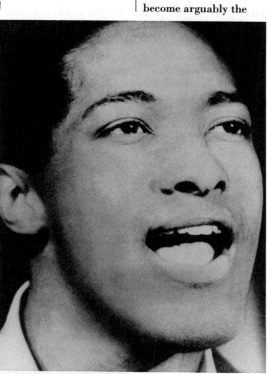

Sam Cooke - shot and killed

Boyer. The coroner returned a verdict of justifiable homicide.

It was a very inglorious end to a brilliant career that had seen Cooke become arguably the most popular black R & B singer in the world during the late 1950s and early 1960s.

He was born in 1931 and started his musical career in a gospel group, The Highway QCs, during his teenage years. Cooke, the son of a preacher, was lead singer of another gospel group, The Soul Stirrers, from 1950 to 1956, when, at the age of 25, he made his first secular recordings under the name of Dale Cook for Specialty Records, the Hollywood label for which Little Richard recorded most of his classic hits.

Cooke was less successful than Richard at Specialty, and in 1957 he moved to Keen Records, for whom he cut ten hits in around two years, including his first No. 1, 'You Send Me', 'Wonderful World' and 'Only Sixteen'. Both the latter songs were later covered by white acts whose singles were bigger hits than the Cooke originals.

After signing to RCA in 1960 the hits continued, including 'Chain Gang' (1960), 'Twistin' The Night Away' (1962), 'Another Saturday Night' (1963) and the posthumous 'Shake' (1965), all of which were US Top 10 hits. In addition, several of his records became the models for covers by the leading groups of the so-called British Invasion.

RAVINGS

1946
The first formal recording session by country-music star Hank Williams (Senior) took place in New York.

★ ★ ★

1972
James Brown was arrested after a concert at Knoxville, Tennessee, and charged with disorderly conduct. When he threatened to sue the local community for $1 million, the charges were dropped.

★ ★ ★

1972

GENESIS MAKES US DEBUT

Genesis (l to r) Rutherford, Banks, Gabriel, Collins

British progressive rock group Genesis made their US concert debut at Brandeis University, Boston, Massachusetts. The fourth line-up of the group had been together for two and a half years, and the fourth Genesis album, *Fox Trot*, had just been released. At the time, Genesis included both Peter Gabriel and Phil Collins, both later superstar solo vocalists, although Collins had joined Genesis as a drummer. After no suitable replacement could be found when Gabriel left the group in 1975, Collins had the unusual distinction of being the lead vocalist as well as the drummer of the band.

ARRIVALS

1915 – Dorothy Laverne (Girls Of The Golden West)
1926 – Big Mama Thornton (Willie Mae Thornton)
1935 – Tom Brumley (Buckaroos/Stone Canyon Band)
1938 – McCoy Tyner
1940 – David Gates (Bread)
1944 – Booker T. Jones
1944 – Brenda Lee (Brenda Mae Tarpley)
1945 – Robert Pickett (Sugarloaf)
1951 – Spike Edney (The Cross)
1953 – Andy Partridge (XTC)
1954 – Jermaine Jackson (Jackson 5)
1954 – Rita Ray (Rocky Sharpe and The Darts)
1958 – Nikki Sixx (Motley Crue)

★ ★ ★

DEPARTURE LOUNGE

1964 – Sam Cooke

★ ★ ★

1968

STONES ROCK 'N' ROLL CIRCUS

The press announcement that The Rolling Stones were both producing and starring in a TV Spectacular to be called *Rock 'n' Roll Circus* promised an extravaganza packed with stars, including Traffic (Steve Winwood's group), Taj Mahal, and Dr John, the extraordinary musical witch doctor from New Orleans. In the event, it also featured such luminaries as John Lennon and Yoko Ono, Eric Clapton, The Who, Jethro Tull and Mick Jagger's then girlfriend, Marianne Faithfull.

An extract of their performance was licensed by The Who and used in their biographical documentary *The Kids Are Alright*, but nothing has ever been publicly seen or heard of the presumably wonderful music that should have been made. One possible explanation is that the events of 1969 – the firing and subsequent death of Brian Jones (which made the group's free concert in Hyde Park almost a wake), the tragedy at Altamont where Meredith Hunter was killed by 'security guards', Marianne Faithfull's overdose in Australia, where Jagger was starring in the Ned Kelly movie – just diverted the group so much that they almost forgot about it, and then did not have time to complete it.

1957

JERRY LEE MARRIES COUSIN MYRA

Piano pumpin' Jerry Lee Lewis married his cousin, Myra Gale Brown, the daughter of the bass player in his band. If some felt that this was not far from incestuous inter-breeding, the furore exploded when it was discovered that Myra was just 13 years old and that he was still married to his first wife, Jane Mitcham. It should be noted that in the deep south of the USA, marriage to a 13-year-old cousin was not considered especially outrageous nor even extraordinary, bigamy however, was.

Jerry Lee and Myra - a cousin, a child and a wife!

1985

SIXTH STONE DIES

Ian Stewart, an original member of The Rolling Stones, died of a heart attack while in the waiting room of his doctor's Harley Street surgery at the age of 47.

Since being told during the 1960s by the group's then manager, Andrew Loog Oldham, that his image (short-haired and burly) was not appropriate to the style Oldham intended to create for the group, he had played piano both on stage and during recording sessions, but was not regarded as a group member, and was in fact employed by the group as personal manager in addition to his musical duties.

In 1986 the group dedicated their first album for Columbia (CBS), *Dirty Work*, to their faithful friend, known as 'the sixth Stone', whom they always called Stu.

RAVINGS

1965
The Beatles played their last concert in Britain, at the Capitol Theatre in Cardiff, Wales

1987
The first picture disc CDs were released, the artists concerned being George Michael and Michael Jackson.

★ ★ ★

1986

JACKIE WILSON TOPS CHART WITH 1958 HIT

Jackie Wilson

Almost two years after he died, eleven years after he fell into a coma and 28 years after the single was first released, Jackie Wilson's 'Reet Petite' re-entered the UK Top 20, which it had left in February 1958, going on to top the UK singles chart for a month.

In February 1987 Wilson's follow-up hit, 'I Get The Sweetest Feeling', reached the UK Top 3, and later that year '(Your Love Keeps Lifting Me) Higher And Higher' also reached the UK Top 20.

Born in Detroit in 1934, Wilson was spotted in a 1951 talent contest by Johnny Otis, who recommended him to Billy Ward and The Dominoes. Wilson joined the latter group as a back-up vocalist behind Clyde McPhatter, and when McPhatter left to launch The Drifters, Wilson took over the lead vocals, but in 1957 embarked on a solo career.

His debut single was 'Reet Petite (The Finest Girl You Ever Want To Meet)', which was a Top 10 hit in Britain, but peaked outside the US Top 50. A follow-up, 'To Be Loved', was a Top 30 hit on both sides of the Atlantic, and in 1959 'Lonely Teardrops' became Wilson's first million seller. That was the song he was performing on stage in New Jersey when he had a heart attack and hit his head as he fell to the ground, suffering brain damage and lapsing into a coma from which he never fully recovered.

1961

BEATLES SIGN MANAGEMENT DEAL WITH BRIAN EPSTEIN

Liverpool group The Beatles agreed to be managed by Brian Epstein. The manager of NEMS, a local record shop, Epstein prided himself on being able to acquire any record requested by his customers, and had first heard of the group when one Raymond Jones asked whether he could get hold of a copy of 'My Bonnie', a single made in Germany by Tony Sheridan and The Beat Brothers (who were actually The Beatles).

Experiencing problems in tracing the record, Epstein made further enquiries and was surprised to discover that the group were actually playing at a local venue, The Cavern, where he saw them perform at a lunchtime session on November 9, 1961. He was impressed with their act, but felt they needed a smarter stage presentation.

ARRIVALS

1942 – Andy Summers (Police)
1944 – Ron Caines (East Of Eden)
1944 – Marti Webb
1948 – Tony Gomez (Foundations)
1948 – Jeff 'Skunk' Baxter (Doobie Brothers/Steely Dan)
1948 – Ted Nugent
1948 – David O'List (Nice/Roxy Music)
1949 – Randy Owen (Alabama)
1949 – Tom Verlaine (Thomas Miller) (Television)
1952 – Alan Love (Opal Butterfly/Merlin)
1954 – Berton Averre (Knack)
1961 – Austin Sorenson (Per Oystein Sorenson) (Fra Lippo Lippi)

★ ★ ★

DEPARTURE LOUNGE

1981 – Pigmeat Markham

★ ★ ★

1974

TAYLOR ABANDONS THE STONES

Mick Taylor, the lead guitarist who replaced Brian Jones in The Rolling Stones, left the group after five years.

Unlike several other members of The Stones, Taylor rarely courted publicity or involved himself in extra-curricular activities, but it was rumoured that he was increasingly unhappy over the refusal of the rest of the group (but mainly Mick Jagger and Keith Richards) to consider his compositions when albums were being recorded.

Mick Taylor

Jagger issued a press statement from Munich, Germany, where the group were working on pre-production of their *Black and Blue album*, which read, 'After five and a half years, Mick wishes a change of scene and wants the opportunity to to try out new ventures, new endeavours. While we are all most sorry that he is going, we wish him great success and much happiness.'

Taylor also issued a statement: 'The last five and a half years with The Stones have been very exciting and proved to be a most inspiring period. As far as my attitude to the other four members is concerned, it is one of respect for them, both as musicians and as people. I have nothing but admiration for the group, but I feel now is the time to move on and do something new.' A few days later, Taylor issued another statement, which read: 'There was no personal animosity in the split, nothing personal at all. I'm very disturbed by the stories going around that it was all to do with credits and royalties, things like that. It had nothing whatever to do with those things.'

1974

BAKER JOINS THE ARMY

Ginger Baker (born Peter Baker), famous for his work with Cream, Blind Faith and Ginger Baker's Airforce (among others), formed a new group with brothers Paul and Adrian Gurvitz, appropriately to be called Baker-Gurvitz Army.

Guitarist Adrian and bass player Paul had first emerged as Gun in 1968 with a UK Top 10 hit, 'Race With The Devil', before forming Three Man Army in 1971, but that group's three albums all failed to chart on either side of the Atlantic. However, the new band achieved more success, their eponymous debut album reaching the album charts in both Britain and the USA, while their second 1975 album, *Elysian Encounter*, again reached the US chart, but after 1976's *Hearts On Fire*, the group seemed to fade.

Baker, Lord of the drums

ARRIVALS		
1911 – Spike Jones (Lindley Armstrong Jones)	1946 – Joyce Vincent (Dawn)	1951 – Mike Scott (Waterboys)
1932 – Charlie Rich	1946 – Jackie McAuley (Them/Poormouth)	★ ★ ★
1943 – Frank Allen (Rebel Rousers/Searchers)	1947 – Patty Duke (Anna Marie Duke)	DEPARTURE LOUNGE
1946 – Jane Birkin	1949 – Cliff Williams (Home/AC/DC)	1963 – Dinah Washington

RAVINGS

1972
Born To Boogie, the film starring Marc Bolan, directed by Ringo Starr and with guest star Elton John, was premiered in London.

1977
Saturday Night Fever, the movie starring John Travolta and with music by The Bee Gees (and others), was premiered in New York. The film's soundtrack album sold 25 million copies.

★ ★ ★

1969
LENNON'S LAST LONDON GIG

The Plastic Ono Band, the group led by John Lennon and Yoko Ono, played their first (and only) concert in Britain at London's Lyceum Ballroom for a charity concert with proceeds destined for UNICEF, the United Nations Children's Fund. The musicians with Lennon and Ono included his fellow Beatle, George Harrison, Eric Clapton, Delaney and Bonnie (with whose band Harrison and Clapton had been guesting on a UK tour), Keith Moon of The Who, and keyboard star Billy Preston, who was signed to Apple Records, the label launched by The Beatles, and who had appeared with the group on the celebrated concert on the roof of the Apple building in Savile Row earlier in the year.

The concert was called *Peace For Christmas*, and a week later, billboards appeared in major cities, including New York, Los Angeles, London, Paris, Berlin, Amsterdam, Tokyo, Athens, Rome and Toronto, proclaiming 'WAR IS OVER! If You Want It – Happy Christmas from John and Yoko'. This message was repeated in 1971 on a single released by The Plastic Ono Band, 'Happy Xmas (War Is Over)', produced by Phil Spector.

RAVINGS

1977
The Who played a private show for fan club members at Shepperton Film Studios, the filmed results of which became part of *The Kids Are Alright*, the feature length documentary on the group.

1979
Jackie Brenston, whose 1951 single, 'Rocket 88', has been cited as the first ever rock 'n' roll record, died of a heart attack at the age of 49.

1959
DON AND PHIL'S DEBUT IN THE BIG APPLE

Everlys - escape from Nashville

The Everly Brothers undertook their first formal recording session outside Nashville when they recorded 'Let It Be Me' at Bell Sound Studios in New York. They enlisted Archie Bleyer, boss of Cadence Records, the label to which Don and Phil were signed, as producer, and Jerry Allison of The Crickets, as drummer on the session.

Originally written by French star Gilbert Becaud as 'Je t'appartiens', the song had been provided with an English lyric and had been a minor US hit in 1957 as 'Let It Be Me' for the little-known Jill Corey, although Don Everly had reportedly first heard it on a Chet Atkins album.

Bleyer wrote a string arrangement for the track, which was the first time The Everlys had used such backing, and it remains one of the duo's best loved early recordings, becoming their eighth US Top 10 single in two and a half years and also reaching the UK Top 20. Its flip side was a song written by Don Everly, 'Since You Broke My Heart', for which Don and Phil added vocals in New York to a backing track made a few days earlier in Nashville.

1974

MOTT HOOPLES ITSELF TO DEATH

After a chequered career lasting five and a half years, Mott The Hoople split up when lead vocalist and frontman Ian Hunter left the band after failing to recover from having collapsed from exhaustion two months before. In 1972 the group had made a previous decision to split, but on that occasion, David Bowie, claiming to be a fan, wrote and produced for them 'All The Young Dudes', which became their first hit.

'All The Young Dudes'

The group survived at that point, but members were regularly leaving thereafter. First to go was keyboard player Verden 'Phally' Allen, who was eventually replaced by two keyboard players, Morgan Fisher (ex-Love Affair) and Mick Bolton. Then in 1973 guitarist Mick

Ralphs left to form Bad Company with Paul Rodgers and Simon Kirke of Free and King Crimson bass player Boz Burrell. He was replaced by ex-Spooky Tooth guitarist Luther Grosvenor (known as Ariel Bender). In July 1974 Mick Bolton left and was replaced by Blue

Weaver (ex-Amen Corner), and two months after that Bender/Grosvenor also departed, at which point Mick Ronson, ex-guitarist with Bowie during the latter's Spiders From Mars period, joined for the group's final single, 'Saturday Gigs'.

Hunter and Ronson

formed the Hunter-Ronson band in early 1975, and bass player Pete 'Overend' Watts, drummer Dale 'Buffin' Griffin and Morgan Fisher resurrected the original parent group, recruiting singer Nigel Benjamin and guitarist Ray Major and abbreviating the name to Mott.

1983

END OF THE ROAD FOR THE WHO

A spokesperson for The Who announced that the group was disbanding. The death of Keith Moon five years earlier had been a blow from which the group had never really recovered, and although substitute

drummer Kenny Jones was probably the best possible substitute, he inevitably lacked the maniacal qualities that had made Moon irreplaceable.

Apart from a number of solo projects of

varying quality and success, the group had recorded two new albums, 1981's *Face Dances ('You Better You Bet')* and 1982's *It's Hard*, but neither seemed to longtime Who fanatics to be among the

group's finest works. In 1984 a live album was released of the group's final concert called *Who's Last*, which failed to reach the Top 40 of the album charts in either Britain or the United States.

The Who decide to call it a day

1988

DISCO STAR SYLVESTER SUCCUMBS

Gay disco star Sylvester (real name Sylvester James) died at the age of 41 of an AIDS-related condition. His best known hit was 1978's 'You Make Me Feel (Mighty Real)', his only UK Top 10 hit.

1973

BOGUS MAC

A group called Fleetwood Mac, assembled by the group's erstwhile manager, Clifford Davis, went on a US tour after the real group, beset at the time by romantic entanglements and other problems, had pulled out of a number of scheduled dates.

Vocalist Dave Walker had joined the band in 1972 after Danny Kirwan, the third and last of the group's original singer/guitarists, had been fired. Walker had met Fleetwood Mac when the latter had toured with his previous group, Savoy Brown, but he only stayed for eight months before apparently forming a group with Kirwan (whom he had replaced), but it was a shortlived affair.

Fleetwood Mac with Bob Weston (wearing a cap)

Talking of affairs, the other problem was that singer/guitarist Bob Weston, who had also joined the band when Kirwan departed, was having an affair with Mick Fleetwood's wife, Jenny (née Boyd). (Jenny was the sister of Patti Boyd, who was married to both George Harrison and Eric Clapton, and was also the subject of Donovan's song 'Jennifer Juniper').

Mick Fleetwood was rather miffed that the new boy was taking such liberties and fired him forthwith, which was inconvenient as Fleetwood Mac were in the middle of a US tour, at which point Davis recruited ex-members of Elmer Gantry's Velvet Opera to finish the tour as Fleetwood Mac.

The result was a bitter legal battle that was reportedly resolved in 1974, when the band moved permanently to the USA and recruited Lyndsey Buckingham and Stevie Nicks, soon afterwards becoming arguably the biggest group in the world.

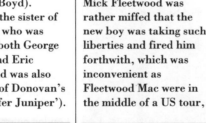

ARRIVALS

1936 – Tommy Steele (Thomas Hicks)
1939 – Eddie Kendricks (Temptations)
1942 – Paul Butterfield
1943 – Dave Dee (David Harman) (DD, D, B, M and T)
1948 – Darryl Way (Curved Air/Sky)
1949 – Paul Rodgers (Free/Bad Company/The Firm)
1950 – Carlton Barrett (Wailers)
1951 – Wanda Hutchinson (Emotions)
1952 – Mickey Jones (Angel)
1953 – Mark Gane (Martha and The Muffins)
1958 – Michael Mills (REM)
1961 – Sarah Dallin (Bananarama)

★ ★ ★

DEPARTURE LOUNGE

1975 – Hound Dog Taylorr
1978 – Don Ellis
1982 – Big Joe Williams

1962

BEATLES DEBUT ON THE BOX

The Beatles made their first British TV appearance on *People and Places*, a show transmitted live from Manchester by Granada, the commercial TV company who transmitted programmes in the north of England. They performed their debut single, 'Love Me Do', which had become their first UK Top 20 hit only days before, and are also believed to have performed cover versions of 'Some Other Guy' (originally recorded by Richard Barrett) and Little Richard's 'Ooh My Soul!'.

As this was the very first broadcast by the group (and it was live), very little documentation has survived about this historic event, although it has been established that the group were paid £35 ($55) for their time and trouble.

RAVINGS

1954
'Shake, Rattle and Roll' by Bill Haley and The Comets became the first rock 'n' roll single to reach the UK chart.

1977
Elvis Costello and The Attractions made their US television debut on *Saturday Night Live*, apparently deputizing for The Sex Pistols.

1983

STONE KEEFE FINALLY MARRIES

Rolling Stone Keith Richards married his longtime girlfriend, Patti Hansen, in Mexico on his 40th birthday, with his partner of 20 years' standing, Mick Jagger, as best man.

Rolling Stone Keith Richards

Richards had lived for all the 1970s with German film star Anita Pallenberg, whom he had first met when she was the girlfriend of Brian Jones. Richards and Pallenberg produced two children, Marlon (born August 1969) and Dandelion (born 1972), but in 1973 things started going badly wrong.

The couple were arrested at their Chelsea home for possession of cannabis and a revolver, but were freed on bail of £1000 ($1500) the following day. Four days after that, Redlands, Richards' country house burnt to the ground, and a few days later, Richards fell asleep in a London hotel and set fire to his room, resulting in the group as a whole being banned from the hotel indefinitely. In October, Richards appeared in court in Nice, France, on drug charges and was given a one-year suspended prison sentence, a heavy fine and barred from returning to France for two years. Just over a week later he was in a London court and received a conditional discharge and a fine for various drugs and firearms offences.

1974 was a bit quieter on the legal front, but in 1975 he was in court in Arizona for dangerous driving and possession of an offensive weapon (a penknife with a device for removing stones from a horse's hoof!) – case dismissed.

1976 brought a third child, a boy named Tara, but in May, Richards fell asleep and crashed his car, which unsurprisingly contained drugs. This was dwarfed by the tragedy of the death of ten-week-old Tara from pneumonia. Perhaps the break with Anita Pallenberg was inevitable.

RAVINGS

1971
Jerry Lee Lewis and his wife, Myra, divorced. Their marriage in 1958, when she was his 13-year-old cousin, caused extreme damage to his career in places where the marriage was seen as illegal due to her age. In fact, the only illegality about the marriage was the fact that he was committing bigamy.

★ ★ ★

ARRIVALS

1941 – Sam Andrew (Big Brother and The Holding Company)
1938 – Chas Chandler (Bryan Chandler) (Animals)
1943 – Keith Richards (Rolling Stones)
1944 – Deke Leonard (Roger Leonard) (Man)
1948 – Buddy Gask (Showaddywaddy)
1950 – Martha Johnson (Martha and The Muffins)
1953 – Bobby Keyes
1956 – Natasha (Natasha England)
1963 – Greg D'Angelo (White Lion)
1966 – Steve Dullaghan

1981

ROD STEWART LEAVES FACES, STARS IN SATELLITE TV SPECIAL

A red-letter day for Rod Stewart, who in 1975 announced that he was leaving The Faces, and in 1981 headlined a concert at Los Angeles Forum that was broadcast live by satellite around the world. His special guest on the TV Special was Tina Turner, who was attempting to revive her career after splitting up with her husband, Ike, five years before, and was without a major record deal at the time.

Nine years later, with Turner established as an international superstar, the two gravel-voiced vocalists duetted on a version of Marvin Gaye and Kim Weston's 'It Takes Two' which made the UK Top 5.

1987

PET SHOP BOYS BY DEMAND

Having performed a fine version of 'Always On My Mind' on a televised show commemorating the tenth anniversary of Elvis Presley's death four months earlier, British electro-pop duo Pet Shop Boys took a recorded version of the song to the top of the British singles chart, where it stayed through into January 1988.

Pet Shop Boy Neil Tennant

It was the duo's third UK No. 1 single in two years, following 'West End Girls' in 1985 and 'It's A Sin' earlier in 1987.

The song was not regarded as one of Presley's greatest classics, having been originally released as the B-side of 'Separate Ways', which just reached the US Top 20 in early 1973. It was written by Wayne Carson Thompson (who had also written 'The Letter', the 1967 million seller by The Box Tops), guitarist Johnny Christopher, and Mark James (writer of 'Suspicious Minds', Elvis Presley's last US No. 1), and was recorded by Brenda Lee in 1972. Willie Nelson made it the title song of his 1982 album, and it became his biggest hit as an artist, winning three Grammy Awards, including Song Of The Year.

ARRIVALS

1915 – Edith Piaf (Edith Giovanna Gassion)
1920 – Little Jimmy Dickens (James Cecil Dickens)
1922 – Eamonn Andrews
1940 – Phil Ochs
1941 – Maurice White (Earth, Wind and Fire)
1944 – Alvin Lee (Ten Years After)
1944 – Zal Yanovsky (Mugwumps/Lovin' Spoonful)
1945 – John McEuen (Nitty Gritty Dirt Band)
1947 – Janie Fricke
1958 – Limahl (Christopher Hamill) (Kajagoogoo)

★ ★ ★

1983

VARIOUS ARTISTS TOP THE ALBUM CHART

In a rare but hugely successful collaboration, EMI and Virgin, two of the leading British record labels, jointly released a 30-track double album titled *Now! That's What I Call Music*, crammed with hits from the year's charts. Including eleven No. 1 hits by such artists as Phil Collins, Duran Duran, UB40, Bonnie Tyler, Culture Club, Rod Stewart, etc., it zoomed to the top of the UK album chart, remaining there for four weeks and even returning to No. 1 for a further week after Paul Young's *No Parlez* briefly overtook it.

This album marked a significant change in the habits of British record-buyers. As more albums in the 'Now' series (and a rival series launched by CBS and WEA titled 'Hits') were released and topped the UK chart, sales of singles decreased. Record-buyers knew that not only would their particular favourite probably appear on a compilation, but that it would be accompanied by another two dozen or more hits, making it economically preferable to wait for the album rather than buy a single. At the start of 1989 the compilers of the UK album chart launched a second album chart for which only compilations were eligible in recognition of the domination of the original album chart by compilations.

BOBBY DARIN DIES

1973

Popular vocal stylist Bobby Darin died of a heart attack at the age of 37 during surgery to repair a heart valve. Artificial valves had been inserted two years earlier, into the singer's heart.

Darin (real name Walden Robert Cassotto) was born in New York's Bronx area and released 40 US hit singles between 1958 and 1969, starting as a vocalist who also wrote songs. His first major success came with 'Splish Splash', a novelty song he co-wrote with famed disc jockey Murray The K, which was a US Top 3 hit in 1958 and sold a million copies. Even before that, he had cut a single of two of his songs, 'Early In The Morning' and 'Now We're One', for Brunswick Records, despite being signed to Atlantic subsidiary Atco. Atco laid claim to the single, which they then reissued and it became a US Top 30 hit. Brunswick, convinced of the potential of the songs, swiftly arranged for Buddy Holly to record and release a single with both songs that became a US Top 40 hit. Still in 1958, Darin returned to the UK Top 10 with 'Queen Of The Hop', a second million

Bobby Darin - dressed to impress

seller, which he also co-wrote.

1959 brought a change of musical direction with 'Dream Lover', a beat ballad rather than his previous R & B flavoured rockers. This became his first UK No. 1 and third million seller and reached the US Top 3, while its follow-up was a sophisticated version of 'Mack The Knife' with a Sinatraesque big band backing, which became his only US No. 1 single and fourth million seller. In 1960, his version of Charles Trenet's 'La Mer' (retitled 'Beyond The Sea' and with lyrics in English) became his fifth million seller. 1962 brought his final major success with 'Things', one of his own compositions and in 1968 he formed his own record company, Direction.

ARRIVALS

1907 – Skeeter Willis (Willis Brothers)
1907 – Paul Francis Webster
1940 – Larry Willis
1944 – Bobby Colomby (Blood, Sweat and Tears)
1947 – Peter Criss (Peter Crisscoula) (Kiss)
1947 – Gigliola Cinquetti

1948 – Stevie Wright (Easybeats)
1957 – Anita Baker
1957 – Billy Bragg
1962 – Ray Coburn (Honeymoon Suite)

★ ★ ★

DEPARTURE LOUNGE

1973 – Bobby Darin

RAVINGS

1952
Elvis Presley sang 'Old Shep' at a Christmas party at his High School in Memphis.

1957
Elvis Presley was given his draft notice to join the US Army for National Service while home at Graceland for Christmas.

★ ★ ★

1975

JOE JOINS EAGLES

With the departure of founder member Bernie Leadon from The Eagles, singer and guitarist Joe Walsh was recruited to join the group who were already extremely successful with four US Top 5 hits during the year: 'Best Of My Love' and 'One Of These Nights' (both No. 1), 'Lyin' Eyes' and 'Take It To The Limit'. With Walsh aboard, the group would go on to even greater success, another two US No. 1s, 'New Kid In Town' and the title track, coming from their fourth album - their first with Walsh - the multi-million selling 'Hotel California'.

Joe Walsh

RICHIE MAKES IT NINE IN A ROW

When his 'Say You, Say Me' topped the US singles chart for four weeks at the end of 1985 and into 1986, compositions by Lionel Richie had topped the US singles chart in nine consecutive years, a truly prodigious achievement by any standards.

This remarkable run of chart-toppers started with 'Three Times A Lady' (1978) and 'Still' (1979), both by The Commodores, the group in which Richie first came to prominence as vocalist and keyboard player, while 1980 brought 'Lady', a chart-topper for country star Kenny Rogers, which was

Lionel - nine years on the trot at the top

written by Richie in only four hours and which he also produced. 1n 1981 he wrote the year's best selling record, 'Endless Love', a duet between Richie and Diana Ross that topped the US chart for nine weeks.

In 1982 Richie finally left The Commodores to embark on his own career, opening his No. 1 chart account as a solo artist with 'Truly'. In 1983, soon after The Mayor of Richie's home town, Tuskegee, Alabama, had declared November 22 Lionel Richie Day, 'All Night Long (All Night)' did the inevitable. 1984's 'Hello' was his first solo single to top the charts in both Britain and the USA, and in 1985 he co-wrote the USA For Africa hit, 'We Are The World', with Michael Jackson. In fact, 'Say You, Say Me' first topped the US chart in 1985, but as it was also the first US No. 1 of 1986, it was the final part of his unique feat.

1983

BARSON'S MADNESS FAREWELL

Madness founder member, keyboard player and main songwriter Mike Barson announced that he was leaving the north London group. Madness were the most successful act of the early 1980s, enjoying 17 UK hit singles from 1979 to 1983 (15 of them Top 10). The group had played its first gig in 1977, and in 1978 vocalist Suggs (real name Graham McPherson)

had joined.

The first hit by Madness was 'The Prince', a tribute to bluebeat star Prince Buster written by saxophonist Lee Thompson, which was released on 2 Tone, the label launched by The Specials, after which Stiff Records signed Madness, releasing all the rest of their hits until shortly after Barson's departure.

RAVINGS

1964
Ode To A High Flying Bird, a largely pictorial tribute to sax genius Charlie Parker by Rolling Stones

drummer Charlie Watts, was published.

1969
Following the dissolution of Blind Faith, drummer Ginger Baker launched his own

group, Airforce, with his ex-colleagues from the shortlived supergroup, Steve Winwood and Ric Grech, along with Denny Laine, Graham Bond, Phil Seamen and others.

ARRIVALS

1926 – Freddie Hart (Fred Segrest)	1942 – Carla Thomas	(The Rumour)
1940 – Paul (Ray Hidebrand) (Paul and Paula)	1943 – Albert Lee	1953 – Betty Wrigh
	1946 – Gwen McCrae	1957 – Allan Johnson
	1946 – Kevin Peek	(Exciter/Real Life)
	1946 – Carl Wilson (Beach Boys)	1957 – Tony Lewis (Outfield)
1940 – Frank Zappa	1948 – Barry Gordon	1964 – Christian James (Halo James)
	1948 – Martin Belmont	

SHAFT MAN HAYES FILES FOR BANKRUPTCY

No hair, no money

Isaac Hayes, who had topped the US singles chart just over five years earlier with 'Theme From Shaft', a hypnotic instrumental that won an Oscar for Best Film Theme of 1971 and Grammy Awards for Best Instrumental Arrangement and Best Engineered Recording, filed for bankruptcy.

First famous as a songwriter in the second half of the 1960s in partnership with David Porter – they wrote and produced a string of hits for Sam (Moore) and Dave (Prater), including 'You Don't Know Like I Know', 'Hold On! I'm A-Comin'', 'When Something Is Wrong With My Baby' and 'Soul Man' (Sam and Dave's biggest hit) – Hayes released his own debut album, *Presenting Isaac Hayes*, in 1967, but it was hardly a success. However, his follow-up album, *Hot Buttered Soul*, a largely orchestral release containing only four tracks, with Hayes himself speaking rather than singing above the music, made the Top 10 of the US album chart and went gold in 1969.

In 1970 his follow-up album, *The Isaac Hayes Movement*, also reached the US Top 10, and a second album that year, *To Be Continued*, reached the US Top 20. Hayes was hot, and when he topped both the singles and album charts with 'Theme From Shaft', it seemed he could do no wrong, following with a late-1971 album, *Black Moses*. Apart from a reissue of his debut album, re-titled *In The Beginning* (which charted second time round, but just failed to make the Top 100), 1972 brought no new album, but two in 1973, both of which went gold: the double live *Live At The Sahara Tahoe* and *Joy*, but thereafter Hayes lost his appeal.

SEGER'S GOLDEN BULLET

Bob Seger, who had been recording for over ten years, achieved his first major US chart success with his eighth album, *Live Bullet*, a double live album that went platinum and became his first to peak inside the Top 50 of the US chart. The album's title referred to his backing group, The Silver Bullet Band, who were widely regarded as one of the finest live bands in the USA during the late 1970s. At around the time *Live Bullet* was certified platinum, *Night Moves*, his follow-up, was released. It also went platinum and gave him his first US Top 10 entry.

Seger - wouldn't you smile?

RAVINGS

Wit And Wisdom Of Ronald Reagan, which contained no sound whatsoever.

★ ★ ★

1973
Stephen Stills was found to be guilty in a paternity suit brought by Harriet Tunis, who lived in Mill Valley near San Francisco.

★ ★ ★

1990
For the second consecutive year, Paula Abdul was the year's Top Female Act in the USA.

★ ★ ★

1980
Stiff Records released an album titled *The*

1964

CHIEF BEACH BOY'S BREAKDOWN

Brian Wilson, *éminence grise* of The Beach Boys (founder, songwriter, producer and group member), was afflicted by a nervous breakdown during a flight from Los Angeles, California, to Houston, Texas, where the group were due to start a tour. He subsequently decided that he would give up stage work, not only because it might help him to avoid stress that might cause further nervous breakdowns, but also because he was experiencing pain in one of his ears (apparently the result either of a fight at school or chastisement from his impatient father).

He was replaced in the touring line-up of the group by session musician Glen Campbell, who worked as a part-time Beach Boy until a permanent replacement was found in April 1964, in the shape of Bruce Johnston, who had worked with film star Doris Day's son, Terry Melcher, in The Rip Chords, another Southern Californian group who, as their name implies, were a surf music group like The Beach Boys.

The Beach Boys when they were...boys (l to r) Brian Wilson, Al Jardine, Dennis Wilson, Mike Love, Carl Wilson

ARRIVALS

1913 – Lulu Belle (Lulu Belle and Scotty) (Myrtle Eleanor Cooper)
1929 – Chet Baker (Chesney Baker)
1932 – Rev. James Cleveland
1935 – Esther Phillips (Esther Mae Jones)
1939 – Johnny Kidd (Frederick Heath)
1940 – Jorma Kaukonen (Jefferson Airplane/Hot Tuna)
1940 – Eugene Record (Chi-Lites)
1941 – Tim Hardin
1945 – Ron Bushy (Iron Buterfly)
1949 – Luther (Ariel Bender) Grosvenor (Spooky Tooth/Mott The Hoople)
1958 – Dave Murray (Iron Maiden)

★ ★ ★

1961

BEATLES IMPRESS DECCA TALENT SCOUT

Liverpool beat group The Beatles played a favourite Merseyside venue, The Cavern Club, where they had appeared many times before. On this occasion, their manager, local record-shop proprietor Brian Epstein, who had first heard of the group only two months before, had invited Mike Smith of Decca Records to watch them perform, and Smith was impressed enough to arrange for them to play a formal audition in London. The audition took place on the first day of 1962, and the four members of the group travelled to Decca's West Hampstead studios.

The group performed 15 songs during the audition, most of which were cover versions, although they interleaved three original songs written by Lennon and McCartney, none of which have appeared on an official Beatles album.

In the event, Decca did not sign The Beatles, instead offering a contract to a group from Essex, Brian Poole and The Tremeloes, on the basis that Poole and Co. were more accessible, living nearer London.

ABBA DUO FILE FOR DIVORCE

1978

Bjorn Ulvaeus and his wife, Agnetha (née Faltskog), both members of ABBA, separated after over seven years of marriage, dispelling the notion that two pairs of romantically involved stars could work together and remain in love.

When the group first briefly convened in November 1970, Ulvaeus and Faltskog were engaged, as were Benny Andersson and Anni-Frid Lyngstad. Although the former couple married before ABBA were well known, their colleagues, who both had children from previous liaisons, were living together as an engaged couple before they married on October 6, 1978, less than three months before Bjorn and Agnetha separated. This was the only short period when ABBA comprised two married couples.

Benny and Anni-Frid announced their divorce on February 14, 1981, two and a half years after their marriage.

Bjorn and Agnetha

RSO MONOPOLY BEGINS

1977

(l to r) Barry, Robin and Maurice Gibb - The Bee Gees

The first of six consecutive US No. 1 singles on one label, RSO Records, reached the top of the chart. This was the greatest monopoly of the pole position by one label to date.

Named from the initial letters of the Robert Stigwood Organisation, the label's biggest stars were The Bee Gees and Eric Clapton. The monopoly lasted until May 20, 1978 – almost five months. It overlapped the domination of the US album chart by another RSO release, the double album soundtrack to the movie *Saturday Night Fever*, which included four of the six consecutive chart-topping singles. In chronological order they were 'How Deep Is Your Love' (Bee Gees, 3 weeks), 'Baby Come Back' (Player, 3 weeks), 'Stayin' Alive' (Bee Gees, 4 weeks), '(Love Is) Thicker Than Water' (Andy Gibb, 2 weeks), 'Night Fever' (Bee Gees, 8 weeks), and 'If I Can't Have You' (Yvonne Elliman, 1 week). All but the hits by Player and Andy Gibb came from *Saturday Night Fever*.

ARRIVALS

1920 – Dave Bartholomew
1924 – Lee Dorsey
1931 – Ray Bryant
1944 – Mike Curb
1944 – Eddie Furey (Fureys)
1945 – Lemmy (Ian Fraser Kilmister) (Motorhead)
1946 – Jan Akkerman (Focus)
1947 – Paul Shuttleworth (Kursaal Flyers)
1957 – Ian Burden (Human League)

★ ★ ★

DEPARTURE LOUNGE

1954 – Johnny Ace

★ ★ ★

RAVINGS

1972
Police in Miami, Florida, cut off the power during the encore of a concert by Manfred Mann's Earth Band, provoking a two-hour riot.

1974
An expensive quartet – James Taylor, Carly Simon, Linda Ronstadt and Joni Mitchell – were spotted singing Christmas carols around Hollywood.

★ ★ ★

ROCK 'N' ROLL'S FIRST CASUALTY

1954

Johnny Ace, one of the most popular black vocalists of the early 1950s, died while playing Russian roulette backstage at Houston City Auditorium in Texas. Ace (real name John Alexander Jr) was born in Memphis, the son of a local preacher. He had been in groups with B. B. King and Bobby 'Blue' Bland, and adopted the name Johnny Ace in 1952. With his band, The Beale Streeters, he topped the US R & B chart for nine weeks with his first single, 'My Song'.

He was only 25 years old and was about to release his seventh hit single, 'Pledging My Love', which became his first (and only) single to reach the Top 20 of the US pop chart, when he pulled the fateful trigger. Many regard his as the first rock 'n' roll death – or suicide.

SMILE STAR DIES

1977

Charlie Chaplin, the silent film star

Sir Charles Chaplin, undoubtedly one of the most famous film stars in history, died at his home in Switzerland at the of 88. While he never claimed or even attempted to be a pop star, he was the composer of 'Smile', a song he wrote for his 1936 movie *Modern Times*, three versions of which were US hits in 1954, by Nat 'King' Cole, Sunny Gale and David Whitfield.

Later versions of the song that entered the US chart include those by Tony Bennett (1959), 'Timi Yuro' (1961), Ferrante and Teicher (an instrumental version in 1962) and Jerry Butler and Betty Everett (a 1965 duet), while Eric Clapton included a short version on a sampler album in the 1970s.

In Britain, Nat 'King' Cole's rendition was the sole version to chart, peaking at No. 2 in 1954.

ARRIVALS

1929 – Billy Horton (Silhouettes)
1937 – O'Kelly Isley (Isley Brothers)
1939 – Bob James
1940 – Pete Brown (Piblokto)
1943 – Trevor Lucas (Eclection/Fairport Convention/Fotheringay)
1944 – John Edwards (Detroit Spinners)
1944 – Henry Vestine (Canned Heat)
1945 – Alice Cooper (Vincent Furnier)
1945 – Noel Redding (Jimi Hendrix Experience)
1954 – Robin Campbell (UB40)
1954 – Annie Lennox (Eurythmics)
1957 – Shane McGowan (Pogues)
1962 – Francis Dunnery (It Bites)

★ ★ ★

DEPARTURE LOUNGE

1977 – Charlie Chaplin

★ ★ ★

RAVINGS

1965
Rubber Soul by The Beatles moved to the top of the UK album chart.

1969
16-year-old Robbie Bachman was given his first drum kit as a Christmas present. In 1972 he became the drummer of his older brother Randy's group, Bachman-Turner Overdrive.

1978
Public Image Ltd., the group formed by John Lydon (aka Johnny Rotten), played their first public concert, at London's Rainbow Theatre.

★ ★ ★

BEATLE PAUL ANNOUNCES ENGAGEMENT

1967

Jane Asher

Paul McCartney was the last of The Beatles to be married and the only member of the 'Fab Four' to be married only once, to Linda Eastman, a union that remains current at the time of writing. However, McCartney had been previously engaged, to actress Jane Asher, and their long-expected engagement took place on Christmas Day 1967. McCartney had been living as a lodger at the Asher family's London home.

During the following July, Jane Asher revealed on *Dee Time*, a popular British TV show fronted by erstwhile disc jockey Simon Dee, that the engagement was off. This was doubtless connected with McCartney's attendance at a Capitol Records convention in Hollywood in June, where he was reported to have become very close to Eastman, with whom he stayed at the Beverly Hills Hotel.

BEATLES TV MOVIE PREMIERED – AUDIENCE BEWILDERED

The famous coach used on 'Magical Mystery Tour'

Magical Mystery Tour, a bizarre TV show featuring The Beatles, was shown for the first time on Boxing Day, when it was correctly anticipated that a huge audience would be watching it.

The programme included a number of the finest songs The Beatles ever wrote, including 'Magical Mystery Tour' itself and 'I Am The Walrus' (included on a double EP, also titled 'Magical Mystery Tour'). The plot (or lack of it) left the vast majority of viewers confused and to some extent disappointed. The concept was, as the title suggested, a mystery tour on a coach containing the four Beatles and other members of the supporting cast, and for five days in September the coach had been driven around Devon and Cornwall, after which it was later taken to a disused airfield in Kent, where empty hangars were used as film studios.

Perhaps the programme's major drawback was that although it was filmed in full colour, very few people in Britain owned colour television sets, and watching in black and white prevented much of its visual appeal from being properly appreciated. Seen subsequently in its full glory, it became clear that this was an ambitious, but largely unsuccessful, enterprise.

ARRIVALS

1939 – Ken Howard
1940 – Phil Spector
1942 – Ernie and Earl Cate (Cate Brothers)
1943 – Ronnie Prophet
1951 – Paul Anthony Quinn (Saxon)

★ ★ ★

RAVINGS

1970
The much praised *All Things Must Pass*, the triple album by George Harrison that many feel remains his finest solo work, entered the UK chart.

1987
'The Tide Is Turning (After Live Aid)', a solo single by Roger Waters, once of Pink Floyd, entered the UK singles chart. It performed poorly, stalling at No. 54

★ ★ ★

POLICE PICK UP POGUE

Shane McGowan, vocalist and main songwriter with London Irish band The Pogues, was arrested for kicking the glass out of a shop window after drinking all day. He was fined £250 ($400) and bound over to keep the peace for a year. A few months earlier, McGowan had collapsed at London's Heathrow Airport and was unable to board a flight to San Francisco where the group were due to support Bob Dylan in a concert. The rest of the group played the show without him, and he was later fired by his colleagues for unreliability.

Formed in 1983 as Pogue Mahone (a Gaelic expression meaning 'kiss my ass'), the group name was abbreviated to The Pogues in 1984 after some radio programmers refused to play their records. Signing with Stiff Records. Their 1984 debut album, *Red Roses For Me*, briefly reached the UK chart, but it was 1985's interestingly titled *Rum, Sodomy and The Lash* (believed to be Winston Churchill's description of life in the Navy) that gave them their first substantial hit, reaching the Top 20 of the UK album chart. Due to Stiff Records going out of business, the next Pogues album, *If I Should Fall From Grace With God*, was not released until early 1988, when it became their first to reach the Top 3 in the UK chart.

Shane McGowan - unreliable?

1976

BLUESMAN KING DIES OF HEART ATTACK

Freddie King, a vocalist and highly rated blues guitarist, died in Dallas, Texas, of a heart attack aggravated by a bloodclot and internal bleeding from ulcers.

One of the kings of The Blues

He had celebrated his 42nd birthday three months earlier.

Born Billy Myles on September 30, 1934 in Gilmer, Texas, he was one of the triumvirate of Kings (the others being B.B. and Albert) who ruled The Blues throughout the 1960s.

During his twenties he moved north to Chicago and worked with Muddy Waters, Memphis Slim, Willie Dixon and others. He was a substantial influence on a generation of British blues guitarists, in particular Eric Clapton, a King

aficionado, who covered King's 'Hideaway' on *Bluesbreakers*, the acclaimed 1966 album made by John Mayall with Clapton as lead guitarist.

King himself was living in obscurity in Texas at that time, but he was rediscovered two years later and toured Britain, which led to his signing with Atlantic Records' subsidiary Cotillion, for whom he recorded two albums released in 1969 and 1970. He then signed to Leon Russell's Shelter label, releasing three more albums – *Getting Ready*, *Texas Cannonball* and *Woman Across The Water*, between 1971 and 1973.

In the early 1970s Eric Clapton recorded King's 'Have You Ever Loved A Woman' on the Derek and The Dominos album, *Layla And Other Assorted Love Songs*, and by 1974 King signed to Robert Stigwood's RSO label, to which Clapton was also contracted, recording two albums, *Burglar* (on which Clapton played) in 1974, and *Larger Than Life* in 1975.

1963

NEWCASTLE R&B GROUP'S RADIO DEBUT

The Animals, a quintet from Newcastle in the north-east of England, made their first radio broadcast on BBC's *Saturday Club*. The group had formed the previous year as the Alan Price Combo, a group that included Price (keyboards), Bryan 'Chas' Chandler (bass) and John Steel (drums), who were joined by local blues singer Eric Burdon and finally by guitarist Hilton Valentine.

The group built up a formidable reputation at the local Club A GoGo, changing their name to The Animals apparently as a result of audience response to their wild stage act. They were spotted by independent record producer Mickie Most, who produced their first two albums

Animals, Eric Burdon (left) and Alan Price (back right)

and first seven hit singles, the second of which was 'House Of

The Rising Sun', which topped the charts on both sides of the Atlantic.

ARRIVALS

1931 – Scotty Moore (Winfield Scott Moore)
1939 – Carl Fisher
1941 – Mike Pinder (Moody Blues)
1941 – Leslie Maguire (Gerry and The Pacemakers)
1944 – Mick Jones (Spooky Tooth/Foreigner)
1944 – Tracy Nelson (Mother Earth)
1948 – Larry Byrom (Steppenwolf)
1950 – Terry Bozzio (Missing Persons)
1952 – David Knopfler (Dire Straits)
1952 – Karla Bonoff
1961 – Youth (Killing Joke)

★ ★ ★

DEPARTURE LOUNGE

1976 – Freddie King
1978 – Bob Luman
1978 – Chris Bell (Big Star)

RAVINGS

1983
In one of the more bizarre mysteries of popular music, vocalist Walter Scott, who had sung on three hits by Bob Kuban and The In-Men in 1966, disappeared. His ex-wife and her husband were charged with his murder when his body was found three years later with a gunshot wound.

1986
Jackie Wilson's reissued 'Reet Petite' topped the UK singles chart, almost three years after his death.

1983

BEACH BOY DROWNS

Dennis Wilson, the only real surfing enthusiast among The Beach Boys, drowned during an incautious dip in the Pacific Ocean from his boat moored in Marina Del Rey, California. He had celebrated his 39th birthday a few weeks earlier and was a strong swimmer, but by all accounts was somewhat incapacitated by alcohol when deciding to enjoy a swim.

Dennis Wilson

A founder member of the group with his brothers Brian and Carl, Dennis was regarded as the sex symbol of the group, for which he played drums. However, he was sometimes inclined towards wild behaviour, and in 1971 had put his hand through a plate-glass window, resulting in serious injuries that prevented him from playing drums for some time. South African Ricky Fataar of Flame, a group signed to Brother Records, the label launched by The Beach Boys, replaced him, playing as a Beach Boy for three years (and later appearing as a member of The Rutles in the spoof TV documentary *All You Need Is Cash*).

Dennis Wilson himself had a brief flirtation with the cinematic art, co-starring with James Taylor in *Two Lane Blacktop*, a 1971 art movie. In 1977 he was the first of The Beach Boys to release a solo album, *Pacific Ocean Blue*, which was a minor chart hit in the USA. In 1982, he fathered a son named Gage by Shawn, the daughter of his Beach Boy colleague Mike Love. He had previously married Karen Lamm, ex-wife of Robert Lamm of Chicago, in 1976.

ARRIVALS

1903 – Earl 'Fatha' Hines
1910 – Billy Williams
1921 – Johnny Otis (John Veliotes)
1938 – Charles Neville (Neville Brothers)
1943 – Chas Hodges (Heads, Hands and Feet/Chas and Dave)
1946 – Edgar Winter
1947 – Dick Diamonde (Easybeats)
1949 – Clive Brooks (Groundhogs)
1950 – Alex Chilton (Box Tops/Big Star)
1951 – Louis McCall (ConFunkShun)
1953 – Richard Clayderman (Phillipe Pages)
1954 – Rosie Vela

★ ★ ★

DEPARTURE LOUNGE

1983 – Dennis Wilson

★ ★ ★

1975

BOOT ON THE OTHER FOOT FOR NUGENT

Fearsome hard-rock guitar hero Ted Nugent, an active supporter of The National Rifle Association in America, who boasted of his prowess at hunting animals for food, using either guns or a bow and arrows, was threatened while playing a concert in Spokane, Washington, by David Gelfer, a member of the audience, who pointed a .44 magnum at him in best Dirty Harry style. Fortunately for Nugent, who earlier that year had disbanded The Amboy Dukes, the group he had led since 1966, the police overpowered the gunman before Nugent 'made his day'. He was charged with 'intimidating with a weapon'. The anti-blood sports lobby noted that now Nugent knew what it was like to be looking down the barrel of a deadly weapon.

Ted Nugent threatens his speakers

RAVINGS

1963
20-year-old Bobby Vee married Karen Bergen in Detroit.

★ ★ ★

1963
Merle Haggard made his first appearance on the US country chart with 'Sing A Sad Song'. Three years earlier he had been released from San Quentin prison, where he served a three-year sentence for burglary.

★ ★ ★

NOT A BAD YEAR ...

Elvis - starting as he means to continue

Elvis Presley ended his first year in the US pop chart with ten singles in the US Top 100, some indication of his incredible impact. During the year, he took 17 separate singles into the US chart, but ten at one time (or 10 per cent of the chart) was his best in a single week's Top 100.

He was not at No. 1 at that time, though, a privileged spot reserved for ten consecutive weeks by Guy Mitchell with 'Singing The Blues'. However, the ten Presley hits included many timeless rock 'n' roll masterpieces, three of which had occupied the No. 1 spot before Mitchell started his residency. 'Hound Dog' and 'Don't Be Cruel' were released as one single, and listed together at No. 1 for eleven weeks between August and November, and both remained in the Hot 100 well into 1957, while 'Blue Moon', which never quite reached the Top 50, was also in the chart for the final three months of 1956. In October, 'Love Me Tender', the title song of Presley's first movie, was released as a single and topped the chart in November and early December, while its flip side, 'Anyway You Want Me (That's How I Will Be)', only entered the chart on its own account in early November, but hung on in until 1957.

In mid November 'Love Me' joined all the other Presley singles in the chart, peaking within the Top 3, although its flip side, 'When My Blue Moon Turns To Gold Again', was slow to reach the chart on its own account, getting there in the first week of December. The ten were completed by three tracks that all entered the chart on December 29: 'Paralysed', 'Poor Boy' (another song from the *Love Me Tender* movie) and 'Old Shep'.

RAVINGS

1967
Singer/guitarist Dave Mason left Traffic, the group launched by Steve Winwood, of which he was a founder member. Traffic did not replace him, continuing as a trio.

1982
A Jamaican postage stamp was issued featuring a picture of Bob Marley, one of the country's most famous sons, who had died the previous year.

★ ★ ★

ARRIVALS

1922 – Rose Lee Maphis
1928 – Bernard Cribbins
1935 – Virgil Johnson (Velvets)
1939 – Ed Bruce
1941 – Ray Thomas (Moody Blues)
1946 – Marianne Faithfull
1947 – Cozy Powell (Colin Flooks)
1950 – Robert Parissi (Wild Cherry)
1951 – Yvonne Elliman
1954 – Roger Voudouris

★ ★ ★

DEPARTURE LOUNGE

1952 – Fletcher Henderson
1967 – Paul Whiteman
1980 – Tim Hardin

★ ★ ★

1980

DEATH OF A TROUBADOUR

Noted singer/songwriter Tim Hardin died of a suspected overdose of heroin in Los Angeles, less than a month after his 39th birthday. Hardin emerged in the mid 1960s as a songwriter with a happy knack of sensitivity, as exemplified by such classics as 'If I Were A Carpenter' (an international hit for Bobby Darin and The Four Tops), 'Reason To Believe' (memorably covered by Rod Stewart and later Wilson Phillips), 'Lady Came From Baltimore' (a Scott Walker cover) and 'Misty Roses' (Colin Blunstone), but after his first two albums, *Tim Hardin* and *Tim Hardin II*, his muse seemed to desert him, and he was never as creative again.

Tim Hardin

1962

TEENAGE STAR LOSES HOUSE AND DOG

18-year-old Brenda Lee (real name Brenda Mae Tarpley) lost her home (valued at $40,000) in a fire that completely destroyed it. She was slightly hurt when she rushed into the house in an unsuccessful attempt to rescue Cee Cee, her poodle, who died from inhaling smoke. Lee also lost stage clothes worth $25,000 that were not insured.

Otherwise, 1962 was a memorable year for the diminutive country singer for more positive reasons – nine hit singles in the US chart, five in its UK equivalent, three US hit albums and one in Britain.

At the start of the year, 'Break It To Me Gently' was a Top 5 single in the USA, then 'Speak To Me Pretty' became her only UK Top 3 hit, but surprisingly was not released in single form in the States. The next US Top 10 hit was 'Everybody Loves Me But You', but in Britain, its B-side in the States, 'Here Comes That Feeling', was a Top 5 hit. 'All Alone Am I' was the US Top 10 single of the year, and the year's third UK Top 10 hit was 'Rockin' Around The Christmas Tree'. With six different singles reaching the Top 10, three on each side of the Atlantic, Brenda Lee had cause for delight, but also confusion. Perhaps this was why she neglected to insure her very valuable wardrobe.

RAVINGS

1973
John McLaughlin and The Mahavishnu Orchestra played their final concert at a hall in Detroit, Michigan.

★ ★ ★

ARRIVALS

1928 – Bo Diddley (Elias Bates McDaniel)
1931 – Skeeter Davis
1933 – Andy Stewart
1937 – John Hartford
1939 – Del Shannon (Charles Westover)
1940 – Kenny Pentifallo (Southside Johnny and The Asbury Jukes)
1942 – Michael Nesmith (Monkees)
1945 – Davy Jones (Monkees)
1946 – Patti Smith
1947 – Jeff Lynne (Idle Race/ELO/Traveling Wilburys)
1949 – Geoff Peacey (Boston Show Band/Lake/Elephant)
1950 – Dave Stewart (Hatfield and The North)
1959 – Tracey Ullman

★ ★ ★

1981

XTC'S USA DEBUT

Regarded as one of Britain's more intriguing new discoveries, XTC, from Swindon in the west of England, played their first US concert in Philadelphia.

Formed in 1977 by singer/guitarist Andy Partridge, Colin Moulding (bass), Terry Chambers (drums) and ex-King Crimson keyboard player Barry Andrews, they were linked by the media with the burgeoning New Wave movement, but proved themselves far more adaptable than many who followed New Wave philosophies.

Signed to Virgin Records, the group released two albums that reached the UK chart in 1978, *White Music* and *Go 2*, but Barry Andrews left the group early in 1979, and was replaced by Dave Gregory.

1979 was the break-through year for XTC, they first released a UK Top 20 single, 'Making Plans For Nigel', although their 1979 album, *Drums and Wires*, was scarcely more of a success than its predecessors. However, XTC's most successful year was certainly 1982, when they released their first Top 10 single, 'Senses Working Overtime', and their first Top 10 album, *English Settlement*.

XTC, 1978

ROCK LEGEND RICK(Y)'S DEATH IN PLANE CRASH

1985

A chartered aeroplane that crashed in Texas contained one of the biggest rock stars of the late 1950s and early 1960s, Rick (or Ricky) Nelson. Also on the aircraft were Nelson's fiancée, Helen Blair, and five other members of his entourage.

After catching fire, it crashed near De Kalb, a small town on the route to Dallas, and rumours were rife that the fire was caused because one of the passengers had been freebasing cocaine, a method of ingesting the drug using naked flame.

It was an inglorious end to a career that had seen Nelson become a rock star overnight, bolstered by regular TV appearances in his family's soap opera, *The Adventures Of Ozzie and Harriet*. After his teenybop fame dissipated in the mid 1960s, Nelson pioneered the fusion of country music with rock, releasing two ground-breaking albums, *Bright Lights and Country Music* (1966) and *Country Fever* (1967), which were every bit as adventurous as the undertakings of Gram Parsons in The International Submarine Band and The Byrds. In the 1970s he led a country/rock group, The Stone Canyon Band, which included Randy Meisner, later a founder member of The Eagles, and Tom Brumley, longtime pedal-steel player in Buck Owens and The Buckaroos.

Rick Nelson pictured on stage in the year of his death

NEW YEAR'S EVE DEBUTANTS

1961,1969

There seems to be a certain logic in playing a debut gig on New Year's Eve – the end of an old regime and the start of a new opportunity. The Beach Boys played their first show under that name on the last day of 1961, at the Ritchie Valens Memorial Concert held at Long Beach, California, for which they received $300. The line-up of the group featured the three Wilson brothers, Brian, Dennis and Carl, their cousin, Mike Love, and Brian's classmate, Al Jardine. Soon after their debut, Jardine left the group for 18 months while he attended dental college, and was replaced by David Marks.

The last day of 1969 brought another

The Beach Boys

significant debut, that of Band Of Gypsys, a group formed by Jimi Hendrix with drummer Buddy Miles and bass player Billy Cox, who played one of their very few live shows at New York's Fillmore East. Unfortunately, Hendrix would not see another New Year's Eve . . .

Acknowledgements

AUTHOR'S ACKNOWLEDGEMENTS

The greatly relieved author wishes to thank the following for their considerable assistance in the completion of this book: Lynda Morrison (registrar of cradle and coffin activity); Dave McAleer for a highly successful trade, Lorraine Dickey, a fellow escapee from the RS syndrome; Emily Hedges for being reasonable and approachable; David Sandison for some days, Alan Clayson for some others; Pete Frame, for starting me on this ridiculous career; Barry Lazell and all the other rock historians whose work has been used as a reference; Terry Cooper of Adams World for speedy disk conversions; Tony Brown; Burning The Stone for the inspiration; the authors of other rock almanacs—no information in this book is culled from a single source, but from at least two, hopefully three or four.

PICTURE ACKNOWLEDGEMENTS

The publishers would like to thank the following sources for their kind permission to reproduce the photographs in this book:
Hulton Deutsch Collection, Hulton Deutsch Collection © Apple Corps Ltd.
London Features International/Adrian Boot, Janet Gough, Anastasia Pantsios, Ebet Roberts.
Pictorial Press/Escott.
Popperfoto.
with special thanks to **REDFERNS/**Richie Aaron, Cyrus Andrews, Bob Baker, Glenn A. Baker Archives, Dick Barnatt, Howard Baum, Colin Beard, Derek Boulton, Gary Brandon, Mike Cameron, Fin Costello, Peter Cronin, Ian Dickson, Erica Echenberg, David Ellis, Colin Fuller, Gems, Suzi Gibbons, Steve Gillett, Tim Hall, Richie Howell, Mick Hutson, Max Jones, Bob King, Neil Kitson, Elliot Landy, Michael Linssen, Mark Marnie, Thomas Meyer/New Eyes, Susan Moore, Steve Morley, Mike Prior, David Redfern, Rick Richards, Ebet Roberts, Tony Russell, Brian Shuel, S&G Press Agency, John Tiberi, Michael Uhl, Bob Willoughby, Val Wilmer, Graham Wiltshire, Bob Vincett.
Retna Pictures Ltd/Robert Mathen.
Rex Features/Crollalanza, Fotex, Dezo Hoffman, J. Lyons, Photoreporters, Richard Young.
Syndication International.